GUILTY PLEAS IN

INTERNATIONAL CRIMINAL LAW

NANCY AMOURY COMBS

Guilty Pleas in International Criminal Law

Constructing a Restorative Justice Approach

STANFORD UNIVERSITY PRESS

Stanford, California 2007

Stanford University Press
Stanford, California
©2007 by the Board of Trustees of the
Leland Stanford Junior University.

Library of Congress Cataloging-in-Publication Data

Combs, Nancy Amoury.
   Guilty pleas in international criminal law : constructing a
restorative justice approach / Nancy Amoury Combs.
      p.   cm.
   Includes bibliographical references and index.
   ISBN-13: 978-0-8047-5351-7 (cloth : alk. paper)
   ISBN-13: 978-0-8047-5352-4 (pbk : alk. paper)
   1. Plea bargaining.   2. International offenses.   3. International
criminal courts—Rules and practice.   I. Title.
KZ6316.C66   2007
345′.072—dc22

                                              2006007572

Printed in the United States of America on acid-free, archival-quality
paper

Typeset by G&S Book Services in 10/14.5 Minion

In memory of my father

Acknowledgments

I am grateful to the many individuals who read and commented on previous drafts, who assisted me in acquiring court documents and other difficult-to-obtain materials, and who were willing to discuss their experiences with guilty-plea processes at the international tribunals. I thank in particular George Aldrich, Stuart Alford, Laurel Baig, François Boudreault, John Braithwaite, Marcel Brus, Douglass Cassel, Bruce Combs, Sylvia de Bertodano, John Dugard, Essa Faal, Alan Gutman, Mark Harmon, Jessica Holmes, Refik Hodzić, Michael Johnson, Nicholas Koumjian, Máximo Langer, Anne Marie van Luijt, Howard Morrison, Daryl Mundis, John Murphy, Gabrielle Kirk McDonald, Andre Nollkaemper, Mohamed Othman, Kimberly Pronk, Flavio Rose, William Schabas, Nico Schrijver, Emir Suljagić, Brenda Sue Thornton, Igor Timofeyev, David Tolbert, Gregory Townsend, Lars Waldorf, Slobodan Zecević, and a host of prosecutors and defense counsel who prefer to remain anonymous. I am likewise grateful for the research assistance of Leah Crosby, Kristina Hofmann, Joseph MacAvoy, Jamie Mickelson, John Newton, Tanner Nielson, Brad Russell, and Michael Sweikar.

Contents

Introduction   1

1. International Criminal Justice Then and Now: The Long Road from Impunity to (Some) Accountability   11

2. Financial Realities: Targeting Only the Leaders   27

3. Do the Numbers Count? The Ends Served by International Criminal Prosecutions in Societies Emerging from Mass Atrocities   45

4. Plea Bargaining at the ICTY   57

5. Plea Bargaining at the ICTR   91

6. Plea Bargaining at the Special Panels in East Timor   114

7. Using Conventional Plea Bargaining to Increase the Number of Criminal Prosecutions for International Crimes   127

8. Plea Bargaining as Restorative Justice: Using Guilty Pleas to Advance Both Criminal Accountability and Reconciliation   136

9. Applying Restorative Principles in the Aftermath of Different Atrocities: A Contextual Approach   155

10. The Minimal Role of Restorative Justice in Current International Criminal Prosecutions   188

Conclusion   223

Notes   229
Bibliography   317
Index   357

Mrs. Plavšić's plea of guilty and acceptance of responsibility represent an unprecedented contribution to the establishment of truth and a significant effort toward the establishment of reconciliation.

—*Prosecutor, International Criminal Tribunal for the former Yugoslavia*

I am speechless. I cannot talk at all, I am shivering. I am completely shaken.

—*Bosnian Muslim woman whose husband and children were killed in a Bosnian Serb ethnic-cleansing campaign, upon learning that Plavšić had received a mere eleven-year prison sentence after pleading guilty, for her implementation of the ethnic cleansing*

Introduction

Fifty years after the victorious allies brought Axis war criminals to justice at the Nuremberg and Tokyo tribunals, the United Nations (U.N.) Security Council established an ad hoc tribunal to prosecute those accused of international crimes in the former Yugoslavia. The years that had elapsed between the creation of the World War II tribunals and the International Criminal Tribunal for the former Yugoslavia (ICTY) saw thousands of atrocities that resulted in millions of deaths but that were followed by virtually no prosecutions. Thus, the establishment of the ICTY, and then a year later, an international tribunal to prosecute those responsible for the slaughter of approximately eight hundred thousand Tutsi in Rwanda (ICTR), was met with great fanfare.[1] The first trial at the ICTY—the prosecution of a low-level sadist named Duško Tadić—similarly garnered enormous scholarly and popular interest[2] and was considered a turning point in the quest to end the impunity that has so often followed mass atrocities.

The early years of the tribunals were fraught with obstacles, many of them exacerbated by the international community's failure to provide adequate financial support to the tribunals. Over the years, the international community came to better fund the tribunals and better assist their enforcement efforts;[3] consequently, a decade after they were established, the ad hoc tribunals have developed into functioning criminal justice institutions. The ICTY and ICTR have also spawned a number of progeny, including the Special Court for Sierra Leone, the Special Panels in the Dili District Court in Timor-Leste (formerly East Timor), the Extraordinary Chambers in the courts of Cambodia, and, most importantly, a permanent International Criminal Court (ICC). Domestic prosecutions of international crimes are also on the rise. Both Chile and Argentina have begun to bring their own offenders to justice after nearly thirty years of impunity,[4] and the courts of Rwanda, Ethiopia, and the states of the former Yugoslavia are trying valiantly to prosecute the perpetrators of their more recent conflicts. In many respects, then, the prospects for bringing international criminals to justice have never appeared better. Although global politics still act as an impediment to many prosecutions, the success of the ICTY in particular has created an awareness of the value and feasibility of criminal accountability.

But at what cost comes this accountability? Although the international community has of late manifested a firm rhetorical commitment to the cause of criminal accountability, its financial commitment to that end has been less than steadfast. Indeed, not long after the international community began providing the ICTY and ICTR with the financial and enforcement support necessary to fulfill their mandates, the U.N. Security Council, led by the United States, began looking for ways to curtail the costs of these institutions. Genocide trials are not cheap: the ICTY and ICTR together employ more than two thousand people and spend more than $200 million per year to prosecute perhaps a dozen people. Not wishing to foot this bill indefinitely, the international community began in 2002 to pressure the tribunals to formulate a completion strategy and to finish their work sooner rather than later. Succumbing to this pressure, the tribunals have drastically reduced the number of investigations they are undertaking; they have made plans to transfer cases to domestic courts, and they have announced optimistic end-dates. Learning from its experience with the budgets of the ICTY and ICTR, the international community, for its part, has imposed tight financial constraints on the tribunals' progeny. The U.N. provided the Special Court for Sierra Leone and the Extraordinary Chambers in the courts of Cambodia, for instance, with only meager budgets and extremely limited mandates that will allow them to prosecute, at most, a dozen defendants. The Special Panels in East Timor were able to prosecute larger numbers of defendants but on a slim $6 million annual budget, which led to due-process problems. Further, the U.N. stopped funding the Special Panels in May 2005 before many of the intended prosecutions could be carried out. Similarly, although the Rome Statute, establishing the ICC, imposes no express quantitative limitations on ICC prosecutions, even before the court formally began its work, insiders had acknowledged that financial constraints would restrict it to prosecuting, at most, six cases per mass atrocity,[5] an estimate that remains accurate some years later.[6] It is not just international tribunals that must contend with severely limited budgets. South Africa's attempt to prosecute apartheid-era criminals who failed to apply for amnesty foundered for lack of resources, while Chile's desire to speed along human-rights cases resulted in a plan to grant immunity to offenders who divulged information about offenses. And Rwanda's ambitious efforts to prosecute every last genocide suspect have been plagued by due-process violations, most of which result from insufficient resources.

It is perhaps too pessimistic to predict that financial constraints will soon render trials for international crimes a thing of the past, but unless drastic changes are made, one can expect international criminal tribunals and their domestic counterparts to limit their prosecutorial efforts to only a small number of offenders, most likely high-level military and political leaders. Mass atrocities do not occur spontaneously but typically are the product of widespread planning and a carefully designed propaganda campaign. The political and military leaders who orchestrate and foment the violence are generally considered the most culpable of offenders; thus, a prosecutorial focus on these individuals is appropriate. Trials of high-level offenders also serve pedagogical and dramaturgical purposes. Mark Osiel, for instance, contends that such "big trials" have the potential to transform societies emerging from large-scale violence by engaging fundamental questions of national identity and collective memory.[7]

Prosecutions of international crimes are also credited with serving a variety of other significant ends. Some—namely, retribution, deterrence, incapacitation, and rehabilitation—are penological goals also understood to be served by the prosecution of domestic crimes. Others satisfy needs specific to societies emerging from the horror of large-scale atrocities. An analysis of these ends and the ways in which they are served by the prosecution of international crimes will be presented in Chapter 3. The analysis reveals that, to the extent these goals are advanced by prosecutions, they are significantly better advanced when a substantial number of prosecutions are undertaken. Indeed, many of the ends that prosecutions are expected to serve are apt to be undermined when criminal justice systems single out only a token few defendants to prosecute.

This book comprehensively examines the ways in which a widespread and systematic effort to obtain guilty pleas can enhance international criminal accountability by increasing the number of prosecutions that feasibly can be undertaken. Prosecutors in common-law states, such as the United States and the United

Kingdom, have for decades engaged in aggressive plea bargaining to obtain guilty pleas as a means of speeding cases through the dockets.[8] Such plea bargaining can take many forms, but the term most typically refers to the prosecutor's offer of some form of sentencing concessions in exchange for the defendant's guilty plea. Approximately 90 percent of American cases are now disposed of by means of guilty pleas.[9] Civil-law states, such as those of Western Europe, have traditionally been more reluctant to resort to non-trial dispositions, but increasingly burdensome caseloads have recently motivated some of these states, such as France and Germany, to make greater use of abbreviated procedures, some of which include bargaining.[10] The need to dispose of cases expeditiously has also lately led international prosecutors to seek guilty pleas from those accused of humankind's most heinous offenses. The ICTY and ICTR, for instance, initially shunned plea bargaining, dismissing it as an unseemly device inconsistent with the tribunals' mandate to impose appropriately severe punishment for the grave crimes within its jurisdiction. But the tribunals have recently been forced to embrace the practice in order to adhere to their completion-date schedules and to gain much-needed evidence about the crimes of high-level offenders. Indeed, the ICTY convicted fifteen defendants in 2003—a record number—but eight of those defendants convicted themselves by means of a guilty plea.[11] Thus, instead of conducting grand, widely publicized human-rights trials—moral dramas pitting defendants with their tales of tragedy against prosecutors seeking to vindicate the dictates of humanity—the ICTY in 2003 disposed of the majority of its cases via an abbreviated proceeding that followed a series of backroom negotiations centering on which charges would be withdrawn, what sentences would be recommended, and how much information defendants would provide.

The tribunals' embrace of plea bargaining has met with nearly unanimous criticism. Victims have condemned the seemingly lenient sentences that have resulted from these plea bargains,[12] and even Serbian liberals, who have supported the ICTY in the past, have denounced the plea bargaining as undermining efforts to encourage Serbs to take responsibility for the atrocities.[13] These international critics have plenty of company in the domestic sphere. American scholarly literature is filled with trenchant and persuasive attacks on plea bargaining, and some commentators on the Continent have begun issuing their own vitriol. Most American critics target the particular problems that result from the way plea bargaining is practiced in the United States, but at least some of the criticism focuses more fundamentally on the undesirability of trading leniency for financial savings; a trade is at the heart of plea bargaining no matter where or how it is practiced. Indeed, returning to the international context, if it is inappropriate for the state of New York to offer a burglar a sentencing discount in exchange for the financial savings of a guilty plea, how much more inappropriate is it for the international community to trade leniency for money with a *génocidaire*?

Analogizing the plea bargaining of international crimes to the plea bargaining of domestic crimes is problematic, however, because the analogy fails to take account of the unique difficulties that plague efforts to bring international criminals to justice. Whereas the prosecution of violent domestic crimes is the norm, the prosecution of international crimes has been the exception. Uganda's Idi Amin, for instance, murdered and expelled many hundreds of thousands of Ugandans and then spent twenty-five years in luxurious exile in Saudi Arabia. Pol Pot led the Khmer Rouge in its killing of up to two million Cambodians in the mid-1970s,[14] yet he died a free man twenty years later. And thus far very few of the Latin American dictators and military commanders at fault in tens of thousands of forced disappearances and tortures during the 1970s and 1980s have suffered criminal sanctions. As David Wippman observed, for most international offenders, the risk of prosecution is "almost the equivalent of losing the war crimes prosecution lottery."[15]

Thus, although plea bargaining is used in relation to both domestic and international crimes to enable the relevant criminal justice system to process its cases more efficiently, domestic criminal justice systems are at least founded on the presumption that violent crime will be investigated and, if appropriate, prosecuted. Indeed, it is this unstated presumption that gives force to the arguments of plea bargaining's opponents. Plea bargaining, domestic critics point out, is a dilution of the full justice that a criminal justice system ought to provide. Institutions prosecuting international crimes must attend as well to these concerns, but they take on entirely different contours because the presumption of prosecution that is so central to domestic criminal justice systems does not exist for international crimes. And it is precisely because most international offenders are not prosecuted that guilty pleas have the potential to play such a valuable role in efforts to end impunity. Indeed, in a realm in which truth-commission reports that merely identify perpetrators are lauded as enhancing accountability, plea bargaining cannot be considered a dilution of full justice, as it is in the domestic sphere, but rather must be understood as presenting a potent opportunity to impose justice on those who otherwise would evade it. Guilty pleas, then, have the potential to broaden substantially the reach of criminal sanctions for international crimes, and, for that reason alone, they should be considered a key feature of any effort to end the impunity that has heretofore been the traditional response to international crimes.

In addition, and although it may seem counterintuitive, guilty pleas also have the potential to advance goals served by a variety of nonprosecutorial mechanisms that have emerged in recent decades to repair the harms wrought by international crimes. Government-funded reparations schemes seek to provide a minimal level of financial assistance to victims of large-scale violence. Symbolic reparations, such as monuments, days of remembrance, and public apologies, serve as official recognition of victim injuries and offender culpability. Truth commissions provide victims with an opportunity to relate their stories to a sympathetic audience and, in the process, create a historical narrative of the suffering. In general, these truth-telling and reparatory mechanisms advance goals that criminal trials either ignore or underemphasize. In this book, I argue that guilty pleas have the potential not only to enhance criminal accountability but also to advance the goals traditionally associated with truth-telling and reparatory processes. The key to this effort lies in incorporating principles drawn from restorative justice into an international guilty-plea system. "Restorative justice" has emerged in domestic criminal justice systems during the past two decades as an alternative to the predominantly retributive focus that pervades those systems. Restorative justice deemphasizes retributive sanctions and places greater weight on "correcting imbalances, restoring broken relationships—with healing, harmony and reconciliation."[16] Restorative-justice programs promote face-to-face contact between victim, offender, and members of the community, during which "offenders are urged to account for their behaviour; victims are encouraged to describe the impact which the crime has had upon them materially and psychologically; and all parties are encouraged to decide upon a mutually agreeable form and amount of reparation—usually including an apology."[17]

Restorative-justice principles have occasionally been invoked in the context of international crimes, but only in relation to nonprosecutorial mechanisms, such as truth commissions and reparations schemes. Restorative-justice principles need not be confined to these spheres, however, and indeed they have a valuable role to play in the prosecution of international crimes. This book constructs an innovative guilty-plea system, through the incorporation of restorative-justice principles, that seeks not only to enable the prosecution of a greater proportion of international offenders but also to advance truth-telling, victim empowerment and healing, and offender reintegration. This guilty-plea system advances penological ends while at the same time promoting the individual and societal reconciliation so desperately needed in regions recently riven by violent conflict.

Chapter 1 traces the development of international criminal law and the creation of international bodies to prosecute violations of that law. Only in the last century have norms prohibiting widespread violence been codified, and even after codification, these laws have been more often ignored than enforced. The establishment of the ICTY in 1993 spawned the creation of a number of other bodies to prosecute international crimes, however, and effected a sea change in prevailing views about the need for and desirability of criminal accountability. Chapter 1 also traces the emergence of various nonprosecutorial mechanisms, such as truth commissions and reparations schemes, and details the goals that they are created to effectuate.

Although theoretically desirable, the prosecution of international crimes gives rise to substantial practical difficulties, not least of which are financial. Chapter 2 examines the financial constraints impeding the prosecution of international crimes. It shows in particular that, given the way in which international tribunals currently operate, they can hope to bring to trial only a miniscule proportion of international offenders. Domestic prosecutions of international crimes cost less, but not substantially less, if they adhere to prevailing due-process standards; thus, they are similarly hampered. Given these financial obstacles, bodies prosecuting international crimes will focus their prosecutorial efforts on senior political and military figures who are considered the most responsible for the atrocities. In many cases, the practical ability to bring these architects of collective violence to justice does not exist, but even when it does, the question remains whether such a limited number of prosecutions is sufficient to satisfy even the most minimal goals that prosecutions of international crimes are designed to serve.

Chapter 3 takes up this theme by exploring the benefits of undertaking a substantial number of prosecutions. International crimes envisage large-scale violence that is at times perpetrated by thousands, even tens of thousands, of offenders. Given the scale of these crimes, resource constraints will prevent the prosecution of many offenders no matter what criminal procedures are utilized. Acknowledging these constraints, Chapter 3 details the purported goals of criminal prosecutions and examines how these goals are in fact served by prosecutions and whether they are better served by prosecuting deeper into the offender class— that is, by prosecuting at least some mid-level and low-level offenders rather than targeting only the leaders. Chapter 3 concludes that these goals not only are better advanced by the prosecution of a substantial number of defendants but that they may be undercut by the selective, token prosecutions that characterize the current approach to international criminal justice.

Chapters 4, 5, and 6 examine one method for increasing the numbers of prosecutions that can be undertaken: the use of plea bargaining to obtain guilty pleas. In particular, these chapters explore in detail the plea bargaining that has taken place at the ICTY, the ICTR, and the Special Panels, and they examine, among other things, the nature of the bargaining that has occurred, the rationales used to justify that bargaining, the effect of bargaining on sentences, the influence of prosecutorial sentencing recommendations after bargaining, and appeals of guilty pleas. This discussion reveals that an evolution has occurred in the practice of plea bargaining: whereas prosecutors made little or no attempt to secure guilty pleas in the early days of the international tribunals, in more recent times, prosecutors have actively sought to induce defendants to plead guilty through the bestowal of more and different kinds of concessions.

Chapter 7 tackles the normative question of whether plea bargaining *should* be practiced when prosecuting international crimes. Domestic plea bargaining gives rise to various distortions and abuses, and the practice is roundly condemned by victims, civil liberties groups, and scholars. Given the problems associated with plea bargaining, one might wonder why anyone would advocate exporting the practice to international tribunals and already troubled domestic criminal justice systems seeking to prosecute the gravest crimes known to humankind. I provide a twofold reason in Chapter 7: namely, that the different contexts in which domestic and international crimes are prosecuted, and the different needs those prosecutions satisfy, render the widely criticized domestic practice of plea bargaining a justifiable—even desirable—choice when the crimes to be prosecuted are international. Turning first to context, I identify the dramatically different political environments in which domestic and international crimes are prosecuted, and I explore the implications of those differences on the feasibility and efficacy of prosecutions. Turning next to the needs of societies emerging from mass violence, I assert that guilty pleas have the potential to benefit such societies by conveying a limited form of truth and acknowledgment; although these values have only minimal import in the context of domestic crimes, they can have profound significance to societies recently torn by large-scale violent conflict.

Chapter 8, then, constructs an innovative guilty-plea system that is designed not only to make feasible more criminal convictions but also to advance the reconciliatory goals more often associated with truth commissions and reparations schemes. I begin the chapter by outlining the theoretical components of the guilty-plea system I envisage. After describing domestic restorative-justice programs and the empirical research that supports the use of restorative processes, I examine at the conceptual level the role that restorative-justice principles might play in the context of international crimes. Next, I flesh out the contours of the proposed guilty-plea system, describing, in particular, its three key features: truth-telling, victim participation, and reparatory obligations.

I conclude Chapter 8 by addressing two of the gravest potential impediments to the success of the guilty-plea system I envisage. First, defendants accused of international crimes may find the mere act of pleading guilty difficult enough without being forced to reveal significant additional information; that is, the disclosure requirements embodied in a restorative-justice approach may be so onerous that they deter defendants from pleading guilty. I propose a sentencing practice that rewards defendants who confess before they are implicated in another offender's confession as one way of obtaining a substantial number of early guilty pleas. The second potential obstacle centers on the fact that plea bargaining is apt to motivate guilty pleas only to the extent that the defendants have reason to fear prosecution and conviction. The problem in the international context is that conducting a substantial number of prosecutions, when politically feasible, is not financially feasible. Indeed, a primary reason that a criminal justice system utilizes plea bargaining in the first place is because it does not possess the resources necessary to conduct a large number of full-scale trials. But the system must appear to be willing and able to do just that, or it will not be able to motivate defendants to plead guilty. Courts prosecuting domestic crimes face this difficulty as well; thus, I offer strategies drawn from domestic court experience. In addition, I advocate a forceful beginning to any prosecutorial endeavor. In particular, I suggest that a criminal justice system prosecuting international crimes use a substantial proportion of its resources to conduct thorough investigations and to arrest and detain large numbers of appropriate suspects at the very outset of its work. Doing so will create a credible threat of sanctions, particularly if arrests are immediately followed by trials for lower-level offenders whose cases are relatively quick and easy to prove.

The guilty-plea model developed in Chapter 8 comprises both restorative and retributive elements; crafting the optimal balance of these elements in a particular guilty-plea system will depend on a number of factors specific to the atrocities in question. These factors include, among others, the victim-perpetrator ratio; the prior relationship, if any, between victims and perpetrators; the nature of the crimes; and the amount of information already available about the crimes and their perpetrators. I explore these and other factors in Chapter 9 by examining four very different atrocities—in Argentina, Bosnia, Rwanda, and East Timor. In the first part, I describe the crimes that took place in each of these locations. Argentine, Rwandan, and East Timorese crimes followed a roughly similar course, but the atrocities occurring during the Bosnian conflict were sufficiently varied that I examine three: the siege of Sarajevo, the massacres at Srebrenica, and the widespread detention of civilians in prison camps. Although every prosecution would benefit by the inclusion of the three key restorative-justice elements— truth-telling, victim participation, and reparations—financial realities require difficult decisions about how and to what extent these restorative elements should be included. To elucidate the factors relevant to such decisions, in the second part of Chapter 9, I consider the degree to which these elements would benefit efforts to prosecute crimes committed in the four locations. Finally, in the third part, I construct optimal guilty-plea processes for each of these atrocities.

Chapter 10 concludes the book by assessing the efforts to obtain guilty pleas at the ICTY, the ICTR, and the Special Panels in East Timor against the model guilty-plea systems previously developed. Finding these efforts lacking, the chapter also evaluates Rwanda's innovative efforts at participatory justice—its *gacaca* courts—and East Timor's Commission for Reception, Truth, and Reconciliation, which contained accountability mechanisms resembling East Timor's traditional criminal justice processes.

CHAPTER ONE

International Criminal Justice Then and Now

The Long Road from Impunity to (Some) Accountability

The Norms of Impunity

The mass atrocities that we would now label crimes against humanity have been committed since the dawn of humankind but have virtually never elicited criminal sanctions. The mid-nineteenth century saw efforts to articulate and codify rules governing the conduct of armed conflict, but these early codification attempts were aimed at the conduct of states.[18] In response to the horrors of World War II, however, the victorious allies established international tribunals at Nuremberg and Tokyo to prosecute the leaders of the defeated Axis powers. The tribunals had jurisdiction over three crimes: crimes against the peace, war crimes, and crimes against humanity,[19] and the convictions they imposed on German and Japanese leaders were considered a watershed in the nascent movement to hold individuals responsible for mass atrocities. Consequently, efforts were made to consolidate these advances. The Genocide Convention[20] was concluded in 1948 to prohibit what has been described as the most heinous international crime, and the entry into force of four Geneva Conventions in 1950 significantly developed and clarified the laws of war and effectively criminalized certain conduct committed during armed conflict.[21] Efforts were made to develop a comprehensive code of international crimes and to establish a permanent international court in which to prosecute those crimes, but these became mired in Cold War politics.[22] The following thirty years did see some codification advances, however, through the conclusion of human-rights treaties, which clarified and strengthened existing prohibitions and established new ones. Widely ratified conventions on slavery,[23] torture,[24] and apartheid,[25] for instance, require states to criminalize these offenses as part of their domestic criminal law.

Despite these advances in codification, the twentieth century saw countless international crimes, resulting in tens of millions of deaths, yet virtually no prosecutions. Stalin's purges, for instance, resulted in as many as twenty million deaths, which have not only gone unpunished, but largely unacknowledged.[26] Idi Amin's regime murdered and expelled hundreds of thousands of Ugandans,[27] yet he died a free man in 2003 after spending twenty-five years in luxurious exile in Saudi Arabia. Former Ethiopian leader Mengistu Haile Miriam presided over a "red terror" in which many thousands of political opponents were killed,[28] yet he lives in high-security comfort in Harare, Zimbabwe. Hissène Habré of Chad, similarly, is considered responsible for tens of thousands of political murders,[29] yet he continues to live freely in Senegal after feeble efforts to bring him to trial collapsed.[30]

That neither these leaders nor their many thousands of accomplices have been brought to justice should come as no surprise. Mass atrocities are typically perpetrated by state actors or undertaken with their complicity; thus, no domestic prosecutions will take place while the repressive regime remains in power. Prosecutions are difficult to initiate even after the old regime gives way because most transitions do not come about through comprehensive military victories but through negotiation processes. During such negotiations, the promise of amnesty and even continued involvement in the successor government are often vital components of the transfer of power; that is, they are crucial carrots used to persuade embattled rulers to relinquish control through a peaceful transition. Further, the new governments of states that transition to democracy through negotiated transfers tend to be politically and militarily weak. They are often under constant surveillance and pressure from military forces, pressure that prevents them from initiating proactive and controversial measures such as criminal prosecutions. As Carlos Nino put it, politicians in these new governments are "so content with the respite from direct authoritarianism that they d[o] not risk debilitating confrontations."[31]

The wave of democratization that swept the countries of Latin America during the past twenty-five years highlights the impunity that is likely to result when amnesties abound[32] and repressive elements of the former government remain entrenched following ostensibly democratic transitions. In Chile, for instance, Augusto Pinochet and the high command of the Chilean armed forces violently deposed Salvador Allende's democratic government in 1973 and established a harsh police state characterized by widespread human-rights violations. Following the worst of the abuses, Pinochet granted himself and his government a blanket amnesty covering all acts committed since the coup that brought him to power.[33] Although Pinochet later lost the presidency,[34] he nonetheless remained commander in chief of the army, and, before relinquishing control, he passed several last-minute laws designed to protect his position, shield the military from prosecutions, and limit the powers of the new government.[35] Given the circumstances of Chile's transition, criminal prosecutions were never seriously considered. The most that Pinochet's successor, Patricio Alywin, had hoped he could accomplish was to hold trials that would be followed up with pardons, but Pinochet's self-granting amnesty initially was an insuperable obstacle even to that limited form of accountability. Not only did Pinochet continue to command the army, but the new government lacked complete control over the Senate because nine of that body's thirty-five members were appointed by Pinochet or institutions that he continued to control pursuant to the Constitution. Further, Alywin could have little hope that the Supreme Court would invalidate the amnesty law since Pinochet had appointed almost all of the justices.[36] Alywin did create a truth commission, but even with respect to this less-threatening form of accountability, Alywin's "tenuous position . . . relative to the Chilean armed forces" prevented him from framing its mandate in terms antagonistic to the former government.[37] The tide has recently begun to turn, however. Now, nearly thirty years after many of the crimes took place, Chilean courts are sidestepping the amnesty and allowing prosecutions against former military officials to go forward.

Guatemala provides a more recent example of a state unable to prosecute its own international crimes. Succumbing to international pressure, Guatemala agreed to prosecute gross human-rights violations after its thirty-six-year civil war left two hundred thousand dead or disappeared and as many as a million and a half displaced.[38] Five years after the war ended, however, prosecutions have occurred with respect to only one massacre out of more than 422, and that case featured only low-level perpetrators.[39] Guatemala's dismal statistics result largely from the fact that the government took no significant steps to remove those responsible for the atrocities from their positions of power.[40] Consequently, intimidation and corruption have stalled most of the prosecutions that have been undertaken, leading to unjustifiable delays, the dismissals of cases, and the disappearance of key evidence.[41]

By the early 1990s, then, impunity appeared to reign. No international forum had been created to prosecute international crimes, and states largely ignored their international obligations to initiate domestic prosecutions of alleged offenders. It was not until the Cold War had ended and the brutal Bosnian war brought images of starving concentration-camp inmates and tales of systematic rape to television sets around the world that the international community took the first steps in fifty years to bring international criminals to justice.

Tentative Steps: Establishing the Ad Hoc Tribunals and Other Institutions to Prosecute International Crimes

Bosnia-Herzegovina's declaration of independence in March 1992 gave rise to a bloody, three-year war that killed approximately two hundred thousand people and dislocated more than two million others, virtually all through the commission of international crimes (see Chapter 9 for more detail on the Bosnian war). The culture of impunity that had so characterized the fifty preceding years seemed initially also to prevail with respect to the Bosnian conflict. Certainly, the international community had no desire to involve itself militarily in the war. Although the U.N. and human-rights organizations began to document the atrocities in 1992 and 1993, the international community made no attempt to use military might to stop the bloodshed.[42] The Security Council did adopt several resolutions and imposed an economic embargo on Serbia, but these had little practical effect.[43] The Security Council also imposed a no-fly zone over Bosnia when Bosnian Serb aircraft began to attack civilian targets by air;[44] but, at the urging of the United Kingdom and France, the clause providing for enforcement of the no-fly zone was omitted from the resolution, and, over the next six months, more than 465 violations of the no-fly zone were documented but ignored.[45]

While the international community was unwilling, until the very end of the war, to exert the military force necessary to end the atrocities, it did take a path-breaking step to put an end to the impunity that has typically followed such crimes. Specifically, in 1993, the Security Council established the ICTY to prosecute those accused of genocide, crimes against humanity, and war crimes in the former Yugoslavia. And a politically improbable step it was. The Security Council first adopted Resolution 780, which established a commission of experts to investigate violations of international humanitarian law.[46] The negotiations leading to Resolution 780 were acrimonious, and the work of the commission itself was viewed with much suspicion by those who believed that the commission's work would undermine efforts to achieve a political settlement.[47] Indeed, fear that the commission's investigations would disrupt the settlement under negotiation led the Security Council to starve the commission of funding and to terminate it prematurely.[48] The subsequent proposal to create an international tribunal to prosecute those responsible for the atrocities also generated considerable opposition, with many arguing that the tribunal would obstruct peace negotiations and others objecting to its establishment by means of a Security Council resolution.[49] It was consequently considered to be "[a]gainst great odds" that the Security Council did eventually create the ICTY.[50]

The road to the creation of an international tribunal for Rwanda featured similar obstacles. In the span of three months, Rwandan Hutu massacred approximately eight hundred thousand Rwandans, most of whom were Tutsi (see Chapter 9 for more details). The international community made no effort to stop the killings, even though it has been estimated that as few as a thousand troops could have brought the violence to an end.[51] Indeed, a U.N. peacekeeping force was stationed in Rwanda when the killings began, and rather than enlarging it, the Security Council reduced it from 1,515 troops to 270.[52] The international community was likewise reluctant at first to become involved in bringing the perpetrators of the bloodshed to justice. In May 1994, the U.N. Commission on Human Rights issued a report stating that "the authors of the atrocities . . . cannot escape personal responsibility for criminal acts carried out, ordered or condoned,"[53] but it stopped short of calling for prosecutions before an international tribunal. The Security Council was equally reluctant to consider establishing an international tribunal for Rwanda and, indeed, was loathe at the outset even to use the term "genocide" to describe the massacres for fear of triggering the obligations under the Genocide Convention.[54] Once additional facts became available, the Security Council was forced to acknowledge that a genocide was indeed taking place, and, over the objection of some members, it also felt compelled to establish a commission of experts, similar to the one it had established for the former Yugoslavia.[55] Only after several months of inaction, during which the new Tutsi-led Rwandan government vacillated about whether or not it wanted an international tribunal, did the Security Council eventually adopt Resolution 955 providing for the creation of the ICTR.[56]

The creation of the ad hoc tribunals for Rwanda and the former Yugoslavia helped to restart the on-again, off-again negotiations regarding a permanent international criminal court. In July 1998, 120 states voted to adopt the Rome Statute of the International Criminal Court,[57] and the ICC opened its doors in July 2002. Likewise, the establishment of the ad hoc tribunals led to the creation of three hybrid domestic-international tribunals, that is, tribunals that have significant international input but that are in one measure or another grafted onto the judicial structure of the states in question. The U.N. and the government of Sierra Leone agreed in 2002, for example, to establish a Special Court for Sierra Leone to prosecute those most responsible for violations of international criminal law and Sierra Leonean law during Sierra Leone's brutal civil war. Similarly, massive violence following East Timor's secession referendum in 1999 led the U.N. to establish Special Panels in the Dili District Court to prosecute those responsible. Finally, Cambodia and the U.N. agreed in 2003 to establish Extraordinary Chambers in the Cambodian judicial system to prosecute leaders of the Khmer Rouge.

The past decade, then, has witnessed a revolution in the then-nearly dead field of international criminal law. The advances, particularly in attitudes about the need and desirability of criminal accountability following international crimes, are nothing less than extraordinary. Criminal accountability is not the only end worth pursuing, however, and the following section will examine certain nonprosecutorial mechanisms, such as reparations schemes and truth-telling commissions, that can also offer vital benefits to societies emerging from large-scale violence.

Nonprosecutorial Mechanisms: Reparations Schemes and Truth-Telling Commissions

In the past few decades, reparatory and truth-telling mechanisms have emerged as common responses to mass atrocities. Occasionally accompanying criminal prosecutions but most often serving as alternatives thereto, reparations schemes and truth commissions seek—in tangible and intangible ways—to assist victims in moving beyond the violence.

Reparations Schemes

Reparations seek to redress victims' suffering through such measures as financial compensation, restitution, symbolic tributes, and apologies. Although monetary payments can never truly compensate for the grave harm inflicted by an international crime—for the rape, the torture, the disappeared child—many victims of gross human-rights abuses have suffered financially as well as physically and emotionally, so compensation, even if only in token form, has traditionally constituted a primary element of many reparations schemes.

History's most sweeping compensatory effort to date has been Germany's payment of tens of billions of dollars for World War II atrocities.[58] Post-Nazi reparations schemes have been smaller in scale; many provided only token sums, and some distinguished arbitrarily among victim classes. Until recently, Chile's compensation scheme, for instance, granted pensions, educational benefits, and exemptions from military service to the families of those killed or disappeared, but it failed to extend compensation to the thousands who were wrongfully detained and tortured but who survived their ordeals.[59] Argentina's reparations scheme cast a broader net, compensating not only for deaths and disappearances but also for unlawful detentions and torture,[60] but payments had to be stopped in 2002 when the government suspended all payments of interest and principal on its foreign and domestic debts, leaving recipients feeling revictimized.[61]

The South African Promotion of National Unity and Reconciliation Act charged the country's Truth and Reconciliation Commission with recommending reparations for those who suffered "a gross violation of human rights."[62] Compensation was thereby excluded for the vast majority of black South Africans who had not been specifically targeted for torture, detention, or the like but who suffered daily the humiliation and degradation, not to mention the economic privations, that apartheid imposed on blacks. The government initially rejected the commission's recommendation of cash payments and indicated that only symbolic reparations would be forthcoming.[63] Succumbing to intense political pressure in April 2003, however, President Thabo Mbeki announced that his government would pay reparations totaling $85 million to the more than nineteen thousand victims who had testified before the Truth and Reconciliation Commission. The sum promised was less than a quarter of the $360 million that the commission had recommended, so some victims deemed the amount insulting.[64]

Other states, particularly those in Eastern Europe, have placed restitution at the center of their reparations schemes. Czechoslovakia, for instance, enacted a law in 1991 that required the return of property that had been obtained by coercive means.[65] Similarly, the unification treaty unifying East and West Germany provided for the return of most confiscated properties to the former owners or their heirs.[66] South Africa likewise enacted the Restitution of Land Rights Act of

1994, which allowed a Land Claims Court to purchase or expropriate a piece of property from its current owner in order to restore the property right of a person wrongfully dispossessed.[67]

Vexing practical problems complicate efforts to provide monetary reparations. Determining which victims should receive compensation and how to quantify their injuries are only the most obvious. Questions relating to the quantity of reparations are particularly thorny because states emerging from collective violence are especially unlikely to possess the financial resources necessary to make even a credible attempt at compensation. Indeed, establishing reparations schemes in depressed economies such as South Africa and the Eastern European countries raises worrisome questions about whether it is appropriate to grant backward-looking remedies such as financial reparations when doing so may impede the state's ability to carry out current, vitally necessary functions. Other value-laden issues concern whether compensation should be paid in cash or its equivalent or rather should take the form of services, such as health care, education, or psychological assistance. Should individual need be considered, with more impoverished victims receiving greater sums, or should classifications be made solely on the basis of injury? Difficult questions of intergenerational justice arise as well when considerable time has elapsed between the injury and the provision of compensation. In particular, when is it just to require those innocent of wrongdoing to assume the financial burden of past wrongs?[68] The United States faced such questions in 1988 when it established a reparations scheme to redress the wrongs visited upon the Japanese Americans who were interned, more than forty years before, during World War II. For a wealthy country like the United States, the scheme was inexpensive, providing only $20,000 for each surviving individual and totaling an estimated $1.2 billion;[69] hence, it was relatively uncontroversial. More recent calls to provide reparations for the injuries inflicted more than one hundred years ago by slavery and the Jim Crow regime give rise to far more heated debates both because the reparations envisaged are typically of a grander scale and because so much time has elapsed that compensation seems less an effort to remedy specific harms and more an attempt at wealth redistribution. Restitution may seem on the surface a more straightforward way of redressing past wrongs, since returning the particular thing wrongfully taken avoids many of the difficult line-drawing problems associated with compensation schemes; but restitutionary measures too can spark controversy, particularly when considerable time has passed and intervening owners are innocent of wrongdoing or when restitutionary schemes, such as those established in Eastern Europe, seek to advance other goals, such as the transition to a market economy.

The provision of reparations can never wholly repair the lives broken by mass atrocities; reparations can, however, advance healing and reconciliation in a variety of ways. The payment of reparations constitutes an acknowledgment of wrongdoing, which victims may find particularly satisfying if it has been preceded by years of denial. At the same time that reparations assign blame, at least in a general sense, they also serve officially to recognize and rehabilitate victims, many of whom have previously been deemed subversives and enemies of the state.[70] The provision of reparations further "draw[s] a line on the past,"[71] advancing political transitions by creating a sharp distinction between the past repressive regime that acted outside the law to injure its citizens and the present democratic regime that uses legally established methods to compensate those who have been harmed. Indeed, the provision of reparations gives recognition to the principle that wrongs must be redressed, a principle that is all but unknown in states emerging from mass violence. And when reparations schemes require payments from specific offenders, through restitutionary measures or through civil actions such as those brought pursuant to the U.S. Alien Tort Claims Act,[72] they also serve retributive goals. Offenders may be forced to relinquish their ill-gotten gains and may be publicly shamed even in cases where they manage to avoid paying the judgments.[73]

Many of these same goals are furthered as well by symbolic reparations, such as commemorative monuments and days of remembrance, and especially by apologies. As noted above, a government's decision to pay monetary reparations itself is an acknowledgment of wrongdoing; thus, it can be understood to constitute an implicit apology. Express apologies arguably carry even greater symbolic value and have in recent years become a popular governmental response to human-rights violations. U.S. presidents Ronald Reagan and George H. W. Bush, for instance, apologized to the Japanese Americans interned during World War II,[74] while President Bill Clinton apologized to the survivors of a U.S. Public Health Service study that withheld proven medical treatment from a group of African American men with syphilis.[75] Canadian leaders have apologized for the suppression of the Aboriginal language and culture. British Prime Minister Tony Blair apologized for his country's role in the mid-nineteenth-century potato famine in Ireland, and Pope John Paul II apologized for Catholic atrocities during the Counter-Reformation.[76] In 1995, Prime Minister Tomiichi Murayama of Japan offered a general apology for World War II suffering caused by Japan,[77] and, more recently, Japan offered a specific apology to China after thirty-six Chinese fell sick following contact with chemical weapons that Japanese soldiers had left in China at the end of World War II.[78]

The current popularity of apologies stems in part from their inexpensive price tag. Martha Minow consequently describes as "most troubling" those apologies "that are purely symbolic, and carry no concrete shifts in resources or practices to alter the current and future lives of survivors of atrocities."[79] Although apologies linked to tangible efforts to repair the harm are certainly more desirable than apologies alone, pure symbolism, in and of itself, can have tremendous significance, as evidenced by the intense opposition that some apologies generate. Croatian president Stjepan Mesić's 2003 apology to "all those who have suffered pain or damage at any time from citizens of Croatia who misused the law or abused their positions" was sharply criticized by some Croatian politicians, who deemed the apology "shameful and humiliating for all Croatian citizens."[80] Heated debates likewise surround the question of whether the U.S. government should apologize for its nineteenth-century practice of slavery.[81] In Japan, Prime Minister Murayama personally apologized to the so-called comfort women, who were kept in sexual servitude by Japanese soldiers during World War II, but the Japanese government notably did not join in the apology.[82] In establishing a reparations scheme for the comfort women, the Japanese government kept similar distance. Although the government established an Asian Women's Fund to provide payments to comfort women as a means of expressing, among other things, the "Japanese people's atonement," the government refused to fund the payments; they were instead funded through private donations.[83] Only six of the five hundred intended recipients accepted payments, with most refusing them because the funds were not provided by the bodies that were actually responsible for the wrongdoing.[84] Symbolism, in and of itself, clearly matters.

Apologies carry the greatest weight when they are made by the individual wrongdoers themselves in the context of continued ethnic or political tension. Witnesses to South Africa's Truth and Reconciliation Commission hearings have described the profound transformations that took place when perpetrators of the most heinous of human-rights abuses apologized to their victims and saw those apologies accepted. Pumla Gobodo-Madikizela, for instance, observed that after Eugene de Kock apologized to the widows of policemen whom de Kock had killed, one widow was "profoundly touched by him" and both "felt that de Kock had communicated to them something he felt deeply and had acknowledged their pain."[85] In a similar vein, Lyn Graybill describes the son of a murder victim who embraced the perpetrator, saying: "You murdered our father. But we forgive you."[86] And when Truth and Reconciliation Commission Chairman Archbishop Desmond Tutu heard General Johan van der Merwe's apology, he deemed it "an incredible moment" and instructed those assembled to "keep quiet a bit and put our heads down for a minute."[87] As Elizabeth Kiss put it: "While the amnesty process did not require perpetrators to apologize for their actions, commission hearings created an opportunity for repentance and forgiveness. The most extraordinary, and publicly celebrated, moments of those hearings occurred when individual victims and perpetrators reached out to one another and achieved some measure of reconciliation."[88]

Expert witnesses testifying on behalf of former Bosnian Serb leader Biljana Plavšić at her ICTY sentencing hearing similarly lauded her apology as especially significant to efforts to bring peace and stability to the region.[89] Martha Minow observes particularly in relation to an individual apology that victims are empowered: they can "accept, refuse, or ignore the apology," and in this way, they "secure a position of strength, respect, and specialness."[90] Even official apologies can resonate with meaning, as occurred when former Chilean president Patricio Alywin "made an emotional appeal, broadcast on national television, in which he begged pardon and forgiveness from the families of the victims." Chilean survivors frequently cite that apology "as a powerful moment after having their claims brushed aside for so many years."[91]

Truth-Telling Commissions

Truth commissions—bodies charged with investigating and publicizing human-rights offenses—have become perhaps the most popular response to collective violence in recent years. More than thirty truth commissions have been established during the past few decades.[92] Many of these, particularly the early ones, were inadequately funded[93] and subject to political manipulation and threats of violence.[94] More recent truth commissions have generally been considered to constitute more-serious attempts to investigate and publicize the truth about the human-rights abuses under their consideration, although some distortions still occur. For instance, although the Guatemalan Truth Commission was able to issue a lengthy and hard-hitting report, concluding that the Guatemalan

government had perpetrated acts of genocide against some Mayan groups,[95] its
work was severely hampered by limited powers, a short period during which to
complete its mandate, and a prohibition against attributing responsibility to individual offenders. Commissioner Christian Tomuschat labeled the commission's
broad mandate combined with its short life span an "almost incomprehensible
contradiction" that Andrew Keller deemed "consistent with the military's goal of
creating a weak commission."[96]

The Commission on the Truth for El Salvador generated considerable attention largely because the U.N. administered it and appointed internationally re-
spected non-Salvadorans to serve as commissioners. The commission, therefore,
functioned with an independence lacking in many domestically administered
commissions.[97] The most notable feature of the commission's report was the fact
that it named the names of those the commission determined to be responsible
for the human-rights abuses.[98] The Salvadoran government made strenuous efforts to prevent the identification of offenders,[99] but the commission's report explained the commissioners' view that "the whole truth cannot be told without
naming names. . . . Not to name names would be to reinforce the very impunity to
which the Parties instructed the Commission to put an end."[100] One of the most
recent truth commission reports, issued by the Sierra Leone Truth and Reconciliation Commission (Sierra Leone TRC), followed the lead of the Commission on
the Truth for El Salvador and likewise named the names of those bearing responsibility for atrocities,[101] a number of whom had contemporaneously been indicted
by the Special Court for Sierra Leone. The report of the Sierra Leone TRC went
on to lay some measure of blame on the U.N. and the international community,
which it found had "abandoned Sierra Leone in its greatest hour of need."[102] The
report made specific findings with respect to youth, children, and women, and it
dispelled some popular beliefs, such as that the desire to exploit diamonds had
caused the conflict.[103] The Sierra Leone TRC also issued the first-ever "Child-
Friendly Version" of its report, which was prepared with the assistance of Sierra
Leonean child victims.

The Truth and Reconciliation Commission (TRC), established in South Africa following the end of apartheid, built on the experience of predecessor commissions but also introduced innovative features that have led many commentators to consider it the most serious attempt to date to investigate and publicize
human-rights offenses.[104] In establishing the TRC, South Africa broke new ground
by granting the commission broad subpoena and search and seizure powers and
by creating a fairly sophisticated witness-protection program that encouraged

fearful witnesses to come forward. Also exceptional was the public nature of the South African process. Some of the previous truth commissions had held public sessions, but the TRC held vastly more, and these proceedings were the subject of intense media coverage. Indeed, two thousand victims and witnesses appeared in public proceedings, and as Priscilla Hayner describes it:

> [M]ost newspapers ran a number of stories on the commission every day, and radio and television news often led with a story on the most recent revelations from the commission's hearings. Four hours of hearings were broadcast live over national radio each day, and a *Truth Commission Special Report* television show on Sunday evenings quickly became the most-watched news show in the country.[105]

The most revolutionary feature of the South African TRC was its ability to grant individual amnesties for politically motivated crimes. One of the key demands of the outgoing National Party leadership during the transition negotiations was for an amnesty, and it was widely believed that failing to concede to this demand would have led to a bloody insurrection. The African National Congress (ANC), which led South Africa's liberation movement, held sufficient power, however, to withstand calls for a blanket amnesty of the sort that General Pinochet imposed on Chile. Instead, the new South African government offered amnesty to those suspected of human-rights abuses, but it tied that amnesty to a truth-telling requirement; specifically, the Promotion of National Unity and Reconciliation Act gave to the TRC the power to grant individual amnesties for political crimes, but only to those who provided a complete accounting of their participation in those crimes.[106]

It became clear early on, particularly in light of the rigorous disclosure requirements imposed on amnesty applicants, that few offenders would apply for amnesty unless they had reason to fear prosecution.[107] Using the threat of prosecution as a "stick" to motivate offenders to come forward proved only partially effective because the government was unable to conduct enough successful prosecutions to make the threat a credible one. As will be described in greater detail in Chapter 2, the government conducted a few high-profile trials for apartheid-related offenses, and these resulted in convictions and lengthy prison sentences, but the trials were protracted and expensive, so very few were undertaken. Some equally high-profile trials resulted in acquittals, which led many senior-level offenders to discount the risk of conviction and consequently to eschew the amnesty process. Many considered the refusal of high-level political and military leaders to seek amnesty to be a significant failure for the TRC,[108] but the TRC did receive more than seven thousand amnesty applications,[109] and, if these applicants had not come forward, "a lot of truth and lot of reality of that time would have been lost."[110]

Although those amnestied were obviously not subject to criminal sanctions, the disclosures they were required to make did expose them to the punishment of public condemnation. For instance, former president P. W. Botha's "public support withered" after extensive information came to light of his "knowledge or approval of a long pattern of state crimes."[111] A number of police officers reported that their marriages failed after they confessed,[112] notorious South African torturer Jeffrey Benzien suffered a nervous breakdown, and other amnestied perpetrators were shunned by their families and friends.[113]

In addition to imposing some accountability, the amnesty process also involved and empowered victims by permitting them to cross-examine amnesty applicants. "Reversing roles, then, torturers and murderers faced interrogation by their former victims and family members."[114] This sort of face-to-face confrontation and engagement, along with many of the TRC's other innovative features, were intended to facilitate reconciliation, one of the TRC's primary goals. Indeed, the TRC is notable among truth commissions for its focus on reconciliation, on healing, and on forgiveness. TRC hearings did appear to advance these goals in certain cases, but other cases featured recalcitrant perpetrators[115] or victims not yet ready to forgive.[116]

Truth-telling inquiries serve a variety of aims critical to societies emerging from collective violence. Truth commissions first and foremost provide an historical account of the period under question. While many of the early truth commissions sought little more than to detail the bare facts of the atrocities, more recent truth commissions have endeavored in addition to elucidate contextual elements of the violence—the historical underpinnings and the role of various social and governmental institutions, among other things. Thus, the South African TRC, for example, held hearings to illuminate the roles of various sectors of civil society—including business, churches, the media, the medical profession, and the legal system—in supporting and perpetuating apartheid.[117] Such an historical account is especially valuable when the crimes themselves have been shrouded in secrecy. The forced disappearances, so widely perpetrated in Latin American dictatorships, for instance, were in particular need of elucidation, since victims were here one minute and gone the next, leaving loved ones with no clue as to their fate or whereabouts. With respect to such clandestine crimes as these, truth

commissions can provide facts of vital consequence to victims' families, including the location of the body,[118] the manner of death, and the reasons for targeting that particular individual. In other cases, truth commissions serve less to
convey knowledge as to officially acknowledge the violence of which everyone
is unofficially aware. Such acknowledgment is critically important to victims,
whose injuries may have been denied or ignored, and it also can help to open the
eyes of bystanders, who turned willfully blind eyes to the violence taking place
around them. Although trials for international crimes are also intended to create
an historical record, many believe that truth commissions more effectively serve
those ends. Martha Minow, for instance, observes that

> [t]he task of making a full account of what happened, in light of the evidence obtained,
> requires a process of sifting and drafting that usually does not accompany a trial. Put-
> ting narratives of distinct events together with the actions of different actors demands
> materials and the charge to look across cases and to connect the stories of victims and
> offenders. Truth commissions undertake to write the history of what happened as a
> central task. For judges at trials, such histories are the by-product of particular moments
> of examining and cross-examining witnesses and reviewing evidence about the respon-
> sibility of particular individuals.[119]

Truth commissions are also more victim-centered than criminal prosecutions
and consequently can create a more hospitable space for victims to relate their
experiences. In particular, truth commissions typically allow victim testimony to
proceed in narrative form, without cross-examination. Some experts assert that
allowing trauma victims to tell their stories to sympathetic listeners enhances
their prospects for healing.[120] The long lines of victims seeking to testify before
many truth commissions evidences the value such testimony must hold for those
who offer it. Efforts, like that of South Africa, to encourage perpetrators to acknowledge their offenses in addition enhance the potential for healing and reconciliation between offenders and victims. Many victims say that they cannot
forgive their perpetrators, let alone reconcile with them, until the perpetrators, at
the least, acknowledge their crimes.[121] Offenders' candid and complete acknowl-
edgments of wrongdoing provide victims with the opportunity to forgive and can
in addition transform the offenders themselves, leading to reconciliation and the
reintegration of the offenders into the community. Truth commissions can facilitate no-less-dramatic conversions in passive supporters of the oppressive regime
who, through the victims' testimonies, must come face-to-face with their own
complicity and shame. During the second week of South African TRC hearings,

Chairman Archbishop Desmond Tutu read an anonymous letter in Afrikaans sent to the commission. Translated, it reads:

> Then I cry over what has happened, even though I cannot change anything. Then I look inside myself to understand how it is possible that no one knew, how it is possible that so few did something about it, how it is possible that often I also just looked on. Then I wonder how it is possible to live with this inner guilt and shame . . . I don't know what to say, I don't know what to do, I ask you to forgive me for this. . . . It isn't easy to say this. I say it with a heart that is broken and tears in my eyes. . . .[122]

Truth commissions, many contend, advance not only individual healing but societal healing as well. Indeed, commentators routinely assert that unless a broken society confronts the horrors of the past, there will be no stable foundation upon which to build a lasting democracy.[123] Truth commissions can expose the multiple causes and conditions contributing to the atrocities and thereby provide the information necessary to inform structural and institutional reforms aimed at preventing future abuses. To the extent that the "truth" reported by a truth commission is widely accepted, it can provide the basis on which opposing parties can govern together without the latent conflicts and resentment that result from past denials and lies. Even when the "truth" expounded is contested, the very dissension that it creates can prove valuable in exposing subjects that were previously taboo and encouraging a dialogue between those holding opposing viewpoints.

Truth commissions have been described as principled compromises on the question of punishment or impunity. As Ruti Teitel put it: "[T]ruth commission[s] emerged as impunity's antidote and amnesty's analogue."[124] On this view, truth commissions serve some of the ends of criminal trials and thus are a better response to mass atrocities than no response at all, but they nonetheless stand as a poor second-best to criminal prosecutions. As the above discussion indicates, however, more recent experience with truth commissions has shown them to constitute another, distinctly valuable response to large-scale violence—in many ways a complement to trials.

This chapter has traced the emergence of various responses to mass atrocities. Criminal prosecutions stand at the center of these responses and are now typically thought to constitute the most potent tool in any effort to impose accountability after mass violence. Criminal prosecutions are expensive, however, and the following chapter will show that as costs rise, enthusiasm for imposing criminal accountability wanes.

CHAPTER TWO

Financial Realities

Targeting Only the Leaders

The rhetoric surrounding international criminal prosecutions is ambitious and idealistic. The ICTY, for instance, was established to "put an end" to the crimes occurring in the former Yugoslavia and to "bring to justice the persons who are responsible for them,"[125] while the ICC was created "to put an end to impunity for the perpetrators of [international] crimes and thus to contribute to the prevention of such crimes."[126] The likelihood that the international tribunals can meet these, or even less-ambitious goals, is a topic for Chapter 3. This chapter sets the stage for that discussion by detailing the financial constraints impeding the prosecution of international crimes. The following sections—which examine the budgetary difficulties of the ad hoc tribunals, the ICC, the hybrid international-domestic tribunals, and domestic criminal justice systems—will show that, given the large number of offenders and the use of criminal procedures that seek to incorporate due-process guarantees, neither international tribunals nor domestic criminal justice systems can hope to prosecute more than a very small proportion of international offenders.

The ICTY and the ICTR

The ICTY and ICTR began their institutional lives inauspiciously. It took more than a year for the Security Council to agree on a prosecutor for the ICTY, for instance, and understaffing at all levels plagued the ICTR for its first few years. A full year after it was created, the ICTR employed only five investigators and prosecutors, when at least one hundred investigators were needed.[127] Moreover, by the end of 1996, more than a third of the investigator positions and nearly half of all professional positions remained vacant.[128] The ICTR's early years were also tarnished by allegations of mismanagement and corruption.[129] Finally, and most importantly, both tribunals were inadequately funded early on. Insufficient resources impeded the tribunals' ability to obtain needed staff and equipment, to conduct investigations, and to protect witnesses and threatened their very survival at times. One ICTR prosecutor colorfully observed that when she arrived in Arusha in 1995, she and her twelve office mates "created makeshift desks by removing doors from their hinges and placing them on crates . . . [and] fought over garbage cans, which [they] used as chairs. "[130]

The tribunals' funding has increased significantly over the years, and the tribunals have lately been considerably more effective. Their prosecutorial arms issue indictments, indicted people are at least sometimes arrested and transferred to the tribunals,[131] trials are held largely in accordance with due-process guarantees appearing in human-rights conventions,[132] and defendants are acquitted or convicted on the basis of reasonably well-established legal principles. That is the good news. The bad news is the time and money needed to achieve those ends. Prosecuting international crimes is a time-consuming, costly affair. The average ICTY and ICTR trial takes seventeen months to complete,[133] costs millions of dollars,[134] and features several hundred witnesses and exhibits and a transcript spanning more than ten thousand pages. For instance, the ICTY's *Kordić & Čerkez* trial lasted twenty months and featured 241 witnesses, 4,665 exhibits, and a transcript of more than 28,000 pages.[135] The *Blaškić* trial lasted more than two years and featured 158 witnesses and more than 1,300 exhibits,[136] while the more recent *Brđanin* case lasted 21 months and featured 221 witnesses and 3,086 exhibits.[137]

Added to the time needed for trials are lengthy pretrial detention periods; some defendants have been detained for up to four years during pretrial, trial, and appellate proceedings,[138] leading commentators to question whether the tribunals are complying with expeditious trial requirements.[139] The reasons why tribunal proceedings take so long and cost so much include the complex nature of international crimes; the physical distance between the tribunals and the locations of the crimes; the difficulty and expense involved in locating witnesses, transferring them to the tribunals, and providing them the necessary protection;

the delays caused by the need for language translation; the refusal of key states to provide access to documents and other evidence; and the robust due-process protections—including the right to appointed counsel—afforded to defendants.[140]

The considerable length and cost of tribunal trials has generated enormous criticism, and the tribunals have consequently taken steps to expedite proceedings. They asked for and received a pool of *ad litem* judges to increase their ability to hear cases, and they have made more efficient use of courtroom space[141] and better use of judicial resources.[142] The prosecutor has made efforts to join related cases.[143] Finally, the tribunals have amended their procedural rules, eliminating many rules drawn from Anglo-American criminal justice systems and replacing them with more efficient procedures derived from continental European criminal justice systems.[144] These efforts to shorten and simplify tribunal proceedings have improved matters, but they have by no means resulted in short, simple proceedings. Indeed, despite the tribunals' considerable efforts, their statistics remain surprisingly bleak: before the ICTY's spate of guilty pleas in 2003, it had spent ten years and nearly $650 million[145] to dispose of eighteen cases. During the ICTR's first ten years, it spent more than $800 million[146] to dispose of nineteen cases, of which four involved guilty pleas.[147]

The sums required to conduct trials before the ICTY and the ICTR have become so large, in fact, that the international community has lately indicated its unwillingness to continue providing them. In particular, the Security Council has pressured the tribunals to formulate a completion strategy that will enable them to close their doors by 2010,[148] and, although the tribunals may not be able to meet this target,[149] they are endeavoring to comply. To that end, the tribunals have adopted a three-pronged approach. First, they have committed to prosecuting only high-level offenders. As a consequence of this more limited focus, prosecutors drastically reduced the number of investigations they planned to conduct,[150] and a 2004 amendment to the ICTY's procedural rules authorizes the judges themselves to confirm that indictments target only high-level offenders.[151]

Second, the tribunals have attempted to dispose of their cases more efficiently by using plea bargaining to obtain guilty pleas. As the ICTY prosecutor announced to the Security Council in 2004: "Great savings of court time have been achieved by guilty pleas, obtained through the active involvement of my Office. We remain open to explore with the defense the possibility of accused persons pleading guilty to all or some of the charges against them."[152]

Finally, the tribunals have formulated a controversial plan to refer many of their cases to domestic courts. The ICTR prosecutor intends to transfer forty-one cases.[153] By the fall of 2005, the prosecutor had transferred the files of fifteen suspects to the courts of Rwanda,[154] which are already overwhelmed by their efforts to prosecute many thousands of genocide suspects. Some ICTR defendants have boycotted their trials to protest the planned transfers, maintaining that they cannot get fair trials in Rwanda.[155] As for the ICTY, in 2000 its judges considered transferring cases to courts in the Balkans, but then rejected that option, maintaining among other things that "the political climate and the issue of the safety of the witnesses, victims, accused and judges" would make referring cases to Balkan courts impossible in the short term.[156] Subsequent pressure from the Security Council, however, led the ICTY judges to conclude that referring a substantial number of its cases to the courts of the states of the former Yugoslavia would be feasible after all. Consequently, since June 2004, the ICTY prosecutor has sought to transfer the cases of a number of Croatian defendants to the courts of Croatia, despite numerous reports that Croatian trials are plagued by ethnic bias.[157] The *Hrastov* case provides an apt example: in *Hrastov*, a Croatian court found the Serb defendant guilty not only of war crimes but also of a five-hundred-year history of Serb crimes against Croatia.[158] Such cases are not anomalies. Indeed, the vast majority of Croatian prosecutions involve Serb defendants accused of committing war crimes against Croats, and the vast majority of these Serb defendants are convicted in absentia.[159] By contrast, many of the few Croatian defendants who are prosecuted are acquitted.[160] Serbian courts arguably suffer from even graver problems, yet ICTY prosecutors have also sought to transfer cases to Serbian courts.[161] Serbia has prosecuted only a handful of war crimes cases in the nearly ten years since the conclusion of the Dayton Accords, and these proceedings have been characterized by sloppy procedures and witness intimidation.[162] In the trial of Sasa Cvjetan, for instance, both the presiding judge and a witness who testified against Cvjetan received numerous death threats. The witness was granted "protective" measures, but these were carried out by police officers sympathetic to the defendant and amounted to near solitary confinement in a small apartment. One human-rights advocate termed the protective measures "mental torture."[163]

The inability of the Bosnian criminal justice system to prosecute international crimes fairly and competently has been too clear to escape notice. "[S]ignificant structural difficulties" plague the courts of Bosnia and Herzegovina, and these include the "excessive compartmentalization of the judicial systems of the Fed-

eration and the Republika Srpska," the lack of cooperation between the two enti-
ties, the political influence brought to bear on judges and prosecutors, the often
"mono-ethnic" composition of the local courts, the difficulty of protecting victims
and witnesses effectively, the court personnel's lack of training, and the backlog of
cases.[164] To ameliorate some of these difficulties, the ICTY has helped to establish
a special chamber within the State Court of Bosnia and Herzegovina. The special
chamber, which opened its doors in March 2005, has jurisdiction over serious violations of international humanitarian law and is staffed, at least for the time being,
by international judges and prosecutors. But the chamber has relied for its operation on foreign donations, and these have diminished sharply of late. The Bosnian
government maintains that it does not have the funds to support the chamber, and
commentators worry that the chamber will soon face a financial crisis.[165]

Also experiencing financial difficulties are the tribunals themselves. During
2004, numerous states failed to make their assessed contributions to the tribunals, causing significant budgetary shortfalls and resulting, among other things,
in a hiring freeze.[166] Indeed, in an October 2004 address, ICTY prosecutor Carla
Del Ponte reported that she had lost nearly 50 percent of her senior legal staff and
more than 40 percent of her senior investigators.[167] The tribunals have observed
that their budget crisis, ironically, is imperiling the completion strategy that, if
adhered to, will ultimately save the international community substantial funds.[168]
But when the tribunals were forced in 2004 to report to the Security Council that,
because of a number of factors outside of their control, they may not finish their
work in accordance with the completion strategy schedule,[169] the Security Council cut them no slack and instead issued Resolution 1534, which reaffirmed "in the
strongest terms" the Security Council's commitment to the timetable articulated
in the completion strategies.[170]

The ICC

The ICC can be expected to fare similarly, if not worse, when it comes to the
time and resources necessary to conduct trials. Indeed, the ICC is apt to suffer
all of the delays and inefficiencies that plague the ad hoc tribunals plus more besides. The ICC's preeminently inefficient feature is its complementarity regime.
The ad hoc tribunals have primacy over national courts; that is, they have the
authority to order national courts to discontinue proceedings and transfer defendants to the tribunals. The ICC, by contrast, operates under the principle of

complementarity, which means that a case is inadmissible before the ICC when it is being investigated or prosecuted by a state that has jurisdiction over it, or when the case has already been investigated and the state has decided not to prosecute. In such circumstances, the ICC may proceed only when the state is "unwilling or unable genuinely" to investigate or prosecute.[171] Although it is appropriate for states to investigate and prosecute international crimes when they are willing and able to do so because states typically have more resources, better developed criminal justice systems, and a greater ability to gather evidence and arrest suspects, the complementarity regime established by the Rome Statute creates enormous practical complications for the efficient processing of ICC cases.

When initiating an investigation, the ICC prosecutor must notify all states parties and those states that would normally exercise jurisdiction over the crime involved. States have one month to inform the prosecutor that they are investigating or have investigated the matter, and they can request the prosecutor to defer to the state's investigation. If the state makes such a request, the prosecutor can apply to the Pretrial Chamber for authorization if the prosecutor wishes to proceed with the investigation, notwithstanding the state's request. Either the state or the prosecutor can appeal the Pretrial Chamber's decision, but the prosecutor must suspend the investigation until the court makes its decision.[172] Other parties may also challenge the jurisdiction of the court or the admissibility of the case, including the defendant and a state from which acceptance of jurisdiction is required,[173] and each challenge is presumably appealable. These challenges have the capacity to delay the work of the ICC considerably not only because of their number but also because the legal questions raised therein are apt to be complex and difficult to decide. Deciding, for instance, whether a state is "unable to conduct a prosecution" may require the court to determine, among other things, the extent to which a state is exercising effective control over its territory, the existence of a functioning law enforcement apparatus, and the state's ability to secure necessary evidence; that is, complicated, fact-based questions that will often be colored by political considerations. Proving that a state is "unwilling" to carry out a prosecution will be no easier. The court may be called upon to determine whether the proceedings are being undertaken "for the purpose of shielding the person concerned from criminal responsibility" or are not being conducted independently or impartially.[174]

Additional inefficiencies will result from the fact that the ICC's workload will be inconstant. Unlike the ad hoc tribunals, which were established after the atrocities had already occurred, the ICC's jurisdiction extends only to crimes occurring after the Rome Statute entered into force. Consequently, the ICC's caseload is indeterminate. It is apt to be small at the outset and fluctuate, perhaps considerably, over the years. With an indeterminate and fluctuating caseload, comes an indeterminate and fluctuating need for staffing. The ICC presidency may propose increasing or decreasing the number of judges when the workload justifies such changes, but any increase or decrease must be approved by a two-third's majority of states parties.[175] Sadly, the experience of the ad hoc tribunals presages an unfortunate lag time between a backlog of cases and the inauguration of new judges to relieve it. The president of the ICTR, for instance, requested a pool of *ad litem* judges on July 9, 2001, but that request was not acted upon until thirteen months had elapsed.[176] Large institutions typically find reducing staff even more problematic, and proposals to reduce the number of ICC judges are apt to give rise to particularly sensitive political issues since states may be tempted to oppose the reductions when they would result in the dismissal of judges who are their nationals.

Levels of nonjudicial staffing are likely to be similarly, if not more, suboptimal because the different cases may require staff having different expertise. Translators pose the most obvious example of this problem. The ICTY and the ICTR have themselves had considerable difficulty keeping up with their need for language translation, even though the languages in need of translating have been known from the tribunals' inceptions. The ICC's difficulties will be all the greater because it will have to acquire the services of different sets of translators to work on cases arising in different parts of the globe. Additionally, the ICC has six official languages—four more than the ad hoc tribunals—into which all judgments and decisions resolving fundamental issues must be translated.[177] Field-office staffing will pose another set of problems. The ad hoc tribunals have used field offices located near crime scenes to provide support for crime-scene investigations and greater access to witnesses, documents, and other evidence. Establishing and staffing such field offices for ICC cases is apt to prove costly and time-consuming because they will have to be created, staffed, and dissolved in numerous locations throughout the world.

The ad hoc tribunals, and especially the ICTY, have experienced considerable difficulty obtaining state cooperation and enforcement of tribunal orders.[178] The ICC is apt to suffer even greater problems because its enforcement powers are less robust than those of the ad hoc tribunals.[179] The Security Council imposed the ICTY on the former Yugoslavia and consequently was able to include a strongly worded provision, stating that states *"shall* cooperate" with the ICTY in the investigation and prosecution of defendants and *"shall* comply without undue delay with any request for assistance or an order issued by a Trial Chamber" (emphasis added).[180] Although the powers the ICTY possesses on paper have rarely translated into full cooperation, the ICC does not even possess such paper powers. Although article 86 of the Rome Statute does require states to "cooperate fully with the Court in its investigation and prosecution of crimes within the jurisdiction of the Court," the statute also contains a number of loopholes and exceptions that will allow states easily to avoid cooperation.[181] The most worrying loophole concerns requests implicating states' national security interests. States parties to the Rome Statute need not comply with requests for cooperation when "the request concerns the production of any documents or disclosure of evidence which relates to its national security."[182] That the request need only "relate[]" to national security to prevent the cooperation obligation from arising shows the potential breadth of this exception. Some states had sought, in addition, the ability to refuse requests on the ground that compliance would be prohibited by national law.[183] Such a broad, potentially devastating, exception was rejected in the end, but the Rome Statute does permit states to refuse a request to cooperate when complying with it would violate "an existing fundamental legal principle of general application."[184]

The Rome Statute fails also to place on states an unqualified obligation to arrest and surrender defendants. States may, for instance, refuse to surrender a person sought by the ICC when the state is under an existing international obligation to extradite the person to another state that is not party to the Rome Statute.[185] The Rome Statute further does not require surrender when the person sought is being proceeded against or serving a sentence in the requested state for a crime different from that for which the ICC seeks him or her.[186] A state may also refuse a request for surrender or other assistance if complying with it would require the state to act inconsistently with its international law obligations pertaining to diplomatic immunity of a person or property of a third state, or if compliance would violate an international agreement pursuant to which the requested state requires the consent of a sending state before surrendering a person of the sending state to the ICC.[187] It is pursuant to this latter provision that the United States has sought to conclude agreements with Rome Statute states parties in an effort to prevent them from transferring American nationals to the ICC.[188] Finally, states can postpone compliance with a request when its immediate execution would interfere with an ongoing investigation or prosecution of a case different from that to which the ICC request relates.[189]

The powers of the ICC are limited in other ways that will also impede the court's functioning. For one thing, the ICC appears to possess no power to subpoena witnesses. Further, the powers of the ICC's prosecutor to conduct on-site investigations without the consent of the state on which the investigation is to take place are severely circumscribed. The Rome Statute does permit the ICC prosecutor to undertake specific investigatory steps on a state's territory without having obtained consent from the state but only if authorized by a Pretrial Chamber, which can give that authorization only after finding that "the State is clearly unable to execute a request for cooperation due to the unavailability of any authority or any component of its judicial system competent to execute the request" using the ordinary channels.[190] One commentator deemed the prosecutor's power one that "is not practicable and cannot be effectively utilized."[191] Finally, even when cooperation is forthcoming, the Rome Statute's frequent references to national procedures are apt to complicate the cooperation process. ICC requests for arrest and surrender, as well as for other forms of assistance, must be in accordance with national procedures.[192] The observation of national procedures seems, on the one hand, a token and harmless nod to state sovereignty, yet it has the potential to increase costs and cause delay, as the ICC will be unable to prepare standard cooperation forms but will instead have to research the (perhaps difficult-to-ascertain) procedures of the numerous states from which it will be seeking assistance.

As noted above, the Rome Statute imposes no express limitations on the number of cases that the ICC can hear, but even before the court formally began its work, insiders had acknowledged that financial constraints would restrict the ICC to prosecuting, at most, six cases per mass atrocity. Similar, if more express, constraints have been imposed on the hybrid international-domestic tribunals of Sierra Leone, East Timor, and Cambodia, which are discussed in the following section.

Hybrid International-Domestic Courts in Sierra Leone, East Timor, and Cambodia

Sierra Leone's eleven-year civil war, with its signature amputations, was unspeakably brutal.[193] The war left as many as two hundred thousand dead, many at the hands of child soldiers, some of whom were only seven years old when they were abducted and forced to fight.[194] After the war ended, the government of Sierra Leone negotiated an agreement with the U.N. secretary-general for the establishment of an independent Special Court.[195] Although the circumstances giving rise to the creation of the Special Court strongly resemble those leading to the establishment of the ad hoc tribunals, the Security Council did not respond in like fashion but rather endeavored to create something of a tribunal-lite. In particular, frustration with the high cost and slow pace of the ICTY and ICTR led the international community to create a "court [that] operates under a tight budget directly controlled by the U.S. and other donor countries, with a three-year timetable and a limited mission."[196] So, unlike the statutes of the ICTY and ICTR, which give those tribunals "the power to prosecute persons responsible for serious violations,"[197] the Security Council insisted on limiting the Special Court's jurisdiction only to those "persons who bear *the greatest responsibility* for serious violations of international humanitarian law and Sierra Leonean law" (emphasis added),[198] a jurisdictional provision that has been interpreted as restricting prosecutions to between twenty and twenty-five individuals.[199] The Security Council failed to provide adequate financing even for this limited mandate, and, as a consequence, the Special Court indicted only thirteen individuals.[200]

Unlike the ICTY and ICTR, which were established by means of Security Council resolutions and thus are subsidiary organs of the U.N., the Special Court is a treaty-based organ and does not receive an assessed share of the U.N. budget. This fact is not coincidental. Indeed, the Security Council insisted that the Special Court be financed through voluntary contributions,[201] and it was the ad hoc tribunals' ever-increasing budgets that led the Security Council to refuse to establish another subsidiary organ.[202] U.N. Secretary-General Kofi Annan strongly objected to voluntary funding, maintaining that a special court "based on voluntary contributions would be neither viable nor sustainable."[203] This prediction came to pass. By 2003, the Special Court faced a financial crisis so severe that its operation could not be guaranteed beyond the end of the year. An appeal for voluntary contributions brought in enough funds to see the court through 2003,[204] but in March 2004, the Special Court faced a $20 million funding shortfall, necessitating the U.N. secretary-general again to appeal to the Security Council to fund the court through assessed rather than voluntary contributions.[205] This appeal went unheeded, and by October 2005, the court was again seeking additional contributions to allow it to continue its work in 2006.[206] The insecure nature of the court's funding has led court staff to devote extensive time to fund-raising rather than to court operations, and it has prevented the hiring of necessary staff since funding for the relevant positions has been uncertain. In August 2004, the Special Court's registrar, Robin Vincent, tendered his resignation, a move prompted in large part by his frustration over the lack of financial support he received.[207]

The Special Court's funding shortfall bodes especially poorly because the court's budget is so spare to begin with. The U.N. secretary-general had originally estimated a first-year budget of approximately $22 million, which is less than one-quarter of the ICTY's and the ICTR's current budgets.[208] But informal consultations indicated that the U.N. could not hope to secure anywhere near that amount from voluntary contributions, so a revised budget was prepared granting the Special Court $16.8 million for its first-year's costs[209] and $56 million for its entire three-year life span.[210] The Special Court currently appears set to continue its work for longer than three years and to cost more than its original budget,[211] but critics nonetheless maintain that the meager budget and the speed with which trials must be conducted threaten to impair important due-process protections in Special Court proceedings. Budgetary constraints, for instance, have in particular hampered witness-protection efforts and the ability of defense counsel and defense investigators to prepare cases for trial.[212]

Similarly, in East Timor, the international community talked the talk of criminal justice but was unwilling to back up that talk with adequate financing. In August 1999, after a referendum in which 78.5 percent of the East Timorese voted against remaining within Indonesia, heavily armed groups favoring the Indonesian retention of East Timor conducted a "scorched earth" campaign during which they "burned and looted entire towns and villages, attacked and killed at random, and kidnapped nearly 200,000 people to the western half of the island that was still controlled by Indonesia."[213] After sending security forces to halt the violence, the Security Council adopted Resolution 1272, establishing the U.N. Transitional Administration in East Timor and empowering it to exercise all legislative and executive authority, including the administration of justice.[214]

Pursuant to that authority, the secretary-general for East Timor created Special Panels for Serious Crimes in the Dili District Court to prosecute particularly serious crimes, including genocide, war crimes, and crimes against humanity.[215] Although the success of the Special Panels was substantially impeded by Indonesia's refusal to cooperate in surrendering suspects,[216] the Special Panels were able to prosecute eighty-seven (mostly low-level) defendants and convict eighty-four of them before the U.N. stopped funding the panels in May 2005.[217] The legal provisions under which these crimes were prosecuted as well as the provisions relating to individual criminal responsibility are nearly identical with those of the ICC, and the Special Panels' procedural rules included the full range of due-process guarantees found in leading human-rights instruments.[218] However, this "state of the art system for prosecuting international crimes"[219] was not matched with the necessary financial support.

At their inceptions, the Special Panels did not possess the resources to employ secretaries, court reporters, stenographers, or law clerks. The absence of support staff meant that judges had to answer their own phones and even move their own furniture, while the absence of court reporters meant that cases were con-ducted without official transcripts.[220] The Special Panels, further, were so severely understaffed in interpreters that many hearings had to be postponed,[221] and some judgments were issued in only one of the panels' official languages, even though judges on that very panel were unable to read the judgment.[222] Interpreters were at times required to work for extensive periods, without breaks, and in some cases, a substantial number of witnesses spoke languages for which there were no official interpreters so that translation had to be performed by interpreters work-ing in the prosecutor's office[223] or even, occasionally, the East Timorese judge on the panel. The dearth of interpreters additionally meant that witness question-ing at times proceeded through multiple translations; for instance, to enable one defense counsel to question a witness in the *Los Palos* case, three interpreters were required, and from the point at which a question was asked until the coun-sel received a reply, six interpretations were made.[224] Further, some interpreters of the less-common East Timorese languages had little experience in transla-tion; one Bunak translator repeatedly summarized the witnesses' testimony in the third person, despite the panels' repeated requests that he instead translate the witness's actual words.

Insufficient resources at the Special Panels also forced prosecutors to charge most of the early defendants with domestic crimes, such as murder, under the In-donesian Criminal Code, rather than charging more time-consuming, difficult-to-prove crimes such as crimes against humanity.[225] Inadequate funding in ad-dition impaired defendants' rights to legal representation. The Special Panels conducted their work on a meager $6.3 million annual budget, and, at the outset, virtually none of those funds were allocated to defense costs. In addition, in the Special Panels' early days, there were less than a dozen public defenders for all of the criminal cases in East Timor, both serious crimes proceedings and ordinary criminal proceedings.[226] As a result, defense attorneys had virtually no ability to undertake investigations in early cases, and indeed, not a single defense witness was called to testify in the first fourteen trials at the Special Panels, not even in the *Los Palos* case, a massive case charging crimes against humanity against ten defendants. As one *Los Palos* defense counsel put it: "We do not have witnesses. We wish we did."[227] He and other defense counsel complained that they lacked both cars and the time to travel to the districts to interview potential witnesses, as well as resources to provide witnesses with transport to court and to pay for their food and lodging while in Dili.[228] In addition, the scarcity of defense counsel led one to send a standardized letter to investigators authorizing the investigators to question his clients when he was not present and including a list of rights to be read to the defendant before the interview.[229]

The Special Panels had difficulty attracting and retaining international judges, and lack of funding proved a substantial cause. The U.N. envisaged establishing two Special Panels, but because it was unable to recruit the requisite number of international judges, only one panel was operational for most of the court's first year.[230] As a result, when that panel would, for some reason, refuse to accept a defendant's guilty plea, that same panel would conduct the defendant's trial.[231] In addition, some trials had to be postponed for lengthy periods of time due to judicial absences. The *Lolotoe* case, for instance, was adjourned for five full months, while the defendants remained in pretrial detention, because, in the words of the chief judge, it proved "impossible . . . to assemble the judges for the continuation of the trial."[232] The inability to attract international judges likewise forced the Appeals Chamber to stop functioning for eighteen months,[233] preventing numerous defendants from appealing their convictions.

Although some improvements were made, most of these problems remained throughout the five-year life span of the Special Panels. The panels continued to struggle in the face of tremendous human and material resource limitations, and the frequent unavailability of judges and interpreters continued to result in postponed trials and excessive pretrial detentions. Plea bargaining became routine at the Special Panels, a development that I will discuss in more detail in Chapter 6, but even with the use of that device, the Special Panels were unable to complete their investigations and prosecutions before U.N. funds ran out in May 2005. Approximately 1,400 people were killed during the 1999 violence in East Timor, yet the ninety-five indictments filed before the Special Panels accounted for only

572 of those murders.[234] Less than a third of the defendants charged in those indictments were able to be brought before the Special Panels while a significant number of crimes were never even investigated,[235] a failure that the U.N. secretary-general attributed to "the need to comply with the deadlines set by the Security Council."[236]

Efforts to prosecute Khmer Rouge leaders in Cambodia have met with similar difficulties. During its approximately four years in power during the 1970s, the Khmer Rouge was responsible for more than two million Cambodian deaths. The Khmer Rouge summarily executed between one hundred thousand and three hundred thousand people and relocated millions of city dwellers to the countryside, which led to the deaths of 1.5 to 2 million people from starvation, disease, and physical exhaustion.[237] Negotiations between the U.N. and the government of Cambodia for a tribunal to prosecute Khmer Rouge leaders began in 1997[238] but stalled five years later, when the U.N. found itself unable to agree to Cambodia's terms. The U.N. believed that the proposed judicial body "would not guarantee the independence, impartiality and objectivity that a court established with the support of the United Nations must have."[239] Negotiations resumed a year later, and this time the U.N. capitulated to many of Cambodia's demands; thus, in March 2003, the parties signed an agreement to establish Extraordinary Chambers in the Courts of Cambodia. Like the Special Court for Sierra Leone, the Extraordinary Chambers will conduct its work for a scant three years and is expected to prosecute only ten or twelve senior Khmer Rouge leaders.[240] The U.N. has estimated that approximately $57 million will be needed to fund the tribunal for its three-year existence,[241] and reminiscent of its position on the Special Court for Sierra Leone, the U.N. General Assembly has again insisted on funding the Extraordinary Chambers through voluntary rather than assessed contributions. Although the $57 million three-year budget constitutes a mere fraction of the sums that the ICTY or the ICTR spend annually, key donors initially refused to contribute, complaining that the price was too high.[242] The U.S. Senate and House of Representatives went so far as to introduce bills prohibiting the United States from providing financial support to the Extraordinary Chambers.[243] Trials were scheduled to begin in 2007, but by February 2006, the Extraordinary Chambers still faced a $9.6 million funding shortfall.[244]

The foregoing indicates that to the extent international criminal prosecutions are politically viable, they will be financially viable only if they are limited to very small numbers. The ICTY and ICTR have had to call off investigations and make plans to send some of their cases to ill-equipped domestic courts; the Special Court for Sierra Leone labors under a severely restricted jurisdictional mandate and does not possess the funds to fulfill even that; the Special Panels in East Timor closed in May 2005 without completing many of the planned prosecutions; and the ICC has opened its doors with the expectation that it can prosecute no more than six cases per atrocity. Since virtually everyone agrees that, if prosecutions must be limited, they should target senior political and military figures, the international prosecution of international crimes currently appears restricted to the high-level architects of the atrocities, leaving mid-level implementers and low-level executioners free from sanctions.

Domestic Prosecutions

Domestic prosecutions of international crimes offer the potential to prosecute a greater proportion of offenders because domestic trials are apt to cost less than their international counterparts. The salaries of court staff and the fees paid to appointed defense attorneys are generally lower in many of the developing nations in which mass atrocities frequently occur, and travel expenses are insignificant compared with the costs incurred by the ad hoc tribunals, which are located far from crime sites. On the other hand, many of the factors that render international prosecutions so expensive also increase the costs of domestic prosecutions of international crimes. International crimes are complex and difficult to prove, whether prosecuted domestically or internationally. To prosecute murder as a crime against humanity, for instance, the prosecution must prove not only that the defendant killed the victim but that the murder took place as part of a widespread or systematic attack against a civilian population. To prosecute grave breaches of the 1949 Geneva Conventions, the prosecution must prove that the offenses took place in the context of an international armed conflict. Proving these contextual elements can take days or weeks of court time. Domestic prosecutions can reduce trial time by charging domestic crimes, such as murder, in lieu of international crimes, but even trials for domestic crimes can be lengthy and costly when they involve high-level offenders who did not themselves perpetrate the violence. In addition, although some domestic prosecutions will not require language translations, many will. South Africa has eleven official languages;[245] although English is the only official language for court proceedings, the fact that many defendants and witnesses do not speak English means that South African proceedings often feature multiple language translations.[246] Similarly, because East Timorese defendants and witnesses may speak Tetum, Indonesian, Portuguese, or any one of a number of local dialects, most of the translation costs required for the cases being heard by the Special Panels would also be incurred if trials were to proceed through purely domestic processes.[247] Finally, witnesses who testify in the prosecutions of international crimes are prone to suffer retaliatory violence, regardless of whether their testimony is heard before an international or domestic court. The ICTY and ICTR allocate a considerable portion of their budgets to victim and witness-protection units, and domestic criminal justice systems must also spend significant funds if they are to provide adequate protection. When one additionally considers that the criminal justice systems of states emerging from widespread violence are often in shambles, it becomes clear that even in those rare cases where political obstacles to domestic prosecutions do not exist, domestic courts may be wholly ill-equipped to undertake such prosecutions.

Financial constraints have already impeded the few domestic prosecutions of human-rights violations that have taken place in recent years. South Africa, for instance, pledged to prosecute offenders who failed to apply for amnesty before that nation's Truth and Reconciliation Commission; it did initially attempt prosecutions, but ultimately their costs proved too high.[248] Although South African prosecutors were able to obtain a conviction against Eugene de Kock for six murders and eighty-three other crimes,[249] his trial lasted eighteen months, featured more than one hundred witnesses, and cost South African taxpayers more than $1.25 million.[250] The trial of former Minister of Defense Magnus Malan and his sixteen codefendants lasted nine months, cost $2 million, and ended in the acquittal of all of the defendants.[251] In a similar vein, Dr. Wouter Basson was acquitted of charges that he supplied deadly drugs to military agents to enable them to murder enemies of the government but only after a trial that lasted thirty months and featured two hundred witnesses and thousands of pages of evidence.[252] The few other high-profile trials undertaken in South Africa were similarly expensive and time-consuming.[253] Even the proceedings against former South African president P. W. Botha for the minor offense of failing to comply with a subpoena issued by the South African TRC, for instance, lasted nearly nine months. Most domestic criminal justice systems would have difficulty sustaining the costs of such prosecutions, and the South African criminal justice system—which has been so underresourced as to be labeled "virtually dysfunctional"[254]—had no hope of doing so. Indeed, in the years following the negotiated transfer, the

South African criminal justice system was unable even to prosecute the vast bulk of the ordinary crimes occurring on the streets of South Africa.[255] Its deficiencies were so severe that many South Africans felt compelled to exercise private vengeance on those suspected of committing crimes.[256] It is not surprising, then, given these circumstances, that South Africa failed to conduct large-scale human-rights prosecutions after the initial, expensive few were completed.

Rwanda's criminal justice system was in a far graver state of disrepair following the shattering violence of 1994; consequently, its early, ambitious attempts to prosecute the more than one hundred thousand genocide suspects were characterized by widespread due-process violations, largely resulting from lack of funding. In many cases, defendants were detained for years in overcrowded prisons. They had no access to legal counsel, and some had never been formally charged or even verbally informed of their alleged crimes.[257] By 2001, the criminal justice system's complete inability to process the genocide cases was apparent and led to the establishment of informal community tribunals, called *gacaca* courts (see Chapter 10).

Insufficient resources have also impeded Ethiopia's effort to prosecute the large-scale atrocities committed during the repressive seventeen-year Dergue regime. During the Dergue rule, tens of thousands of Ethiopians were tortured, murdered, or disappeared, and the transitional government that assumed power after the Dergue was overthrown in 1991 promptly arrested approximately two thousand former government officials. A Special Prosecutor's Office was created to handle these prosecutions, but its lack of resources and the inexperience of its staff have impeded its ability to carry out its work.[258] No defendants were charged until the end of 1994[259]—more than three years after their arrests. Nongovernmental organizations (NGOs) expressed concern in addition that defendants had not been provided with adequately resourced defense counsel and that the government had interfered with defense counsel's access to defendants.[260] Although prosecutors had amassed a large quantity of physical and testimonial evidence, its financial inability to conduct appropriately expeditious trials that comport with due-process guarantees led Human Rights Watch to suggest the use of plea bargaining to dispose of cases.[261] Prosecutors apparently have not followed that advice: by 2004 approximately one thousand defendants remained imprisoned pending trial,[262] and trials continue to date.[263]

In Chile, domestic prosecutions were initially foreclosed by the blanket amnesty that General Pinochet granted himself and his underlings. In recent years, however, judges have sidestepped the amnesty by holding that "disappearances" in which the fate of the victim is unknown are ongoing crimes that fall outside of the time period covered by the amnesty.[264] In consequence, hundreds of former military officials are now eligible for prosecution,[265] and some have already been sentenced to terms of imprisonment.[266] Because these trials moved slowly and featured evidentiary impediments, Chile's then president Ricardo Lagos proposed a bill in 2003 that would have granted immunity to people who came forward of their own accord to divulge information about the crimes and that would have granted reduced or commuted sentences to those who provided information on the whereabouts or fate of the "disappeared."[267] Victims opposed these measures,[268] and the bill was defeated in March 2005, but many believe that such accommodations will be necessary if successful prosecutions are to take place.[269]

A final fact bedeviling domestic efforts to prosecute international crimes concerns the large number of offenders who are typically implicated in such crimes. Because most international crimes are perpetuated by hundreds if not thousands of individuals, even well-resourced criminal justice systems will rarely have the means to prosecute every last offender. Lines must be drawn, and those lines, in many cases, will assign a substantial portion of offenders to the impunity column. It nonetheless remains vitally important to critically evaluate where those lines should fall. In a numerical sense, the question may be whether to prosecute six offenders, sixty, six hundred, or six thousand. In a more analytical sense, the question may be whether to prosecute only those who masterminded the atrocities and implemented them at the highest levels of authority or whether to extend prosecutions to those closer to the ground—to local leaders who carried out local implementation and to at least some low-level offenders who themselves killed, raped, tortured, and otherwise destroyed lives. The following chapter examines these questions by exploring the ways in which criminal prosecutions serve or fail to serve the goals they are intended to advance. The chapter reaches the somewhat self-evident conclusion that more is better when it comes to the prosecution of international crimes. More interestingly, the chapter explores *why* more is better and how conducting only a few, token prosecutions may as easily undermine those efforts.

CHAPTER THREE

Do the Numbers Count?

*The Ends Served by International Criminal Prosecutions
in Societies Emerging from Mass Atrocities*

The Nuremberg and Tokyo tribunals were expected to usher in an era of accountability for international crimes, but although the fifty years that elapsed after the creation of those tribunals saw many thousands of international crimes, virtually no criminal prosecutions took place. The importance of the ICTY's creation in 1993, then, cannot be overestimated; a veritable revolution in attitudes regarding the need for criminal accountability following mass atrocities has been wrought in little more than a decade. However, as Chapter 2 demonstrated, the "criminal accountability" currently being sought is being sought from only a small proportion of offenders. Prosecutions of international crimes are said to advance a variety of penological goals, including retribution, deterrence, incapacitation, and rehabilitation. Prosecutions are further said to promote other ends of value specifically to societies recently torn by large-scale violence, such as encouraging acceptance of the rule of law, minimizing the likelihood of collective blame, and creating an accurate historical record. Whether the prosecution of international crimes advances any or all of these goals has lately been subject to question, but assuming for the sake of argument that they do, then the question arises as to whether these goals are advanced when prosecutions are limited to a small number of (usually) high-level offenders. The following discussion suggests that, although in many cases the ends served by international prosecutions are nominally the same as the ends served by the prosecution of domestic crimes, in fact, these goals take on different contours in the context of large-scale violence—differences that indicate an especially compelling need for a substantial number of prosecutions. The discussion further reveals that undertaking a substantial number of prosecutions is all the more necessary when attempting to serve purposes specifically designed to benefit conflict-riven societies. In sum, for prosecutions to come close to generating the benefits for which they are credited, there must be an expansion of the selective, token prosecutions that characterize the current approach to international criminal justice.

Retribution

Retributive theories of justice posit that punishment is a necessary and appropriate response to wrongdoing, not because the punishment deters future crimes or leads to any other desirable societal end, but because wrongs must be denounced and those who perpetrate them punished. Retribution, then, is not future-oriented but rather focuses on the past and demands that each and every wrong that deserves punishment receive punishment.[270] It almost goes without saying, therefore, that since retribution requires that all wrongs be punished, the greater the percentage of wrongs that are punished, the better retributive goals are served. The theoretical requirement that punishment attend each and every wrong routinely gives way, however, to practical realities. No criminal justice system is able to prosecute all crimes, and criminal justice systems seized with international crimes are even less equipped than most to approximate comprehensiveness. But the fact that universal prosecution is unattainable cannot justify a prosecutorial scheme that sets out to prosecute only the tiniest proportion of offenders. Such a scheme, indeed, stands as a mockery of the retributive ideal.

Although certain research suggests that victims are not as retributive as is popularly believed,[271] victims of international crimes do typically express a desire for some retribution. Sanja Ivković's study of victim perceptions in the Balkans, for instance, showed that the overwhelming majority of victims surveyed advocated punishment for those who had committed international crimes on retributive grounds, that is, because "[e]veryone should pay for the crimes they have committed."[272] The retribution desired by most victims of international crimes is not focused on the leaders who orchestrated the atrocities but rather is aimed primarily at the so-called "low-level perpetrators," those who generate little interest at the international tribunals but whom victims perceive to be directly responsible for bringing life, as they knew it, to an end. While most commentators agree that the senior political and military leaders—those who plan the atrocities and use hate-based propaganda to incite ordinary, law-abiding people to brutalize former friends and neighbors—carry the greatest responsibility for the crimes, this reality is not the reality most compelling to victims. Although it is the Slobodan Miloševićs and Charles Taylors of the world who orchestrate the conflicts, the nightmares of victims are peopled not by leaders such as they but by the Sierra Leonean rebel who amputated the victim's arm, or by the Bosnian Serb prison guard who forced the victim to castrate his own son. When victims desire personal vengeance, it is these low-level offenders on whom they set their sights.

Although victims' desires for retribution cannot be given undue weight when determining the appropriate scope of prosecutions, the current approach to international criminal justice threatens to ignore victims' views entirely. Criminal prosecutions are optimistically credited with substituting for and thus helping to prevent vigilantism,[273] but if they are to serve that function, they must run sufficiently broad and deep actually to quell the vengeful inclinations of a substantial number of victims. The need to bring retribution into the individual towns and villages that have been shattered by violence is especially pressing because in many cases, after the atrocities cease, victims must continue to coexist in those same towns and villages with those who inflicted the harms. A man who is forced to interact with his mother's rapist at the local market, or his son's murderer at the village well, may not be able to suppress his desire for private vengeance. Indeed, in defending her early attempts to prosecute a range of both high-level and low-level perpetrators at the ICTY and ICTR, Prosecutor Carla Del Ponte made just this point, arguing that unless local leaders are also prosecuted, "the ordinary population will not come to terms with the past, and the process of reconciliation and building a stable peace will suffer accordingly."[274]

Deterrence

Deterring the commission of future crimes is a key justification for the imposition of criminal sanctions for domestic crimes, and supporters of trials for international crimes similarly credit those proceedings with helping to deter future atrocities. The Security Council established the ICTY while the Yugoslavian conflict was still underway with the express goal of deterring international crimes,[275] and both it and the ICTR consider deterrence to be one of their most important ends.[276] Similarly, the Rome Statute establishing the ICC cites deterrence as a reason for creating that institution.[277]

Despite the optimistic rhetoric, systems of international criminal justice are not sufficiently pervasive or mature to act as effective deterrents. The threat of an ICTY prosecution seemingly deterred none of the major actors in the Yugo-slavian conflict. The Bosnian war's single most horrific crime—the execution of approximately seven thousand men and boys in Srebrenica—occurred in 1995, two years after the ICTY was created. Three years after that, Slobodan Milošević launched an expulsion campaign against Kosovar Albanians with full knowledge that the crimes fell within the ICTY's jurisdiction. That the existence of interna-tional tribunals has failed to deter mass atrocities should come as no surprise. Criminal justice experts assert that deterrence is effected not primarily by the severity of punishment but by the certainty of punishment.[278] That is, the more likely offenders consider prosecution to be, the more likely they are to be de-terred from committing offenses. Since most international offenders know with near certainty that they will never face prosecution, the trials that do take place have little, if any, deterrent effect. Although the developments in international criminal justice over the past ten years have put the architects of mass atrocities at marginally greater risk, the sad fact remains that most atrocities will go unpun-ished. The same political and military impediments to prosecutions that resulted in widespread impunity throughout the years since World War II will continue to hinder efforts to prosecute human-rights abusers, if perhaps to a slightly lesser degree. The international community's recent willingness to send former Libe-rian president Charles Taylor into comfortable exile despite the fact that the Spe-cial Court for Sierra Leone had issued a warrant for his arrest only underscores the fact that in many cases peace continues to be bought at the price of justice.

Because many instances of collective violence will be followed by no prosecu-tions, it arguably becomes all the more crucial, for deterrence purposes, to prose-cute well those instances of collective violence that do prove themselves politically amenable to criminal prosecution. Although the nascent state of international criminal justice mechanisms renders it unrealistic to expect substantial deter-rence to result from the prosecution of international crime, prosecuting a signifi-cant number of low-level and mid-level offenders of one atrocity could have some deterrent effect on soldiers in neighboring armies who have little personal stake in the underlying hostilities but great personal stake in avoiding a prison sentence. Deterrence of mid-level and low-level offenders is furthermore of no small con-sequence given their vital importance to any plan to conduct widespread human-rights abuses. For mass atrocities to be carried out, leaders must enlist the ser-vices of hundreds or thousands—indeed, sometimes tens of thousands—of their citizens. Rwandan officials required the help of more than one hundred thousand

Hutu to exterminate approximately eight hundred thousand Tutsi and moderate Hutu in the spring of 1994. Deterring those on the ground, then, can substantially reduce the violence. Indeed, John Braithwaite and Brent Fisse have demonstrated in an analogous setting that the most effective way to deter corporate crime is to focus deterrence efforts not on the criminal who has the most to gain from the crime but on "a softer target" who has preventative capabilities.[279] Deterring low-level offenders is a difficult task because, under the best of circumstances, a significant percentage of them will not be prosecuted and because genocidal leaders make use not only of potent racist propaganda and misinformation to incite their citizens to violence, but also threats and incentives. But a prosecutorial strategy that targets not only those who masterminded the violence but at least some of those who carried it out must be considered a vital first step in encouraging defiance among individuals who might otherwise be inclined to blindly follow genocidal orders.

Prosecuting low-level defendants might additionally help to deter high-level architects of violence by making it more likely that these leaders too will be convicted. The Nazis left Nuremberg prosecutors a voluminous paper trail, but more recent *génocidaires* have learned that relying on oral orders and obscuring the relevant chains of command prove a safer course. So, prosecutors seeking to implicate Slobodan Milošević in the Bosnian atrocities, for instance, were forced to gain information from sometimes-hostile insider witnesses.[280] These witnesses face condemnation and perhaps even violent retaliation for providing the information prosecutors seek; thus, such witnesses are not apt to make damaging disclosures unless they face some other threat—such as the threat of prosecution—through which that information can become a commodity for trade. Tribunals, such as the Special Court for Sierra Leone, which has indicted all of thirteen people, have little hope of gaining such information because they have no credible "stick" by which to threaten low-level offenders who are not otherwise inclined to disclose it.

Incapacitation

The ICTY has stated that imposing long prison sentences on tribunal defendants enables the tribunal "to protect society from the hostile, predatory conduct of the guilty accused."[281] When the tribunals prosecute high-level offenders, however, it is not only the hostile and predatory conduct of the *accused* themselves that the tribunals incapacitate but, more importantly, the accused's ability to incite hostile and predatory conduct in others. Indeed, in candid moments, ICTY employees acknowledge that a primary function of the tribunal is to get nationalists such as Slobodan Milošević and Vojislav Šešelj off the street, as it were; that is, to remove them from the realm of national politics where they would otherwise continue to sow the seeds of ethnic and religious hatred.[282] In a similar vein, the arrests of high-level Rwandan officials responsible for the 1994 genocide helped to prevent further violence by incapacitating their military attacks against Rwanda's postgenocide government.[283] And the lengthy failure to arrest former Liberian president Charles Taylor enabled him to continue to promote violence in Liberia from his Nigerian exile. While in exile, Taylor reportedly continued to control the government army, communicating by cell phones with commanders and receiving ministers.[284]

With respect to domestic crimes, more convictions means better incapacitation because more offenders are incapacitated. However, in the international sphere, the incapacitation returns of increasing convictions are diminishing because many perpetrators of international crimes do not need to be incapacitated. Most low-level perpetrators of international crimes are people who were formerly law-abiding and who would have remained law-abiding had large-scale ethnic, religious, or nationalist conflict not intruded into their villages, towns, and lives.[285] That is, many low-level perpetrators are not violent people, but rather are people who became violent because of the violence that ripped through their regions. Without relieving such offenders of responsibility for their crimes, it remains the case that imprisoning them serves little the end of incapacitation because such offenders do not need to be removed from society. Once the large-scale contextual violence ceases, so too does their individual violence. The Rwandan genocide starkly highlights this phenomenon, for there a substantial portion of the previously law-abiding population picked up machetes and slaughtered their neighbors, daily from dawn till dusk. Spurred on by threats, incentives, and inflammatory radio broadcasts that portrayed Tutsi as "cockroaches" bent on destroying Hutu, more than one hundred thousand Hutu wielded their machetes and "went to work," as the slaughter was euphemistically described, butchering every Tutsi they could find in an effort to eliminate them from the face of the earth.[286] Imprisoning more than one hundred thousand formerly law-abiding Rwandans, as the Tutsi-led Rwandan government did in the years following the genocide, may serve some penological goals, but incapacitation is not likely to be one of them.

The goal of incapacitation can be advanced, however, by increasing the number of prosecutions targeting mid-level perpetrators—those offenders who held positions of local or regional leadership—because their status could enable them to assume greater power in the future and to stoke the passions underlying the violence. The international criminal bodies, as they are currently operating, have only limited ability to target these mid-level offenders, even though removing them from the local political scene by imprisonment could well advance regional peace and security.

Rehabilitation

A state that seeks to rehabilitate its criminals is a state that seeks to transform them from people who break the law into people who respect and comply with the law; that is, the state seeks to bring those who have strayed from legal and societal norms back into the fold. Rehabilitation plays an entirely different role in the context of international crimes because international crimes are committed within a fold that is itself outside the fold. In other words, because societies riven by violent conflict are typically governed by hate-based norms, the actions of international offenders often not only fail to breach prevailing moral standards but in fact exemplify them. Journalist Philip Gourevitch observed, for instance, that during the Rwandan genocide, "the work of the killers was not regarded as a crime in Rwanda; it was effectively the law of the land."[287] Thus, rehabilitating international offenders envisages a renunciation not only of their own behavior but also of the norms of the twisted society from which that behavior sprang.

Rehabilitation has been largely abandoned as a penological goal in the United States,[288] but when it was in vogue, it centered primarily on providing treatment to incarcerated offenders in an effort to prevent recidivism. As noted in the discussion of incapacitation, recidivism is not so pressing a problem in the international context. International offenders are not likely to repeat their offenses, with or without treatment, absent the context of violent conflict in which the original offenses took place. International offenders are, however, apt to retain the deeply held racist, nationalistic, or religious views that motivated their offenses, and these views can not only impede reconciliation but, under certain circumstances, can precipitate future conflict. How one goes about rehabilitating violent ultranationalists, for instance, is far beyond the scope of this book. Suffice it to say that attempting to counteract the hate-based misinformation on which their actions are founded and seeking to promote empathy and dialogue between conflicting groups are efforts that may have a rehabilitory effect both on individual offenders and on the society as a whole.

Domestic rehabilitation efforts traditionally have taken place while offenders are incarcerated, so, assuming that the rehabilitation efforts are efficacious,[289] the more offenders who can be incarcerated, the more rehabilitation that will be achieved. The approach used for domestic crimes may not succeed when the offenders are guilty of international crimes, however, given the political context in which international crimes take place. The widespread incarceration of Hutu in Rwanda, for instance, has likely increased group cohesiveness and ethnic hatred, as most Hutu view the imprisonment as victor's justice, rather than the imposition of the rule of law.[290] Indeed, given the nature of the rehabilitation required in the context of international crimes, it may be that rehabilitation efforts must begin earlier, not at incarceration, but during the criminal prosecution itself. If so, the relevant question may not be how many prosecutions take place, but what kinds of prosecutions take place. Criminal trials, particularly those conducted pursuant to adversarial procedures, do not typically promote self-reflection, empathy, or candid dialogue, but rather require litigants to call all doubts in their own favor in order to present their "best case" to the fact-finder. Adversarial proceedings, thus, do not encourage defendants to engage in honest self-examination, but rather encourage them to frame their actions in the most defensible light. A large-scale effort to obtain guilty pleas might, by contrast, encourage the kind of critical self-evaluation desirable for purposes of rehabilitation.

Whether it *will* so encourage honest reflection is a far more difficult question to answer and one that will be taken up in Chapter 7. Many critics of domestic plea bargaining maintain that trading leniency for self-conviction inspires in defendants not insightful self-awareness but resentful cynicism about the criminal justice system and a belief that they have "gotten away with something."[291] At the same time, the anguished testimony of some South African amnesty applicants, who were required to make full and public disclosure of their crimes to receive amnesty, evidences the transformations that can result from a candid acknowledgment of wrongdoing, even when compulsorily made. In most cases, the racist or nationalist views that motivated the lower-level offenders to pick up their weapons against their neighbors were purposely and systematically inculcated by leaders and mass media. The public renunciation of these views, especially when proffered to obtain benefits, will not likely carry the same didactic force as the original hate propaganda, but it can create a space to express differing viewpoints and to begin to undermine the demonization of the victim class that precipitated the conflict.

Goals Specific to Societies Emerging from Large-Scale Violence

In addition to the penological goals described above that are also implicated in the prosecution of domestic crime, the prosecution of international crime is said to advance ends particularly valuable to societies that have been ruptured by widespread violence. Serving these ends, however, typically requires the undertaking of more than a mere token number of prosecutions.

Prosecutions of international crimes are understood, for instance, to affirm the rule of law, an affirmation desperately needed in states where governmental lawlessness has been the norm.[292] However, whether the prosecution of international offenders does indeed signify a society's adherence to (or the international community's imposition of) the rule of law depends, at least to some extent, on how many prosecutions take place. In particular, the decision to prosecute only a handful of offenders does not manifest an embrace of the rule of law. As Ruti Teitel put it, "Fundamental to the rule of law is the notion that the law applies with equal force and obligation to all."[293] Legal norms prohibiting violent behavior, for instance, are norms of universal applicability that should be universally enforced. Practical impediments preclude the universal enforcement of legal norms, both in the domestic context, where, for instance, nonviolent property crimes routinely go uninvestigated and unprosecuted, and in the international context, where the large number of offenders can quickly overwhelm the capabilities of most criminal justice systems. A criminal justice system need not prosecute all of the crimes within its jurisdiction to be perceived as adhering to the rule of law, but undertaking a mere token number of prosecutions while leaving the vast bulk of offenders unthreatened could do more to undermine acceptance of the rule of law than to advance it. Citizens accustomed to governmental corruption and lawlessness are likely to view such token prosecutions as more of the same rather than as a break with the past. Teitel compares the thousands of World War II prosecutions with the far smaller number of ICTY prosecutions and observes that "the highly selective prosecutions of the ICTY seem to circumscribe the very rule of law that they are designed to instantiate. The policy of selective prosecutions thus underscores the elusive quality of the transformative project of the ICTY, a project that gestures toward a liberal rule of law which the project can bring itself at most merely to symbolize."[294] Undertaking token prosecutions in addition raises the risk of creating martyrs of the few who are brought to justice. Martha Minow observes that in such situations "[t]he distinction between law and politics seems all but erased and the truth-seeking process seems subordinated to public spectacle and symbolic governmental statements—and thus perpetrators begin to look like victims of the prosecutorial regime."[295]

Because prosecutions assign blame to specific offenders, they are said to diminish the victims' propensity to blame collectively all those in the offenders' group. That is, by individualizing justice, criminal prosecutions enable victims to pinpoint their anger at particular perpetrators and discourage them from demonizing entire racial or religious groups. As Martha Minow puts it, a prosecution's "emphasis on individual responsibility offers an avenue away from the cycles of blame that lead to revenge, recrimination, and ethnic and national conflicts."[296] Justice is not likely to be individualized, however, unless a sufficient number of individuals are in fact brought to justice. A small number of prosecutions—targeting only those in senior leadership positions—is not apt to serve this goal, and, in fact, such prosecutions could be seen, counterproductively, as evidencing the blameworthiness of the entire group. It bears repeating that no matter what procedures are used, many international offenders will go unprosecuted, so many victims will be denied the satisfaction of seeing punished the people who directly caused their injuries. That said, a broader prosecutorial strategy that targets at least some mid-level government officials and low-level sadists will enhance efforts to direct victims' wrath at appropriate targets.

Trials also serve a truth-telling function, even if only as a subsidiary aim, and for this reason, the ad hoc tribunals consider one of their primary purposes to be the creation of an historical record. The ICTY's first judgment in the *Tadić* case, for instance, contains a lengthy discussion of the historical and contextual elements framing both the larger conflict that enveloped Bosnia-Herzegovina and much of the former Yugoslavia, as well as the regional conflict in Opstina Prijedor, the scene of Tadić's crimes.[297] The ICTY's efforts notwithstanding, it is widely acknowledged that criminal trials are not the most effective vehicles for the explication of historical truth. Jurisdictional requirements frequently force prosecutors to focus on certain types of evidence and tell certain aspects of stories that effectively minimize other equally important aspects.[298] Further, a trial's focus on select individuals impedes its ability to elucidate the complex events and relationships that culminate in large-scale violence. Finally, procedural rules designed to protect defendants' rights often serve to obscure rather than reveal relevant facts. What little capacity trials do have to create an accurate and nuanced historical record is further limited when prosecutions are few and target only high-level defendants. As Mark Osiel observes, "the past can have little relevance to the present when it is understood as a story about how the evil few led the innocent many astray."[299]

Finally, trials of international crimes pit good against evil in a courtroom morality play. Indeed, at their most theoretical, trials allow the prosecution and defense to present competing visions of reality, which thereby encourage a candid dialogue about the conflict, its causes, and its effects. Mark Osiel argues that a "traumatized society that is deeply divided about its recent past can greatly benefit from collective representations of that past, created and cultivated by a process of prosecution and judgment, accompanied by public discussion about the trial and its result."[300] Osiel consequently has developed a provocative theory about the value of human-rights prosecutions, maintaining that they can be instrumental in the formation of collective memory and social solidarity. Osiel contends that trials of large-scale atrocities should be "unabashedly designed as monumental spectacles," for when trials are "effective as public spectacle, [they] stimulate discussion in ways that foster the liberal virtues of toleration, moderation, and civil respect."[301] Osiel believes that the law's traditional concern with retribution and deterrence should be deemphasized in the aftermath of large-scale brutality because in that context, "the need for public reckoning with the question of how such horrific events could have happened is more important to democratization than the criminal law's more traditional objectives."[302] According to Osiel, trials of widespread human-rights violations "present moments of transformative opportunity in the lives of individuals and societies."[303] These moments should be capitalized on in order to inculcate principles of liberal morality. To that end, Osiel asserts, judges and prosecutors should pay "close[] attention to the 'poetics' of legal storytelling, i.e., to the way in which an experience of administrative massacre can be framed within the conventions of competing theatrical genres."[304] The judicial task should be to "employ the law of evidence, procedure, and professional responsibility to recast the courtroom drama in terms of the 'theater of ideas,' where large questions of collective memory and even national identity are engaged."[305]

Osiel's focus on the way criminal prosecutions are conducted may seem to have little relevance to the question of how many prosecutions should be undertaken. The trials Osiel envisages are the monumental ones—the Nuremberg and

Tokyo trials, the Argentine junta trial, Israel's trial of Adolf Eichmann. It is these well-publicized trials of well-known personages that have the greatest capacity to create collective memory and effect transformative change. Osiel's insights are not completely without relevance to my discussion, however, because they can be applied to efforts designed to increase the number of prosecutions that can be undertaken. Defendants' guilty pleas can be viewed purely in market terms, as cut-and-dried exchanges in which defendants agree to self-convict solely to obtain sentencing concessions. Or that act of pleading guilty can be viewed as a transformative experience in which defendants acknowledge their culpability and renounce their behavior. Chapter 8 will expand on this insight and will contend that judges and prosecutors who wish to use plea bargaining as a means of increasing criminal accountability in the international realm will do well to heed Osiel's advice to attend to "the 'poetics' of legal storytelling," that is, to construct a guilty-plea system that self-consciously seeks to advance peace and reconciliation.

Summary

The foregoing discussion reveals that increasing the proportion of international offenders who are prosecuted better serves most of the goals that those prosecutions are intended to advance. As importantly, perhaps, the discussion also indicates that undertaking a very small number of prosecutions can prove counterproductive; that is, it can undermine rather than advance some of the aims of criminal prosecutions. So far, then, the terrain is not especially controversial. While human-rights advocates of a few decades ago sought to persuade the international community and states to prosecute *some* international offenders, with that aim achieved, today's human-rights advocates should be trying to persuade the powers-that-be to conduct more criminal prosecutions—a substantial number, not just a token few. That pitch, however, is a hard sell. The most recently established international tribunals—the Special Court for Sierra Leone, the Extraordinary Chambers, and the ICC—have targeted only a very small number of high-level offenders. The ICTY, ICTR, and Special Panels cast a broader net but have had financial difficulty prosecuting their larger pools of indictees and have lately resorted to plea bargaining to assist them in carrying out their prosecutions. The following three chapters describe and analyze the plea bargaining that has taken place at these institutions as a precursor to evaluating in Chapter 7 whether efforts to obtain guilty pleas for international crimes are justified.

CHAPTER FOUR

Plea Bargaining at the ICTY

The international criminal tribunals established in the 1990s were created amidst a heady optimism and no small measure of naiveté. While the mandates of the tribunals' progeny have been carefully circumscribed from their outsets, the ICTY, ICTR, and Special Panels were not initially so constrained. The statutes of the ICTY and ICTR, for instance, provide, rather vaguely, that those tribunals are to prosecute "persons responsible for serious violations of international humanitarian law,"[306] while Regulation 2000/15 of the U.N. Transitional Administration of East Timor (UNTAET), establishing the Special Panels, likewise contained no limiting language.[307] Although these bodies investigated and ultimately indicted only a small percentage of the individuals responsible for the relevant crimes, they each did indict more than a handful of suspects.[308] Commentators have criticized the seemingly random nature of the indictments, particularly those emanating from the ICTY, which seemed initially to target high-level offenders, low-level offenders, and a host of offenders in between with little apparent scheme or strategy. At the time the indictments were issued, however, the tribunals operated without any express completion date so that the prosecution of a substantial number of indictees of all levels seemed feasible. That perception of feasibility declined in recent years as the U.N. Security Council made plans to stop funding the Special Panels in May 2005 and began seeking the closure of the ICTY and ICTR. As noted in Chapter 2, the advent of these completion dates motivated the tribunals to adopt docket-clearing strategies, one of which has been plea bargaining.

After a brief description of guilty-plea procedures at the current international tribunals, this chapter will analyze the plea-bargaining and guilty-plea practices of the ICTY. Then Chapters 5 and 6 will provide a similar analysis regarding these practices of the ICTR and the Special Panels.

Guilty-Plea Procedures at the International Tribunals

Although it was not expected at their inceptions that the ICTY and ICTR would heavily utilize plea bargaining, the tribunals' initial set of procedural rules did envisage the possibility of a defendant pleading guilty. Consequently, unlike many continental European criminal justice systems that contain no procedure for defendants to waive their rights to a trial, Rule 62 of the ICTY's and ICTR's Rules of Evidence and Procedure provides that when defendants are brought to a Trial Chamber for their initial appearance, the Trial Chamber shall call upon them "to enter a plea of guilty or not guilty on each count."[309] The procedural rules, as initially promulgated, contained no further guidance regarding guilty pleas, and when the ICTY's first case involved a defendant who desired to plead guilty, that lack of guidance proved problematic. Dražen Erdemović was charged with one count of a crime against humanity, and in the alternative, one count of a violation of the laws or customs of war. In his initial appearance before the Trial Chamber, Erdemović pled guilty to the count of a crime against humanity. The Trial Chamber accepted Erdemović's guilty plea, dismissed the alternative war-crimes count, and sentenced him to ten years' imprisonment.[310] Erdemović appealed on a number of grounds, and the Appeals Chamber took the opportunity to set forth what it described as the "pre-conditions" that must be satisfied before a Trial Chamber can accept a guilty plea: that the guilty plea be voluntary, informed, and unequivocal.[311] These requirements and an additional requirement that the plea be supported by a sufficient factual basis were later included in an amendment to the ICTY's and ICTR's procedural rules.[312] In subsequent amendments to the procedural rules, the ICTY and ICTR each added a provision governing the conclusion of plea agreements. The rule authorizes prosecutors to enter into plea agreements wherein the prosecution agrees to amend the indictment, to submit that a specific sentence or sentencing range is appropriate, or to decline to oppose the defendant's sentencing request. The rule further provides that the plea agreement will not be binding on the Trial Chamber but must be made known to it.[313]

The Special Court for Sierra Leone has not yet received any guilty pleas, but because its procedural rules are identical to those of the ICTR, any guilty pleas it might receive must also satisfy the conditions described above. As for the Special Panels in East Timor, its procedural rules governing guilty pleas are nearly identical to those of the ICC. Like the ICTY and ICTR, the ICC and the Special Panels require that guilty pleas be informed, voluntary, and supported by the facts of the case. The rules of the ICC and Special Panels, however, bestow on judges greater authority over the guilty-plea process. In particular, the rules provide that where the court is convinced that a more thorough presentation of the facts is required in the interests of justice, particularly taking account of the interests of victims, the court can request the prosecutor to present additional evidence, including the testimony of victims, or it can conduct a full-scale trial. The procedural rules of the ICC and Special Panels further state that "[a]ny discussions between the Prosecutor and the defence regarding modification of the charges, the admission of guilt or the penalty to be imposed shall not be binding on the Court."[314] At the time of this writing, the ICC has had no occasion to interpret this rule because it has obtained custody over only one defendant, and he has not pled guilty.[315] The Special Panels, by contrast, had frequent recourse to the guilty-plea procedures during its life span because many East Timorese defendants entered ambiguous guilty pleas that either were not entirely consistent with the charges or that suggested confusion about the consequences of the guilty pleas. These will be discussed in Chapter 6; the following section examines the plea-bargaining and guilty-plea practices that have developed at the ICTY.

Plea Bargaining at the ICTY

Early Guilty Pleas

Although the ICTY's procedural rules have always envisaged the possibility of guilty pleas, in its early years the ICTY made no particular effort to encourage defendants to plead guilty. Indeed, when the tribunal was first established, plea bargaining was considered a distasteful and unnecessary procedural device. Few defendants were in the dock at that time, so little pressure existed to expedite proceedings through the use of bargaining. In addition, the vital task with which the tribunals had been entrusted—to bring justice to war-torn lands through the prosecution of those responsible for mass atrocities—seemed too noble to be sullied by bargaining. For that reason, when the United States proposed a provision in the tribunal's procedural rules authorizing the prosecution to grant defendants full or partial testimonial immunity in exchange for their cooperation, the proposal was rejected.[316] Then-ICTY president Antonio Cassese put it thus: "The persons appearing before us will be charged with genocide, torture, murder, sexual assault, wanton destruction, persecution and other inhuman acts. After due reflection, we have decided that *no one* should be immune from prosecution for crimes such as these, no matter how useful their testimony may otherwise be." [317] Whether or not the ICTY now provides testifying defendants full-scale immunity is not currently clear;[318] what is clear is that the ICTY provides testifying defendants, and even defendants who have no information about which to testify, significant sentence reductions for pleading guilty. Nineteen ICTY defendants pled guilty between 1994 and 2005,[319] with eleven of those defendants tendering their guilty pleas just since May 2003.[320] During these eleven years and nineteen guilty pleas, a profound transformation has occurred in the way that guilty pleas are obtained and rewarded at the ICTY.

The ICTY's first two guilty pleas were not obtained through plea bargaining at all. The first ICTY defendant to plead guilty was Dražen Erdemović, a Bosnian Croat foot soldier who had only reluctantly joined the Bosnian Serb army just before that army launched the Srebrenica massacres (which are discussed in Chapter 9). Within the span of a few days in July 1995, Bosnian Serb forces summarily executed more than seven thousand Bosnian Muslim men and boys in the area of Srebrenica. Erdemović and his fellow soldiers shot and killed approximately twelve hundred Muslims during a five-hour period, with Erdemović killing approximately seventy of them.[321] Erdemović stated that he initially refused to carry out the executions but was threatened with instant death. He was told, "If you don't wish to do it, stand in line with the rest of them and give others your rifle so that they can shoot you." [322]

The ICTY had never heard of Dražen Erdemović until Erdemović brought himself and the massacre in which he participated to the tribunal's attention. While in Belgrade, Erdemović made several attempts to contact the tribunal, mostly through journalists to whom he told his story, and these attempts led Yugoslav authorities to arrest him.[323] He was subsequently transferred to the tribunal[324] and, as noted above, he was charged with one count of a crime against humanity, and in the alternative, one count of a violation of the laws or customs of war. Immediately upon his arrival at the tribunal, Erdemović provided the prosecution with a great deal of information about the Srebrenica massacres,[325] and, on his initial appearance before the Trial Chamber, he pled guilty to the count of a crime against humanity.[326] Erdemović testified on behalf of the prosecution in a number of cases,[327] and he repeatedly expressed remorse about what had happened at Srebrenica.[328] As noted above, Erdemović was initially sentenced to ten years' imprisonment, but the Appeals Chamber vacated his guilty plea, determining that it was not informed. After Erdemović subsequently expressed his willingness to plead guilty to the war-crimes charge, he and prosecutors entered into a plea agreement in which both parties agreed that "seven years' imprisonment would be an appropriate sentence in this case."[329] Despite the appearance of a bargain, however, prosecutors repeatedly informed the Trial Chamber that Erdemović proffered his guilty plea without any offer or expectation of leniency.[330]

The ICTY's next guilty plea, tendered by Bosnian Serb Goran Jelisić, also was not brought about through plea bargaining. Jelisić was the de facto commander of the Luka detention camp, the camp to which Muslim men were transported and imprisoned following the Serbs' May 1992 attack on Brčko, in northeastern Bosnia. Jelisić presented himself to his Muslim detainees and later to the tribunal as the "Serbian Adolf" and allegedly told the detainees that 70 percent of them were to be killed and the remaining 30 percent beaten. Jelisić reportedly declared that he had to execute twenty to thirty people in a morning before being able to drink his coffee and allegedly kept detainees informed of the running count of Muslims that he had killed.[331] In an amended indictment, Jelisić was charged with one count of genocide and thirty-nine counts of crimes against humanity and violations of the laws or customs of war.[332] Jelisić pled not guilty to the count of genocide, but, after he indicated his willingness to plead guilty to thirty-one of the war-crimes and crimes-against-humanity counts, the parties prepared an "Agreed Factual Basis for the Guilty Pleas to be Entered by Goran Jelisić," and the prosecution dropped the eight remaining war-crimes and crimes-against-humanity counts.[333] In the "Agreed Factual Basis," Jelisić admitted to killing thirteen people, severely beating some of his victims with truncheons and clubs before killing them. He also admitted to inflicting bodily harm on four people and stealing money from the Luka camp detainees.[334]

The Trial Chamber held a trial on the genocide count and acquitted Jelisić after hearing only the prosecution's submissions.[335] At the presentencing hearing on the counts to which Jelisić had pled guilty, the prosecution sought a sentence of life imprisonment, the harshest sentence available at the ICTY.[336] By seeking a life sentence for Jelisić, the prosecution patently provided Jelisić nothing for his guilty plea. Indeed, according to one of Jelisić's lawyers, Jelisić pled guilty over his lawyers' objections on the mistaken belief that his guilty plea would be considered substantial cooperation with the prosecution.[337] In fact, prosecution lawyers told Jelisić that they would offer him nothing for his plea, and true to their word, they sought the harshest available sentence. The prosecution did withdraw eight of the thirty-nine counts of war crimes and crimes against humanity, but according to the prosecution it did so as a result of evidentiary deficiencies, not to grant Jelisić a concession.[338] The Trial Chamber likewise gave Jelisić nothing for his guilty plea. Although it did not impose on Jelisić a life sentence, it came close, sentencing him to forty years' imprisonment for the crimes to which he had pled guilty.[339] The Trial Chamber asserted that it "considered [Jelisić's] guilty plea out of principle," but it went on to observe that Jelisić was fully aware of photographs that showed him committing some of the crimes and "demonstrated no remorse . . . for the crimes he committed." Accordingly, the Trial Chamber accorded "only relative weight to his plea."[340]

The seventeen guilty pleas that followed Jelisić's did involve plea bargaining, but the nature and scope of the bargaining has changed dramatically over the years. Stevan Todorović's plea, the first to result from bargaining, seemed in many respects idiosyncratic. Todorović was allegedly arrested by means of kidnapping and delivered to NATO forces in Bosnia-Herzegovina (SFOR).[341] He consequently challenged the legality of his arrest and, in doing so, obtained an order from the Trial Chamber requiring SFOR and the states participating in SFOR to provide Todorović with wide-ranging and potentially embarrassing information about his arrest.[342] NATO and the United States, among other states, vehemently objected to the order; soon after, the prosecution offered Todorović a sentencing discount to secure his guilty plea and the withdrawal of his troublesome challenge to his arrest. After *Todorović*, the rate of guilty pleas remained slow and relatively stable until 2003, when eight cases were disposed of by means of guilty pleas, double the number of trials that took place during that year.[343] That increase resulted from a variety of factors, but most prominent was the prosecution's intense need to adhere to the tribunal's completion schedule. That need has manifested itself not only in a greater willingness to plea bargain cases that in past years would have gone to trial but also in an increase both in the kinds of plea bargaining practiced and in the value of the concessions bestowed on defendants who plead guilty.

The Introduction of Charge Bargaining

In the first several ICTY plea bargains, negotiations took place over sentencing recommendations only. When a prosecutor is engaged in charge bargaining, by contrast, he or she will agree not to charge certain crimes or to dismiss charges already brought in exchange for the defendant's guilty plea. Although some of the plea agreements in the early ICTY cases saw the withdrawal of certain charges, those withdrawals did not constitute bargaining over charges because the withdrawn charges were either not supported by sufficient evidence, or their withdrawal did not affect the factual basis of the conviction or the eventual sentence imposed. As noted above, the prosecution's withdrawal of eight charges in the *Jelisić* case resulted from evidentiary deficiencies. Prosecutors in *Todorović*, moreover, withdrew a whopping twenty-six of the twenty-seven original counts, but the withdrawals did not constitute charge bargaining because the one count to which Todorović pled guilty was the most serious of the charges, and it contained the factual allegations appearing in all of the withdrawn charges.

In 2002, however, ICTY prosecutors introduced charge bargaining in the case of Milan Simić. Simić had been indicted in the same indictment that charged Stevan Todorović and others with atrocities committed in the area of Bosanski Šamac. After Bosnian Serb forces took over Bosanski Šamac, Simić was appointed president of the executive board of the Bosanski Šamac Assembly, and in that position, he apparently implemented the policies and regulations of the Serb Crisis Staff and War Presidency and was responsible for the governmental affairs of the municipality.[344] Simić was charged with one count of persecution as a crime against humanity and two counts of torture as crimes against humanity, two counts of inhumane treatment as a crime against humanity, and two counts of cruel treatment as a violation of the laws and customs of war.[345]

The persecution count alleged that Simić participated in a number of persecutory acts including the unlawful detention and confinement of Bosnian Croat and Bosnian Muslim civilians in inhumane conditions, the torture and beating of Bosnian Croat and Bosnian Muslim civilians, and the implementation of orders of the Serb Crisis Staff, which infringed on the basic and fundamental rights of Bosnian Croat and Bosnian Muslim civilians. The counts of torture, inhumane treatment, and cruel treatment related to beatings that Simić, along with his subordinates, inflicted on five Bosnian Muslims and Croats. The counts alleged that on two occasions, Simić went to the primary school in Bosanski Šamac, which was serving as a prison camp, and brutally beat five men who were detained there.[346] About a year after these events, Simić was rendered a paraplegic after he was shot in an assassination attempt.[347] He not only lost the use of both legs, he also lost a kidney, leaving him prone to a variety of infections, and he has virtually no use of one arm. Consequently, he cannot move a wheelchair without assistance, and because he cannot move the upper part of his body while in bed, he suffers continually from bedsores.[348]

Simić, along with his codefendants, proceeded to trial in September 2001. Simić's medical condition complicated the conduct of the trial from the outset. At first, the Trial Chamber held sessions only in the mornings to accommodate Simić's medical needs; later, the tribunal provided a nurse to assist him and a suitable bed on which he could rest during breaks, and these provisions allowed the Trial Chamber to sit for an additional hour in the afternoon. Finally, in February 2002, the tribunal installed a video link and a two-way telephone link between the ICTY's detention unit and the courtroom.[349]

Eight months into the trial, in May 2002, Simić pled guilty to two counts of torture as crimes against humanity. Simić refused to provide the prosecution with information for use in other cases, and the plea agreement contains a specific provision prohibiting the prosecution from seeking to produce that agreement into evidence as an exhibit against the remaining defendants in the case.[350] The counts to which Simić pled guilty related to the beatings of the five men, and in exchange for Simić's guilty plea, the prosecution dropped the remaining five charges.[351] Four of those charges related to inhumane and cruel treatment. The withdrawal of those charges was of no value to Simić because they related to the same conduct as that to which he pled guilty, and the crime to which he pled—torture—is arguably more serious than the crimes that were the subject of the withdrawn counts. Withdrawing the charges of persecution, by contrast, did amount to a substantial concession. That charge encompassed conduct for which Simić did not plead guilty, and the conduct itself was far more serious than the conduct that Simić admitted. Specifically, in charging Simić with persecution, the prosecution contended that he participated, in his role as president of the executive board, in the illegal arrests, detentions, and inhumane treatment visited upon the thousands of Bosnian Muslim and Bosnian Croat citizens of Bosanski Šamac. In other words, Simić pled guilty to a charge involving five victims while the prosecution withdrew charges involving thousands of victims. Further, putting aside the particular facts of this case, the withdrawn crime—persecution as a crime against humanity—is considered to deserve more severe punishment than torture or other crimes against humanity because persecution, unlike other crimes against humanity, requires a showing of discriminatory intent.[352]

At first glance, the prosecution's willingness to withdraw the persecution charge against Simić appears inexplicable. Substantial evidence apparently supported the charge, and Simić's guilty plea did not save the prosecution substantial resources since Simić's codefendants continued to contest their guilt at trial. Simić found himself in a unique and advantageous position, however, as a result of his medical condition. His medical needs had substantially slowed the trial, so the prosecution chose to withdraw a provable charge against him as a means of speeding up the trial.[353] The charge bargaining that took place in *Simić*, in turn, affected the resulting sentence bargaining. Both parties agreed to request a sentence of imprisonment of between three and five years.[354] Such a low sentencing range would have been unthinkable had Simić also pled guilty to the count of persecution given the grave and far-reaching conduct encompassed in that count. Perhaps trying to compensate for the considerable charging and sentencing concessions that it had bestowed on Simić, the prosecution submitted a hard-hitting sentencing brief, which urged the Trial Chamber to find numerous aggravating factors and no mitigating factors. In particular, the prosecution contended that Simić's guilty plea should be given "virtually no weight, if any" because it occurred so late in the proceedings and because Simić's refusal to cooperate indicated that "Milan Simić has a limited interest in the scope of the truth of the crimes committed in Bosanski Šamac."[355] The prosecution did uphold its end of the bargain, however, and recommended a five-year sentence, which is precisely what the Trial Chamber imposed.

Charge bargaining also played a prominent role in the next three guilty pleas, those of Biljana Plavšić, Momir Nikolić, and Dragan Obrenović, because in all three cases, prosecutors agreed to withdraw charges of genocide, the gravest of the crimes within the tribunal's jurisdiction.[356] Plavšić was copresident of the Serbian Republic of Bosnia and Herzegovina and had been instrumental in promoting and implementing the Bosnian Serbs' ethnic-cleansing campaign; Nikolić and Obrenović were Bosnian Serb military officers who had helped to implement the mass executions at Srebrenica. The withdrawal of the genocide charges was particularly valuable to Nikolić and Obrenović because the ICTY had previously found the Srebrenica killings to have constituted a genocide.[357] In pleading guilty, all three defendants admitted to the same conduct that formed the basis of the withdrawn charges, so the withdrawals did not distort the factual bases for the convictions as it had in *Simić*. The withdrawals did, however, have a significant effect on sentencing; the only ICTY defendant to be convicted of genocide at that time, Radislav Krstić, had received a forty-six-year prison sentence,[358] and virtually all of the ICTR defendants convicted of genocide have received life sentences.[359] By contrast, after withdrawing the genocide charges against Plavšić, prosecutors recommended a sentence of between fifteen and twenty-five years' imprisonment,[360] and the Trial Chamber sentenced her to eleven years in prison.[361] As for Obrenović and Nikolić, the prosecution recommended sentences of between fifteen and twenty years' imprisonment,[362] and the Trial Chamber imposed seventeen- and twenty-seven-year sentences, respectively.[363]

In more recent times, ICTY prosecutors have not engaged in the sort of blatant charge bargaining featured in *Simić*, perhaps because ICTY Trial Chambers have criticized the practice when it results in a distortion of the historical facts. The *Momir Nikolić* Trial Chamber, for instance, drew a distinction between the charge bargaining of domestic crimes and that of international crimes, observing that "[a]lthough it may seem appropriate to 'negotiate' a charge of attempted murder to a charge of aggravated assault, any 'negotiations' on a charge of genocide or crimes against humanity must be carefully considered and be entered into for good cause." The Trial Chamber went on to note that, because the prosecution has a duty to prepare an indictment only after determining that a prima facie case exists, "[o]nce a charge of genocide has been confirmed, it should not simply be bargained away" because when a prosecutor "make[s] a plea agreement such that the totality of an individuals [*sic*] criminal conduct is not reflected or the remaining charges do not sufficiently reflect the gravity of the offences committed by the accused, questions will inevitably arise as to whether justice is in fact being done."[364]

Charge bargaining that distorts the historical record of the crime is indeed undesirable, but it is not always easy to determine when such bargaining has occurred. The plea bargain concluded in the *Miodrag Jokić* case, for instance, appeared to be a factually distortive charge bargain but in fact was not. In 1991, Jokić was a commander of the Yugoslav Navy, and in that position, he participated in a military campaign directed at the then-municipality of Dubrovnik, Croatia. The first amended indictment charged Jokić and his two codefendants, Pavle Strugar and Vladimir Kovacević, with nine counts of violations of the laws and customs

of war for the unlawful shelling of the Old Town section of Dubrovnik on December 6, 1991, as well as for unlawful shelling that occurred in the Old Town
and in other Dubrovnik locations on October 7, 23, and 24, 1991, and November 8
through 13, 1991. The indictment alleged that as a result of this shelling, 42 civilians were killed, 177 were wounded, and a host of buildings were damaged or
destroyed.[365] Upon Jokić's guilty plea, prosecutors withdrew all of the charges relating to the shellings that took place in October and November 1991 and filed a
second amended indictment that contained charges relating only to the shelling of
the Old Town on December 6, 1991.[366] The December 6 shelling was the most dramatic of the originally charged offenses. Its target was a UNESCO World Cultural
Heritage site, and the shelling drew sharp condemnation from the international
community. But only 2 of the 42 alleged civilian deaths and 3 of the 177 alleged
civilian injuries occurred on December 6.[367] Given these circumstances, the withdrawal of the charges relating to the October and November shellings strongly
suggested charge bargaining. An examination of the indictments of Jokić's former codefendants, Strugar and Kovacević, however, shows that it was not. On
the same day that the prosecution withdrew the charges against Jokić, it likewise
sought to amend the indictments against Strugar and Kovacević, despite the fact
that neither of these two defendants had pled guilty.[368] Prosecutors apparently
decided to forego those charges because they either lacked sufficient evidence or
decided that their limited resources would be better spent on other cases.

The case of Miroslav Deronjić also gave rise to suspicions of charge bargaining,
but these too may be unfounded. Deronjić, a Bosnian Serb, had been a secondary
school teacher in Srebrenica before turning to politics in 1990. During the war in
Bosnia, Deronjić held a series of political offices in the Serbian Democratic Party
of Bosnia and Herzegovina. For instance, after Bosnian Serb forces took over the
municipality of Bratunac, Deronjić served as the president of three crisis staffs
and as a member of the War Commission of the municipality.[369] Deronjić began
cooperating with the prosecution in 1997, five years before he was indicted,[370]
and during a series of interviews before and after his indictment, Deronjić provided ICTY prosecutors with substantial information regarding the formulation
and implementation of the Bosnian Serbs' ethnic-cleansing campaign in Eastern
Bosnia, the arming and assistance provided to Bosnian Serbs by Serbian special
forces and paramilitaries, and the identities of people involved in the Srebrenica massacres. In order to induce Deronjić to speak openly, ICTY prosecutors
provided him with a signed "Agreement of the Parties," in which prosecutors

promised that nothing Deronjić said would be used against him in ICTY proceedings.[371] Although the information Deronjić provided during these interviews persuaded the Trial Chamber's presiding judge that Deronjić should have been indicted for crimes relating to the Srebrenica massacres as well as to the overall ethnic-cleansing campaign in Bratunac municipality,[372] the prosecution declined to indict him for these crimes and instead indicted him only for ordering an attack on the undefended Muslim town of Glogova.[373] The prosecutor denied that an indictment against Deronjić regarding the Srebrenica massacres would have been appropriate.[374] With respect to the prosecution's failure to indict Deronjić for his involvement in the larger ethnic-cleansing campaign in Bratunac municipality, the prosecutor admitted that the indictment was a "limited" one but asserted that, because ICTY trials can take more than two years to complete, the prosecutor had purposely chosen to limit the indictment "for purposes of resolving this case quickly in order to fulfill the mandate of" the tribunal.[375] Apparently unimpressed with this reasoning, Presiding Judge Wolfgang Schomburg, in his dissenting opinion, decried what he considered to be selective charging, maintaining that the prosecution had "arbitrarily present[ed] facts, selected from the context of a larger criminal plan and, for unknown reasons, limited to one day and to the village of Glogova only."[376]

Judge Schomburg suspected that charge bargaining had also occurred in relation to the charges involving Deronjić's participation in the May 1992 attack on Glogova,[377] but prosecutors and defense counsel vehemently denied it. With respect to the attack on Glogova, prosecutors initially charged Deronjić with six counts: one count of persecution as a crime against humanity, one count of murder as a crime against humanity, one count of murder as a violation of the laws and customs of war, and three counts of violations of the laws and customs of war relating to the destruction of cities, towns, or villages, destruction of institutions dedicated to religion, and an attack on an undefended village.[378] When Deronjić agreed to plead guilty, the prosecution withdrew all of the counts except the most serious—that of persecution as a crime against humanity—and it withdrew its allegations that Deronjić was liable under article 7(3) of the statute of the tribunal for superior responsibility. Additionally, the amended indictment filed in response to the guilty plea failed to include a number of seemingly trivial factual assertions that had appeared in the previous indictments.[379] None of these alterations seemed noteworthy, but Judge Schomburg identified a factual omission that troubled him, and he pressed the prosecution on it: the initial indictment and the amended indictment charged that Deronjić had been physically present when one Bosnian Muslim was executed and when the bodies of fifteen other Bosnian Muslims were dumped into a river. By contrast, the indictment to which Deronjić pled guilty omitted this allegation.[380] When Judge Schomburg sought "clarification" as to Deronjić's role and intentions regarding the killings by asking the prosecution whether it possessed supporting material that Deronjić was in fact present as had been initially alleged, the prosecutor pronounced himself "quite uncomfortable" with having a public discussion of such a question with the court.[381] Deronjić's defense counsel maintained that the defense team had substantial and compelling evidence that Deronjić was in another location at the relevant time, and the prosecution withdrew the allegation in acknowledgment of the strength of this evidence.[382]

A factually distortive charge bargain may also have occurred in the *Mrđa* case, though again, it is difficult to tell. Certainly, a charge bargain occurred. Darko Mrđa was a member of the Prijedor Police "Intervention Squad." In August 1992, Mrđa and others followed the orders of their superiors and loaded more than two hundred non-Serb male prisoners onto two buses. The prisoners were told that they were going to be exchanged for Serb prisoners. Instead, Mrđa and other members of the Serb forces took the men to a cliff at Koricanske Stijene, forced them to kneel at the edge of the cliff, and then shot them so that their bodies fell into the ravine below. All but twelve of the prisoners were killed.[383] Mrđa was initially indicted on three counts: extermination as a crime against humanity, inhumane acts as a crime against humanity, and murder as a violation of the laws or customs of war.[384] In exchange for Mrđa's guilty plea, prosecutors withdrew the most serious charge of extermination, and Mrđa pled guilty only to the lesser charges of murder as a violation of the laws and customs of war and inhumane acts as a crime against humanity.[385] That withdrawal did not alter the factual basis for the conviction, but the amended indictment to which Mrđa pled guilty also omitted certain factual allegations that had appeared in the original indictment. In particular, the initial indictment stated that Mrđa "was in command" of the police unit and that he had ordered the separation and killing of the men. The indictment also asserted that, after forcing prisoners to kneel at the edge of the cliff, Mrđa said, "Here is where we do the exchange, the living for the living and the dead. . . ." The factual basis to which Mrđa attested in support of his guilty plea does not contain those facts. Mrđa specifically said that he had been prepared to plead guilty sooner, but he could not admit those facts.[386] Interestingly, however, and perhaps unbeknownst to Mrđa, the facts remain in the amended indictment to which Mrđa pled guilty.[387]

In the rare case, the withdrawal of one charge pursuant to a plea bargain can pave the way for conviction on a more-serious charge. The early indictments against Dragan Nikolić, commander of the Sušica camp, for instance, included a charge that he raped a teenaged girl—Saha Berbić—nearly every night for two months.[388] During plea negotiations, Nikolić vehemently denied committing the rapes, and although he expressed a willingness to plead guilty to all of the other counts in the indictment, he refused to plead guilty to the rape charge. Berbić had been killed by other individuals upon the closing of the Sušica camp, and prosecutors had no eyewitness to the rapes. Given the evidentiary weakness of the Berbić rape charge and Nikolić's protestations of innocence, prosecutors decided to replace the original rape charge with a charge that Nikolić had facilitated the rapes of many women and girls detained at Sušica camp by removing them or allowing them to be removed by camp guards, soldiers, and others for purposes of rape.[389] The subsequent charge, to which Nikolić readily pled guilty, could well be considered more grave given Nikolić's authority over the camp and the large numbers of victims involved.

The *Miroslav Bralo* plea agreement gave rise to an even rarer occurrence: there, prosecutors added a charge and significant facts to the defendant's indictment after the defendant indicated a desire to plead guilty. Bralo was a member of the Jokers, a special-forces unit of the Bosnian Croat Defense Council that attacked Bosnian Muslim villages in 1993. Prosecutors initially charged Bralo with using Muslim civilians as "human shields" by forcing them to dig trenches on the front line, with killing three men near the village of Kratine, and with brutally and repeatedly raping a Muslim woman in front of other soldiers and thereafter confining her for approximately two months, during which time she was repeatedly raped by other members of the Jokers.[390]

In anticipation of Bralo's guilty plea, the prosecution not only failed to withdraw any charges, it *added* a charge of persecution as a crime against humanity, a charge more serious than the charges for which Bralo had initially been indicted. The prosecution was able to add that charge because Bralo himself revealed that, in addition to the crimes appearing in the indictment, he also participated in the ethnic cleansing of the village of Ahmići. In particular, Bralo disclosed that he burned down houses, destroyed a mosque, and committed or helped to commit seventeen additional murders.[391] As a result of Bralo's admissions, the prosecution engaged in the opposite of charge bargaining, and—for the first time in ICTY history—it presented a defendant preparing to plead guilty with an indictment containing more and more serious charges than that which had initially been prepared against him.[392]

The Evolution of Sentence Bargaining

Like charge bargaining, sentence bargaining at the ICTY has also undergone an evolution. In the early days of ICTY plea bargaining, prosecutors offered modest sentencing concessions to defendants pleading guilty, so modest indeed that, in some cases, it was not clear that there existed any sentencing differential between conviction after trial and conviction after a guilty plea. The ICTY's first plea bargain, in the *Todorović* case, was something of an exception. There, the prosecution agreed to recommend a sentence not exceeding twelve years' imprisonment, which was quite lenient compared with similar, contemporaneous cases. Todorović, who served during the war as police chief of Bosanski Šamac, pled guilty to persecution as a crime against humanity. He admitted to participating in the takeover and ethnic cleansing of Bosanski Šamac and Odžak and the subsequent detention of non-Serbs. He also admitted to personally killing one man, beating several others, and ordering six men to perform fellatio on one another.[393] Duško Tadić had received a twenty-year sentence for fairly similar conduct, and he did not hold a superior position, as did Todorović.[394] However, as noted above, the concessions the prosecution offered to Todorović appeared to be driven largely by its desire to rid itself of Todorović's embarrassing challenge to the legality of his arrest.

The prosecution's recommended sentences in the next four guilty-plea cases, by contrast, did not seem especially lower than the sentences that likely would have been imposed after trial. As noted above, Milan Simić received a five-year sentence after pleading guilty to torturing five men. Simić received a tremendous benefit when the prosecution withdrew the persecution charge against him, but the sentence he received for the crimes to which he pled guilty did not seem to be much, if any, reduced. There is no question that Simić and his companions severely mistreated the victims. They beat them with instruments on various parts of their bodies, including their genitals. They forced one of the victims to pull down his pants, they threatened to cut off his penis, and they pushed a gun into his mouth while Simić himself fired gunshots over the victim's head.[395] As depraved as this behavior was, however, it was probably less brutal than the typical

ICTY crime, and the incidents were isolated ones. Further, one week after these events took place, Simić returned to the detention center, apologized to the victims, and took two of them out of the detention center to buy them food and cigarettes and to allow them to change their clothes.[396] Under these circumstances, a five-year sentence, though lenient, does not appear to reflect a substantial sentence bargain.

The defendants in the *Sikirica* case pled guilty in September 2001, and they seemed to garner even less for their guilty pleas. The case centered on the infamous Keraterm detention camp and it featured three defendants: Duško Sikirica, who was Keraterm's commander of security, and Damir Došen and Dragan Kolundžija, who served as shift leaders. Keraterm detainees were kept in appalling conditions and were regularly beaten and killed, by guards and by outsiders given entry by guards. After the trial was mostly completed, all three defendants pled guilty to persecution as a crime against humanity, acknowledging varying levels of culpability. The persecution count alleged persecution by five methods: (1) murder; (2) torture and beating; (3) sexual assault and rape; (4) harassment, humiliation, and psychological abuse; and (5) confinement in inhumane conditions. Sikirica acknowledged participating in all of those methods and in particular admitted to personally killing one detainee; Došen admitted to participating in the second, fourth, and fifth methods; and Kolundžija admitted only to the fifth method.[397] All three defendants acknowledged the murders and beatings that took place at Keraterm and the inhumane conditions prevailing,[398] but the plea agreements also noted the defendants' limited responsibilities. Pursuant to the plea agreement, the prosecution recommended sentences between ten and seventeen years' imprisonment for Sikirica, between five and seven years' imprisonment for Došen, and between three and five years' imprisonment for Kolundžija.[399] The prosecution recommended the maximum sentence for each defendant.[400] The Trial Chamber sentenced Sikirica, Došen, and Kolundžija to fifteen, five, and three years' imprisonment, respectively.[401]

Since the *Sikirica* defendants did not plead guilty until the trial was nearly completed, the prosecution did not gain very much in resource savings by the guilty pleas. One can therefore presume that the prosecution consequently offered the *Sikirica* defendants less generous concessions than it would have to defendants who pled guilty before the trial began. That said, the *Sikirica* bargain is nonetheless notable in how little it provided the defendants. The ICTY had earlier sentenced Croatian prison camp commander Zlatko Aleksovski to a two-and-one-half-year prison sentence after trial, which the Appeals Chamber subsequently increased to seven years' imprisonment.[402] The conditions prevailing in the Keraterm camp concededly were worse than those at the Kaonik prison, at which Aleksovski was a commander; yet even without a guilty plea, the Trial Chamber's initial two-and-one-half-year sentence for Aleksovski was substantially lower than the prosecution's recommendation for Sikirica. As another example, Hazim Delić, deputy commander of the Čelebići prison camp, was convicted of brutally murdering two detainees, raping and torturing two more, and torturing numerous others, some by means of an electric shock device.[403] Delić received a sentence of twenty years' imprisonment after trial, which was reduced on appeal to eighteen years' imprisonment;[404] that is, after a full-blown trial, Delić received a sentence only slightly higher than the prosecution's maximum recommendation for Sikirica, for crimes arguably involving greater harm. Similarly, Dragoljub Prcać was an administrative aide at the notorious Omarska camp. Prcać, like Kolundžija, held a position of authority in a brutal detention center but was not himself convicted of inflicting any direct harm.[405] Without pleading guilty, Prcać was sentenced to five years' imprisonment;[406] that is, Prcać received a sentence at the upper end of the prosecution's sentencing recommendation for Kolundžija. This similarity in sentences is even more startling because substantial evidence had been produced in the *Sikirica* trial regarding Kolundžija's kindness to prisoners and the efforts he had made to assist them.[407]

The ICTY's sentencing practice following guilty pleas appeared to undergo a dramatic change with the guilty plea of Biljana Plavšić. As copresident of the Serbian Republic of Bosnia and Herzegovina, Plavšić played a leading role in encouraging and implementing the Bosnian Serbs' ethnic-cleansing campaign, which resulted in the expulsion of hundreds of thousands of Bosnian Muslims and Croats.[408] Approximately 850 Muslim- and Croat-occupied villages were destroyed entirely and no longer exist.[409] In many municipalities, virtually all non-Serbs were killed or forced to flee. Before the war, for instance, approximately 15,000 Muslims and Croats lived in the Foca municipality; 434 remained in 1997. Similarly, approximately 53,000 non-Serbs resided in the Prijedor municipality before the war; by 1997, less than 4,000 were left.[410] The indictment against Plavšić pointed to thirty-seven municipalities in particular, and the evidence showed that, to encourage non-Serbs to leave, Serbian forces killed approximately 50,000 non-Serbs and destroyed more than one hundred mosques and Catholic churches.[411]

The factual basis to Plavšić's guilty plea distinguishes between the roles played by the various Bosnian Serb leaders in the ethnic cleansing; in particular, it states that Radovan Karadžić and Momčilo Krajišnik exercised primary control over the Bosnian Serb power structures and provided primary direction to municipal leaders who were charged with implementing the persecutory campaign. Plavšić played a lesser role, but she did support the government and military in the ethnic cleansing by serving as a copresident and by inviting Serbian paramilitaries to assist in the violence. She also made public pronouncements encouraging the forcible expulsions on the grounds that certain territories were "Serbian by right" and that Serbs were in danger of genocide at the hands of Bosnian Muslims and Croats. Finally, when evidence of the crimes came to light, Plavšić participated in a cover-up.[412]

Plavšić's plea deal was unusual in many ways. As noted above, as part of the plea agreement prosecutors withdrew genocide charges against her, a concession that appeared on its face to be substantial but that may have been of relatively little consequence because the only ICTY defendants who thus far have been convicted of genocide were those who had been involved in the Srebrenica massacres. Prosecutors therefore may have perceived little chance of convicting Plavšić of genocide. Whatever its import, the withdrawal of the genocide charge was apparently the only concession Plavšić received. A provision in her plea agreement states that "the Prosecutor has made no promises to Biljana Plavšić in order to induce her to change her plea . . . from not guilty to guilty,"[413] and her lawyer publicly stated that "there is no agreement, nor have there been any discussions, between Mrs. Plavšić and the Office of the Prosecution regarding sentencing. Mrs. Plavšić understands, as the Agreement itself specifically provides, that she is subjecting herself to a possible sentence of life imprisonment." The prosecution did not recommend a life sentence but instead recommended a sentence of between fifteen and twenty-five years' imprisonment,[414] a range that had the potential to effectively constitute a life sentence because Plavšić was seventy-two years old at the time of sentencing. The Trial Chamber, however, sentenced her to a mere eleven years in prison.[415] The sentence horrified Bosnian Muslims,[416] and the ICTY's president enraged victims further by sending Plavšić to serve her sentence in Sweden, where she is housed in an apparently luxurious minimum-security prison featuring sauna, solarium, massage room, horse-riding paddock, and other amenities.[417]

Nine guilty pleas followed Plavšić's in quick succession, and many have featured lenient—some would argue, unseemly—sentence recommendations, particularly compared with previous ICTY cases, even previous cases involving guilty pleas. Ranko Češić, for instance, was a member of the Bosnian Serb Police Reserve Unit at the Brčko Police Station, the same camp at which Goran Jelisić acted as de facto commander. Češić was tasked, among other things, with arresting specified non-Serbs and bringing them to the police station or to the Luka detention camp. Češić admitted to personally killing ten people and to forcing two brothers to perform fellatio on one another;[418] that is, he admitted to crimes roughly comparable to the thirteen murders that Jelisić admitted when he pled guilty. Both men pled guilty, but Jelisić's plea, coming before the rush to close the tribunal, gained him nothing. The prosecution recommended a life sentence for Jelisić,[419] and the Trial Chamber imposed a near equivalent by sentencing him to forty years in prison.[420] Češić was of a subordinate position to Jelisić, so one would expect him to receive a lower sentence, but compared with Jelisić, Češić received an extremely attractive plea deal even taking that fact into account. In the plea agreement it concluded with Češić, the prosecution promised to recommend a sentence of between thirteen and eighteen years' imprisonment, and the Trial Chamber sentenced him to an eighteen-year term.[421]

Other examples of relative leniency abound. The contrast has already been drawn between the seventeen- and twenty-seven-year sentences that Dragan Obrenović and Momir Nikolić received, respectively, for their roles in implementing the Srebrenica massacres and the forty-six-year term a Trial Chamber imposed on Radislav Krstić. Admittedly, Krstić, as deputy commander of the Drina Corps, should be considered more culpable given his position of greater responsibility, but the span between a seventeen-year sentence and a forty-six-year sentence is vast. Similarly, Predrag Banović, a guard at the same Keraterm camp where Sikirica, Došen, and Kolundžija committed their crimes, pled guilty in June 2003 to participating in beating five prisoners to death and participating in twenty-seven other beatings and shootings.[422] Even after a guilty plea, prosecutors recommended a seventeen-year sentence for Sikirica when he committed only one murder, while they recommended a seven-year sentence for Došen when he was not personally implicated in any serious violence.[423] Concededly, Sikirica and Došen held positions of greater responsibility than did Banović, but all three were relatively low-level offenders, and Banović's crimes were vastly more numerous and brutal; thus, one might have expected Banović to receive a sentence greater than Došen's and perhaps equal to Sikirica's, particularly since those defendants also pled guilty. Instead, in exchange for Banović's guilty plea, the prosecution and defense agreed to recommend a mere eight-year term of imprisonment for Banović, which the Trial Chamber duly imposed.[424] The relative

leniency of Banović's eight-year sentence is further highlighted when it is compared with the twenty-year sentence that the ICTY contemporaneously imposed
after a trial on Mitar Vasiljević, who, like Banović, participated in the killing of
five people.[425]

Prosecutorial sentence recommendations indeed became so lenient during
2003 that some ICTY trial judges led a backlash. As early as the *Simić* case,
Trial Chambers were indicating some hesitancy about adhering to prosecutorial
sentencing recommendations born out of plea negotiations. In *Simić*, the Trial
Chamber did sentence the defendant to five years' imprisonment, a term within
the three-to-five-year sentencing range recommended by the prosecution, but it
made clear in doing so that its decision was based on exceptional circumstances
present in that case. In particular, after observing that Milan Simić was "a senior
public official in Bosanski Šamac and he committed acts of torture in the primary school while serving as President of the Executive Board of the municipality," the Trial Chamber "condemned in the highest degree" Simić's crimes and
noted that "[u]nder ordinary circumstances a long custodial sentence, even up
to the remainder of his life, would have been appropriate."[426] Although the Trial
Chamber did take account of Simić's guilty plea and the remorse he had showed
victims, it indicated that its decision not to impose a long custodial sentence had a
great deal to do with Simić's severe medical condition, which it termed an "exceptional circumstance."[427] The Trial Chamber thus suggested that, absent Simić's
medical condition, it would have sentenced Simić outside the range to which
Simić and the prosecution had agreed in the plea deal.

In sentencing within the prosecution's recommended range, the *Simić* Trial
Chamber followed the practice of Trial Chambers in preceding guilty-plea cases.
In particular, the Trial Chambers imposed sentences in accordance with prosecutorial recommendations in the cases of the first nine defendants to tender
guilty pleas.[428] In December 2003, however, a Trial Chamber in the *Momir Nikolić*
case rejected the prosecution's recommendation of a fifteen-to-twenty-year sentence. Nikolić was chief of intelligence and security of the Bratunac Brigade
during the Srebrenica massacres, and he pled guilty to persecution as a crime
against humanity for helping to coordinate and organize the operation in which
Bosnian Muslim women and children were transported to Muslim-held territory,
while Bosnian Muslim men were transported to the various locations at which
they were executed. Some months after the executions, Nikolić also assisted in
the effort to conceal the bodies of the Bosnian Muslim men by exhuming and

reburying the remains.[429] At the plea hearing, Presiding Judge Liu Daqun expressed some discomfort with guilty pleas in general, querying the prosecution, for instance, as to how the defendant could be deprived of such fundamental rights as the right "not to be compelled to testify against himself or to confess guilty [sic], the right to be tried without undue delay, [and] the right to testify or to remain silent at trial." When the prosecution explained that the waiver of those rights was part and parcel of a guilty plea, Judge Liu opined that some of those rights are so fundamental that they might be considered inalienable, even by the defendant himself.[430]

That same discomfort with guilty pleas was also reflected in the Trial Chamber's sentencing judgment. There, the Trial Chamber considered the broad question of whether plea agreements are appropriate in cases involving serious violations of international humanitarian law. In addition to the above-mentioned concerns that the Trial Chamber raised about charge bargaining, it also noted that guilty pleas eliminate public trials, and these trials, the chamber opined, give rise to "a more complete and detailed historical record than a guilty plea" and they permit victims to participate in the criminal process. The Trial Chamber also expressed concern about the inequality inherent in plea bargaining; it noted in particular that some defendants are offered greater concessions because they provide important information to the prosecution while other defendants gain no such benefits because they have no such information to disclose. At the same time, the Trial Chamber acknowledged the benefits of plea bargaining. It recognized, for instance, that guilty pleas save resources, help to prevent subsequent denial of the crime, and have the potential to enhance peace-building and reconciliation. The Trial Chamber concluded that guilty pleas made pursuant to plea agreements may be appropriate in certain instances but must be regarded with caution and used only when doing so would further the interests of justice.[431] Apparently deciding that the sentencing range recommended by the prosecution—fifteen to twenty years' imprisonment—did not further the interests of justice, the Trial Chamber sentenced Nikolić to twenty-seven years' imprisonment. In imposing this harsher-than-recommended sentence, the chamber emphasized that Nikolić had played a substantial and enthusiastic role in ensuring the success of the Srebrenica massacres and that he had been evasive and not entirely forthcoming when testifying in the trial of his codefendants.[432] As will be discussed in more detail in Chapter 10, Nikolić initially lied to prosecutors about certain details of the massacres, a fact noted by the Trial Chamber.

Eight days later, the same Trial Chamber sentenced Momir Nikolić's codefendant, Dragan Obrenović, to seventeen years' imprisonment after his guilty plea,[433] a term that was well within the prosecution's fifteen-to-twenty-year sentence recommendation. Proponents of tribunal plea bargaining breathed a sigh of relief and considered Nikolić's sentence to be an aberration resulting from Nikolić's lack of candor. In fact, although both the *Obrenović* and *Momir Nikolić* cases involved the Srebrenica massacres, the defendants' involvement in those massacres differed markedly, and the Trial Chamber's imposition of a longer-than-recommended sentence on Nikolić did not constitute an aberration but rather reflected the chamber's willingness to consider all of the circumstances of each case and to consider—independently of the prosecution's recommendation—what sentence those circumstances justify. The *Obrenović* Trial Chamber apparently concluded that the prosecution's recommendation reflected an appropriate sentence.

Obrenović was a major in the Bosnian Serb Army, and at the time of the Srebrenica massacres, he held the position of chief of staff and deputy commander at the Zvornik Brigade. A few weeks after Momir Nikolić pled guilty, Obrenović followed suit, also pleading guilty to persecution as a crime against humanity. Obrenović was not himself present during the Srebrenica executions; rather, at the time they took place, Obrenović was leading soldiers in heavy fighting at the front line.[434] Obrenović was, however, aware of the plan to execute the Bosnian Muslims, and he released a few soldiers under his command to help organize and implement the killings.[435]

The Trial Chamber commented that, had there been no aggravating or mitigating circumstances to consider, Obrenović's sentence should fall in the range of twenty to forty years' imprisonment.[436] The chamber did, however, identify numerous mitigating circumstances, including most importantly Obrenović's guilty plea, his remorse about the crimes, and his cooperation with the prosecution.[437] Indeed, the Trial Chamber's overall view of Obrenović seemed to differ considerably from its view of his codefendant Momir Nikolić. Whereas the Trial Chamber called into question Nikolić's honesty and candor, it specifically observed that during Obrenović's testimony in the *Blagojević* case, "Obrenovic answered each question as clearly and precisely as he could, regardless of whether it was asked by the Prosecution, defense counsel or the Trial Chamber."[438] In addition, whereas the Trial Chamber observed that Nikolić's involvement with the Srebrenica massacres was enthusiastic and proactive, it characterized Obrenović's involvement as composed primarily of his failure to stop the executions.[439] The

Trial Chamber further lauded Obrenović's decision to plead guilty, finding that it reflected his "unreserved acceptance of his individual criminal responsibility."[440] Finally, the Trial Chamber concluded that Obrenović took important steps toward his rehabilitation that should mitigate his sentence.[441] In particular, the chamber pointed to the fact that Obrenović cooperated with ICTY prosecutors before his indictment; he agreed to answer questions, and he allowed prosecutors to search the premises of the Zvornik Brigade, knowing that the search would likely yield information that would incriminate him. Obrenović went so far as to offer to surrender should an indictment be issued against him.[442]

The Trial Chamber's sentencing of Obrenović to a prison term within the prosecution's recommended range placed the *Obrenović* case squarely among all of the ICTY's previous guilty-plea cases except that of *Momir Nikolić*. Eight days after the *Obrenović* judgment was issued, however, a different ICTY Trial Chamber spurned the prosecution's recommendations, this time in the case of Dragan Nikolić (no relation to Momir). In addition to serving as commander of the brutal Sušica detention center, where murders, beatings, and rapes occurred daily, Dragan Nikolić admitted to beating nine men to death, torturing five more, and facilitating countless rapes.[443] Nikolić's crimes were particularly depraved: Nikolić would

> brutally and sadistically beat the detainees. He would kick and punch detainees and use weapons such as iron bars, axe handles, rifle butts, metal "knuckles," truncheons, rubber tubing with lead inside, lengths of wood and wooden bats to beat the detainees. . . . When detainees who were being beaten begged to be shot, [Nikolić] would reply: "A bullet is too expensive to be spent on a Muslim."[444]

After engaging in months of vigorous bargaining with the defense, the prosecution eventually agreed to recommend a fifteen-year sentence for Nikolić, but the Trial Chamber sentenced him to twenty-three years' imprisonment, a term more than 50 percent longer than the sentence for which Nikolić had bargained. The Trial Chamber did not seek to justify its decision to impose a longer-than-recommended sentence on Nikolić by blaming the defendant's evasiveness or by identifying any other post-crime behavior or characteristic, as the *Momir Nikolić* Trial Chamber had done. Instead, the *Dragan Nikolić* Trial Chamber simply expressed its view that a fifteen-year sentence is too short for the crimes Nikolić committed. Before deciding on a sentence, the chamber had commissioned the Max Planck Institute to submit an expert report detailing various countries' sentencing laws as applied to cases of serious, violent crimes disposed of via guilty pleas. The report indicated that the sentencing laws of most countries provide that a single act of murder can be punished by either life imprisonment or the death penalty.[445] Given the extreme depravity of Nikolić's crimes, the Trial Chamber unhesitatingly asserted that, considering only the gravity of the crime and the aggravating circumstances, "no other punishment could be imposed" upon Nikolić except a life sentence.[446] The Trial Chamber went on, then, to consider a number of mitigating factors, including Nikolić's guilty plea; in doing so, it observed that the Max Planck report found that in all of the major legal systems of the world, guilty pleas or confessions serve to reduce a defendant's sentence.[447] The existence of these mitigating factors, however, did not convince the Trial Chamber that Nikolić's sentence should be reduced to fifteen years' imprisonment, as recommended by the prosecution. It held instead that the "brutality, the number of crimes committed and the underlying intention to humiliate and degrade would render a sentence such as [the prosecution] recommended unjust." Rather, the chamber concluded that it was "not only reasonable and responsible, but also necessary in the interests of the victims, their relatives and the international community, to impose a higher sentence than the one recommended by the Parties."[448]

ICTY Trial Chambers sentenced within the prosecution's recommended ranges in the next four cases to be disposed of by guilty pleas, all of which were handed down in March 2004. The crimes of Ranko Češić, Darko Mrđa, Miodrag Jokić, and Miroslav Deronjić have all been described above. In its plea agreement with Češić, the prosecution agreed to recommend a sentence of between thirteen and eighteen years' imprisonment, and, rather than making a specific recommendation, the prosecution simply advised the Trial Chamber to impose a sentence that fell somewhere within that range.[449] The chamber sentenced Češić to eighteen years' imprisonment.[450] In Mrđa's plea agreement, both parties agreed to recommend a sentence of between fifteen and twenty years' imprisonment,[451] and the Trial Chamber sentenced Mrđa to a term of seventeen years.[452] Jokić's plea agreement required the prosecution to recommend a sentence of ten years' imprisonment, and it permitted Jokić to seek a shorter sentence.[453] He sought a two-year term,[454] and the Trial Chamber sentenced him to seven years in prison.[455]

Prosecutors recommended a ten-year sentence for Deronjić, which the Trial Chamber duly imposed, but it did so over the vehement dissent of the presiding judge, Wolfgang Schomburg. Judge Schomburg concluded that Deronjić deserved a sentence of no less than twenty years' imprisonment, reasoning that even when one considered only the "fragments of facts" presented by the prosecution, they showed that Deronjić was a high-ranking perpetrator who had committed "heinous and long planned crimes" which "do not allow for a sentence of only ten years, which may possibly even be a *de facto* deprivation of liberty of only six years and eight months, taking into account the possibility of an early release."[456] Judge Schomburg concluded that a sentence of less than twenty years' imprisonment "could be seen as an incentive for politicians, who might in [the] future find themselves in a similar situation as Miroslav Deronjić was as of December 1991, to act in the same manner." Such a politician, according to Judge Schomburg, "would believe that he/she could buy him/herself more or less free by admitting some guilt and giving some information to the then competent prosecutor."[457]

After adhering to prosecutorial sentencing recommendations in the four cases handed down in March 2004, a Trial Chamber in the *Milan Babić* case once again rejected the sentence to which the parties had agreed. Milan Babić, a Croatian Serb and a dentist by profession, became a prominent political figure in the Serbian Democratic Party in Croatia during the early 1990s. Based in Knin, an industrial town in the region of Krajina, Babić held a series of high-level positions, serving as president of the Municipal Assembly of Knin, president of the Serbian National Council, and president of the Temporary Executive Council of the "Serbian Autonomous District," among other positions.[458] After Croatia declared its intention to secede from the Federal Republic of Yugoslavia, Babić became concerned about the discrimination that Croatian Serbs might suffer in a new Croatian state, so he advocated the creation of an independent Serbian state in Krajina, and, to advance this goal, he sought the help of Slobodan Milošević.[459]

As an initial matter, Babić apparently sought to obtain autonomy for Croatian Serbs through peaceful means, but there developed a "parallel structure" of authority whose members answered directly to Milošević and who chose to use violence to obtain that goal. In particular, beginning in the summer of 1991, Serbian Croat forces, under the direction of the parallel structure and assisted by the Yugoslav Army, launched an ethnic-cleansing campaign designed to forcibly remove Croat and other non-Serb populations from the region. This campaign resulted in the deaths of more than 230 Croats, the illegal incarceration of several hundred Croats and other non-Serbs, and untold property damage.[460] Babić apparently had no effective control over this parallel structure, and he apparently was not the architect of the ethnic-cleansing campaign; nonetheless, he cooperated with this structure by providing material, logistical, and political support for the military takeover of the territories in Krajina and by making ethnically biased and inflammatory speeches that frightened Croatian Serbs and helped to convince them that they would be safe only in a state of their own.[461]

Babić voluntarily brought himself before the prosecution in the fall of 2001 after his name appeared in an indictment against Milošević. Babić subsequently engaged in extensive interviews with the prosecution and eventually provided detailed and useful testimony in the Milošević case.[462] His testimony was so useful, indeed, that many commentators were surprised when ICTY prosecutors chose to indict Babić in November 2003.[463] That indictment charged Babić with one count of persecution as a crime against humanity and four counts of violations of the laws and customs of war, and it alleged that he committed these crimes through his participation in a joint criminal enterprise or, alternatively, as an aider and abettor.[464] Two months later, Babić agreed to plead guilty to aiding and abetting the one count of persecutions, but when presented with a plea agreement in which Babić admitted that crime, the Trial Chamber expressed concern that Babić may have understated his actual criminal liability by admitting only to aiding and abetting the crimes; as a consequence, the parties subsequently presented to the chamber a revised plea agreement in which Babić's participation in the crime was characterized as coperpetratorship.[465] The plea agreement required prosecutors to withdraw the less-serious charges of violations of the laws and customs of war, and it required prosecutors to recommend a sentence of no more than eleven years' imprisonment.[466]

The "Factual Statement" appended to Babić's plea agreement was unusual. Prior ICTY factual statements were composed of admissions inculpating the defendant; Babić's factual statement contained some of those, but it also contained numerous assertions that functioned to minimize his role in the crimes and his ultimate culpability. The "Factual Statement," for instance, reported that Babić's crimes were driven by his fear that Croatian Serbs would suffer discrimination at the hands of the Croats, and it legitimized that fear by asserting that Babić had fallen prey to a "media campaign directed by Belgrade that portrayed the Serbs in Croatia as being threatened with genocide by the Croat majority."[467] The "Factual Statement" also emphasized that Babić did not share the goals of those in the parallel structure who sought to obtain autonomy for Croatian Serbs through force, and it asserted that several of Babić's decisions or appointments were made "under pressure from Milošević" or only to "ratif[y] a decision made in Belgrade."[468]

The Trial Chamber did not consider these assertions persuasive. Finding that Babić's participation in the joint criminal enterprise was substantial, the chamber concluded that "Babić's role . . . was [not] as limited as the parties claim it was" and that he himself may not have recognized "the full significance of the role he played in Croatia in that period."[469] The Trial Chamber was also not convinced of the appropriateness of the prosecution's sentencing recommendation. As noted above, prosecutors had agreed in Babić's plea agreement to seek a sentence of no longer than eleven years' imprisonment. In previous guilty-plea cases, prosecutors had sought the longest sentence permissible under the plea agreement. In *Babić*, by contrast, prosecutors advocated a sentence of "below 11 years." The prosecutor emphasized: "I stress here the word 'below.'"[470] The Trial Chamber declined to comply, however, and sentenced Babić to thirteen years' imprisonment, concluding that a sentence of eleven years "would not do justice."[471]

Almost certainly as a consequence of the Trial Chambers' imposition of longer-than-agreed-to sentences in *Dragan Nikolić*, *Momir Nikolić*, and *Babić*, more than a year-and-a-half elapsed after Babić's guilty plea before another ICTY defendant elected to plead guilty. By the time that Miroslav Bralo and Ivica Rajić tendered their guilty pleas in the summer and fall of 2005, however, prosecutors had another weapon in their bargaining arsenal—the threat to transfer a case to the courts of Bosnia.

ICTY prosecutors had indicted Miroslav Bralo in 1995, but they kept the indictment under seal.[472] Two years later, while unaware of the indictment, Bralo attempted to surrender to U.N. peacekeepers. He told them that he had killed at Ahmići and could no longer live with his conscience,[473] and he provided them with a bundle of documents of interest to ICTY prosecutors.[474] The peacekeepers declined to arrest Bralo, however, because his name did not appear on their list of indicted people.[475] Bralo subsequently surrendered to the Bosnian Croat army and was held under house arrest for two years until he was able to escape.[476] In October 2004, the ICTY unsealed Bralo's indictment, and he immediately surrendered to the tribunal.[477] Eight months after that, Bralo pled guilty[478] and issued a public apology for his crimes.[479] He also provided prosecutors with a statement in addition to the factual basis of his guilty plea that revealed facts incriminating Bosnian Croat general Tihomir Blaškić and other Bosnian Croat officials.[480] Bralo additionally helped mine-clearing officials in identifying areas containing mines, and he assisted in efforts to locate and exhume the bodies of victims of the ethnic cleansing at Ahmići. As a result of the information Bralo provided, Bosnia's Federal Commission of Missing Persons was able to exhume the remains of numerous victims.[481]

Bralo's plea agreement states that "no promises or inducements have been made by the Prosecutor to induce Miroslav Bralo to enter this Agreement."[482]

This provision is reminiscent of the *Plavšić* plea agreement, which similarly provided that "the Prosecutor has made no promises to Biljana Plavšić in order to induce her to change her plea . . . from not guilty to guilty."[483] It is true that *Plavšić* prosecutors had not committed to a particular sentencing recommendation, but they had agreed to withdraw charges of genocide against Plavšić, a withdrawal that might have had a considerable effect on sentencing. By contrast, as noted in the discussion on charge bargaining, Bralo pled guilty to *more* crimes than those for which he was initially charged. In addition, his plea agreement, like Plavšić's, contains no promises regarding sentence recommendations. As Bralo's defense counsel put it: "The passage which is sometimes included in such plea agreements marked 'Consideration' has been excised altogether because there is none. The Prosecution has made no promise to the Defendant."[484]

That the prosecution indeed had made no promises to Bralo became abundantly clear once the prosecution announced its sentence recommendation for Bralo. Although the norm at the ICTY is for the Trial Chambers to impose a sentence from which a defendant might be granted early release in accordance with the laws of the state of imprisonment, *Bralo* prosecutors asked the Trial Chamber to order that Bralo serve "a minimum term of 25 years."[485] Since ICTY defendants typically serve their terms in states that release criminal defendants once they have served one-half to two-thirds of their sentences, *Bralo* prosecutors were effectively recommending that the ICTY sentence Bralo to a forty- or fifty-year term of imprisonment,[486] which is a particularly harsh sentence given Bralo's low-level status. Bralo prosecutors, in addition, took a narrow view of his efforts to cooperate with the prosecution. As noted above, Bralo provided the prosecution with a supplemental statement and documents that the prosecution has used in other ICTY cases.[487] Bralo has also offered to be deposed under oath,[488] but he was not willing to meet privately with the prosecution because he feared that his family would suffer retaliation.[489] In the prosecution's view, Bralo's assistance did not rise to the level of substantial cooperation, which, pursuant to Rule 101 of the ICTY's Rules of Evidence and Procedure, would be a mitigating factor in sentencing.[490] The Trial Chamber agreed with the prosecution that Bralo did not substantially cooperate, but it did deem his cooperation "moderate" and gave him some credit for it.[491] The Trial Chamber also rejected the prosecution's request to impose a mandatory minimum term on Bralo.[492] Rather, it imposed a sentence of twenty years' imprisonment after determining that a sentence of at least twenty-five years would have been warranted absent Bralo's guilty plea, his remorse, his voluntary surrender, and the other mitigating circumstances that the Trial Chamber took into account.[493]

The *Bralo* case is in many ways reminiscent of *Erdemović*. Both Bralo and Erdemović were low-level offenders, and both pled guilty without receiving any concrete sentencing concessions from the prosecution.[494] In addition, both defendants attempted to surrender to authorities, claiming to have incriminating information about more senior offenders. But while Erdemović succeeded in expeditiously presenting himself before the ICTY, providing the prosecution with vital information about the Srebrenica massacres and testifying in numerous cases, Bralo did not. And that difference might account for the very different treatment that the two defendants received from the prosecution. In addition, although Bralo, like Erdemović, did not receive any concrete sentencing concessions from the prosecution in exchange for his guilty plea, Bralo's guilty plea did garner him a benefit that was not available at the time that Erdemović pled guilty. As a result of Bralo's low-level status, his case was considered a likely candidate for transfer to the Special War Crimes Court in Sarajevo. Many ICTY defendants have vehemently opposed the transfer of their cases to Bosnia,[495] and by pleading guilty, Bralo eliminated the possibility of a Bosnian prosecution. Even if Bralo's guilty plea was motivated by a desire to avoid transfer to Bosnia, his plea provides an outstanding example of the kinds of elements that a guilty-plea process should include. In Chapter 8, I argue that guilty pleas that incorporate such restorative-justice principles as truth-telling, apologies, and reparations can enhance peace-building and reconciliation following large-scale violent conflict. Bralo's guilty plea includes these features and consequently was enthusiastically welcomed by victims.[496]

Ivica Rajić tendered the next and most recent ICTY guilty plea, and he presents the more typical case of a defendant seeking concrete advantage in exchange for his self-conviction. Rajić was a commander in the Bosnian Croat army. In October 1993, he ordered his subordinates, who he knew had previously committed atrocities against Bosnian Muslims, to attack the Bosnian Muslim town of Stupni Do and to arrest and detain military-aged men in the town of Vareš.[497] The forces under Rajić's command destroyed Stupni Do: they killed at least thirty-seven villagers, sexually assaulted numerous women, and razed the village.[498] In Vareš, Rajić's forces apprehended more than 250 Muslim men, ill-treated them, and detained them in deplorable conditions.[499] Rajić eluded an ICTY arrest warrant for more than eight years, and when he was finally apprehended in June 2003, he pled not guilty to all the charges against him.[500] A little more than two years later, in

July 2005, prosecutors filed a motion to have Rajić's case transferred to the Bosnian courts, a motion that Rajić firmly opposed.[501] Two months later, Rajić agreed to plead guilty to four of the ten counts against him.[502] After doing so, however, Rajić repeatedly tried to minimize his responsibility for the crimes and distance himself from his own admissions, a topic that will be taken up in Chapter 10.

Although prosecutors withdrew six counts, Rajić obtained no benefit from the withdrawals because the withdrawn crimes were no more serious than the crimes to which Rajić pled guilty, and the facts contained in the withdrawn charges were also contained in the charges to which Rajić pled guilty. As for sentencing concessions, prosecutors agreed to recommend a sentence of between twelve and fifteen years' imprisonment,[503] a recommendation that appears moderately discounted in light of ICTY precedents. Perhaps the most important benefit Rajić obtained by pleading guilty, however, was the resolution of his case by the ICTY and not the courts of Bosnia. Although upon judicial questioning, both Rajić and the prosecution denied that Rajić's guilty plea was motivated by a desire to avoid a transfer to the Bosnian courts, the timing of the plea gave rise to doubts.[504] As the date for the ICTY's closure draws nearer, it may be that the prosecution's threat to seek transfer of a case to a judicial system believed to be more harsh than the ICTY represents its most potent bargaining tool in the guilty-plea process.

Appeals in ICTY Guilty-Plea Cases

The first two ICTY defendants to plead guilty appealed after their convictions. While Erdemović's appeal, as discussed above, raised interesting legal issues about the nature of guilty pleas and led the Appeals Chamber to vacate his guilty plea and remit the case to the Trial Chamber,[505] the second appeal—brought by Goran Jelisić—merely challenged his sentence, a challenge that failed, even though the Appeals Chamber agreed with Jelisić that the Trial Chamber had erroneously convicted him of killing fourteen people when, in fact, he had pled guilty to killing only thirteen.[506] In an effort to prevent guilty-plea defendants from launching similar time-consuming appeals to their sentences, ICTY prosecutors began including in subsequent plea agreements a provision preventing either party from appealing a sentence, if the sentence falls within the range of sentences that the parties agreed upon in the plea agreement.[507] Consequently, no appeals were brought in *Todorović*, *Simić*, and *Obrenović*. The plea agreements of Momir Nikolić and Dragan Nikolić likewise prevented them from appealing if they were sentenced in accordance with the prosecution's recommendation, but since they were not, those defendants could and did appeal. In recent times, defendants have been less amenable to waiving their right to appeal; consequently, no appeal prohibition was included in the plea agreements of Banović, Mrđa, Rajić, Deronjić, Babić, and Jokić,[508] and the latter three defendants did file appeals following their sentencing.[509] As a consequence, the Appeals Chamber of late has been well-occupied with appeals to sentences in guilty-plea cases.

Given the similarity of the Trial Chambers' sentencing analysis in guilty-plea cases, it should come as no surprise that there also exists a similarity in the defendants' challenges to these sentences. In particular, guilty-plea defendants have typically claimed that the Trial Chambers inappropriately assessed aggravating and mitigating circumstances. With respect to the former, Deronjić, for instance, asserted that the factors that the Trial Chamber considered to be aggravating were already subsumed in the offense to which he pled guilty,[510] while Babić argued that the Trial Chamber erred in considering his leadership position as an aggravating factor.[511] Dragan Nikolić, for his part, maintained that the Trial Chamber erred by holding that Nikolić enjoyed his criminal acts and that the beatings he administered had had "'all the making of *de facto* attempted murder.'"[512] When it has come to challenging the Trial Chambers' assessment of mitigating factors, some defendants have claimed that the chambers did not pay due attention to the value of their guilty pleas,[513] their personal or family circumstances,[514] or their remorse.[515] Given that the Trial Chambers possess tremendous discretion in sentencing, these challenges were unlikely to succeed under any circumstances, and in some cases, the defendants' allegations were directly contradicted by the clear text of the Trial Chambers' judgment.[516]

The guilty-plea defendants who have lately appealed their sentences have also asserted—in so many words—that they did not get the benefit of their plea bargain. Consequently, in addition to the specific challenges regarding aggravating and mitigating circumstances, most recent appeals have also featured the allegation, phrased in a variety of ways, that the Trial Chamber's view of the defendant's overall culpability inappropriately diverged from that which formed the basis of the plea agreement. In some cases, the divergence has related only to technical legal issues. In *Jokić*, for instance, both the prosecutor and defense asserted on appeal that the Trial Chamber had erred in finding Jokić partially liable pursuant to article 7(1) of the ICTY statute and partially liable under article 7(3) of the statute, which provides for superior responsibility.[517] More frequently, however, the divergence relates more fundamentally to an assessment of the gravity of the crime and the defendant's role in that crime. In *Babić*, for instance, the defense and prosecution had agreed that, although Babić held the highest political office in the region, his role in and control over the ethnic-cleansing campaign was very limited. On the basis of the facts to which Babić pled guilty, however, the Trial Chamber disagreed with the parties' characterization and found that Babić's participation in the joint criminal enterprise was "substantial."[518] Babić appealed and unsurprisingly maintained that the chamber had abused its discretion by failing to give sufficient weight to the facts agreed upon in the plea agreement.[519] Deronjić likewise appealed in part on the basis that the Trial Chamber had "expanded, amended and modified the facts contained in the second amended indictment and the factual basis."[520] He further maintained, in another ground of appeal, that the Trial Chamber "insinuate[d] his criminal responsibility for additional crimes not covered by the Second Amended Indictment," which, he maintained, constituted an "attempt to picture him as a vicious man."[521] Deronjić's defense counsel indicated that Deronjić was very upset by the chamber's conclusions. According to defense counsel, Deronjić had admitted many inculpatory facts from his first interviews with prosecutors and was willing to acknowledge fully the crimes that he committed. But he was not willing to accept inappropriate responsibility, which he felt that the Trial Chamber had imposed on him.[522]

Because the Trial Chambers possess tremendous sentencing discretion, the defendants have little about which they can legitimately complain, so their grounds of appeal have a nitpicky flavor to them. As noted above, Deronjić asserted that the Trial Chamber reached conclusions not specifically contained in the "plea agreement package." That assertion is certainly weighty, but in attempting to support it, Deronjić raised a host of alleged factual mistakes, the bulk of which, even if they were mistakes, were exceedingly trivial in the grand scheme of Deronjić's overall culpability. For instance, although Deronjić admitted to participating in the disarming of the population of the municipality of Bratunac as a whole, he argued that the Trial Chamber erred in finding that he had "joined the mission" to disarm the population of the specific village of Glogova, which is part of the municipality of Bratunac. In another similarly trivial-seeming allegation, Deronjić claimed that, because the Trial Chamber mentioned the Muslims of Glogova who were put on buses and transported to Muslim-held territory, the chamber "insinuate[d]" that Deronjić was criminally responsible for the fate of those Muslims.[523]

Jokić's grounds for appeal read similarly. Although the Trial Chamber sentenced him to seven years' imprisonment, which is three years less than the maximum ten-year term the prosecution could recommend, Jokić nonetheless appealed, maintaining, among other things, that the chamber had abused its discretion and caused a miscarriage of justice by failing to hold that Jokić's health and family circumstances—the fact that his daughter is ill and unable to care for herself—was an exceptional circumstance.[524] Babić, for his part, went so far as to seek to invalidate his guilty plea on the ground that the Trial Chamber had coerced him into pleading guilty as a coperpetrator by declining to accept his guilty plea as an aider or abettor.[525] On its face, the claim appears weighty, but not only did the evidence conclusively show the voluntariness of Babić's plea, but his own counsel conceded on appeal that it is "very difficult to discern the difference" between liability as an aider and abettor and the liability to which Babić in fact pled guilty.[526] As will be discussed in more detail in Chapter 10, allegations such as these reduce the reconciliatory impact of guilty pleas and cast doubt on the remorseful sentiments that ICTY defendants now routinely express.

The prosecution has supported many of the defendants' grounds for appeal. The *Dragan Nikolić* prosecution and defense were in accord, for instance, in asserting that when a Trial Chamber declines to follow a joint sentencing recommendation, it is obliged to provide a substantial explanation as to the basis for the departure.[527] Likewise, the Momir Nikolić prosecution and defense agreed that a mistranslation of defense counsel remarks could have prejudiced the Trial Chamber against Nikolić, and they agreed that the Trial Chamber had erred in its evaluation of Nikolić's testimony against other defendants.[528] And the *Babić* prosecution supported defense allegations that the Trial Chamber had erred in failing to consider as mitigating circumstances Babić's good conduct before and after the crime and in concluding that Babić had played a more substantial role in the joint criminal enterprise than the parties had asserted.[529] Indeed, in the *Babić* appeal, the prosecution joined with the defendant to seek the less-than-eleven-year sentence that the prosecution had originally urged upon the Trial Chamber.[530] By contrast, in *Jokić*, although the prosecution agreed with the defense that the Trial Chamber had erred in its conclusions regarding the basis of Jokić's conviction, the prosecution asserted that the error had no material effect on sentencing.[531] Presumably, the primary difference between the two cases is that the *Babić* Trial Chamber imposed a harsher-than-recommended sentence on Babić, whereas the *Jokić* Trial Chamber sentenced in accordance with the prosecution's recommendations. Even if the prosecution is not in fact displeased with a harsher-than-recommended sentence in a given case, its interest lies in convincing the Trial Chamber to sentence in accordance with the prosecution's recommendations because it is only through the chambers' adherence to the prosecution's recommendations that the promise of a particular recommendation will persuade defendants to plead guilty.[532]

If the ICTY Trial Chambers have failed to pay due attention to that reality, the Appeals Chamber has not. Whereas the Appeals Chamber has dismissed the appeals of those guilty-plea defendants who were sentenced to terms within the ranges appearing in their plea agreements, it has seen fit to reduce the sentences of two of the three guilty-plea defendants who were sentenced to terms outside of the agreed-upon ranges.[533] In *Momir Nikolić*, the Appeals Chamber reduced Nikolić's sentence by a sizable seven years after finding that the Trial Chamber had erred in double counting Nikolić's role in the atrocities, had failed adequately to support its assessment of Nikolić's cooperation with the prosecution, and may have been influenced by a mistranslation of defense counsel's remarks.[534] In reducing Nikolić's sentence from twenty-seven to twenty years' imprisonment, the Appeals Chamber bestowed on him a sentence within the range for which he had bargained. The only error that the Appeals Chamber was able to identify in the *Dragan Nikolić* case was that, in sentencing Nikolić to a term eight years longer than the term jointly recommended by the prosecution and defense, the Trial Chamber had attached too much weight to the possibility of Nikolić's early release.[535] The Appeals Chamber reduced Nikolić's sentence by only three years for that error, but even that reduction seemed questionable, as pointed out by Judge Mohamed Shahabuddeen in dissent. By sentencing outside the agreed-upon ranges in the *Momir Nikolić*, *Dragan Nikolić*, and *Babić* cases, ICTY Trial Chambers discouraged subsequent defendants from pleading guilty. The Appeals Chamber's subsequent sentence reductions in two of those cases ameliorated the influence of the Trial Chambers' decisions and helped to pave the way for future guilty pleas.

Other Aspects of the Evolution of ICTY Plea Bargaining

The ICTY's practice of plea bargaining has also evolved in other ways. For one thing, in recent times, the prosecution has required most defendants to cooperate with the prosecution by providing information and testifying in appropriate cases. Recent guilty-plea defendants have also made a point of expressing remorse when it has come time for sentencing. Finally, an evolution has occurred in the rationales the ICTY invokes to justify its practice of plea bargaining. All of these developments will be discussed in detail in Chapter 10, which will assess how the ICTY's recent practice of plea bargaining measures up to the restorative-justice guilty-plea system that I will develop in Chapters 8 and 9.

CHAPTER FIVE

Plea Bargaining at the ICTR

The ICTY and the ICTR each began its institutional life with a defendant who pled guilty, and the tribunals' subsequent practice of plea bargaining has also followed a roughly similar path. Both tribunals obtained their early guilty pleas without the promise of sentencing concessions and under somewhat idiosyncratic circumstances. However, because both tribunals have labored of late under intense Security Council pressure to complete their work, they have begun to use plea bargaining in a deliberate and systematic way to encourage defendants to plead guilty. As Chapter 4 recounts, the ICTY has had considerable success in this endeavor, disposing of the cases of nineteen defendants by means of guilty pleas. The ICTR was slower to get started. During its first nine years of operation, it received only three guilty pleas. However, during the eighteen months between December 2004 and May 2006, ICTR prosecutors persuaded three more defendants to plead guilty and persuaded two high-level offenders to provide incriminating evidence against their former accomplices. To obtain the evidence and the guilty pleas, prosecutors had to offer defendants substantial sentencing and charging concessions. The concessions were so substantial, in fact, that they have sparked something of a backlash. Trial chambers have refused to enforce some of the terms of these deals, and the Rwandan government has harshly condemned them. The ICTR is learning, as the ICTY did before it, that aggressive efforts to obtain incriminating information and guilty pleas are likely to provoke both judicial resistance and vociferous criticism.

A discussion of the three early ICTR guilty pleas is next, and it is followed by an examination of the ICTR's more recent and aggressive efforts to obtain

guilty pleas and incriminating evidence. The chapter concludes with an analysis
of ICTR plea bargaining, past and present.

Early ICTR Guilty Pleas: Few Incentives

The first three ICTR guilty pleas were tendered by the highest-ranking political official in Rwanda, a low-level killer who surrendered himself to the ICTR and
never would have been indicted otherwise, and an idealistic Belgian journalist
who had emigrated to Rwanda just a few months before the genocide. In other
words, the first three guilty-plea cases at the ICTR featured defendants in idiosyncratic circumstances that were unlikely to be replicated. In those early days,
ICTR prosecutors, like their ICTY counterparts, did little to encourage defendants to plead guilty.

The Kambanda Case

The ICTR obtained its first guilty plea from Jean Kambanda, who had been the
prime minister of the interim government that presided over Rwanda during the
1994 genocide. Kambanda was not one of the architects of the genocide, but he
admitted to actively implementing it by, among other things, distributing weapons and ammunition, setting up roadblocks to capture Tutsi, and using media
broadcasts to incite and encourage the massacres.[536] In July 1997, Kambanda was
arrested in Kenya.[537] He engaged in interviews with the prosecution before a lawyer had been appointed for him,[538] and he reportedly left these interviews believ-
ing that he would receive a sentence of no more than three years' imprisonment if
he pled guilty.[539] Kambanda entered into a plea agreement with the prosecution
in April 1998, pleading guilty to genocide and crimes against humanity. If he had
received any sentencing promises, however, they did not make their way into
his plea agreement. Indeed, the agreement expressly stated that the parties had
made "no agreements, understandings or promises" with respect to Kambanda's
sentence.[540]

Even if no promises had been made to Kambanda, it is customary for prosecutors to recommend a discounted sentence following a guilty plea. Kambanda's
guilty plea might have been expected to earn him especially significant concessions as a result of his high-level position. In *Plavšić*, for instance, the ICTY emphasized that Plavšić's former position as copresident of the Serbian Republic of
Bosnia and Herzegovina enhanced the reconciliatory and truth-telling value of

her guilty plea.[541] Further, Kambanda tendered his guilty plea before the completion of any ICTR trials; thus, his guilty plea, coming so early in the life of the tribunal, had the potential to set a powerful example for other defendants to follow. Finally, Kambanda provided prosecutors with a treasure trove of valuable information, including ninety hours of recorded testimony for use in subsequent trials of senior political and military leaders.[542] The prosecution described this information as "invaluable,"[543] and Kambanda promised to testify for the prosecution at those trials.[544] Such cooperation is also ordinarily rewarded with a sentence reduction.

Despite these considerations, the prosecution asked the Trial Chamber to impose a life sentence on Kambanda[545]—the harshest sentence the ICTR can impose. Unfortunately for Kambanda, the very same factors that could be marshaled to justify a significantly reduced sentence for Kambanda likely persuaded prosecutors to recommend a term of life imprisonment. Kambanda was the second highest-ranking political authority in Rwanda during the genocide, and although his high-level status rendered his guilty plea all the more significant, that same status made him seem especially deserving of a life sentence. That perception carried all the more significance because Kambanda was convicted at the very outset of the ICTR, so the disposition of his case garnered particularly intense publicity. The prosecution did try to ameliorate the effect of its harsh sentencing recommendation by suggesting that any future application for pardon or commutation of sentence "be considered favorably on the basis of past, current and future significant cooperation extended to the prosecution,"[546] but further it was not willing to go. The Trial Chamber acceded to the prosecution's recommendation and sentenced Kambanda to life imprisonment.[547] Although the Trial Chamber acknowledged that Kambanda's guilty plea constituted a mitigating factor, it concluded that the aggravating circumstances surrounding his crimes "negate[d] the mitigating circumstances."[548]

Outraged, Kambanda ceased cooperating with the prosecution, and he appealed, seeking to quash his guilty plea and proceed to trial.[549] Kambanda maintained, among other things, that he had not received competent legal advice and that he had been inappropriately detained in isolation in a safe house five hundred kilometers from the detention facility where the other ICTR defendants were held.[550] The Appeals Chamber rejected his appeal,[551] and Kambanda was sent to Mali to serve his sentence. Negotiations between the prosecution and Kambanda about the location of Kambanda's detention and about his request for a sentence revision resumed in 2004 when the prosecution again sought to obtain Kambanda's testimony in upcoming cases, but as of this writing no agreement has been reached.[552]

The Serushago Case

When Omar Serushago pled guilty to genocide and crimes against humanity in December 1998, he became only the third defendant to be convicted by the ICTR and the second to be convicted by means of a guilty plea. Serushago entered his guilty plea three months after Kambanda received his life sentence, but Serushago's decision to plead guilty was made long before the decision in *Kambanda* was handed down. The genocide was implemented largely at the hands of a militia called *Interahamwe*,[553] and Serushago commanded a small group of this militia. Serushago supervised a roadblock at which Tutsi were detained and killed, and he admitted to personally killing four people.[554] While living in Nairobi in April 1997, Serushago approached ICTR prosecutors and provided them with information that led, among other things, to the arrest of several high-ranking ICTR defendants, including Kambanda and Georges Ruggiu,[555] who will be discussed next. More than a year later, in July 1998, Serushago voluntarily surrendered to the ICTR even though he had not been indicted by the tribunal.[556]

Once Serushago arrived in Arusha, prosecutors hurriedly prepared a five-count indictment, charging him with one count of genocide and four counts of murder, extermination, torture, and rape as crimes against humanity.[557] At his first appearance, Serushago pled guilty to four of the five counts, and prosecutors withdrew the rape count.[558] The withdrawal of the rape count was somewhat curious: given Serushago's provision of information and his voluntary surrender without an indictment, it must have been clear to prosecutors that Serushago intended to plead guilty once an indictment was prepared. Under these circumstances, one might have expected the parties to consult about the charges to which Serushago would be willing to plead guilty before the indictment was issued. However, the parties apparently did not. Indeed, once indicted, Serushago vehemently objected to the rape charge, and his counsel was apparently so convinced that Serushago would be acquitted of rape that he threatened to proceed to trial on the rape charge after pleading guilty to the other charges. Prosecutors maintain that they included the rape charge because they initially believed it to be supported by sufficient evidence, but they subsequently determined that it was not, so they withdrew the count.[559] In subsequent testimony in the "Media Trial," however, Serushago indicated that he and another Rwandan offender "were incit-ing the killing of the Tutsis and their rape."[560]

Serushago, like Kambanda, received no written promises regarding the pros-ecution's sentence recommendation; indeed, with regard to sentencing, Serush-ago's plea agreement provides only that it "is at the entire discretion of the Trial Chamber."[561] When the time came to recommend a sentence, however, the pros-ecution did provide Serushago some consideration for his plea. Because Serush-ago was a low-level defendant whose case had not generated significant publicity, prosecutors—and the Trial Chamber for that matter—likely felt more able than in *Kambanda* to discount Serushago's sentence without concern that that dis-count would give rise to disastrous publicity. The prosecution accordingly praised Serushago's substantial cooperation and recommended a sentence of not less than twenty-five years' imprisonment.[562] At the time the prosecution made that recommendation, it had made sentencing recommendations in three previous cases, and in all three cases, it had recommended life sentences, which the Trial Chambers then imposed.[563] In every subsequent case that has gone to trial, the prosecution has likewise recommended a life sentence.[564] Thus, the prosecution's twenty-five-year sentence recommendation in *Serushago* seems clearly to reflect a discount for his guilty plea and cooperation, as does the fifteen-year sentence that the Trial Chamber in fact imposed.[565] Indeed, although four other ICTR defen-dants have now received more lenient sentences than Serushago, three of them also pled guilty.[566] In sentencing Serushago, the Trial Chamber had little to say about Serushago's guilty plea, although it duly noted the plea as a mitigating factor.[567]

The Ruggiu *Case*

Belgian defendant Georges Ruggiu is the only non-Rwandan to be indicted by the ICTR. Ruggiu had developed an interest in Rwanda and its politics in the early 1990s when he became friends with Rwandan students who were his neigh-bors in Belgium.[568] He subsequently participated in Belgian political debates re-garding Rwanda and met with Rwandan president Juvénal Habyarimana several times. Ruggiu became radically opposed to the Rwandan Patriotic Front (RPF), which had been engaged in an armed conflict with the Hutu-led Rwandan gov-ernment. In late 1993, Ruggiu moved to Rwanda apparently to marry[569] and to work as a journalist and broadcaster for the *Radio Television Libre des Mille Col-lines* (RTLM). During the spring of 1994, RTLM broadcasts, including those of Ruggiu, incited the population to kill Tutsi. ICTR prosecutors indicted Ruggiu on six counts: conspiracy to commit genocide, direct and public incitement to commit genocide, complicity in genocide, and murder, persecution, and extermination as crimes against humanity.[570]

A year after the genocide, Ruggiu wrote a book in which he proclaimed his innocence and asserted that RTLM broadcasts were intended to mobilize Rwandans against the RPF, not against Tutsi civilians.[571] Not surprisingly, then, after he was arrested, Ruggiu pled not guilty, and he subsequently contended that he remained convinced of his innocence until one of his codefendants made a public speech to the other ICTR detainees, informing them that the Rwandan violence had in fact been a planned genocide. Ruggiu reported that this news greatly distressed him and motivated him to engage in interviews with the prosecution.[572] He then reported undertaking a process of serious reflection after which he recognized his moral responsibility to tell the truth and to plead guilty.[573] Nearly three years after he was arrested, then, in May 2000, Ruggiu pled guilty to direct and public incitement to commit genocide and persecution as a crime against humanity.[574]

During plea negotiations, Ruggiu's lawyers made efforts to wring from prosecutors firmer sentencing guarantees than they had provided Kambanda and Serushago.[575] These efforts appeared to fail: Ruggiu's plea agreement, like Kambanda's and Serushago's, contained no promises regarding the prosecution's sentencing recommendation.[576] At the same time, the recommendation that the prosecution did submit to the Trial Chamber clearly reflected a discount as a result of Ruggiu's guilty plea. In particular, the prosecutor asked the Trial Chamber to impose a twenty-year prison sentence on Ruggiu, which is the shortest sentence ICTR prosecutors had theretofore ever recommended. In doing so, the prosecutor expressly stated that she would have recommended a life sentence had Ruggiu proceeded to trial.[577]

Ruggiu's Trial Chamber was likewise willing to reward Ruggiu for his self-conviction. Recall that the *Kambanda* Trial Chamber sentenced Kambanda to the harshest sentence available to it. The *Serushago* Trial Chamber did appear to discount Serushago's sentence as a result of his guilty plea, but the chamber did not discuss in any detail the mitigating role that Serushago's guilty plea played in his sentence. The *Ruggiu* Trial Chamber, by contrast, expressly extolled the value of guilty pleas and commended those who chose to tender them. The chamber lauded Ruggiu's guilty plea for "spar[ing] the Tribunal a lengthy investigation and trial" and for reflecting Ruggiu's "acknowledgement of his mistakes," which, according to the Trial Chamber, constituted "a healthy application of reason and sentiment." Most importantly, the chamber announced to other defendants that "some form of consideration" would be shown to defendants who plead guilty "in order to encourage other suspects and perpetrators of crimes to come forward."[578] The Trial Chamber then sentenced Ruggiu to twelve years' imprisonment, a sentence that was subsequently blessed by the prosecution. Although the government of Rwanda sharply criticized Ruggiu's sentence, the ICTR's chief of prosecutions described it as "a good gesture for other accused who would also wish to plead guilty and accept responsibility for their crimes."[579] The blessing given to guilty pleas did not, however, motivate a spate of defendants to confess their crimes. In fact, after Ruggiu, no ICTR defendant tendered a guilty plea for four-and-one-half years until Vincent Rutaganira pled guilty in December 2004.

Recent ICTR Guilty Pleas and Other Negotiations: The Introduction of Aggressive Charge Bargaining and Sentencing Bargaining

By November 2005, after approximately ten years in existence, the ICTR had disposed of the cases of twenty-six defendants, four of whom had pled guilty. Only three years remained, then, before the tribunal was required to complete its trials. The trials of twenty-six other defendants were ongoing at that time, and seventeen defendants were awaiting trial. Nineteen additional defendants remained at large. Some of these cases were slated for transfer to domestic courts, but most were to remain at the ICTR.[580] Given the tribunal's pace during its first ten years, the prospect that it could wrap up its trials by the end of 2008 looked dim indeed.

Aware of these realities, ICTR prosecutors have, for several years now, offered defendants substantial sentencing concessions to persuade them to plead guilty. But these efforts largely failed. As just noted, four-and-a-half years passed after Ruggiu's guilty plea, during which time no ICTR defendant was willing to plead guilty. In another work, I explored the reasons why ICTR defendants refused to tender guilty pleas. In particular, I determined that while most ICTR defendants would be happy enough to receive a sentence discount, they were not willing to plead guilty to genocide to get it. By and large, ICTR defendants deny that the Rwandan violence constituted a genocide. In their view, the violence took place in the context of the long-running war between the government of Rwanda and Ugandan Tutsi rebel forces. Although they acknowledge that atrocities were perpetrated against the Tutsi in Rwanda, they consider those atrocities the excesses of a legitimate and spontaneous national defense effort, not the elements of genocide.[581]

That the massacres in Rwanda did in fact constitute a genocide is a well-established fact in the international community. In addition, all of the ICTR defendants who have been convicted after trial have been convicted of genocide.[582] Not surprisingly, then, for most of the ICTR's existence, prosecutors have been unwilling to withdraw genocide charges in order to procure guilty pleas. With the trial-completion deadline fast approaching, however, prosecutors have lately been forced to do just that. Indeed, in order to obtain guilty pleas in recent cases, prosecutors have not only withdrawn genocide charges but they have radically revised the factual bases for the convictions. Prosecutors have additionally offered other substantial benefits to defendants who would provide incriminating evidence against high-level offenders. Negotiating with ICTR prosecutors has proved a risky business, however. One ICTR defendant turned up dead following his provision of evidence to the prosecution, and two others saw their agreements with the prosecution unravel at the hands of Trial Chambers. A discussion of the ICTR's newfound willingness to bargain over anything and everything follows.

The Rutaganira Case

Vincent Rutaganira was a low-level government official, who served as *conseiller* of the Mubuga sector from 1980 to 1994. The prosecutor's charges against him concerned a massacre of Tutsi that took place at the church in Mubuga. During three days in April 1994, between four thousand and five thousand Tutsi who had sought refuge in the church were butchered. The indictment against Rutaganira charged that he and two others had ordered the attack on the church and had personally participated in the killings. On the basis of these allegations, the indictment charged Rutaganira with six counts: genocide, extermination as a crime against humanity, murder as a crime against humanity, inhumane acts as a crime against humanity, a violation of article 3 common to the Geneva Conventions, and a violation of Additional Protocol II to the 1949 Geneva Conventions.[583]

Rutaganira fled Rwanda after the massacres and was still at large at the time the prosecutor issued the indictment against him in 1996. In February 2002, Rutaganira voluntarily surrendered to the tribunal,[584] and by the time he pled guilty, eight-and-one-half years after his indictment, the prosecution was prepared to take a very different view of the crimes he had committed. In particular, in his plea agreement, Rutaganira admitted only to omissions; that is, he denied ordering the attack on the church and participating in the attack, the charges that had formed the basis for his indictment. Rather, he admitted only that he was aware that Tutsi civilians had gathered in the church, that assailants were gathering near the church before the attack took place, and that "despite the fact that he was *conseiller* of Mubuga *secteur* he failed to protect the Tutsi who had sought refuge" in the church.[585] As part of the plea agreement, Rutaganira pled guilty to only one count: aiding and abetting extermination as a crime against humanity on the basis of his omissions. Pursuant to the plea agreement, the prosecution did not seek merely to withdraw the remaining counts of genocide, crimes against humanity, and war crimes, but rather asked the court to acquit Rutaganira of those counts because, the prosecution maintained, there did not exist sufficient evidence to convict him. As for Rutaganira's sentence, the prosecution agreed in the plea agreement to recommend a term of between six and eight years' imprisonment and further agreed to recommend that Rutaganira serve his sentence either in a European country or in the kingdom of Swaziland. Finally, the plea agreement made clear that Rutaganira would not cooperate with the prosecution.[586]

Rutaganira represents the first case of obvious sentence bargaining at the ICTR since it is the first case in which the prosecution was willing to commit to recommending a specific range of sentences in exchange for the defendant's guilty plea. *Rutaganira* appears to represent the first ICTR charge bargain, but in this case, appearances are probably deceiving. Although there is no question that Rutaganira admitted to facts substantially less serious than those that formed the basis of his indictment, it appears that the prosecution was willing to accept Rutaganira's meager admissions because it truly did not have the evidence to prove the original charges at trial. The prosecution said as much during Rutaganira's sentencing hearing, admitting that its "chance[] of success in proving all the charges against him was . . . extremely low" because the prosecutor was "not in possession of any evidence . . . which indicates that Mr. Rutaganira himself was implicated in the planning of the said attack, . . . nor does [the Prosecutor] possess any evidence . . . indicating that Mr. Rutaganira's role in the said attack at Mubuga church was premeditated."[587]

The evidence and testimony at Rutaganira's sentencing hearing supported the prosecution's representations. Witnesses testified, for instance, that Rutaganira and his wife had hidden two Tutsi girls and a Tutsi woman in their home during the massacres, despite the fact that the Rutaganiras themselves would have been killed had their assistance to the three Tutsi become known.[588] Another Tutsi witness testified that Rutaganira had saved her life by telling assailants that she was a Hutu, while others testified that Rutaganira had been on very good terms with Tutsi before the killings, acting as a godfather to a number of Tutsi children and asking Tutsi to be godparents to some of his children.[589] Finally, Mrs. Rutaganira returned to the same town in Rwanda in which the Mubuga church massacres took place, and she was appointed deputy mayor for Women's Development. That she holds a political position in Rwanda's current Tutsi-led government provides further support for the prosecution's assertions that no compelling evidence exists linking Rutaganira with the planning or execution of the killings at the Mubuga church.

Thus, the dramatic difference between the factual basis of Rutaganira's indictment and the factual basis of his guilty plea appears to have resulted from evidentiary insufficiencies rather than from charge bargaining. Rutaganira's plea deal might nonetheless be considered a charge bargain, however, because the prosecution asked the Trial Chamber to acquit Rutaganira of the remaining charges of crimes against humanity and war crimes for lack of evidence.[590] Extermination as a crime against humanity—the crime to which Rutaganira pled guilty—is a more-serious crime than murder as a crime against humanity because extermination requires proof of "an element of mass destruction which is not required for murder."[591] Therefore, if the prosecution possessed sufficient evidence to convict Rutaganira of aiding and abetting extermination as a crime against humanity, that evidence must have been sufficient to convict him of aiding and abetting in murder and inhumane acts as crimes against humanity. It is not surprising that the prosecution would desire to eliminate those charges once Rutaganira pled guilty to extermination: all of the counts related to the same conduct that formed the basis for the extermination charge, and, in those circumstances, prosecutors commonly withdraw counts that are less serious than the counts to which the defendant pleads guilty. The distinctive feature of *Rutaganira*, however, is that the prosecution did not seek merely to withdraw the less-serious counts but rather to have the Trial Chamber acquit Rutaganira of those counts on the basis of insufficient evidence. That request is implausible on its face, given Rutaganira's guilty plea to the more-serious crime of extermination.

Implausible or not, the request was of vital significance to Rutaganira because the government of Rwanda has attempted to prosecute ICTR defendants for crimes for which they have not been tried at the ICTR. For instance, in the *Bagambiki et al.* case, ICTR prosecutors declined to charge Bagambiki with rape even though it possessed evidence of his involvement in rape and sexual violence.[592] After the ICTR acquitted Bagambiki of the charges that had been brought against him,[593] the government of Rwanda sought his arrest so that it could try him for rape.[594] Rutaganira thus desired an acquittal on the remaining charges of crimes against humanity and war crimes as a means of preventing a subsequent Rwandan prosecution.

The *Rutaganira* Trial Chamber acceded to the prosecution's request and acquitted Rutaganira of the charges to which he did not plead guilty, holding that where the prosecutor admits that he has no proof supporting his indictment, and no other evidence exists in the record to establish the defendant's responsibility, then the Trial Chamber may determine that there exists no legal grounds for finding the defendant guilty.[595] In sentencing Rutaganira, the Trial Chamber took into account various mitigating factors, including his guilty plea, his voluntary surrender, the assistance he gave to some victims, his expression of remorse, and the fact that he did not actively participate in the killings. The Trial Chamber sentenced Rutaganira to six years' imprisonment,[596] the shortest sentence theretofore imposed by the ICTR.

The Bisengimana *Case*

Paul Bisengimana provided the ICTR with its next guilty plea, and the first at the ICTR to be obtained through the aggressive use of charge bargaining. Bisengimana was *bourgmestre* of Gikoro commune, where on April 13, 1994, more than one thousand Tutsi were massacred in the Musha church.[597] The prosecution's initial indictment against Bisengimana charged him with thirteen counts of genocide, crimes against humanity, and war crimes[598] for having helped to plan and implement the massacres at the Musha church and in Gikoro commune generally. The indictment portrayed Bisengimana as an active and enthusiastic participant in planning and executing the genocide. In particular, the indictment alleged that Bisengimana armed and trained *Interahamwe* militia during the months preceding the genocide and that he encouraged and ordered Hutu to rape and kill Tutsi once the genocide had begun.[599] The indictment also charged Bisengimana with personally raping and killing Tutsi.[600] As for the Musha church massacre, the indictment charged Bisengimana with transporting arms and men to the church, with personally participating in the killings, and with directing burials in mass graves.[601]

In September 2005, the prosecution moved to amend Bisengimana's indictment. The amended indictment, which charges Bisengimana with five counts of genocide and crimes against humanity,[602] omits some of the allegations that had appeared in the initial indictment,[603] but it retains many others and adds new allegations besides. The amended indictment, like the original indictment, paints Bisengimana as actively organizing and participating in the massacres. For instance, the amended indictment charged him with "spearheading a campaign of the destruction of Tutsi homes and the killing of Tutsi civilians" in the Gikoro commune[604] by, among other things, "launch[ing] an attack on Tutsi civilians taking refuge in [the] Musha church."[605] The amended indictment asserts that, during the attack, Bisengimana cut off the arms of a Tutsi man named Rusanganwa, after which Rusanganwa bled to death.[606] Among other new allegations, the amended indictment also charged Bisengimana with launching an attack on the Tutsi civilians seeking refuge at the Ruhanga Protestant church and school, a massacre that had not been mentioned in the initial indictment.[607] In both Bisengimana's initial and amended indictments, he is alleged to have committed many of his crimes with Laurent Semanza, formerly the *bourgmestre* of Bikumbi commune. The ICTR convicted Semanza of genocide in 2003, and during his trial, witnesses testified as to Bisengimana's involvement in some of the incidents described in Bisengimana's indictments.[608]

In October 2005, a month after the prosecution amended its indictment against Bisengimana, the parties entered into a plea agreement in which Bisengimana agreed to plead guilty to aiding and abetting two of the five charges in his amended indictment: murder and extermination as crimes against humanity.[609] In exchange for Bisengimina's guilty plea, the prosecution agreed to withdraw and seek his acquittal on the charges of genocide, complicity in genocide, and rape as a crime against humanity, and it agreed to recommend a sentence of between twelve and fourteen years' imprisonment.[610] Finally, the prosecution promised to support Bisengimana's request to serve his sentence in a European country.[611]

The facts contained in Bisengimana's plea agreement bear little resemblance to the facts alleged in the amended indictment filed only a month before the conclusion of the plea agreement. Whereas both the initial and amended indictments portray Bisengimana as actively planning and executing the raping and killing sprees, the plea agreement depicts him only as a passive observer. No longer is

Bisengimana arming and training *Interahamwe* militia; in the plea agreement, he is merely "aware that weapons such as guns and grenades were distributed to *Interahamwe* militia . . . at the Musha church by members of the Rwandan army."[612] No longer is Bisengimana launching attacks and participating in massacres. In his plea agreement, Bisengimana admits only to being "present" during the attack on the Musha church.[613] As for the attack on the Ruhanga church, the plea agreement does not even acknowledge Bisengimana's presence there. He admits only that he "he took no active steps to protect the Tutsi refugees."[614] Bisengimana likewise admits only that he was present at the murder of Rusanganwa, not that he himself hacked off the man's limbs.[615] Under the plea agreement, Bisengimana's criminal liability stems not from his commission of any criminal acts, then, but from his failure to prevent and punish those acts. Bisengimana acknowledges in the plea agreement that, as *bourgmestre* of Gikoro, he was responsible for enforcing local laws and for ensuring peace, public order, and the safety of people and property. He admits that by virtue of his position, he had a duty to prevent the murders or punish their perpetrators and that he failed to do so.[616] He also acknowledges that his presence at the massacre sites "had an encouraging effect on the perpetrators and [gave] them the impression that he endorsed the killing[s]."[617]

The *Bisengimana* case appears to constitute the ICTR's first factually distortive charge bargain. As just noted, the facts appearing in Bisengimana's indictment differ dramatically from the facts appearing in his plea agreement. Whereas in the indictment, Bisengimana planned massacres, trained and armed militias, and himself raped and murdered, in the plea agreement, his involvement was limited to that of a passive observer whose position obligated him merely to prevent the crimes. The facts in *Rutaganira* likewise changed markedly between the indictment and the plea agreement, but in *Rutaganira*, the prosecution stated outright that it lacked the evidence to prove the facts and charges that were subsequently withdrawn, and this assertion was supported by the evidence that was presented at Rutaganira's sentencing hearing. Charles Adeogun-Phillips was the lead prosecutor in both *Bisengimana* and *Rutaganira*, but in *Bisengimana*, Adeogun-Phillips was far less forthcoming about the evidence that the prosecution did or did not possess. At one point during the sentencing hearing, Adeogun-Phillips indicated that he lacked evidence to prove the three charges on which he sought Bisengimana's acquittal;[618] however, at other points, he appeared to acknowledge that the request for acquittal was a consequence of the plea negotiations.[619]

Presumably, Adeogun-Phillips was unwilling to assert clearly and forthrightly that the prosecution lacked sufficient evidence to convict Bisengimana because such a claim would be difficult to sustain. For one thing, more than five years after issuing the initial indictment and just a month before entering into the plea agreement, the prosecution filed an amended indictment that contained detailed allegations of Bisengimana's eager participation in the massacres. If the prosecution did not have evidence to support these allegations, then one has to ask why it amended the indictment to include them. Second and more importantly, a spate of witnesses in the *Semanza* trial testified not only as to Bisengimana's presence during the massacres but also as to his active involvement, and that testimony directly supports many of the allegations appearing in Bisengimana's indictment. *Semanza* witness VC, for instance, testified that Bisengimana introduced Semanza at a February 2004 meeting as an "important personality" to whose message the audience should listen carefully. According to VC, Semanza then told the audience that the Tutsi of the region would be killed and thrown into nearby lakes so that they would return to their ancestors in Ethiopia.[620] *Semanza* witness VF testified that Bisengimana and police came to her hill and shot at her and other Tutsi on the morning of April 10, 1994.[621] Witness VA testified to overhearing a conversation between Bisengimana and Semanza during which Semanza suggested burning down the Musha church to kill the refugees inside. According to witness VA, Bisengimana expressed reluctance to destroy the church because he had been baptized and married there, so he proposed starving to death the Tutsi refugees instead.[622] Witness VA also testified that she saw Bisengimana hack off Rusanganwa's arm and leg.[623]

The *Semanza* Trial Chamber was persuaded by much of this testimony. It found, for instance, that Bisengimana, Semanza, and others went to the Musha church on April 8 or 9, 1994, in order to assess the situation shortly after the refugees began arriving there. The Trial Chamber further accepted the testimony of witnesses who claimed to have seen Semanza and Bisengimana gathering local *Interahamwe* militia in preparation for the attack on the Musha church.[624] The Trial Chamber further found that Semanza, "Bisengimana and others . . . returned to the church with *Interahamwe*, soldiers, and gendarmes on 13 April 1994 around midmorning. These assailants proceeded to attack the refugees in the church with gunfire and grenades."[625] During the trial, Semanza's defense counsel tried to portray Bisengimana as the person primarily responsible for the genocide in Gikoro,[626] and the Trial Chamber seemed receptive to such an argument: after surveying the evidence, it found that "the Prosecutor did not introduce sufficient evidence to prove that [Semanza] worked in close cooperation with Bisengimana to organize the massacre at Musha church,"[627] thus suggesting that it was Bisengimana who had organized the massacre there.

The *Semanza* testimony and findings along with the prosecution's issuance of the amended indictment render implausible any suggestion that the prosecution agreed to withdraw charges in *Bisengimana* because it lacked evidence to prove those charges. This fact did not go unnoticed by the *Bisengimana* Trial Chamber. Indeed, the charge bargain in *Bisengimana* was so blatant that it seemed to provoke in the Trial Chamber hostility toward Bisengimana's plea deal in its entirety. The Trial Chamber reportedly refused the parties' numerous requests to discuss the provisions of the plea agreement prior to its conclusion. And once the plea agreement was concluded, the Trial Chamber refused to accept Bisengimana's guilty plea, holding that the factual discrepancies between the amended indictment and the plea agreement had "an impact on the equivocal or unequivocal nature of the plea."[628]

In response to the Trial Chamber's rejection of the guilty plea, the prosecution again amended the indictment, this time deleting the allegations of Bisengimana's active participation in the bloodshed. This amended indictment contained the same five counts as its predecessor: genocide; complicity in genocide; and murder, extermination, and rape as crimes against humanity.[629] At a December hearing, Bisengimana pled guilty to aiding and abetting murder and extermination as crimes against humanity and not guilty to the two counts of genocide and the count of rape as a crime against humanity.[630] As he had done in *Rutaganira*, the *Bisengimana* prosecutor asked the Trial Chamber to acquit Bisengimana of the genocide and rape charges, but this Trial Chamber refused. Although it granted the prosecution's request to withdraw the charges, it rejected the request for an acquittal, holding that "there isn't adequate reason to justify acquittal."[631] That decision, though sound as a legal matter, is highly worrisome for Bisengimana given Rwanda's efforts to prosecute ICTR defendants such as Emmanuel Bagambiki. The Trial Chamber's refusal to acquit Bisengimana leaves him vulnerable to a Rwandan prosecution.

Not only was the Trial Chamber unwilling to accede to the prosecution's charging requests, it also rejected its sentencing recommendation. As noted above, Bisengimana's plea agreement permitted the parties to recommend sentences of between twelve and fourteen years' imprisonment, and the prosecution sought a fourteen-year term.[632] Noting Bisengimana's official position and the fact that more than one thousand people were killed in his presence at the Musha church, the Trial Chamber chose to sentence outside of the parties' agreement and imposed on Bisengimana a fifteen-year term of imprisonment.[633] Given the Trial Chamber's evident hostility to Bisengimana's plea agreement, neither the prosecutor nor the defense counsel was surprised by the Trial Chamber's imposition of a harsher-than-agreed-upon sentence,[634] but both parties decried it, maintaining that it will discourage other ICTR defendants from pleading guilty.[635] The government of Rwanda, for its part, expressed satisfaction with Bisengimana's sentence but condemned the ICTR for withdrawing the genocide charges.[636]

However disappointed the parties might have been about the Trial Chamber's refusal to sentence within the agreed-upon range, the fact remains that Bisengimana's charge bargain garnered for him a significant sentence reduction. Semanza received a twenty-five-year sentence,[637] and other ICTR defendants convicted of similar crimes received sentences of equal or greater length. For instance, the ICTR's first defendant, Jean-Paul Akayesu, was, like Bisengimana, a *bourgmestre*, and he too was charged with encouraging and participating in massacres of Tutsi.[638] Akayesu in fact appears a more sympathetic figure than Bisengimana because considerable evidence was presented at his trial suggesting that before April 18, 1994, he attempted to prevent the killings in his commune. The evidence indicated that Akayesu began participating in the genocide after that date only because the *Interahamwe* threatened him with death if he failed to do so.[639] For his involvement in the killings in Taba commune, Akayesu was convicted of one count of genocide, one count of direct and public incitement to genocide, and seven counts of crimes against humanity;[640] he was sentenced to life imprisonment.[641] Compared with Akayesu, then, Bisengimana's longer-than-recommended sentence was short indeed.

The Serugendo Case

During the spring of 2006, prosecutors and defense counsel in the *Serugendo* case observed with concern Trial Chamber II's resistance to the *Bisengimana* plea bargain.[642] Serugendo was indicted in July 2005 on five counts: genocide, conspiracy to commit genocide, complicity in genocide, direct and public incitement to genocide, and persecution as a crime against humanity.[643] The indictment alleged that Serugendo was a founding member of both the *Interahamwe* militia and the RTLM radio station, whose broadcasts incited the killing of Tutsi. According to the indictment, Serugendo, along with others, organized rallies and political meetings designed to indoctrinate and incite *Interahamwe* to kill Tutsi.[644] The indictment further charged Serugendo with traveling through the streets of Kigali during the genocide, ordering *Interahamwe* to kill Tutsi and praising the killers for their "good work."[645] As for RTLM, Serugendo was a member of its steering committee and served as its technical chief.[646] The indictment alleged that Serugendo was aware of and encouraged RTLM's genocidal broadcasts, and that as a result of his position at the radio station, he exercised authority over its employees.[647] Serugendo was arrested in September 2005 and pled not guilty to the five charges in his indictment.[648]

By the spring of 2006, rumors were circulating that the prosecution was engaged in plea negotiations with Serugendo, but little was known of them. Indeed, Serugendo appeared at a closed hearing on March 15, 2006, that was not even listed on the tribunal's calendar.[649] At some point during the spring, Serugendo and the prosecution apparently concluded a plea agreement, but the existence of that agreement was not disclosed until the day before Serugendo's sentencing hearing. As part of the plea agreement, Serugendo agreed to plead guilty to two of the five counts against him: direct and public incitement to commit genocide and persecution as a crime against humanity.[650] He also agreed to cooperate with the prosecution, and his cooperation reportedly "fills 200 pages."[651] Prosecutors dropped the remaining three charges and agreed to recommend a sentence of between six and ten years' imprisonment.[652]

Serugendo had recently been diagnosed with a terminal illness, and, at his sentencing hearing, held on June 1, 2006, he was not able to stand without assistance or to read his statement of remorse. Consequently, during his sentencing hearing, prosecutors accepted the possibility of a sentence of less than six years' imprisonment or even of a transfer to a hospital prison ward in Europe.[653] As a result of Serugendo's deteriorating health, the Trial Chamber issued an oral judgment the very next day, sentencing him to six years' imprisonment. In reaching its sentence, the Trial Chamber took account of various mitigating circumstances, including Serugendo's guilty plea, his remorse, his substantial cooperation with the prosecution, and his poor health.[654] As of this writing (only a week after the judgment was announced), the ICTR has not made available Serugendo's plea agreement, the transcripts of his hearings, or the Trial Chamber's judgment. What is clear even without any documents is that Serugendo received substantial concessions for his guilty plea. If his actions during the genocide in any way resembled those charged against him in his indictment, he could have expected to receive a lengthy sentence, perhaps life imprisonment, following a trial.

Negotiations for Information

ICTR prosecutors have lately been negotiating not only to obtain guilty pleas but also to obtain incriminating evidence against high-level offenders. Two ICTR defendants, Michel Bagaragaza and Juvénal Uwilingiyimana, were members of the so-called akazu, the inner circle surrounding former Rwandan president Habyarimana's family. Members of the akazu are believed to have organized the genocide; thus, Bagaragaza and Uwilingiyimana were believed to have information of tremendous value to ICTR prosecutors.[655] In exchange for this insider evidence, the prosecution apparently promised to shield Bagaragaza and Uwilingiyimana from ICTR prosecutions. The two men took the bargain, but as matters currently stand, neither man got what he was hoping for.

The Bagaragaza *Case.* Michel Bagaragaza was the former head of Rwanda's powerful tea industry and a close friend of former President Habyarimana. In an indictment confirmed in July 2005, prosecutors charged Bagaragaza with three counts: genocide, conspiracy to commit genocide, and complicity in genocide. The indictment alleged that Bagaragaza helped to plan the extermination of the Tutsi and that he helped to implement that plan by making speeches inciting others to genocide, by making financial contributions to the *Interahamwe*, and by ordering his tea factory employees to provide *Interahamwe* members with fuel and transportation to massacre sites.[656] Bagaragaza voluntarily surrendered to the ICTR in August 2005, but before doing so, he entered into an agreement with the prosecution in which he promised to provide an extensive statement that would incriminate himself and other members of the akazu. In exchange, the prosecution promised to seek the transfer of Bagaragaza's case to a national court.[657] After Bagaragaza's surrender, he was immediately sent to the ICTY's detention facilities in The Hague because his cooperation with the prosecution made it too dangerous to detain him with the other ICTR defendants in Arusha. His family was sent to the United States.[658]

In February 2006, prosecutors requested that the Trial Chamber transfer Bagaragaza's case to the courts of Norway.[659] Because Norwegian courts do not have jurisdiction over genocide, Bagaragaza was to be prosecuted there on charges of domestic homicide, for which the maximum sentence is twenty-one years.[660]

As noted in Chapter 2, the ICTY and ICTR added provisions to their procedural rules that permit them to transfer cases to national jurisdictions. Such transfers were considered necessary to enable the tribunals to complete their work on schedule. The *Bagaragaza* prosecutors further observed that a trial in Norway would help to educate people about the Rwandan genocide and to prevent similar tragedies in the future.[661] Although prosecutors did not say so, one has to assume that the lenient maximum sentence that Norwegian courts could have imposed on Bagaragaza and Norway's practice of releasing prisoners after they have served only half of their sentences[662] also made Norway a particularly attractive trial location for prosecutors seeking to induce Bagaragaza to provide them with information. Most Rwandan defendants convicted by the ICTR have been sent to serve their sentences in Mali, where amenities are few and defendants have no guarantee of early release.

Norway, indeed, was such an attractive trial location that the government of Rwanda vehemently opposed Bagaragaza's transfer there. Rwanda argued that the maximum prison sentence to which Bagaragaza would be subject in Norway was patently inadequate, and it sought transfer of the case to its own courts.[663] Rwanda requested leave to appear before the Trial Chamber to present its complaints officially, but the Trial Chamber denied Rwanda's request because it had not been made in a timely fashion. However, the Trial Chamber denied the prosecution's request for transfer, even without the benefit of Rwanda's official input because Norwegian courts do not have jurisdiction over the crimes for which Bagaragaza was charged. Under the circumstances, the Trial Chamber held, "Bagaragaza's alleged criminal acts cannot be given their full legal qualification."[664] The Trial Chamber's decision places Bagaragaza and the prosecution in a difficult position. Bagaragaza has already upheld his end of the bargain; he has provided incriminating evidence to the prosecution and he has testified in a recent trial. The ball is now in the prosecution's court to find a trial location that is both desirable to Bagaragaza and acceptable to the Trial Chamber.

The Uwilingiyimana *Case.* In his interviews with the prosecution, Bagaragaza implicated other members of the akazu, one of whom was Juvénal Uwilingiyimana, a former minister of commerce and director of Rwanda's Office of Tourism and National Parks during the genocide.[665] Prosecutors issued a sealed indictment against Uwilingiyimana in June 2005, charging him with helping to plan and implement the genocide by allowing militia members to train in Rwanda's dense forests and by ordering executions at roadblocks once the genocide had begun.[666] The ICTR issued an arrest warrant against Uwilingiyimana in August of that year. Uwilingiyimana reportedly had valuable information implicating other members of the akazu,[667] so when he indicated a willingness to reveal that information, prosecutors agreed to hold the arrest warrant in abeyance.

Prosecutors interviewed Uwilingiyimana in Lille, France, throughout the fall of 2005.[668] On November 21, 2005, Uwilingiyimana failed to arrive for a scheduled meeting with prosecutors, and his family reported him missing soon thereafter. On November 28, a letter allegedly written by Uwilingiyimana was posted to the Internet. The letter accused ICTR prosecutors and investigators of threatening him with bodily harm if he failed to cooperate and of pressuring him to lie about his former associates in order to confirm the prosecutors' allegations.[669] ICTR prosecutors denied that the letter was authentic, but Uwilingiyimana's family insisted that it was.[670] In response to the letter and Uwilingiyimana's failure to appear for his interview, ICTR prosecutors unsealed the indictment against him and made public Uwilingiyimana's written agreement to cooperate. In the latter document, Uwilingiyimana stated that he had "not been pressurized" and had not received any threats or promises from the ICTR to induce him to collaborate with them.[671]

On December 17, 2005, Uwilingiyimana's badly decomposed body was found in a Belgian canal.[672] Tests conducted by Belgian authorities were inconclusive as to the cause of his death.[673]

A Summary of the ICTR's Practice of Plea Bargaining: Troubling Success in the Midst of Troublesome Challenges

The ICTR's practice of plea bargaining has undergone a dramatic evolution in recent times. In the early days, ICTR prosecutors did not practice plea bargaining—or they at least did not admit to practicing it—as a means of motivating defendants to plead guilty. Kambanda reportedly believed that he had been promised a sentence discount in exchange for his guilty plea, but no such promise appeared in his plea agreement, and prosecutors instead asked the Trial Chamber to impose on Kambanda the harshest available sentence. Prosecutors similarly declined to make Serushago any written promises regarding his sentence. In the end, the prosecution did appear to discount the sentence it recommended for Serushago on the basis of his guilty plea, and the Trial Chamber likewise saw fit to impose on him a relatively lenient sentence. Both the prosecution and the Trial Chamber acknowledged that guilty pleas are considered mitigating factors in sentencing, but that was the extent of the discussion.

By the time Ruggiu decided to plead guilty, ICTR prosecutors were still unwilling to commit to recommending a specific sentence or range of sentences; however, they were willing to publicly acknowledge that the sentence they had chosen to recommend for Ruggiu had been discounted as a result of his guilty plea. Had Ruggiu been convicted at trial, the prosecution would have recommended a life sentence, the prosecutor announced. Instead, she recommended a twenty-year sentence. The *Ruggiu* Trial Chamber likewise was willing expressly to acknowledge that it had discounted Ruggiu's sentence in consequence of his guilty plea, and it went further by generally praising the benefits brought about through guilty pleas and by announcing its willingness to reward them. That is, the Trial Chamber advised defendants who were considering guilty pleas that the Trial Chambers would reduce their sentences, regardless of whether or not they had received any specific promises from the prosecution.

In the years following Ruggiu's April 2000 guilty plea, prosecutors reportedly made substantial efforts to induce ICTR defendants to plead guilty. Prosecutors expressed their willingness to bargain not only over the sentence recommendations but additionally over the location of the defendant's detention after conviction.[674] Ruggiu, Rutaganira, and Bisengimana all benefited from this latter sort of bargaining as prosecutors supported their requests to serve their sentences in Europe.[675]

The offer of substantial sentencing discounts and attractive detention locations was nevertheless insufficient to motivate ICTR defendants to plead guilty. Rather, as explored elsewhere, it was the withdrawal of genocide charges that ICTR defendants most desired. Until very recently, however, that sort of charge bargaining was the one form of bargaining in which ICTR prosecutors were unwilling to engage. And I for one expected it to stay that way. In the manuscript that I submitted to my editor in December 2005, I wrote:

> The nature of Rwandan violence effectively prevents prosecutors from engaging in charge bargaining. The Rwandan massacres are well-accepted to have constituted a genocide; ICTR judgments, the judgments of other courts, and virtually all commentators have labeled the massacres a genocide. Under these circumstances, ICTR prosecutors have little ability to withdraw genocide charges without infuriating the current government of Rwanda and generating scathing publicity.

The plea bargains concluded during the winter and spring of 2006 proved my prediction wrong, but while the ICTR's willingness to engage in charge bargaining contravened my expectations, the reaction to that charge bargaining did not. As I predicted, Rwanda has harshly condemned the ICTR's current willingness to withdraw charges of genocide, and that in itself is worrisome for the ICTR because the ICTR's ability to conduct its trials depends a great deal on its willingness to placate Rwanda. Rwanda has flexed its figurative muscles effectively on a number of occasions. In 1999, for instance, when the ICTR Appeals Chamber dismissed with prejudice the indictment of Jean-Bosco Barayagwiza and ordered him released after determining that his rights had been violated,[676] Rwanda sharply denounced the decision and suspended all dealings with the ICTR, going so far as to refuse to issue a visa to the tribunal's chief prosecutor, Carla del Ponte.[677] Relations normalized after the Appeals Chamber reconsidered its decision and reinstated Barayagwiza's indictment,[678] but a new crisis erupted when del Ponte announced that her office would begin investigating the war crimes and crimes against humanity allegedly committed by soldiers of the current Rwandan government. Rwanda retaliated by preventing ICTR witnesses from traveling to Arusha, and trials stalled.[679] Del Ponte acknowledged Rwanda's power when she observed, "If I don't get cooperation from Rwanda, . . . I can first open the door at the detention center and set them all free and then second I can close the door to my office because without them I cannot do anything at all."[680] Del Ponte felt that power firsthand when she was relieved of her post, largely as a result of Rwanda's efforts to oust her.[681]

A desire to placate Rwanda may have underlay the Trial Chambers' refusals to enforce prosecutorial promises in *Bisengimana* and *Bagaragaza*, but whatever the chambers' motivations, their actions place the prosecution in a difficult bind. Required to complete its trials in an impossibly short time frame, the prosecution has understandably turned to plea bargaining. Efforts to procure guilty pleas with the same sort of concessions that motivated ICTY defendants to plead guilty failed, however, so ICTR prosecutors understandably turned to more aggressive—and distortive—forms of bargaining. The concessions offered as a result of this bargaining have proved appealing to ICTR defendants, but that appeal will be short-lived if the Trial Chambers refuse to convey them. Bisengimana pled guilty expecting that his sentence would not exceed fourteen years' imprisonment. Instead, he received a fifteen-year term and faces the possibility of a Rwandan prosecution if he lives beyond his ICTR sentence. Bagaragaza provided prosecutors with information expecting that he would be tried in a European court that features lenient sentences, comfortable prison conditions, and generous parole practices. It is too soon to know what treatment Bagaragaza will eventually receive, but the Trial Chamber's unwillingness to transfer his case to Norway casts a cloud over prosecutorial efforts to conclude similar agreements with other defendants. ICTY defendants abruptly stopped pleading guilty once the Trial Chambers began sentencing outside of the recommended range, and there is reason to believe that ICTR defendants will be similarly deterred.

Indeed, ICTR defendants may need particular assurance that their concessions will be forthcoming given the danger facing defendants who plead guilty or provide evidence to the prosecution. As noted above, Kambanda complained on appeal about his detention in a safe house five hundred kilometers from the U.N. detention facility in Arusha, but he was detained there largely because detention with the other ICTR defendants was deemed too dangerous for a defendant who was cooperating with the prosecution. Similarly, once Ruggiu began cooperating with the prosecution, other ICTR defendants started threatening him, so he had to be moved to a different wing of the detention facility.[682] And Bagaragaza never even got to Arusha. He was taken directly to detention facilities in The Hague following his voluntary surrender. Kambanda, Serushago, and Ruggiu also insisted that the prosecution provide protection—including the possibility of relocation—to their families,[683] and Serushago repeatedly asked for security for himself when he appeared in court.[684] The sad fate of Juvénal Uwilingiyimana suggests that the fears of these ICTR defendants are justified, but for the prosecution, they make concluding a plea agreement even more difficult.

CHAPTER SIX

Plea Bargaining at the Special Panels in East Timor

In 2001 the United Nations established Special Panels for Serious Crimes to prosecute crimes relating to East Timor's 1999 vote of independence from Indonesia. From their inception to their closure in 2005, the panels convicted eighty-four defendants, and as time went on, an increasingly large proportion of those convictions came about by means of guilty pleas. After an overview of criminal prosecutions at the Special Panels and an overview of the panels' early guilty-plea cases, this chapter will trace the evolution that has occurred in plea bargaining over the panels' life span.

Overview of Criminal Prosecutions and Early Guilty Pleas

Following the violence that engulfed East Timor in the fall of 1999, the U.N. established the U.N. Transitional Administration in East Timor (UNTAET) as a peacekeeping mission to administer East Timor until its independence was viable.[685] As part of its administration, UNTAET established Special Panels for Serious Crimes, granting them jurisdiction to prosecute those accused of genocide, war crimes, and crimes against humanity, along with certain violent domestic crimes, such as murder, sexual offenses, and torture.[686] The prosecutorial arm of the Special Panels, known as the Serious Crimes Unit, issued its first indictments in 2000, and virtually all of its early indictments charged domestic crimes, under the Indonesian Criminal Code, rather than international crimes. Subsequent indictments charged crimes against humanity, and by the time of its closure in May 2005, the Serious Crimes Unit had indicted 391 individuals.[687] The Special Panels tried eighty-seven of these defendants, acquitting three and convicting eighty-four of at least some of the charges leveled against them.[688] Virtually all of the defendants convicted were low-level Timorese militia members—typically illiterate farmers.[689] A majority of the remaining indictees—and all of the high-level indictees—live in Indonesia,[690] which refused to surrender them. Thus, the Special Panels obtained custody over only low-level offenders.

Upon apprehension, virtually all Special Panels defendants immediately admitted to participating in the crime for which they were charged, but virtually all of them also maintained that they did so because they were forced, or at least ordered, by a militia leader or an Indonesian military official.[691] The Special Panels' first case is prototypical: the defendant, João Fernandes, pled guilty to murder, admitting that he killed a village chief but asserting that he did so on the orders of a militia commander and the Indonesian military.[692] The panel accepted Fernandes's guilty plea and sentenced him to twelve years' imprisonment.[693] Fernandes appealed and showed his and his defense counsel's unfamiliarity with the consequences of guilty pleas by claiming, among other things, that he should not have been convicted because one of the proven facts of his conviction was that he had acted under orders, so that the killing did not result from his deliberate and premeditated action. The appeals court affirmed the conviction, holding that the fact that the defendant acted under someone else's orders did not exclude his own criminal responsibility.[694] In a separate opinion, however, appeals court judge Egonda-Ntende called the Special Panels' guilty-plea procedure into serious question. In particular, Judge Egonda-Ntende maintained that the presiding judge had failed to ensure that Fernandes understood the consequences of his guilty plea. The presiding judge had merely asked Fernandes, an illiterate farmer, if he understood the consequences of the plea, and the judge was satisfied when Fernandes responded, "yes, I am aware." In Judge Egonda-Ntende's view, merely repeating the words of the statute was insufficient; rather, the presiding judge should have asked Fernandes a series of questions, the responses to which would have revealed whether Fernandes did or did not actually understand the consequences of the plea.[695] Judge Egonda-Ntende was also critical of the presiding judge's attempt to ensure that Fernandes's plea was voluntary and informed. Judge Egonda-Ntende maintained, for instance, that the presiding judge's questions relating to the voluntariness of the plea "could have been better framed," and he criticized the fact that the presiding judge referred to witness statements and original testimony of witnesses interchangeably.[696]

Following *Fernandes*, and perhaps as a result of Judge Egonda-Ntende's guidance, the Special Panels appeared to treat defendant admissions more cautiously. After conducting an almost incomprehensible plea colloquy with defendant João da Costa in the *Los Palos* case, the panel declined to accept his guilty plea. Indeed, ten cases of individual defendants and one case of multiple defendants followed *Fernandes*, and all of these featured defendants who admitted to participating in the crimes for which they were charged but who also claimed to have done so under orders or as a result of duress. In all but one of these cases, the Special Panels declined to treat such admissions as guilty pleas, instead finding, for instance, that "there was no admission of guilt in the Defendant's statement . . . because the Defendant did not agree totally with the charges put forward by the Public Prosecutor."[697] This caution proved advisable, particularly given the confusion exhibited by many defense counsel and defendants regarding the distinction between duress, which the Special Panels treat as a defense, and superior orders, which can constitute only a mitigating factor in sentencing.[698] Indeed, in the *Gaspar Leki* case, the defendant pled guilty to murder because he shot and killed a man who had been hiding in the bushes. The panel initially accepted the guilty plea, and only as a result of further questioning did it learn that, although the defendant had been ordered to shoot anything that moved, he believed that he was shooting a wild pig in the bush. Since the element of deliberate intent to commit murder was called into question, the panel reversed its decision to accept the guilty plea and proceeded to trial.[699] That few of these early cases were resolved by guilty pleas was of comparatively little financial import because these early Special Panels' trials took very little time; they sometimes lasted only one day or consumed two or three sessions at the longest.[700] Thus, guilty pleas would have resulted in only minimal time and resource savings.

Subsequent trials took considerably longer, however. For one thing, prosecutors began bringing charges of crimes against humanity, rather than the easier-to-prove domestic crimes. In addition, some of the Special Panels' later indictments featured allegations of command responsibility, the proof of which requires additional witness testimony, and they featured multiple defendants, each of whom might be charged with a number of crimes taking place in more than one location. Thus, in later cases, prosecutors tried more crimes; had more theories of liability to prove in each case; and, because the crimes charged were crimes

against humanity, had to prove not only the defendant's commission of the underlying offense, say murder or imprisonment, but also that the offense took place
in the context of a widespread or systematic attack directed against a civilian
population.[701] Proving the contextual elements of crimes against humanity took
less time at the Special Panels than at other international criminal tribunals,
largely because Special Panels' judges were willing to substantially rely on media
and NGO reports to conclude that the events of 1999 were part of a widespread
and systematic attack on a civilian population.[702] Indeed, in the Special Panels'
first case involving allegations of crimes against humanity, the *Los Palos* case,
defense counsel appeared virtually to concede the existence of the contextual elements of crimes against humanity as well as the existence of an armed conflict,[703]
which the panel seemed intent on establishing even though it is not one of the elements of crimes against humanity as defined in the Special Panels' legislation.[704]
Nonetheless, the additional complexity of these cases has resulted in longer trials.
For instance, the *Los Palos* case featured ten defendants and was conducted over
thirty-five sessions that took place over four months.[705] The duration of later Special Panels' trials increased further still because as time went on, a greater proportion of the Special Panels' resources were allocated to defense counsel; thus, while
the early cases featured no defense cases to speak of, later defendants had the benefit of counsel who called witnesses, made objections, and filed motions—that is,
defense counsel who engaged in activities that protected their clients' rights but
that also lengthened the duration of trials. Consequently, the *Lolotoe* case, featuring three defendants, required forty-two sessions conducted over the course of
thirteen months.[706]

   As the duration of Special Panels' trials increased, efforts to obtain guilty pleas
to eliminate the need for those trials intensified. By the time the Special Panels
closed, about 50 percent of its cases had been disposed of by means of guilty
pleas,[707] and many of these cases featured the same due-process difficulties that
first appeared in the João *Fernandes* case. In particular, many defendants pled
guilty without any real awareness of what they were doing or of the consequences
of their pleas. For instance, in June 2003, when the Special Panel asked Benjamin
Sarmento if he wanted to plead guilty, he seemed to indicate that he did, but
he repeatedly asserted that he had been ordered to commit the crimes, making
such statements as: "People send us to kill. That's why we did it. That is like we
accept our guilty" and "This charge, I accept, because they told me to do it. That's
why I accept. But the problem is that for me to think about doing it, I wouldn't

have done it. That is because I was told to do it."[708] Despite the obvious ambiguities in Sarmento's admissions, the panel accepted his guilty plea, making no attempt to inform him of the consequences of his action. A few minutes later, Sarmento's codefendant Romeiro Tilman also attempted to plead guilty, and his responses were even more equivocal. Tilman apparently held a victim down while someone else killed him. When asked if he was prepared to plead guilty, Tilman responded:

> I agree. This is not because of what I wanted, but because those in charge forced me. I did it. It is not that I used a knife, or a machete to kill. I didn't. The commander of militia forced me. I was scared of death. My colleague did it. And I have been in jail for over 3 years. This wrong is not mine. The person who did this is not here. And I, have come to accept my wrong. . . . I feel that I am wrong because I held with my hands.[709]

Because Tilman claimed to have been forced to commit the crime, the court adjourned to allow him to consult with his lawyer. Returning from his consultation, Tilman said simply, "I am guilty."[710]

Jhoni Franca's guilty-plea colloquy followed a similar pattern. Franca entered into a written plea agreement whereby he pled guilty to four counts of imprisonment and one count of torture as crimes against humanity. During the plea colloquy, Franca admitted to three of the counts, but he emphatically denied the remaining two counts of imprisonment. Franca's lawyer then requested an opportunity to speak with Franca, and, after their conversation, Franca admitted to the two imprisonments, stating that he had previously been confused but "now we have agreed together that I am ready and available to admit my responsibility because I have already signed the agreement acknowledging my responsibility."[711] The panel then accepted Franca's plea even though the reason he proffered for admitting his responsibility—the fact that he had already signed the agreement—should not have alleviated any doubts about whether the guilty plea was informed and voluntary.

As guilty pleas became more prevalent at the Special Panels, an evolution occurred, similar to that seen at the ICTY, in the kinds of plea bargaining practiced, in the sophistication of the resulting agreements, and in the sentencing practices that the panels utilized to encourage future guilty pleas. As the following discussion will show, plea bargaining was not practiced during the first few years of the Special Panels' existence, yet it eventually became a fundamental feature of the panels' guilty-plea processes.

The Evolution of Plea Bargaining

The Special Panels' first guilty plea, tendered by João Fernandes, was not the result of plea bargaining. Fernandes engaged in no negotiations with prosecutors[712]
but rather made a spontaneous and possibly ill-advised confession. The same can
be said about the next guilty plea, that of Joni Marques, who tried to plead guilty
to three counts but whose admissions were sufficiently unclear that the panel
accepted his guilty plea only as to one count. Marcurious José de Deus entered
the Special Panels' third guilty plea in April 2002, and neither it nor the guilty
plea of Augusto Dos Santos, which was entered one month later, appeared to
result from negotiations. The introduction of better-resourced defense counsel at
the end of 2002, however, put an end to such spontaneous confessions. Because
these defense counsel routinely advised their clients to say nothing and plead not
guilty, prosecutors in later cases were forced to negotiate with defendants if they
wanted to obtain guilty pleas.

These negotiations occasionally featured charge bargaining and invariably featured sentence bargaining and a written plea agreement that memorialized the
parties' understanding. These agreements followed a standard form that contained
provisions setting forth the defendant's admissions, his willingness to waive various rights by pleading guilty, and his assertion that the plea was knowing, voluntary, and supported by adequate evidence. The agreements also set forth the sentence recommendation that the parties agreed upon, and it listed any charges that
the prosecution had agreed to withdraw in exchange for the defendant's plea.[713]

Most of the negotiations that culminated in plea agreements centered on the
prosecution's sentence recommendations, which were relatively lenient; toward
the end of the Special Panels' life, they hovered at about seven years' imprisonment
for one murder as a crime against humanity. The results of these plea negotiations
carried considerable weight because the Special Panels never imposed a sentence
longer than that recommended by the prosecution. In an effort to introduce some
uniformity into the negotiations, Deputy Prosecutor for Serious Crimes Nicholas
Koumjian introduced guidelines at the end of 2003 that provided ranges of appropriate sentence recommendations for guilty pleas made before trial and after
trial. Although prosecutors apparently tried to reach agreements that fell within
the guidelines, they had the flexibility to negotiate outside of them, if circumstances warranted.[714] Circumstances apparently did frequently warrant negotiating outside of the bargaining ranges; in the *Ludji & Pereira* case, for instance,

prosecutors agreed to recommend a mere three-year sentence after José Pereira pled guilty to one murder as a crime against humanity.[715] Indeed, the guidelines, which are fairly general in any event, appear never to have been strictly adhered to, and because the length of sentences declined over time, some defense counsel believed that the guidelines were out-of-date soon after they were promulgated.

More controversial is the question of whether charge bargaining took place at the Special Panels. Prosecutors routinely withdrew charges when the conduct forming the basis for the charges was already reflected in other counts to which the defendant had pled guilty. So, for instance, when Jhoni Franca pled guilty to four counts of imprisonment and one count of torture as crimes against humanity, the prosecutor withdrew one count of persecution and two counts of inhumane acts as crimes against humanity, since the latter counts concerned the same conduct that formed the basis of the former counts. As noted in the discussion in Chapter 4 on the ICTY, this sort of charge bargaining does not distort the factual basis of the conviction because, although charges are dropped, the guilty plea continues to reflect the defendant's actual conduct. However, Special Panels prosecutors also withdrew charges reflecting conduct different from that forming the basis of the guilty plea. In both the *Benjamin Sarmento* case and the *Abilio Mendez Correia* case, for instance, the prosecution dropped charges of murder as crimes against humanity for the killing of two people whose deaths were not otherwise represented in the guilty plea. Prosecutors maintained that such withdrawals were not driven by a desire to secure guilty pleas but came about because the evidence supporting the charges was insufficient.[716] The judgment in the *Martins and Gonçalves* case supports this explanation. In *Martins*, the prosecutor withdrew one count of murder as a crime against humanity for the killing of three people and one count of deportation as a crime against humanity. Although these withdrawals appeared to be part of a plea bargain, the panel observed that they "could not [have been] wiser, since [it] is clear that a similar case would not have much hope of a positive result for the Prosecutor, given the vagueness of the statements on the issues."[717] Nonetheless, defense counsel often viewed the withdrawal of charges as part of a charge-bargaining process, a perception that was enhanced when the prosecution waited until the last stage of the negotiations to withdraw the charges.[718] Adding to that impression, the prosecution, in its own Serious Crimes Unit update, described the withdrawal of charges in the *Correia* case and the *de Carvalho* case as being "due to" their guilty pleas.[719]

Examining the Special Panels' sentencing practices one sees that the panels never imposed a sentence on a guilty-plea defendant longer than that recommended by the prosecution. That, however, was perhaps the only stable feature of the panels' sentencing policy; a brief summary of the sentences imposed in guilty-plea cases highlights their lack of uniformity. As noted above, João Fernandes, the first defendant to plead guilty, did not negotiate with the prosecution over its sentencing recommendation. The panel nonetheless ostensibly gave Fernandes credit for the guilty plea in that it treated the plea as a mitigating factor in sentencing. The panel also considered the superior orders pursuant to which Fernandes committed the crime a mitigating factor, and it sentenced him to twelve years' imprisonment for the one murder.[720] Following the *Fernandes* decision, the Special Panels conducted trials in a number of cases featuring similar facts. In particular, Carlos Soares, Manuel Bere, Agustinho da Costa, and Augusto Tavares each were convicted of one murder after a trial, and each had the benefit of superior orders as a mitigating factor. These cases, thus, resembled *Fernandes* in every respect except for Fernandes's guilty plea. Soares, Bere, da Costa, and Tavares received prison sentences of fifteen-and-one-half, fourteen, fifteen, and sixteen years, respectively. Because these sentences are approximately 20 percent longer than Fernandes's sentence, one might assume that the panel had discounted Fernandes's sentence by 20 percent on the basis of his guilty plea; however, another defendant, Jose Valente, was convicted of one murder following trial, and without the benefit either of superior orders or a guilty plea, he received a sentence of twelve-and-one-half years' imprisonment,[721] only six months longer than the sentence imposed on Fernandes. Further, Joseph Leki was convicted of committing four murders—three more than Fernandes—and with superior orders as a mitigating factor, he received a sentence of thirteen years' imprisonment,[722] just one year longer than Fernandes's sentence.

The sentences imposed on the ten defendants convicted in the *Los Palos* case similarly fail to reveal the quantum of discount, if any, that the Special Panels bestowed on defendants pleading guilty. Nine of the *Los Palos* defendants were members of the Team Alfa militia, while the tenth, Joni Marques, was one of Team Alfa's commanders. Several of the defendants made inculpatory statements at the start of the trial, admitting, for instance, to participating in some of the crimes but maintaining that they had not performed all of the acts for which they had been charged or asserting that they had participated in the crimes under threat of death. The *Los Palos* indictment charged Marques with seven counts, and in his opening statement, Marques attempted to plead guilty to three of the counts. The panel declined to accept two of the attempted guilty pleas because Marques's admissions did not precisely match the charges, but it did accept the third, which related to the murders of nine clergy and journalists.[723] In its sentencing, the panel considered as a mitigating circumstance Marques's guilty plea,[724] but its judgment gives little indication of what benefit Marques received in exchange for that guilty plea.

The panel determined that Marques was "in charge" of the operation to kill the clergy and journalists, and, while acknowledging that the plan itself was drafted by Indonesian officers, it considered Marques's supervision of the plan's implementation to be an aggravating factor. The panel sentenced Marques to nineteen years' imprisonment for this count, which is the same sentence that the panel imposed on two of Marques's codefendants, neither of whom had a leadership role in the operation.[725] The mitigating effect of Marques's guilty plea, then, seems to have functioned to negate the aggravating effect of his supervisory role in the killing operation; however, it is not clear what the aggravating effect of Marques's supervisory role would have been since a comparison of the sentences that the panel imposed on Marques and his codefendants on the other counts is not very illuminating. Marques, for instance, was convicted on another count of ordering a murder, while codefendant João da Costa was convicted of physically assisting in that murder. The panel considered Marques's supervisory role as an aggravating factor, and he received a nineteen-year sentence, while da Costa, who was not considered a supervisor, received a seventeen-year sentence.[726] The comparison is not very useful, however, because the two defendants were involved in the murder in very different ways and because the panel also considered da Costa "one of the leaders in arresting the victim," so da Costa's sentence may also have been enhanced to some degree as a result of his role in the arrest.

A possibly more useful comparison can be made from the sentences the *Los Palos* panel imposed on a count involving the expulsion of civilians and the destruction of villages. The panel determined that, although there existed insufficient evidence to prove that Marques had burned any houses himself, Marques was present when the expulsions and house-burnings took place, and his presence was that of a commander.[727] The panel considered his supervisory position as an aggravating factor and sentenced him to seven years' imprisonment for this count. It went on to find that codefendant Paolo da Costa himself burned houses and expelled villagers, but it found that he did so pursuant to the superior orders of Marques. In sentencing Paolo da Costa, then, the panel not only did not consider any aggravating factors with respect to a leadership role but considered as a mitigating factor the superior orders under which Paolo da Costa committed the crime.[728] Yet the panel sentenced Paolo da Costa to six years' imprisonment,[729] a term only one year shorter than the term it imposed on Marques. Again, the facts underlying the two convictions are by no means identical, but the sentences do suggest that Marques's supervisory role did not earn him a significant sentence increase. To the extent, then, that Marques's guilty plea for the killing of clergy and journalists merely negated the sentence enhancement for his supervisory role, one can surmise that Marques's guilty plea benefited him little.

The Special Panels' sentencing practice in guilty-plea cases appeared to undergo a dramatic change following the guilty plea of Marcurious José de Deus. De Deus pled guilty to one murder that appeared similar in relevant respects to the murders described in the *Fernandes, Soares, Bere, Agustinho da Costa,* and *Tavares* cases. The panel considered as mitigating factors not only de Deus's guilty plea and superior orders but also his apology to the family of the victim,[730] and it sentenced him to a mere five years' imprisonment. One month later, Augusto Dos Santos likewise pled guilty to one murder, and he too received a five-year sentence after the panel took account of his guilty plea, remorse, and superior orders as mitigating factors.[731] The panel did not say anything to indicate why the *de Deus* and *Dos Santos* sentences were so low, nor was there any indication that the prosecution's views accorded with that of the Trial Chamber. Indeed, in *Dos Santos,* the prosecutor asked for a "high" sentence, noting that the defendant murdered an old man and did so in a cruel manner.[732] Early Special Panels cases, therefore, featured somewhat arbitrary sentencing practices whereby some defendants pleading guilty appeared to gain considerable sentencing discounts while others received little or no leniency, with no explanation given for the disparate treatment.

In its June 2003 opinion in the *Agustinho Atolan* case, the Special Panels attempted to explain its sentencing policy and in particular to set forth a specific sentencing discount to be applied to defendants pleading guilty. Atolan pled guilty to one count of murder as a crime against humanity, and the defense and prosecution agreed to recommend a seven-year prison sentence. After surveying analogous past cases, the panel concluded that the Special Panels' practice was to sentence defendants convicted of one murder following a trial to a prison term of between twelve and sixteen years.[733] The panel went on to praise defendants who, "being regretful, [choose] a procedural option which spares time and resources of the Court," and it asserted that if such defendants were to receive an appropriate "advantage" in exchange for their guilty plea, then their sentences should be halved. To support the need for a substantial discount, the panel observed: "A less drastic approach proved to be useless: after the first decision of the Special Panel, in the *João Fernandes* case, where the Court took a less lenient decision, more than one year elapsed before a second guilty plea was submitted."[734] Consequently, after concluding that it would have sentenced Atolan to a fourteen-year prison term had the case proceeded to trial, the panel sentenced him to seven years,[735] the exact sentence recommended by the prosecutor.

Six months later a panel composed of Dora Martins De Morais, Antonio Helder Viera do Carmo, and Francesco Florit adhered to the framework articulated in *Atolan* when it decided the *Martins & Gonçalves* case. In that case, Anastacio Martins pled guilty to one count of murder as a crime against humanity for the killing of three people, while his codefendant, Domingos Gonçalves, proceeded to trial and was also convicted of one count of murder as a crime against humanity for the killing of three people along with one count of deportation as a crime against humanity. Cutting and pasting several paragraphs from the *Atolan* case, the panel held that a guilty plea should normally result in a 50 percent reduction in sentence. The panel then determined that a single brutal murder of the sort Martins committed would warrant a sixteen-year prison term following a trial, while Martins's three murders would have resulted in a twenty-three-year sentence had he proceeded to trial. Discounting Martins's sentence by half, then, the panel sentenced him to eleven-and-one-half years' imprisonment, which was within the eight-to-twelve-year range recommended by the prosecution.[736] Gonçalves did not plead guilty, so he was in line to receive a twenty-three year sentence for the three murders he committed and an additional year of imprisonment for the deportation count. Although Gonçalves did not receive any discount for a guilty plea, the panel did consider, in mitigation, his low rank and the current difficulties he and his family faced: namely, that he was unemployed and that he "has lost a leg, cut by his own wife; his wife is mad; his children are young and his mother is very old."[737] In light of these mitigating factors, the panel sentenced Gonçalves to fifteen years' imprisonment.[738]

Despite the potential benefits of a clear rule, such as the 50 percent discount articulated in *Atolan*, the rule did not appear to have been followed in a substantial number of subsequent cases. My conclusion is tentative because the Special Panels' reasoning about sentencing is not always apparent; some judgments are not available in English, and in other cases, the panels issued only three- or four-page "Dispositions of the Decision," which do little more than state the defendants' crimes and the sentences imposed for those crimes.[739] At the same time, none of the prosecutors, defense counsel, or NGO staff whom I interviewed seemed particularly familiar with the 50-percent-discount rule, suggesting that prosecutorial recommendations played a far more influential role in sentencing.

However limited the effect of the 50-percent-discount rule, its very articulation reflected the Special Panels' keen interest in encouraging guilty pleas. Setting forth a clear range of sentences that would be imposed after a trial and promising defendants who pled guilty a substantial discount from those sentences were steps well-calculated to motivate a large number of defendants to enter guilty pleas. But the otherwise arbitrary nature of the Special Panels' sentencing practices undercut these efforts. For instance, one Special Panel not only failed to follow the *Atolan* panel's 50-percent-discount rule but contemporaneously imposed a number of lenient sentences following trials. Indeed, a month after the *Martins & Gonçalves* decision, this panel convicted Damiao Da Costa Nunes of two counts of murder as crimes against humanity and one count of persecution as a crime against humanity. Although the panel concluded that there existed no mitigating factors, it nonetheless sentenced Da Costa Nunes to a total of ten-and-one-half years' imprisonment for all of the counts.[740] The panel's sentencing in some subsequent cases has been similar.[741]

Imposing lenient sentences following trials undermined efforts to obtain guilty pleas and was particularly detrimental to the Special Panels since they had an enhanced need for summary dispositions as they brought their operations to a close. In anticipation of the May 2005 closure of the Special Panels, the Security Council required the prosecution to complete its investigations by November 2004. Long before November 2004, then, the prosecution had already completed numerous investigations, but it was unable to issue indictments in these cases because there was not sufficient time to hold trials before May 2005. These cases could have gone forward, however, if some of the cases then pending before the panels had been resolved through guilty pleas.

Summary of the Plea Bargaining of International Crimes

This chapter and Chapters 4 and 5 have described and analyzed the practice of plea bargaining at the ICTY, the ICTR, and the Special Panels; that is, the practice of plea bargaining at the only recent international tribunals to conduct more than a handful of prosecutions. In another work, I analyzed the functional and ideological roles that plea bargaining plays in various domestic jurisdictions to create a framework for evaluating the emergence of plea bargaining in the realm of international crimes.[742] In that work, I concluded that the ICTY and ICTR have a strong functional need for summary methods of case disposition. Although some features of the tribunals' structure and ideology seem to militate against the practice of plea bargaining, other features would encourage it, and I concluded that the tribunals' compelling functional need to dispose of cases expeditiously suggested that they would, over time, more frequently resort to plea bargaining.

That prediction proved true with respect to the ICTY and the Special Panels, though the latter was not included in the previous study because its work had not yet begun in earnest. Certain ideological commitments of ICTR defendants have acted to discourage many of them from pleading guilty,[743] but notwithstanding that fact approximately 25 percent of ICTR convictions have resulted from guilty pleas.[744] Like it or not, then, guilty pleas are apt to become a pervasive feature of any international criminal justice system that seeks to prosecute more than a miniscule number of offenders. Whether we should like it or not is the question to which Chapter 7 now turns.

Using Conventional Plea Bargaining to Increase the Number of Criminal Prosecutions for International Crimes

Plea bargaining is now a pervasive feature of Anglo-American criminal justice systems, but this was not always the case. Indeed, before the nineteenth century, guilty pleas were virtually unknown in British and American criminal proceedings. Early British trials in particular, were short, summary proceedings; consequently, prosecutors had little incentive to induce defendants to waive their right to a trial. The introduction of a series of adversarial features—most notably complex evidentiary rules and the use of defense counsel—transformed the theretofore summary jury proceedings into more time-consuming, complex events dominated by professional advocates. Because this transformation significantly lengthened the time necessary to conduct a trial, an alternative procedure—the guilty plea—gained popularity as a means of disposing of cases more expeditiously.[745] To encourage defendants to plead guilty, prosecutors offered defendants some form of sentencing concession in exchange for the defendants' guilty pleas. As noted in the Introduction, guilty pleas procured by plea bargaining have, since then, become the most prevalent means of disposing of American criminal cases.

In addition to its prevalence, plea bargaining has also become one of the most disreputable features of the American criminal justice system, and a summary description of some of the abuses to which the practice gives rise quickly reveals why.[746] American prosecutors frequently rely on charge bargaining of the sort that distorts the historical record of proceedings. Some prosecutors, for instance, systematically overcharge defendants so as to be able to withdraw charges during the bargaining process. Albert Alschuler, a leading critic of plea bargaining, describes prosecutors who "charge robbery when they should charge larceny from the person, [who] charge grand theft when they should charge petty theft, [who] charge assault with intent to commit murder when they should charge some form of battery."[747] Other prosecutors issue accurate indictments but, as a result of the bargaining process, agree to withdraw charges in a way that understates the actual criminal responsibility. So, "[g]uns are 'swallowed' as armed robberies become unarmed robberies; burglaries committed at night are transformed through prosecutorial wizardry to burglaries during the day; and defendants solemnly affirm that they have driven the wrong way on one-way streets in towns without one-way streets."[748] Plea bargaining also encourages prosecutors and defense attorneys to misrepresent facts and to bring frivolous motions, all in the hope of obtaining a better plea. Prosecutors might, for instance, conceal fatal defects in the case, such as that a critical witness has died, will not testify, or cannot be found.[749] Defense attorneys, for their part, frequently demand jury trials when they have no interest in trying the case before a jury, and they often file numerous pretrial motions in an effort to enhance their own bargaining positions.[750] Finally, as a result of the way in which most appointed counsel are compensated, American plea bargaining gives rise to conflicts of interest whereby defense counsel feel compelled to pressure their clients to plead guilty regardless of whether it is in their best interests to do so. Retained defense attorneys, for instance, typically obtain a flat fee, paid up front, for their representation.[751] That fee is always sufficient, and frequently generous, for the work involved in securing a guilty plea,[752] but it is often woefully inadequate as compensation for taking a case to trial.[753] Appointed counsel, for their parts, are typically paid either a flat fee or an hourly rate with a ceiling. Whichever form the compensation takes, the amounts are embarrassingly low. Because the compensation caps are almost always the same regardless of whether the defendant pleads guilty or goes to trial, appointed defense counsel have powerful incentives to dispose of as many cases as possible by guilty plea.[754] As Chad Baruch notes, court-appointed defense attorneys and those paid a flat fee who proceed to trial "take[] the risk of earning as little as one or two dollars per hour."[755]

Regulatory efforts can ameliorate some of these abuses, but even then the trade of sentence leniency for financial savings remains problematic on penological grounds. If a defendant who pleads guilty committed the crime for which he or she was charged, then, as a result of the concessions bestowed through plea bargaining, the defendant receives less punishment than the legislature has deemed penologically adequate.[756] If the defendant is innocent, as some defendants who plead guilty apparently are,[757] then the defendant suffers undeserved punishment. Either way, justice is not done or seen to be done. As a result of these practical and conceptual flaws, American plea bargaining has been harshly condemned by victims, civil liberties groups, and the vast majority of scholars who have studied the practice.[758] Why, then, would anyone advocate exporting the much maligned practice of plea bargaining to international tribunals and already-troubled domestic criminal justice systems seeking to prosecute the gravest crimes known to humankind?

The answer to that question is twofold: the *different contexts* in which domestic and international crimes are prosecuted and the *different needs* those prosecutions satisfy render the widely criticized domestic practice of plea bargaining a justifiable—even desirable—choice when the crimes to be prosecuted are international. Turning first to context, the political environments in which domestic crimes and international crimes are prosecuted differ markedly. Domestic critics of plea bargaining consider it justice on the cheap—an unfortunate dilution of the full justice that a criminal justice system ought to provide. This view is in many respects accurate, and a primary reason that it is accurate is that most domestic criminal justice systems are founded on the presumption that violent crimes will be investigated, and when possible, prosecuted. Given this presumption of prosecution, it is not surprising that the plea bargaining of domestic crimes is resisted and viewed as an undesirable accommodation to expediency. However, the presumption of prosecution that is so central in the context of domestic crimes simply does not exist for international crimes. As Chapter 2 detailed, prosecutions for international crimes have been the exception, not the rule. As cynical commentators have put it: if you "kill one person, you go to prison; kill 20, you go to an insane asylum; kill ten thousand, and you get invited to a peace conference."[759] That adage highlights the political and military impediments to prosecuting international crimes, but as the ad hoc tribunals and their progeny have learned, financial impediments can prove just as constraining. Even the wealthiest criminal justice system in the world could not hope to provide full-scale trials to the more than one hundred thousand people accused of genocide in Rwanda, say, or even the ten thousand people suspected of committing international crimes in Bosnia. Expeditious alternatives must be found if more than a small fraction of these defendants are to be held criminally accountable. Seen in this light, the use of plea bargaining in the context of international crimes does not constitute an unfortunate dilution of justice but rather presents a potent opportunity to impose justice on those who would otherwise evade it.

Indeed, plea bargaining for international crimes can be seen as the step beyond that taken by the South African TRC. Although the TRC granted offenders immunity from prosecution, it did so only after receiving the offenders' full and complete confessions. Plea bargaining similarly trades jail time for truth, but unlike the amnesty offered by the South African TRC, plea bargaining does not trade away *all* of the jail time. Instead of offering defendants immunity, plea bargaining offers them a sentencing discount. Thus, a plea-bargaining system such as the one I describe below is the deal that South Africa's democratic government would have liked to strike if it had had the political and military strength to do so. And such a deal would have provided far greater satisfaction to victims. As vast an improvement as the South African TRC was over previous truth commissions, it is nonetheless considered a failure among many South Africans.[760] Multiple reasons exist for this dissatisfaction, but one of the most important relates to the TRC's perceived failure to "do justice,"[761] a failure that plea bargaining would help to remedy.

Plea bargaining, then, has the valuable potential to enhance what limited criminal accountability can currently be imposed in the context of international crimes. A second reason to advocate its use in that context relates to the needs of societies emerging from mass violence, and in particular the need for truth-telling and acknowledgment. Although the primary function of guilty pleas is to serve as the basis for defendants' convictions, those guilty pleas, assuming they are made by people who are in fact guilty, also constitute a limited form of truth-telling because, through the guilty plea, defendants admit that they committed the crimes to which they pled guilty. In the context of domestic crime, that limited form of truth-telling has little effect because it conveys little noteworthy information. When a woman reports her car missing from its parking spot, for instance, few question that a car has been stolen; a defendant's guilty plea to that theft conveys only that the defendant was the person who stole the car. International crimes, by contrast, are routinely and repeatedly denied. Latin American forced disappearances exemplify the secrecy that can surround international crimes; and even crimes of enormous scale, crimes that cannot possibly be concealed— like the execution of the more than seven thousand Bosnian Muslim men and boys at Srebrenica—can be said never to have happened. Thus, in the context of international crimes, the mere act of pleading guilty—of admitting that a crime occurred and that the defendant is responsible—can have a powerful impact on victims and survivors. Indeed, after former Bosnian Serb Army officers Momir Nikolić and Dragan Obrenović pled guilty in May 2003 to helping implement the Srebrenica massacres, one survivor described feeling a sense of relief that he had not known since the executions took place.[762] In the same vein, the president of the Ahmići municipality—which Miroslav Bralo participated in ethnically cleansing—lauded Bralo's guilty plea, saying:

> I am asked about the impact that [Bralo's guilty plea] will have on relations in this area. I say it will have a fantastic effect. We are now twelve years after Ahmici. If five or six or seven years ago there were people like Miroslav Bralo who would say they had done this and this, and that and that happened, it would now be much better for people to live at peace with one another here, and move from the hard positions against each other. They, the actors, the perpetrators, they are often the only ones who really know just what happened. It is time to clear their consciences and I am glad that those with some decency are now telling their crimes.[763]

Likewise, many victims praised Biljana Plavšić's guilty plea for its contribution to "the eventual process of reconciliation."[764] The acknowledgment that is inherent in a guilty plea can prove profoundly meaningful to victims and conflict-riven societies.

The "price" that must be paid for guilty pleas is sentence leniency, but in the international context, this price is no cost at all. By enabling more prosecutions to take place, plea bargaining will in most cases increase the overall punishment imposed in the context of each mass atrocity.[765] Further, even if the overall quantity of punishment were to remain the same following plea bargaining, that punishment would better serve its intended ends because it would be distributed over a larger number of defendants. As noted in Chapter 3, deterrence is better effected by certain punishment than by severe punishment; plea bargaining increases the number of criminal prosecutions, thereby making punishment that much more certain. Although in the international context deterrence is a thin reed upon which to justify the imposition of criminal sanctions, whatever value deterrence has in this realm will be enhanced by imposing criminal punishment on a larger pool of defendants.

Even if a particular plea-bargaining scheme were to result in less overall punishment per atrocity, the benefits gained by imposing that punishment on a larger number of offenders would likely justify the scheme. For one thing, the imposition of criminal sanctions in the international realm serves to counteract the culture of impunity that has prevailed with respect to international crimes. Punishing a substantial number of offenders, even if the punishment imposed on each is penalogically inadequate by any of the traditional measures, nonetheless drives home the point that international crimes do attract (at least some) sanctions. Prosecuting a substantial number of offenders also enhances short-term peace-building by paving the way for refugees and displaced persons to return to their homes. In many areas of Bosnia, for instance, refugee returns have been impeded by the fact that war criminals remain in positions of financial and police power in ethnically cleansed regions. As one commentator put it: "Refugees won't return home while the people who drove them away are still around. . . . That's the final point of ethnic cleansing."[766] Imposing even relatively short prison sentences on these offenders removes them from their positions of power and allows victims to return and resume their lives.

Although granting leniency in exchange for guilty pleas is apt to enhance criminal accountability in the international context, the perception of that leniency—particularly among victims—is just the opposite. Victims were outraged when the ICTY sentenced Predrag Banović to a mere eight years' imprisonment after he pled guilty to beating five prisoners to death and participating in twenty-seven other beatings and shootings.[767] The popular reaction was worse still to the ICTY's imposition of an eleven-year sentence on Biljana Plavšić after she pled guilty to implementing an ethnic-cleansing campaign that left tens of thousands dead and hundreds of thousands expelled from their homes. Although victim perception cannot control the decisions of a criminal justice system—after all, victims of domestic crimes also routinely complain about leniency in sentencing—the horror that greeted some of the ICTY sentences also cannot be cavalierly dismissed. Prosecutions of international crimes advance not only penological goals but didactic and reconciliatory goals, and these latter goals are undermined by widespread victim dissatisfaction. In particular, although the use of plea bargaining may enhance accountability and truth-telling, these benefits will have limited effect if they are drowned out, as it were, by victim outrage over sentencing.

Ameliorating this outrage, therefore, must be a primary concern for anyone considering the use of plea bargaining for international crimes. I propose two ways of reducing victim dissatisfaction with the sentencing concessions that must be bestowed to obtain guilty pleas. The first concerns the severity of the sentences imposed following full-scale trials, and the second relates to the creation of appropriate expectations.

A plea-bargaining scheme must offer some leniency if it is to persuade defendants to plead guilty, but how much leniency is a question of vital significance and can be seriously considered only in the context of particular atrocities. Answers to such questions as how many offenders were involved, what kind of crimes were committed, how much is already known about the crimes, and what resources exist for prosecutions will help to define the value to be ascribed to guilty pleas and the concomitant reward that should be offered in exchange. Rwanda, for instance, is faced with an impossible caseload and possesses only the most meager of resources; Rwandan defendants who confess, then, are not surprisingly favored with generous sentencing discounts, as will be discussed in more detail in Chapter 10.

How resentful victims will become as a result of these discounts will largely depend on the baseline sentences imposed absent a guilty plea. In other words, Bosnian victims were not outraged because Plavšić received a certain percentage discount from an ideal sentence; they were outraged because she was sentenced to a mere eleven years of imprisonment for her high-level role and substantial involvement in the ethnic-cleansing campaign. Similarly, victims decried Banović's eight-year sentence because it constituted "shamefully small punishment" for the large number of brutal crimes that he committed. Eight years in prison is eight years longer than most international criminals spend behind bars, yet sentences such as Banović's, which appear spectacularly lenient compared with those handed out for less-serious domestic crimes, run the risk of trivializing prosecutorial efforts and undermining the notion that international crimes are humankind's gravest.

Although, in the eyes of victims, no sentence will constitute adequate punishment for the harms inflicted in the context of mass atrocities, a practice of imposing lengthy prison sentences after trial can serve to acknowledge the severity of the crimes while at the same time providing an appropriately high baseline from which to discount sentences following guilty pleas. The ICTR has already taken this path, sentencing most of its convicted defendants to life imprisonment.[768] Similarly, Rwanda has established *gacaca* courts, which must sentence murderers who fail to confess to prison terms of up to thirty years.[769] The ICTY, by contrast, has imposed life imprisonment in only one case, and it was reduced to a forty-year term on appeal.[770] The ICTY has, in addition, imposed sentences of between forty and forty-six years in three additional cases,[771] but two of those sentences were also reduced on appeal,[772] and most ICTY sentences have been considerably shorter in the first instance. Further, it has been the practice of the ICTY to release defendants after they have served two-thirds of their sentences.[773] That the ICTY has imposed lenient sentences is not surprising given the belief, held by many Western Europeans, that a life sentence constitutes cruel and unusual punishment.[774] This view emerged in the context of domestic crime, however, where murder and multiple murders, in particular, are exceptional occurrences. Whatever the merits of such a position in the domestic context, it seems ill-advised in the international context where some defendants will be responsible for dozens or even hundreds of deaths. Specifically, in cases involving murder, life imprisonment should be the presumptive sentence. A plea-bargaining discount, then, to a term of twenty years' imprisonment will bestow a significant benefit on most defendants[775] without running so great a risk of trivializing the crimes and embittering victims.

A second way of reducing public dissatisfaction with plea bargaining relates to the creation of public expectations. In particular, a guilty-plea system will be more favorably perceived if those perceiving it have realistic expectations about the goals it is seeking to accomplish and the political context in which those goals must be pursued. Victims' reactions to the South African TRC, on the one hand, and the ICTY, on the other, exemplify this point. South African victims were largely accepting of their TRC, even though it exempted confessing defendants from *all* punishment, not just from a portion of it, whereas Bosnian victims have sharply condemned the sentencing discounts that the ICTY has offered confessing defendants. These differing reactions stem primarily from the different contexts in which the two institutions were created and the way in which those contexts shaped victim expectations. The TRC was a negotiated solution, and South African victims recognized the compromise embodied in the TRC to be necessary to accomplish a peaceful transition. The ICTY, by contrast, was anything but negotiated. The international community imposed the ICTY on the former Yugoslavia; thus, no compromises were initially apparent in the ICTY's mandate, and victims and commentators came to expect the tribunal to dispense full justice to each individual brought before it. Financial constraints have lately forced the ICTY to engage in sentencing compromises; however, these constraints have not been well-publicized, and victims have been left feeling shortchanged.

For guilty pleas to provide optimal benefits, plea bargaining must be understood by the relevant constituencies for what it is: a compromise measure that allows for the prosecution of a greater percentage of criminal defendants. In particular, any international criminal justice system that plans to use plea bargaining should showcase the practice as an integral feature of the system from the outset. Victims and other interested parties must understand that offenders who confess will receive sentencing discounts, and they must understand why those confessions justify sentencing rewards. Victims must be made to see that insisting on full-scale trials and full punishment will result in considerably fewer prosecutions and less overall punishment. A candid dialogue about the goals of criminal prosecutions and the financial constraints that limit their attainment will diminish the likelihood of subsequent dissatisfaction and provide victims with a realistic understanding of the prosecutorial endeavor.

These suggestions—regarding the severity of the baseline sentences and the appropriate expectations that must be inculcated in victims—will help to reduce victim dissatisfaction with the discounted sentences that result from traditional plea bargaining of the sort currently practiced in the United States and at the ICTY. The following chapter constructs an innovative guilty-plea system designed not just to increase the number of prosecutions that can take place but also to advance long-term reconciliation in regions recently torn by violent conflict. The values added through such a system will additionally help to legitimize plea bargaining, so that it is viewed less as an unseemly cost-cutting measure and more as a key element in a society's effort to move beyond large-scale violence.

CHAPTER EIGHT

Plea Bargaining as Restorative Justice

Using Guilty Pleas to Advance Both Criminal Accountability and Reconciliation

Chapter 7 described the benefits that can result from the conventional practice of plea bargaining in the context of international crimes. Specifically, the use of plea bargaining creates an opportunity to prosecute offenders who would otherwise remain free, and it conveys a limited amount of truth and acknowledgment about the crimes committed. Guilty pleas have the capacity to advance not only these aims but also reconciliatory goals that are better associated in the international context with nonprosecutorial mechanisms, such as truth commissions and reparations schemes. In the context of domestic crimes, these goals have recently begun to be pursued through restorative-justice processes. This chapter explores the incorporation of restorative-justice principles to efforts to prosecute international crimes and the key role that guilty pleas can play in that incorporation.

The Theory

As its name indicates, restorative justice aims to correct imbalances and restore broken relationships through healing, harmony, and reconciliation.[776] The needs of victims constitute a central focus for restorative justice; thus, instead of asking the primary question of a conventional criminal justice system—what should be done with the offender?—restorative justice asks what should be done for the victim. At the same time, restorative justice emphasizes the community's ongoing relationship with offenders. Offenders are not to be viewed as "people who are different from ourselves and who do not properly belong in our society";[777]

rather, they are considered part of the community even if they need to be moni-tored and to be made aware of the harm they have caused. To advance these mul-tiple goals, restorative-justice programs promote face-to-face contact between offenders and victims, and preferably also family members and other interested members of the community. At such meetings, "offenders are urged to account for their behaviour; victims are encouraged to describe the impact which the crime has had upon them, materially and psychologically; and all parties are en-couraged to decide upon a mutually agreeable form and amount of reparation—usually including an apology."[778] Through restorative-justice programs, then, all of the individuals with an interest in the crime come together and seek to col-lectively determine how to address the harms caused by the crime and their implications for the future.

Empirical research into restorative justice is still in its early stages, but stud-ies consistently show that those who participate in restorative-justice programs come away more satisfied than those whose cases proceed through the ordinary court system. In particular, restorative-justice processes appear to respond better to participants' needs and desires. John Braithwaite describes "an overwhelming amount of evidence" showing that victim, offender, community, and police satis-faction with restorative justice processes "is extremely high, typically 90%–95%, and in some studies even higher. . . . Moreover, for cases randomly assigned to conference rather than court, perceptions of fairness and overall satisfaction are higher in conference than in court cases for all types of participants."[779] Barton Poulson similarly observes that restorative justice outperforms court procedures on almost every variable for victims and offenders.[780]

Although victims are popularly viewed as punitive, seeking retribution above all else, research now indicates that many victims place considerable—in some cases predominant—weight on other values, including information, participa-tion, material reparation, and symbolic reparation, which includes apologies.[781] Victims participating in restorative-justice programs have the opportunity to tell their stories, express their feelings, and question offenders about issues that in-terest or worry them. Such victims, not surprisingly, are more likely to feel that their needs and views have been taken into account.[782] Mark Umbreit notes that "[v]ictims frequently report that while restitution was the primary motivator for them to participate in [victim-offender mediation], what they appreciated most about the program was the opportunity to talk with the offender."[783] Victims par-ticipating in restorative-justice programs also report feeling less fear and anger about the crime and less concern about revictimization than victims who proceed through ordinary court processes. Indeed, one study indicated that victims of violent crime whose cases had proceeded through the ordinary court system were five times as likely to believe that they would be revictimized as victims who had participated in restorative-justice processes.[784] In addition, offenders are far more likely to apologize during a restorative-justice proceeding than a conventional court proceeding,[785] and the value of sincere apologies to both victims and offenders is extraordinary.[786] At least one study reports that, to many victims, an apology is more important than tangible reparation.[787] Restorative-justice processes aim to reconcile offender and victim, and genuine expressions of remorse are the first and essential step in that reconciliation process.

Offenders, for their parts, also report greater satisfaction with restorative-justice processes.[788] Like victims, offenders who participate in restorative-justice programs are more likely to feel that their stories have been heard and their needs considered.[789] Most importantly, the victim-offender interactions that form the basis of restorative-justice processes are designed to instill in offenders a greater appreciation for the harms that they have caused.[790] Studies indicate that offenders employ a variety of psychological techniques to shield themselves from an awareness of the full human consequences of their behavior.[791] That sort of denial is harder for offenders to sustain when they must come face to face with victims and listen to them describe the injuries they have suffered. These interactions help offenders to see their victims as human beings, equal to themselves; the interactions likewise encourage victims to view their offenders as real people, people who cannot be excused for their crimes but who do have explanations to offer. Preliminary research also indicates a reduction in recidivism rates after offenders participate in a restorative-justice program.[792]

The foregoing discussion indicates that the use of restorative-justice measures has the potential to improve markedly the performance of a domestic criminal justice system. Restorative-justice procedures have been used primarily for non-violent crimes, and one might assume that they would be less efficacious in the context of violent crime on the theory that the graver the injury a victim suffers, the more that victim will desire retribution over the values advanced by restorative-justice programs. In particular, restorative-justice programs primarily utilize material and symbolic reparations to restore victims, and one would expect that these reparatory measures would have little restorative value in the context of violent crime. The research conducted thus far, however, does not bear out this view. The few studies that have examined the effectiveness of re-storative-justice processes following severely violent crime have reported positive results.[793] Indeed, some studies have shown that restorative justice is more effective at reducing violent crime than at reducing petty property crime.[794] Heather Strang and Lawrence Sherman speculate that the greatest benefit from restorative justice may be found in the most serious crimes: "It appears that the higher level of emotional engagement by victims and offenders in these kinds of encounters is the 'engine' leading to the emotions of empathy and remorse which may be the essential ingredients for reduced reoffending."[795]

A study of victim-offender mediation in Texas and Ohio showed "that many of the principles of restorative justice can be applied in crimes of severe violence, including murder, with clear effectiveness in supporting both the process of victim healing and offender accountability."[796] In the Texas and Ohio programs, family members of the murder victims had typically initiated the meetings and did so primarily because they sought information from offenders and an opportunity to describe to offenders the impact of the crimes. Offenders agreed to participate for a number of reasons, including a desire to apologize to victims, a desire to assist in the victim's healing process, and a desire to assist in their own reha-bilitation and healing.[797] Not all victims were able to forgive their offenders, but offenders who were forgiven found it a very moving and motivating experience. As one offender put it: "If you murder somebody's child, and they forgive you, if she can forgive me, I can forgive. I made a commitment. I'm not gonna mess up."[798] In all, victims, family members of victims, and offenders reported an ex-tremely high level of satisfaction with their participation in the program. Seventy-seven of seventy-eight participants reported that they were satisfied, and seventy-one selected the highest rating, "very satisfied."[799] In addition, all of the initial participants reported that the sessions were very healing,[800] and, astonishingly, 80 percent of all participants reported that their involvement in the program had had a life-changing effect.[801] Similar results were obtained through a Wiscon-sin restorative-justice program that brought together victims and offenders of severely violent crime.[802]

As the authors of the study on the Texas and Ohio programs report:

> Victims/family members and offenders alike reported feeling more at peace and better able to cope with their lives. For the 30 victims and family members, letting go of hate, obtaining answers, placing the anger where it belongs, having a human encoun-ter, and/or experiencing the offender's ownership and remorse have been important

factors. The 33 offenders pointed to being accountable, seeing their victim as a person, understanding the impact of their actions, being able to give something back, feeling the victim/family member's opinion of them had changed for the better, and being more open to feelings.[803]

These studies relating to violent domestic crime indicate that restorative-justice values might usefully inform efforts to prosecute international crimes, although questions remain about the nature of the sanctions to be imposed through restorative processes. Domestic restorative-justice programs typically culminate in a reparations plan that imposes certain financial and/or service obligations on offenders, but not severe burdens such as long-term imprisonment. Because most domestic restorative-justice programs center on petty crimes, there exists a reasonable potential that financial and service-oriented reparations can substantially repair the relevant harms. Such measures are apt to be considered wholly inadequate, by contrast, in the context of severely violent crimes. Indeed, much of the research indicating that restorative processes benefit victims and offenders of violent domestic crimes does not address the question of punishment because the victim-offender mediations studied in that research took place long after the offender was sentenced to long-term imprisonment or even death. It is by no means clear that the programs would have so satisfied victims if the programs had resulted in a significant diminution of incarceration.

Even in the context of the domestic restorative-justice programs involving petty crimes, a debate among restorative-justice theorists exists as to whether the burdens imposed on offenders through restorative justice constitute punishment in the retributive sense or are in fact alternatives to punishment. For instance, John Braithwaite, the restorative-justice movement's most well-known and influential proponent, urges that punishment be minimized to the greatest degree possible. Braithwaite and others maintain that punishment results in a variety of unfortunate consequences;[804] consequently, they urge restorative measures as an alternative to traditional punishment. Other commentators, by contrast, espouse the view that not only are restoration and retribution compatible but that restoration requires retribution.[805] That view has appeal, particularly in the context of international crimes, which typically feature large-scale violence. Crimes of this magnitude cry out for onerous sanctions, justified at least in part on retributive principles. In addition, the underdeveloped nature of international criminal justice apparatuses cautions against eschewing retributive punishment even if restoration could be accomplished without it. For most of human history, international crimes have been followed by no sanctions whatever. The "culture of impunity" surrounding international crimes has begun to erode in recent years, and it would be profoundly unwise to impair this erosion by declining to impose retributive punishment in circumstances in which its imposition would be feasible.

In the international context, a criminal justice system that imposes retributive sanctions pursuant to restorative processes would provide divided societies with optimal benefits. The linchpin to such a system is the guilty plea. Most domestic restorative-justice programs require defendants to admit their guilt, on the rather obvious ground that defendants cannot be in an appropriate frame of mind to accept responsibility and/or make amends if they continue to contest having committed the crime in the first place. Having pled guilty, then, a domestic defendant in a jurisdiction that offers restorative-justice alternatives would have a choice between having the case proceed through ordinary court processes or participating in a restorative-justice program. For international crimes, I propose incorporating restorative-justice principles into guilty-plea processes. In particular, I propose conditioning acceptance of a defendant's guilty plea on the completion of certain restorative obligations; in this way, defendants who wish to obtain the sentencing benefits that typically flow from a guilty plea will have to engage in a restorative process designed to advance peace and reconciliation between individual victims and offenders and between their respective groups. The following section sketches the contours of a guilty-plea system conducted pursuant to restorative-justice principles.

The Practice

A guilty-plea system that embodies restorative-justice principles would bear little resemblance to the guilty-plea processes currently in use in most domestic criminal justice systems, including the American criminal justice system. In particular, a restorative-justice guilty-plea system would differ from current processes with respect to the amount and type of information obtained, the level of victim participation, and the imposition of reparatory obligations. Turning first to truth-telling, as already noted, every guilty plea that reflects the defendant's actual commission of a crime conveys some information; a restorative-justice approach to guilty pleas would seek, however, to obtain more and different kinds of information. In particular, a restorative-justice approach would require defendants pleading guilty to provide a full and complete accounting of their crimes as part of a guilty plea. That accounting has the potential to benefit prosecutors, victims and family members of victims, and offenders.

First, a full accounting of the crime would in many cases reward prosecutors with information implicating other, perhaps more-senior, offenders. Such information can be of vital importance to the success of efforts to prosecute high-level offenders who orchestrated but did not actually execute the crimes. As Chapter 10 will describe, ICTY prosecutors have required many plea-bargaining defendants to provide information about the crimes of their associates and superiors and to testify in the trials of those individuals. The information revealed through these processes has proved instrumental in enabling ICTY prosecutors to prosecute senior military and political figures.

A complete accounting also has the potential to provide family members with crucial details about the crimes, such as the location of the body, the cause of death, and the events that took place during their loved one's final days or hours. This information is of vital consequence to family members, many of whom cannot begin to move beyond their tragedy without it. Psychologist Teufika Ibrahimefendić testified during the ICTY's *Krstić* trial about the women and children who lost their male relatives during the Srebrenica massacres:

> The fact that they do not know the truth—even the worst truth, would be better for them than this uncertainty, this constant, perpetual uncertainty as to what happened to their loved ones, because they keep waiting, they're waiting for something. They cannot begin life, they cannot face up with the reality of the death of a missing person. They only remember the moment they bade farewell, the moment when they agreed to meet in a spot that would be safe.[806]

Ibrahimefendić's expert opinion about the devastating effects of uncertainty was poignantly confirmed for the Trial Chamber in that case by the testimony of a Bosnian Muslim mother whose fourteen-year-old son had been pulled from her arms when the women and children had been separated from the men and boys at Srebrenica. Even though the executions of Bosnian Muslim men and boys from Srebrenica had been widely documented and was certainly known to the witness, when the judge asked her whether she had anything to say or ask of the defendant, she said:

> I would like to appeal to you to ask Mr. Krstić, if you can, whether there is any hope for at least that little child that they snatched away from me, because I keep dreaming about him. I dream of him bringing flowers and saying, "Mother, I've come." I hug

him and say, "Where have you been, my son?" and he says, "I've been in Vlasenica all this time." So I beg you, if Mr. Krstić knows anything about it, about him surviving some place. . . .[807]

Other parents have reconciled themselves to the deaths of their children but are still consumed with questions. South African mother Joyce Mthimkulu put it thus: "'If they can just show us the bones of my child, I'll be grateful. Where did they leave the bones of my child? Where did they take him? Who handed him over to them? What did they do to him?"[808]

Finally, an accounting would constitute a powerful acknowledgment of wrongdoing. Commentators have noted that truth commission reports often serve less to impart knowledge to victims about the crimes that took place than to constitute official—and much needed—acknowledgment that crimes did take place and that victims were harmed.[809] Admissions made in the context of guilty pleas may prove even more valuable to victims since the acknowledgment of wrongdoing is made by wrongdoers themselves, rather than an outside body.[810] Offenders, too, benefit when they are able to acknowledge the wrongs they have committed, among other reasons, because, as already noted, "for the offender to acknowledge responsibility . . . , he must first acknowledge the victim as a real individual."[811]

While the quantity and content of the information disclosed is of vital significance, the process by which information is disclosed can prove just as significant on a restorative-justice model. A defendant pleading guilty in the United States, for instance, is questioned by a judge to determine whether the defendant is making the plea knowingly, voluntarily, and unequivocally and whether the plea satisfies any other requirements the jurisdiction imposes. In the United States, these plea colloquies are perfunctory affairs; questions are mechanically posed, answers are monosyllabically provided, and all of the participants seek to get the proceedings over with as quickly as possible. By contrast, the primary purpose of a restorative-justice guilty-plea hearing would not be to satisfy certain minimal requirements, but to learn all that can be learned from the defendant and to publicize that information to the greatest degree and the greatest effect. The South African TRC provides a useful model in this regard. Although the TRC's Amnesty Committee may have granted amnesty to certain applicants who failed to make full disclosure,[812] little question exists that the TRC obtained and publicized a tremendous quantity of information and made significant efforts to investigate cases, in part to determine whether amnesty applicants were making full disclosure and, if they were not, to encourage them to do so.

Turning to victim participation, domestic guilty-plea colloquies typically do not include victim input; sentencing hearings frequently do, but even there, the victim's role is limited and carefully defined. A restorative-justice approach to guilty pleas would promote more and more-varied victim involvement. In domestic restorative-justice programs, victims are encouraged to describe both the material and emotional harms they have suffered and to describe how they wish those harms to be repaired. Doing so not only helps victims to feel that their needs and views have been taken into account, but it helps offenders to appreciate the consequences of their actions and encourages them to view victims as valuable individuals. The South African TRC permitted victims to confront and question those who had wronged them, and at least some guilty-plea proceedings could permit similar victim involvement. Widespread victim participation was feasible in the South African context because many South African crimes featured one defendant for perhaps a handful of victims. Other mass atrocities feature considerably more victims per perpetrator, and in those cases, logistics may prevent many victims from personally participating. Victim-offender interactions should be encouraged whenever possible, however, because they not only benefit victims and offenders in the ways described above, but they also give rise to a different and more nuanced kind of truth-telling; while judges ask questions to determine whether the legal elements of the crime have been satisfied, and truth commissioners ask questions they believe of interest to society in general, victims seek information specific to their own needs and experiences. These questions and the answers they elicit, though at times idiosyncratic, provide valuable insights into how the crimes are perceived by those most affected.

Turning to reparations, most domestic restorative-justice programs require offenders to provide material and/or symbolic reparations. Apologies are a particularly potent form of symbolic reparations. They are considered an essential first step in the reparations process, and many victims desire apologies more than material reparations.[813] Genuine apologies may be all the more potent in the context of international crimes because they can signify not only remorse over the particular wrongdoing but a change of attitude about the conflict and the victim class. Apologies, for that reason, can serve vital pedagogical and dramaturgical purposes in societies riven by ethnic or religious conflicts. The apparent transformation of former Bosnian Serb leader Biljana Plavšić, for instance, exemplifies this phenomenon. While leading an ethnic-cleansing campaign that resulted in the deaths of more than one hundred thousand Bosnian Muslims and Croats,

Plavšić was considered among the most rabid of Serb nationalists. She termed the purge of non-Serbs "a natural phenomenon"[814] and described Muslims as "'a genetic defect on the Serbian body.'"[815] In pleading guilty, however, Plavšić apologized, acknowledging that "many thousands of innocent people were the victims of an organized, systematic effort to remove Muslims and Croats from the territory claimed by Serbs." At the time, she said, she had convinced herself that the ethnic-cleansing plan was a matter of survival and self-defense. She came later to acknowledge, however, that she and other Bosnian Serb leaders had "led an effort which victimised countless innocent people . . . and violated the most basic duty of every human being, the duty to restrain oneself and to respect the human dignity of others."[816] Plavšić's apology was widely publicized, and, although Bosnian victims subsequently decried the lenient sentence Plavšić received, most were moved and gratified by her apology.[817] In a similar vein, post-apartheid South Africa's efforts to transform attitudes about blacks and their role in society were immeasurably enhanced by the public apologies proffered by some TRC amnesty applicants. These apologies and the responses they elicited were widely broadcast and discussed.

Although sincere apologies constitute a valuable reconciliation tool, not all apologies are sincere. Indeed, given the rabid racist and nationalistic ideology that fuels much international crime, it is perhaps too optimistic to expect that many offenders will be able sincerely to regret their crimes soon after they have committed them. But a guilty-plea system that presents offenders with the concrete harms resulting from their crimes—the widow who cannot feed her family without her murdered husband's income, the mother who dreams nightly of the son who was snatched from her arms before being executed—can hope to reach the conscience of offenders and humanize victims in a way that contradicts the racist ideology. Whether this sort of guilty-plea system will effect such a transformation in a majority of cases cannot be known, and the question arises whether a guilty-plea system should require defendants to apologize or encourage them to do so through the bestowal of sentencing concessions. Most domestic restorative-justice programs do require defendants to apologize, and the ICTY and other international tribunals encourage apologies by regarding remorse as a mitigating factor in sentencing.

Some commentators question the reconciliatory value of required or rewarded apologies,[818] and indeed some believe that apologies perceived to be insincere may be more damaging than restorative. At least one psychological study supports this view by suggesting, somewhat analogously, that the perceived honesty of those providing an explanation as a conflict-management strategy is a critical component of the explanation's effectiveness.[819] Lee Taft has argued, in addition, that the moral process of apology is potentially corrupted when apologies are rewarded or required.[820] Of course, the gravity of these concerns will depend in part on the means used to obtain the apologies; in particular, the greater the coercion employed, the greater the skepticism that is likely to greet the apology. Thus, the perceived sincerity of required apologies is apt to be lower than that of apologies that are merely rewarded by sentencing discounts; similarly, larger sentencing discounts are likely to undermine the perceived sincerity of apologies more than smaller discounts will. The reception that will greet an apology is also likely to be influenced by the role that apology has traditionally played in the society in question. Although the Japanese criminal justice system, for instance, rewards apologies and other displays of remorse with substantial benefits,[821] those apologies do not consequently appear to be undermined in the view of the public, probably because apologies are an entrenched feature of virtually every aspect of Japanese life.[822] If apologies are to be rewarded, then, it is these factors that must be carefully considered both in designing the rewards and in explaining them to victims and the public.

The enormous potential value of most apologies, in my view, justifies carefully crafted efforts to encourage them. For one thing, the concern that victims will be more likely to reject apologies that appear self-serving may not be a substantial one. Psychological studies have shown that victims who fail to accept apologies are viewed negatively and that victims consequently face strong social pressure to accept apologies, even when the apologies are reasonably perceived to be insincere.[823] Erin Ann O'Hara and Douglas Yarn, moreover, utilized evolutionary biology to explain apology as an adaptive strategy that encourages survival through cooperation; on this theory, humans have developed an emotional and cognitive bias to seek and grant forgiveness, a bias that may encourage reconciliation even when the proffered apology is not heartfelt.[824] Further, even if an apology is insincere at the time it is uttered, the mere act of making it can begin a process that leads to genuine remorse. Finally, encouraged or even coerced apologies may be valuable in the context of international crimes precisely because there is so little that otherwise can be done at a practical level to repair the harms wrought by mass violence. Because every effort seems so patently inadequate, every effort that has even the smallest potential to enhance reconciliation should be favorably considered.

Most domestic restorative-justice programs also impose on offenders material reparations obligations, such as restitution or community service. Since many of the crimes channeled through domestic restorative-justice processes are relatively minor, the reparatory obligations imposed on offenders usually constitute credible attempts to restore victims to their previous positions. When the crime at issue is rape, torture, or worse yet, murder, no financial payment or service requirement will come close to repairing the harm. Because material reparations are so wholly inadequate in the context of grave crimes, it may seem as though they are not worth pursuing, but, in fact, quite the opposite is true.

For one thing, some victims value financial reparations over incarceration. As South African Eunice Miya put it, after her son was killed in a massacre by South African police: "Going to jail is useless. . . . The . . . [perpetrators] must just support our children's children."[825] Further, many survivors of large-scale violence suffer tremendous financial privations as a result of their victimhood. Many ethnically cleansed Bosnians, for instance, lost all of their material possessions upon their expulsion; often those returning home have found only the charred remains of their houses. And victims who were severely beaten, tortured, or raped often bear physical and emotional scars that subsequently prevent them from engaging in gainful employment. The reparations that can feasibly be required of offenders, many of whom will themselves be impoverished, cannot be expected to improve dramatically the financial lot of such victims, but they can help in small and symbolic ways. A Bosnian Serb who is required to spend one day per week assisting in the reconstruction of a home he burned down provides his victims more than mere financial support; by undertaking such a reparatory effort, offenders acknowledge and publicize their wrongdoing in an especially tangible way. Harvard psychiatrist Judith Herman opines that victims value this sort of restitution far more than reparations from the state. Victims want to have "'a sense that the people who did the damage are made to give something back, or to try to clean up the mess that they made.'"[826]

Indeed, such reparations benefit not only victims and the community, but also offenders because they enhance offender reintegration. Societies in general, and victim groups in particular, are more welcoming of offenders who have made some attempt to right their wrongs, and offenders gain a greater appreciation for the harm they have caused when they undertake some attempt—financial or otherwise—to repair that harm. At the same time, reparations obligations must take into account the factual context of the crimes. When imposing community-service requirements on Hutu killers, the Rwandan government chose not to require Hutu to perform services directly to Tutsi survivors because doing so was apt to rekindle painful memories of the Tutsi's past use of oppressive community-service requirements as a means of subjugating the Hutu, memories that might reinflame ethnic tensions.[827]

As will now be obvious, many key features of the restorative-justice guilty pleas just described appear in one or another of the traditional responses to mass atrocities, namely, conventional criminal trials, truth commissions, and reparations schemes. Criminal trials impose accountability on offenders; truth commissions encourage victims to describe the harm that they have suffered; and reparations schemes provide much-needed financial assistance to victims. Pursuing these values in independent bodies, however, considerably dilutes their impact. Recent truth commissions, for instance, have effectively disseminated the truth as it is perceived by victims, but most have failed entirely to include the perpetrator's perspective.[828] Without the threat of prosecution to encourage their testimony, most offenders choose to keep their own counsel, and crucial details about victims remain hidden to family members; crucial insights into the motivation of perpetrators, which could help to prevent future atrocities, go unexplored; and crucial interactions between victims and offenders—such as apologies and acceptance—fail to take place. Without the participation of offenders, the truth that is reported is not the complete truth, and the reconciliation that takes place is but partial.

Criminal prosecutions, for their part, also function most efficaciously when informed by the truth that only offenders can provide. Many prosecutions cannot proceed at all without the evidence of coperpetrators or underlings. Insufficient evidence poses an especially acute problem for those seeking to prosecute high-level defendants who may appear insulated from the ghastly deeds by several levels of intermediary perpetrators. Moreover, as a systemic matter, efforts to undertake a significant number of prosecutions are likely to fail as a result of resource constraints. Thus, if justice—and by that I mean more than token justice—is to be done, it must be facilitated by defendants who are willing to confess. The monetary payments made pursuant to government-funded reparations schemes are welcome both as financial assistance and as implicit acknowledgment of wrongdoing, but their reconciliatory potential would be greatly enhanced by offender contributions, both to the material reparations and, when possible, in the form of symbolic reparations, such as apologies.

South Africa did amalgamate many of these values in the three bodies that comprised its TRC. The TRC's Human Rights Violations Committee invited victims to tell their stories; the Amnesty Committee required offenders to reveal their crimes and permitted some victim-offender questioning; and the Reparation and Rehabilitation Committee made recommendations to the government regarding reparations. Commentators quickly seized on these values to pronounce the TRC a restorative-justice process,[829] and that label is not entirely misplaced. However, the TRC's adoption of certain restorative practices did not spring from a principled commitment to the values of restorative justice but from political weakness. Indeed, the TRC's political inability to hold confessing offenders criminally or civilly accountable in even the smallest way undermined both the claim that it did justice in any form and its own potential to advance reconciliation.

Potential Obstacles

A restorative-justice guilty-plea system can provide many benefits to societies emerging from mass violence, but is such a system feasible to implement? A number of objections may be raised, but the following two are perhaps the most compelling. First, defendants accused of international crimes may find the mere act of pleading guilty difficult enough without being forced to reveal significant additional information; that is, the disclosure requirements inherent in a restorative-justice approach might deter a substantial number of defendants from pleading guilty, thus dooming the project to failure. Second, plea bargaining is apt to motivate guilty pleas only to the extent that the defendants pleading guilty have reason to fear prosecution and conviction. Thus, for a plea-bargaining system to be viable, the criminal justice system in which the plea bargaining takes place must have the political and financial ability to credibly threaten prosecutions, even though the political will ultimately to fund those prosecutions may not exist.

Turning to the first problem, asking defendants to reveal all that they know about their own crimes and those of their associates is asking a lot. Defendants who make full disclosure may justifiably fear retaliation against themselves or their families. Those back home often view the mere act of pleading guilty a betrayal; revealing damaging particulars is apt to prove all the more risky. The first three ICTR defendants to plead guilty, as well as some ICTY defendants, insisted that the tribunals provide them and their families with substantial protection, including relocation. As a Croatian reporter observed about a recent ICTY defendant who pled guilty: "The question is where Ivica Rajić will be able to live once he has served his sentence. I sincerely doubt it that those whom he has got into trouble will leave him alone for as long as he lives."[830] Such concerns are by no means exaggerated. As noted above, after providing ICTR prosecutors with incriminating evidence about high-level Rwandan offenders, Juvénal Uwilingiyimana went missing in November 2005, and his body was later found in a Belgian canal.[831] Several ICTR witnesses and their families have also been murdered by Hutu extremists, even though they were purportedly under ICTR protection.[832] Any criminal justice system prosecuting international crimes must be prepared to provide substantial protection to those who plead guilty and implicate other offenders. Violence suffered by confessing defendants and their families is not only tragic for the individuals involved, but it has the potential to destroy the guilty-plea system by deterring other defendants from pleading guilty.

Fear of retaliation will not be the only deterrent. Making the complete disclosures that I have described will require defendants to engage in a level of critical self-examination that will prove excruciating to many. American defendants participating in a typical guilty-plea colloquy can grunt a "yes" or "no" to most of the perfunctory questions asked of them. Such colloquies do not require defendants to think very hard, to engage very deeply, or to critically examine their actions in any meaningful way. The guilty-plea scheme that I envisage, by contrast, requires all of those things, and requires it in a context in which it is even more difficult to provide. A domestic defendant who pleads guilty to car theft admits only that he or she stole a car. An international defendant who pleads guilty to persecution as a crime against humanity must call into question, at least nominally, a host of deeply held beliefs that the defendant may prefer to leave unscrutinized. Even those most committed to the racist or nationalist ends that motivated their actions must recognize, at some level, the evil inherent in torturing a fellow human being, or, worse yet, in extinguishing a life. A guilty-plea system embodying restorative-justice principles would not be satisfied with a summary description of the crime but would require the defendant to disclose sufficient information to satisfy the victims' and survivors' need to know and to prompt critical self-inquiry and appropriate shame. How did you torture John Smith? What did he do when you placed the plastic bag over his head? What were you trying to gain by these actions? How do you feel about them now? The anguish that many South African amnesty applicants exhibited in answering questions such as these evidences both the understandable reluctance of human beings to face piercing questions about their own unspeakable behavior as well as its transformative potential.[833]

Thus, asking defendants to open themselves to such potentially searing experiences may, in many cases, be asking too much. Prosecutors of domestic crimes can typically increase the number of guilty pleas by increasing the sentencing concessions that they offer. Similarly, one might expect that more substantial sentencing concessions would be required to motivate defendants to provide the requirement-laden guilty pleas that I advocate. South Africa, however, offered the ultimate sentencing concession—freedom from all punishment, criminal or civil—in exchange for full disclosure, yet many offenders refused the bargain, preferring instead to risk a criminal prosecution. That the risk was not a substantial one in South Africa explains the willingness of many offenders to gamble, and it highlights the fact that, to be successful, a guilty-plea scheme must be backed up by a credible threat of prosecution. The South African experience also demonstrates that factors such as how interrelated the crimes are and which defendants choose initially to come forward have considerable influence on whether future defendants are motivated to plead guilty.

In South Africa, for instance, just when it looked as though no one but low-level offenders would seek amnesty, five mid-level police officers confessed to involvement in forty apartheid-era murders. In their amnesty applications, these officers implicated General Johan van der Merwe, maintaining that he had ordered them to fire on civilians during a 1992 demonstration. Van der Merwe then sought amnesty himself, and he in turn implicated two cabinet-level officials and asserted that former president P. W. Botha had personally ordered the bombing of a church headquarters.[834] A similar phenomenon occurred in the ICTY's *Sikirica* case (see Chapter 4). As noted there, the case centered on the Keraterm prison camp and featured three defendants—Duško Sikirica, Keraterm's commander of security, and Damir Došen and Dragan Kolundžija, two of Keraterm's shift commanders.[835] Sikirica was considered the most culpable of the three and was charged not only with war crimes and crimes against humanity but also with genocide and complicity to genocide. Kolundžija, by contrast, was considered the least culpable; although he was charged with crimes against humanity as a result of the inhumane conditions under which prisoners were detained, prosecutors acknowledged that Kolundžija did not himself mistreat any prisoners and in fact made significant efforts to relieve their suffering.[836] Once Kolundžija—the least culpable defendant—pled guilty and acknowledged the conditions prevailing in the Keraterm camp, the remaining defendants presumably felt they had little choice but to follow suit, and, within a few days, they too pled guilty.[837] The snowball effect, then, may help to motivate even the most reluctant defendants to disclose their wrongdoing.

The second, and more grave, obstacle threatening the guilty-plea system I envisage relates to financing—not the financing of the guilty-plea procedure, but of the trials that stand as its alternative. The South African experience demonstrates that most defendants will not confess their crimes unless motivated by a credible threat of prosecution. The problem in the context of international crimes is that such prosecutions are not economically feasible. Indeed, the primary reason for conducting plea bargaining in the first place is that the international community (in the case of international tribunals) or domestic criminal justice systems either are not willing or are not able to devote the resources necessary to conduct a significant number of full-scale trials. But the system must appear to be willing and able to do just that, or it will not be able to motivate guilty pleas.

Domestic criminal justice systems regularly face and surmount this problem. Indeed, the criminal justice system of one of the wealthiest nations in the world—the United States—is able to credibly threaten individual defendants with trials even though, as currently operating, the system would come to a grinding halt if significant numbers of defendants began insisting on trials.[838] As then Chief Justice Warren Burger calculated more than thirty years ago, "[a] reduction from 90 per cent to 80 per cent in guilty pleas requires the assignment of twice the judicial manpower and facilities—judges, court reporters, bailiffs, clerks, jurors and courtrooms. A reduction to 70 per cent trebles this demand."[839] The system's dependence on plea bargaining has not been lost on American public defenders, who, as a result of their large caseloads and organized structure, have the ability to organize "general strikes," during which all of their clients insist on a trial. The mere threat of a general strike is often enough to compel prosecutorial concessions.[840] General strikes are rarely used, however, primarily because they require individual defendants to act as sacrificial lambs for the benefit of the defendant class. In particular, in order to persuade prosecutors and judges of their resolve, some defendants must proceed to trial, and these defendants will receive significantly longer sentences than they would have had they pled guilty. Few adequately informed defendants will be willing to spend an extra ten or fifteen years in prison to benefit complete strangers. Thus, at least in the domestic context, as long as prosecutors can persuade individual defendants that they, personally, are at risk of prosecution, that threat generally provides defendants with sufficient motivation to consider a guilty plea.

The analogy to domestic-court experience is not perfect, however. The most ambitious general strikes in the domestic context encompass the defendants of, say, one city, and the goal of the strike is to secure additional leniency, not to de-

stroy the system altogether. International defendants, by contrast, could reasonably conclude that their refusal to enter guilty pleas will completely destroy the
system; that is, that it will result in the prosecution of few or none because the system financially is incapable of trying a significant number of defendants. International defendants are also more likely to band together in this way because they
are more likely to share deeply held ideological views and because many of them
will actually know one another and thus may form a cohesive group. In certain
circumstances, cash-strapped international tribunals may be able to sidestep this
problem by threatening to send cases to less-desirable domestic courts. As it pre-
pares to close its doors in the next few years, the ICTY has begun to transfer some
of its cases to special chambers of the courts of Bosnia-Herzegovina. The prospect
of ending up before a Bosnian court, and in particular while housed in a dangerous Sarajevo prison, has reportedly motivated a number of ICTY defendants to
plead guilty.[841]

Most international tribunals do not possess this weapon and neither do domestic criminal justice systems seeking to prosecute international crimes. These
bodies can still motivate a substantial number of guilty pleas, though, by wisely
using what funds are available and carefully orchestrating the timing of prosecutions. In particular, a domestic or international criminal justice system seeking
to motivate guilty pleas should use a substantial proportion of its resources to
conduct thorough investigations and to arrest and detain large numbers of appropriate suspects at the outset of the prosecutorial endeavor. Doing so will create
a credible threat of sanctions, particularly if arrests are immediately followed by
trials for low-level offenders whose cases are relatively quick and easy to prove.
Such a forceful beginning can act to put pressure on defendants to consider guilty
pleas; as noted above, guilty pleas beget more guilty pleas, particularly when those
pleading guilty must reveal substantial information implicating other offenders.
As Chapter 10 will describe, the Rwandan criminal justice system was entirely
unable to provide trials to all of the 130,000 detained genocide suspects, but its
long-term detention of these individuals without prospect of trial motivated a
substantial number of them to confess through Rwanda's *gacaca* process. Rwanda's treatment of its genocide suspects blatantly violated prevailing due-process
standards and should not be emulated; at the same time, conducting widespread
arrests of individuals for whom there truly exists substantial evidence of criminal
wrongdoing is entirely appropriate. Many of these offenders may have to be released eventually if financial constraints prevent them from being tried in a timely

manner, but one can hope that, in the meantime, a substantial number of them will choose to plead guilty and in doing so will motivate other guilty pleas.

Summary

This chapter has constructed an innovative model of plea bargaining that locates the practice simultaneously within the realm of such mechanisms as truth commissions, reparations schemes, and conventional criminal justice systems. Although the primary function of plea bargaining is to increase the number of convictions that prosecutors can obtain, if practiced on a restorative-justice model, plea bargaining has the additional potential to advance many of the ends typically served by the nonprosecutorial methods referred to above. Plea bargaining can increase the amount and kinds of information available to victims and society, as prosecutors use the lure of leniency to persuade defendants to disclose the details of their crimes. Guilty-plea hearings can empower victims by allowing them to participate in ways that would be inappropriate in the context of an ordinary criminal prosecution. Although even restorative-justice guilty-plea proceedings cannot be conducted in the manner of truth-commission hearings, whose primary purpose is to provide victims a safe place to tell their stories, they can permit some victims some time to present the information most important to them and to seek desired information from offenders. These victim-perpetrator interactions can advance individual reconciliation, between the particular victims and perpetrators, and societal reconciliation, as the insights revealed through these interactions enable different sectors of society to reach a better understanding of the crimes and their societal impact.

Restorative justice promotes a number of values simultaneously, but the relative emphasis to place on each element will depend, in the international context, on the particular circumstances of the atrocity. Truth-telling might be a preeminent goal in the aftermath of some conflicts, for instance, while other conflicts will call for a greater emphasis on criminal accountability. The following chapter explores ways in which various restorative values must be balanced through an examination of four very different atrocities.

CHAPTER NINE

Applying Restorative Principles in the Aftermath of Different Atrocities

A Contextual Approach

I began this book with the observation that financial constraints will in most instances prevent the prosecution of the vast majority of international criminals unless alternatives to full-scale trials are utilized. I continued by exploring the benefits of prosecuting a larger proportion of offenders and identifying plea bargaining as a means of effecting more prosecutions without increasing the overall financial costs of the prosecutorial endeavor. I then examined in more detail the value of plea bargaining in the context of international crimes, and in particular, I constructed a model guilty-plea system that would aim both to increase the number of prosecutions that can take place and to enhance peace-building and reconciliation efforts. Such a guilty-plea system would seek simultaneously to advance retributory and restorative goals. This chapter will explore the different balances between restoration and retribution that might optimally be struck for different atrocities.

Advancing both retributive and restorative goals can be of considerable value to societies emerging from widespread violence, but those goals conflict when it comes to resource allocation. A guilty-plea system aiming solely to increase the number of criminal prosecutions, for instance, would permit guilty pleas to be entered with the most minimal inquiry consistent with due-process standards, and it would seek to obtain from defendants only the information and testimony likely to be useful in subsequent prosecutions. By contrast, if guilty pleas are to advance truth-telling in a broader sense, and other restorative-justice values such as victim participation, offender reintegration, and individual and societal reconciliation, a more complex, and costly, model must be utilized. Proceedings that feature detailed offender confessions, victim questioning, and the develop-ment of reparatory obligations take time and cost money, time and money that could be used to prosecute additional offenders.

Crafting the most desirable balance between retribution and restoration in a guilty-plea system will hinge on a number of factors specific both to the inter-national crimes in question and the cultures of the offenders and victims. How much truth must be sought from offenders may depend on how much informa-tion is already available about the crimes. How much weight to place on apologies may be influenced by cultural views about the way apologies are made, received, and valued in the society in question.[842] The size and makeup of the offender and victim populations will also be important guides in determining how many pros-ecutions to undertake. Were the offenses carried out by a large number of per-petrators against mostly anonymous victims? If so, perhaps the need for truth-telling and victim involvement is not acute, and the guilty-plea system should devote most of its resources toward obtaining convictions. This chapter will ex-amine these issues in the context of four very different atrocities—in Argentina, Bosnia, Rwanda, and East Timor—in order to explore how different restorative elements might optimally coalesce in different factual settings.

Whatever the precise contours of the balance ultimately chosen, it is impera-tive that the guilty-plea system contain substantial restorative-justice elements. For one thing, a tendency exists, particularly among human-rights activists, to overestimate the value of prosecutions and to undervalue the less obvious bene-fits provided by nonprosecutorial measures. Thus, even in situations in which the benefits of restorative-justice measures appear limited, it may be wise to include them. More importantly, and as alluded to above, restorative-justice elements should be included in a guilty-plea system because they legitimize the plea bar-gaining that is the essential prerequisite to obtaining guilty pleas. Ordinary plea bargaining—by which a defendant receives a sentencing discount for the mere act of self-conviction—breeds contempt. American victims hate it, and Bosnian victims hate it. Citizens of even the wealthiest nations recognize that resources are limited and that different societal needs must be balanced, so that not ev-ery offender can be prosecuted, nor can each receive the optimal level of pun-ishment. Most people further recognize, particularly in the context of societies emerging from mass violence, that convicting five offenders and sentencing each to ten years' imprisonment is likely to better serve the goals of criminal law than convicting one offender, sentencing that one person to life imprisonment, and leaving the remaining four offenders unpunished. Despite this recognition, there remains a trenchant unseemliness about subjecting justice to calculations and a severe risk that these sorts of calculations will further embitter victims. Kenneth Kipnis, a leading American critic of plea bargaining, has argued that punishments should be deserved and that bargains are out of place in a context where people are to get what they deserve.[843] Kipnis's argument has validity, but it assumes a retributory model of criminal punishment that does not exhaust the possibilities. When the model is expanded to include not only retribution and the other traditional goals of criminal law but also restorative-justice values, the significance of guilty pleas—and the methods used to motivate them—emerge. For this reason, some restorative-justice elements should be included in every guilty-plea system concerned with international crimes, *and* these elements should be well-publicized, for they will legitimize what might otherwise be viewed solely as a distasteful cost-cutting mechanism.

A Summary of Four Atrocities

Detailed histories have been written about the violent conflicts that engulfed Argentina, Bosnia, Rwanda, and East Timor. The following summary treatment is intended only to provide a sufficient basis for examining how different restorative and retributive features might optimally be balanced in different factual contexts.

Argentina

Twentieth-century Argentine history is replete with coups, but the coup that deposed Isabel Perón in 1976 ushered in a particularly violent and repressive military regime. Eager to stamp out a real or perceived threat from leftist guerrillas, the military unleashed a brutal campaign, targeting "subversives" who were believed to oppose the military's rabidly anti-communist view of Western Christian civilization. Central to the military's "dirty war" was its widespread use of "disappearances," during which government agents abducted, tortured, and usually killed suspected subversives.[844] The disappearances followed a similar pattern. Civilian authorities, such as the police, were warned to steer clear of the targeted area. An armed task force would then burst into the victim's home, usually in the wee hours of the morning, ransack the house, and load the victim into an unmarked car. The attackers would then drive the then-hooded victim to a clandestine detention center where the victim was made to suffer ghastly torture methods.[845] Some prisoners were detained for years, others were immediately tortured to death, while still others were killed through mass executions. To prevent detection of these activities, the Argentine military "disappeared" the bodies. A large number of victims were thrown, still alive, from airplanes over the sea,[846] and their remains have never been recovered. Many of those killed through mass executions had their heads and hands cut off so that their bodies could not be identified.[847] Although these activities were carefully organized and thoroughly documented within governmental apparatuses, they were nonetheless carried out with the utmost external secrecy. The government categorically denied the existence of the detention centers at which tens of thousands were imprisoned,[848] and, by "disappearing" the victims' bodies, no evidence was left to be discovered. Families of the disappeared filed habeas corpus petitions in droves, but "from 1973 on, judges did not manage to locate or rescue a single one of the many disappeared."[849]

In all, between ten thousand and thirty thousand people were disappeared at the hands of the Argentine military.[850] Victims came primarily from the blue-collar working class and certain sectors of the middle class, especially students, professionals, and white-collar employees. Nearly a third of the victims were women,[851] and most victims were young: 71 percent were thirty years old or younger, and 83 percent were younger than thirty-five years of age.[852] Although a small percentage of victims were active in left-wing guerrilla organizations, the vast majority had little or no connection to any illegal activities.[853] The perpetrators, for their part, numbered approximately one thousand.[854]

The families of the disappeared remain devastated by these crimes. As Argentina's Truth Commission reported:

> First it was the people, their absence giving hope to the relatives that the kidnap victim would be freed and return; then the concealment and destruction of documentation, which undoubtedly existed in every case, prolonging the uncertainty about what had happened; and finally, the nameless bodies, without identity, driving people distraught at the impossibility of knowing the specific fate of their loved one. It was a bottomless pit of horror....
>
> [The disappearances had the effect] of paralysing public protest, of ensuring the silence of the relatives. By giving them hope that their loved ones might be alive, in

the nebulous category of missing persons, an ambiguity was created which forced the relatives into isolation, frightened to do anything which might annoy the government. They were terrified by the mere idea that their own actions might decide whether their son, daughter, father or brother joined the lists of the dead. . . .

Lastly, at the heart of this policy of total disappearance lay the prevention by every possible means of solidarity being shown by the population in general, with all the protests and demands this would lead to within the country, and the knowledge abroad that behind the façade of a fight against a terrorist minority lurked genocide.[855]

The fact that the Argentine junta perpetrated its repression by means of disappearances has, in the view of many, impeded reconciliation. As human-rights activist Emilio Mignone put it: "Exiles come back or stay abroad, but are alive. . . . Dead are buried and we pay them homage, according to our customs. But the disappeared are neither dead nor alive. They constitute a tragedy, something that has wounded Argentine society and that makes reconciliation difficult."[856] Argentine journalist Hector Verbitsky agreed, observing "After someone takes away your daughter, tortures her, disappears her, and then denies ever having done it— would you ever want to 'reconcile' with those responsible? The word makes no sense here. The political discourse of reconciliation is profoundly immoral, because it denies the reality of what people have experienced."[857] Also impeding reconciliation is the unrepentant attitude of the military. Most members of the armed forces continue to believe that their actions were justified by the threat posed by the left. Following a transition to democracy in 1983, nine leaders of the military were prosecuted and convicted for their roles in the atrocities. In the face of military unrest, these leaders and others awaiting prosecution were soon pardoned,[858] and on the date of his release from prison, the first president of the military junta, Jorge Rafael Videla, "wrote a public letter to the high command stating that the Army had been wrongly accused and that it deserved an apology and vindication from society."[859] Similarly, Julio "El Turco Julian" Simón appeared on television maintaining "that all of his victims were dangerous terrorists" and said that he would commit the same actions against them again, if given the chance.[860]

Bosnia

From 1945 until 1990, Yugoslavia was composed of six republics: Bosnia-Herzegovina, Croatia, Montenegro, Serbia, Slovenia, and Macedonia. Although most of the people of the different regions of Yugoslavia share a common language and physical appearance, religious differences and divergent historical experi-

ences led to the growth of strong, separate ethnic identities.[861] After World War
II, Josip Broz Tito emerged as leader of a unified Yugoslavia, and most accounts
credit him with containing ethnic tension by use of stern repression at the hands
of secret police.[862] However, Tito's death in 1980, followed by economic difficulties
and the end of communist rule, set the stage for rising nationalism and ethnic
friction. Slobodan Milošević capitalized on rising Serbian nationalism to become Serbian Communist Party chief in 1986, and he attempted to create a more
centralized Yugoslavia under Serbian dominance. The leaders of the other republics resisted Milošević's efforts, and in 1991 the republics began declaring
independence from the Federal Republic of Yugoslavia. Macedonia's secession
was peaceful, and Slovenia secured its independence after only ten days of fighting. The war in Croatia, however, was longer and bloodier, leading to more than
ten thousand deaths and six hundred thousand displaced persons.[863] But it was
Bosnia-Herzegovina's declaration of independence in March 1992 that gave rise
to the most fierce and protracted fighting.[864]

Unlike the other republics, which were predominantly populated by one ethnic group, Bosnia-Herzegovina had substantial Serbian, Muslim, and Croatian
populations.[865] The Serbs living in Bosnia had opposed independence, and after
proclaiming the formation of an independent Serbian Republic of Bosnia and
Herzegovina, they began launching attacks on Bosnia's Croatian and Muslim
populations. Assisted by the Serb-dominated Yugoslav National Army, the Bosnian Serbs implemented a plan to create a "Greater Serbia" by occupying and
"cleansing" non-Serbs from areas which formed a corridor linking Serbia with
parts of Bosnia-Herzegovina and Croatia that were populated by Serbs.[866] Using
methods reminiscent of the Nazis, the Serbs engaged in mass forced population
transfers of non-Serbs in convoys of cattle trucks; they organized massacres and
destroyed entire towns and more than one thousand major historical, religious,
and cultural monuments in Bosnia and Croatia; they systematically raped Muslim women and girls; and they established more than four hundred prison camps
where tens of thousands of Bosnian Muslims and Croats were beaten, tortured,
and killed, while others died from malnutrition and disease brought on by the
appalling conditions prevailing in the camps. M. Cherif Bassiouni and Peter
Manikas describe the Serbian attacks aimed at ethnic cleansing as following "a
similar pattern":

> First, Bosnian Serb paramilitary forces, often with the assistance of the JNA [Yugoslav
> People's Army], seized control of the area. In many cases, Serb residents were told

to leave the area before the violence began. The homes of non-Serb residents were targeted for destruction and cultural and religious monuments—especially churches and mosques—were destroyed. Second, the area fell under the control of paramilitary forces who terrorized the non-Serb residents with random killings, rapes, and looting. Third, the seized area was administered by local Serb authorities, often in conjunction with paramilitary groups. During this phase, non-Serb residents were detained, beaten, and sometimes transferred to prison camps where further abuse, including mass killings, occurred. Non-Serb residents were often fired from their jobs and their property was confiscated. Many were forced to sign documents relinquishing their rights to their homes before being deported to other areas of the country.[867]

Bosnian Muslim and Bosnian Croat forces were weaker than those of the Bosnian Serbs, but they could be similarly brutal when they had the opportunity.[868] Fighting continued until 1995 when the presidents of Croatia, Bosnia-Herzegovina, and the Federal Republic of Yugoslavia entered into the Dayton Peace Accords.[869] In total, the Bosnian war resulted in tens of thousands of rapes,[870] approximately two hundred thousand deaths, and the forced relocation of more than two million people.[871] The number of offenders has been estimated at ten thousand.[872]

Whereas the Argentine forced disappearances and the Rwandan and East Timorese violence described below were fairly uniform in their basic contours, the Bosnian war featured several different kinds of atrocities—including the prison camps, the siege of Sarajevo, and the mass execution at Srebrenica. Each is summarily described here.

Prison Camps. As part of their ethnic-cleansing campaign, Bosnian Serb forces took over municipalities and regions and, after gaining control, interned Muslim and Croats—primarily men and boys—in brutal prison camps. Conditions in these camps were inhuman.[873] Prisoners were provided scant water and food; they frequently received only one meal per day, which was often spoiled or otherwise inedible. Because prisoners received only starvation rations, they frequently lost between forty-five and sixty-five pounds of body weight during their detentions.[874] The camps were horribly overcrowded. In some camps, prisoners had no room to lie down and were forced to sleep on top of one another. Facilities for personal hygiene were virtually nonexistent. Many camps had no toilet facilities and no washing facilities; consequently, dysentery and lice were widespread.

In addition to the suffering caused by deplorable conditions, prisoners were subjected to frequent torture, sexual assaults, and beatings that in many cases resulted in death.[875] Beatings would be administered for purposes of interrogation as well as entertainment. Events at the Omarska camp were typical:

> [G]roups from outside the camp would appear, would call out particular prisoners from their rooms and attack them with a variety of sticks, iron bars or lengths of heavy electric cable. Sometimes these weapons would have nails embedded in them so as to pierce the skin. On occasions knives would be used to slash a prisoner's body.[876]

Most murder victims were killed one at a time at the camps, but a few mass executions also took place. At the Keraterm camp in July 1992, for instance, a machine gun was placed in front of Room 3. The doors were locked, gas was thrown into the room, and, when prisoners tried to break down the door, soldiers responded with gunfire, killing more than 125 of them.[877] In a massacre at the Omarska camp, also in July 1992, nearly 200 prisoners were shot and killed during the course of a single night.[878]

Siege of Sarajevo. For more than three-and-one-half years, Serb forces numbering some thirteen thousand held Bosnia's largest city, Sarajevo, under siege.[879] The forces positioned themselves in the hills overlooking the city and launched a campaign of terror by means of indiscriminate shelling and sniper attacks against civilians. Holed up in a high-rise building in a Sarajevo suburb, Serb snipers were able to target civilians attempting to traverse various thoroughfares in the center of the city. People trying to cross a frequently attacked bridge, for example, were forced to hide behind a tree or a wall and then jump up and run, trying to evade the expected gunfire.[880] Automobile accidents abounded, as frightened drivers sped through dangerous intersections.[881] Serbs also routinely targeted shelling against civilians. Ambulances and funerals became such regular targets that ambulances began avoiding main roads, and funerals were held only at night.[882] The shellings averaged from two hundred to one thousand per day,[883] and because civilians were attacked "'more or less every day, if not every day,'"[884] they stayed indoors whenever possible. "They learned to move around as little as possible, rarely leaving their apartments: some old people were 'literally dying of malnutrition because they were too terrified to come out.'"[885] By the end of the war, the siege had killed approximately twelve thousand civilians, as many as sixteen hundred of them children.[886]

Srebrenica. In July 1995, Bosnian Serb forces captured and occupied the predominantly Bosnian Muslim town of Srebrenica.[887] Within a few days, Serb forces had separated the men from the women and children and had transported the women and children across battle lines into Bosnian-Muslim–held territory. The Bosnian Muslim men were loaded onto buses and transported to various detention sites, where they were systematically executed by firing squads. Groups of ten were lined up, ordered to turn their backs, and then shot.[888] In the course of a few days, Bosnian Serb forces executed more than seven thousand men and boys, burying their bodies in mass graves. To prevent their detection, these graves were excavated a few months later and the bodies reburied in different locations.[889] Nine years after the executions, about five thousand bodies had been recovered but only about twelve hundred had been identified through DNA techniques.[890] Until very recently, Bosnian Serbs categorically denied that the executions took place; they maintained, rather, that the killings were fabricated or insisted that, if Muslims were killed, they were killed in combat or by other Muslims. In this vein, a 2002 report issued by the Documentation Center of the Republika Srpska Bureau of Government purportedly designed to "'present the whole truth about crimes committed in Srebrenica region [sic]'" stated that "'the number of Muslim soldiers who were executed by Bosnian Serb forces for personal revenge or for simple ignorance of international law would probably stand at less than 100.'"[891] It was not until more than nine years after the massacres that Bosnian Serb leaders finally acknowledged the atrocities,[892] and that acknowledgment came only after the imposition of intense international pressure.[893]

Rwanda

In 1994, large-scale ethnic violence engulfed Rwanda, a small country in the Great Lakes region of Africa.[894] Rwanda's population is composed of two predominant groups, the Hutu and the Tutsi. The Tutsi minority had ruled Rwanda for centuries, but in 1959 the Hutu took control of the country and thereafter unleashed a series of massacres against the Tutsi that drove nearly one hundred thousand Tutsi into exile in neighboring countries. By the late 1980s, the number of Tutsi in exile had grown to approximately six hundred thousand, and the exiled Tutsi had formed an army, the Rwandan Patriotic Front (RPF). During the early 1990s, the RPF and the Rwandan government, then led by Hutu President Habyarimana, engaged in several military clashes, and after fighting to a standstill, the parties entered into the Arusha Accords in 1993. The accords provided, among other things, for a new transitional government, with a prime minister acceptable to both sides, and for multiparty general elections with the full participation of the RPF.

Both sides soon began to undermine the accords, and President Habyarimana in addition attempted to unify Hutu and shore up their support by creating a common enemy—the Tutsi. Tutsi civilians living in Rwanda were equated with RPF soldiers and with centuries-old Tutsi oppressors. Tutsi devils were reported to be lurking in the villages, waiting to retake control of the country by perpetrating genocide on Hutu. By December 1990, the newspaper *Kangara*

> had begun charging that the Tutsi had prepared a war that "would leave no survivors." Another pamphlet . . . declared in February 1991 that the RPF planned "to restore the dictatorship of the extremists of the Tutsi minority," by "a genocide, the extermination of the Hutu majority." As the conflict progressed, the warnings became increasingly explicit and hysterical. By mid-1993, propagandists were asserting, "We know that they have attacked us with the intention of massacring and exterminating 4.5 million Hutu and especially those who have gone to school."[895]

The government made the Tutsi threat appear all the more real by staging phony attacks allegedly perpetrated by Tutsi. For instance, the military "staged a fake assault on the important Bigogwe military camp." The "attack" was so believable that in one commune the *bourgmestre* had trouble persuading the Hutu not to flee but instead to stay and attack their Tutsi neighbors.[896] The government also used radio and newspapers to spread its virulent message of hate,[897] and it ensured broad dissemination by distributing radios free to local authorities.[898] Long before the massacres began, the government drew up lists of people to be killed and established a training camp for Hutu militia to indoctrinate them in ethnic hatred and instruct them on methods of mass murder. The government also distributed millions of dollars' worth of firearms and machetes throughout the country.[899] By late March 1994, Hutu extremists were determined to slaughter massive numbers of Tutsi and Hutu political opponents. As Philip Gourevitch describes it: "The dead had seen their killers training as militias in the weeks before the end, and it was well known that they were training to kill Tutsis; it was announced on the radio, it was in the newspapers, people spoke of it openly."[900]

In April 1994, a plane carrying President Habyarimana was shot down, and, blaming the Tutsi for the assassination,[901] Hutu soldiers, the militia, and the Presidential Guard immediately began to hunt down and kill Tutsi and moderate Hutu. Within an hour of Habyarimana's death, roadblocks had been established to catch and kill Tutsi who were trying to flee, and armed forces were conducting house-to-house searches, seeking Tutsi and targeted individuals, such as politicians, journalists, and civil-rights activists. At the genocide's outset, small bands of assailants killed individual victims where they found them, but soon after, efforts were made to drive large numbers of Tutsi out of their homes and into large buildings—schools, churches, and the like—where they could be exterminated through large-scale operations.[902] Most victims were hacked to death by machetes,[903] but when a large number of victims congregated in one location, authorities often called in military units to use mortar shells or hand grenades. These attacks left tens of thousands of bodies often piled four and five feet high, and many of these were thrown into rivers.[904]

Rwanda's political tradition, according to some scholars, was characterized for centuries by a "systematic, centralized and unconditional obedience to authority,"[905] which well served those organizing the genocide. The leaders of the genocide appropriated the well-established military, administrative, and political hierarchies and were consequently able to mobilize efficient, comprehensive massacres. Although the military and the militia took the initial lead in the extermination, the scale of the killings required the mobilization of hundreds of thousands of ordinary civilians, "tens of thousands to actually slaughter and the others to spy, search, guard, burn, and pillage."[906] The interim government that assumed power following the death of President Habyarimana instructed the political administration in carrying out this mobilization. Prefects transmitted orders from the interim government while *bourgmestres* and their subordinates did the actual work of mobilizing the people. These local leaders went house to house, signing up all of the adult men and posting "work" schedules at public notice areas. They transported assailants to massacre sites, supervised the killings, and generally ensured the smooth functioning of the genocide.[907]

Many ordinary Hutu participated voluntarily, indeed enthusiastically, in the massacres.[908] Government propaganda had succeeded in demonizing Tutsi to such a degree that many Hutu believed that their only choice was to kill or be killed by Tutsi.[909] In addition to this fear, the scarcity of land in Rwanda motivated some Hutu to kill their Tutsi neighbors in an effort to gain their victims' property.[910] At the same time, not all Hutu were willing executioners. To motivate widespread participation, authorities offered considerable rewards, including cash payments, food, drink, and other material incentives. These incentives were insufficient in some cases, and authorities were then forced to use threats of violence. Prefects and *bourgmestres* opposed to the killings were murdered, and civilians who refused to search for Tutsi were threatened with severe sanctions, including death.[911] Although tens of thousands of Hutu refused to participate in the extermination and thus saved Tutsi lives,[912] a stunning number of Hutu—more than one hundred thousand—either killed, facilitated the killings, or stood by silently while the genocide took place.

The massacres of Tutsi and moderate Hutu continued for one hundred days, during which time five hundred thousand to one million people were murdered. The killings came to an end only when the RPF defeated the Rwandan army in July 1994.[913]

East Timor

East Timor had been a Portuguese colony for more than 450 years when, in 1974, Portugal began considering dismantling its colonies, including East Timor.[914] Before Portugal could take any action, however, Indonesia invaded East Timor in December 1975 and soon after formally annexed the territory, proclaiming East Timor the twenty-seventh province of Indonesia.[915] Indonesia's invasion and subsequent twenty-four-year occupation were brutal: more than two hundred thousand Timorese—about a third of the preinvasion population—unnecessarily lost their lives during these years, a death toll that some scholars have labeled genocidal.[916] By 1999, however, Indonesia's continued military presence in East Timor had led to trenchant international criticism and a financial drain on Indonesia's fragile economy. As a consequence, then Indonesian president B. J. Habibie agreed with Portugal and the U.N. on a consultation process whereby a referendum would be held permitting East Timorese to vote either to become independent or to remain within Indonesia, bearing a special autonomous status.[917]

The months before the ballot saw considerable violence, aimed at intimidating the East Timorese population into voting to remain within Indonesia. The Indonesian military (TNI) established, funded, and armed local militias, typically made up of illiterate East Timorese peasants, instructing them to brutalize and in many cases kill proindependence supporters and their families.[918] In one of the worst preelection acts of violence, Indonesian military forces and local militia attacked a large group of civilians who had taken refuge in the Liquica church, killing at least twenty-five of them.[919] Despite the intimidation, when East Timorese went to the ballots on August 30, 1999, 78.5 percent of them voted for independence.[920] After the result was announced, the violence, which had theretofore primarily targeted known supporters of independence, became large-scale and indiscriminate. Indonesian-sponsored militia groups wreaked devastation on East Timor, killing some 1,400 people, raping and torturing countless more, and forcibly deporting approximately 250,000 to Indonesian-controlled West Timor.[921] The physical violence perpetrated on victims was particularly brutal. Militia members used primitive weapons such as machetes and spears to kill their victims and, in many cases, mutilated them before killing them. A favorite tactic, for instance, involved cutting off the victim's ear and forcing him or her to eat it.[922] Virtually all of the East Timorese who participated in the violence maintained that they did so because they were forced to or at least ordered to by militia leaders or the Indonesian military. The postelection "scorched earth" campaign also led to unparalleled property destruction. Entire villages were razed, and virtually every aspect of East Timor's infrastructure was destroyed.[923] Of particular relevance here, virtually all court buildings were in rubble after the referendum, and all court equipment, furniture, registers, records, and archives as well as law books and case files were lost or burned. In addition, during the Indonesian occupation, judges, lawyers, and prosecutors had been installed by Indonesia, and all of them returned to Indonesia following the referendum.[924]

To put an end to the violence, the Security Council sent a multinational force to restore order and keep peace.[925] The U.N. thereafter established UNTAET as a peacekeeping mission to administer East Timor until its independence was viable.[926] A key element of UNTAET's mandate involved the monumental task of establishing a judicial system from scratch. The effort got off to a slow start. For several months after the referendum, for instance, UNTAET had no contact with areas outside of East Timor's capital city, Dili.[927] Thus, the majority of East Timorese had no access to any judicial system. Thereafter, UNTAET did take steps to construct courthouses, police stations, and prisons as well as to appoint and train police officers, prosecutors, and judges,[928] but these efforts have not come close to creating for East Timor a viable justice system capable of serving the country's needs. Resources are extremely scarce, and this shortage of funds hampers East Timor's judicial system in every aspect of its work. A shortage of judges has plagued the courts since their inception and has caused district courts to cease functioning for months at a time.[929] Indeed, the problem became acute in July 2003, when nine judges traveled to Portugal for a year-long training project.[930] More worryingly, it was announced in January 2005 that all twenty-two East Timorese probationary judges failed their written competence examinations.[931] Like the Special Panels for Serious Crimes (see Chapter 2), the district courts also suffer from a severe shortage of translators and interpreters. Many court staff cannot speak the national languages of East Timor,[932] and there is a complete lack of interpreters in the courts of Baucau, Oecusse, and Suai.[933] Most East Timorese are unaware of the shortcomings in their judicial system because the location of the courts leaves East Timorese entirely unable to access the courts even if they were adequate. UNTAET Regulation 2000/11 called for the establishment of eight district courts,[934] but, as a result of the scarcity of qualified legal personnel, only four have been established,[935] and these are often located far from the populations they are intended to serve. The Suai District Court, for instance, presents an especially egregious example because it currently operates not from Suai but from Dili, apparently because there are no public defenders in Suai.[936] Many crime victims have no means of traveling to the courts; no vehicles can pass during some periods of heavy rain, and when roads are passable, vehicles are so scarce that in some criminal cases, victims, witnesses, and even perpetrators must be transported to court in the same vehicle.[937]

These manifest failures of the formal justice system might be devastating to the inhabitants of many countries, yet they barely have been noticed in many areas of East Timor because most East Timorese prefer, in any event, to have their crimes and other disputes addressed through so-called "local justice" mechanisms. Local justice has been practiced in East Timor since "time immemorial."[938] It constituted the primary means of conflict resolution throughout the 450 years of Portuguese colonization and the twenty-four years of Indonesian occupation,[939] and it likewise stands as the means by which most current disputes are resolved.[940] Local justice practices vary considerably from region to region in East Timor, but some underlying principles of justice and social interaction that pervade most of the local systems can be identified.[941]

Most accounts of East Timorese local justice emphasize its interrelation with other features of the East Timorese sociocosmic system. Among the most crucial features of this system are blood kinship and the relationships built through marriage. East Timorese marriages are arranged in accordance with certain social rules, most important of which is that the consummation of a marriage requires an exchange of goods, described as a "bride price." The wife's family (the Wife Giver) and the husband's family (the Wife Taker) engage in a well-established exchange and are thereafter ordered in a hierarchical relationship with one another.[942] An individual belongs not only to a Wife Giver or Wife Taker family but also to a "sacred house," which traces the individual's lineage to the common ancestor who founded the house. Each sacred house is headed by an elder, who is responsible for contacting the ancestors and for the various aspects of ceremonial life. In addition to the elder, who is the ritual authority of the community, each community has one or a series of political authorities. The *liurai,* for instance, constitutes the highest political authority in some communities and must liaison between the community and the outside world, including governmental authorities or, in the past, colonial powers.[943] The *liurai* typically assigns legal tasks to a *lian nain,* but, with respect to many disputes, the *lian nain* need not become involved. Conflicts that occur between family members, for instance, are brought for resolution to the head of the family. When a conflict occurs between members of two families, the elders of those families meet to resolve the dispute.[944] Only if these authorities do not succeed in resolving the conflict do the *lian nain* or other community leaders become involved.[945] In such an instance, village authorities may convene a meeting of village elders, in which community participation is encouraged.[946]

"Crimes" and other transgressions of the social order are understood by East Timorese as disruptions of the cosmic flow of values. Consequently, the appropriate punishment for such transgressions aims to restore the imbalance of values that has occurred.[947] When one person harms another, for instance, a debt is created, and that debt accrues not just to the individual who perpetrated the offense but to the offender's family and, in some instances, to his or her community.[948] Thus, crime is not perceived as an individual matter but rather as a problem that has the potential to threaten the entire community.[949] According to one scholar, East Timorese "would be afraid not to follow their customs, as it could prove very dangerous to them and their families not to do so. The idea that mystical sanctions are likely to be imposed by the ancestors or the spirits remains a very strong force."[950] Because crime is conceived as creating an imbalance of values, the punishment meted out through local justice seeks primarily to replace values and to reestablish the correct exchange, which will, in turn, reinforce the sociocosmic order.[951] As Dionísio Babo-Soares puts it, "the East Timorese conception of reconciliation forms part of a grand process that aims to link the past and the future" and "is an evolving process which seeks ultimately to achieve a stable social order within society."[952]

The East Timorese conception of justice, therefore, is not solely or even primarily about punishing the offender; rather, it seeks first and foremost to compensate the victim and the victim's family, whose honor has been damaged, as a means of reestablishing balance.[953] In cases of theft, for instance, the offender must compensate the victim for the stolen goods and pay additional compensation. If a house is destroyed, the family of the perpetrator must compensate the victims for everything that was in the victims' house, or, if they are unable to do so, the victims are entitled to the perpetrator's belongings. Even a murder may result in compensation being paid by the murderer to the victim's family.[954] Restoring the social order requires not only compensation but reconciliation, which is understood to involve the offender's public acknowledgment of wrongdoing, an apology, and the victim's forgiveness.[955] A successful reconciliation signifies that the conflict has been resolved and that both sides are again engaged in a peaceful relationship; if reconciliation fails to occur, by contrast, East Timorese believe that the social order remains imbalanced and the community's well-being subject to threat. A reconciliation process typically culminates in a ceremony that centers around a communal meal, including the alcoholic beverage *tuak*, which is typically provided by the offender.[956] Because compensation and reconciliation constitute the central features in the East Timorese conception of justice, detention is rarely imposed on offenders. Indeed, in the eyes of many East Timorese, detention constitutes no punishment at all because prisoners are fed and housed in jail and in some cases can avoid their compensation obligation.[957] In addition, the potential harm to the community that results from a transgression of the social order is in no way addressed by the offender's incarceration.

Restorative-Justice Values in Different Factual Contexts

Prosecutions for each of the atrocities described above would benefit by the inclusion of the restorative-justice elements appearing in most domestic restorative-justice programs. However, as discussed above, because international crimes typically feature so many offenders and so few resources with which to prosecute them, hard decisions must be made about the extent to which various restorative elements should be included. To elucidate the factors relevant to such decisions, this section will examine the degree to which the inclusion of the three primary restorative-justice elements—truth-telling, victim participation, and reparations—would benefit the prosecution of crimes committed in Argentina, Bosnia, Rwanda, and East Timor. The value of these elements will depend in part on the time that has elapsed between the crimes and their prosecution. A society will likely have less need for truth-telling procedures to be included in prosecutions, for instance, when prosecutions occur many years after the crime was committed because, during that time, considerable information about the crimes will likely have been revealed through other mechanisms. In order to provide a relevant comparison among the atrocities, this section will assume that prosecutions take place within a few years after the commission of the crimes.

Truth-telling

The mere act of pleading guilty constitutes a minimal form of truth-telling because, by pleading guilty, the defendant acknowledges that a crime took place and that the defendant was a perpetrator of that crime. Restorative-justice processes aim to elucidate more than the mere minimum quantity of facts necessary to support a guilty plea; rather, they encourage defendants to reveal all relevant information about the crimes in question. By obtaining and publicizing this information, a restorative-justice guilty-plea system can advance truth-telling in three ways. First, it can provide specific factual details about the crime, often of vital significance to victim families, such as how the victim was killed, what treatment he or she received before dying, where the body is now, and why this particular victim was selected. Second, revelations made by defendants may constitute official acknowledgment of the crime that can help to undercut long-standing denials of criminal wrongdoing. Finally, these revelations can provide information useful for prosecuting other, often more senior, defendants.

These different kinds of "truth" will benefit post-atrocity societies to differing degrees depending on the circumstances surrounding the atrocity and, in particular, depending on how much truth is already known about the crimes. Revelations conveying the factual details of the crimes will be far more valuable in the context of a crime that has been carefully concealed—an Argentine disappearance, for instance—than it will be in the context of a crime for which most details are already known—an East Timorese massacre, say, that took place in full public view. To this day, thousands of Argentine families do not know what happened to the relative who was yanked from his or her home by government agents, let alone why that person was selected for disappearance in the first place. The same uncertainties do not plague most East Timorese survivors because many of them witnessed firsthand the deaths of their loved ones.

Similarly, a society's need for the acknowledgment that can be conveyed through a defendant's confession will vary according to how much has already been acknowledged. In Bosnia, for instance, little acknowledgment of any sort took place for a number of years after the war. Most Bosnian Serbs continued to deny, most fundamentally, that atrocities even took place: the prison camps at which thousands of non-Serbs were murdered or died from malnutrition or disease have been known to Serbs as "collection centers" or "centers for the protection of the population." Denial about the prison camps is so entrenched that many Serbs actually believe that photographs of starving prisoners depict people who were sick before entering the camp.[958] Similarly, until November 2004, the Srebrenica deaths, if they were acknowledged at all, were said to have taken place during armed conflict by enemy combatants. By contrast, the Argentine crimes, along with similar offenses committed in other Latin American countries, were widely documented and publicized soon after their commission[959] so that, even just a few years after the democratic transitions, perpetrators could no longer categorically deny their occurrence; offenders continued, however, steadfastly to defend their actions as justified in light of the threat posed by leftist guerrillas.[960] The above-described letter written by former Argentine president Jorge Rafael Videla exemplifies this phenomenon, as do more recent statements by General Pinochet of Chile in which he described himself as a "patriotic angel" and asserted not only that he had nothing for which to apologize, but that he himself should be the recipient of an apology.[961] Peruvian general Roberto Clemente Noel's 2003 pronouncements are of a similar vein. Clemente Noel, for instance, pronounced himself "proud" of his wartime past, which he described as filled with heroism and sacrifice, despite the findings of a recent Peruvian truth commission that he was responsible for tortures and extrajudicial executions at a notorious military base.[962] Offenders such as these have the ability to resist acknowledging their crimes primarily because they continue to hold some political or military power in their countries. In Rwanda, by contrast, Tutsi forces completely defeated the Hutu extremists who organized the genocide, so the new Rwandan government has had the political ability to officially acknowledge and condemn the crimes. Some of this acknowledgment has come about through the government's efforts to prosecute more than one hundred thousand offenders; additionally, evidence of the violence is never far from sight because the country remains dotted with genocide "memorials"—piles of decomposing bodies that have been left where they fell.[963]

The third sort of truth revealed by restorative-justice procedures concerns information relevant to the prosecution of other offenders, and this information will also have greater or lesser value depending on the circumstances surrounding the atrocity. ICTY prosecutors, for instance, have had considerable difficulty linking political and military leaders with particular crimes because the structures of Bosnian civil and military authority became blurred during the war. In the *Delalić* case, for example, ICTY prosecutors were unable to prove that Zejnil Delalić acted as commander of the Čelebići prison camp;[964] they were likewise unable to prove in the *Kvočka* case that Dragoljub Prcać held the position of deputy commander of the Omarska camp.[965] ICTY prosecutors have begun, therefore, to rely heavily on the testimony of subordinates in their prosecutions of high-level and sometimes even mid-level offenders (see Chapter 10).[966] Likewise, East Timorese militias were hastily organized, and their activities were orally directed by members of the Indonesian military. Implicating even the mid-level offenders who instructed the militias in the choice of targets, for instance, requires the testimony of low-level militia members.

By contrast, the hierarchy of the Argentine military is well-established, and the forced disappearances were so uniform and systematic that one can infer that they were authorized by high-ranking officials.[967] As one low-level Argentine navy officer pointed out, "a gang of ten guys can[not] succeed in mobilizing airplanes belonging to the coast guard and the navy."[968] Even in the context of Argentine crimes, however, evidentiary uncertainties can arise because the orders for criminal activity were given orally; thus, when high-level Argentine junta members were convicted in 1985, it was at least partially on the basis of subordinate testimony.[969] Those prosecuting Rwandan crimes have perhaps the least need for the testimony of low-level perpetrators. A genocide on the scale of Rwanda's requires such careful organization, planning, and broad civilian participation that it cannot be carried out in secret. The plan to exterminate the Tutsi was implemented through well-established hierarchical structures and was so well-publicized that radio broadcasts frequently identified the names and sometimes the locations of Tutsi to be killed.[970] The public nature of the crimes and well-established structures through which they were carried out consequently render the testimony of subordinates less important in the Rwandan context, but even there it has certain value because the general chaos surrounding the Rwandan killings along with the lack of credibility of some victim testimony can leave prosecutors with evidentiary insufficiencies.[971]

Victim Participation

The feasibility of victim participation will depend primarily on the victim-perpetrator ratio; in particular, a high victim-perpetrator ratio will render widespread victim participation a practical impossibility.[972] When victim participation is feasible, it can serve two related goals. First, as discussed above, victim questioning can lead to the revelation of information that may not come to light through ordinary truth-telling efforts. The truth-telling procedures that would be utilized by a restorative-justice guilty-plea system would themselves be rigorous, but victims are nonetheless apt to seek idiosyncratic information that may not otherwise be revealed. Such information is most likely to be sought when the crimes were committed in secrecy and when they took place against individual victims over a protracted period of time. The Argentine forced disappearances, for instance, fit this model. In particular, the fact that most Argentine murder victims were neither immediately killed nor killed in a uniform fashion, as were victims in Rwanda or Srebrenica, for instance, makes it more likely that family members would ask detailed questions about the treatment their loved ones received before their deaths, as well as about the precise causes of their deaths.

Second, permitting victims to question offenders empowers victims and legitimates them vis-à-vis offenders. Victim questioning will be most meaningful in this regard when the victim had personal contact with offenders during the crime. The few victims who survived the Srebrenica executions,[973] for instance, would have little to say to members of the firing squad charged with their extermination because they had no meaningful contact with their would-be executioners. The Bosnians beaten and tortured in prison camps and the East Timorese mutilated by militia members, by contrast, may well appreciate an opportunity to confront and question those who brutalized them. Such interactions are apt to be all the more powerful when victims and offenders knew one another before the conflict, as did many Bosnian prisoners and prison guards and East Timorese victims and offenders,[974] or when their relationship was characterized by a substantial power imbalance that was overcome following the atrocities, as was the case in South Africa. Indeed, by confronting their former torturers in the South African TRC, black apartheid victims turned the tables on their tormentors and—by extension—on oppressive white society as a whole. Mass atrocities are typically carried out at least nominally on ideological grounds, and giving victims the floor, as it were, constitutes a powerful way of vindicating their inherent humanity and contradicting the dehumanizing message underpinning the atrocity.

Reparations

Symbolic reparations made by offenders, particularly apologies, are powerful tools for reconciliation. Further, unlike many of the restorative features discussed above, the inclusion of mechanisms to promote apologies is also logistically straightforward and inexpensive. Because apologies are so valuable and their inclusion will not appreciably diminish the number of offenders who can be prosecuted, apologies should be encouraged in the context of virtually all mass atrocities. That said, apologies are apt to be most valuable in communities where widespread denial about the crimes continues to exist, and they are apt to be most meaningful when offender and perpetrator knew one another before the conflict. The perception and value of apologies will, in addition, vary to some degree among different cultures, and those administering a guilty-plea system must be attuned to these cultural variations so that apologies can be elicited and conveyed in a way that will maximize their reconciliatory potential. That an apology is a key feature of East Timorese local justice processes, for instance, means that its value in that context is particularly high.

Requiring offenders to pay material reparations enhances the prospects for reconciliation by benefiting victims while at the same time making offenders aware, in an especially concrete way, of the harm that they have caused. Virtually all instances of mass atrocity place grave financial burdens on victims, but even among victims of severe violence, some distinctions can be drawn. Crimes such as the Srebrenica massacres, which targeted male heads-of-households, had a devastating financial effect on survivors. To this day, many Srebrenica widows live in cramped "collective centers" and rely on the inadequate pensions of their late husbands to survive.[975] By contrast, Argentine forced disappearances were disproportionately perpetrated against young people, many of whom were not family wage-earners; their deaths did not impose on their families the same degree of financial loss. Crimes involving the destruction and theft of property—such as the looting and burning down of houses that were part and parcel of the Bosnian Serbs' ethnic-cleansing campaign and the devastation in East Timor—seem especially amenable to financial reparations because the material value of the harm can be more objectively ascertained. A society's tradition of imposing reparations obligations on offenders is also relevant in determining their appropriateness in a given context. Because a compensation obligation is the primary component of the East Timorese response to crime, the failure to include a reparatory element would likely undermine the perceived legitimacy of any prosecution.

Despite the beneficial potential of reparations obligations, they will not prove feasible to impose in most instances because the victim-offender ratio in most international crimes is too high. Some Rwandan offenders killed several thousand people,[976] and even those Bosnian offenders directly responsible for a mere dozen deaths cannot be expected to make financial payments to victims unless the offenders happen to possess extraordinary wealth. Service obligations can, however, be imposed in cases featuring either a large number of victims per offender or an impoverished offender. The required service obligations ideally would be rendered directly to victims, if the number of victims permits it and if victims desire it, and the obligations would preferably bear some relationship to the crime or the harm caused by the crime.

The Contours of Optimal Restorative-Justice Guilty-Plea Systems in the Argentine, Bosnian, Rwandan, and East Timorese Contexts

In exploring the various aims that would be advanced by a restorative-justice guilty-plea system, the foregoing section identified the different ways in which those aims function and might be valued in the aftermath of different atrocities. Advancing truth-telling may be a worthy goal in virtually all instances, but the kind of truth that will be revealed will vary with the circumstances of the crime, as will the capacity of that truth to promote individual and societal reconciliation. The foregoing section, then, sought to use the concrete examples of atrocities in Argentina, Bosnia, Rwanda, and East Timor to explore the kind of assessments that must take place when striking the appropriate balance between restorative and retributive goals. This section relies on the insights of the previous section to present general descriptions of guilty-plea systems appropriate for the atrocities under discussion. Efforts have already been made to obtain guilty pleas for Bosnian, Rwandan, and East Timorese crimes, as discussed in Chapters 4, 5, and 6, and the following discussion will refer to these guilty-plea practices where relevant.

To present a useful comparison, this section must largely ignore the sort of political constraints that can significantly impair efforts to undertake criminal prosecutions. Imposing criminal accountability will not be politically viable either internationally or domestically in the context of many atrocities, but that fact must be set aside if any sort of theoretical framework is to be developed. At the same time, the political constraints that might in the real world prevent the undertaking of prosecutions cannot be ignored entirely, because those same considerations will influence the contours of a guilty-plea system appropriate for that particular society. A guilty-plea system developed to process Argentine disappearances, for instance, will be largely shaped by the secrecy that surrounds those crimes. That secrecy persisted because the Argentine military continued to wield considerable power long after the country transitioned to democracy. Thus, although this section will not specifically consider whether, in a particular political climate, prosecutions would occur in the first place, it will take note of less decisive political constraints that would influence the development of an optimal guilty-plea procedure. Because restorative-justice guilty-plea systems are amenable to implementation by both an international tribunal and a domestic criminal justice system, this section also will not consider the level of resources possessed by the body undertaking the prosecutions in determining the appropriate balance to be struck among various values. Clearly, Argentina has a greater financial ability to undertake domestic prosecutions than does East Timor, but both Argentine and East Timorese crimes might be prosecuted by international bodies whose budgets might themselves differ considerably. Finally, to simplify the analysis, this section will also assume, perhaps contrary to fact in some cases, the general desirability of retributive punishment and the particular desirability of prosecuting as many offenders as possible. Restorative elements, therefore, will be assessed in a given context in light of the fact that their inclusion will result, negatively, in fewer overall prosecutions. Finally, the descriptions that follow are, of necessity, summary; they sketch optimal guilty-plea systems for the four atrocities in broad outline but do not delve into many of the more nuanced details.

Argentina

Argentine crimes present a particularly compelling case for the inclusion of substantial restorative-justice elements in a guilty-plea scheme. For one thing, the fact that Argentine crimes were committed by a relatively small number of offenders—about one thousand—makes it more likely that retributive aims can be fulfilled despite the inclusion of restorative-justice features. Further, the secrecy surrounding the fate of the victims and the refusal of most offenders to acknowledge the wrongfulness of their actions render particularly valuable measures aimed at encouraging apologies and at advancing the three different kinds of truth-telling described earlier—divulging facts, acknowledging the wrong, and inculpating superiors. As for victim participation, many of the victims who were released alive would benefit from the opportunity to confront and question those responsible for their mistreatment. The majority of Argentine victims were killed, however, and, while this fact would ordinarily diminish the importance of victim participation since the victims themselves can do no questioning, the secrecy surrounding the crimes and the considerable time that elapsed between the abductions and the victims' eventual deaths increase the likelihood that family members would seek information from offenders that might not emerge during ordinary criminal proceedings.

An optimal guilty-plea system addressing Argentine crimes, then, would devote considerable time and resources to obtaining from defendants all relevant information about their crimes and about the military structures in which those crimes took place. Because many Argentine offenders continue to maintain that most victims were leftist subversives who posed a substantial threat to the nation, the guilty-plea system would seek in particular to learn why various victims had been targeted as a means of vindicating the vast bulk who had no direct ties to leftist guerrillas. Publicizing the information received from offenders would pierce the secrecy surrounding the crimes and pave the way for other offenders to acknowledge their wrongful conduct. The need for that acknowledgment is so strong in the Argentine context that devoting considerable efforts to encouraging defendants to apologize would also be beneficial. Given the intransigence of many offenders, such apologies, if perceived to be sincere, would send a potent reconciliatory message.

Although the prosecution of Argentine crimes would initially benefit greatly from the inclusion of a substantial number of restorative features, the value of these features would diminish over time. As the truth becomes known and as offenders begin to acknowledge the wrongfulness of their actions, the societal value of these confessions and apologies would diminish because they would be perceived as cumulative.[977] This diminishing-returns effect would occur in the context of all mass atrocities, but it is apt to be especially marked in the Argentine context because the crimes were conducted in a relatively uniform way and because, even if offenders make full disclosure, much will remain unknowable. That is, although not all Argentine murder victims were dropped from airplanes, a substantial proportion were, so the value of learning specific details about the dropping of a particular victim into the sea will diminish over time. In addition, although learning from a particular offender the fate of a loved one will provide some measure of closure to friends and families, it will not provide what many friends and families seek most: a body to bury. Because so many Argentine crimes featured the destruction or permanent concealment of the victim's body, the truth that can emerge from a restorative-justice process concerned with Argentine crimes is by necessity limited, and its value may thus diminish sharply over time.

Bosnia

Ideally, the restorative-justice elements included in a guilty-plea system prosecuting Bosnian crimes would vary depending on the nature of the atrocity at issue. The prosecution of crimes occurring during the siege of Sarajevo would, for instance, present the least need for restorative-justice features. The need to obtain information about the crimes is minimal in this context: it is, for instance, a well-known fact that Serb soldiers, stationed in high-rise buildings, were firing on civilians. The acknowledgment that would result from a rigorous truth-telling endeavor would also be of limited value because only limited acknowledgment is possible in this context, as a few examples from other atrocities show. For instance, as a result of the widespread denial surrounding the Srebrenica massacres, acknowledgment in that context would constitute official acceptance that Bosnian Serb forces executed many thousands of defenseless Bosnian Muslim men and boys. The acknowledgment that might emerge from restorative-justice processes concerned with Argentine disappearances would be more limited because the commission of those disappearances has already been officially accepted, but it would nonetheless convey the important fact that most victims were innocent of any wrongdoing. Acknowledgment in the context of the Sarajevo crimes would be yet more limited still. It has never been questioned that the Sarajevan civilians shot at or shelled were victims of Serb forces. Nor has it been in doubt that these victims were innocent civilians. Serb offenders have maintained only that civilian injuries were the incidental effects of a legitimate military campaign.[978] So, the only acknowledgment possible in the Sarajevan context is the acknowledgment that civilians were purposefully targeted to spread terror among the population—an acknowledgment of relatively limited significance.

With respect to information implicating superiors, although every prosecution has some need for such information, the fact that the siege crimes were perpetrated by soldiers engaged in a clear military offensive means that prosecutors can more easily tie the crimes of subordinates to their superiors through well-defined military hierarchies. Since victims were not individually "selected" and did not have any meaningful contact with their offenders before, during, or after the crimes, the prosecution of these crimes probably would not give rise to a considerable number of questions or a substantial desire for victim participation. Finally, although apologies have reconciliatory potential in virtually every context, that potential in the Sarajevo context is more limited than in most because victims and offenders had no previous relationship and in most cases did not even live in the same community before the conflict. Material reparations also are of value in virtually every instance, but nothing about the victims of the Sarajevo siege suggests that they have a more pressing need for reparations than any other victims of violence.

Restorative-justice features would provide greater benefits in the prosecutions of Srebrenica offenders. The Bosnian Serbs' steadfast denial of the massacres created a pressing need for all three kinds of truth-telling. The need for acknowledgment is perhaps foremost, but offender confessions would also provide valuable information about the locations of victims' bodies, many of which remain unfound, and would help to inculpate high-level offenders who are not tied to the executions through any documentary evidence or established military hierarchy. Victim participation would not be of significant value in the Srebrenica context because virtually all of the victims were killed and were killed in a quick and uniform way that does not give rise to substantial uncertainty on the parts of family members. The value of apologies in Srebrenica, by contrast, is apt to be considerable because many victims and perpetrators grew up in the region and some knew one another before the conflict.[979] Momir Nikolić, who helped implement the Srebrenica massacres, for instance, was a schoolteacher before the war and taught some of the men and boys who were later executed.[980] Efforts to require offenders to provide material reparations would also be particularly beneficial because the victims were the male heads-of-household in traditional Muslim families, and their deaths have left their families financially devastated. The high victim-perpetrator ratio means that reparations, if feasible at all for offenders to provide, would feature only token sums, but even these could offer much-needed assistance.

Prosecutions of crimes that took place at Bosnian prison camps would benefit most from the inclusion of restorative-justice elements. The need for truth-telling in all of its forms is especially compelling with respect to these crimes. Basic details of the crimes have not yet come to light. Many prisoners who entered the camps have never been seen again, leaving loved ones in the dark about the victims' ultimate fate and the location of their remains. Even ICTY prosecutors have been unable to identify many of the victims of the crimes for which they have charged defendants. In the *Češić* case, for instance, prosecutors charged Ranko Češić with killing two unnamed individuals and misidentified one of Češić's other murder victims.

Serb denial about the true purpose of the camps and the conditions that prevailed within them is widespread, so truth-telling efforts would also serve as official and much-needed acknowledgment. In addition, the uncertain organizational structure of the camps' leadership and the ready access given to unaffiliated outside groups bent on mistreating prisoners render offender testimony of particular value to prosecutors wishing to convict coperpetrators or superiors. Allowing victim participation would also enhance reconciliation efforts, particularly because many victims and offenders lived in the same community and knew one another before the conflict. These previous relationships enhance victims' desire for involvement, and the fact that those who were killed or died in the camps did so after lengthy periods of confinement is likely to engender numerous questions from family members. The benefits of both symbolic and material reparations in this context are also apt to be considerable. The previous relationship existing between many victims and perpetrators enhances the significance of sincere apologies, just as they also enhanced the emotional pain caused by the crimes. That previous relationship will also render more meaningful any efforts to provide material reparations. Although most of the harms that victims suffered are not especially amenable to monetary quantification or redress through service obligations, most of the crimes were perpetrated by not-impecunious offenders against a victim population that suffered tremendous financial losses as a result of the ethnic cleansing that formed the core feature of the conflict.

An analysis of the Bosnian conflict indicates that a guilty-plea system designed to convict the maximum number of offenders while advancing reconciliation to the greatest possible degree would have the flexibility to treat different atrocities within a single conflict in the way most likely to meet the system's multifarious goals. Past experience, however, indicates that most criminal justice procedures are not so readily adaptable, and, even if they were, that adaptation might give rise to claims of inequity as some defendants would be required to fulfill truth-telling and other obligations not required of other defendants. If we assume instead a uniform guilty-plea system for Bosnian crimes that features the same procedures in every case, then the foregoing analysis indicates that the system should emphasize restorative elements to a substantial degree, but not the degree justified in the Argentine context. For one thing, the considerably greater number of offenders in the Bosnian conflict—approximately ten thousand—raises more pressing concerns that the use of restorative features will substantially undercut the system's ability to prosecute a reasonable proportion of offenders. In addition, as has been described, the need for restorative-justice features is simply not as great when it comes to some Bosnian crimes. At the same time, as Chapter 10 will reveal, the inclusion of very few restorative-justice elements in ICTY efforts to obtain guilty pleas presents problems of its own. In sum, an optimal guilty-plea system for use across the spectrum of Bosnian crimes would require perpetrators to disclose all the details of their offenses, even though the details of some crimes would already have been widely publicized. Defendants also would be strongly encouraged to apologize and would be required to make material reparations whenever feasible. The optimal level of victim participation will necessarily depend on the number of people victimized by a particular offender and the nature of the crime, but efforts would be made to allow at least one victim to question each offender, if only for the sake of symbolism.

Rwanda

At first glance, the Rwandan genocide presents the least compelling case of the four atrocities under study for the inclusion of substantial restorative-justice features. For one thing, the sheer number of offenders would seem to argue in favor of establishing an efficient, streamlined guilty-plea system that emphasizes criminal accountability over other values. Indeed, because so many Rwandans participated in the genocide—more than one hundred thousand and as many as one million by some estimates—a large proportion of offenders will go unpunished no matter what prosecutorial mechanisms are used.[981] Restorative-justice measures, then, must prove particularly valuable if they are to justify the "costs" they impose in terms of forsaken prosecutions. This substantial value is also not apparent at first glance. The truth-telling function of restorative justice, for instance, offers some benefits in the Rwandan context but fewer than is the norm for mass atrocities because much is already known about the Rwandan genocide. The extermination of the Tutsi was publicly encouraged by the government and a topic of broad popular interest long before the killings actually began. When the massacres did commence, they occurred in full public view. Granted, many survivors were in hiding when their family members were hacked to death, so they might benefit from hearing offender confessions that contain details about the crimes. But unlike many of the crimes committed in Argentina and Bosnia, there exists at least the possibility in Rwanda that other members of the community who were not in hiding could provide relevant details.

The acknowledgment that results from offender confessions also is not a particularly valuable commodity in the Rwandan context, since the new Rwandan government completely vanquished its genocidal predecessor and immediately and officially acknowledged the crimes when it took power. Some information provided by defendants would assist in prosecuting high-level offenders since orders were issued orally and prosecutors have had some difficulty tracing chains of command. But even those benefits hold less value in Rwanda than in the context of other mass atrocities because the Rwandan crimes were of a uniquely public nature and were committed through a relatively clear organizational structure that has at least to some degree assisted prosecutors in connecting the high-level architects of the genocide to the crimes on the ground.

On the surface, then, the foregoing factors appear to argue for a relatively streamlined guilty-plea system that aims to process offenders as quickly and efficiently as possible. A closer look at these factors and at other restorative-justice values reveals, however, that restorative justice in fact has a vital role to play in helping Rwanda move beyond its genocide. In particular, although the large number of Rwandan offenders does mean that a substantial proportion will not be prosecuted and particularly not if restorative-justice procedures are used, it means more fundamentally that a stunning percentage of Hutu were involved in the genocide in one or another capacity, and that fact must inform the nature of the prosecutorial enterprise at its most fundamental level. As journalist Philip Gourevitch put it: "the work of the killers was not regarded as a crime in Rwanda; it was effectively the law of the land."[982] Although it is not true that when everyone is guilty, no one can be held responsible, it is true that when a substantial portion of the population is guilty, notions of responsibility stretch and distort; in such a context, imposing retributive punishment may be of less long-term value than are efforts aimed at reconciling individuals, enhancing understanding, and rebuilding communities.

The restorative role of victim-offender dialogue is apt to be especially significant in the Rwandan context because offenders and survivors are forced to interact with one another on a daily basis. Hutu and Tutsi speak the same language, worship in the same churches, and share the same social customs. Most importantly, unlike Bosnians, who now live in ethnically "pure" pockets segregated from their wartime enemies, Hutu and Tutsi live among one another in small, rural communities.[983] Further, many murdered Tutsi were killed by people from their own communities, and, because most survivors are too impoverished to move, they must regularly interact with their loved ones' murderers. In such a setting, restorative-justice processes offer tremendous potential for advancing individual and societal healing and reconciliation. Although everyone in Rwanda knows in broad outline what happened in the spring of 1994, many do not know why it happened or, more importantly, the effects these events continue to have on those in their community. An optimal restorative-justice process in Rwanda would aim to bring communities together to discuss the crimes and their consequences for all concerned. One cannot expect such discussions to eliminate the intense animosity that was inculcated in Hutu and Tutsi in the years before the genocide, but it would, at the least, provide opportunities for civil dialogue. These opportunities may prove particularly valuable in the Rwandan context because Rwandans are reported to be reluctant to discuss emotional issues.

Victim-offender dialogue may also prove of key import in determining a Rwandan offender's true culpability. As noted above, many Hutu who killed did not do so willingly, and even Hutu who were enthusiastic participants in the genocide were themselves the victims of a relentless media campaign against the Tutsi that was particularly potent because it was broadcast to a largely uneducated peasant population that did not have the benefit of unbiased media sources to counteract the hate. On the one hand, this is nothing new: large-scale violence is virtually always governmentally organized and spurred on by government-backed hate propaganda. Argentine naval officer Adolfo Scilingo, who eventually broke rank with his military colleagues and confessed to having thrown live prisoners out of airplanes, for instance, seemed genuinely to believe that his actions were lawful and justified because they were authorized by the Argentine Navy.[984] War criminals throughout history have unconvincingly alleged that they were forced to do their dirty deeds. Yet, the evidence indicates that a claim of compulsion has considerable credibility in a significant number of Rwandan cases, and this claim may be better explored through restorative rather than retributive processes. In between the two extremes of those who killed gleefully and those who killed under threat of death are a substantial proportion of offenders whose culpability is less well-defined. The potential for restorative-justice processes to

elucidate these matters should not be overstated given the ease of claiming coercion, but some victim-offender dialogue will allow for some nuanced explorations of these issues, explorations that may prove impossible within the confines
of an ordinary criminal proceeding.

The provision of reparations, both symbolic and material, also has considerable potential to enhance reconciliation in Rwanda. Apologies will be of key
importance given the day-to-day proximity of victims and offenders and their
relationships before and after the genocide. Few offenders would have the means
to provide material reparations, but Rwanda does have a tradition of imposing
community-service requirements, and these existing structures could be used to
impose reparatory obligations on offenders. These structures must be deployed
with care, however, because the community-service requirement has been abused
on numerous occasions in Rwanda's past. As noted above, requiring Hutu to perform services directly to Tutsi might revive memories of past Tutsi oppression,
some of which involved the exploitation of the community-service requirement.

East Timor

Restorative-justice proponents frequently seek to legitimize modern restorative-justice processes by observing that traditional societies have used these
processes for centuries.[985] Although differences between traditional restorative
practices and their modern incarnations certainly exist, the fact is that, for many
centuries, the vast majority of crimes and other conflicts in East Timor have been
addressed by means of local justice practices that share many features with Western restorative-justice programs. The atrocities in East Timor, then, present the
most compelling case for the inclusion of restorative-justice elements, of the four
atrocities under study, for the simple reason that most East Timorese not only expect the inclusion of these features as part and parcel of an appropriate response
to crime but would consider a criminal justice system that failed to include them
illegitimate and potentially threatening. In the East Timorese worldview, merely
incarcerating offenders fails to appropriately reconcile victims, offenders, and
their relevant communities, and that failure could leave the communities vulnerable to harm. The inclusion of substantial restorative features would—in East
Timor as everywhere else—reduce the number of prosecutions that can occur,
but that reduction would have fewer deleterious consequences in East Timor than
elsewhere because local justice processes already exist in East Timor to address
the crimes that go unprosecuted by the formal justice system. Indeed, as I will

discuss in greater detail in Chapter 10, East Timor's internationally sponsored Commission for Reception, Truth, and Reconciliation used local justice mechanisms to impose some accountability on offenders of less-serious East Timorese crimes.

The inclusion of restorative-justice elements would be of substantial value in the East Timorese context even in the absence of widespread community expectation of their inclusion. Turning first to truth-telling, considerable information about the crimes came to light soon after their commission. Many attacks were committed in broad view by perpetrators who were known to victims and witnesses.[986] Further, the violence that occurred after the referendum, though devastating, was relatively short-lived, and the rapid arrival of the U.N. peacekeeping forces prevented the concealment of many crimes. At the same time, the bodies of some of the victims of large-scale massacres have yet to be discovered because they were transported to undisclosed locations or dumped in rivers.[987] The absence of the victims' remains, which is devastating enough for Western families, arguably carries even greater significance for the East Timorese, since they conduct elaborate funeral rites that require the presence of a corpse.[988]

The acknowledgment that results from truth-telling would not be of vital importance in East Timor because the immediate arrival of the peacekeeping force enabled the crimes in their general form to be investigated, acknowledged, and publicized. The ability to obtain details about high-level perpetrators and chains of command, however, would substantially benefit East Timorese prosecutions. Although the considerable involvement of the Indonesian military in the atrocities has been well-established in general outline, Indonesia's refusal to transfer suspects or evidence means that only limited information has come to light about the specifics of that involvement. Indeed, some question exists as to whether the East Timorese militia instigated the violence and were supported only by rogue elements in the Indonesian military or whether the Indonesian military itself was the primary force behind the atrocities. Most commentators consider the latter view more plausible,[989] a position supported by the Serious Crimes Unit's February 2003 indictment of eight high-ranking Indonesian officials including General Wiranto, defense minister and commander of the Indonesian Armed Forces.[990] The Special Panels for East Timor were unable to prosecute these suspects as a result of Indonesia's refusal to surrender them, but if such prosecutions ever were to be undertaken, their success would be based in large part on the testimony of lower-level defendants.

Victim participation would also be of considerable value in the East Timorese context for reasons in addition to the community's expectation of victim and community involvement. The victim-perpetrator ratio in East Timor is relatively low (for mass atrocities), so victim-perpetrator questioning is logistically feasible. The fact that many victims and offenders knew one another before the crimes— indeed, some were even related[991]—would enhance the value of victim-offender interactions. These interactions would also assist in efforts to explore the nature of the offenders' culpability, an important question since virtually all low-level offenders have claimed to have acted under compulsion. Finally, most of the violence in East Timor was committed through the use of primitive weapons such as machetes and spears. Victims and family members are apt to be more desirous of questioning offenders who perpetrated their violence in direct and proximate ways than of offenders who wrought harms through more remote means.

The value of including reparations in prosecutions of East Timorese atrocities derives primarily from the central role that reparations play in the East Timorese conception of justice. To the East Timorese, there is no justice without compensation, nor is there reconciliation—a crucial component of East Timorese justice— without public acknowledgment of fault.[992] For these reasons, criminal prosecutions of international crimes in East Timor are apt to possess little legitimacy unless their punishment includes the imposition of reparatory obligations for offenders. Imposing such obligations on East Timorese offenders is fortunately fairly straightforward because an exchange of goods features in virtually every aspect of East Timorese relations.

Summary

The relative value of various restorative-justice elements can vary considerably depending on a host of contextual features relating to the nature of the atrocity, the nature of the society in which the atrocity took place, and the nature of post-atrocity events. Because the inclusion of restorative-justice measures reduces a criminal justice system's financial ability to prosecute offenders, issues such as those explored must be carefully weighed when crafting an optimal restorative-justice guilty-plea system in any given situation.

The Minimal Role of Restorative Justice in Current International Criminal Prosecutions

Chapter 9 examined the ways that restorative and retributive elements might optimally coalesce in model guilty-plea systems addressing crimes in Argentina, Bosnia, Rwanda, and East Timor. Actual guilty-plea processes are being used in the prosecutions of crimes that occurred in the latter three locations, and this chapter will evaluate those processes in light of the restorative-justice models just constructed. First, I will consider the extent to which, if any, the guilty-plea processes of the ICTY, the ICTR, and the Special Panels include the three primary restorative-justice features—victim participation, truth-telling, and reparatory measures. I will conclude that restorative-justice elements play only a minimal role in the guilty-plea processes of these institutions. Next, I will explore two innovative local justice mechanisms, in Rwanda and East Timor, that impose accountability on offenders through processes that seek to blend restorative and retributive features.

Restorative Elements in ICTY Guilty-Plea Processes

As Chapter 4 described, the ICTY's practice of plea bargaining has undergone a marked evolution from a rarely used, somewhat suspect procedural device to a well-accepted case disposition mechanism. Concomitant with that evolution in practice has come an evolution in the rationales used to justify the ICTY's practice of plea bargaining. In the early days of ICTY plea bargaining, the parties and the Trial Chambers justified the bestowal of sentencing concessions primarily on the ground that guilty pleas saved the tribunal time and resources. In *Er-demović*, for instance, Judges Gabrielle Kirk McDonald and Lal Chand Vohrah asserted that guilty pleas benefit the public by "minimising costs, in the saving of court time and in avoiding the inconvenience to many, particularly to witnesses." Judges McDonald and Vohrah observed that these benefits are particularly valuable in the context of international criminal cases because these cases, "by their inherent nature, are very complex and necessarily require lengthy hearings if they go to trial under stringent financial constraints arising from allocations made by the United Nations itself dependent upon the contributions of States."[993] The Trial Chambers also noted the truth-telling value of guilty pleas[994] and the fact that guilty pleas eliminate the need for victims to travel to The Hague to testify,[995] and in one case, a Trial Chamber asserted that guilty pleas demonstrate a defendant's honesty.[996] But the primary emphasis was on the financial savings brought about by pleas. These rationales served tolerably well. Because the ICTY's early guilty pleas were infrequent and did not result in substantial sentencing discounts, they did not give rise to considerable opposition, and neither the prosecution nor the Trial Chambers had need to formulate more elaborate justifications in defense of them.

The spate of defendants pleading guilty in 2003 and the more generous sentencing concessions bestowed on these defendants, by contrast, have generated enormous opposition, even among some members of the ICTY bench. Presumably as a result of this opposition, ICTY prosecutors and Trial Chambers discovered the language of restorative justice; that is, although not termed as such, the ICTY began invoking restorative-justice principles in defense of its plea bargaining, particularly in cases featuring especially lenient sentencing recommendations. Gone—ostensibly—is the belief that guilty pleas should be rewarded primarily for the financial savings they bring about. The *Momir Nikolić* Trial Chamber, for instance, acknowledged that "the savings of time and resources due to a guilty plea has [sic] often been considered as a valuable and justifiable reason for the promotion of guilty pleas." However, the Trial Chamber concluded that it could not "fully endorse this argument" because "in cases of this magnitude, where the Tribunal has been entrusted by the United Nations Security Council—and by extension, the international community as a whole—to bring justice to the former Yugoslavia through criminal proceedings that are fair, in accordance with international human rights standards, and accord due regard to the rights of the accused and the interests of victims, the saving of resources cannot be given undue consideration or importance."[997] Similarly, the *Deronjić* Trial Chamber surveyed the purposes and justifications for plea bargaining in domestic jurisdictions and contrasted them with the very different goals of the international tribunals: "[I]n contrast to national legal systems where the reasons for mitigating a punishment on the basis of a guilty plea are of a more pragmatic nature, the rationale behind the mitigating effect of a guilty plea in this Tribunal is much broader, including the fact that the accused contributes to establishing the truth about the conflict in the former Yugoslavia and contributes to reconciliation in the affected communities."[998]

Thus, instead of emphasizing the more "pragmatic" rationales, such as resource savings, that are now relegated to the realm of domestic criminal justice systems, the ICTY has lately justified the practice of plea bargaining primarily on the ground that obtaining guilty pleas advances truth and enhances reconciliation and peace-building efforts in the Balkans, goals that are not mere ideals but that form the crux of the tribunal's mandate.[999] *Plavšić* was the first case in which this rationale appeared, and there the prosecution, eager to justify its lenient sentencing recommendation, lauded Plavšić's guilty plea, as "an unprecedented contribution to the establishment of truth and a significant effort toward the advancement of reconciliation."[1000] The prosecution moreover took the theretofore unheard-of step of presenting joint witnesses with the defense to testify about the contribution Plavšić's guilty plea made to peace-building efforts in Bosnia.[1001] The prosecution took the same approach in the *Obrenović* and *Momir Nikolić* cases. In *Obrenović*, the prosecution asserted that Obrenović's guilty plea "represents a significant contribution to the establishment of truth and a significant effort toward the advancement of reconciliation,"[1002] and the prosecution's closing arguments in both *Obrenović* and *Momir Nikolić* centered almost exclusively on the truth-telling and reconciliatory value of the defendants' guilty pleas.[1003] Similarly, in *Babić*, commentators noted that "the prosecution and defense are practically on the same side."[1004] At Babić's sentencing hearing, "lawyers for the prosecution and the defence repeatedly echoed each other's arguments,"[1005] and both sides were so eager to praise Babić's guilty plea that it was frequently difficult to distinguish the prosecution's position from that of the defense. In his closing arguments, Babić's defense attorney even quoted from the prosecution's opening statement, observing that the prosecution had addressed the point "in a more thorough and eloquent fashion than I would have been able."[1006]

The ICTY's recent implicit embrace of restorative-justice principles is welcome. Indeed, it is the thesis of this book that guilty pleas often possess greater potential to restore and reconcile than full-scale trials. For that potential to be realized, however, the ICTY must do more than just talk about the reconciliatory value of guilty pleas; it must, in addition, incorporate into the processes by which defendants plead guilty features such as those drawn from restorative justice that are designed to enhance reconciliation. Restorative-justice elements have begun to appear in ICTY guilty-plea processes, but they have not been incorporated to the degree necessary to provide the benefits currently attributed to them, particularly given the bitterness spawned by the ICTY's lenient sentencing practice. An examination of the ICTY's practice of plea bargaining in light of three key restorative-justice values now follows.

Victim Involvement

Victims play little or no role in the ICTY's plea-bargaining processes nor could they. Victim involvement would impair the confidentiality of the plea negotiations and thereby deter defendants from engaging in them. Because ICTY trials are held before a relatively small number of professional judges, defendants cannot take the chance that the judges will become aware of plea negotiations because those very same judges will try the defendants if the negotiations fail to result in an agreement.

ICTY victims could be involved in the sentencing of guilty-plea defendants, yet no victim testified at nine of the last eleven sentencing hearings for ICTY defendants who pled guilty.[1007] When victims do testify before the ICTY, they typically present their information to the Trial Chamber and do not interact with the defendant. The sentencing hearing for Dragan Nikolić, the former commander of the Sušica prison camp, proved an exception to that rule, however, and demonstrated the potential value of victim-offender interactions. In Dragan Nikolić's sentencing hearing, prosecutors called to testify Habiba Hadzić, a sixty-year-old woman who had been detained at the camp. Hadzić's sons had also been imprisoned at Sušica, and the last time she saw them was when she was transferred out of Sušica. Midway through her testimony, Hadzić made clear that she longed to know what had happened to her sons.[1008] At the conclusion of her testimony, when asked whether she would like to say anything to the judges about her experiences at Sušica, Hadzić briefly responded to that question but then, without invitation, proceeded to ask Nikolić himself a question: "I would just like to ask

Dragan to tell me where [my sons] are, in which mass grave, so that their mother could give them a dignified funeral. I want to give them a proper burial, and then I can go away myself."[1009] After consulting with his lawyer, Nikolić told Hadzić that her sons had been taken in a group of about forty people to Debelo Brdo and there were "liquidated." Nikolić went on to inform her that her sons' identifications had been removed but that he remembered that one of them was wearing a denim jacket and trousers and his body might therefore be identified by his clothing.[1010] Learning where, how, and when her sons were killed and the likely location of their remains was of profound significance to Hadzić. She obtained this information only because the prosecution saw fit to include her in the sentencing hearing and, even then, only because she herself stepped out of the traditionally defined witness's role and confronted the defendant.

Truth-telling

As previous chapters have discussed, various forms of truth can emerge from guilty pleas. Defendants who plead guilty can provide facts about the crimes that are of particular interest to victims, they can provide information inculpating other defendants, and they can speak the truth in their acknowledgment of their culpability. Recent ICTY guilty pleas have advanced each of these kinds of truth to some degree, but ICTY prosecutors have put the bulk of their efforts into obtaining information inculpating other defendants. Although in early cases, prosecutors were willing to enter into plea agreements without any promise of insider testimony,[1011] in nine of the last eleven plea agreements, prosecutors have required defendants to provide information regarding the crimes of other perpetrators.[1012] In many cases, plea-bargaining defendants have been required to meet with prosecutors "as often as necessary"[1013] and to testify against other ICTY defendants now or in the future, if asked to do so by the prosecution.[1014] To ensure that defendants are sufficiently candid and forthcoming, the prosecution has, in some cases, requested that their sentencing be postponed until after they had testified in other cases.[1015] Only after the prosecution had evaluated the testimony was it willing to make its sentencing recommendations to the Trial Chamber.[1016] That the Trial Chambers also place considerable value on a defendant's willingness to provide insider testimony is evidenced by the fact that the *Momir Nikolić* chamber sentenced Nikolić to a prison term seven years longer than the longest sentence in the prosecution's recommended range largely because it determined that his testimony in the *Blagojević* case was evasive and not entirely forthright.[1017]

The prosecution's efforts to obtain inculpatory information through the use of plea agreements has borne considerable fruit. Most recent defendants pleading guilty have provided the prosecution with information, and six such defendants have provided substantial testimony in one or more ICTY trials. In 2003, Dragan Obrenović and Momir Nikolić each testified for seven days in the *Blagojević* case,[1019] and both men affirmed their testimony in the *Krstić* appeal hearing.[1020] Miodrag Jokić testified for five days in the *Strugar* trial,[1021] and Milan Babić testified for a grueling eleven days in the *Milošević* case.[1022] Miroslav Deronjić, labeled by his attorney as a "crown witness" for the prosecution,[1023] testified in a record four cases,[1024] spending literally weeks on the ICTY stand. Most recently, Ivica Rajić, who pled guilty in October 2005, is scheduled to testify at the joint trial of Jadranko Prlić, Bruno Stojić, Slobodan Praljak, Milivoj Petković, Valentin Ćorić, and Berislav Pušić,[1018] some of whom were his superiors in the Bosnian Croat army.

The revelations made during the testimony of these defendants have been invaluable to prosecutors. At the time he appeared in the *Milošević* case, Milan Babić was perhaps the highest-level insider to testify, and he provided a crucial link between Milošević and the Croatian Serbs' effort to ethnically cleanse Croats from the Serbian Autonomous Region of the Krajina in Croatia. Journalists labeled Babić's testimony "the Prosecution's smoking gun,"[1025] and prosecutors themselves considered Babić's testimony so valuable that they agreed to give up fourteen planned witnesses—approximately 20 percent of the total number of witnesses for the Croatian phase of the case—in exchange for two additional days of direct examination of Babić.[1026] Lead prosecutor Geoffrey Nice said this case could "almost be proved with [this] one witness."[1027] The testimony of Miroslav Deronjić has likewise been tremendously important to the prosecution. In the *Milošević* case, Deronjić provided crucial information about Serbia's arming of the Bosnian Serbs, and he linked Milošević to that effort.[1028] In *Krajišnik*, Deronjić provided a painstaking and detailed account of how the policies promulgated by high-level Bosnian Serb politicians were implemented at the local level and led eventually to the expulsion and murder of thousands of Muslim civilians.[1029]

Rajić's testimony promises to be equally valuable since Rajić possesses insider information about Croatia's involvement in the Bosnian war and about the crimes of his superiors in the Bosnian Croat army,[1030] matters that Rajić has already alluded to in the factual basis of his guilty plea.[1031] Rajić's case indeed highlights the need for such insider information because it shows the lengths that some governments are willing to go to cover up international crimes. After Rajić's forces destroyed Stupni Do, Rajić's superiors issued a written order instructing Rajić to investigate the crimes. Rajić was told orally, however, not to conduct the investigation because the order was issued only to appease the international community. Rajić and his superiors thereafter participated in a cover-up of the crimes. He was told to change his name, and while the international community was led to believe that he had been discharged from the Bosnian Croat army, he was instead promoted to the rank of active colonel under his assumed name.[1032]

Although insider testimony at the ICTY has unquestionably facilitated the prosecution of high-level defendants and revealed information of interest to the communities in question, a desire for the sentencing concessions that are provided in exchange for such testimony can motivate defendants to lie. Momir Nikolić, for instance, initially told prosecutors that he had ordered and supervised executions at Sandici and the Kravica warehouse—two of the largest execution sites of the Srebrenica massacres—when, in fact, he was not even present when the executions took place.[1033] Nikolić admitted lying soon after he had done so and said that he had fabricated the story because he had so wanted the plea agreement to succeed.[1034] In a similar vein, Miroslav Deronjić also admitted to lying to prosecutors in initial interviews, maintaining that he did so in part because he feared for his safety and that of his family.[1035] In addition, Deronjić later admitted to gleaning some factual details that he had provided to prosecutors from other ICTY detainees.[1036] The problem is not unique to the ICTY. Under the U.S. Sentencing Guidelines, defendants charged with federal crimes could obtain the most sizable sentence reductions by providing "substantial assistance in the investigation or prosecution of another person who has committed an offense."[1037] Federal defendants were often so desirous of obtaining the sentencing concessions bestowed on those who cooperate that they would compete with one another to be first to the prosecutor's door or to provide the most "useful" information.[1038] These incentives also frequently motivated defendants to embellish the truth, to resolve questionable issues in favor of the prosecution, or to lie outright, a 1999 study found.[1039]

In early ICTY guilty-plea cases, the Trial Chambers expressed concern about these sorts of conflicts of interest. The *Todorović* plea agreement contains a provision allowing prosecutors to reinstate the entire indictment against Todorović if he failed to fulfill his obligations under the plea agreement. This provision troubled Judge David Hunt, who repeatedly expressed his concern that Todorović's testimony in subsequent cases would lack credibility because Todorović stood to have his plea agreement dissolved if he did not "fulfil his obligations."[1040] Such concerns now seem almost quaint. The *Momir Nikolić* Trial Chamber did object to a provision in Nikolić's plea agreement that permitted the prosecution to withdraw the genocide charges only upon the sentencing of Nikolić,[1041] but both that Trial Chamber and others have been willing to postpone the sentencing of guilty-plea defendants until after the defendants have testified in other cases precisely so as to determine the defendant's level of cooperation. They do so apparently without excessive worry that sequencing the events in that way will encourage defendants to embellish their testimony to gain favor from the prosecution and the Trial Chamber. Indeed, when Momčilo Krajišnik's defense counsel highlighted the problem by filing a motion seeking to postpone Deronjić's testimony in *Krajišnik* until after Deronjić had been sentenced, the Trial Chamber rejected the motion. The chamber noted, among other things, that a professional bench would be less likely to be misled by a witness and that, even after sentencing, defendants might be tempted to misrepresent facts.[1042] The Trial Chamber's last point is quite true: defendants might be motivated to embellish their testimony even after sentencing because that testimony can provide the basis for a motion for early release.[1043]

Putting aside for the moment the troubling aspects of insider testimony, the prosecution's efforts to obtain such testimony has had the beneficial effect of revealing substantial information about the crimes themselves and some details of particular relevance to victims. For instance, as part of their guilty pleas, Dragan Obrenović and Momir Nikolić submitted "Statements of Facts," which are lengthy, detailed documents describing the preparation and implementation of the Srebrenica massacres and the roles the defendants played in those events. Most importantly to victims, perhaps, Nikolić revealed the locations of two hitherto unknown mass graves.[1044] Deronjić's factual basis similarly provides a detailed account of the ethnic-cleansing plan and its implementation in the Bratunac municipality in general and in the town of Glogova in particular.[1045] He also gave prosecutors a seventy-one-page document that was valuable primarily for the prosecution of other high-level offenders but that also provided some details of special concern to victims.[1046]

Because the prosecution's primary, if not exclusive, interest is in obtaining information relevant to pending or future ICTY trials, it has made little effort to obtain information from plea-bargaining defendants who do not possess such information. In particular, prosecutors have made virtually no attempt to obtain information of sole relevance to victims' families—information, for instance, relating to the location of particular bodies or the reasons why this or that victim was targeted.[1047] For this reason, the plea agreements of low-level defendants who have little information valuable to future ICTY cases have tended to be short, cursory documents. The factual basis of Ranko Češić's plea agreement, for instance, is barely two pages long, and its contents appear to be cut and pasted almost verbatim from Češić's indictment. Worse still, the indictment itself was incomplete and partially inaccurate. It charged Češić with killing two unnamed individuals, and these individuals remained unnamed in the factual basis for Češić's guilty plea.[1048] The indictment misidentified another murder victim—a mistake that was carried over into the factual basis.[1049] The prosecutor labeled the misidentification a "housekeeping matter[]," and the indictment and factual basis for the guilty plea were quickly amended during Češić's sentencing hearing.[1050] In a similar vein, although Predrag Banović's factual basis does contain a reasonable amount of information regarding the conditions prevailing in the Keraterm camp, at which he was a guard, Banović also personally participated in beating five people to death and severely beating twenty-seven more, and these crimes receive little attention in the factual basis, which merely incorporates information appearing in Banović's indictment.[1051]

Even some high-level offenders have concluded plea agreements without providing prosecutors virtually any details about the crimes to which they pled guilty. Biljana Plavšić, for instance, whose political position and role in the ethnic-cleansing campaign gave her insights into every aspect of its planning and implementation, concluded a plea agreement with a scant five-page factual basis that presents only the briefest sketch of the atrocities and of Plavšić's role in committing them. Victims groups have vehemently protested the dearth of facts contained in such plea agreements. Family members of the approximately two hundred men executed at Koricanske Stijene, for instance, expressed outrage at the plea agreement that ICTY prosecutors concluded with Darko Mrđa precisely because it failed to require Mrđa to reveal the locations of the victims' bodies.[1052] Similarly, when the victims group Women from Podrinje protested Deronjić's lenient ten-year sentence, it did so in part on the ground that "[t]he victims have not found . . . peace even after 12 years, because not even 1% of the victims from Bratunac have been found."[1053]

Perhaps as a result of these complaints, ICTY Judge Schomburg has recently made efforts both to publicize whatever truth the prosecution has managed to glean and to press defendants to reveal yet more information. In both the *Dragan Nikolić* and *Deronjić* cases, for instance, Judge Schomburg read, slowly and deliberately, the full text of the indictments during the defendants' guilty-plea hearing. After nearly every paragraph, Judge Schomburg asked the defendants, "is that correct?," thereby forcing them to specifically admit the details of the brutal conduct for which they had been convicted.[1054] In the *Deronjić* plea hearing, Judge Schomburg additionally read out the factual basis in open court.[1055] Deronjić testified as a witness in his own sentencing hearing, and there Judge Schomburg questioned him vigorously through forty pages of transcript, requiring Deronjić to clarify and significantly expand on statements appearing in the factual basis for his guilty plea.[1056] Additionally, the Trial Chamber was sufficiently concerned about "material discrepancies" between that factual basis and Deronjić's statements in other cases that it called a supplemental sentencing hearing to resolve the issues.[1057] In a similar vein, after Keraterm camp guard Predrag Banović pled guilty, prosecutors received a phone call from the wife of a man killed at Keraterm. She was distressed upon hearing of the guilty plea and feared that her husband's suffering and death would not be acknowledged. Consequently, during the guilty-plea hearing, the prosecutor read out the names of the victims to pay them respect and to acknowledge "that ultimately these proceedings are about people who suffered at the Keraterm camp."[1058]

The Trial Chambers' limited efforts both to publicize the information revealed through guilty pleas and to force guilty-plea defendants to publicly acknowledge their wrongdoing are welcome because some ICTY defendants who ostensibly admit their culpability when pleading guilty seem reluctant to internalize that culpability. Ivica Rajić's sentencing brief, for instance, contained assertions that blatantly contradicted the factual basis that Rajić submitted with his plea agreement. For instance, in the sentencing brief, Rajić suggested that the murder victims in Stupni Do numbered only seventeen, even after acknowledging that in "the plea agreement, we agreed to . . . 36 victims."[1059] Similarly, Rajić quibbled over the number of combatants among the victims. Although the plea agreement states that approximately six of the thirty-eight victims were combatants,[1060] Rajić subsequently maintained that the "majority" of victims were soldiers.[1061] He also admits in the plea agreement to participating in a cover-up of the crimes.[1062] Rajić later contended, however, that he participated in the cover-up only because he was ordered to do so.[1063]

Other guilty-plea defendants have also made vague references to duress when it came time to be sentenced, though they offered no evidence that they committed their crimes under compulsion. Ranko Češić's sentencing brief, for instance, notes without elaboration that Češić killed the victims under superior orders and would have been killed himself had he not followed those orders.[1064] Darko Mrđa's sentencing brief similarly states that Mrđa was only following orders when he participated in the execution of more than two hundred men, and "failure to follow those orders would have resulted in serious consequences for Mrđa."[1065] And Banović's sentencing brief states that Banović "did not find a way to resist the power of his superiors nor the force of those who wilfully barged into the camp, committed crimes, and forced him and others to commit crimes, too." As if this claim were not sufficiently inconsistent with Banović's guilty plea, the brief goes on to assert that, although Banović is "of the opinion that he did not kill anyone while beating him, he admitted that he had reason to believe that the injuries that the participants in the crime inflicted to prisoners resulted in death of a victim [*sic*], so he admitted that he was capable of committing a crime."[1066] The prosecutor was so disturbed by the inconsistency between these statements and Banović's admission of guilt that she raised with the Trial Chamber the question of whether Banović's plea was unequivocal.[1067]

The Trial Chamber itself in the *Mrđa* case highlighted the material inconsistencies between Mrđa's guilty plea and the statements he subsequently made to a court-appointed psychologist. Mrđa, for instance, admitted in his factual basis that he personally selected "men of military age with the awareness and expectation that these men would be killed." When subsequently describing the events to the psychologist, however, Mrđa at one point stated that he selected the men and only later found out that they were to be killed. At another point, Mrđa stated that "some people were chosen," without stating who did the choosing.[1068] Mrđa also admitted in the factual basis to participating in the shooting and killing of some of the victims, yet he initially told the psychologist that he was shooting without aiming at people and later said that "[d]uring the time he held the gun in his hands, approximately 10 people were hit by bullets." As the Trial Chamber summarized it: "a picture is created that Mr. Mrđa was standing there with his weapon and while he was standing there, ten people were killed? By whom? Not by Mr. Mrđa; Mr. Mrđa, who did not aim at persons?"[1069]

Despite the fact that the inconsistencies in *Mrđa* and *Banović* were raised during the sentencing hearings, which those defendants attended, the Trial Chambers did not make any effort to query the defendants as to what they thought that they had done and to what they believed themselves to be pleading guilty. Rather, in *Mrđa*, defense counsel simply urged the Trial Chamber to rely on the plea agreement in case of inconsistencies, an answer that immediately satisfied the Trial Chamber.[1070] Banović's defense counsel likewise hastily assured the chamber that he did not intend to call the plea agreement into question, and that ended the matter.[1071] In *Rajić*, the Trial Chamber did not even seek assurances from defense counsel. Instead, at the sentencing hearing, the Trial Chamber summarily dismissed the inconsistent assertions, stating:

> [I]n your submission now you have made a number of points that are in contradiction with the facts as they have been agreed to in the plea agreement. . . . [W]e, as the Trial Chamber, are bound by these facts and . . . we can't re-open a discussion on a number of items that you would now want to bring under our attention or facts that you would wish to put in a different light.[1072]

The Trial Chambers' treatment of the inconsistencies in these cases may have been appropriate since the inconsistencies may have been more a reflection of overzealous defense counsel than defendants unwilling to internalize their crimes. At the same time, a restorative-justice approach would have sought to determine the genesis of the inconsistencies and, if they originated with the defendant, to engage the defendant and encourage him to face up to his wrongdoing. Instead, the Trial Chambers made no effort to learn what the defendants actually believed about their role and culpability in the crimes but focused solely on confirming that the legal basis for the conviction—the guilty plea—was unequivocal and therefore valid. Although there was good reason to worry that the defendants had failed to come to terms with the crimes they committed, that fact was not relevant. As long as the Trial Chamber was satisfied that the plea agreement still governed, the matter was closed.

Apologies

Studies of domestic restorative-justice programs indicate that apologies constitute a key element in the effort to advance reconciliation between victims and offenders. The ICTY has always encouraged defendants to apologize by considering remorse a mitigating factor in sentencing. Virtually all of the ICTY defendants pleading guilty to date have made statements of remorse at their sentencing hearings, but early statements of remorse did not sound especially remorseful. The bulk of Todorović's statement, for instance, dealt not with Todorović's remorse but with the deprivations that war had brought to his town and the difficulties that he himself had suffered as a result of the war. Todorović further sought to diminish his responsibility by claiming that he never wanted to be police chief but that "destiny or a set of unfortunate circumstances put [him] in that position, and at the worst possible time, the time of war."[1073] Finally, although Todorović pled guilty to beating one man to death, severely beating numerous others, and sexually assaulting others still, he said nothing of those acts but rather noted only that "he lacked courage to prevent the illegal and inhuman activities that were going on."[1074] The *Sikirica* defendants appeared to model their statements on Todorović's, so their statements had similar failings. Duško Sikirica, commander of the Keraterm camp, for instance, pled guilty to killing one man, but he failed to mention that fact in his statement of remorse and rather spoke only of his omissions and the compulsion under which he acted. He said in part:

> Before the war in Bosnia, we all lived together in good neighbourly relations regardless of who or what we were. Prijedor was a good place to live in . . . the former Yugoslavia and to live together. I had many friendships, many of which transcended ethnic differences. When the war broke out, we had to go where we were told to go because we had no choice. We could [*sic*] refuse to obey orders—do I have to repeat? Unfortunately, when the war broke out, we had to go where we were told to go. We didn't have much choice. We could either obey orders, refuse to obey them, or desert. I was sent to Keraterm, although I would have preferred to go somewhere else at the time, because to go and work in Keraterm was the worst thing that could have happened to me. . . . After I saw and I understood the consequences, I wish to tell the Trial Chamber that I deeply regret everything that happened in Keraterm while I was there. I feel only regret for all the lives that have been lost and the lives that were damaged in Prijedor, in Keraterm, and unfortunately, I contributed to the destruction of these lives. I am especially sorry that I did not have enough moral courage and power to prevent some or all of the terrible things that happened. I would like to be able to turn back the clock and act differently.[1075]

Darko Mrđa's "statement of remorse" manifested a similar unwillingness to face up to his crimes[1076] while, even more troublingly, Ivica Rajić used his statement to paint himself as a heroic peacemaker who "played a key role in stopping this completely senseless conflict" and who "stood up to lawlessness, very often at the risk of [his] own life."[1077] Such statements as these breed contempt, not reconciliation.

The good news is that most of the more recent ICTY defendants to plead guilty have issued statements of remorse that in fact convey remorseful sentiments. Ranko Češić, for instance, stated:

> First of all, without any false sentiments, I wish to express my deep remorse for all the evil I have done. Words such as "remorse" are insufficient to express what somebody like me feels. Looking back in time after so much time has elapsed since I committed those crimes, there is an enormous difference between my state of mind now and then. Now I would never do the things I did then, the things that took place in a time of euphoria, a time when all human dignity was abolished.
>
> Before the trial, I pleaded guilty to the counts of the indictment, and I did my best to help the Office of the Prosecutor and the Tribunal to bring to light a small part of the overall truth, the part that refers to my actions.
>
> Your Honors, I will do anything to bring back the past and not to do what I have done. Since this is not possible, all that is left for me is to feel the deepest remorse for what I have done. To this I would like to add that I did not want to bring my friends and relatives here to say nice things about me because I didn't want to increase the pain of the victims and their families, out of respect for the deceased.
>
> I hope that my sincere remorse, which I feel deeply, will help to prevent similar things from happening in the future, and I wish to say that any people that experiences war is unfortunate, and people who live through this and families who have suffered pain feel this deeply. I want to say that I hope nobody will ever do the things that I have done and that prison is not the only punishment for me, because it is even harder to go on living with this feeling of guilt.[1078]

In a similar vein, Dragan Nikolić asserted:

> I repent sincerely.
>
> I genuinely repent. I am not saying this *pro forma*, this repentance and contrition comes from deep inside me, because I know most of those people from the earliest stage. I want to avail myself of this opportunity to say to all of those whom I hurt, either directly or indirectly, that I apologize to everyone who spent any time in Sušica, be it a month or several months. I would like, now that I have this opportunity to speak in public, to make even those victims feel the sincerity of my apology and my repentance, even those who were never at the Sušica camp and who are now scattered all over the word [sic] as a result of that conflict and the expulsions which made it impossible for them to return home.[1079]

The Trial Chambers have uniformly found these statements of remorse sincere and treated them as mitigating factors,[1080] even when prosecutors opposed such treatment.[1081] Guilty-plea defendants lately have been so keen to be perceived as remorseful that some of those who have appealed their sentences have taken the opportunity to express their remorse a second time at the appeals hearing,[1082] perhaps hoping for an additional sentence reduction on appeal.

Despite the genuine sound of these apologies, doubts remain about their impact and their sincerity. Predrag Banović's statement of remorse was moving,[1083] but Bosnian speakers immediately recognized that it was almost certainly written by someone else: when reading the statement, the uneducated Banović followed the words with his finger and mispronounced some of the more complex words.[1084] Milan Babić's apology to his "brother Croats" also failed to impress many in Croatia, "where his reconciliatory tone has been viewed as an insincere attempt to save his own skin."[1085] Access to information about the ICTY is limited in the states of the former Yugoslavia, so many victims are not even aware of the defendants' apologies, or if they are aware, know only that the defendant apologized but have no information about what he or she said.[1086] Even victims who have information about the apologies are understandably skeptical about their sincerity. ICTY defendants pleading guilty in recent times have garnered tremendous sentencing discounts and other benefits in exchange for their guilty pleas. If these benefits are sufficiently desirable to have motivated some defendants to misrepresent facts, they are certainly attractive enough to encourage defendants to feign remorse. However, as discussed earlier, the same concerns arise in the context of domestic restorative-justice programs and will in any setting in which apologies are rewarded or required.

Restorative Elements in ICTR Guilty-Plea Processes

Victim Involvement

Rwandan victims, like Yugoslav victims, are afforded little or no role in the ICTR's guilty-plea processes. Victims do not participate in the plea-bargaining process, and in none of the ICTR cases to be disposed of by guilty plea did victims testify at the sentencing hearings. To be fair, though, it is not clear that victims could have played a meaningful role in some of those hearings. The crimes committed in those cases featured many thousands of victims, and in *Kambanda*, *Ruggiu*, and *Rutaganira*, the defendants' criminal actions were far removed from the scenes of the massacres. Thus, victim testimony at the sentencing hearings of these defendants would have neither assisted the tribunal significantly nor constituted the sort of valuable victim involvement discussed throughout this book.

That said, the ICTR has made little effort to connect with Rwandan victims even when doing so would provide victims with substantial benefits. The ICTR has translated only a few of its judgments into Kinyarwanda, the local language; it should come as no surprise, then, that more than ten years after the ICTR was established, many Rwandans remain substantially unaware of its work.[1087] Six years after it was created, the ICTR did establish an outreach office in Kigali to publicize tribunal proceedings, but that office has done virtually nothing to educate the majority of Rwandans who live in rural areas. Indeed, most visitors to the center are lawyers, researchers, or university students, not genocide survivors.[1088] As Samantha Power observed:

> The [ICTR] is a world away from the people whom international justice claims to serve. The rare Rwandan who tries to visit the UN court must take a bus through four countries to get there—from Kigali, Rwanda, to Kampala, Uganda, to Nairobi, Kenya, to Arusha, Tanzania. The journey takes two days, and costs around $40 for the bus ticket and $20 for a Kenyan transit visa. This is more than most Rwandans earn in a month.[1089]

Whatever value victim participation might have in the Rwandan context, in guilty-plea cases or otherwise, the ICTR has done little to capture it. The ICTR's efforts in this regard stand in stark contrast to the Rwandan government's *gacaca* proceedings, which will be discussed later in this chapter, because *gacaca*, at least in its conception, envisages a substantial role for victims.

Truth-telling

The ICTR's commitment to truth-telling broadly resembles that of the ICTY. Like their counterparts in The Hague, ICTR prosecutors have made substantial efforts to obtain from guilty-plea defendants information that is useful to prosecuting other defendants. However, whereas ICTY prosecutors have been quite successful in obtaining useful information, ICTR prosecutors have had much more difficulty. Of the six ICTR defendants to plead guilty, two—Rutaganira and Bisengimana—refused entirely to cooperate with the prosecution.[1090] Rutaganira held such a low political position in Rwanda that he may not have had access to much information of value to the prosecution in any event. Moreover, Rutaganira's codefendants had been tried several years before Rutaganira surrendered to the ICTR, so the information he did possess was likely to be of little relevance by the time he could have made it available to prosecutors. Bisengimana, by contrast, likely does know a great deal that would be useful to ICTR prosecutors. Bisengimana committed his crimes with both Laurent Semanza, who has already been convicted, and Juvénal Rugambarara, who has not. Rugambarara succeeded Semanza as *bourgmestre* of Bikumbi commune,[1091] and the ICTR has charged him with participating with Bisengimana and Semanza in many of the same events that formed the basis for those defendants' convictions.[1092] At Semanza's trial, prosecutors labeled Semanza, Bisengimana, and Rugambarara "the evil troika,"[1093] and there is little question that, had he wanted to, Bisengimana could have assisted the prosecution in its case against Rugambarara.

All the four remaining guilty-plea defendants have ostensibly cooperated with the prosecution, yet the value of that cooperation is in some cases questionable. As noted in Chapter 5, the most recent ICTR defendant to plead guilty—Joseph Serugendo—provided prosecutors with approximately two hundred pages of incriminating information,[1094] but Serugendo's bleak medical outlook makes it unlikely that he will be able to testify for the prosecution in future cases. Omar Serushago and Georges Ruggiu also provided prosecutors with considerable inculpatory information about other ICTR defendants, but in the end, that information proved less useful than it had initially seemed.

As noted in Chapter 5, Serushago gave prosecutors a great deal of information before his indictment, and some of this information led to the arrests of a number of high-level offenders. Serushago continued cooperating throughout his plea negotiations, and in his plea agreement, he implicated no fewer than twenty-nine named individuals.[1095] He described various meetings, for instance, and named the high-level political leaders and local authorities who conducted those meetings.[1096] Serushago also volunteered the names of the militiamen most involved in the massacres in the Gisenyi prefecture.[1097] Whereas that information was sufficiently specific as to be potentially useful, Serushago's plea agreement also contained statements that were so broad as to be of little value. For instance, his plea agreement concludes with the expansive declaration that "[m]ilitary officers, members of the Interim Government, militia leaders and Civilian authorities, planned, prepared, instigated, ordered, aided and abetted their subordinates and others in carrying out the massacres of the Tutsi population and their 'accomplices.'"[1098] Other inculpatory statements in Serushago's plea agreement were cut and pasted from his indictment, so they did not provide prosecutors with new information.

Serushago promised to follow up these statements with trial testimony,[1099] and although he did testify in the so-called Media Trial,[1100] his testimony did prosecutors little good. The judges in the Media Trial criticized Serushago's testimony for its many "inconsistencies and contradictions."[1101] For instance, he initially told prosecutors that one of the defendant's victims was a woman or a boy; while testifying at trial, however, he steadfastly maintained that the victim had been a man. Serushago also testified that a certain Colonel Rwendeye attended two death squad meetings in 1993 and 1994. Confronted with evidence that Rwendeye had died in 1990, Serushago rejected that evidence and instead maintained that Rwendeye had died at the end of 1992. When it was pointed out that Serushago's revision nonetheless made Rwendeye "the only dead man at the meeting,"[1102] Serushago tried to deny his own testimony, claiming that he had testified that the meetings had taken place at the end of 1992 and 1993. The Trial Chamber recounted numerous other inconsistencies and contradictions to support its ultimate conclusion that Serushago was "confused and at times incomprehensible in his testimony."[1103] As a consequence, the chamber deemed Serushago's testimony to be "not consistently reliable" and accepted it only to the extent that it was corroborated by other testimony.[1104]

As for Ruggiu, his plea agreement spans thirty pages, but the first several pages read more like diary entries than legal provisions in that they explicate in substantial detail the factors motivating Ruggiu's decision to plead guilty as well as his hopes for the reconciliatory effect of his guilty plea.[1105] Subsequent pages of Ruggiu's plea agreement contain "admissions" about the genocide, but they are so broad and vague as to be virtually useless to the prosecution. Ruggiu "admit[ted]," for instance, "that *all* [RTLM] broadcasts were directed towards rallying the population against the 'enemy,' the RPF and those who were considered to be allies of the RPF" (emphasis added).[1106] In a similar vein, Ruggiu acknowledged "that RTLM broadcast extremist Hutu . . . ideology" and that RTLM broadcasts "incited young Rwandans, *Interahamwe* militiamen and soldiers to take part in armed conflict against the 'enemy' and its accomplices, [and] to kill and inflict serious bodily and mental harm on Tutsi and moderate Hutu." Going on to issue a sweeping indictment, Ruggiu asserted in his plea agreement "that RTLM broadcasters, including himself, together with RTLM managerial and editorial staff, bear full responsibility for the 1994 massacre of Tutsi and Hutu opposition party members."[1107] Statements such as these are welcome acknowledgment for victims, but they provide little assistance to the prosecution. Moreover, Ruggiu's subsequent testimony in the Media Trial, was even less credible than Serushago's. While on the stand, Ruggiu admitted to lying to prosecutors in his early interviews,[1108] and the remainder of his testimony was so riddled with inconsistencies that the Trial Chamber rejected it "in its entirety."[1109]

In Jean Kambanda's initial interviews with the prosecution, by contrast, he provided prosecutors with information far more valuable than the vague, unsupported assertions appearing in Ruggiu's plea agreement. In fact, Kambanda provided prosecutors with ninety hours of recorded testimony that included, in the prosecution's words, direct evidence "of such key facts" as the meeting between the "Council of Ministers and *Prefets* . . . where the topic of massacres committed against the civilian population was raised; the contents of deliberations and decisions agreed upon by consensus in the numerous closed sessions of the Cabinet; [and] the involvement of Ministers, senior Military officers and *Prefets*" in the commission of crimes within the tribunal's jurisdiction.[1110] The prosecution labeled Kambanda's information "invaluable,"[1111] and a review of the portions of Kambanda's disclosures that are revealed in Linda Melvern's account of the Rwandan genocide supports that description.[1112] The testimony that Kambanda promised subsequently to provide might likewise have been invaluable, but the prosecution lost its opportunity to acquire that testimony when it recommended that Kambanda receive a life sentence. Upon learning of that recommendation, Kambanda immediately stopped cooperating with the prosecution, and its subsequent efforts to obtain his further assistance have thus far proved unavailing.

Prosecutors may have seen greater success in obtaining inculpatory information from such defendants as Michel Bagaragaza and Juvénal Uwilingiyimana, who did not plead guilty. As members of the akazu, Bagaragaza and Uwilingiyimana were well-positioned to have information of vital significance to the prosecution, and there is reason to believe that the prosecution received at least some of that information. Certainly, it is unlikely that prosecutors would have requested to transfer Bagaragaza's case to Norway had he not provided them with valuable information. As for Uwilingiyimana, a Toronto newspaper reported that, at the time he went missing, he was on the verge of signing a ninety-two-page document in which he answered various questions posed by the prosecution. How useful Uwilingiyimana's evidence would have been, though, is open to question. Recall that a letter attributed to Uwilingiyimana appeared on the Internet and accused ICTR investigators of threatening him with bodily injury if he did not convey the information they needed to prove their cases. If that letter was authentic, then Uwilingiyimana's statements to the prosecution were valueless. In addition, after Uwilingiyimana's death, defense counsel in the *Karemera et al.* case sought the disclosure of the information that Uwilingiyimana had provided prosecutors, claiming that it would help to exculpate their clients. Defense counsel revealed that they too had interviewed Uwilingiyimana and had intended to call him as a witness.[1113] As defense counsel Peter Robinson put it, "His death actually does more harm to us than the prosecution."[1114] These conflicting accounts of Uwilingiyimana's evidence and loyalties suggest that he may have been tailoring his story to suit the needs of his listeners. Consequently, his "assistance" to the prosecution may well have proved no more helpful than that of Serushago and Ruggiu before him.

Even though their efforts have largely failed, ICTR prosecutors have at least tried to obtain from guilty-plea defendants inculpatory information about other defendants. By contrast, prosecutors have made little or no attempt to obtain information that would be of exclusive interest or value to survivors. The plea agreements of ICTR guilty-plea defendants, for instance, typically contain no information about victims. Serushago killed only four people, but even his plea agreement does not identify those victims. Chances are, of course, that neither Serushago nor anyone else even knows the identities of his specific victims, and it would be more ludicrous still to attempt to identify the victims of such high-ranking officials as Kambanda, since their crimes—in orchestrating and implementing the genocide—affected all of the victims. The difficulty, then, of obtaining information useful to victims in the context of such widespread and anonymous violence as that which took place in Rwanda must be taken into account when assessing those efforts.

However, whereas failing to obtain information useful to victims may not be worrisome in certain contexts, distorting the information already available is. As Chapter 5 discussed, ICTR prosecutors have shown newfound willingness to withdraw genocide charges and dramatically amend indictments to induce defendants to plead guilty. That prosecutors would resort to such tactics is understandable given the pressure they are under to adhere to the tribunal's completion strategy and the difficulty they have had in persuading defendants to plead guilty in exchange for sentencing concessions alone. But the fact remains that such measures distort the historical record and consequently undermine truth-telling and reconciliation efforts.

Apologies

The ICTR's experience with statements of remorse mirrors that of the ICTY. The first ICTR defendant to plead guilty, Jean Kambanda, issued no statement of remorse. Throughout Kambanda's interviews with the prosecution, he appeared completely unrepentant,[1115] and when asked during his sentencing hearing if he had anything to say, Kambanda declared simply, "I have nothing further to add." Although both the prosecution and defense urged the Trial Chamber to interpret Kambanda's guilty plea as an expression of remorse, the chamber declined to do so, observing that "remorse is not the only reasonable inference that can be drawn from a guilty plea." The chamber went on in an incriminatory tone: "Jean Kambanda has offered no explanation for his voluntary participation in the genocide; nor has he expressed contrition, regret or sympathy for the victims in Rwanda, even when given the opportunity to do so by the Chamber, during the hearing of 3 September 1998."[1116]

Kambanda's decision to remain silent clearly did not bolster his chances of receiving a sentence discount, a lesson that was well-learned by subsequent guilty-plea defendants, all of whom have expressed their remorse. Bisengimana's statement seemed carefully scripted. In stating his remorse, Bisengimana took great pains to acknowledge only those omissions that formed the basis for his guilty plea.[1117] Rutaganira likewise "begged forgiveness of the families of the victims," stating that he "regret[ted] not having been able to save the people in the Church" and that he would "never forget the horrible sight [he] saw the day after the attacks."[1118] Ruggiu, for his part, "plead[ed]" with the families of the victims to "understand that I greatly regret and sincerely what happened in Rwanda in 1994,"[1119] and Serushago had to choke back tears when he asked for forgiveness.[1120]

Although these statements of remorse might be viewed solely as calculating attempts to obtain leniency, that is not necessarily the way that victims view them. Helena Cobban writes of a Rwandan businessman, identified by the pseudonym B.V., who criticizes virtually every aspect of the justice that is meted out at the ICTR. There was, however, "one moment in all the years of the ICTR's work that gave B.V. and his friends some real satisfaction," and this moment came when Serushago made his confession in open court:

> B.V. had seen Serushago's statement on television, and he remembered it clearly even five years after the event: "Serushago cried. He pleaded for forgiveness. He showed remorse," he said. . . . "Rwandese liked to see the way Serushago acted," B.V. told me.

He contrasted Serushago's behavior—and the popular reaction to it—with that of the most prominent suspect to plead guilty at ICTR, Jean Kambanda. . . [who] notably failed to express any remorse. "Kambanda just admitted he had committed the crimes, and thought that was enough," B.V. said. "And he didn't even understand why, after he had done that, he got a life sentence."[1121]

Restorative Elements in Special Panels Guilty-Plea Processes

Truth-telling and Victim Involvement

The Special Panels made little effort in any of their cases to develop or publicize an historical record of the atrocities. As Chapter 2 described, the panels were inadequately funded throughout their existence, and they simply did not have the resources to advance truth-telling in any meaningful way. Judges for the Special Panels were not assisted by secretaries or law clerks, so when they issued judgments at all, those judgments featured only very brief statements of fact, virtually all of which had been cut and pasted from the indictments. As time went on, moreover, the panels dispensed even with issuing judgments; in their later years, the panels disposed of many cases by means of oral decisions or "Dispositions of the Decision," which did not include any facts. In addition, even though the Special Panels were required to make a transcript publicly available, they often failed to do so.[1122] After defendants in the *Los Palos* case filed a notice of appeal, the court of appeal ordered the court registry to provide the official trial record, but there is no indication that the registry ever did so.[1123] Similarly, the defense counsel in the *José Cardoso* case filed a notice of appeal in April 2003 but had been unable to provide a written appeal statement by June 2004 because no transcript was available.

Given the Special Panels' general failure to develop the historical record, it should come as no surprise that the prosecution and the panels likewise failed to generate considerable information through the use of guilty pleas. According to the Serious Crimes Unit's chief of prosecutions, prosecutors sought to obtain as much information as they could when they interviewed any defendant, but they made no special efforts to obtain information from defendants who pled guilty, and they certainly did not condition a sentence recommendation on a guilty-plea defendant's willingness to cooperate with the prosecution. Indeed, the chief of prosecutions reported that, because the standard plea agreement provided that defendants could be prosecuted for crimes not covered by the agreement, prosecutors would not have expected defendants to disclose information because doing so might put them at risk of a subsequent prosecution.[1124]

The prosecution's lack of interest in defendant information, while unfortunate, is understandable given the context in which the Special Panels operated. Only in recent years have the better-funded ICTY prosecutors begun conditioning their sentencing recommendations on the defendants' provision of information, and the information they have sought almost exclusively concerned other ICTY cases involving high-level defendants. Because the Special Panels had no ability to arrest any high-level defendants, the sort of information that is of substantial value at the ICTY was worth little at the Special Panels. Further, most of the defendants that the Special Panels were able to prosecute were low-level militia members who had no valuable information to provide prosecutors in any event.[1125]

The Special Panels were also entirely unable to involve victims in their proceedings, whether those proceedings involved guilty pleas or not.[1126] Most East Timorese live in remote villages and did not have the means to travel to the Special Panels' proceedings in Dili. In addition, the Special Panels had no public information program, and because many villagers are illiterate, the scant media reports on the Special Panels that did exist would not have helped them.[1127] Indeed, communication is so limited in East Timor that, when defendants were arrested from villages, most villagers had no idea where they were taken or what fate befell them; as far as the villagers were concerned, the defendants simply disappeared.[1128] Further, the few East Timorese who made efforts to attend Special Panels' proceedings faced considerable obstacles. During the first few days of the *Los Palos* case, for instance, East Timorese were prevented from entering the court building because they lacked U.N. identity cards. Although this policy was soon changed and guards were instructed to grant the public access, mistakes were occasionally made throughout the trial, and interested people were prevented from attending. In addition, even when the doors were not barred, victims and witnesses were nonetheless indirectly prevented from attending the proceedings because the panels never published their court dates.[1129] Many of the East Timorese who surmounted these sorts of hurdles and did manage to attend a court session faced disappointment nonetheless because the proceedings were not translated into a language they understood. In the *Carlos Soares* case, for instance, four members of the defendant's family traveled from the villages to hear the defense's closing statements in the case but did not understand a word of it because it was read in Portuguese, and no English or Tetum translation was provided.[1130] The panels suffered from a scarcity of interpreters throughout their existence so that defendants themselves were often unable to follow the proceedings in their entirety because the overworked interpreters routinely failed to translate exchanges between judges and counsel.[1131]

Reparations and Apologies

The Special Panels did require some defendants to pay the costs of the proceedings,[1132] but they imposed no obligations to make material reparations to victims. As for apologies, a few of the later guilty-plea defendants made statements of remorse. Some of these were very brief. Augusto Dos Santos, for instance, stated: "I did not know that man. He did no wrong to me. I am sorry."[1133] Other statements placed more emphasis on the pressure exerted on the defendant to commit the crimes than on the defendant's remorse for having committed them. Sabino Leite's statement comprised approximately forty-five sentences, for instance, but in only one did he express remorse for the harm he inflicted. In the remainder of his statement, he informed the judges of his low-level status, the compulsion under which he acted, the difficulty his family faces while he is in prison, and his desire to be immediately released. Indeed, after stating that he felt remorse for his actions, Leite went on to say that the time he had already spent in prison served to pay for his "mistakes," and he asked the judges to release him immediately. He concluded his statement by reiterating this request: "I repeat, I would like to be released this second."[1134] Jhoni Franca's statement was similar: it featured one or two sentences of remorse amidst approximately fifty sentences of justifications.[1135] The available evidence indicates that many Special Panels defendants did act under extreme compulsion, so it is understandable that they would emphasize that fact in their statements. At the same time, statements that seek primarily to justify defendants' behavior do little to advance reconciliation between victims and offenders. The point is a small one in any event because even if these statements had been better drafted, they nonetheless would have had little or no impact because victims were unaware of them.

In sum, then, Special Panels' guilty pleas served only one purpose—efficiency: that is, they resulted in a more expeditious resolution of cases. However, unlike some ICTY cases that make unsupportable claims about the reconciliatory value of their guilty pleas, the Special Panels were forthright about their practical focus. As the *Atolan* panel put it:

> The fact that the decision of the accused to plead guilty came at the end of a moral process of remorse, as a way to reconcile himself "with his Timorese brothers as well as with God" (words by the learned Counsel) is, in itself, of minor importance. What matters is the practical reflex of this internal drive or, in other words, the cooperation with the Prosecution during the inquiry and with the Court, pleading guilty.[1136]

Reconciliation and Restoration through Rwanda's Domestic Guilty-Plea Procedures and Its *Gacaca* Courts

The ICTR guilty-plea procedures discussed above contain few restorative elements; Rwanda, however, has made some of its own efforts to encourage defendants to self-convict. After the genocide, the new Tutsi-led Rwandan government embarked on the largest-scale national criminal prosecution effort in history. By 1998, Rwanda had arrested and imprisoned approximately 130,000 people on genocide charges[1137] and had adopted Organic Law No. 08/96 (Organic Law) to govern the prosecution of these suspects. The Organic Law classified offenders into four categories depending on their level of culpability. Category 1 perpetrators include those who had planned, instigated, or organized the genocide along with notorious murderers who distinguished themselves by their excessive malice. Category 2 perpetrators include lower-level murderers, the "foot soldiers" of the genocide. Category 3 perpetrators are those who committed serious assaults, and Category 4 perpetrators committed property offenses.[1138]

Recognizing that it could not hope to provide full-scale trials to 130,000 defendants, the Rwandan government included in the Organic Law an innovative guilty-plea procedure that offers reduced sentences primarily to perpetrators who fall into Categories 2 and 3.[1139] The penalty reductions are significant. For instance, the law provides that Category 2 defendants will receive a sentence of life imprisonment if convicted following trial but will receive a sentence of seven to eleven years' imprisonment if they plead guilty before prosecution and a sentence of twelve to fifteen years' imprisonment if they plead guilty after having been accused.[1140] To obtain these sentence reductions, defendants must do more than just plead guilty, though; in addition, they must provide "a detailed description" of all of their offenses, "including the date, time and the scene of each act, as well as the names of victims and witnesses, if known," along with information relating to accomplices, conspirators, and "all other information useful to the exercise of public prosecution."[1141] Defendants are also required to apologize for their offenses.[1142] The Rwandan guilty-plea procedure, then, incorporates many of the restorative features examined throughout this book.

The guilty-plea process has functioned as intended in a small proportion of cases. Some defendants have confessed their crimes, pled guilty, identified their coperpetrators, and apologized to victims.[1143] And some victims have received not only apologies but much-desired information. One twenty-two-year-old Tutsi woman, who watched a defendant murder her family, desperately wanted to know where the bodies had been buried. Upon her request, the defendant disclosed this information through the guilty-plea process, and the victim stated that it "was some kind of closure to me."[1144] Cases like this have been rare, however. Initially, few defendants chose to confess, largely because they were unaware of the guilty-plea procedure and the sentencing benefits it bestows on defendants.[1145] After the genocide, only a handful of practicing lawyers remained in Rwanda, and virtually none of them would agree to represent genocide suspects.[1146] Because few defendants had legal representation, and the prosecution failed to convey to defendants even the most basic information about their cases, a large proportion of defendants did not even know with what crimes they had been charged, let alone how to take advantage of a complex guilty-plea procedure.[1147]

Another impediment to pleading guilty was fear of retaliation: the Rwandan guilty-plea procedure required confessing defendants to name coconspirators and accomplices, among others, but it provided for no witness-protection mechanism to prevent reprisals.[1148] Indeed, while a defendant's confession was under review, the defendant remained detained in the same facilities that housed those prisoners implicated in the defendant's confession.[1149] Further, and particularly early on, there existed no organized procedure for communicating a defendant's confession.[1150] In some cases the confession had to be conveyed through the informal prison hierarchy and thus was made known to those inclined to retaliate. Some prisoners refused to confess not so much because they feared retaliation but because they did not feel that they had done anything wrong. Some of these prisoners were indeed factually innocent, but even those who had committed crimes often did not believe themselves to be morally culpable because the previous government had encouraged their crimes.[1151]

Given these difficulties, it is not surprising that only 500 prisoners of the approximately 130,000 detained confessed in 1997.[1152] Confessions increased following the widely publicized April 1998 executions of twenty-two convicted Hutu, so that seven thousand confessions had been received by September 1998,[1153] and twenty thousand by 2000. Rwandan courts had great difficulty processing these confessions, however. The hearing and review process proved slow and cumbersome, and a scarcity of personnel ensured that at any given time only one-fourth of the confessions were verified by the Public Prosecution Department. Thus, although five hundred defendants confessed throughout 1997,[1154] by the middle of that year, only twenty-five of them had been accorded reduced sentences on the basis of their guilty pleas.[1155]

Rwanda's initial guilty-plea system consequently failed to speed cases through the system. Nine years after the genocide, Rwanda had managed to dispose of the cases of only sixty-five hundred defendants with more than one hundred thousand still awaiting trial.[1156] Calculating that it would take more than two hundred years to try all of the prisoners using conventional methods, the Rwandan government began plans to transform a precolonial, community-based system of dispute resolution, known as *gacaca*, into a centrally managed system for trying genocide cases. In precolonial times, *gacaca* was used to resolve small-scale disputes, typically involving property rights, marital disputes, inheritance questions, and the like. Using traditional *gacaca*, village elders, called *Inyangamugayo*, would convene all parties to the dispute to mediate solutions and reintegrate offenders into the community. In 2001, the Rwandan government adapted traditional *gacaca* by enacting a law establishing approximately eleven thousand *gacaca* jurisdictions to prosecute genocide and crimes against humanity.[1157] The government professed its hope that *gacaca* would establish the truth about the genocide, would impose deserved criminal sanctions, and would promote national reconciliation by reintegrating guilty parties into society.[1158]

The government amended the original *gacaca* law in 2004, altering the structure of the *gacaca* jurisdictions. *Gacaca* jurisdictions are now divided into three levels—cell, sector, and sector courts of appeal. Each *gacaca* jurisdiction is charged with specific tasks. Approximately 9,500 cell-level *gacacas* must investigate and record the crimes that took place within a cell and must try suspects accused of property crimes. The 1,550 sector-level *gacacas* try Category 2 suspects and hear appeals from certain cell-level decisions. Finally, the courts of appeal hear appeals of sector-level *gacaca* decisions.[1159] The work of the *gacacas* will proceed in three stages. Cell-level *gacacas* will begin the process by investigating the crimes. Specifically, during the first phase, cell-level *gacacas* must prepare lists of people killed as a result of the genocide, forms detailing the damage suffered by cell residents, and lists of accused people.[1160] These investigations will form the basis for later prosecutions, but they also advance *gacaca*'s truth-telling and reconciliation missions by establishing a historical record of the genocide and allowing those who have suffered losses to feel that their grievances have been taken into account. During the second phase, cell-level *gacacas* must collect information relevant to the accusation of suspects and, using that information, must sort suspects into the three categories of offenders.[1161] During the third and final phase, suspects will be tried in the appropriate *gacaca*. In 2002, a pilot phase was begun wherein *gacaca* was introduced in 10 percent of the country; the process was launched nationwide in January 2005. The first trials in the pilot sectors began March 10, 2005,[1162] while trials in the rest of the country began in the spring of 2006.

In its conception, Rwanda's *gacaca* experiment contains a unique blend of retributive and restorative elements. *Gacaca* jurisdictions have the authority to impose severe criminal sanctions, including sentences of thirty years' imprisonment.[1163] At the same time, *gacaca* also seeks to enhance truth-telling and reconciliation through use of the guilty-plea procedure contained in the 1996 Organic Law, with modifications that provide for even greater leniency to confessing offenders. In particular, Category 2 suspects who confess prior to their *gacaca* trial will not only receive reduced prison sentences but will also be eligible to have half of their sentences commuted to community service.[1164] To obtain these concessions, suspects must not only, as before, make full and complete confessions and apologize, but must also reveal the location of the remains of their victims.[1165]

These confessions, along with virtually all of the work of the *gacacas*, are intended to take place in front of and with the participation of the entire community. The work of cell-level *gacacas* is conducted before their General Assemblies, which are composed of all cell inhabitants older than eighteen years. Each *gacaca* also contains a bench, with nine judges and four deputies, and a coordinating committee, with five members.[1166] Thus, the *gacacas*' judicial staff alone numbers nearly 170,000 Rwandans.[1167] A *gacaca* session cannot be convened without the attendance of at least seven judges and one hundred members of the General Assembly.[1168] The gathering of information and the investigation of suspects, therefore, is intended to be informed by substantial community participation. Even ascertaining simple factual details, such as who lived in the cell before the genocide, involves the entire community; in some cells, each household was requested to bring a list of their pregenocide members, and in others, *gacaca* leaders prepared the lists and discussed them during the assembly.[1169] Creating lists of accused was somewhat chaotic given the wide community participation. A Penal Reform International Report illustrated the painstaking nature of a simple census process in areas where many inhabitants are illiterate: "People came with small pieces of paper, with a few (incomplete) names scribbled down which were often difficult to read, to recall the persons living in each household. Full names and ages were often unknown and memory gaps were frequent."[1170] However, despite the inefficiency and chaos caused by the community participation, that very participation offered the potential to legitimize the lists.

Confessions, too, are often delivered in front of the very communities in which the crimes took place and with the participation not only of victims' families but defendants' families and other suspects whom defendants may need to implicate if their confessions are to be complete. Confessions made in such a context can be interactive. Community members may provide their own recollection of events and may question suspects: "Why is this story different from what you said last time?"[1171] and "You told us you had 15 bullets on the first day and that you only killed one person. What did you do with the remaining bullets?"[1172] Through these interactions, survivors may face down murderers in front of the community in which they murdered: During a *gacaca* in Kigese, for instance, one woman, "looking straight ahead and not at the man being cross-questioned, said to him, 'You killed my son.' After a rambling denial from him, she spoke again, calm and determined: 'You killed my son.'"[1173] The theory of *gacaca* is that such structured, yet informal, face-to-face encounters enable survivors to convey what is meaningful to them and have it heard in the communities in which their lives gain meaning. As Allison Corey and Sandra Joireman describe it, the active participation of survivors "contributes to political and personal reconciliation within the Rwandan population, since people are given the opportunity to confront their attackers, tell their stories and express pent-up emotions all in a secure environment."[1174] *Gacaca* also requires offenders to face the very people harmed by their actions and have those actions and that harm exposed before their friends and family. That exposure has at least the potential to shame suspects in reintegrative ways that do not occur in the context of formal courtroom proceedings.

Although the theoretical benefits of mechanisms like *gacaca* that seek to balance and blend retributive and restorative aims are compelling, their practical implementation can prove a challenge. For that reason, among others, some commentators are decidedly pessimistic about *gacaca*'s prospects for achieving its stated ends.[1175] *Gacaca*'s real-world problems are unquestionably numerous and daunting, and while some could be easily remedied, others are entrenched in the socioeconomic context in which *gacaca* must be carried out. For instance, a significant proportion of *gacaca* judges are illiterate,[1176] and even those who can read and write have had difficulty mastering the material they must learn because they had, at most, thirty-six hours of training.[1177] More worryingly, some judges have themselves been accused of genocide-related crimes; nearly twelve hundred judges resigned in June 2005 as a result of such allegations.[1178] Other judges are viewed as biased because they have relatives in prison or because they are survivors and are assumed to reflexively promote survivor interests.[1179] *Gacaca*'s jurisdiction is itself biased, which causes tremendous disillusionment among Hutu. In putting an end to the genocide, the Tutsi-led RPF committed many crimes of its own against Hutu—killing many tens of thousands of them[1180]—yet the Tutsi-dominated Rwandan government has not placed these crimes within *gacaca*'s jurisdiction.[1181] Hutu victims, then, have no hope of seeing their perpetrators prosecuted; consequently, many Hutu see their participation in *gacaca* as satisfying a governmentally imposed obligation, not as "a process that truly serves each community as much as it depends upon all of them."[1182]

Gacaca's most notable failing concerns its core element—community participation. After initial enthusiasm about *gacaca*, attendance dropped off.[1183] Dissatisfaction with *gacaca*'s one-sidedness accounts for the failure of some Rwandans to participate, while fear accounts for much of the rest. Tutsi survivors fear violence from those whom they accuse; Hutu witnesses fear that the information they provide will be used subsequently to prosecute them; and the families of perpetrators fear that confessions by those perpetrators will result in retaliation against *them*.[1184] Indeed, during the spring of 2005, thousands of Hutu fled Rwanda for neighboring countries, and rumors circulated that some of those departing feared being accused of genocide through *gacaca*.[1185] The economic consequences of *gacaca* participation also deter Rwandans from attending. Ninety percent of Rwandans are subsistence farmers who must eke out a living by working their fields or performing itinerant labor. Attending a *gacaca* session requires Rwandans to forego their usual livelihood, which is a sacrifice that not all are willing or able to make.[1186] Attendance has become so poor in some cells that authorities have taken to using coercive measures to compel attendance,[1187] and the 2004 amendments to the *gacaca* law authorize *gacaca* courts to impose criminal sanctions on those who refuse to testify as to what they know.[1188]

Confessions have increased since the introduction of *gacaca*, though *gacaca*'s inception coincided with more robust independent efforts by prosecutors to obtain guilty pleas, so the increase in confessions is not necessarily entirely attributable to *gacaca*.[1189] Whatever the cause, by late 2004 approximately sixty-five hundred detainees had confessed,[1190] and these confessions, along with the government's January 2003 decision to release very young, elderly, and ill prisoners, brought freedom to tens of thousands. These confessions, though, are implicating scores of additional suspects. Extrapolations from the confessions obtained during *gacaca*'s pilot phase suggest that as many as one million additional suspects might be identified through *gacaca*.[1191] Thus, a process designed to clear the prisons appears poised to fill them up again. An additional problem regarding *gacaca* confessions concerns their completeness; Penal Reform International reported that some prisoners confess to crimes less serious than those they actually committed or admit only those crimes for which they are already sure to be convicted. Throughout the world, confessing defendants seek to understate their criminal liability, but *gacaca* participants are more able to succeed in their efforts because *gacaca* courts have made no effort to verify the truthfulness or completeness of confessions.[1192] Some Rwandan prisoners additionally make "arrogant" confessions, speaking "in a loud aggressive voice, a stream of words expressed without any visible sign of feeling or remorse, ending in vociferous attempts to pressure the victims to pardon them immediately, on the spot."[1193] Finally, human-rights organizations are quick to point out *gacaca*'s due-process failings and, in particular, the fact that defendants are provided no right to legal counsel.[1194]

Although responsibility for some of *gacaca*'s problems must fall to Rwanda's current Tutsi-led government,[1195] many of *gacaca*'s failings are no worse than one might expect to encounter in a desperately impoverished country seeking accountability and reconciliation after a cataclysm of violence that extinguished nearly a million lives. It would be a miracle if issues such as these did not arise, given Rwanda's extreme poverty and high illiteracy rate, problems that render it a challenge merely to compile lists of pregenocide and postgenocide cell residents. Although the practical impediments to achieving *gacaca*'s goals seem at times insurmountable, its theoretical underpinnings are sound, and it is these underpinnings that should inform future transitional justice projects. As they play out during the coming years, *gacaca* proceedings will likely exemplify both the promise of criminal justice measures that aim to blend restorative and retributive features and the obstacles they must surmount.

Reconciliation and Restoration through East Timor's Commission for Reception, Truth, and Reconciliation

Although the Special Panels failed entirely to include restorative features in their prosecutions, many less-serious offenses in East Timor have nonetheless been addressed through restorative processes that have been initiated in local communities and incorporated into East Timor's innovative truth commission.

After the 1999 violence, tens of thousands of East Timorese who had participated in militia activities fled to West Timor and remained there, fearful of the reception that would greet them if they were to return home.[1196] The continuing presence of a large number of refugees in West Timor was considered a security threat to East Timor, so serious efforts were made to facilitate their peaceful return.[1197] In particular, different types of grassroots reconciliation processes have been convened since 2000 to welcome refugees. In some cases, refugees are brought back by family members, while in others a village or district will arrange to meet members of their communities living in the refugee camps and will bring them back under the auspices of local political authorities. In either case, refugees participate in a ceremonial handover, which takes place at the border. During this handover, refugees are expected to face their communities and confess their offenses. A local team evaluates these confessions, verifying them with available witnesses. An elected representative of the refugees or an elder also issues a confession on behalf of the group. After receiving that confession, the community members who are present can address complaints to particular individuals, and a discussion typically ensues. Upon arriving home, refugees participate in a welcoming ceremony, which also features confessions and apologies. Often the ceremony will culminate in an exchange of betel nut or an "oath of blood," in which each side drinks the other's blood.[1198]

Also to advance reconciliation, UNTAET established a Commission for Reception, Truth, and Reconciliation in July 2001, which is generally known by the Portuguese acronym CAVR.[1199] CAVR operated for two years, during which time it investigated the human-rights violations that had occurred within the context of political conflicts in East Timor between 1974 and 1999.[1200] To fulfill its mandate, CAVR took nearly eight thousand statements from victims[1201] and held a series of well-attended public meetings centering on specific instances of violence, such as internal political conflict between 1974 and 1976,[1202] famine and forced displacement during the late 1970s and early 1980s,[1203] and women in conflict.[1204] CAVR was also tasked with preparing a comprehensive report detailing the information it gathered and making recommendations for preventing future human-rights violations.[1205] In most respects, then, CAVR is fairly similar to a number of previous truth commissions, but it differs from them markedly in its inclusion of a Community Reconciliation Process (CRP), which, like the grassroots initiatives described above, is intended to facilitate refugee returns and to reconcile perpetrators of less-serious crimes with their victims.

Offenders[1206] wishing to participate in the CRP began the process by submitting to CAVR a written statement that contained, among other things, a full description of the relevant acts, an admission of responsibility for those acts, and a renunciation of the use of violence to achieve political objectives.[1207] UNTAET granted the CRP jurisdiction, as it were, only over less-serious crimes; consequently, after an offender submitted a statement, a copy was sent to the Office of the General Prosecutor to give the prosecutor the opportunity to exercise jurisdiction if the prosecutor considered the offenses too serious to be processed through the CRP.[1208]

If the Office of the General Prosecutor waived its right to prosecute, then the regional commissioner of CAVR scheduled a public hearing on the matter. Although the relevant UNTAET regulation appears to envisage that a hearing would be convened for each individual offender,[1209] most CRP hearings featured multiple offenders, in some cases as many as twenty.[1210] CRP hearings were presided over by a panel that included community representatives and that was chaired by the CAVR regional commissioner. Traditional community leaders were typically not appointed to the CRP panel but often functioned in an oversight capacity, and their eventual endorsement of a particular hearing bestowed on it considerable legitimacy.[1211] During a CRP hearing, the panel would hear from the offenders, the victims, and community members.[1212] At the start of a hearing, a CRP official would read the offender statements that had been submitted for that hearing; next, the offender was given an opportunity to make an oral statement. Some offenders issued very brief statements while others spoke at length.[1213] In making some of these statements, it was evident that offenders "were 'lowering themselves' before their communities, and that the hearing was at one level a public process of shaming, that concluded with the official re-admittance of the [offenders] back into the family."[1214] The public accounting required by the hearing was emotional and difficult for some offenders. "[M]any looked . . . uncomfortable throughout the proceedings."[1215]

After offenders made their statements, they were subject to questioning from the CRP panel and from victims and community members. Although offenders were technically required to disclose all relevant information about their offenses, including information about other offenders,[1216] in many instances, little interrogation about these matters took place. Rather, victim questioning in particular tended to focus on idiosyncratic issues of importance to the victim. For instance, one victim, who had been beaten by an offender, did not ask the offender for information about the other person who had beaten him but wanted instead to know what had happened to his sacred sword that had been stolen during the incident. Similarly, some community members asked questions relevant to the offender's actions while others used the opportunity to ascertain whether the offender had any information about an unrelated offense that had been perpetrated on the questioner.[1217] Following the hearing, the panel was required to determine an appropriate act of reconciliation, which, if the offender agreed to it, would be memorialized in a Community Reconciliation Agreement. In some cases, the panel included service requirements, such as four days of labor to build a community hall, the planting of trees for ten days on church land, or the cleaning of church land for one day a week for several months. In other cases, offenders were required to compensate their victims through the transfer of livestock.[1218] However, the majority of offenders were required only to apologize and promise not to engage in future violence.[1219] In addition to setting forth the act of reconciliation, Community Reconciliation Agreements also included a description of the offenders' acts, a record of their acceptance of responsibility, and their apologies.[1220]

CRP processes concluded in the spring of 2004 and were considered a success. The CRP expected to receive approximately one thousand statements from offenders, and in the end, it received more than fifteen hundred, a 50-percent increase over projections. Indeed, the popularity of the program resulted in a large backlog of cases for the CRP as it was concluding its operations, and this backlog required CRP officials to rush through the caseload in ways that may have impaired the hearings' quality to some extent.[1221] As a result of substantial outreach efforts,[1222] the hearings generated considerable community interest and were usually well-attended. An average of two hundred to three hundred people attended the hearings in Bobonaro, for instance, while another hearing saw more than five hundred attendees and another more than one thousand.[1223] Although not all victims and community members were satisfied with the process, and some in particular complained that the acts of reconciliation were not commensurate with the harms done, victim and community approval remained generally high. A CRP internal review completed in March 2004 found high levels of forgiveness among victims,[1224] with some victims clearly expressing the importance to them of confronting and questioning offenders.[1225] Indeed, this review determined that the level of victim satisfaction and forgiveness had far less to do with what act of reconciliation was imposed than with the perceived comprehensiveness and truthfulness of the offender's confession.[1226] The CRP's success in incorporating substantial features of local justice legitimized the process and enhanced victim and community satisfaction with the eventual results.

As noted above, UNTAET deemed the CRP appropriate only for relatively minor crimes, such as theft, minor assault, the killing of livestock, and arson that did not result in death or injury.[1227] These guidelines were not always followed, however, and in some cases the CRP did address serious crimes.[1228] As troubling as this is to some commentators, the failure to process other serious crimes through the CRP has proved more troubling to local communities because most of the offenses deemed too serious for the CRP have not been addressed in any manner whatsoever because East Timor's underdeveloped, underresourced criminal justice system has not had the capacity to undertake the prosecutions. Thus, there currently exists the disquieting likelihood that perpetrators of the most serious crimes will face no justice at all, a prospect that has deeply distressed many victims. East Timor's experience, then, highlights a central thesis of this book: that in many cases doing some "justice," even if it is inadequate by usual standards, brings considerable benefits, particularly when the likelihood exists that arguably more appropriate measures will not prove feasible.

Conclusion

Weighing the value of various responses to mass atrocities is an unfulfilling exercise. To a population shattered by widespread murders, rapes, abductions, and torture, no response can be an adequate response. No amount of money, truth-telling, or criminal sanctions can come close to repairing lives ruptured by violence. "Reconciliation," a six-syllable word that can be hard to say, is even harder to achieve, a fact evidenced by the chaos and violence that continue to plague many areas that had formerly experienced war and had ostensibly put their conflicts behind them.

Despite the inherent inadequacy of remedial measures, anecdotal evidence suggests that which measures are chosen and how they are implemented do in fact matter. Societies torn apart by mass violence benefit when truth is told, when reparations are provided, and when perpetrators suffer criminal punishment. Victims will often be dissatisfied with the amounts of these commodities handed out following mass atrocities: many South African victims believe that perpetrators disclosed some details but not all of them;[1229] victims routinely complain about the amounts of reparations they receive;[1230] and few victims consider any prison sentence adequate punishment for the perpetration of one, let alone many, murders.[1231] Attempting to redress the harms resulting from international crimes, therefore, is an unsatisfying task that can realistically aim to provide only a small measure of comfort and vindication amidst widespread sorrow, despair, and frustration.

The plea-bargaining system developed in this book is designed to enhance that small measure of comfort and vindication. It is premised on the belief that, even in a context in which a large proportion of offenders will not be prosecuted, increasing the number of offenders who do face criminal sanctions enhances the ability of those prosecutions to serve the penological goals that they are credited with serving. It is further premised on the belief that the way in which guilt is determined has a crucial significance for the way in which that guilt is perceived by the relevant parties. In particular, defendants who acknowledge their atrocities rather than deny the obvious, who accept responsibility rather than blame their enemies, and who apologize to victims rather than continue to demonize them stand a better chance of reintegrating and advancing peace efforts. These reconciliatory values come with a price tag, however—sentencing discounts—which some believe is a price too high. Sentence discounts are most problematic when they are bestowed for the mere act of self-conviction, but even when prosecutors utilize a restorative-justice guilty-plea system such as I have developed here, a careful balance must be struck between leniency and the reconciliatory benefits that the leniency purchases, for offering leniency in too large a quantity is likely to impair the very reconciliation that the system seeks to advance. The ICTY can praise to the skies Biljana Plavšić's guilty plea, but when it sentenced her to a mere eleven-year prison term, of which she will serve at most two-thirds and in a posh Swedish prison, the ICTY contributed more to enhancing bitterness than reconciliation.

Even if seemingly appropriate balances can be crafted in various factual contexts, both practical and theoretical objections to the provision of sentencing discounts still exist. Many objections to the practice of plea bargaining appear on the foregoing pages. A few prosecutors have distorted the facts of the crimes in order to obtain guilty pleas; a few defendants have been caught lying in an effort to secure more favorable plea agreements; and a good number of East Timorese defendants have pled guilty without any real awareness of the nature of the crimes to which they were pleading guilty, let alone the consequences of their guilty pleas. These issues can be addressed to a greater or lesser extent through regulation, but the theoretical objections remain. Domestic critics of plea bargaining have argued that punishments should be deserved and that bargains are out of place in a context where people are to get what they deserve. Defendants who plead guilty and obtain sentencing concessions, however, never receive the penologically appropriate punishment that the legislature has mandated. Such concerns are magnified in the context of international crimes because the crimes are so grave. No adequate punishment exists for those who participate in large-scale murders, rapes, and the like, and discounting an already inadequate sanction can seem all the more troubling. In the foregoing pages, I have suggested focusing not on the egregious nature of the crimes, but on the historical and political contexts in which the response to those crimes will be developed. Despite the gravity of international crimes, the vast majority have and will go unpunished. As a consequence, I have argued that the exceptionality of prosecutions for international crimes goes a long way toward justifying sentencing discounts; that is, I have advanced a half-a-loaf theory which posits that sentencing discounts are theoretically and practically less disquieting in a context in which few offenders receive any punishment at all than they are in a system that has the political and financial capacity to impose appropriate punishment on most offenders. In other words, context matters.

An examination of context could, however, lead to the opposite conclusion. One could assert, by contrast, that it is precisely because these trials are so rare, precisely because they have been preceded by so many centuries of impunity, that the few that are now undertaken must be undertaken with the greatest possible care. According to this view, those prosecuting international crimes must be all the more intent on adhering to the highest due-process standards and on imposing appropriately harsh punishment consistent with those standards, rather than engaging in unseemly bargaining and handing out discounts mandated by political constraints. Although according to this view, few trials will be undertaken now, they will stand as exemplars for succeeding generations when, one can hope, political considerations will not hold such sway, and the prosecution of international crimes is the norm, not an aberration.

Although this argument has surface appeal, it does not give sufficient weight to the importance of truth-telling and reparations, values that a grant of leniency can advance. Putting those values aside, moreover, I am also not convinced that the gold-standard trial model currently in use at the ICTY, for instance, has any hope of ever becoming a viable means of disposing of significant numbers of cases involving international crimes. The international community's response to the ICTY's expenditures certainly provides no reason to expect that it will. More tellingly, American trials take less time and cost less money than international trials, yet still they are provided to a mere 10 percent of American criminal defendants. European countries that once eschewed any sort of trial negotiations are now utilizing bargaining practices that bear a substantial resemblance to plea bargaining, as their trial procedures have become more complex and their caseloads more burdensome.[1232] The American public holds plea bargaining in contempt, and citizens of European countries have likewise expressed discomfort with the increasing prevalence of bargaining in their criminal justice systems; yet, the negotiations go on. Consequently, if a wealthy country like the United States refuses to spend the funds necessary to provide its own violent nationals with full-scale trials, despite public disapproval, how much more unlikely is it that it will contribute substantial resources to provide full-scale trials to a large number of violent offenders half a world away? Equally, if a wealthy country like the United States cannot see fit to allocate sufficient funds to provide full-scale trials to its small number of violent offenders, how much more unlikely is it that developing nations, which face pressing demands in health, education, and police protection, among many others, will be able to provide full-scale trials to many thousands of offenders?

As these questions indicate, there is no greater chasm than that which divides what should be done to redress the harms caused by international crimes and what will be done. The guilty-plea system developed here aims at narrowing that chasm, if but a little.

REFERENCE MATTER

Notes

BOOK EPIGRAPHS: Prosecutor v. Plavšić, Case No. IT-00-39&40/1-S, Prosecution's Brief on the Sentencing of Biljana Plavšić (Nov. 25, 2002) Daria Sito-Sucic, *Muslim Victims Outraged, Say Plavšić Sentence Low*, REUTERS, Feb. 27, 2003.

Introduction

1. The ICTY's first prosecutor, Richard Goldstone, hailed the tribunals as "a tremendous and exciting step forward," Richard Goldstone, *Conference Luncheon Address*, 7 TRANSNAT'L L. & CONTEMP. PROBS. 1, 2 (1997), while Payam Akhavan described the establishment of the ICTY and ICTR as "an unprecedented institutional expression of the indivisibility of peace and respect for human rights" that "represents a radical departure from the traditional realpolitik paradigm which has so often and for so long ignored the victims of mass murder and legitimized the rule of tyrants in the name of promoting the purported *summum bonum* of stability." Payam Akhavan, *Justice and Reconciliation in the Great Lakes Region of Africa: The Contribution of the International Criminal Tribunal for Rwanda*, 7 DUKE J. COMP. & INT'L L. 325, 327 (1997).

2. *See, e.g.*, MICHAEL P. SCHARF, BALKAN JUSTICE (1997); Jose E. Alvarez, *Rush to Closure: Lessons of the Tadić Judgment*, 96 MICH. L. REV. 2031 (1998); Sanja Kutnjak Ivković, *Justice by the International Criminal Tribunal for the Former Yugoslavia*, 37 STAN. J. INT'L L. 255, 331 (2001) (describing the media frenzy at the opening of the Tadić trial); Kellye L. Fabian, Note and Comment, *Proof and Consequences: An Analysis of the Tadić & Akayesu Trials*, 49 DEPAUL L. REV. 981 (2000).

3. Allison Marston Danner, *When Courts Make Law: How the International Criminal Tribunals Recast the Laws of War*, 59 VAND. L. REV. 1, 25 (2006).

4. After less than a month in office, Argentine president Néstor Kirchner purged the military high command, announced a willingness to extradite human-rights offenders wanted in other countries, and called on the Argentine Supreme Court to declare amnesty laws and pardons unconstitutional. Larry Rohter, *Now the Dirtiest of Wars*

Won't Be Forgotten, N.Y. TIMES, June 18, 2003, at A4. First, Mexico agreed to extradite an Argentine ex-navy officer to stand trial in Spain on charges of genocide and terrorism. Diego Cevallos, *Rights-Mexico: Extradition of Accused Argentine Torturer Approved*, INTERPRESS SERVICE, June 10, 2003. Next, Kirchner prepared to extradite Argentine military officers to various European countries that are seeking to prosecute them. Rohter, *supra*; Damian Wroclavsky, *Argentina Says It Would Extradite "Angel of Death,"* REUTERS, Oct. 11, 2003. In August of 2003, the Argentine Senate overwhelmingly voted to repeal the amnesty laws that had put an end to trials in the 1980s, Reed Lindsey, *Taking on the Past, Argentina Repeals Amnesty*, BOSTON GLOBE, Aug. 22, 2003, at A12, and in June 2005, the Argentine Supreme Court struck down the amnesties, holding that they were contrary to current international law norms requiring states to protect human rights and punish abuses, Hector Tobar, *Argentine Court Voids Amnesty in Dirty War*, L.A. TIMES, June 15, 2005, at A9.

In Chile, courts are sidestepping the amnesty law that ostensibly prevents prosecutions, and they are allowing prosecutions against former military officials to go forward. Approximately 160 former members of the military are now on trial, and a handful have already been convicted. *See* Sebastian Brett, *Justice a Step Closer in Chile*, THE OBSERVER, May 30, 2004 ("Of more than 200 former officers now facing trials, 15 have received jail sentences, including Pinochet's former intelligence chief, Manuel Contreras."); Louise Egan, *Victims: Chile's Human Rights Plan Soft on Military*, REUTERS, Aug. 13, 2003; *see also* Ellen Lutz & Kathryn Sikkink, *The Justice Cascade: The Evolution and Impact of Foreign Human Rights Trials in Latin America*, 2 CHI. J. INT'L L. 1, 24 (2001) (noting that "[s]ince Pinochet's arrest, twenty-five Chilean officers have been arrested on charges of murder, torture, and kidnapping" and describing a 1999 Chilean Supreme Court case holding the amnesty law inapplicable in cases of disappearances).

5. ICLN Conference, *Establishing the International Criminal Court*, The Hague, Dec. 16–18, 2002 (comments of Sam Muller, ICC Advance Team coordinator).

6. In March 2005, the ICC's deputy prosecutor in charge of investigations confirmed that the ICC would be capable of prosecuting only a handful of perpetrators per mass atrocity. Serge Brammertz, Speech, *Challenges Faced during an Investigation*, Grotius Center, The Hague, Mar. 10, 2005.

7. MARK OSIEL, MASS ATROCITY, COLLECTIVE MEMORY, AND THE LAW 39 (1997).

8. *See* Nancy Amoury Combs, *Copping a Plea to Genocide: The Plea Bargaining of International Crimes*, 151 U. PA. L. REV. 1, 9–28, 46–47 (2002) [hereinafter Combs, *Copping a Plea to Genocide*].

9. WAYNE R. LaFAVE ET AL., CRIMINAL PROCEDURE 21–22 (3d ed. 2000) (observing that no more than 15 percent of felony charges and only 3 percent to 7 percent of misdemeanor charges are likely to be resolved by trial); Stephanos Bibas, *The Right to Remain Silent Helps Only the Guilty*, 88 IOWA L. REV. 421, 422 (2003) (reporting that only 6 percent of felony cases proceed to trial); George Fisher, *Plea Bargaining's Triumph*, 109 YALE L.J. 857, 1012 (2000) (noting that in modern American courtrooms, "guilty plea rates above ninety or even ninety-five percent are common"). As Stephanos Bibas puts it, "Our world is no longer one of trials, but of guilty pleas." Stephanos Bibas, *Judicial Fact-Finding and Sentence Enhancements in a World of Guilty Pleas*, 110 YALE L.J. 1097, 1150 (2001).

10. *See* Combs, *Copping a Plea to Genocide, supra* note 8, at 40–43.

11. Guilty pleas were offered by Predrag Banović, *see* Prosecutor v. Meakić et al., Case No. IT-02-65-PT, Joint Motion for the Consideration of a Plea Agreement between Predrag Banović and the Office of the Prosecutor, Annex 1 (June 18, 2003) [hereinafter Banović Plea Agreement]; Momir Nikolić, Prosecutor v. Momir Nikolić, Case No. IT-02-60-PT, Joint Motion for Consideration of Plea Agreement between Momir Nikolić and the Office of the Prosecutor, Annex A, Amended Plea Agreement (May 7, 2003) [hereinafter Momir Nikolić Plea Agreement]; Dragan Obrenović, Prosecutor v. Dragan Obrenović, Case No. IT-02-60-PT, Joint Motion for Consideration of Plea Agreement between Dragan Obre-nović and the Office of the Prosecutor, Annex A, Plea Agreement (May 20, 2003) [here-inafter Obrenović Plea Agreement]; Dragan Nikolić, Prosecutor v. Dragan Nikolić, Case No. IT-94-2-S, Sentencing Judgement, para. 35 (Dec. 18, 2003) [hereinafter Dragan Nikolić Sentencing Judgement]; Darko Mrđa, Prosecutor v. Mrđa, Case No. IT-02-59-S, Sentenc-ing Judgement, para. 4 (Mar. 31, 2004) [hereinafter Mrđa Sentencing Judgement]; Mio-drag Jokić, Prosecutor v. Jokić, Case No. IT-01-42/1-S, Sentencing Judgement, paras. 7–11 (Mar. 18, 2004) [hereinafter Jokić Sentencing Judgement]; Miroslav Deronjić, Prosecutor v. Deronjić, Case No. IT-02-61-PT, Plea Agreement (Sept. 29, 2003) [hereinafter Deronjić Plea Agreement]; and Ranko Češić, Prosecutor v. Češić, Case No. 95-10/1-PT, Plea Agree-ment (Oct. 8, 2003) [hereinafter Češić Plea Agreement].

12. *See, e.g.*, Dario Sito-Sucic, *Muslim Victims Outraged, Say Plavšić Sentence Low*, RE-UTERS, Feb. 27, 2003; Amra Kebo, *Regional Report: Plavšić Sentence Divides Bosnia*, IWPR's TRIBUNAL UPDATE, No. 302, Feb. 24–28, 2003; Emir Suljagić & Amra Kebo, *Mrda Guilty Plea Sparks Anger*, IWPR's TRIBUNAL UPDATE, No. 322, Aug. 1, 2003; *Bosnian Women's Association Calls Serb Camp Guard Sentence "Insult,"* BBC WORLDWIDE MONITOR-ING, Oct. 29, 2003; *Bosnian Muslims Protest "Shameful" War Crimes Sentence*, AGENCE FRANCE-PRESSE, Oct. 29, 2003; Nerma Jelacić & Chris Stephen, *Anger at Short Sentence for Prison Killer*, IWPR's TRIBUNAL UPDATE, No. 331, Nov. 1, 2003.

13. *See* Milanka Saponja-Hadzić, *Hague Deals Reduce Impact*, IWPR's TRIBUNAL UP-DATE, No. 321, July 24, 2003.

14. For a discussion of large-scale human-rights abuses in other Asian countries, see CARLOS SANTIAGO NINO, RADICAL EVIL ON TRIAL 26–30 (1996); LEO KUPER, GENOCIDE: ITS POLITICAL USE IN THE TWENTIETH CENTURY 79–80, 150–54 (1981); Belinda A. Aquino, *The Human Rights Debacle in the Philippines, in* IMPUNITY AND HUMAN RIGHTS IN IN-TERNATIONAL LAW AND PRACTICE 231 (Naomi Roht-Arriaza ed., 1995); Niall MacDermot, *Crimes against Humanity in Bangladesh*, 7 INT'L. LAW. 476 (1973).

15. David Wippman, *Atrocities, Deterrence, and the Limits of International Justice*, 23 FORDHAM INT'L L.J. 473, 477 (1999).

16. 1 Truth and Reconciliation Commission of South Africa Report, Chap. 1, para. 36 and Chap. 5, para. 70 (2003). Similarly, restorative justice is understood to emphasize "re-pair of social connections and peace rather than retribution against the offenders." MAR-THA MINOW, BETWEEN VENGEANCE AND FORGIVENESS: FACING HISTORY AFTER GENO-CIDE AND MASS VIOLENCE 92 (1998). Restorative justice has been said to comprise three dimensions: "the central and elevated role of the victim, the general focus on repair, and the procedural emphasis on seeking mutual involvement and support for the three

co-participants and explicitly promoting the role of each in producing justice outcomes." Willie McCarney, *Restorative Justice: An International Perspective* 3 J. CENTER FOR FAMILIES, CHILD. & CTS. 3, 5 (2001).

17. GERRY JOHNSTONE, RESTORATIVE JUSTICE: IDEAS, VALUES, DEBATES 1 (2002); *see also* Stephen P. Garvey, *Restorative Justice, Punishment, and Atonement*, 2003 UTAH L. REV. 303, 314; Mark S. Umbreit et al., *The Impact of Victim-Offender Mediation: Two Decades of Research*, FED. PROBATION, Dec. 2001, at 29, 29 [hereinafter Umbreit et al., *The Impact of Victim-Offender Mediation*].

Chapter 1

18. Beginning with the Geneva Convention of 1864, Geneva Convention for the Amelioration of the Condition of the Wounded of Armies in the Field, Aug. 22, 1864, 18 Martens Nouveau Recueil (ser. 1) 607, and followed by the 1868 St. Petersburg Declaration, Declaration Renouncing the Use, in Time of War, of Explosive Projectiles under 400 Grammes Weight, Nov. 29, 1868, 18 Martens Nouveau Recueil (ser. 1) 474, and the 1874 Declaration of Brussels, Project of an International Declaration Concerning the Laws and Customs of War, Aug. 27, 1874, 4 Martens Nouveau Recueil (ser. 2) 219, states primarily of the Western Hemisphere began to regulate the conduct of armed conflict. The Hague Peace Conferences of 1899 and 1907 advanced this movement by further developing and codifying the principles previously articulated. *See, e.g.*, Convention (No. IV) Respecting the Laws and Customs of War on Land, with Annex of Regulations, Oct. 18, 1907, 36 Stat. 2277, T.S. No. 539. For insightful analyses of the developments since the Hague Peace Conferences in each of the areas addressed by the conferences, see Symposium, *The Hague Peace Conferences*, 94 AM. J. INT'L L. 1 (2000).

19. Agreement for the Prosecution and Punishment of the Major War Criminals of the European Axis Powers, art. 6, Aug. 8, 1945, 54 Stat. 1544, 82 U.N.T.S. 280; Charter of the International Military Tribunal for the Far East, art. 5, Jan. 19, 1946, T.I.A.S. No. 1589, 4 Bevans 20 (as amended, Apr. 26, 1946, 4 Bevans 27).

20. Convention on the Prevention and Punishment of the Crime of Genocide, Dec. 9, 1948, 102 Stat. 3045, 78 U.N.T.S. 277. For a comprehensive treatment of the history and current contours of the crime of genocide, see WILLIAM A. SCHABAS, GENOCIDE IN INTERNATIONAL LAW (2000). For an interesting account of Raphael Lemkin's role in developing the concept and the prohibition of genocide, see SAMANTHA POWER, A PROBLEM FROM HELL 31–78 (2002).

21. Geneva Convention for the Amelioration of the Condition of the Wounded and Sick in Armed Forces in the Field, art. 50, Aug. 12, 1949, 6 U.S.T. 3114, 75 U.N.T.S. 31; Geneva Convention for the Amelioration of the Condition of the Wounded, Sick and Shipwrecked Members of Armed Forces at Sea, art. 51, Aug. 12, 1949, 6 U.S.T. 3217, 75 U.N.T.S. 85; Geneva Convention Relative to the Treatment of Prisoners of War, art. 130, Aug. 12, 1949, 6 U.S.T. 3316, 75 U.N.T.S. 135; Geneva Convention Relative to the Protection of Civilian Persons in Time of War, art. 147, Aug. 12, 1949, 6 U.S.T. 3516, 75 U.N.T.S. 287.

22. In 1947, the U.N. General Assembly asked the International Law Commission (ILC) to begin work on a Code of Offenses against the Peace and Security of Mankind,

G.A. Res. 177 (II), U.N. Doc. A/CN.4/4 (1947), and a draft was completed in 1954, Int'l Law Comm'n, *Report of the International Law Commission on the Work of Its Sixth Session*, U.N. Doc. A/2693 (June 3–July 28, 1954), *reprinted in* [1954] 2 Y.B. Int'l L. Comm'n 140, U.N. Doc. A/CN.4/SER.A/1954. By the time the draft was finished, however, political interest in prosecuting international crimes had already begun to fade as hostilities erupted in Korea, and the other major powers began to accuse one another of crimes against the peace. *Draft Code of Offenses against the Peace and Security of Mankind*, 80 AM. SOC'Y. INT'L PROC. 120, 125 (1986) (remarks of Sharon A. Williams) [hereinafter Draft Code]; D. H. N. Johnson, *The Draft Code of Offences against the Peace and Security of Mankind*, 4 INT'L & COMP. L. Q. 445, 451 (1955). The draft was further criticized for failing to define aggression. *Draft Code, supra* at 121 (remarks of Stephen C. McCaffrey). The task of defining aggression became mired in Cold War politics; it was not until 1974 that the General Assembly adopted a resolution defining "aggression," G.A. Res. 3314 (XXIX), U.N. Doc. A/9631 (Dec. 14, 1974), and it was not until 1996 that the ILC adopted a final text of the draft code on offenses, Int'l Law Comm'n, *Report of the International Law Commission on Its Forty-eighth Session*, para. 50, U.N. Doc. A/51/10 (6 May–26 July 1996).

The U.N. General Assembly asked the ILC to examine the establishment of an international criminal court, G.A. Res. 260B (III), U.N. Doc. A/760, at 12–13 (1948), and the ILC submitted a draft to the General Assembly in 1953. However, the U.N. tabled these efforts pending the completion of the *Draft Code of Offenses against the Peace and Security of Mankind*, which, as noted above, was itself tabled pending agreement on the definition of aggression. M. Cherif Bassiouni, *From Versailles to Rwanda in Seventy-Five Years: The Need to Establish a Permanent International Criminal Court*, 10 HARV. HUM. RTS. J. 11, 53 (1997).

23. *See* 1956 Supplementary Convention on the Abolition of Slavery, the Slave Trade, and Institutions and Practices Similar to Slavery, art. 6, Sept. 7, 1956, 18 U.S.T. 3201, 266 U.N.T.S. 3; 1950 Convention for the Suppression of the Traffic in Persons and of the Exploitation of the Prostitution of Others, arts. 1–2, Mar. 21, 1950, 96 U.N.T.S. 271, 274.

24. *See* Convention against Torture and Other Cruel, Inhuman or Degrading Treatment or Punishment, art. 4, Dec. 10, 1984, 1465 U.N.T.S. 85, 113, G.A. Res. 39/46, U.N. Doc. A/39/51 (1984).

25. International Convention on the Suppression and Punishment of the Crime of Apartheid, art. III, Nov. 30, 1973, 1015 U.N.T.S. 243.

26. *See* ROBERT CONQUEST, THE GREAT TERROR: STALIN'S PURGE OF THE THIRTIES 699–713 (rev. ed. 1973); ROBERT CONQUEST, THE GREAT TERROR: A REASSESSMENT 486–87 (1990). Leo Kuper, however, maintains that the death toll was much higher than twenty million. KUPER, *supra* note 14, at 97. Subsequent Soviet leaders Khrushchev and Gorbachev formed commissions to investigate illegal activity under Stalin, but the results of these investigations remained largely secret. Kathleen E. Smith, *Destalinization in the Former Soviet Union, in* IMPUNITY AND HUMAN RIGHTS IN INTERNATIONAL LAW AND PRACTICE 113, 117 (Naomi Roht-Arriaza ed., 1995); *see also* CONQUEST, STALIN'S PURGE OF THE THIRTIES, *supra* at 11.

27. For a discussion of the difficulty in ascertaining the numbers of Ugandan victims of different kinds of violence, see Louise Pirouet, *Refugees in and from Uganda in the*

Post-Colonial Period, in UGANDA NOW 239, 246–50 (Holger Bernt Hassen & Michael Twaddle eds., 1988). For a discussion of Uganda's expulsion of Asians, see EXPULSION OF A MINORITY: ESSAYS ON UGANDAN ASIANS (Michael Twaddle ed., 1975).

28. Michael J. Bazyler, *Reexamining the Doctrine of Humanitarian Intervention in Light of the Atrocities in Kampuchea and Ethiopia,* 23 STAN. J. INT'L L. 547, 554–69 (1987).

29. Inbal Sansani, *The Pinochet Precedent in Africa: Prosecution of Hissène Habré,* HUM. RTS. BRIEF, Vol. 8, No. 2, at 32, 32 (2001); Reed Brody, *The Prosecution of Hissène Habré—An "African Pinochet,"* 35 NEW ENG. L. REV. 321, 321–23 (2001).

30. Ten years after Habré took up residence in Senegal, a Senegalese prosecutor indicted him for torture on the basis of a suit brought by his victims. Senegal's new president removed the judge on the Habré case a few days before the court ruled, and the Appeals Chamber then quashed the indictment. Brody, *supra* note 29, at 321, 326, 329–30; Sansani, *supra* note 29, at 33–34.

31. NINO, *supra* note 14, at 32.

32. Brazil's amnesty, for instance, covered both those who had committed political crimes and military and police agents who had violated human rights. NINO, *supra* note 14, at 33–34; Roseann M. Latore, *Coming Out of the Dark: Achieving Justice for Victims of Human Rights Violations by South American Military Regimes,* 25 B.C. INT'L & COMP. L. REV. 419, 425 (2002). El Salvador granted perpetrators an amnesty only days after the release of a truth commission report naming the perpetrators. Margaret Popkin & Naomi Roht-Arriaza, *Truth as Justice: Investigatory Commissions in Latin America, in* 1 TRANSITIONAL JUSTICE: HOW EMERGING DEMOCRACIES RECKON WITH FORMER REGIMES 262, 283 (Neil J. Kritz ed., 1995); Douglass W. Cassel, Jr., *International Truth Commissions and Justice, in* 1 TRANSITIONAL JUSTICE: HOW EMERGING DEMOCRACIES RECKON WITH FORMER REGIMES 326, 327 (Neil J. Kritz ed., 1995). In Uruguay, the two major political parties enacted a blanket amnesty, relinquishing the state's right to prosecute crimes committed before March 1985 by military and police officials either for political reasons or in fulfillment of their functions. Uruguayan citizens challenged the amnesty law, but after a government-backed scare campaign in which General Hugo Medina asserted that the country would be threatened if the amnesty were overturned, a majority voted to maintain the amnesty law. ALEXANDRA BARAHONA DE BRITO, HUMAN RIGHTS AND DEMOCRATIZATION IN LATIN AMERICA: URUGUAY AND CHILE 126–27 (1997). More recently, in 1995, the Peruvian Congress enacted a blanket amnesty, covering both common and military crimes originating from the "fight against terrorism" between May 1980 and June 1995 but granting immunity only to "the Military, Police, or Civilian Personnel." William W. Burke-White, *Reframing Impunity: Applying Liberal International Law Theory to an Analysis of Amnesty Legislation,* 42 HARV. INT'L L.J. 467, 486–87 (2001). *See also* Douglass Cassel, *Lessons from the Americas: Guidelines for International Response to Amnesties for Atrocities,* L. & CONTEMP. PROBS., Autumn 1996, at 197, 200–01.

33. Law of Amnesty, No. 2.191 (Apr. 18, 1978) (Chile).

34. Pinochet had drafted a constitution that envisaged the country passing to a protected democracy under the tutelage of the military. According to one commentator: "Pinochet's men designed and scheduled the transfer of power to civilian hands on their

terms, and put themselves in position to secure significant advantages within the new democratic order." David Pion-Berlin, *To Prosecute or to Pardon? Human Rights Decisions in the Latin American Southern Cone, in* 1 TRANSITIONAL JUSTICE: HOW EMERGING DEMOCRACIES RECKON WITH FORMER REGIMES 82, 89–90 (Neil J. Kritz ed., 1995). The constitution provided for a plebiscite to determine whether Pinochet should remain in power, and in 1988, a narrow majority rejected the continuation of his rule. BARAHONA DE BRITO, *supra* note 32, at 98; NINO, *supra* note 14, at 37.

35. BARAHONA DE BRITO, *supra* note 32, at 105; Mark Ensalaco, *Truth Commissions for Chile and El Salvador: A Report and Assessment*, 16 HUM. RTS. Q. 656, 657 & n.3 (1994).

36. NINO, *supra* note 14, at 37.

37. Ensalaco, *supra* note 35, at 662.

38. THE GUATEMALAN COMMISSION FOR HISTORICAL CLARIFICATION, *Guatemala: Memory of Silence*, at I, paras. 2, 66, *available at* http://shr.aaas.org/guatemala/ceh/report/english/intro.html [hereinafter Guatemalan Truth Commission Report]. Guatemala did subsequently adopt a partial amnesty law, but it excluded from the amnesty crimes of genocide, torture, and forced disappearance as well as crimes that are not subject to a statute of limitations or that do not permit the extinction of criminal responsibility. Raquel Aldana-Pindell, *In Vindication of Justiciable Victims' Rights to Truth and Justice for State-Sponsored Claims*, 35 VAND. J. TRANSNAT'L L. 1399, 1480 n.479 (2002) (translating the provisions of the amnesty law).

39. Nathanial Heasley et al., *Impunity in Guatemala: The State's Failure to Provide Justice in the Massacre Cases*, 16 AM. U. INT'L L. REV. 1115, 1120 (2001).

40. Aldana-Pindell, *supra* note 38, at 1489; Andrew N. Keller, *To Name or Not to Name? The Commission for Historical Clarification in Guatemala, Its Mandate, and the Decision Not to Identify Individual Perpetrators*, 13 FLA. J. INT'L L. 289, 290 (2001).

41. Heasley et al., *supra* note 39, at 1150–51.

42. Bosnia's president, Alija Izetbegović, asked for the deployment of preventative peacekeepers in 1991, and he pleaded for preventative NATO air strikes when fighting broke out in 1992, but those requests fell on deaf ears. Even after reports of Serb-run death camps became known, the United States was not inclined to act, and Britain and France insisted on limiting international action in Bosnia to a relief effort assisted by the U.N. Protection Force. WARREN ZIMMERMANN, ORIGINS OF A CATASTROPHE: YUGOSLAVIA AND ITS DESTROYERS xii, 172, 215 (rev. ed. 1999); SCHARF, *supra* note 2, at 30–32.

43. Resolution 764 reaffirmed that all parties to the Yugoslav conflict were required to comply with international humanitarian law and that those who committed or ordered the commission of grave breaches of the Geneva Conventions were individually responsible for war crimes. S.C. Res. 764, para. 10, U.N. Doc. S/RES/764 (July 13, 1992). Resolution 771, issued in August 1991, required member states to report violations of international humanitarian law to the Security Council. S.C. Res. 771, para. 5, U.N. Doc. S/RES/771 (Aug. 13, 1992). The Security Council's economic embargo against Serbia was riddled with loopholes, at Russia's insistence, which allowed Serbia to circumvent it easily. SCHARF, *supra* note 2, at 34.

44. S.C. Res. 781, U.N. Doc. S/RES/781 (Oct. 9, 1992).

45. SCHARF, *supra* note 2, at 35–36. It was not until March 1993 that the Security Council authorized NATO to enforce the no-fly zone, and it was not until nearly a year later that NATO would finally take action to shoot down Serb aircraft violating the ban. *Id*. at 36.

46. S.C. Res. 780, para. 2, U.N. Doc. S/RES/780 (Oct. 6, 1992).

47. The commission's second chairman, M. Cherif Bassiouni, maintained that U.N. officials were fearful of the Commission because they believed "that the top priority of the Security Council is to achieve a political settlement, and that everything that impedes this goal should really be checked." IAIN GUEST, ON TRIAL: THE UNITED NATIONS, WAR CRIMES, AND THE FORMER YUGOSLAVIA 93–94 (1995).

48. M. CHERIF BASSIOUNI & PETER MANIKAS, THE LAW OF THE INTERNATIONAL CRIMINAL TRIBUNAL FOR THE FORMER YUGOSLAVIA 207 (1996). The international community's failure to support the commission led its first chairman, Fritz Karlshoven, to resign in protest. The commission's subsequent chairman, M. Cherif Bassiouni, was able to get the commission's work underway by relying on volunteer attorneys and law students and $800,000 he obtained in grants from various foundations. SCHARF, *supra* note 2, at 46–47.

49. BASSIOUNI & MANIKAS, *supra* note 48, at 202–03; THEODOR MERON, WAR CRIMES LAW COMES OF AGE 282 (1998); Anthony D'Amato, Editorial Comment, *Peace vs. Accountability in Bosnia*, 88 AM. J. INT'L L. 500, 500–02 (1994); Ivan Simonović, *The Role of the ICTY in the Development of International Criminal Adjudication*, 23 FORDHAM INT'L L.J. 440, 444–45 (1999).

50. SCHARF, *supra* note 2, at xv; *see also* Christian Tomuschat, *International Criminal Prosecution: The Precedent of Nuremberg Confirmed*, 5 CRIM. L.F. 237, 237 (1994) ("One may call it truly amazing that the international community, acting through the Security Council, has been able to set up two international criminal jurisdictions in the recent past.").

51. Ruth Wedgewood, *The Evolution of United Nations Peacekeeping*, 28 CORNELL INT'L L.J. 631, 638 (1995).

52. VIRGINIA MORRIS & MICHAEL P. SCHARF, 1 THE INTERNATIONAL CRIMINAL TRIBUNAL FOR RWANDA 59–60 (1998) [hereinafter MORRIS & SCHARF, ICTR]. For a description of the U.N. decision-making that led to the withdrawal, see LINDA MELVERN, CONSPIRACY TO MURDER: THE RWANDAN GENOCIDE 179–81, 186–88, 196–203, 214–20 (2004).

53. Report of the United Nations Commissioner for Human Rights, Mr. José Ayala Lasso, on his Mission to Rwanda, 11–12 May 1994, at para. 32, U.N. Doc. E/CN.4/S-3/3 (1994).

54. POWER, *supra* note 20, at 359.

55. *Report of the Secretary-General on the Establishment of the Commission of Experts pursuant to paragraph 1 of Security Council Resolution 935 (1994) of 1 July 1994*, U.N. Doc. S/1994/879 (July 26, 1994).

56. Rwanda had initially proposed the establishment of an international tribunal and had participated in the deliberations on the ICTR statute, but it ultimately voted against Security Council Resolution 955 establishing the ICTR and leveled a number of criticisms against the tribunal, including its inability to impose the death penalty and its location in

Tanzania rather than in Rwanda. *See generally,* Payam Akhavan, Current Developments, *The International Criminal Tribunal for Rwanda: The Politics and Pragmatics of Punishment,* 90 AM. J. INT'L L. 501, 504–08 (1996).

57. Rome Statute of the International Criminal Court, July 17, 1998, U.N. Doc. A/Conf.183/9 [hereinafter Rome Statute].

58. Germany provided both restitution for war-related property confiscations and compensation to victims of Nazi persecution. The Federal Compensation Law, pursuant to which Germany compensated victims of the Nazis, was sweeping in its coverage. It provided compensation for "physical injury and the loss of freedom, property, income, professional, or financial advancement if the loss resulted from persecution for political, social, religious, or ideological reasons." RUTI G. TEITEL, TRANSITIONAL JUSTICE 122–23 (2000).

59. *See* Naomi Roht-Arriaza, *The Need for Moral Reconstruction in the Wake of Past Human Rights Violations: An Interview with José Zalaquett, in* HUMAN RIGHTS IN POLITICAL TRANSITIONS: GETTYSBURG TO BOSNIA 195, 198 (Carla Hesse & Robert Post eds., 1999); BARAHONA DE BRITO, *supra* note 32, at 206. Chile had provided health benefits for torture victims, however. Roht-Arriaza, *supra* at 198. Following the publication of a report that documented thousands of state-sponsored tortures, Chilean president Ricardo Lagos, in November 2004, offered pensions to the more than twenty-eight thousand torture victims. *Chile Torture Victims Win Payout,* BBC NEWS, Nov. 29, 2004.

60. HORACIO VERBITSKY, THE FLIGHT: CONFESSIONS OF AN ARGENTINE DIRTY WARRIOR 166 (1996) (Afterward by Juan E. Méndez describing the reparations plan).

61. Larry Rohter, *Argentine Default Reopens "Dirty War" Wounds,* N.Y. TIMES, Mar. 12, 2002; Christina M. Wilson, Note, *Argentina's Reparation Bonds: An Analysis of Continuing Obligations,* 28 FORDHAM INT'L L.J. 786, 792–93 (2005). Only in March 2005 did Argentina reach a settlement in which it agreed to pay creditors, at most, thirty cents on each dollar. Larry Rohter, *Argentina Announces Deal on Its Debt Default,* N.Y. TIMES, Mar. 4, 2005.

62. Promotion of National Unity and Reconciliation Act, No. 34 of 1995, at Preamble and Ch. 5, *available at* www.doj.gov.za/trc/legal/act9534.htm [hereinafter South African TRC Act].

63. Wendy Orr, *Reparation Delayed Is Healing Retarded, in* LOOKING BACK, REACHING FORWARD: REFLECTIONS ON THE TRUTH AND RECONCILIATION COMMISSION OF SOUTH AFRICA 239, 246–47 (Charles Villa-Vicencio & Wilhelm Verwoerd eds., 2000); Catherine Jenkins, *After the Dry White Season: The Dilemmas of Reparation and Reconstruction in South Africa,* 16 S. AFRICAN J. HUM. RTS. 415, 476 (2000).

64. Ginger Thompson, *South Africa to Pay $3900 to Each Family of Apartheid Victims Families,* N.Y. TIMES, Apr. 16, 2003. For a detailed discussion of the effort to provide reparations in South Africa, see Erin Daly, *Reparations in South Africa: A Cautionary Tale,* 33 U. MEM. L. REV. 367 (2003).

65. *Law on Extrajudicial Rehabilitation ("Large Restitution Law")* (Czech and Slovak Federal Republic 1991), *reprinted in* CENTRAL AND EASTERN EUROPEAN LEGAL TEXTS (March 1991).

66. Federal Republic of Germany and German Democratic Republic, Treaty on the Establishment of German Unity, art. 41 and Annex III, *done at* Berlin, Aug. 31, 1990, *reprinted in* 30 I.L.M. 457 (1991).

67. Restitution of Land Rights Act 22 of 1994, *assented to* Nov. 17, 1994.

68. For a careful treatment of the questions that arise and their implications, see TEITEL, *supra* note 58, at 139.

69. Civil Liberties Act of 1988, Pub. L. No. 100-383, 102 Stat. 903 (1988) (codified at 50 U.S.C. § 1989B [2000]).

70. The Guatemalan Truth Commission Report stated, for instance, that the "State also tried to stigmatise and blame the victims and the country's social organisations, making them into criminals in the public eye and thus [turning them] into 'legitimate' targets for repression." Guatemalan Truth Commission Report, *supra* note 38, at Conclusions I, para. 49. As Naomi Roht-Arriaza put it: "[I]n Latin America, *por algo sera* ("they must have done something") was the watchword among the silent and terrorized majority watching their neighbors and colleagues disappear. Those killed were often derided as subversives and terrorists, worthy of no better fate." Naomi Roht-Arriaza, *Reparations Decisions and Dilemmas*, 27 HASTINGS INT'L & COMP. L. REV. 157, 160 (2004). The South African committee charged with making reparations recommendations was named the Reparation and Rehabilitation Committee precisely because reparations do act to rehabilitate victims in the political sphere. *See* TEITEL, *supra* note 58, at 137.

71. TEITEL, *supra* note 58, at 137.

72. 28 U.S.C. § 1350 (2000). *See also* Torture Victims Protection Act of 1991, Pub. L. No. 102-256, 106 Stat. 73 (1992), which authorizes civil suits against anyone who, under color of law of any foreign nation, tortures or summarily executes another person.

73. Plaintiffs in American civil suits have had difficulty collecting their judgments because defendants seldom have assets in the United States. *See* John F. Murphy, *Civil Liability for the Commission of International Crimes as an Alternative to Criminal Prosecution*, 12 HARV. HUM. RTS. J. 1, 49 (1999).

74. President Reagan issued a statement that read: "No payment can make up for those lost years. What is most important in this bill has less to do with property than with honor. For here we admit wrong." President Bush sent individual letters of apology to survivors. MINOW, *supra* note 16, at 112–13.

75. President William J. Clinton, Remarks in Apology for Study Done in Tuskegee (May 16, 1997), *available at* http://www.cmh.pitt.edu/presremarks.html.

76. MINOW, *supra* note 16, at 113–14.

77. *See* Onuma Yasuaki, *Japanese War Guilt and Postwar Responsibilities of Japan*, 20 BERKELEY J. INT'L L. 600, 606 (2002).

78. Norimitsu Onishi, *Japan Apologizes to China for Injuries from Remnants of War*, N.Y. TIMES, Aug. 13, 2003, at A5.

79. MINOW, *supra* note 16, at 112.

80. *Apologies All Around*, TRANSITIONS ONLINE (Prague), Sept. 15, 2003; *Political Parties in Croatia Differ on President's Apology for War Crimes*, BBC WORLDWIDE MONITORING, Sept. 12, 2003.

81. *See, e.g.*, Daniel W. Shuman, *The Role of Apology in Tort Law*, 83 JUDICATURE 180, 186 (2000); Chad W. Bryan, *Precedent for Reparations? A Look at Historical Movements for Redress and Where Awarding Reparations for Slavery Might Fit*, 54 ALA. L. REV. 599, 599–600 (2003). A 1995 suit brought by African American plaintiffs seeking, among other things, an apology for slavery was dismissed for lack of standing, Cato v. United States, 70 F. 3d 1103, 1111 (1995), and a bill introduced into the House of Representatives in 1997 calling for an apology for slavery, H.R. Res. 96, 105th Cong. (1997), similarly went nowhere, which is not surprising, given that contemporaneous polls showed that 61 percent of those polled opposed the government's issuing an apology, Bryan, *supra* at 605–06.

82. *See* Mark S. Ellis & Elizabeth Hutton, *Policy Implications of World War II Reparations and Restitution as Applied to the Former Yugoslavia*, 20 BERKELEY J. INT'L L. 342, 349 n.37 (2002).

83. Maki Arakawa, *A New Forum for Comfort Women: Fighting Japan in United States Federal Court*, 16 BERKELEY WOMEN'S L.J. 174, 183 (2001).

84. MINOW, *supra* note 16, at 105.

85. PUMLA GOBODO-MADIKIZELA, A HUMAN BEING DIED THAT NIGHT: A SOUTH AFRICAN STORY OF FORGIVENESS 14 (2003).

86. LYN S. GRAYBILL, TRUTH & RECONCILIATION IN SOUTH AFRICA: MIRACLE OR MODEL? 48 (2002).

87. MINOW, *supra* note 16, at 77.

88. Elizabeth Kiss, *Moral Ambition Within and Beyond Political Constraints: Reflections on Restorative Justice, in* TRUTH V. JUSTICE 68, 82 (Robert I. Rotberg & Dennis Thompson eds., 2000).

89. *See* Prosecutor v. Plavšić, Case No. IT-00-39&40/1-S, Transcript, at 593 (Dec. 17, 2002) (testimony of Alex Boraine).

90. MINOW, *supra* note 16, at 115.

91. PRISCILLA B. HAYNER, UNSPEAKABLE TRUTHS: FACING THE CHALLENGE OF TRUTH COMMISSIONS 26 (2002). Other, more recent, official apologies include the "appeal for forgiveness made by the President of [Guatemala] on 29 December 1998, and the partial appeal for forgiveness made by the Guatemalan National Revolutionary Unity on 19 February 1998." Guatemalan Truth Commission Report, *supra* note 38, at II, and Croatian president Sanader's apology for his country's World War II atrocities, *Sanader Condemns "Croatia's Auschwitz*," AGENCE FRANCE-PRESSE, Mar. 16, 2004 (on file with author). Srebrenica victims' and survivors' groups have sought "a public apology" for the crimes committed at Srebrenica, *see Mothers' Association Urges Re-examination of All Aspects of Srebrenica Massacre*, BBC WORLDWIDE MONITORING, Oct. 10, 2003, showing the importance of symbolic gestures even as a response to unspeakable brutality.

92. The Secretary General, *The Rule of Law and Transitional Justice in Conflict and Post-Conflict Societies*, delivered to the Security Council, para. 50, U.N. Doc. S/2004/616 (Aug. 23, 2004) [hereinafter *The Rule of Law and Transitional Justice*]. Priscilla Hayner documents twenty-one truth commissions in her definitive work on the subject: these truth commissions investigated atrocities in Argentina, Bolivia, Burundi, Chad, Chile, El Salvador, Ecuador, Haiti, Germany, Guatemala, Nepal, Nigeria, Sierra Leone, Sri Lanka,

South Africa, Uganda, Uruguay, and Zimbabwe. Uganda saw two truth commissions, one in 1974 and one in 1986, while South Africa saw three, two established by the African National Congress (ANC) to investigate abuses in ANC detention camps and the very famous South African Truth and Reconciliation Commission, which was tasked with investigating gross human rights abuses that took place during the apartheid era. HAYNER, *supra* note 91, at 32–71. *See also* KENNETH CHRISTIE, THE SOUTH AFRICAN TRUTH COMMISSION 54–55, 58–59 (2000) (comparing and contrasting nineteen truth commissions).

93. The truth commission established by the Philippines was created without staff or budget and was quickly overwhelmed by a large number of complaints. The Ugandan Truth Commission established in the 1980s was likewise handicapped by insufficient resources, as was the Chadian Truth Commission, which lacked appropriate vehicles and office space, Priscilla B. Hayner, *Fifteen Truth Commissions—1974 to 1994: A Comparative Study*, 16 HUM. RTS. Q. 597, 620, 623–24 (1994); BARAHONA DE BRITO, *supra* note 32, at 25.

94. The Uruguayan Truth Commission and the first Ugandan Truth Commission operated in difficult political circumstances. The Chadian commission "received threats from former security personnel who had been rehired into the new intelligence service" that were sufficiently intimidating that three-fourths of the original commissioners had to be replaced, while the Ugandan truth commissioners "were targeted by the state in apparent reprisal for their work," with one losing his employment, another framed with murder charges and sentenced to death, and a third having to flee the country to avoid arrest. Hayner, *Fifteen Truth Commissions*, *supra* note 93, at 612–13, 616, 624.

95. Guatemalan Truth Commission Report, *supra* note 38, at Conclusions II, para. 111.

96. Keller, *supra* note 40, at 300–01.

97. The commission nonetheless had difficulty obtaining relevant documents, including those detailing the United States' support of the El Salvadoran government. The commission also had difficulty persuading victims and witnesses to testify publicly because they feared retaliation, so the commission consequently was compelled to take confidential testimony. Thomas Buergenthal, *The United Nations Truth Commission for El Salvador*, 27 VAND. J. TRANSNAT'L L. 497, 507, 510, 513 (1994); U.N. Commission on the Truth for El Salvador, *Report of the Commission on the Truth for El Salvador: From Madness to Hope*, 23–24, U.N. Doc. S/25500, Annexes (1993) (English version) [hereinafter El Salvador Truth Commission Report].

98. The Chadian Truth Commission was the first to publish names. *See* Hayner, *Fifteen Truth Commissions*, *supra* note 93, at 625. The Honduran report took an intermediate approach: it focused on the institutional responsibility of the army high command and certain special units but did name the names of the heads of those units as potential targets of a judicial investigation. Popkin & Roht-Arriaza, *supra* note 32, at 281.

99. Buergenthal, *supra* note 97, at 520.

100. El Salvador Truth Commission Report, *supra* note 97, at 25. Some commentators have argued that naming "culprits who ha[ve] not defended themselves and were not obliged to do so [is] the moral equivalent to convicting someone without due process." José Zalaquett, *Introduction to* 1 Report of the Chilean National Commission on Truth and Reconciliation xxxii (Philip Berryman trans., 1993).

101. *See, e.g.*, Sierra Leone Truth and Reconciliation Commission Report, Vol. 2, Ch. 2, paras. 5, 145, 155, 156, 172, 206, 228, 261, 330, 363 (2004), *available at* http://www .trcsierraleone.org/pdf/FINAL%20VOLUME%20TWO/VOLUME%202.pdf [hereinafter Sierra Leone TRC Report].

102. *Id.* at para. 405.

103. *Id.* at paras. 36, 444–552.

104. Books describing the South African TRC include CHRISTIE, *supra* note 92; DOR- OTHY SHEA, THE SOUTH AFRICAN TRUTH COMMISSION (2000); ANTIJE KROG, COUNTRY OF MY SKULL: GUILT, SORROW, AND THE LIMITS OF FORGIVENESS IN THE NEW SOUTH AFRICA (1999); LOOKING BACK, REACHING FORWARD: REFLECTIONS ON THE TRUTH AND RECONCILIATION COMMISSION OF SOUTH AFRICA (Charles Villa-Vicencio & Wilhelm Verwoerd eds., 2000); JILLIAN EDELSTEIN, TRUTH & LIES: STORIES FROM THE TRUTH AND RECONCILIATION COMMISSION IN SOUTH AFRICA (2002).

105. HAYNER, *supra* note 91, at 42.

106. South African TRC Act, *supra* note 62, at arts. 18–20. For a more detailed treat- ment of the TRC's amnesty powers and decisions, see Ronald Slye, *Justice and Amnesty, in* LOOKING BACK, REACHING FORWARD: REFLECTIONS ON THE TRUTH AND RECONCILI- ATION COMMISSION OF SOUTH AFRICA 174 (Charles Villa-Vicencio & Wilhelm Verwoerd eds., 2000). For a more detailed discussion of the requirements for amnesty, see Emily H. McCarthy, Symposium Note, *South Africa's Amnesty Process: A Viable Route toward Truth and Reconciliation?*, 3 MICH. J. RACE & L. 183, 203–39 (1997).

107. HAYNER, *supra* note 91, at 43; SHEA, *supra* note 104, at 14–15; Charles Villa-Vicen- cio, *Why Perpetrators Should Not Always Be Prosecuted: Where the International Criminal Court and Truth Commissions Meet*, 49 EMORY L.J. 205, 209 (2000).

108. *See* CHRISTIE, *supra* note 92, at 140; HAYNER, *supra* note 91, at 43.

109. KROG, *supra* note 104, at 158.

110. Colleen Scott, *Combating Myth and Building Reality, in* LOOKING BACK, REACH- ING FORWARD: REFLECTIONS ON THE TRUTH AND RECONCILIATION COMMISSION OF SOUTH AFRICA 107, 109 (Charles Villa-Vicencio & Wilhelm Verwoerd eds., 2000).

111. HAYNER, *supra* note 91, at 44.

112. David Goodman, *Why Killers Should Go Free: Lessons from South Africa*, 22 WASH. Q. 1, 6 (1999).

113. Kiss, *supra* note 88, at 77.

114. *The Role of Forgiveness in the Law*, Symposium, 27 FORDHAM URB. L.J. 1347, 1403 (2000) (comments of Martha Minow). *But see* KROG, *supra* note 104, at 95 (describing Jef- frey Benzien's amnesty hearing in which Benzien within the first few minutes "manage[d] to manipulate most of his victims back into the roles of their previous relationship— where he has the power and they the fragility").

115. Kiss, *supra* note 88, at 77; KROG, *supra* note 104, at 119. David Goodman, for in- stance, describes Jacques Hecter's "flat, emotionless" apology, and his subsequent asser- tion that "I'm not really fuckin' sorry for what I did. . . . And I'd do it again if the circum- stances called for it." Goodman, *supra* note 112, at 4.

116. As one South African perpetrator commented, "[t]he victims' lawyer says we must talk to them, but it is difficult . . . because every time we say we're sorry, they shake their

heads and say they don't accept it." KROG, *supra* note 104, at 117. *See also* Paul Lansing & Julie C. King, *South Africa's Truth and Reconciliation Commission: The Conflict between Individual Justice and National Healing in the Post-Apartheid Age*, 15 ARIZ. J. INT'L & COMP. L. 753, 772 (1998); Robyn Dixon, *A Decade after Apartheid: The Official Truth Falls Short for Many*, L.A. TIMES, May 30, 2004, at A5 (reporting on a victim who refused to "have a beer" with the person who murdered his mother and sister). Some victims resented what they perceived as pressure to forgive. *See* Charles Villa-Vicencio, *Getting on with Life: A Move towards Reconciliation, in* LOOKING BACK, REACHING FORWARD: REFLECTIONS ON THE TRUTH AND RECONCILIATION COMMISSION OF SOUTH AFRICA 199, 201 (Charles Villa-Vicencio & Wilhelm Verwoerd eds., 2000). Although Alex Boraine asserted that it was not the intention of the TRC to demand forgiveness, ALEX BORAINE, A COUNTRY UNMASKED 356 (2000), some commentators believe that the TRC did just that. Stuart Wilson, *The Myth of Restorative Justice: Truth, Reconciliation and the Ethics of Amnesty*, 17 S. AFR. J. HUM. RTS. 531, 548 (2001).

117. The TRC institutional hearings had mixed results. The legal hearings were particularly disappointing because judges refused to appear. Kiss, *supra* note 88, at 78; *see generally* DAVID DYZENHAUS, JUDGING THE JUDGES, JUDGING OURSELVES: TRUTH, RECONCILIATION AND THE APARTHEID LEGAL ORDER (1998). For a description of the business hearings, see KROG, *supra* note 104, at 314–17.

118. For a description of the exhumations carried out by the South African TRC, see KROG, *supra* note 104, at 271–72. Krog also reports on the request of a South African widow "for something to bury—even if it was just a piece of bone or a handful of ash." *Id.* at 44.

119. MINOW, *supra* note 16, at 59–60.

120. For a discussion of the healing experiences of some victims who testified at the South African TRC, see HAYNER, *supra* note 91, at 138–39. Elizabeth Kiss further reports that "after testifying before the [South African] TRC, one . . . man, blinded as the result of an assault by a police officer, replied, 'I feel what has been making me sick all the time is the fact that I couldn't tell my story. But now . . . it feels like I got my sight back by coming here.'" Kiss, *supra* note 88, at 72; Antije Krog reproduces a letter from a victim who, after testifying before the South African TRC stated, "It's as if I have been freed from a prison that I've been in for eighteen years." KROG, *supra* note 104, at 191–93.

Some psychologists are skeptical, however, that a one-time catharsis can result in long-term psychological healing. HAYNER, *supra* note 91, at 139; Brandon Hamber, *Does the Truth Heal? A Psychological Perspective on Political Strategies for Dealing with the Legacy of Political Violence, in* BURYING THE PAST: MAKING PEACE AND DOING JUSTICE AFTER CIVIL CONFLICT 155, 160 (Nigel Biggar ed., 2003). Further, relating the brutal details of their mistreatment in one sitting without psychological support leaves some victims at serious risk for developing post-traumatic stress disorder. HAYNER, *supra* note 91, at 139.

121. HAYNER, *supra* note 91, at 164.

122. KROG, *supra* note 104, at 62.

123. *See* HAYNER, *supra* note 91, at 30, 155; TEITEL, *supra* note 58, at 69; Kiss, *supra* note 88, at 71–72; Robert I. Rotberg, *Truth Commissions and the Provision of Truth, Jus-*

tice, and Reconciliation, in TRUTH V. JUSTICE 3, 6 (Robert I. Rotberg & Dennis Thompson eds., 2000).

124. TEITEL, *supra* note 58, at 79.

Chapter 2

125. S.C. Res. 808, at 2, U.N. Doc. S/RES/808 (Feb. 22, 1993).

126. Rome Statute, *supra* note 57, at Preamble.

127. Catherine Cissé, *The International Tribunals for the Former Yugoslavia and Rwanda: Some Elements of Comparison*, 7 TRANSNAT'L L. & CONTEMP. PROBS. 103, 114 (1997).

128. HUMAN RIGHTS FIRST, A HUMAN RIGHTS FIRST REPORT ON THE ICTR AND NATIONAL TRIALS, at IV(A) (1997), *available at* http://www.humanrightsfirst.org/pubs/descriptions/rwanda.htm.

129. In 1997, the U.N. Office of Internal Oversight Services issued a report criticizing the ICTR's administration and management, finding, among other things, that not a single administrative area of the ICTR registry "functioned effectively." *Financing the International Criminal Tribunal, Report of the Secretary-General on the Activities of the Office of Internal Oversight Services*, para. 9, U.N. Doc. A/51/789 (Feb. 6, 1997).

130. Sara Darehshori, *Inching toward Justice in Rwanda*, N.Y. TIMES, Sept. 8, 1998.

131. For a discussion of the difficulties the ICTY has faced in obtaining custody over defendants, see Gabrielle Kirk McDonald, *Problems, Obstacles and Achievements of the ICTY*, 2 J. INT'L CRIM. JUST. 558, 559–67 (2004). During 2005, the ICTY began experiencing considerably greater success in obtaining custody over indicted people. From November 2004 to June 2005, the tribunal obtained custody over twenty-two suspects, Press Release, ICTY, Statement by Judge Theodor Meron, President, International Criminal Tribunal for the former Yugoslavia, to the Security Council, TM/MOW/976e (June 13, 2005) [hereinafter Meron June 2005 Statement to the Security Council], a development that resulted largely from the economic pressure that the international community in general and the European Union in particular exerted on the states of the former Yugoslavia to cooperate with the tribunal. *See* Bogdan Ivanisević and Géraldine Mattioli, Human Rights Watch, *Real Progress in The Hague*, Mar. 29, 2005, http://hrw.org/english/docs/2005/03/29/serbia10386.htm.

132. *See Secretary-General's Report on Aspects of Establishing an International Tribunal for the Prosecution of Persons Responsible for Serious Violations of International Humanitarian Law Committed in the Territory of the former Yugoslavia*, para. 106, U.N. Doc. S/25704 (1993), *reprinted in* 32 I.L.M. 1159 (1993).

133. Press Release, ICTY, Address by His Excellency, Judge Claude Jorda, President of the International Criminal Tribunal for the Former Yugoslavia, to the United Nations Security Council, JDH/P.I.S./708-e (Oct. 30, 2002), *available at* http://www.un.org/icty/pressreal/p708-e.htm. Before 2002, the average ICTR trial lasted between one and two years. Statement by the President of the ICTR to the United Nations General Assembly, Oct. 28, 2002, *available at* http://69.94.11.53/ENGLISH/speeches/pillay281002ga.htm

[hereinafter ICTR President's 2002 General Assembly Statement]. More recent large-scale ICTR trials are now taking longer to complete.

134. Together the ICTY and ICTR spend approximately $250 million per year. ICTY at a Glance, General Information, updated May 8, 2006 (noting a budget for 2006–07 of $276,474,100), *available at* http://www.un.org/icty/glance-e/index.htm; Coalition for International Criminal Justice, Frequently Asked Questions -ICTR, http://www.cij.org/index.cfm?fuseaction=faqs&tribunalID=2#q7 (noting a budget of $255,909,500 for 2004–05). Before and after the recent spate of guilty pleas at the ICTY, each tribunal would render judgments in perhaps two to five cases in a typical year. Eleventh Annual Report of the International Tribunal for the Prosecution of Persons Responsible for Serious Violations of International Humanitarian Law Committed in the Territory of the Former Yugoslavia since 1991, para. 49, U.N. Doc. A/59/219, S/2004/627 (Aug. 13, 2004) (reporting that the Trial Chambers rendered two final judgments on the merits and nine sentencing judgments following guilty pleas); Ninth Annual Report of the International Tribunal for the Prosecution of Persons Responsible for Serious Violations of International Humanitarian Law Committed in the Territory of the Former Yugoslavia since 1991, Summary, U.N. Doc. A/57/379-S/2002/985 (Aug. 14, 2002) (reporting that Trial Chambers had issued five judgments during the year) [hereinafter ICTY 2002 Annual Report]; Tenth Annual Report of the International Criminal Tribunal for the Prosecution of Persons Responsible for Genocide and Other Serious Violations of International Humanitarian Law Committed in the Territory of Rwanda and Rwandan Citizens Responsible for Genocide and Other Such Violations Committed in the Territory of Neighbouring States between 1 January and 31 December 1994, paras. 10, 21, U.N. Doc. A/60/229-S/2005/534 (Aug. 15, 2005) (reporting the Trial Chambers disposed of three cases during the year, one of which was disposed of by means of a guilty plea) [hereinafter ICTR 2005 Annual Report]; Seventh Annual Report of the International Criminal Tribunal for the Prosecution of Persons Responsible for Genocide and Other Serious Violations of International Humanitarian Law Committed in the Territory of Rwanda and Rwandan Citizens Responsible for Genocide and Other Such Violations Committed in the Territory of Neighbouring States between 1 January and 31 December 1994, para. 4, U.N. Doc. A/57/163-S/2002/733 (July 2, 2002) (indicating that no judgments were issued that year) [hereinafter ICTR 2002 Annual Report]; Sixth Annual Report of the International Criminal Tribunal for the Prosecution of Persons Responsible for Genocide and Other Serious Violations of International Humanitarian Law Committed in the Territory of Rwanda and Rwandan Citizens Responsible for Genocide and Other Such Violations Committed in the Territory of Neighbouring States between 1 January and 31 December 1994, para. 1, U.N. Doc. A/56/351-S/2001/863 (Sept. 14, 2001) (reporting that one Trial Chamber judgment was issued).

135. Prosecutor v. Kordić, Case No. IT-95-14/2-T, Judgement, para. 3 (Feb. 26, 2001).

136. Prosecutor v. Blaškić, Case No. IT-94-14-T, Judgement, para. 19 (Mar. 3, 2000) [hereinafter Blaškić Judgement].

137. Prosecutor v. Brđanin, Case No. IT-99-36-T, Judgement, Annex B, para. 1180 (Sept. 1, 2004). ICTR trials have typically featured fewer witnesses. *See* Prosecutor v. Akayesu, Case No. ICTR-96-4-T, Judgement, para. 24 (Sept. 2, 1998) (reporting that forty-one wit-

nesses were heard and 155 exhibits introduced) [hereinafter Akayesu Judgement]. Prosecutor v. Elizaphan and Gérard Ntakirutimana, Case Nos. ICTR-96-10 & ICTR-96-17-T, Judgement and Sentence, para. 26 (Feb. 21, 2003) [Ntakirutimana Judgement] (Feb. 21, 2003) (reporting that forty-three witnesses were heard and 149 exhibits were admitted); Nahimana Judgement, *supra* note 3, at para. 53 (noting that ninety-three witnesses were heard in a case involving three defendants).

138. *Completion Strategy of the International Criminal Tribunal for Rwanda*, U.N. Doc. S/2003/946, para. 15, Enclosure to Letter from Erik Møse, President, ICTR, to the Secretary General, Letter Dated October 3, 2003, Annex (Oct. 6, 2003) (reporting, in 2003, on a defendant who had been in custody since 1999) [hereinafter ICTR Completion Strategy Letter].

139. *See* Ralph Zacklin, *The Failings of Ad Hoc International Tribunals*, 2 J. INT'L CRIM. JUST. 541, 543 (2004); INTERNATIONAL CRIMINAL TRIBUNAL FOR RWANDA: TRIALS AND TRIBULATIONS, § 3 (Apr. 1, 1998), *available at* http://web.amnesty.org/ai.nsf/index/ior400 031998?OpenDocument&of=THEMES/INTERNATIONAL+JUSTICE; ICTR President's 2002 General Assembly Statement, *supra* note 133.

140. *See* Combs, *Copping a Plea to Genocide, supra* note 8, at 94–102.

141. In particular, they conduct more than one trial in each courtroom, holding proceedings in some cases in the mornings and in others in the afternoons. ICTR President's 2002 General Assembly Statement, *supra* note 133; ICTR 2002 Annual Report, *supra* note 134, at paras. 2–3.

142. The tribunals now permit certain proceedings to be held before one judge rather than a three-judge panel, and they permit other tasks to be performed by senior legal officers, rather than judges. In July 2001, for instance, the ICTY's Rule 65*ter* was amended to authorize a senior legal officer to perform some of the functions previously assigned to the pretrial judge. The ICTR has revised its procedural rules to allow a trial to proceed with a substitute judge if a sitting judge falls ill or is unable to attend for any other reason. ICTR R.P. & EVID. 15*bis* (2003).

143. Fifth Annual Report of the International Criminal Tribunal for the Prosecution of Persons Responsible for Genocide and Other Serious Violations of International Humanitarian Law Committed in the Territory of Rwanda and Rwandan Citizens Responsible for Genocide and Other Such Violations Committed in the Territory of Neighbouring States between 1 January and 31 December 1994, paras. 138–39, U.N. Doc. A/55/435-S/2000/927 (Oct. 2, 2000). Not all of these efforts have been successful. The prosecutor had difficulty joining ICTY cases because, during its early years, the ICTY did not have custody over a large percentage of its indictees. The ICTR did have custody over most of its indictees and thus was able to join related cases, but the cases became so large and unwieldy that the ICTR has, in general, reverted to trying single-defendant cases.

144. *See* Combs, *Copping a Plea to Genocide, supra* note 8, at 70–78; Daryl A. Mundis, *From 'Common Law' towards 'Civil Law': The Evolution of the ICTY Rules of Procedure and Evidence*, 14 LEIDEN J. INT'L L. 367 (2001).

145. ICTY at a Glance, General Information, http://www.un.org/icty/glance-e/index .htm (follow General Information hyperlink).

146. Coalition for International Criminal Justice, *supra* note 134.

147. ICTR 2005 Annual Report, *supra* note 134, at Summary.

148. *See* S.C. Res. 1503, U.N. Doc. S/RES/1503 (Aug. 28, 2003); S.C. Res. 1534, U.N. Doc. S/RES/1534 (Mar. 26, 2004).

149. In June 2005, the president of the ICTY informed the U.N. Security Council that trials could not be completed by 2008, as the Security Council had instructed, but would of necessity continue into 2009. Meron June 2005 Statement to the Security Council, *supra* note 131.

150. Press Release, ICTY, *Address by the Prosecutor of the International Criminal Tribunals for the Former Yugoslavia and Rwanda, Mrs. Carla del Ponte, to the United Nations Security Council*, JJJ/P.I.S/.709-e (Oct. 30, 2002), *available at* http://www.un.org/icty/pressreal/p709-e.htm [hereinafter Del Ponte 2002 Address]; ICTY 2002 Annual Report, *supra* note 134, at para. 6. For a discussion of the ICTR's reduction in investigations, see Letter dated 30 April 2004, from the President of the International Criminal Tribunal for the Prosecution of Persons Responsible for Genocide and Other Serious Violations of International Humanitarian Law Committed in the Territory of Rwanda and Rwandan Citizens Responsible for Genocide and Other Such Violations Committed in the Territory of Neighbouring States between 1 January and 31 December 1994 addressed to the President of the Security Council, paras. 6, 30, U.N. Doc. S/2004/341, (May 3, 2004) [hereinafter ICTR April 2004 letter to the Security Council].

151. ICTY R.P. & EVID. 28 (2004). For additional commentary on the rule and on the controversy it generated in the Office of the Prosecutor, see Daryl A. Mundis, *The Judicial Effects of the "Completion Strategies" on the* Ad Hoc *International Criminal Tribunals*, 99 AM. J. INT'L L. 142, 147–50 (2005).

152. Press Release, ICTY, Address by Carla Del Ponte, Chief Prosecutor of the International Criminal Tribunal for the Former Yugoslavia to the United Nations Security Council, CT/P.I.S./863-e (June 30, 2004).

153. ICTR April 2004 letter to the Security Council, *supra* note 150, at paras. 36–38; ICTR Completion Strategy Letter, *supra* note 138, at para. 23.

154. ICTR 2005 Annual Report, *supra* note 134, at Summary.

155. Sukhdev Chhatbar, *Priest Dismisses Rwanda Genocide Charges, Says He's Praying for the Victims*, CANADIAN PRESS, Sept. 27, 2004; Modestus Kessy, *Genocide Suspects Call Off Protest*, THE SUNDAY OBSERVER (Tanzania), Sept. 26, 2004.

156. *Report on the Operation of the International Criminal Tribunal for the Former Yugoslavia Submitted by Judge Claude Jorda, President, on Behalf of the Judges of the Tribunal*, paras. 47–54, U.N. Doc. A/55/382-S/2000/865, Annex I (May 12, 2000) *available at* http://www.un.org/icty/pressreal/RAP000620e.htm.

157. A June 2004 report from the Organization for Security and Co-operation in Europe (OSCE), for instance, concluded that "there is a considerable lack of impartiality amongst parts of the judiciary." ORG. FOR SEC. & CO-OPERATION IN EUR. MISSION TO CROATIA: SUPPLEMENTARY REPORT: WAR CRIME PROCEEDINGS IN CROATIA AND FINDINGS FROM TRIAL MONITORING, 13 (June 22, 2004) [hereinafter OSCE, SUPPLEMENTARY

REPORT]; *see also* Human Rights Watch, *Croatia: Conviction Spotlights Justice Failings*, July 19, 2004, *available at* http://hrw.org/english/docs/2004/07/19/croati.9083.htm.

158. OSCE, SUPPLEMENTARY REPORT, *supra* note 157, at 13.

159. ORG. FOR SEC. & CO-OPERATION IN EUR., MISSION TO CROATIA: BACKGROUND REPORT: DOMESTIC WAR CRIME TRIALS 2003, 6–7, June 22, 2004. The percentage of Serb defendants convicted is also considerably higher than the percentage of Croat defendants convicted. *Id.* at 7.

160. *See Croatia's Top Court Orders War Crimes Retrial*, REUTERS, Aug. 19, 2004; Human Rights Watch, *Croatia: Conviction Spotlights Justice Failings, supra* note 157, at 1.

161. *See* Prosecutor v. Kovacević, Case No. IT-01-42/2-I, Order on the Prosecutor's Request for Referral to National Authorities under Rule 11 *bis* (Jan. 20, 2005) [hereinafter Kovacević 11*bis* request].

162. Milanka Saponja-Hadzić, *Serbia Tries Hague's Patience*, IWPR's TRIBUNAL UPDATE, No. 362, June 11, 2004.

163. Natasa Kandić, *How to Protect Witnesses Who Are Seen by Public and Police as Traitors*, Feb. 6, 2004 (on file with author).

164. Press Release, ICTY, Address by his Excellency, Judge Claude Jorda, President of the International Criminal Tribunal for the Former Yugoslavia, to the United Nations Security Council, JDH/P.I.S./690-e (July 26, 2002), *available at* http://www.un.org/icty/pressreal/p690-e.htm. For further discussion of the failings of the Bosnian courts, see Amnesty International, *Bosnia-Herzegovina: Memorandum to the High Representative of Bosnia-Herzegovina*, AI Index: EUR 63/009/2002, Aug. 1, 2002, *available at* http://web.amnesty.org/library/endindex (at Search by AI index, enter EUR63/009/2002) [hereinafter *Memorandum to the High Representative*].

165. *Bosnian State Judiciary Faces Funding Crisis as Donations Dwindle*, BBC MONITORING EUROPE, June 4, 2006 (providing translated transcript of Bosnian television report). Even when foreign donations were relatively plentiful, the funding provided for the protection of victims and witnesses was inadequate. *See* AMNESTY INTERNATIONAL, REPORT 2004—BOSNIA AND HERZEGOVINA, *available at* http://web.amnesty.org/report2004/bih-summary-eng; Human Rights Watch, *The Trial of Dominik Ilijasević*, BALKANS JUSTICE BULLETIN, Jan. 2004, *available at* http://hrw.org/backgrounder/eca/balkans0104.htm, Such funding inadequacies are particularly problematic because virtually all war crimes trials that have taken place to date in Bosnia have featured harassment and intimidation of witnesses. Merdijana Sadović, *Teething Problems for Bosnian Courts*, IWPR's TRIBUNAL UPDATE, No. 358, May 15, 2004.

166. Assessments and Report of Judge Theodor Meron, President of the International Criminal Tribunal for the Former Yugoslavia, provided to the Security Council pursuant to paragraph 6 of Security Council Resolution 1534, paras. 56–61, U.N. Doc. S/2004/420, Enclosure (May 24, 2004) [hereinafter President Meron's May 2004 Letter to the President of the Security Council].

167. *Impunity Bears the Germ of Future Conflicts*, SENSE NEWS AGENCY, Oct. 11, 2004.

168. President Meron's May 2004 Letter to the President of the Security Council, *supra* note 166, at paras. 58–59; Press Release, ICTR, President and Prosecutor Update Security Council on Completion Strategy, ICTR/INFO-9-2-394(a).EN (July 6, 2004).

169. ICTR Completion Strategy Letter, *supra* note 138 at Summary.

170. S.C. Res. 1534, *supra* note 148.

171. Rome Statute, *supra* note 57, at Preamble, para. 10 & art. 17(1).

172. *Id.* at arts. 18(1), (2), (4), 19(7).

173. *Id.* at art. 19(2).

174. *Id.* at art. 17(2)(a), (c).

175. *Id.* at art. 36(2).

176. S.C. Res. 1431, U.N. Doc. S/RES/1431 (Aug. 14, 2002).

177. Rome Statute, *supra* note 57, at art. 50(1). For a discussion of the negotiations regarding the translation of ICC documents, see Socorro Flores Liera, *Publications, Languages, and Translation, in* THE INTERNATIONAL CRIMINAL COURT: ELEMENTS OF CRIMES AND RULES OF PROCEDURE AND EVIDENCE 314, 314 (Roy S. Lee ed., 2001). Determining, during the Preparatory Commission on the Rules of Procedure and Evidence, which judgments were to be considered important enough to translate into all six languages again highlighted the question of cost, with some delegations favoring a very limited approach. *Id.* at 315.

178. *See generally* Combs, *Copping a Plea to Genocide, supra* note 8, at 66–69. For a discussion of the ad hoc tribunals' powers to compel cooperation, see GÖRAN SLUITER, INTERNATIONAL CRIMINAL ADJUDICATION AND THE COLLECTION OF EVIDENCE: OBLIGATIONS OF STATES 15–39 (2002).

179. For a comparison of the enforcement powers of the ICC and those of the ad hoc tribunals, *see generally* Thomas Henquet, *Mandatory Compliance Powers* vis-à-vis *States by the* Ad Hoc *Tribunals and the International Criminal Court: A Comparative Analysis*, 12 LEIDEN J. INT'L L. 969 (1999). For a thorough discussion of the ICC's enforcement powers, see SLUITER, *supra* note 178, at 40–46.

180. Statute of the International Criminal Tribunal for the Former Yugoslavia, art. 29(2), *adopted by* S.C. Res. 827, U.N. Doc. S/RES/827 (May 25, 1993); *amended by* S.C. Res. 1166, U.N. Doc. S/RES/1166 (May 13, 1998); *amended by* S.C. Res. 1329, U.N. Doc. S/RES/1329 (Nov. 30, 2000); *amended by* S.C. Res. 1411, U.N. Doc. S/RES/1411 (May 17, 2002); *amended by* S.C. Res. 1431, U.N. Doc. S/RES/1431 (Aug. 14, 2002), *amended by* S.C. Res. 1481, U.N. Doc. S/RES/1481 (2003) [hereinafter ICTY Statute].

181. For a discussion of states' obligations to cooperate with the ICC, see Phakiso Mochochoko, *International Cooperation and Judicial Assistance, in* THE INTERNATIONAL CRIMINAL COURT: THE MAKING OF THE ROME STATUTE 305 (Roy S. Lee ed., 1999).

182. Rome Statute, *supra* note 57, at art. 93(4). The ICTY and ICTR have had difficulty obtaining information regarding Yugoslavian and Rwandan military information, but, unlike the ICC prosecutor, at least their prosecutors can complain to the Security Council since the states of the former Yugoslavia and Rwanda have an obligation to provide such information. *See* Del Ponte 2002 Address, *supra* note 150.

183. Mochochoko, *supra* note 181, at 308.

184. Rome Statute, *supra* note 57, at art. 93(3).

185. *Id*. at art. 90(6).

186. In that case, the state must "consult with the court," *id*. at art. 89(4), and can surrender the person on a temporary basis, attaching the conditions it chooses, ICC R.P. & Evid. 183, but the Rome Statute does not require the state to surrender the person at all.

187. Rome Statute, *supra* note 57, at arts. 98(1), 98(2).

188. Nearly one hundred states have concluded such agreements with the United States. *See* Coalition for the International Criminal Court, *Status of U.S. Bilateral Immunity Agreements*, Apr. 14, 2006, *available at* http://www.iccnow.org/documents/CICCFS_BIAstatusCurrent.pdf.

189. Rome Statute, *supra* note 57, at art. 94(1).

190. *Id*. at arts. 54(2), 57(3)(d), 99(4). For discussions concerning the negotiations regarding on-site investigations, see WILLIAM A. SCHABAS, AN INTRODUCTION TO THE INTERNATIONAL CRIMINAL COURT 104 (2001); Fabricio Guariglia, *Investigation and Prosecution, in* THE INTERNATIONAL CRIMINAL COURT: THE MAKING OF THE ROME STATUTE 227, 231 (Roy S. Lee ed., 1999).

191. SCHABAS, *supra* note 190, at 105 (quoting Fabricio Guariglia).

192. Rome Statute, *supra* note 57, at arts. 89(1), 91(2)(c), 99(1).

193. For a comprehensive account of the atrocities, see Sierra Leone TRC Report, *supra* note 101. For an account of the formation and activities of the Revolutionary United Front, see Ibrahim Abdullah & Patrick Muana, *The Revolutionary United Front of Sierra Leone, in* AFRICAN GUERRILLAS 172 (Christopher Clapham ed., 1998).

194. Diane Marie Amann, *Medium As Message in Sierra Leone*, 7 ILSA J. INT'L & COMP. L. 237, 238 (2001); *see also* HUMAN RIGHTS WATCH, *Getting Away with Murder, Mutilation, Rape* (1999), *available at* http://www.hrw.org/reports/1999/sierra.

195. President Kabbah sent a letter to the U.N. secretary-general asking for U.N. assistance in establishing a criminal tribunal for Sierra Leone. Annex to the Letter dated 9 August 2000, from the Permanent Representative of Sierra Leone to the United Nations addressed to the President of the Security Council, U.N. Doc. S/2000/786 Annex (Aug. 10, 2000). The Security Council consequently adopted Resolution 1315, stating that "the situation in Sierra Leone continues to constitute a threat to international peace and security in the region," and it directed the secretary-general to negotiate with the government of Sierra Leone regarding the Special Court. S.C. Res. 1315, 2 & para. 1, U.N. Doc. S/RES/1315 (Aug. 14, 2000).

196. Jess Bravin, *Tribunal in Africa May Serve as Model for Trial of Hussein*, WALL ST. J., Feb. 12, 2003; *see also* Zacklin, *supra* note 139, at 545 (labeling the Special Court for Sierra Leone as "the victim of the ICTY/ICTR experience").

197. ICTY Statute, *supra* note 180, at art. 1; S.C. Res. 955, Annex, art. 1, U.N. Doc. S/RES/955 (Nov. 8, 1994) [hereinafter ICTR Statute].

198. Letter dated December 22, 2000, from the President of the Security Council addressed to the Secretary-General, para. 2, U.N. Doc. S/2000/1234 (Dec. 22, 2000), *available at* http://documents-dds-ny.un.org/doc/UNDOC/GEN/N00/812/77/pdf/N0081277.pdf?OpenElement [hereinafter Sierra Leone Letter to the Security Council]; Statute of

the Special Court for Sierra Leone, art. 1, Jan. 16, 2002, *available at* http://www.sc-sl.org/ scsl-statute.html.

199. Daryl A. Mundis, *New Mechanisms for the Enforcement of International Humanitarian Law*, 95 AM. J. INT'L L. 934, 936 (2001); *U.N. War Crimes Court to Try 20 Suspects in Sierra Leone*, N.Y. TIMES, Jan. 4, 2002, at A8.

200. Two of the indictees, including rebel leader Foday Sankoh, died while in custody. Somini Sengupta, *African Held for War Crimes Dies in Custody of a Tribunal*, N.Y. TIMES, July 31, 2003, at A6.

201. Sierra Leone Letter to the Security Council, *supra* note 198, at para. 2; Agreement between the United Nations and the Government of Sierra Leone on the Establishment of a Special Court for Sierra Leone, art. 6, Jan. 16, 2002, *available at* http://www.specialcourt .org/documents/Agreement.htm.

202. Zacklin, *supra* note 139, at 545.

203. *Report of the Secretary-General on the Establishment of a Special Court for Sierra Leone*, para. 70, U.N. Doc. S/2000/915 (Oct. 4, 2000) [hereinafter *Report on the Establishment of a Special Court for Sierra Leone*].

204. AMNESTY INTERNATIONAL & JUDICIAL SYSTEM MONITORING PROGRAMME INDONESIA & TIMOR-LESTE, JUSTICE FOR TIMOR-LESTE: THE WAY FORWARD, § 11.4, AI Index: ASA 21/006/2004, Apr. 1, 2004 [hereinafter JUSTICE FOR TIMOR-LESTE].

205. Elisabeth Schreinemacher, *Sierra Leone War-Crimes Court Running Out of Money*, MAIL & GUARDIAN, OCT. 6, 2005; *see also Sierra Leone War Crimes Prosecutors Gather Witnesses Ahead of Trials*, AGENCE FRANCE-PRESSE, May 5, 2004; *Annan Proposes Assessed Dues to Close Sierra Leone Court's Budget Gap*, U.N. NEWS CENTRE, Mar. 11, 2004, *available at* http://www.un.org/apps/news/storyAr.asp?NewsID=10044&Cr=sierra&Cr1= &Kw1=assessed&Kw2=dues&Kw3=sierra.

206. Thierry Cruvellier, *Sierra Leone: The Cost of a Mixed Model*, INT'L JUST. TRIB., No. 27, June 13, 2005.

207. *Sierra Leone: Special Court Registrar Announces Resignation but Urged to Stay*, IRIN NEWS, Aug. 4, 2004.

208. *Report on the Establishment of a Special Court for Sierra Leone*, *supra* note 203, at para. 58.

209. Letter dated 12 July 2001 from the Secretary-General addressed to the President of the Security Council, at 2, U.N. Doc. S/2001/693 (July 12, 2001).

210. William A. Schabas, *The Relationship between Truth Commissions and International Courts: The Case of Sierra Leone*, 25 HUM. RTS. Q. 1035, 1040 (2003).

211. Cruvellier, *supra* note 206.

212. *See* HUMAN RIGHTS WATCH, Vol. 16, No. 8(A), BRINGING JUSTICE: THE SPECIAL COURT FOR SIERRA LEONE, ACCOMPLISHMENTS, SHORTCOMINGS AND NEEDED SUPPORT, 21–31.

213. Hansjörg Strohmeyer, *Collapse and Reconstruction of a Judicial System: The United Nations Missions in Kosovo and East Timor*, 95 AM. J. INT'L L. 46, 50 (2001) [hereinafter Strohmeyer, *Collapse and Reconstruction of a Judicial System*].

214. S.C. Res. 1272, para. 1, U.N. Doc. S/RES/1272 (Oct. 25, 1999).

215. UNTAET Regulation No. 2000/11 on the Organization of the Courts in East

Timor, § 9 UNTAET/REG/2000/11 (Mar. 6, 2000); UNTAET Regulation No. 2000/15 on the Establishment of Panels with Exclusive Jurisdiction over Serious Criminal Offenses, § 1.3 UNTAET/REG/2000/15 (June 6, 2000) [hereinafter UNTAET Reg. 2000/15].

216. By December 2004, the Special Panels had indicted 370 individuals, Press Release, Serious Crimes Unit, SCU Indicts Suai Church Massacre Commanders (Nov. 30, 2004), but at least 281 of them were residing in Indonesia, and that country has refused to surrender them, JUDICIAL SYSTEM MONITORING PROGRAMME, JSMP ISSUE REPORT, THE FUTURE OF THE SERIOUS CRIMES UNIT, JSMP ISSUE REPORT, Jan. 2004, at 10 [hereinafter THE FUTURE OF THE SERIOUS CRIMES UNIT]; JUSTICE FOR TIMOR-LESTE, *supra* note 204, at § 4.1. Indonesia has itself conducted domestic prosecutions of Indonesians accused of international crimes relating to Timorese independence, but these have been dismissed as shams. *See* JUSTICE FOR TIMOR-LESTE, *supra* note 204, at §§ 5–9; William J. Furney, *East Timor Atrocities: Submit to International Tribunal*, STRAITS TIMES (Singapore), Aug. 15, 2003.

217. JUDICIAL SYSTEM MONITORING PROGRAMME, THE FUTURE OF SERIOUS CRIMES (delivered by Tiago A. Sarmento, Victoria University, June 16–18, 2005) [hereinafter *The Future of Serious Crimes*].

218. *See* UNTAET Regulation No. 2000/30 on Transitional Rules of Criminal Procedure, UNTAET/REG/2000/30 (as amended by Regulation 2001/25 of September 14, 2001).

219. Suzannah Linton, *Cambodia, East Timor and Sierra Leone: Experiments in International Justice*, 12 CRIM. L.F. 185, 205 (2001) [hereinafter Linton, *Experiments*].

220. David Cohen, *Seeking Justice on the Cheap: Is the East Timor Tribunal Really a Model for the Future?* in ASIA PACIFIC ISSUES NO. 61, at 5–6 (EAST-WEST CENTER 2002); *see also* Prosecutor v. Francisco Dos Santos Laku, Dili District Court, Special Panels for Serious Crimes, Case No. 8/2001, Judgement at 2 (July 25, 2001); Prosecutor v. Carlos Soares, Dili District Court, Special Panels for Serious Crimes, Case No. 12/2000, Judgement at 2 (May 31, 2001) [hereinafter Carlos Soares Judgement]; Prosecutor v. Joseph Leki, Dili District Court, Special Panels for Serious Crimes, Case No. 5/2000, Judgement at 2 (June 11, 2001) [hereinafter Joseph Leki Judgement].

221. Suzanne Katzenstein, Note, *Hybrid Tribunals: Searching for Justice in East Timor*, 16 HARV. HUM. RTS. J. 245, 251-52 (2003); Judicial System Monitoring Programme, *Special Panels for Serious Cases—Weekly Report 27–31 January 2003* (Jan. 27–31, 2003), *available at* http://www.jsmp.minihub.org/Reports/spscweeksumm/SPSC27-31Jan03jr10feb03.pdf.

222. *See* Lino de Carvalho v. Prosecutor General, Court of Appeal of East Timor, Criminal Appeal No. 25 of 2001, Judgement of Fredrick Egonda-Ntende, para. 1 (Oct. 29, 2001); Julio Fernandes v. Prosecutor General, Court of Appeal of East Timor, Criminal Appeal No. 7 of 2001, Judgement of Fredrick Egonda-Ntende, para. 36, (June 29, 2001).

223. JUDICIAL SYSTEM MONITORING PROGRAMME, THE GENERAL PROSECUTOR V. JONI MARQUES AND 9 OTHERS (THE LOS PALOS CASE): A JSMP TRIAL REPORT, at § 3.2.1.2. (Mar. 2002) [hereinafter JSMP, THE LOS PALOS CASE REPORT].

224. *Id.* at §§ 3.2.4.2, 3.2.4.3.

225. Suzannah Linton, *Correspondents' Reports, in* 2 Y.B. OF INT'L HUM. LAW 471, 481 (2000). Indeed, when the court asked the prosecutor in the *João Fernandes* case "why the

accused is charged with one murder since the evidences [*sic*] in the file show that there were more victims," the prosecutor responded, among other things, that the accused is already detained, and the prosecutor needed to seek "quick justice." Prosecutor v. João Fernandes, Dili District Court, Special Panels for Serious Crimes, Case No. 01/00.C.G.2000, Judgement at para. 5 (Jan. 25, 2001) [hereinafter João Fernandes Judgement].

226. JSMP, The Los Palos Case Report, *supra* note 223, at §§ 2.2.2, 3.1.2. And few, if any, of these defenders had significant experience. All of the East Timorese defenders in the *Los Palos* case had only recently completed their law degrees from universities in Indonesia, and none of them had practiced law before their appointment to the case. *Id.* at § 3.2.2.2.

227. "Los Palos" Case Trial Notes, Oct. 4, 2001, at 343.

228. JSMP, The Los Palos Case Report, *supra* note 223, at § 3.2.2.1.

229. *Id.* § 3.12.

230. Another impediment has been the government of Timor-Leste's insistence that judges should be from civil-law states and should speak Portuguese. *Id.*

231. Suzannah Linton & Caitlin Reiger, *The Evolving Jurisprudence and Practice of East Timor's Special Panels for Serious Crimes on Admissions of Guilt, Duress and Superior Orders*, 4 Y.B. of Int'l Hum. L. 167, 185 (2001).

232. Judicial System Monitoring Programme, The Lolotoe Case: A Small Step Forward § 3.1, (July 2004), *available at* http://www.jsmp.minihub.org/Reports/ jsmpreports/Lolotoe%20Reports/Lolotoe%20report%20-%20FINAL.pdf   [hereinafter The Lolotoe Case: A Small Step Forward].

233. Judicial System Monitoring Programme, *Departure of International Judge Means Special Panels for Serious Crimes in East Timor Unable to Function*, Apr. 21, 2003, *available at* http://www.jsmp.minihub.org/News/News/21_04_03nb.htm.

234. Phillip Rapoza, J. Special Panel for Serious Crimes, The Serious Crimes Process in Timor-Leste: Accomplishments, Challenges and Lessons Learned, Speech delivered at the International Symposium on U.N. Peacekeeping Operations in Post-Conflict Timor-Leste: Accomplishments and Lessons Learned (Apr. 28, 2005).

235. Judicial System Monitoring Programme, *The Special Panels for Serious Crimes Hear Their Final Case*, Justice Update, Issue 12/2005 (2005), *available at* http://www.jsmp .minihub.org/Justice%20update/2005/May%202005/050520_JSMP_JUissue12(e).pdf.

236. Public Statement, Amnesty International, Justice for Timor-Leste: Victims Await Further Action from the Security Council to Ensure Perpetrators Are Held to Account, (Apr. 29, 2005).

237. *See generally*, Ben Kiernan, The Pol Pot Regime: Race, Power, and Genocide in Cambodia under the Khmer Rouge, 1975–1979 (1996). For a description of the killings, see Hurst Hannum, *International Law and Cambodian Genocide: The Sounds of Silence*, 11 Hum. Rts. Q. 82, 89–91, 93–94 (1989). For a description of the evacuation of Phnom Penh, see Power, *supra* note 20, at 88.

238. Pressure from the special representative secretary-general for human rights in Cambodia led the Cambodian government to ask the U.N.'s assistance in bringing members of the Khmer Rouge to justice. Linton, *Experiments*, *supra* note 219, at 187-88;

Craig Etcheson, *The Persistence of Impunity in Cambodia, in* REINING IN IMPUNITY FOR
INTERNATIONAL CRIMES AND SERIOUS VIOLATIONS OF FUNDAMENTAL HUMAN RIGHTS:
PROCEEDINGS OF THE SIRACUSA CONFERENCE 17–21 SEPTEMBER 1998, at 231, 239 (Chris-
topher C. Joyner ed., 1998).

239. Hans Corell, U.N. Legal Counsel, *Negotiations Between the U.N. and Cambodia
Regarding the Establishment of the Court to Try Khmer Rouge Leaders,* statement at a press
briefing at U.N. Headquarters in New York (Feb. 8, 2002), *available at* http://www.un.org/
News/dh/infocus/cambodia/corell-brief.htm.

240. Agreement between the United Nations and the Royal Government of Cambodia
Concerning the Prosecution Under Cambodian Law of Crimes Committed during the
Period of Democratic Kampuchea, arts. 1, 5(3), 6(3), June 6, 2003; David Scheffer, *A Rare
Chance to Try These Architects of Atrocity,* FINANCIAL TIMES (LONDON), Aug. 16, 2004;
Richard Woodd & Vong Sokheng, *US Senate Moves to Block KR Trial Funds,* PHNOM
PENH POST, Oct. 8, 2004.

241. Woodd & Sokheng, *supra* note 240.

242. Scheffer, *supra* note 240; Alan Sipress, *Khmer Rouge Trials Stalled by Political
Deadlock,* WASH. POST, May 5, 2004, at A24.

243. S. 2812 § 554(e), 108th Cong. (2004); H.R. 4818, § 5054(e), 108th Cong. (2004).

244. Ek Madra, *U.N., Cambodia Look to Khmer Rouge Trial in 2007,* REUTERS,
Feb. 9, 2006.

245. S. Afr. Const., Ch. 1, § 6(1); Max Loubser, *Linguistic Factors into the Mix: The
South African Experience of Language and the Law,* 78 TUL. L. REV. 105, 106 (2003).

246. The Magnus Malan trial, for instance, was conducted in Afrikaans and English
while a Zulu translator interpreted the testimony for the seven black defendants who were
charged with being triggermen. Andrew Maykuth, *A Watershed Trial in South Africa:
Did an Ex-Defense Minister and Others Train an Apartheid Hit Squad?,* PHILADELPHIA
INQUIRER, Apr. 22, 1996, *available at* http://www.maykuth.com/Africa/malan422.htm.

247. For a discussion of East Timor's many languages, see James J. Fox, *Tracing the
Path, Recounting the Path: Historical Perspectives on Timor, in* OUT OF THE ASHES: DE-
STRUCTION AND RECONSTRUCTION OF EAST TIMOR 1, 3–5, 19 (James J. Fox & Dionísio
Babo-Soares eds., 2003).

248. For a discussion of the costs of these high-profile South African trials, see
HAYNER, *supra* note 91, at 89–90; Paul van Zyl, *Justice without Punishment: Guaranteeing
Human Rights in Transitional Societies, in* LOOKING BACK, REACHING FORWARD: REFLEC-
TIONS ON THE TRUTH AND RECONCILIATION COMMISSION OF SOUTH AFRICA 42, 45–46
(Charles Villa-Vicencio & Wilhelm Verwoerd eds., 2000) [hereinafter Van Zyl, *Justice
Without Punishment*].

249. De Kock is popularly blamed for at least seventy murders. *See* Jeremy Gordin,
Foreword to EUGENE DE KOCK, A LONG NIGHT'S DAMAGE 13, 19 (1998).

250. AMNESTY INTERNATIONAL & HUMAN RIGHTS WATCH, TRUTH AND JUSTICE:
UNFINISHED BUSINESS IN SOUTH AFRICA, 10–11, AI Index: AFR 53/001/2003 (Feb. 2003)
[hereinafter TRUTH AND JUSTICE]; MARTIN MEREDITH, COMING TO TERMS: SOUTH AF-
RICA'S SEARCH FOR TRUTH 370 (1999); Paul van Zyl, *Dilemmas of Transitional Justice: The*

Case of South Africa's Truth and Reconciliation Commission, 52 J. INT'L AFF. 647, 653 n.15 (1999) [hereinafter Van Zyl, *Dilemmas of Transitional Justice*]; *State to Halt Legal Aid for "Third Force,"* MAIL & GUARDIAN (S. Afr.), Apr. 4, 1997.

251. Van Zyl, *Dilemmas of Transitional Justice, supra* note 250, at 653; Goodman, *supra* note 112, at 174. Various explanations have been offered for the prosecution's failure to secure convictions in the Malan trial, including prosecutorial incompetence and/or a desire to protect apartheid-era criminals. *See* DYZENHAUS, *supra* note 117, at 119–20. For an analysis of the conduct of the trial, see generally Howard Varney & Jeremy Sarkin, *Failing to Pierce the Hit Squad Veil: An Analysis of the* Malan *Trial*, 10 SOUTH AFRICAN J. CRIM. L. 141 (1997).

252. TRUTH AND JUSTICE, *supra* note 250, at 11–12.

253. Van Zyl, *Justice without Punishment, supra* note 248, at 45.

254. Van Zyl, *Dilemmas of Transitional Justice, supra* note 250, at 651.

255. *Id.* at 651–53; AMNESTY INTERNATIONAL, THE CRIMINAL JUSTICE SYSTEM AND THE PROTECTION OF HUMAN RIGHTS IN SOUTH AFRICA: THE ROLE OF THE PROSECUTION SERVICE, 5, AI Index: AFR 53/001/1998 (Feb. 11, 1998) [hereinafter AMNESTY INTERNATIONAL, THE CRIMINAL JUSTICE SYSTEM].

256. AMNESTY INTERNATIONAL, THE CRIMINAL JUSTICE SYSTEM, *supra* note 255, at 5; David Beresford & Rehana Rossouw, *Generals Avoid Justice as System Struggles to Cope*, MAIL & GUARDIAN (S. Afr.), Sept. 29, 1995.

257. *See generally* AMNESTY INTERNATIONAL, RWANDA: THE TROUBLED COURSE OF JUSTICE, AI Index: AFR 47/010/2000 (Apr. 4, 2000).

258. HUMAN RIGHTS WATCH AFRICA, Vol. 6 No. 11: ETHIOPIA: RECKONING UNDER THE LAW 11–12, 15–16 (Dec. 1994) [hereinafter HUMAN RIGHTS WATCH, ETHIOPIA].

259. AMNESTY INTERNATIONAL, ETHIOPIA, ACCOUNTABILITY PAST AND PRESENT: HUMAN RIGHTS IN TRANSITION 46 (Apr. 1995) [hereinafter AMNESTY INTERNATIONAL, ETHIOPIA].

260. HUMAN RIGHTS WATCH, ETHIOPIA, *supra* note 258, at 33–35; AMNESTY INTERNATIONAL, ETHIOPIA, *supra* note 259, at 50.

261. HUMAN RIGHTS WATCH, ETHIOPIA, *supra* note 258, at 26–27.

262. U.S. DEP'T OF STATE, COUNTRY REPORTS ON HUMAN RIGHTS PRACTICES – 2004: ETHIOPIA, § e, *available at* http://www.state.gov/g/drl/rls/hrrpt/2004/41603.htm.

263. *Court Sentences Former Regime's Security Chief to Death*, ETHIOPIAN HERALD, Aug. 11, 2005.

264. *Chile: Court Ruling May Define Future of Rights Prosecutions*, HUMAN RIGHTS WATCH NEWS, May 27, 2004, *available at* http://www.hrw.org/english/docs/2004/05/27/ chile8622.htm; Lutz & Sikkink, *supra* note 4, at 24.

265. Eva Vergara, *Chilean President Plans to Up Reparations*, A.P., Aug. 13, 2003; Stacie Jonas, *The Ripple Effect of the Pinochet Case*, HUM. RTS. BRIEF, Vol. 11, No. 3, at 36, 36 (2004).

266. Brett, *supra* note 4.

267. HUMAN RIGHTS WATCH, DISCREET PATH TO JUSTICE?: CHILE THIRTY YEARS AFTER THE MILITARY COUP, Briefing Paper, at 2–3 (Sept. 2003), *available at* http://hrw.org/ backgrounder/americas/chile/chile0903.pdf [hereinafter DISCREET PATH TO JUSTICE?];

see also Egan, *supra* note 4; *Redressing Injustices of the Past Back on Chile's Agenda*, TAIPEI TIMES, Sept. 8, 2003, at 7.

268. The Association of Relatives of Disappeared Detainees, the main organization representing the relatives of the "disappeared," labeled President Lagos's proposals "a disgrace" and asserted that they constituted a "new form of promoting the most flagrant impunity in an underhand way." DISCREET PATH TO JUSTICE?, *supra* note 267, at 10 n.26; *see also* Egan, *supra* note 4. Jonas, *supra* note 265, at 37.

269. Egan, *supra* note 4.

Chapter 3

270. Philosopher Jean Hampton constructs a more positive, victim-centered view of retribution that is founded on the equal dignity of all people. In Hampton's view, it is through retribution that the community uses its power to "deny the wrongdoer's prior claim of superiority." Retribution, therefore, seeks to diminish wrongdoers to "a level that is correct and equal to the level of their victims." JEFFRIE G. MURPHY & JEAN HAMPTON, FORGIVENESS AND MERCY 137–38 (1988).

271. *See* Elmar G. M. Weitekamp, *Research on Victim-Offender Mediation: Findings and Needs for the Future, in* VICTIM-OFFENDER MEDIATION IN EUROPE: MAKING RESTORATIVE JUSTICE WORK 99, 105 (The European Forum for Victim-Offender Mediation and Restorative Justice ed., 2000).

272. Ivković, *supra* note 2, at 323, 301. And it was by no means token punishment that they advocated. More than 90 percent of respondents advocated either the death penalty or life imprisonment and had little interest in prison sentences shorter than twenty-five years. *Id.* at 323. In a similar vein, Munira Subašić, representing the Mothers of Srebrenica and Zepa, asserted during a 2003 conference, that the twenty-seven-year sentence imposed on Momir Nikolić for his role in the Srebrenica executions constituted a "reward." As she put it, "270 years would not be enough." Conference, Plea Agreements and Guilty Pleas at the ICTY and Related Practice in National Systems, Dec. 5–6, 2003, Sarajevo, Bosnia-Herzegovina [hereinafter Comment of Munira Subašić].

273. *See* BORAINE, *supra* note 116, at 293; Carla Hesse & Robert Post, *Introduction* to HUMAN RIGHTS IN POLITICAL TRANSITIONS: GETTYSBURG TO BOSNIA 13, 16 (Carla Hesse & Robert Post eds., 1999); Report of the International Tribunal for the Prosecution of Persons Responsible for Serious Violations of International Humanitarian Law Committed in the Territory of the Former Yugoslavia since 1991, para. 15, U.N. Doc. A/49/342, S/1994/1007 (Aug. 29, 1994) [hereinafter ICTY 1994 Annual Report].

274. Press Release, ICTY, Address to the United Nations Security Council by the Prosecutor of the International Criminal Tribunals for the Former Yugoslavia and Rwanda, Carla Del Ponte, to the U.N. Security Council, GR/P.I.S/642-E.p642-e.htm Nov. 27, 2001. How well retributory goals are served cannot be measured solely by reference to the number of prosecutions undertaken but also must consider the quantity of punishment imposed. A society that prosecutes every last offender does not necessarily serve well the goal of retribution if it must, as a consequence, reduce the sanctions to token punish-

ments. In other words, depending on the society in question, victims' appropriate desire for vengeance might be better satisfied by a smaller number of prosecutions that result in appropriately lengthy prison sentences than by a far larger number of prosecutions that are followed by patently trivial sanctions. Indeed, as will be discussed in Chapter 5, one task for those seeking to use plea bargaining to increase the number of prosecutions is to find an appropriate balance between the quantity of offenders prosecuted and the severity of punishment imposed.

275. ICTY 1994 Annual Report, *supra* note 273, at para. 13.

276. Prosecutor v. Aleksovski, Case No. IT-95-14/1-A, Judgement, para. 179, 185 (Mar. 24, 2000) [hereinafter Aleksovski Appeal]; Prosecutor v. Kambanda, Case No. ICTR-97-23-S, Judgement and Sentence, para. 28 (Sept. 4, 1998) [hereinafter Kambanda Judgement]. For an argument that at least one ICTY Trial Chamber overemphasized the goal of deterrence in sentencing, see Shahram Dana, *Revisiting the* Blaškić *Sentence: Some Reflections on the Sentencing Jurisprudence of the ICTY*, 4 INT'L CRIM. L. REV. 321, 330–31, 344, 347 (2004).

277. Rome Statute, *supra* note 57, at Preamble.

278. *See* ANDREW VON HIRSCH ET AL., CRIMINAL DETERRENCE AND SENTENCE SEVERITY 5 (1999). This view extends back at least as far as the eighteenth century when Cesare Beccaria propounded it. *See* Guyora Binder, *Punishment Theory: Moral or Political?*, 5 BUFF. CRIM. L. REV. 321, 336 (2002).

279. BRENT FISSE & JOHN BRAITHWAITE, CORPORATIONS, CRIME AND ACCOUNTABILITY 219–21 (1993).

280. *See* Prosecutor v. Milošević, Case No. IT-02-54, Transcript, at 16727 (Feb. 21, 2003).

281. Prosecutor v. Delalić and Others, Case No. IT-96-21-T, Judgement, para. 1232 (Nov. 16, 1998) [hereinafter Delalić Judgement].

282. *See* Prosecutor v. Momir Nikolić, Case No. IT-02-60/1-S, Sentencing Judgement, para. 60 (Dec. 2, 2003) [hereinafter Momir Nikolić Sentencing Judgement]. In 2002, Šešelj received a million votes in a failed presidential election, "signaling that nationalists still enjoy considerable support in Serbia, more than two years after Milošević was ousted from power by a pro-Western coalition." Katarina Kratovac, *Thousands Bid Farewell to Ultranationalist War Crimes Suspect*, A.P., Feb. 23, 2003.

283. Payam Akhavan, *Beyond Impunity: Can International Criminal Justice Prevent Future Atrocities?*, 95 AM. J. INT'L L. 7, 7, 23 (2001); Mark A. Drumbl, *Rule of Law Amid Lawlessness: Counseling the Accused in Rwanda's Domestic Genocide Trials*, 29 COLUM. HUM. RTS. L. REV. 545, 601 (1998) [hereinafter Drumbl, *Rule of Law*]. For a detailed description of the activities of the Hutu insurgents living in refugee camps, see GÉRARD PRUNIER, THE RWANDA CRISIS: HISTORY OF A GENOCIDE 312–17 (1995).

284. *See* Eric Witte, *The Cost of Impunity for Liberian Ex-Leader*, IWPR AFRICAN REPORTS, No. 44, Oct. 17, 2005; Emily Wax, *In Exile, Taylor Exerts Control: Liberian Ex-President Exercises Influence from Nigeria*, WASH. POST, Sept. 17, 2003, at A17. Even criminal arrest may not be sufficient to eliminate the destructive influence of war criminals. A number of ICTY indictees have lately run for office, including some who are in ICTY detention. The ICTY's registrar consequently prohibited the indictees from campaigning from the ICTY's detention center. *See Restrictions on Vojislav Šešelj's Communication Privileges Extended*, SENSE NEWS AGENCY, June 10, 2004; Press Release, ICTY, Registry

Imposes Communications Restrictions on Detainees with Regard to Political Campaigning in the Media from the Tribunal's Detention Unit, JL/P.I.S./810-e (Dec. 12, 2003). By contrast, a Trial Chamber in October 2005 permitted indicted Kosovar politician Ramush Haradinaj to engage in certain political activities in Kosovo while on provisional release. Prosecutor v. Haradinaj et al., Decision on Defence Motion on Behalf of Ramush Haradinaj to Request Re-assessment of Conditions of Provisional Release Granted 6 June 2005, Case No. IT-04-84-PT (Oct. 12, 2005).

285. Indeed, some of the most brutal perpetrators of international crimes showed no previous proclivity toward violence. ICTY defendant Dragan Nikolić, commander of the Sušica prison camp, for instance, beat to death nine detainees, sometimes kicking them, sometimes punching them, and sometimes using metal pipes and wooden boards, yet before the atrocities he had no prior criminal record and "'was a gainfully employed resident of Vlasenica who was well-liked by many of the victims.'" *See* Dragan Nikolić Sentencing Judgement, *supra* note 11, at paras. 7, 71–86, 262. Similarly, Predrag Banović beat five detainees to death and severely beat twenty-five others and shot two more, yet he had no prior criminal record and had worked as a waiter. Prosecutor v. Banović, Case No. IT-02-65-1-S, Sentencing Judgement, paras. 1, 29–30, 74 (Oct. 28, 2003) [hereinafter Banović Sentencing Judgement]. Darko Mrđa, likewise, had no criminal record before he participated in the executions of more than two hundred Muslim men by the Ilomska River. *See* Mrđa Sentencing Judgement, *supra* note 11, at paras. 10, 88, 91.

286. For a discussion of the concept of "work" during the Rwandan genocide, see MELVERN, *supra* note 52, at 191–92. And work it was. Many Hutu killers described the exhaustion that followed hours of hacking. *See* Erin Daly, *Between Punitive and Reconstructive Justice: The Gacaca Courts in Rwanda*, 34 N.Y.U. J. INT'L L. & POL. 355, 363 (2002). "Survivors and other witnesses . . . speak of the killers approaching the destruction of the crowds at a church, hospital, or hilltop as a piece of work to be kept at until finished. One compared killers to government workers putting in a day at the office; another likened them to farmers spending a day at labor. In case after case, killers quit at day's end, to go home and feast on food and drink they had pillaged or been given, ready to come back the next morning, rested and fit for 'work.'" ALISON DES FORGES, HUMAN RIGHTS WATCH, LEAVE NONE TO TELL THE STORY: GENOCIDE IN RWANDA 212 (1999) [hereinafter LEAVE NONE TO TELL THE STORY].

287. PHILIP GOUREVITCH, WE WISH TO INFORM YOU THAT TOMORROW WE WILL BE KILLED WITH OUR FAMILIES: STORIES FROM RWANDA 123 (1998).

288. Weitekamp, *supra* note 271, at 102.

289. Such an assumption may not be warranted. *See* Darren Bush, *Law and Economics of Restorative Justice: Why Restorative Justice Cannot and Should Not Be Solely About Restoration*, 2003 UTAH L. REV. 439, 457.

290. *See* AFRICAN RIGHTS, GACACA JUSTICE: A SHARED RESPONSIBILITY 28 (January 2003) [hereinafter GACACA JUSTICE]. "Many detainees see themselves as prisoners of war, simply ending up on the losing side." Drumbl, *Rule of Law*, *supra* note 283, at 607.

291. Albert W. Alschuler, *Implementing the Criminal Defendant's Right to Trial: Alternatives to the Plea Bargaining System*, 50 U. CHI. L. REV. 931, 933 (1983).

292. MINOW, *supra* note 16, at 25; TEITEL, *supra* note 58, at 56; Stephan Landsman,

Alternative Responses to Serious Human Rights Abuses: Of Prosecution and Truth Commissions, 59 L. & CONTEMP. PROBS. 81, 83 (1996); *The Rule of Law and Transitional Justice*, *supra* note 92, at para. 39.

293. *See* Ruti Teitel, *Bringing the Messiah through the Law*, *in* HUMAN RIGHTS IN POLITICAL TRANSITIONS: GETTYSBURG TO BOSNIA 177, 188 (Carla Hesse & Robert Post eds., 1999).

294. *Id.*

295. MINOW, *supra* note 16, at 45.

296. *Id.* at 40; *see also* Richard J. Goldstone, *50 Years after Nuremberg: A New International Criminal Tribunal for Human Rights Criminals*, *in* CONTEMPORARY GENOCIDES: CAUSES, CASES, CONSEQUENCES 215, 215-16 (Albert J. Jongman ed., 1996).

297. *See* Prosecutor v. Tadić, Case No. IT-94-1-T, Opinion and Judgement, paras. 130–92 (May 7, 1997) [hereinafter Tadić Judgement].

298. Crimes within the jurisdiction of the Nuremberg Tribunal, for instance, were defined with a nexus to the waging of aggressive war. Thus, the story told by the Nuremberg judgment is far more a story about Germany's crime against the peace than about its extermination of six million Jews.

299. OSIEL, *supra* note 7, at 158.

300. *Id.* at 39.

301. *Id.* at 2–3.

302. *Id.* at 2.

303. *Id.*

304. *Id.* at 3.

305. *Id.*

Chapter 4

306. ICTY Statute, *supra* note 180, at art. 1; ICTR Statute, *supra* note 197, at art. 1.

307. UNTAET Reg. 2000/15, *supra* note 215, at § 1.1.

308. The ICTY has indicted 162 individuals; the ICTR has indicted 83 individuals; and the Special Panels for Serious Crimes indicted a whopping 391 individuals in 95 indictments, though the vast majority of Special Panels' indictees were located in Indonesia, where there was no chance of obtaining custody over them.

309. ICTY R.P. & EVID. 62(iii); ICTR R.P. & EVID. 62(A)(iii) (Oct. 6, 1995).

310. Prosecutor v. Erdemović, Case No. IT-96-22-T, Sentencing Judgement, paras. 3, 10, and text accompanying n.141 (Nov. 29, 1996) [hereinafter Erdemović Sentencing Judgement].

311. Prosecutor v. Erdemović, Case No. IT-96-22-A, Joint Separate Opinion of Judge McDonald and Judge Vohrah, para. 8 (Oct. 7, 1997) [hereinafter Erdemović, Joint Separate Opinion of Judge McDonald and Judge Vohrah].

312. *See* ICTY R.P. & EVID. 62*bis* (Dec. 4, 1998); ICTR R.P. & EVID. 62(B)(iii) (July 1, 1999). According to the rules, the plea will be supported by a sufficient factual basis as long as there is no material disagreement between the parties about the facts of the case.

313. ICTY R.P. & EVID. 62*ter* (Dec. 13, 2001); ICTR R.P. & EVID. 62*bis* (May 27, 2003).

314. Rome Statute, *supra* note 57, at art. 65; UNTAET Regulation 2000/30, On Transitional Rules of Criminal Procedure, art. 29A, Sept. 25, 2000.

315. *DR Congo Rebel in Landmark Trial*, BBC NEWS, Mar. 20, 2006.

316. *Prosecuting and Defending Violations of Genocide and Humanitarian Law: The International Tribunal for the Former Yugoslavia*, 88 PROC. AM. SOC. INT'L L. 239, 248 (1994) (remarks of Steven J. Lepper).

317. SCHARF, *supra* note 2, at 67. As then judge Gabrielle Kirk McDonald remembers, Judge Georges Abi-Saab insisted that because the crimes within the tribunal's jurisdiction are *jus cogens*, the tribunal had an obligation to prosecute them. Interview with Gabrielle Kirk McDonald, former president of the ICTY, The Hague (Sept. 15, 2003).

318. Rumors abound, for instance, that insider witnesses are informally granted immunity.

319. These are Dražen Erdemović, Erdemović Sentencing Judgement, *supra* note 310, at para. 3; Goran Jelisić, Prosecutor v. Jelisić, Case No. IT-95-10-T, Judgement, para. 11 (Dec. 14, 1999) [hereinafter Jelisić Judgement], Stevan Todorović, Prosecutor v. Todorović, Case No. IT-95-9/1, Sentencing Judgement, para. 5 (July 31, 2001) [hereinafter Todorović Sentencing Judgement], Duško Sikirica, Damir Došen, Dragan Kolundžija, Prosecutor v. Sikirica et al., Case No. IT-95-8-T, Sentencing Judgement, paras. 12–15 (Nov. 13, 2001) [hereinafter Sikirica Sentencing Judgement], Milan Simić, Prosecutor v. Milan Simić, Case No. IT-95-9/2-S, Sentencing Judgement, paras. 9–16 (Oct. 17, 2002) [hereinafter Simić Sentencing Judgement], Biljana Plavšić, Prosecutor v. Plavšić, Case No. IT-00-39&40/ 1-S, Sentencing Judgement, para. 5 (Feb. 27, 2003) [hereinafter Plavšić Sentencing Judgement], Dragan Obrenović, Prosecutor v. Obrenović, Case No. IT-02-60/2-S, Sentencing Judgement, para. 10 (Dec. 10, 2003) [hereinafter Obrenović Sentencing Judgement], Momir Nikolić, Momir Nikolić Sentencing Judgement, *supra* note 282, at para. 12; Darko Mrđa, Mrđa Sentencing Judgement, *supra* note 11, at para. 5, Miodrag Jokić, Jokić Sentencing Judgement, *supra* note 11, at paras. 7–14, Predrag Banović, Banović Sentencing Judgement, *supra* note 285, at para. 13; Dragan Nikolić, Dragan Nikolić Sentencing Judgement, *supra* note 11, at para. 36, Ranko Češić, Prosecutor v. Češić, Case No. IT-95-10/1-S, Sentencing Judgement, para. 4 (Mar. 11, 2004) [hereinafter Češić Sentencing Judgement], Miroslav Deronjić, Prosecutor v. Deronjić, Case No. IT-02-61-S, Sentencing Judgement, para. 19 (Mar. 30, 2004) [hereinafter Deronjić Sentencing Judgement], Milan Babić, Prosecutor v. Babić, Case No. IT-03-72-I, Amendment to the Joint Motion for Consideration of Plea Agreement between Milan Babić and the Office of the Prosecutor Plea Agreement (Jan. 22, 2004) [hereinafter Babić Plea Agreement], Miroslav Bralo, Prosecutor v. Bralo, Case No. IT-95-17-PT, Plea Agreement (July 18, 2005) [hereinafter Bralo Plea Agreement]; Ivica Rajić, Case No. IT-95-12-PT, Confidential Plea Agreement (Oct. 25, 2005) [hereinafter Rajić Plea Agreement].

320. Dragan Obrenović and Momir Nikolić pled guilty in May 2003. Predrag Banović pled guilty in June 2003. Darko Mrđa pled guilty in July 2003, and Miodrag Jokić pled guilty in August 2003. Miroslav Deronjić and Dragan Nikolić pled guilty in September 2003. Ranko Češić pled guilty in October 2003, Milan Babić pled guilty in January 2004, Miroslav Bralo pled guilty in July 2005, and the last ICTY defendant to plead guilty to date, Ivica Rajić, did so in October 2005.

321. Prosecutor v. Erdemović, Case No. IT-96-22-T*bis*, Sentencing Judgement, para. 15 (Mar. 5, 1998) [hereinafter Erdemović Second Sentencing Judgement].

322. Erdemović Sentencing Judgement, *supra* note 310, at para. 80.

323. Prosecutor v. Erdemović, Case No. IT-96-22-T*bis*, Transcript, at 33, 44–45 (Jan. 14, 1998) [hereinafter Erdemović Transcript], *available at* http://www.un.org/icty/transe22/980114it.htm.

324. Erdemović Sentencing Judgement, *supra* note 310, at para. 2; Erdemović Transcript, *supra* note 323, at 25–26.

325. Erdemović Transcript, *supra* note 323, at 35–38.

326. Erdemović Sentencing Judgement, *supra* note 310, at paras. 3, 10.

327. *Id.* at para. 6. Prosecutor v. Krstić, Case No. IT-98-33, Judgement, para. 234 (Aug. 2, 2001) [hereinafter Krstić Judgement].

328. Erdemović Transcript, *supra* note 323, at 48.

329. Erdemović Second Sentencing Judgement, *supra* note 321, at para. 18(d).

330. Erdemović Transcript, *supra* note 323, at 29, 38, 46.

331. Jelisić Judgement, *supra* note 319, at paras. 102–03.

332. Prosecutor v. Jelisić, Case No. IT-95-10-PT, Amended Indictment, paras. 16–41 (Mar. 3, 1998).

333. Jelisić Judgement, *supra* note 319, at paras. 8, 10–11, 24.

334. *Id.* at paras. 3, 38, 12–11, 19.

335. *Id.* at para. 15. The Appeals Chamber subsequently reversed the Trial Chamber's conclusion that the evidence was not sufficient to sustain a conviction on genocide. However, it did not send the case back to the Trial Chamber for a new trial. Prosecutor v. Jelisić, Case No. IT-95-10-A, Appeal, paras. 57, 73–77 (July 5, 2001).

336. Jelisić Judgement, *supra* note 319, at para. 119; Prosecution v. Jelisić, Case No. IT-95-10-T, Transcript, at 3070, 3132 (Nov. 25, 1999).

337. Telephone Interview with Nicola Kostić, ICTY defense counsel (Oct. 25, 2001).

338. Telephone Interview with Terree Bowers, former ICTY senior trial attorney (Oct. 30, 2001).

339. Jelisić Judgement, *supra* note 319, at para. 139.

340. *Id.* at para. 127.

341. *See* Christopher M. Supernor, *International Bounty Hunters for War Criminals: Privatizing the Enforcement of Justice*, 50 A.F.L. REV. 215, 217 n.11 (2001); Marlise Simons, *War Crimes Court Takes It Easy on a Cooperative Bosnian Serb*, N.Y. TIMES, Aug. 1, 2001, at A4. A regional court in Serbia subsequently convicted nine people of "kidnapping for money." *9 Convicted of Kidnap of War-Crimes Suspect*, N.Y. TIMES, Dec. 12, 2000, at A15; see also Prosecutor v. Todorović, Case No. IT-95-9/1, Transcript, at 786 (Dec. 13, 2000).

342. Sean D. Murphy ed., *Contemporary Practice of the United States Relating to International Law*, 95 AM. J. INT'L L. 387, 401 (2001).

343. The four trials led to the conviction of seven defendants: Blagoje Simić, Miroslav Tadić, and Simo Zarić, *see* Prosecutor v. Simić et al., Case No. IT-95-9-T, Judgement (Oct. 17, 2003); Milomir Stakić, *see* Prosecutor v. Stakić, Case No. IT-97-24-T, Judgement (July 31, 2003) [hereinafter Stakić Judgement]; Mladen Naletilić and Vinko Martinović,

see Prosecutor v. Naletilić & Martinović, Case No. IT-98-34-T, Judgement (Mar. 31, 2003); and Stanislav Galić, *see* Prosecutor v. Galić, Case No. IT-98-29-T, Judgement (Dec. 5, 2003) [hereinafter Galić Judgement].

344. Prosecutor v. Simić et al., Case No. IT-95-9, Fourth Amended Indictment, para. 2 (Jan. 9, 2002); Prosecutor v. Milan Simić, Interview with Milan Simić, at 15 (Mar. 2, 1998), *reprinted as* Annex A to Prosecutor's Brief on the Sentencing of Milan Simić.

345. Prosecutor v. Simić et al., Case No. IT-95-9, Fourth Amended Indictment, paras. 16, 24–26 (Jan. 9, 2002).

346. Simić Sentencing Judgement, *supra* note 319, at para. 11.

347. *Id.* at para. 7.

348. Telephone Interview with Slobodan Zecević, ICTY defense counsel (Dec. 17, 2002).

349. Simić Sentencing Judgement, *supra* note 319, at paras. 7–8.

350. Prosecutor v. Milan Simić, Case No. IT-95-9/2-T, Prosecutor's Brief on the Sentencing of Milan Simić, para. 50 (July 15, 2002) [hereinafter Simić, Prosecutor's Sentencing Brief].

351. Simić Sentencing Judgement, *supra* note 319, at paras. 10, 22.

352. *See* Todorović Sentencing Judgement, *supra* note 319, at paras. 32, 113.

353. Interview with BH, Sarajevo, Bosnia (Dec. 4, 2003).

354. Simić Judgement, *supra* note 319, at para. 13.

355. Simić, Prosecutor's Sentencing Brief, *supra* note 350, at para. 54.

356. Plavšić and Nikolić had been charged with genocide while Obrenović had been charged with complicity to commit genocide.

357. The ICTY has acquitted several defendants of genocide, *see* Jelisić Judgement, *supra* note 319, at para. 108; Stakić Judgement, *supra* note 343, at para. 560, Prosecutor v. Sikirica, Case No. IT-95-8-T, Judgement on Defence Motions to Acquit, para. 97 (Sept. 3, 2001), and has thus far determined that genocide took place only in relation to the Srebrenica massacres, Krstić, *supra* note 327, at para. 598; Prosecutor v. Krstić, Case No. IT-98-33-A, Judgement, paras. 5–38 (Apr. 19, 2004) [hereinafter Krstić Appeal].

358. Krstić Judgement, *supra* note 327, at para. 727. The Appeals Chamber reduced Krstić's sentence to a term of thirty-five years because it set aside his conviction as a participant in a joint criminal enterprise to commit genocide and convicted him rather of aiding and abetting genocide. Krstić Appeal, *supra* note 357, at Disposition.

359. The following ICTR defendants received life sentences: Jean Paul Akayesu, Prosecutor v. Akayesu, Case No. ICTR-96-4-T, Sentence (Oct. 2, 1998) [hereinafter Akayesu Sentence]; Juvénal Kajelijeli, Prosecutor v. Kajelijeli, Case No. ICTR-98-44A-T, Judgement and Sentence (Dec. 1, 2003) [hereinafter Kajelijeli Judgement and Sentence]; Jean Kambanda, Kambanda Judgement, *supra* note 276; Jean de Dieu Kamuhanda, Prosecutor v. Kamuhanda, Case No. ICTR-95-54A-T, Judgement and Sentence (Jan. 22, 2004) [hereinafter Kamuhanda Judgement and Sentence]; Clément Kayishema, Prosecutor v. Kayishema, Case No. ICTR-95-1-T, Judgement and Sentence (May 21, 1999); Alfred Musema, Prosecutor v. Musema, Case No. ICTR-96-13-A, Judgement and Sentence (Jan. 27, 2000) [hereinafter Musema Judgement and Sentence]; Ferdinand Nahimana, Nahimana Judge-

ment, *supra* note 3; Hassan Ngeze, Prosecutor v. Ngeze, Case No. ICTR-99-52-T, Judgement and Sentence (Dec. 3, 2003); Eliezer Niyitegeka, Prosecutor v. Niyitegeka, Case No. ICTR-96-14-T, Judgement and Sentence (May 16, 2003) [hereinafter Niyitegeka Judgement and Sentence]; George Rutaganda, Prosecutor v. Rutaganda, Case No. ICTR-96-3, Judgement and Sentence (Dec. 6, 1999) [hereinafter Rutaganda Judgement and Sentence]. Jean-Bosco Barayagwiza would have received a life sentence, but the Trial Chamber reduced his sentence to thirty-five years' imprisonment to remedy the prosecution's violation of his procedural rights. Nahimana Judgement, *supra* note 3, at para. 1106.

360. Prosecutor v. Plavšić, Case No. IT-00-39&40/1-S, Prosecution's Brief on the Sentencing of Biljana Plavšić (Nov. 25, 2002) [hereinafter Plavšić Prosecution's Sentencing Brief], at para. 43.

361. Plavšić Sentencing Judgement, *supra* note 319, at para. 132.

362. Momir Nikolić Plea Agreement, *supra* note 11, at para. 4(a); Obrenović Plea Agreement, *supra* note 11, at para. 4(a).

363. *See* Obrenović Sentencing Judgement, *supra* note 319, at para. 156; Momir Nikolić Sentencing Judgement, *supra* note 282, at para. 183.

364. Momir Nikolić Sentencing Judgement, *supra* note 282, at para. 65.

365. Prosecutor v. Strugar et al., Case No. IT-01-42, Amended Indictment (Mar. 31, 2003). The initial indictment charged Jokić with fifteen counts of violations of the laws and customs of war and one count of a grave breach of the Geneva Conventions of 1949 for military activities that took place between October 1 and December 31, 1999. Prosecutor v. Strugar et al., Case No. IT-01-42, Indictment (Feb. 22, 2001).

366. Prosecutor v. Jokić, Case No. IT-01-42, Second Amended Indictment (Aug. 27, 2003).

367. *Id.* at para. 14.

368. Prosecutor v. Strugar, Case No. IT-01-42-T, Judgement, Annex IV, para. 488 (Jan. 31, 2005) [hereinafter Strugar Judgement]. The amended indictments against Strugar and Kovacević, like Jokić's amended indictment, do not include allegations relating to the October and November 1991 incidents of shelling. Whereas Jokić's amended indictment relates only to the events of December 6, 1991, the amended indictments against Strugar and Kovacević allege crimes occurring between December 6 and December 31, 1991. Prosecutor v. Strugar & Kovacević, Case No. IT-01-42, Second Amended Indictment (Oct. 17, 2003). Strugar was convicted following a trial of holding superior responsibility for the shelling that occurred to the Old Town on December 6, 1991. Strugar Judgement, *supra* at para. 446. Kovacević was deemed unfit to enter a plea because of a psychiatric illness and was sent to Serbia for treatment. In January 2005, prosecutors moved to transfer his case to the courts of Serbia, a motion that remains under consideration by the Trial Chamber. Kovacević 11*bis* request, *supra* note 161.

369. Deronjić Sentencing Judgement, *supra* note 319, at paras. 8–9, 48.

370. Prosecutor v. Deronjić, Case No. IT-02-61-S, Miroslav Deronjić's Sentencing Brief, paras. 64–67, 69 (Dec. 18, 2003).

371. Prosecutor v. Deronjić, Case No. IT-02-61-S, Dissenting Opinion of Judge Schomburg, para. 12 (Mar. 30, 2004) [hereinafter Deronjić Dissent].

372. *Id.* at para. 9.

373. Prosecutor v. Deronjić, Case No. IT-02-61-I, Indictment (July 3, 2002) [hereinafter Deronjić Indictment]; Deronjić Sentencing Judgement, *supra* note 319, at para. 44.

374. Prosecutor v. Deronjić, Case No. IT-02-61-S, Transcript, at 99 (Jan. 27, 2004). Telephone Interview with Mark Harmon, ICTY prosecutor (Feb. 24, 2005). Harmon vehemently rejected any suggestion that a charge bargain had taken place in the *Deronjić* case.

375. Prosecutor v. Deronjić, Case No. IT-02-61-S, Transcript, at 314 (Mar. 5, 2004).

376. Deronjić Dissent, *supra* note 371, at para. 4.

377. Deronjić Sentencing Judgement, *supra* note 319, at para. 44.

378. Prosecutor v. Deronjić, Case No. IT-02-61-PT, Amended Indictment, paras. 29–55 (Nov. 29, 2002) [hereinafter Deronjić Amended Indictment].

379. For instance, the first two indictments charged Deronjić with participating in a joint criminal enterprise that was in existence from April 9 to May 9, 1992, *id.* at para. 5, while the second amended indictment reduced the time span of the joint criminal enterprise to the period between "the end of April 1992 to 9 May 1992," Prosecutor v. Deronjić, Case No. IT-02-61-PT, Second Amended Indictment, para. 5 (Sept. 29, 2003) [hereinafter Deronjić Second Amended Indictment]. In another minor difference, the first two indictments asserted that, after Bosnian Muslims were instructed to appear at a meeting at the community building in Glogova, Deronjic directed the assembled villagers to relinquish their weapons. Deronjić Amended Indictment, *supra* note 378, at para. 8(b). The Second Amended Indictment, by contrast, asserts only that "the residents of Glogova were told to turn in their weapons," without naming Deronjić as the person issuing the order. Deronjić Second Amended Indictment, *supra* at para. 8(b).

380. *See* Deronjić Indictment, *supra* note 373, para. 23. Deronjić Amended Indictment, *supra* note 378; Deronjić Second Amended Indictment, *supra* note 379, at para. 35.

381. Prosecutor v. Deronjić, Case No. IT-02-61-S, Transcript, at 301–03 (Mar. 5, 2004).

382. Telephone Interview with Slobodan Zecević, ICTY defense counsel (Sept. 1, 2005).

383. Mrđa Sentencing Judgement, *supra* note 11, at para. 10.

384. Prosecutor v. Mrđa, Case No. IT-02-59-I, Indictment, para. 17 (Apr. 16, 2002).

385. *See* Prosecutor v. Mrđa, Case No. IT-02-59-PT, Transcript, at 86–87 (July 24, 2003).

386. Prosecutor v. Mrđa, Case No. IT-02-59-S, Darko Mrđa's Sentencing Brief, para. 42 (Oct. 13, 2003) (on file with author) [hereinafter Mrđa's Sentencing Brief]; Prosecutor v. Mrđa, Case No. IT-02-59-S, Transcript, at 178 (Oct. 22, 2003).

387. Prosecutor v. Mrđa, Case No. IT-02-59-S, Amended Indictment, paras. 13, 15 (Aug. 4, 2003).

388. Prosecutor v. Dragan Nikolić, Case No. IT-94-2-PT, Second Amended Indictment, paras. 21–22 (Jan. 7, 2002).

389. Prosecutor v. Dragan Nikolić, Case No. IT-94-2-PT, Third Amended Indictment, paras. 21–22 (Oct. 31, 2003).

390. Prosecutor v. Bralo, Case No. IT-95-17-PT, Indictment, paras. 21, 25 (Nov. 2, 1995) [hereinafter Bralo Initial Indictment].

391. Prosecutor v. Bralo, Case No. IT-95-17-PT, Factual Basis, paras. 8–17 (July 18, 2005).

392. Some of the details regarding Bralo's infamous rape of so-called Witness A that had appeared in the initial indictment, however, failed to appear in the amended indictment. For instance, the initial indictment alleged that Bralo raped Witness A anally, required her thereafter to "lick his penis clean," and put his revolver in her mouth during the rapes, Bralo Initial Indictment, *supra* note 390, at paras. 21, 25, allegations that did not appear in the amended indictment.

393. Todorović Sentencing Judgement, *supra* note 319, at para. 9.

394. Also by way of comparison, Jelisić, who pled guilty without the benefit of a plea bargain, received a forty-year sentence. Jelisić Judgement, *supra* note 319, at para. 139. Jelisić admitted to killing thirteen people, *id.* paras. 3, 28, whereas Todorović admitted only to one murder, but the difference between a twelve and forty year sentence is vast.

395. Simić Sentencing Judgement, *supra* note 319, at para. 11.

396. Prosecution v. Simić et al., Case No. IT-95-9, Transcript, at 2741–43 (Oct. 23, 2001); Prosecution v. Simić et al., Case No. IT-95-9, Transcript, at 3364–66 (Nov. 2, 2001).

397. Sikirica Sentencing Judgement, *supra* note 319, at paras. 18, 21, 26, 32.

398. Prosecutor v. Kolundžija, Case No. IT-95-8-T, Admitted Facts Relevant to the Plea Agreement for Dragan Kolundžija, para. 3 (Sept. 4, 2001) [hereinafter Kolundžija Plea Agreement]; Prosecutor v. Došen, Case No. IT-95-8-T, Joint Submission of the Prosecution and the Accused Damir Došen Concerning a Plea Agreement and Admitted Facts, paras. 8–10 (Sept. 6, 2001) [hereinafter Došen Plea Agreement]; Prosecution v. Sikirica, Case No. IT-95-8-T, Joint Submission of the Prosecution and the Accused Duško Sikirica Concerning a Plea Agreement and Admitted Facts, paras. 8–10 (Sept. 6, 2001) [hereinafter Sikirica Plea Agreement].

399. Sikirica Sentencing Judgement, *supra* note 319, at paras. 25, 31, 37.

400. Prosecutor v. Sikirica, Case No. IT-95-8-T, Transcript, at 5687 (Oct. 8, 2001); Sikirica Sentencing Judgement, *supra* note 319, at para. 42.

401. Sikirica Sentencing Judgement, *supra* note 319, at para. 245.

402. Aleksovski Appeal, *supra* note 276, at para. 191.

403. Delalić Judgement, *supra* note 281, at para. 1253.

404. Prosecutor v. Mucić, Case No. IT-96-21-T*bis*-R117, Sentencing Judgement, para. 44 (Oct. 9, 2001).

405. The prosecution accused Prcać of personal involvement in certain brutalities but failed to prove its allegations. Prosecution v. Kvočka et al., Case No. IT-98-30/1-T, Judgement, paras. 451–63 (Nov. 2, 2001) [hereinafter Kvočka Judgement].

406. *Id.* at para. 726.

407. Sikirica Sentencing Judgment, *supra* note 319, at paras. 33–35.

408. Plavšić Prosecution's Sentencing Brief, *supra* note 360, at para. 14.

409. Plavšić Sentencing Judgement, *supra* note 319, at para. 32.

410. *Id.* at paras. 38–39.

411. *Id.* at paras. 41–44.

412. Prosecution v. Krajišnik & Plavšić, Case No. IT-00-39&40-PT, Factual Basis for Plea of Guilt, paras. 16–17, 20 (Sept. 30, 2002) [hereinafter Plavšić Plea Agreement]; Plavšić Sentencing Judgement, *supra* note 319, at paras. 14, 17.

413. Plavšić Plea Agreement, *supra* note 412, at para. 7.

414. Plavšić Prosecution's Sentencing Brief, *supra* note 360, at para. 43; Prosecutor v. Plavšić, Case No. IT-00-39&40/1-S, Transcript, at 638 (Dec. 18, 2002).

415. Plavšić Sentencing Judgement, *supra* note 319, at para. 134.

416. Sito-Sucic, *supra* note 12; Kebo, *supra* note 12.

417. Patrick McLoughlin, *Serb War Criminal Plavšić Goes to Swedish Jail*, REUTERS, June 27, 2003. Even Swedish prison guards objected when Plavšić was granted special privileges including private accommodation with a toilet and extended recreation time, and when she was presented a birthday cake to celebrate her birthday. Patrick McLoughlin, *War Criminal's Conditions Rile Guards*, REUTERS, Aug. 1, 2003. Plavšić, by contrast, has claimed that, in an effort to coerce her to testify against Slobodan Milošević, "bad air from a nearby factory is being pumped into her cell, causing her lungs to bleed." *Serb Leader Alleges Prison Conspiracy*, THE INDEPENDENT (London), Oct. 18, 2003; *Former Bosnian Serb President Complains about Prison Conditions in Sweden*, AGENCE FRANCE-PRESSE, Oct. 17, 2003.

418. Češić Sentencing Judgement, *supra* note 319, at paras. 7, 9–17.

419. Jelisić Judgement, *supra* note 319, at para. 119; Prosecution v. Jelisić, Case No. IT-95-10-T, Transcript, at 3070, 3132 (Nov. 25, 1999).

420. Jelisić Judgement, *supra* note 319, at para. 139.

421. Češić Plea Agreement, *supra* note 11, at para. 11; Češić Sentencing Judgement, *supra* note 319, at para. 111.

422. Banović Sentencing Judgement, *supra* note 285, at paras. 29–30.

423. Sikirica Sentencing Judgement, *supra* note 319, at paras. 25, 31.

424. Banović Sentencing Judgement, *supra* note 285, at paras. 94, 96.

425. Prosecutor v. Vasiljević, Case No. IT-98-32-T, Judgement, paras. 96–111 (Nov. 29, 2002). Vasiljević participated in the so-called Drina River incident in which Serbian paramilitaries, among others, brought seven Bosnian Muslim men to the bank of the Drina River and shot them at close range. Five died.

426. Simić Sentencing Judgement, *supra* note 319, at para. 115.

427. *Id.* at para. 116.

428. In the first round of sentencing in *Erdemović*, the prosecution recommended a sentence not exceeding ten years, Erdemović Sentencing Judgement, *supra* note 310, at text accompanying n.140, and the Trial Chamber sentenced Erdemović to ten years' imprisonment, *id.* at text accompanying n.141. In the second round of sentencing, the parties agreed in a plea agreement "that seven years' imprisonment would be an appropriate sentence," Erdemović, Second Sentencing Judgement, *supra* note 321, at para. 18, but the Trial Chamber sentenced Erdemović to five years' imprisonment, *id.* at para. 23. In *Jelisić*, the prosecution asked for a sentence of life imprisonment, Jelisić Judgement, *supra* note 319, at para. 119, and the Trial Chamber sentenced Jelisić to forty years' imprisonment, *id.* at para. 139. In *Todorović*, the parties entered into a plea agreement prohibiting the prosecution from recommending a sentence in excess of twelve years' imprisonment. Todorović Sentencing Judgement, *supra* note 319, at para. 11. The prosecution recommended a sentence of twelve years' imprisonment, *id.* at para. 22, and the Trial Chamber sentenced Todorović to ten years' imprisonment, *id.* at para. 115. In *Sikirica*, the parties entered into

plea agreements in which the prosecution agreed not to recommend sentences exceeding seventeen, seven, and five years' imprisonment for Sikirica, Došen, and Kolundžija, respectively. Sikirica Sentencing Judgement, *supra* note 319, at paras. 25, 31, 37. The prosecution recommended the maximum sentences for each defendant, *id.* at para. 42, and the Trial Chamber sentenced Sikirica, Došen, and Kolundžija to fifteen, five, and three years' imprisonment, respectively, *id.* at para. 245. As discussed in the text, in *Milan Simić*, the parties entered into a plea agreement in which they each agreed to recommend a sentence of not less than three and not more than five years' imprisonment, Simić Sentencing Judgement, *supra* note 319, at para. 13. The prosecution recommended a five-year sentence, *id.* at para. 30, and the Trial Chamber imposed a five-year sentence, *id.* at para. 122. In *Plavšić*, the prosecution recommended a sentence of between fifteen and twenty-five years' imprisonment, Plavšić Prosecution's Sentencing Brief, *supra* note 360, at para. 43, and the Trial Chamber imposed an eleven-year sentence, Plavšić Sentencing Judgement, *supra* note 319, at para. 132. Finally, in *Banović*, the prosecutor and defense both agreed to recommend an eight-year sentence for Banović, Banović Sentencing Judgement, *supra* note 285, at para. 11, and that is the term that the Trial Chamber imposed, *id.* at para. 96.

429. *See generally* Prosecution v. Momir Nikolić, Case No. IT-02-60-PT, Joint Motion for Consideration of Plea Agreement between Momir Nikolić and the Office of the Prosecutor, at Tab A to Annex A, Statement of Facts and Acceptance of Responsibility (May 7, 2003).

430. Prosecutor v. Momir Nikolić, Case No. IT-02-60-PT, Transcript, at 285–86 (May 6, 2003).

431. Momir Nikolić Sentencing Judgement, *supra* note 282, at paras. 57–73.

432. *Id.* at paras. 156, 176–79.

433. Obrenović Sentencing Judgement, *supra* note 319, at para. 156.

434. *Id.* at para. 87.

435. *Id.* at para. 85; Prosecution v. Obrenović, Case No. IT-02-60-T, Joint Motion for Consideration of Plea Agreement between Dragan Obrenović and the Office of the Prosecutor, at Tab A to Annex A, Statement of Facts As Set Out by Dragan Obrenović (May 20, 2003).

436. Obrenović Sentencing Judgement, *supra* note 319, at para. 90.

437. *Id.* at para. 141. Of lesser importance, the Trial Chamber also considered as mitigating circumstances Obrenović's offer of voluntary surrender, his comportment at the U.N. detention center, and his personal circumstances. *Id.*

438. *Id.* at para. 128.

439. *Id.* at para. 151.

440. *Id.* at para. 116.

441. *Id.* at paras. 142–46.

442. *Id.* at para. 105.

443. Dragan Nikolić Sentencing Judgement, *supra* note 11, at paras. 56–60, 66–104.

444. *Id.* at paras. 189, 192.

445. *Id.* at para. 172.

446. *Id.* at para. 214.

447. *Id.* at paras. 227–32.

448. *Id.* at para. 281 and Disposition.

449. Prosecutor v. Češić, Case No. IT-95-10/1-S, Prosecution's Sentencing Brief, at para. 67 (Nov. 12, 2003) [hereinafter Češić, Prosecution's Sentencing Brief]; Prosecutor v. Češić, Case No. IT-95-10/1-S, Transcript, at 114 (Nov. 27, 2003).

450. Češić Sentencing Judgement, *supra* note 319, at 111.

451. Prosecutor v. Mrđa, Case No. IT-02-59-PT, Transcript, at 81–82 (July 24, 2003).

452. Mrđa Sentencing Judgement, *supra* note 11, at para. 129.

453. Prosecutor v. Jokić, Case No. IT-01-42-PT, Transcript, at 139 (Aug. 27, 2003).

454. Prosecutor v. Jokić, Case No. IT-01-42/1-S, Miodrag Jokić's Sentencing Brief, para. 69 (Nov. 14, 2003).

455. Jokić Sentencing Judgement, *supra* note 11, at para. 116.

456. Deronjić Dissent, *supra* note 371, at paras. 2, 5.

457. *Id.* at para. 19.

458. Prosecutor v. Babić, Case No. IT-03-72-I, Amendment to the Joint Motion for Consideration of Plea Agreement between Milan Babić and the Office of the Prosecution Pursuant to Rule 62 *ter*, at Tab 1, Factual Statement, para. 5 (Jan. 22, 2004) [hereinafter Babić Factual Statement].

459. Prosecutor v. Babić, Case No. IT-03-72-S, Sentencing Judgement, paras. 20, 23 (June 29, 2004) [hereinafter Babić Sentencing Judgement].

460. *Id.* at para. 51.

461. *Id.* at para. 24.

462. Prosecutor v. Babić, Case No. IT-03-72-S, Transcript, at 206 (Apr. 2, 2004).

463. *See* Milanka Saponja-Hadzić, *Surprise at Babić Indictment*, IWPR's Tribunal Update, No. 334, Nov. 22, 2003.

464. Prosecutor v. Babić, Case No. IT-03-72-I, Indictment, paras. 4, 13–16 (Nov. 6, 2003).

465. Prosecutor v. Babić, Case No. IT-03-72-I, Transcript, at 29 (Jan. 27, 2004); Babić Sentencing Judgement, *supra* note 459, at paras. 6–8.

466. Babić Plea Agreement, *supra* note 319, at para. 4.

467. Babić Factual Statement, *supra* note 458, at para. 6.

468. *Id.* at paras. 26–27.

469. Babić Sentencing Judgement, *supra* note 459, at paras. 57, 98.

470. Prosecutor v. Babić, Case No. IT-03-72-S, Transcript, at 191 (Apr. 2, 2004).

471. Babić Sentencing Judgement, *supra* note 459, at paras. 101–02.

472. Press Release, ICTY, Indictment Against Miroslav Bralo Made Public, JL/P.I.S./902-e, Oct. 13, 2004.

473. Prosecutor v. Bralo, Case No. IT-95-17-S, Sentencing Brief on Behalf of Miroslav Bralo, para. 13 (Nov. 25, 2005) [hereinafter Bralo's Sentencing Brief]; Prosecutor v. Bralo, Case No. IT-95-17-S, Sentencing Judgement, para 69 (Dec. 7, 2005) [hereinafter Bralo Sentencing Judgement].

474. Bralo Sentencing Judgement, *supra* note 473, at para. 77.

475. Bralo's Sentencing Brief, *supra* note 473, *at* paras. 13–16; John Pomfret & Lee Hockstader, *In Bosnia, a War Crimes Impasse*, Wash. Post, Dec. 9, 1997, at A1.

476. Bralo's Sentencing Brief, *supra* note 473, at para. 17.

477. *Id.* at para 97.

478. According to defense counsel, Bralo immediately made clear his intention to plead guilty not only to the crimes in the indictment but to the crimes in Ahmići for which he had not been charged. Counsel advised Bralo, however, to enter not guilty pleas until the defense and prosecution could draft a factual basis that reflected the whole of his criminal liability. Bralo's Sentencing Brief, *supra* note 473, at para. 23.

479. Prosecutor v. Bralo, Case No. IT-95-17-A, Appeal Brief on Behalf of Miroslav Bralo, Appendix C, Apology (May 26, 2006) [hereinafter Bralo's Appeal Brief].

480. *Id.* at Appendix D, Declaration of Supplemental Statement of Miroslav Bralo.

481. *Id.* at Appendix F, Statement of Zaim Kablar; Bralo Sentencing Judgement, *supra* note 473, at 67.

482. Bralo Plea Agreement, *supra* note 319, at para. 9.

483. Plavšić Plea Agreement, *supra* note 412, at para. 7.

484. Bralo's Sentencing Brief, *supra* note 473, at para. 26; Prosecutor v. Bralo, Case No. IT-95-17-PT, Transcript, at 35 (July 19, 2005) (prosecutor informing the Trial Chamber that there are "no promises or inducements made by the Prosecutor's office in respect of securing the pleas that Mr. Bralo intends to tender to this Court").

485. Prosecutor v. Bralo, Case No. IT-95-17-S, Prosecution's Sentencing Brief, para. 97 (Oct. 10, 2005) [hereinafter Bralo Prosecution's Sentencing Brief].

486. Prosecutor v. Bralo, Case No. IT-95-17-S, Transcript, at 114 (Oct. 20, 2005).

487. Bralo Sentencing Judgement, *supra* note 473, at para. 77.

488. Bralo's Appeal Brief, *supra* note 479, at para. 54.3; Bralo Sentencing Judgement, *supra* note 473, at para. 74.

489. Bralo Sentencing Judgement, *supra* note 473, at para. 78.

490. *Id.* at para. 75.

491. *Id.* at para. 81.

492. *Id.* at para. 94.

493. *Id.* at para. 95.

494. By the time Erdemović pled guilty for the second time, the prosecution and defense had entered into a plea agreement providing that the parties would jointly recommend a sentence of seven years' imprisonment, Erdemović Second Sentencing Judgement, *supra* note 321, at para. 18(d).

495. *See, e.g.,* Prosecutor v. Janković, Case No. IT-96-23/2-PT, Decision on Referral of Case under Rule 11 *bis*, para. 16 (July 22, 2005).

496. Prosecutor v. Bralo, Case No. IT-95-17-A, Appeal Brief on Behalf of Miroslav Bralo, Appendix E, Apology, Statement of Mehmed Ahmić (May 26, 2006) [hereinafter Mehmed Ahmić Statement].

497. Prosecutor v. Rajić, Case No. IT-95-12-PT, Factual Basis, paras. 15–19 (Oct. 25, 2005) [hereinafter Rajić Factual Basis].

498. Prosecutor v. Rajić, Case No. IT-95-12-S, Sentencing Judgement, paras. 29, 42, 49 (May 8, 2006) [hereinafter Rajić Sentencing Judgement].

499. Rajić Factual Basis, *supra* note 497, at para. 28; Prosecutor v. Rajić, Case No. IT-95-12-PT, Amended Indictment, para. 15 (Jan. 13, 2004).

500. Rajić Sentencing Judgement, *supra* note 498, at paras. 2–4.

501. *See* Prosecutor v. Rajić, Case No. IT-95-12-PT, Decision for Further Information in the Context of the Prosecutor's Motion for Referral of the Case under Rule 11*bis* (Sept. 8, 2005).

502. Rajić pled guilty to four Grave Breaches of the Geneva Conventions: willful killing, inhuman treatment, appropriation of property, and extensive destruction not justified by military necessity and carried out unlawfully and wantonly. Rajić Plea Agreement, *supra* note 319, at para. 4.

503. *Id.* at para. 18(a).

504. Prosecutor v. Rajić, Case No. IT-95-12-S, Transcript, at 206, 255 (April 7, 2006).

505. Prosecutor v. Erdemović, Case No. IT-96-22-A, Judgement, para. 20 (Oct. 7, 1997).

506. The Appeals Chamber held that the Trial Chamber's sentence rested on "the totality of the criminal conduct of the accused," and it concluded that the totality of that conduct was not "materially affected by the Trial Chamber's error of convicting [Jelisić] of one additional murder." Prosecutor v. Jelisić, Case No. IT-95-10-A, Judgement, paras. 93–94 (July 5, 2001).

507. *See* Todorović Judgement, *supra* note 319, at para. 11; Simić Judgement, *supra* note 319, at para. 117; Obrenović Plea Agreement, *supra* note 11, at para. 14.

508. Bralo's plea agreement also does not contain an appeal provision, but that is because the prosecution in *Bralo* made no promises regarding sentence recommendations.

509. The *Rajić* Sentencing Judgement was issued only two weeks before the date of this writing, so it is not yet clear whether Rajić will appeal his sentence.

510. Prosecutor v. Deronjić, Case No. IT-02-61-A, Judgement on Sentencing Appeal, para. 100 (July 20, 2005) [hereinafter Deronjić Appeals Judgement].

511. Prosecutor v. Babić, Case No. IT-03-72-A, Judgement on Sentencing Appeal, para. 78 (July 18, 2005) [hereinafter Babić Appeals Judgement].

512. Prosecution v. Dragan Nikolić, Case No. IT-94-2-A, Judgement on Sentencing Appeal, paras. 23–42 (Feb. 4, 2005) [hereinafter Dragan Nikolić Appeals Judgement].

513. *Id.* at paras. 49–56; Babić Appeals Judgement, *supra* note 511, at paras. 67–68; Prosecutor v. Momir Nikolić, Case No. IT-02-60/1-A, Judgement on Sentencing Appeal, para.74 (Mar. 8, 2006) [hereinafter Momir Nikolić Appeals Judgement].

514. Prosecutor v. Jokić, Case No. IT-01-42/1-A, Transcript, at 316, 321–24 (Apr. 26, 2005); Deronjić Appeals Judgement, *supra* note 510, at para. 147; Babić Appeals Judgement, *supra* note 511, at paras. 76–77.

515. Dragan Nikolić Appeals Judgement, *supra* note 512, at para. 57; Babić Appeals Judgement, *supra* note 511, at para. 71; Momir Nikolić Appeals Judgement, *supra* note 513, at para. 116.

516. *See* Babić Appeals Judgement, *supra* note 511, at paras. 68, 70, 72, 74–75, 77; Dragan Nikolić Appeals Judgement, *supra* note 512, at paras. 53, 56, 59; Prosecutor v. Jokić, Case No. IT-01-42/1-A, Judgement on Sentencing Appeal, para. 49 (Aug. 30, 2005).

517. Prosecutor v. Jokić, Case No. IT-01-42/1-A, Transcript, at 316, 345–47 (Apr. 26, 2005).

518. Babić Sentencing Judgement, *supra* note 459, at para. 57; *see also id.* at para. 79.

519. Babić Appeals Judgement, *supra* note 511, at para. 34.

520. Deronjić Appeals Judgement, *supra* note 510, at III.

521. *Id.* at 55.

522. Telephone Interview with Slobodan Zecević, ICTY defense counsel (Sept. 1, 2005).

523. Deronjić Appeals Judgement, *supra* note 510, at paras. 28–29, 59–60.

524. Prosecutor v. Jokić, Case No. IT-01-42-PT, Order on Miodrag Jokić's Motion for Provisional Release, paras. 4, 28 (Feb. 20, 2002); Prosecution v. Jokić, Case No. IT-01-42/1-A, Transcript, at 321–23 (Apr. 26, 2005).

525. Babić Appeals Judgement, *supra* note 511, at para. 8.

526. Prosecution v. Babić, Case No. IT-03-72-A, Transcript, at 33–34 (Apr. 25, 2005).

527. Prosecutor v. Dragan Nikolić, Case No. IT-94-2-A, Prosecution Respondent's Brief, paras. 8, 10(f) (Aug. 9, 2004); Prosecutor v. Dragan Nikolić, Case No. IT-94-2-A, Transcript, at 35, 48 (Nov. 29, 2004).

528. Momir Nikolić Appeals Judgement, *supra* note 513, at paras. 71, 105, 109.

529. Prosecution v. Babić, Case No. IT-03-72-A, Transcript, at 21, 25 (Apr. 25, 2005).

530. *Id.* at 37.

531. Prosecution v. Jokić, Case No. IT-01-42/1-A, Transcript, at 358–59 (Apr. 26, 2005).

532. *See generally,* Nancy Amoury Combs, *Procuring Guilty Pleas for International Crimes: The Limited Influence of Sentencing Discounts,* 59 Vand. L. Rev. 69 (2006) [hereinafter Combs, *Procuring Guilty Pleas for International Crimes*].

533. The third defendant, Milan Babić, did persuade the Appeals Chamber that the Trial Chamber had erred in failing to consider his post-crime peace-building efforts, but the Appeals Chamber nonetheless declined to reduce his sentence, finding that "in the context of the complete picture of the Appellant's conduct that was before the Trial Chamber, the Appeals Chamber is not persuaded that the Trial Chamber would have, or that it should have, issued a different sentence" had it considered Babić's peace-building efforts. Babić Appeals Judgement, *supra* note 511, at paras. 53–61. Whereas the *Momir Nikolić* and *Dragan Nikolić* Trial Chambers had sentenced those defendants to seven and eight years longer than the terms agreed upon in their respective plea agreements, the *Babić* Trial Chamber had sentenced Babić to a term only two years longer than that appearing in the plea agreement. Because the discrepancy was small, the Appeals Chamber may have felt more comfortable letting the Trial Chamber's sentence stand.

534. Momir Nikolić Appeals Judgement, *supra* note 513, at paras. 57–63, 68–73, 86–115.

535. Dragan Nikolić Appeals Judgement, *supra* note 512, at paras. 96–97.

Chapter 5

536. Prosecutor v. Kambanda, Case No. ICTR-97-23-1, Plea Agreement between Jean Kambanda and the Office of the Prosecutor, paras. 23–40 (Apr. 29, 1998) [hereinafter Kambanda Plea Agreement]; Kambanda Judgement, *supra* note 276, at para. 39.

537. Kambanda Judgement, *supra* note 276, at para. 1.

538. Jean Kambanda v. Prosecutor, Case No. ICTR 97-23-A, Provisional Appellant's Brief and Motions for Extension of the Time-Limits and for Admission of New Evidence on Appeal Pursuant to Rules 115 and 116 of the Rules of Procedure and Evidence, paras. 3–6 (Mar. 29, 2000) [hereinafter Kambanda's Appeals Brief].

539. Telephone Interview with SK (Dec. 1, 2004); Telephone Interview with Howard Morrison, ICTR defense counsel (Dec. 2, 2004); Interview with BM, Nov. 8, 2004, The Hague.

540. Kambanda Judgement, *supra* note 276, at para. 48; *see also* Prosecutor v. Kambanda, Case No. ICTR-97-23-I, Transcript, at 6 (Sept. 3, 1998).

541. Plavšić Sentencing Judgement, *supra* note 319, at para. 80.

542. Prosecutor v. Kambanda, Case No. ICTR-97-23-I, Prosecutor's Pre-Sentencing Brief at 22–23 (Aug. 31, 1998) [hereinafter Kambanda Prosecutor's Pre-Sentencing Brief].

543. *Id.; see also* Prosecutor v. Kambanda, Case No. ICTR-97-23-I, Transcript, at 12 (Sept. 3, 1998).

544. Kambanda Plea Agreement, *supra* note 536, at para. 42; *see also Lawyer for the Former Rwandan Prime Minister Argues for Light Sentence,* INTERNEWS, Sept. 4, 1998 (reporting prosecutor's comments that Kambanda would testify in the genocide trials of other government and military leaders), *available at* http://www.internews.org/activities/ICTR_reports/ICTRNewsSep98.html.

545. Kambanda Judgement, *supra* note 276, at para. 60.

546. Kambanda Prosecutor's Pre-Sentencing Brief, *supra* note 542, at 2.

547. Kambanda Judgement, *supra* note 276, at Verdict.

548. *Id.* at para. 62.

549. Kambanda v. Prosecutor, Case No. ICTR-97-23-A, Judgement, para. 3 (Oct. 19, 2000) [hereinafter Kambanda Appeals Judgement].

550. Kambanda's Appeals Brief, *supra* note 538, at paras. 2–10.

551. Kambanda Appeals Judgement, *supra* note 549, at para. 126.

552. Telephone Interviews with SK (December 1 and 10, 2004).

553. *Interahamwe* means "those who fight together."

554. Prosecutor v. Serushago, Case No. ICTR-98-39-S, Sentence, para. 25 (Feb. 5, 1999) [hereinafter Serushago Sentence].

555. *Id.* at para. 32; Prosecutor v. Serushago, Case No. ICTR-98-39, Transcript, 11 (Jan. 29, 1999) [hereinafter Serushago Transcript].

556. Serushago Sentence, *supra* note 554, at paras. 1, 34.

557. Prosecutor v. Serushago, Case No. ICTR-98-37-I, Indictment (Oct. 8, 1998).

558. Serushago Sentence, *supra* note 554, at paras. 2–4; Prosecutor v. Serushago, Case No. ICTR-98-37, Plea Agreement between Omar Serushago and the Office of the Prosecutor (Dec. 4, 1998) [hereinafter Serushago Plea Agreement].

559. Telephone interview with Mohamed Othman, former ICTR prosecutor (Aug. 27, 2005).

560. Lars Waldorf, *Memoirs of a Snitch,* DIPLOMATIE JUDICIAIRE, Nov. 27, 2001.

561. Serushago Plea Agreement, *supra* note 558, at para. 13.

562. Serushago Transcript, *supra* note 555, at 10–12, 15.

563. Kambanda Judgement, *supra* note 276, at para. 60 and Verdict; Akayesu Sentence, *supra* note 359; Prosecutor v. Kayishema & Ruzindana, Case No. ICTR 95-1-T, Judgement, at Sentence paras. 25, 27–28 (May 21, 1999) [hereinafter Kayishema & Ruzindana Judgment].

564. *See* Musema Judgement and Sentence, *supra* note 359, para. 994; Rutaganda Judgement and Sentence, *supra* note 359, at para. 464; Niyitegeka Judgement and Sentence, *supra* note 359, at para. 489; Ntakirutimana Judgement, *supra* note 137, at paras. 888–90; Nahimana Judgement, *supra* note 3, at para. 1097; Prosecutor v. Gacumbitsi, Case No. ICTR-2001-64-T, Judgement, para. 338 (June 17, 2004) [hereinafter Gacumbitsi Judgement]; Prosecutor v. Ntagerura et al., Case No. ICTR-99-46-T, Judgement and Sentence, para. 815 (Feb. 25, 2004) [hereinafter Ntagerura et al. Judgement]; Kajelijeli Judgement and Sentence, *supra* note 359, at para. 956; Prosecutor v. Ndindabahizi, Case No. ICTR-2001-71-I, Judgement and Sentence, para. 503 (July 15, 2004) [hereinafter Ndindabahizi Judgement]; Prosecutor v. Semanza, Case No. ICTR-97-20-T, Judgement and Sentence, para. 558 (May 15, 2003) [hereinafter Semanza Judgement]. The Trial Chamber did not report the prosecution's sentence recommendation in the *Kamuhanda* case. However, the fact that the chamber sentenced Kamuhanda to life imprisonment strongly indicates that the prosecution recommended a life sentence in that case as well. *See* Kamuhanda Judgement and Sentence, *supra* note 359, at para. 770.

565. Serushago Sentence, *supra* note 554, at Verdict.

566. The other defendant, Elizaphan Ntakirutimana, was sentenced to ten years' imprisonment, but his advanced age and poor health contributed to the leniency of the sentence. *See* Ntakirutimana Judgement, *supra* note 137, at paras. 898, 921.

567. Serushago Sentence, *supra* note 554, at para. 35.

568. Prosecutor v. Ruggiu, Case No. ICTR-97-32-I, Judgement and Sentence, para. 38 (June 1, 2000) [hereinafter Ruggiu Judgement]. At Ruggiu's presentencing hearing, his lawyer maintained that Ruggiu "had come to know Rwanda through highly partisan friends who gave him a biased idea of the political situation in the country." *How Belgian Journalist Became Involved in Hate Media*, INTERNEWS, May 15, 2000, *available at* http://www.internews.org/activities/ICTR_Reports/ICTRNewsMay00.html; *see also* Prosecution v. Ruggiu, Case No. ICTR-97-32, Transcript, at 109–12 (May 15, 2000) [hereinafter Ruggiu Transcript].

569. Ruggiu Transcript, *supra* note 568, at 113.

570. Prosecutor v. Ruggiu, Case No. ICTR-97-32-I, Amended Indictment, 12-15 (Dec. 18, 1998).

571. *I Lied in My Book to Protect RTLM, Says Convicted Radio Presenter*, HIRONDELLE NEWS AGENCY, Feb. 28, 2002.

572. Ruggiu Transcript, *supra* note 568, at 47–56. It later was revealed that Ruggiu lied to prosecutors in some of these early interviews. *Convicted Ex-Radio Presenter Has Mental Problems, Defence Suggests*, HIRONDELLE NEWS AGENCY, Mar. 5, 2002.

573. Prosecutor v. Ruggiu, Case No. ICTR-97-32-DP, Plea Agreement between Georges Ruggiu and the Office of the Prosecutor, para. 4 (Apr. 11, 2000) [hereinafter Ruggiu Plea Agreement].

574. *Id.* at para. 2; Ruggiu Judgement, *supra* note 568, at para. 10 and Verdict.

575. *Hate Radio Presenter Set to Plead Guilty to Genocide Charges*, HIRONDELLE NEWS AGENCY, May 9, 2000.

576. Prosecutors emphasized this point, both in the press, *see Portrait of Georges Ruggiu, Journalist Who Incited Genocide*, HIRONDELLE NEWS AGENCY, May 14, 2000, and to the Trial Chamber, *see* Ruggiu Transcript, *supra* note 568, at 66.

577. Ruggiu Transcript, *supra* note 568, at 188, 190.

578. Ruggiu Judgement, *supra* note 568, at paras. 53, 55.

579. *Rwanda Unhappy with Ruggiu Sentence*, HIRONDELLE NEWS AGENCY, June 1, 2000.

580. Letter dated 5 December 2005 from the President of the International Criminal Tribunal for the Prosecution of Persons Responsible for Genocide and Other Serious Violations of International Humanitarian Law Committed in the Territory of Rwanda and Rwandan Citizens Responsible for Genocide and Other Such Violations Committed in the Territory of Neighbouring States between 1 January and 31 December 1994 addressed to the President of the Security Council, U.N. Doc. S/2005/782, Summary (Dec. 14, 2005).

581. *See generally Combs, supra* note 532, at 100–24.

582. Gacumbitsi Judgement, *supra* note 564, at para. 334; Ntagerura et al. Judgement, *supra* note 564, at para. 806 (convicting Imanishimwe); Kamuhanda Judgement and Sentence, *supra* note 359, at para. 750; Nahimana Judgement, *supra* note 3, paras. 1092–94; Kajelijeli Judgement and Sentence, *supra* note 359, at para. 942; Niyitegeka Judgement and Sentence, *supra* note 359, at para. 480; Semanza Judgement, *supra* note 564, at para. 553; Ntakirutimana Judgement, *supra* note 137, at paras. 877–78 (Feb. 21, 2003); Ndindabahizi Judgement, *supra* note 564, at para. 495; Ruggiu Judgement, *supra* note 568, at Verdict; Musema Judgement and Sentence, *supra* note 359, at Verdict; Rutaganda Judgement and Sentence, *supra* note 359, at Verdict; Kayishema & Ruzindana Judgement, *supra* note 563, at Verdict, para. 2; Serushago Sentence, *supra* note 554, at Verdict; Kambanda Judgement, *supra* note 276, at Verdict; Akayesu Judgement, *supra* note 137, at Verdict.

583. Prosecutor v. Kayishema et al., Case No. ICTR-95-1-I, First Amended Indictment, para. 54 (Apr. 29, 1996).

584. Prosecutor v. Rutaganira, Case No. ICTR-95-1C-T, Transcript, at 9 (Jan. 17, 2005).

585. *Id.* at 13.

586. *Id.* at 5–6, 10, 27.

587. *Id.* at 10.

588. *Id.* at 20, 24–25, 29.

589. *Id.* at 15–16, 20, 24.

590. The prosecution also asked the Trial Chamber to acquit Rutaganira of genocide, but that request is in keeping with the factual basis of Rutaganira's guilty plea. One cannot commit genocide without having the specific intent to commit genocide. Thus, because Rutaganira admitted only to failing to protect the Tutsi, the prosecution did in fact lack sufficient evidence to convict him of genocide.

591. Akayesu Judgement, *supra* note 137, at para. 591.

592. The prosecution's failure to bring rape charges, and later to add rape charges once evidence of rape was presented at trial, generated widespread controversy. *See* Binaifer Nowrojee, *"Your Justice Is Too Slow?" Will the ICTR Fail Rwanda's Rape Victims?* Occasional Paper 10, UNITED NATIONS RESEARCH INSTITUTE FOR SOCIAL DEVELOPMENT 14–17 (Nov. 2005).

593. Ntagerura et al, Judgement, *supra* note 564, at para. 805.

594. *Rwanda: Government Wants Acquitted Bagambiki to Surrender in Order to Face Rape Trial*, HIRONDELLE, May 4, 2006.

595. Prosecutor v. Rutaganira, Case No. ICTR-95-1C-T, Sentencing Judgement, para. 104 (Mar. 14, 2005).

596. *Id.* at Sentence.

597. Prosecutor v. Bisengimana, Case No. ICTR-00-60-T, Judgement and Sentence, paras. 1, 4 (Apr. 13, 2006) [hereinafter Bisengimana Judgement].

598. Bisengimana's indictment charges him with one count of genocide, one count of complicity in genocide, one count of conspiracy in genocide, one count of direct and public incitement to genocide, one count of murder as a crime against humanity, one count of extermination as a crime against humanity, one count of torture as a crime against humanity, one count of rape as a crime against humanity, one count of inhumane acts as a crime against humanity, and three counts of violations of the Geneva Conventions. Prosecutor v. Bisengimana, Case No. ICTR-2000-60-I, Indictment (July 1, 2000).

599. *Id.* at paras. 3.14, 3.21(i), 3.22, 3.27, 3.28, 3.29, 3.31.

600. *Id.* at paras. 3.26, 3.39, 3.45.

601. *Id.* at paras. 3.33, 3.35, 3.40, 3.41.

602. The amended indictment charged Bisengimana with one count of genocide, one count of complicity in genocide, one count of murder as a crime against humanity, one count of extermination as a crime against humanity, and one count of rape as a crime against humanity. Prosecutor v. Bisengimana, Case No. ICTR-00-60-1, Amended Indictment (Oct. 31, 2005).

603. For instance, the amended indictment no longer contained the claim that Bisengimana personally committed rape. *Id.*

604. *Id.* at para. 16.

605. *Id.* at para. 21.

606. *Id.* at para. 22.

607. *Id.* at para. 26–28.

608. Semanza Judgement, *supra* note 564, at paras. 166, 169, 170, 174, 180, 196–97.

609. Prosecutor v. Bisengimana, Case No. ICTR-2000-60-I, Joint Motion for Consideration of a Guilty Plea Agreement between Paul Bisengimana and the Office of the Prosecutor, para. 5 (Nov. 30, 2005).

610. Prosecutor v. Bisengimana, Case No. ICTR-2000-60-I, Plea Agreement between Mr. Paul Bisengimana and the Office of the Prosecutor, paras. 46, 48 (Oct. 19, 2005) [hereinafter Bisengimana Plea Agreement]. The English version of the plea agreement requires the prosecution to recommend a sentence of between eleven and fifteen years' imprison-

ment, while the French version requires a recommendation of between twelve and fourteen years. The parties agreed that the French version is correct. Prosecutor v. Bisengimana, Case No. ICTR-2000-60-S, Transcript, at 47 (Jan. 19, 2006).

611. *Id.* at para. 49.

612. Bisengimana Plea Agreement, *supra* note 610, at para. 34.

613. *Id.* at para. 35.

614. *Id.* at para. 42.

615. *Id.* at para. 37.

616. *Id.* at para. 29.

617. *Id.* at para. 36.

618. Prosecutor v. Bisengimana, Case No. ICTR-2000-60-I, Transcript, at 21 (Nov. 17,
2005) ("And it will suffice to say that the paragraphs in the agreement . . . [are] indicative
of the current state of affairs regarding the evidence available to the Prosecutor at this
stage.").

619. *Id.* at 22. Later, after receiving harsh criticism from the government of Rwanda,
the prosecution asserted as a general matter that genocide charges are withdrawn only
when "it would difficult to prove beyond a reasonable doubt the role that the particular
accused person played in the perpetration of the genocide." *ICTR and Rwanda Argue over
Plea Bargains*, HIRONDELLE NEWS AGENCY, Apr. 22, 2006.

620. Prosecutor v. Semanza, Case No. ICTR-97-20-T, Transcript, at 44–49 (Nov. 7,
2000).

621. Prosecutor v. Semanza, Case No. ICTR-97-20-T, Transcript, at 26–27 (Dec. 6,
2000); Semanza Judgement, *supra* note 564, at para. 150.

622. Prosecutor v. Semanza, Case No. ICTR-97-20-T, Transcript, at 60–61 (Mar. 7,
2001); *id.* at para. 166.

623. *Id.* at para. 170.

624. *Id.* at paras. 196–97.

625. *Id.* at para. 196.

626. Defense counsel emphasized Bisengimana's active participation in the genocide
during closing arguments, Prosecutor v. Semanza, Case No. ICTR-97-20-T, Transcript,
at 182–83 (June 18, 2002), and he elicited testimony from Semanza that Bisengimana took
orders from no one, Prosecutor v. Semanza, Case No. ICTR-97-20-T, Transcript, at 64–65
(Feb. 27, 2002).

627. Semanza Judgement, *supra* note 564, at para. 207.

628. Prosecutor v. Bisengimana, Case No. ICTR-2000-60-I, Transcript, at 26 (Nov. 17,
2005).

629. Prosecutor v. Bisengimana, Case No. ICTR-00-60-1, Amended Indictment
(Nov. 23, 2005).

630. Prosecutor v. Bisengimana, Case No. ICTR-2000-60-I, Transcript, at 12–13
(Dec. 7, 2005).

631. *Id.* at 13–14, 18.

632. Bisengimana Judgement, *supra* note 597, at paras. 186. Not surprisingly, Bisengimana asked for a twelve-year sentence; *id.* at para. 188.

633. *Id.* at para. 202. Although Bisengimana pled guilty to both murder and extermination as crimes against humanity, the Trial Chamber convicted him only of extermination, finding that the count of murder is included in the crime of extermination. *Id.* at paras. 96–104.

634. *ICTR/Bisengimana—Former Mayor Who Pleaded Guilty Sentenced to 15 Years,* HIRONDELLE NEWS AGENCY, Apr. 13, 2006.

635. *See Sentence against Bisengimana to Discourage Further Confessions,* HIRONDELLE NEWS AGENCY, Apr. 20, 2006.

636. *ICTR and Rwanda Argue over Plea Bargains,* HIRONDELLE NEWS AGENCY, Apr. 22, 2006.

637. Semanza Judgement, *supra* note 564, at para. 590.

638. Prosecutor v. Akayesu, Case No. ICTR-96-4-I, Amended Indictment, paras. 12–23 (June 17, 1997).

639. Akayesu Judgement, *supra* note 137, at paras. 184, 187, 193.

640. *Id.* at Verdict.

641. Akayesu Sentence, *supra* note 359.

642. *Sentence against Bisengimana to Discourage Further Confessions,* HIRONDELLE NEWS AGENCY, Apr. 20, 2006; *ICTR/Judges/Prosecution—ICTR Hampers Prosecution Strategy Again,* HIRONDELLE NEWS AGENCY, May 25, 2006.

643. Prosecutor v. Serugendo, Case No. ICTR-2005-84-I, Corrigendum of Indictment, at I (July 21, 2005).

644. *Id.* at para. 27.

645. *Id.* at paras. 21, 25.

646. *Id.* at paras. 10–11.

647. *Id.* at para. 30.

648. Sukhdev Chhatbar, *Rwandan Pleads Innocent to Genocide Charge,* A.P., Sept. 30, 2005.

649. Thierry Cruvellier, *Confessions—A Key to Wrapping Up Trials in ICTR,* INT'L JUST. TRIB., Mar. 27, 2006.

650. Press Release, ICTR, Joseph Serugendo Sentenced to Six Years Imprisonment, ICTR/INFO-9-2-478.EN (June 2, 2006) [hereinafter Serugendo Press Release].

651. *ICTR/Serugendo—Serugendo's Guilty Plea Bargain Settled on a Prison Sentence of 6 to 10 Years,* HIRONDELLE NEWS AGENCY, June. 1, 2006.

652. *Id.*

653. *Id.*

654. *Id.;* Serugendo Press Release, *supra* note 650.

655. *Prosecutor Steps Up Pressure on the Akazu,* INT'L JUST. TRIB., Dec. 5, 2005; *ICTR/Uwilingiyimana—Uwilingiyimana's Death Threatens to Hamper Prosecutor's Work,* HIRONDELLE NEWS AGENCY, Jan. 17, 2006.

656. Prosecutor v. Bagaragaza, Case No. ICTR-2005-86-R11*bis,* Decision on the Prosecution Motion for Referral to the Kingdom of Norway, para. 1, May 19, 2006 [hereinafter Bagaragaza Rule 11*bis* Decision].

657. *Id.* at para. 2.

658. *ICTR: Looking for the Secrets of the Akazu*, INT'L JUST. TRIB., Sept. 12, 2005.

659. Bagaragaza Rule 11*bis* Decision, *supra* note 656, at para. 3.

660. *Id.* at para. 9.

661. *Id.* at para. 7.

662. Mary Margaret Penrose, *Lest We Fail: The Importance of Enforcement in International Criminal Law*, 15 AM. U. INT'L L. REV. 321, 382 n.225 (2000).

663. *Tribunal Throws Out Motion to Have Bagaragaza's Transfer to Norway*, HIRONDELLE NEWS AGENCY, May 19, 2006.

664. Bagaragaza Rule 11*bis* Decision, *supra* note 656, at para. 16.

665. *Prosecutor Steps Up Pressure on the Akazu*, INT'L JUST. TRIB., Dec. 5, 2005.

666. Karen Palmer, *Justice in Jeopardy*, TORONTO STAR, Mar. 27, 2006.

667. *ICTR/Uwilingiyimana—Uwilingiyimana's Death Threatens to Hamper Prosecutor's Work*, HIRONDELLE NEWS AGENCY, Jan. 17, 2006.

668. *Former Rwandan Minister's Body Found in Belgium*, ASHEVILLE GLOBAL REPORT, No. 363, Dec. 29–Jan. 4 2006; *ICTR/Uwilingiyimana—Many Questions in Arusha after the Announcement of Uwilingiyimana's Death*, HIRONDELLE NEWS AGENCY, Dec. 23, 2005.

669. Letter of Juvénal Uwilingiyimana, *available at* http://cirqueminime.blogcollective.com/blog/_archives/2005/12/27/1523635.html.

670. Radio interview of Uwilingiyimana's son, Eric Migamba, by Phil Taylor, Jan. 9, 2006, available at http://www.taylor-report.com/audio/index.php?month=2006-01. *See also* Gilbert Dupont, Mutilé et éviscéré, LA DERNIERE HEURE, Dec. 24, 2005.

671. *ICTR/Uwilingiyimana—Many Questions in Arusha after the Announcement of Uwilingiyimana's Death*, HIRONDELLE NEWS AGENCY, Dec. 23, 2005.

672. *The Uwilingiyimana Mystery*, INT'L JUST. TRIB., Jan. 23, 2006.

673. Gilbert Dupont, *Rien ne contredit le suicide*, LA DERNIERE HEURE, Feb. 7, 2006.

674. *See* Combs, *Procuring Guilty Pleas for International Crimes*, *supra* note 532.

675. At the time of this writing, however, none of the defendants has yet been transferred. Status of Detainees, *available at* http://69.94.11.53/default.htm.

676. Prosecutor v. Barayagwiza, Case No. ICTR-97-17-AR72, Decision (Nov. 3, 1999).

677. Franck Petit, *Cameroonian Intrigues*, INT'L JUST. TRIB., Mar. 5, 2001; *ICTR/Prosecution—Synthesis: Prosecutors at the ICTR*, HIRONDELLE NEWS AGENCY, Oct. 28, 2003.

678. Prosecutor v. Barayagwiza, Case No. ICTR-97-17-AR72, Decision (Prosecutor's Request for Review or Reconsideration) (March 31, 2000).

679. *ICTR/Prosecution—Synthesis: Prosecutors at the ICTR*, HIRONDELLE NEWS AGENCY, Oct. 28, 2003; *ICTR/Rusatira—General Rusatira's Release Heightens Tension Between Rwanda and the ICTR*, HIRONDELLE NEWS AGENCY, Oct. 29, 2003.

680. J. Coll Metcalf, *An Interview with United Nations' Chief War Crimes Prosecutor, Carla del Ponte*, INTERNEWS, Feb. 15, 2000.

681. *Rwanda Pressing UN to Drop Del Ponte As Prosecutor: Spokeswoman*, AGENCE FRANCE-PRESSE, July 24, 2003.

682. Ruggiu Transcript, *supra* note 568, at 50–52.

683. Kambanda Prosecutor's Pre-Sentencing Brief, *supra* note 542; Serushago Plea Agreement, *supra* note 558, at para. 45; Ruggiu Plea Agreement, *supra* note 573, at para. 226.

684. *See* Mary Kimani, *Former Rwandan Militia Leader Asks for the Forgiveness of Rwanda*, INTERNEWS, Jan. 29, 1998, *available at* http://internews.org/activities/ICTR_reports/ICTRnewsJAN99.html.

Chapter 6

685. S.C. Res. 1272, U.N. Doc. S/RES/1272 (Oct. 25, 1999).

686. UNTAET Reg. 2000/15, *supra* note 215.

687. Megan Hirst & Howard Vareny, International Center for Transitional Justice, *Justice Abandoned? An Assessment of the Serious Crimes Process in East Timor* 8 (June 2005).

688. *The Future of Serious Crimes*, *supra* note 217.

689. Some defendants, however, led Timorese militia groups, *see, e.g.*, Prosecutor v. João Franca da Silva, Dili District Court, Special Panels for Serious Crimes, Case No. 04a/2001, Judgement, at para. 46 (Dec. 5, 2002); Prosecutor v. Manuel Gonçalves Bere, Dili District Court, Special Panels for Serious Crimes, Case No. 10/2000, Judgement, at 6 (May 15, 2001) [hereinafter Bere Judgement], but such offenders nonetheless had little status and authority compared with Indonesian military leaders.

690. JUSTICE FOR TIMOR-LESTE, *supra* note 204, at § 3.3, § 4.1; *The Future of Serious Crimes*, *supra* note 216, at 10.

691. *See, e.g.*, Prosecutor v. Julio Fernandes, Dili District Court, Special Panels for Serious Crimes, Case No. 02 C.G. 2000, Judgement, at 4 (Mar. 1, 2000) [hereinafter Julio Fernandes Judgement]; Prosecutor v. Carlos Soares Carmona, Dili District Court, Special Panels for Serious Crimes, Case No. 03 C.G. 2000, Judgement at 3–4 (Apr. 19, 2001) [hereinafter Carmona Judgement]; Bere Judgement, *supra* note 689, at 5; Carlos Soares Judgement, *supra* note 220, at 4; Joseph Leki Judgement, *supra* note 220, at 2; Prosecutor v. Jose Valente, Dili District Court, Special Panels for Serious Crimes, Case No. 3/2001, Judgement, at 2 (June 19, 2001) [hereinafter Jose Valente Judgement]; Prosecutor v. Agustinho da Costa, Dili District Court, Special Panels for Serious Crimes, Case No. 07/2000, Judgement, at 8 (Oct. 11, 2001).

692. João Fernandes Judgement, *supra* note 225, at paras. 12–15.

693. *Id.* at Verdict.

694. João Fernandes v. Prosecutor, Court of Appeal of East Timor, Criminal Appeal No. 2001/02, at 4–5, 8 (June 29, 2001).

695. João Fernandes v. Prosecutor, Court of Appeal of East Timor, Criminal Appeal No. 2001/02, Judgement of Egonda-Ntende, J., at 20 (June 29, 2001).

696. *Id.* at 21–22.

697. Carmona Judgement, *supra* note 691, at 2; *see also* Jose Valente Judgement, *supra* note 691, at 2.

698. UNTAET Reg. 2000/15, *supra* note 215, at §§ 19(d), 21.

699. Linton & Reiger, *supra* note 231, at 17–18. (The Special Panels refer to the defendant in this case as Gaspar Leki and at other times as Gaspar Leite). Leki was eventually convicted of negligence causing death and sentenced to eleven months' imprisonment. Prosecutor v. Gaspar Leki, Dili District Court, Special Panels for Serious Crimes, Case No. 05/2001, Judgement, at para. 61 (Sept. 14, 2002).

700. The following trials were each conducted over the course of one day. Julio Fernandes Judgement, *supra* note 691, at 2; Carmona Judgement, *supra* note 691, at 2; Bere Judgement, *supra* note 689, at 4. The Joseph Leki trial was held over two sessions. Joseph Leki Judgement, *supra* note 220, at 2.

701. UNTAET Reg. 2000/15, *supra* note 215, at § 5.1.

702. In some crimes against humanity cases, the language of the judgments on the question of whether there had been a widespread or systematic attack on a civilian population was cut and pasted from the indictments. *Compare* Deputy General Prosecutor for Serious Crimes against Damiao Da Costa Nunes, Dili District Court, Special Panels for Serious Crimes, Case No. 1/2003, Indictment, paras. 1–7 (Dec. 17, 2002) *with* Prosecutor v. Damiao Da Costa Nunes, Dili District Court, Special Panels for Serious Crimes, Case No. 1/2003, Judgement, at paras. 37–44 (Dec. 10, 2003) [hereinafter Da Costa Nunes Judgement]. When the panels did cite outside sources, they typically relied on the reports of international organizations. *See* Prosecutor v. Joni Marques et al., Dili District Court, Special Panels for Serious Crimes, Case No. 09/2000, Judgement, para. 686 (Dec. 11, 2001) [hereinafter Los Palos Judgement]. The standard plea agreement form used at the Special Panels requires defendants to admit that their crimes were "committed as part of a widespread or systematic attack against a civilian population with knowledge of the attack." *See* Prosecutor v. Abilio Mendez Correia, Dili District Court, Special Panels for Serious Crimes, Case No. 19/2001, Admissions by Abilio Mendez Correia, para. 2(b) (Mar. 2, 2004) [hereinafter Correia Plea Agreement]. Even in full-scale trials, the parties have often agreed on the existence of these elements. *See* da Costa Nunes Judgement, *supra* at para. 37.

703. Los Palos Judgement, *supra* note 702, at paras. 680–91.

704. UNTAET Reg. 2000/15, *supra* note 215, at § 5 (1999).

705. Los Palos Judgement, *supra* note 702, at para. 13.

706. THE LOLOTOE CASE: A SMALL STEP FORWARD, *supra* note 232, at § 2.2.

707. Telephone Interview with Nicholas Koumjian, deputy prosecutor for serious crimes, Special Panels for Serious Crimes (July 29, 2004); Telephone Interview with Alan Gutman, defense counsel, Special Panels for Serious Crimes (July 30, 2004).

708. Special Panels for Serious Crimes, Prosecutor v. Benjamin Sarmento et al., Court Record, at 11 (June 30, 2003) (on file with author).

709. *Id.* at 16.

710. *Id.* at 17.

711. THE LOLOTOE CASE: A SMALL STEP FORWARD, *supra* note 232, at § 2.5.2.2.

712. Telephone Interview with Essa Faal, chief of prosecutions, Special Panels for Serious Crimes (July 30, 2004).

713. *See, e.g.*, Correia Plea Agreement, *supra* note 702, at paras. 2, 3, 6, 9. In addition,

the plea agreements provide that neither party will appeal if the panel sentences in accordance with the agreed-upon recommendation. *See, e.g., id.* at para. 9(2). They also warn defendants that the panel may, despite the sentencing recommendation, impose a prison term of up to twenty-five years, and that the prosecution is free to prosecute the defendant for any criminal conduct not addressed in the agreement. *See, e.g., id.* at paras. 4, 5.

714. Telephone Interview with Essa Faal, chief of prosecutions, Special Panels for Serious Crimes (July 30, 2004).

715. Telephone Interview with Alan Gutman, defense counsel, Special Panels for Serious Crimes (July 30, 2004); *see also* Serious Crimes Unit indictee file, http://socrates .berkeley.edu/~warcrime/Serious%20Crimes%20Unit%20Files/suspects/MVIS-65KAKY .html.

716. Telephone Interview with Nicholas Koumjian, deputy prosecutor for serious crimes, Special Panels for Serious Crimes (July 29, 2004); Telephone Interview with Essa Faal, chief of prosecutions, Special Panels for Serious Crimes (July 30, 2004); *see also* Office of the Deputy General Prosecutor for Serious Crimes Timor Leste, *Serious Crimes Unit Update,* at 7 (Apr. 30, 2004) [hereinafter *Serious Crimes Unit Update*].

717. Prosecutor v. Anastacio Martins and Domingos Gonçalves, Dili District Court, Special Panels for Serious Crimes, Case No. 11/2001, Judgement, at 3-4 (Nov. 13, 2003) [hereinafter Martins and Gonçalves Judgement].

718. Telephone Interview with Alan Gutman, defense counsel, Special Panels for Serious Crimes (July 30, 2004).

719. *Serious Crimes Unit Update, supra* note 716, at 7–8.

720. João Fernandes Judgement, *supra* note 225, at para. 20 and Verdict.

721. Jose Valente Judgement, *supra* note 691, at 11–12. Valente did admit "some facts before the Court and freely cooperated with the Public Prosecutor about his involvement in becoming a member of Team Ratih/Panah," *id.* at 11, but the same could be said of most of the defendants discussed thus far.

722. Joseph Leki Judgement, *supra* note 220, at 11–12.

723. Los Palos Judgement, *supra* note 702, at paras. 70, 892. Marques's admissions even with respect to that count did not precisely match the prosecution's allegations because Marques denied that he was the commander of Team Alfa. *Id.* at para. 67. The panel apparently considered the charges and the admissions a close-enough fit, however, and it made its own finding that, despite his protestations to the contrary, Marques was in fact a commander. *Id.* at para. 921.

724. *Id.* at para. 1069. The panels also considered as a mitigating factor the inculpatory statements that Marques made that did not rise to the level of a guilty plea. *Id.* at para. 1055.

725. *Id.* at paras. 1068, 1071, 1077, 1084. The Panel imposed eighteen-year sentences on three other codefendants, *id.* at paras. 1091, 1098, 1113, and a seventeen-year sentence on a final codefendant, *id.* at para. 1106.

726. *Id.* at paras. 1012–23.

727. *Id.* at para. 796.

728. *Id.* at para. 1035.

729. *Id.* at para. 1037.

730. Prosecutor v. Marcurious José de Deus, Dili District Court, Special Panels for Serious Crimes, Case No. PID.C.G/13/2001, at III.1.22, Sentence (Apr. 18, 2002).

731. Prosecutor v. Augusto Dos Santos, Dili District Court, Special Panels for Serious Crimes, Case No. 06/2001, Judgement, at paras. 60, 66 (May 14, 2002) [hereinafter Augusto Dos Santos Judgement].

732. The defendant beat the victim "to death, and when he didn't die, he took a sharp piece of wood and hit him in the ears." *Id.* at para. 55.

733. Prosecutor v. Agustinho Atolan, Dili District Court, Special Panels for Serious Crimes, Case No. 3/2003, Judgement, at 6 (June 9, 2003) [hereinafter Agustinho Atolan Judgement]. Without further explanation, the panel asserted that the sentences imposed on three defendants that fell outside this range were justified by "specific reasons." *Id.* at 7.

734. *Id.* at 7.

735. *Id.* at 8.

736. Martins and Gonçalves Judgement, *supra* note 717, at 17–18.

737. *Id.* at 18.

738. *Id.* at 19.

739. *See, e.g.,* Prosecutor v. Abilio Mendes Correia, Dili District Court, Special Panels for Serious Crimes, Case No. 19/2001, Disposition of the Decision (Mar. 3, 2004); Prosecutor v. Benjamin Sarmento et al., Dili District Court, Special Panels for Serious Crimes, Case No. 18/2001, Disposition of the Decision Relating to the Conviction of the Accused Benjamin Sarmento and Romeiro Tilman (July 16, 2003); Prosecutor v. Domingos Mendonça, Dili District Court, Special Panels for Serious Crimes, Disposition of the Decision, Case No. 18a/2001 (Oct. 13, 2003).

740. Da Costa Nunes Judgement, *supra* note 702, at paras. 65–76, Disposition. Judge Blunk dissented to the sentence, asserting that "[s]entencing an accused who has committed Murder as a Crime against Humanity by his own hands to only 8 years imprisonment fails to meet" the goals of deterrence, retribution, reconciliation, and reprobation. Prosecutor v. Damiao Da Costa Nunes, Dili District Court, Special Panels for Serious Crimes, Case No. 04a/2001, Dissenting Opinion of Judge Siegfried Blunk (Dec. 10, 2003).

741. For instance, the panel sentenced Umbertus Ena after a trial to eleven years' imprisonment for two counts of murder as crimes against humanity and one count of inhumane acts as a crime against humanity. *Serious Crimes Unit Update, supra* note 716, at 8. The panel also convicted Marcelino Soares after a trial of one count of murder as a crime against humanity, one count of torture as a crime against humanity, and one count of persecution as a crime against humanity. After determining that the defendant not only failed to express regret but that he "appeared pleased with himself, when the victims of his torture testified to his savage cruelty, and showed the severe wounds inflicted by him," the panel sentenced him to nine, six, and three years' imprisonment, respectively, on each of the counts and a total of eleven years' imprisonment. Prosecutor v. Marcelino Soares, Dili District Court, Special Panels for Serious Crimes, Case No. 11/2003, Judgement, at Disposition (Dec. 11, 2003).

742. *See generally* Combs, *Copping a Plea to Genocide, supra* note 8.

743. *See* Combs, *Procuring Guilty Pleas for International Crimes, supra* note 532.

744. By May 2006, the ICTR had convicted twenty-four defendants, five of them through guilty pleas.

Chapter 7

745. *See generally* Combs, *Copping a Plea to Genocide, supra* note 8, at 9–16.

746. Plea bargaining is the subject of a vast quantity of scholarly and popular criticism. *See, e.g., id.* at 4 n.13.

Plea bargaining is none too popular in other countries either. For works critical of Australian plea bargaining, see Kathy Mack & Sharyn Roach Anleu, *Sentence Discount for a Guilty Plea: Time for a New Look*, 1 FLINDERS J. L. REFORM 123, 124 (1997); Kathy Mack & Sharyn Roach Anleu, *Choice, Consent and Autonomy in a Guilty Plea System*, 17 L. IN CONTEXT 75 (1999); John Willis, *New Wine in Old Bottles: The Sentencing Discount for Pleading Guilty*, 13 L. IN CONTEXT 39, 72 (1995). For criticism of British plea bargaining, see *Murder Sentence Changes Unveiled*, BBC NEWS, Sept. 20, 2004; Lincoln Archer, *"We Feel We've Been Robbed,"* BBC NEWS, Sept. 20, 2004.

747. Albert W. Alschuler, *The Prosecutor's Role in Plea Bargaining*, 36 U. CHI. L. REV. 50, 89–90 (1968) [hereinafter Alschuler, *Prosecutor's Role*].

748. Albert W. Alschuler, *The Trial Judge's Role in Plea Bargaining, Part I*, 76 COLUM. L. REV. 1059, 1141 (1976).

749. Alschuler, *Prosecutor's Role, supra* note 747, at 65–67; *see also* William F. McDonald et al., *Prosecutorial Bluffing and the Case against Plea-Bargaining, in* PLEA BARGAINING 1, 9 (William F. McDonald & James A. Cramer eds., 1980); Fred C. Zacharias, *Justice in Plea Bargaining*, 39 WM. & MARY L. REV. 1121, 1149 (1998).

750. Alschuler, *Prosecutor's Role, supra* note 747, at 56, 80; *see also* Kenneth Kipnis, *Criminal Justice and the Negotiated Plea*, 86 ETHICS 93, 94 (1976).

751. David Lynch, *The Impropriety of Plea Agreements*, 19 LAW & SOC. INQUIRY 115, 123, and n.9 (1994).

752. Albert W. Alschuler, *The Defense Attorney's Role in Plea Bargaining*, 84 YALE L.J. 1179, 1182–84 (1975) [hereinafter Alschuler, *Defense Attorney's Role*].

753. Stephen J. Schulhofer, *Plea Bargaining as Disaster*, 101 YALE L.J. 1979, 1988 (1992) [hereinafter Schulhofer, *Plea Bargaining as Disaster*]; Stephen J. Schulhofer, *A Wake-Up Call from the Plea Bargaining Trenches*, 19 LAW & SOC. INQUIRY 135, 138 (1994); Alschuler, *Defense Attorney's Role, supra* note 752, at 1181–1206.

754. Schulhofer, *Plea Bargaining as Disaster, supra* note 753, at 1989.

755. Chad Baruch, *Through the Looking Glass: A Brief Comment on the Short Life and Unhappy Demise of the Singleton Rule*, 27 N. KY. L. REV. 841, 850 (2000).

756. For an expansion of this argument, see Kipnis, *supra* note 750, at 104; *see also* Kenneth Kipnis, *Plea Bargaining: A Critic's Rejoinder*, 13 LAW & SOC'Y REV. 555, 558–59 (1979).

No one denies the difficulty in determining what is the "just sentence" in any given circumstance, but opponents of plea bargaining contend that plea bargaining violates many of its qualities. Albert Alschuler, for instance, asserts that

[o]ne aspect of a just sentence is that it respects the principle of equality, and, at least as an initial matter, we are offended when defendants of equal culpability are treated differently simply because they have made differing tactical decisions. Although attaching weight to these decisions might serve some social purpose, we sense that this purpose is not, or should not be, what sentencing is about. Moreover, a just sentence must be the product of a just process—one that focuses "on the merits" rather than on extraneous social objectives.

Albert W. Alschuler, *The Changing Plea Bargaining Debate*, 69 CAL. L. REV. 652, 680 (1981).

757. *See* John Baldwin & Michael McConville, *Plea Bargaining and Plea Negotiation in England*, 13 LAW & SOC'Y REV. 287, 296 (1979). Aogán Mulcahy describes a 1992 survey of the Crown Court that showed that barristers believed that 6 percent of their clients who pled guilty may have been innocent. Aogán Mulcahy, *The Justifications of "Justice": Legal Practitioners' Accounts of Negotiated Case Settlements in Magistrates' Courts*, 34 BRIT. J. CRIMINOLOGY 411, 413 (1994).

758. Plea bargaining and bargaining analogues are on the rise in Western European countries that had not previously utilized these procedures, *see* Combs, *Copping a Plea to Genocide*, *supra* note 8, at 39–45, and Europeans too have vigorously criticized the practice, *see, e.g.*, Mirjan Damaška, *Models of Criminal Procedure*, 51 ZBORNIK PRAVNOG FAKULLETA U ZAGREBU 477, 483 (2001); Richard S. Frase & Thomas Weigend, *German Criminal Justice as a Guide to American Law Reform: Similar Problems, Better Solutions?*, 18 B.C. INT'L & COMP. L. REV. 317, 344–45 (1995); Joachim Herrmann, *Bargaining Justice— A Bargain for German Criminal Justice?*, 53 U. PITT. L. REV. 755, 756 (1992); Heike Jung, *The Criminal Process in the Federal Republic of Germany—An Overview, in* THE CRIMINAL PROCESS AND HUMAN RIGHTS: TOWARD A EUROPEAN CONSCIOUSNESS 59, 61–62 (Mireille Delmas-Marty & Mark A. Summers eds., 1995).

759. *See* Reed Brody, *Idi Amin at Death's Door: Despots Should Not Rest in Peace*, INT'L HERALD TRIB., July 25, 2003.

760. HAYNER, *supra* note 91, at 156; KROG, *supra* note 104, at 385.

761. Although South Africans generally recognize that the truth and reconciliation process was not intended to result in widespread prosecutions—that is, that South Africans bought a peaceful transition with the price of criminal justice—that bargain still rankles many victims. Stuart Wilson, for instance, describes a survey conducted by the Center for the Study of Violence and Reconciliation which showed that "'justice and punishment was still favoured as a way of dealing with the perpetrators over amnesty.'" Wilson, *supra* note 116, at 551. Elizabeth Kiss repeats a common refrain among observers of the TRC's work: "We've heard the truth. There is even talk of reconciliation. But where's the justice?" Kiss, *supra* note 88, at 68.

Another contributing factor to the perception of failure is that the TRC did not motivate enough offenders to confess. As detailed above, virtually no high-level military or government officials sought amnesty, and the primary reason they failed to do so was that the threat of prosecution was not sufficiently threatening. The South African experience demonstrates the obvious: that most offenders will not confess to wrongdoing unless they are threatened with sanctions and, moreover, unless that threat of sanctions is a credible one.

762. Emir Suljagić, *Truth at The Hague*, N.Y. TIMES, June 1, 2003. The mayor of Srebrenica likewise lauded Nikolić's guilty plea, opining that "[o]nly by recognising and admitting the real and whole truth about [Srebrenica] and other crimes in BH can trust be rebuilt among the citizens of BH." Momir Nikolić Sentencing Judgement, *supra* note 282, at para. 147.

763. Mehmed Ahmić Statement, *supra* note 496.

764. Sito-Sucic, *supra* note 12; *see also* Daniel Simpson, *U.N. Tribunal, with Surprise Guilty Plea, Rivets Bosnians*, N.Y. TIMES, Oct. 4, 2002 (reporting one Bosnian Muslim's view that "[i]t's a big step forward that she admitted guilt").

765. The reason that plea bargaining will in most cases increase the overall punishment imposed is because plea bargaining results in sentence discounts that are smaller than the financial discounts it affords. If we assume, for instance, that the average defendant receives a 50 percent sentence discount for pleading guilty, then overall punishment will increase with the introduction of a guilty-plea system as long as guilty pleas result in a more than 50 percent financial savings over trial. Given the tremendous costs of trials at the international tribunals, the proportional savings produced by a guilty plea in virtually every instance will far exceed the proportional discounts to sentences afforded to defendants pleading guilty.

766. Beth Kampschror, *Bosnia to Try Its War Criminals, But Is New Court Up to the Job?*, CHRISTIAN SCIENCE MONITOR, Dec. 23, 2003.

767. *Bosnian Women's Association Calls Serb Camp Guard Sentence "Insult,"* BBC WORLDWIDE MONITORING, Oct. 29, 2003; *Bosnian Muslims Protest "Shameful" War Crimes Sentence*, AGENCE FRANCE-PRESSE, Oct. 29, 2003; Jelacić & Stephen, *supra* note 12.

768. The ICTR imposed life sentences on Akayesu, Kajelijeli, Kamuhanda, Kayishema, Musema, Nahimana, Ngeze, Niyitegeka, and Rutaganda.

769. Organic Law No. 16/2004 Establishing the Organisation, Competence, and Functioning of *Gacaca* Courts Charged with Prosecuting and Trying the Perpetrators of the Crime of Genocide and Other Crimes against Humanity Committed between October 1, 1990 and December 31, 1994, arts. 72–73 [hereinafter 2004 Revised *Gacaca* Law].

770. Prosecutor v. Stakić, Case No. IT-97-24-A, Judgement, at Disposition (Mar. 22, 2006).

771. The ICTY sentenced Goran Jelisić to forty years' imprisonment, Jelisić Judgement, *supra* note 319, at para. 139; the ICTY sentenced Tihomir Blaškić to forty-five years' imprisonment, Blaškić Judgement, *supra* note 136, at Disposition, and it sentenced Radislav Krstić to forty-six years' imprisonment, Krstić Judgement, *supra* note 327, at para. 727.

772. The Appeals Chamber reduced Blaškić's sentence from forty-five to nine years' imprisonment after finding for Blaškić on several of his grounds for appeal, *see* Prosecutor v. Blaškić, Case No. IT-95-14-A, Appeal Judgement, at Disposition (July 29, 2004), and it reduced Krstić's sentence from forty-six to thirty-five years' imprisonment, Krstić Appeal, *supra* note 357, at Disposition.

773. *Bosnian Serb "Monster" Todorović to Be Released from Prison*, AGENCE FRANCE-PRESSE, June 29, 2005; *Blaškić's Sentence Cut Down from 45 to 9 Years in Prison*, SENSE

News Agency, July 29, 2004. The ICTY's practice is in keeping with that of the Western European countries in which ICTY defendants are serving their sentences.

774. Donald P. Kommers, The Constitutional Jurisprudence of the Federal Republic of Germany 314–20 (1989); William A. Schabas, *Sentencing by International Tribunals: A Human Rights Approach*, 7 Duke J. Comp. & Int'l L. 461, 480 (1997). Indeed, concerns were raised during the Rome Conference that some states would be unable to transfer indictees to the ICC because it can sentence defendants to life imprisonment. William A. Schabas, *Follow up to Rome: Preparing for Entry into Force of the International Criminal Court Statute*, 20 Hum. Rts. L.J. 157, 158 (1999).

775. Some defendants, like the seventy-two-year-old Plavšić, are of such an advanced age that only the most lenient of sentences will motivate them to plead guilty because they will likely die before they can serve a justifiable sentence. A disproportionate number of these defendants are apt to be high-level offenders, since people generally do not obtain high-level positions until they are middle-aged or older.

Chapter 8

776. A sampling of the literature focusing on various aspects of restorative justice includes John Braithwaite, Restorative Justice and Responsive Regulation (2002); Michael Braswell et al., Corrections, Peacemaking and Restorative Justice (2001); Elizabeth Elliott, New Directions in Restorative Justice: Issues, Practice, Evaluation (2005); Roger Graef, Why Restorative Justice? Repairing the Harm Caused by Crime (2000); Johnstone, *supra* note 17; Declan Roche, Accountability in Restorative Justice (2003); Heather Strang, Repair or Revenge: Victims and Restorative Justice (2002); Heather Strang, Restorative Justice: Philosophy to Practice (2000); Dennis Sullivan & Larry Tifft, Restorative Justice: Healing the Foundations of our Everyday Lives (2001); Mark S. Umbreit et al., Victim Meets Offender: The Impact of Restorative Justice and Mediation (1994); Lode Walgrave, Restorative Justice and the Law (2002); Critical Issues in Restorative Justice (Howard Zehr & Barbara Toews eds., 2004); Restorative Justice & Criminal Justice: Competing or Reconcilable Paradigms? (Andrew von Hirsch et al. eds., 2003); Victim-Offender Mediation in Europe: Making Restorative Justice Work (The European Forum for Victim-Offender Mediation and Restorative Justice ed., 2000).

777. David Cayley, The Expanding Prison: The Crisis in Crime and Punishment and the Search for Alternatives 32 (1998) (quoting D. Faulkner).

778. Johnstone, *supra* note 17, at 1. The most popular restorative-justice processes are victim-offender mediation and family group conferencing. McCarney, *supra* note 16, at 6; Joanna Shapland, *Restorative Justice and Criminal Justice: Just Responses to Crime? in* Restorative Justice & Criminal Justice: Competing or Reconcilable Paradigms? 195, 197 (Andrew von Hirsch et al. eds., 2003) (also describing sentencing circles). Victim-offender mediation brings "victims and offenders face-to-face in a safe, structured facilitated dialogue." Mara Schiff, *Models, Challenges and the Promise of Restorative Conference Strategies, in* Restorative Justice & Criminal Justice: Competing

OR RECONCILABLE PARADIGMS? 315, 318 (Andrew von Hirsch et al. eds., 2003). Family group conferencing comprises a number of distinctive models, including the New Zealand model, the Wagga model, neighborhood sanctioning boards, and circle sentencing. McCarney, *supra* note 16, at 6. Family group conferences are similar to victim-offender mediations but are attended by a larger group of people, including interested community members and those concerned about the well-being of either the victims or offender. All of the participants are invited to contribute to the problem-solving process. *Id.* at 6; Schiff, *supra* at 320.

779. John Braithwaite, *A Future Where Punishment Is Marginalized: Realistic or Utopian?*, 46 UCLA L. REV. 1727, 1744 (1999)) [hereinafter Braithwaite, *A Future Where Punishment Is Marginalized*].

780. *See* Barton Poulson, *A Third Voice: A Review of Empirical Research on the Psychological Outcomes of Restorative Justice*, 2003 UTAH L. REV. 167, 180. *See also* UMBREIT, *supra* note 776, at 21–23, 75–82; Umbreit et al., *The Impact of Victim-Offender Mediation*, *supra* note 17, at 30.

781. UMBREIT, *supra* note 776, at 10–13; John Braithwaite, *Restorative Justice: Assessing Optimistic and Pessimistic Accounts*, 25 CRIME & JUST. 1, 24 (1999) [hereinafter Braithwaite, *Restorative Justice*]. Roger Graef reports that "[o]f victims taking part in mediation, 73% wanted an apology, 80% said they wanted answers, and 90% wanted to tell the offender about the impact of the crime. The number of victims who wanted restitution was much lower: 65%." GRAEF, *supra* note 776, at 27.

782. Poulson, *supra* note 780, at 184–85.

783. Umbreit et al., *The Impact of Victim-Offender Mediation*, *supra* note 17, at 31.

784. Heather Strang & Lawrence W. Sherman, *Repairing the Harm: Victims and Restorative Justice*, 2003 UTAH L. REV. 15, 29–31; Poulson, *supra* note 780, at 195–98. For further discussions of anger and fear reductions in victims following restorative-justice processes, see BRAITHWAITE, *supra* note 776, at 52; *see also* Kathleen Daly, *Mind the Gap: Restorative Justice in Theory and Practice, in* RESTORATIVE JUSTICE & CRIMINAL JUSTICE: COMPETING OR RECONCILABLE PARADIGMS? 219, 230 (Andrew von Hirsch et al. eds., 2003).

785. Poulson reports that "offenders were 6.9 times more likely to apologize to the victim in restorative justice settings than in court," Poulson, *supra* note 780, at 189, while Strang and Sherman report that "[e]ighty-six percent of Canberra victims attending restorative justice conferences received apologies from their offenders, in comparison to only 16% of victims whose cases were disposed of in court." Strang & Sherman, *supra* note 784, at 28.

786. BRAITHWAITE, *supra* note 776, at 52; Stephanos Bibas & Richard A. Bierschbach, *Integrating Remorse and Apology into Criminal Procedure*, 114 YALE L.J. 85, 90 (2004). Tort victims likewise desire apologies and indeed are more likely to initiate lawsuits when they have not received apologies. *See* Erin Ann O'Hara & Douglas Yarn, *On Apology and Consilience*, 77 WASH. L. REV. 1121, 1122–25 (2002).

787. GRAEF, *supra* note 776, at 27, 47.

788. Braithwaite, *Restorative Justice*, *supra* note 781, at 26–27; Poulson, *supra* note 780, at 193.

789. Poulson, *supra* note 780, at 182–85.

790. JOHNSTONE, *supra* note 17, at 99–102; Paul H. Robinson, *The Virtues of Restorative Processes, the Vices of "Restorative Justice,"* 2003 UTAH L. REV. 375, 375; Robert F. Cochran, Jr., *The Criminal Defense Attorney: Roadblock or Bridge to Restorative Justice,* 14 J. L. & RELIGION 211, 212 (1999–2000). Restorative-justice proponents maintain that offenders gain other benefits from restorative processes, including "an increased sense of respect." Strang & Sherman, *supra* note 784, at 37.

791. HOWARD ZEHR, CHANGING LENSES: A NEW FOCUS FOR CRIME AND JUSTICE 40–41 (1990); Braithwaite, *Restorative Justice, supra* note 781, at 47.

792. See BRAITHWAITE, *supra* note 776, at 55–66; UMBREIT, *supra* note 776, at 24; Bush, *supra* note 289, at 441; Barbara Hudson, *Victims and Offenders, in* RESTORATIVE JUSTICE & CRIMINAL JUSTICE: COMPETING OR RECONCILABLE PARADIGMS? 177, 189 (Andrew von Hirsch et al. eds., 2003) (discussing studies); William R. Nugent et al., *Participation in Victim-Offender Mediation and the Prevalence and Severity of Subsequent Delinquent Behavior: A Meta-Analysis,* 2003 UTAH L. REV. 137, 163; Poulson, *supra* note 780, at 199; Umbreit et al., *The Impact of Victim-Offender Mediation, supra* note 17, at 32. For a discussion of recidivism reduction through restorative justice in Austria and the United Kingdom, see Christa Pelikan, *Victim-Offender Mediation in Austria, in* VICTIM-OFFENDER MEDIATION IN EUROPE: MAKING RESTORATIVE JUSTICE WORK 125, 148–49 (The European Forum for Victim-Offender Mediation and Restorative Justice ed., 2000); Marian Liebmann & Guy Masters, *Victim-Offender Mediation in the UK, in* VICTIM-OFFENDER MEDIATION IN EUROPE: MAKING RESTORATIVE JUSTICE WORK 337, 365 (The European Forum for Victim-Offender Mediation and Restorative Justice ed., 2000).

793. Umbreit et al., *The Impact of Victim-Offender Mediation, supra* note 17, at 33; Mark S. Umbreit & Betty Vos, *Homicide Survivors Meet the Offender prior to Execution: Restorative Justice through Dialogue,* 4 HOMICIDE STUD. 63, 64 (2000); Mark S. Umbreit, *Violent Offenders and Their Victims, in* MEDIATION AND CRIMINAL JUSTICE 99 (Martin Wright & Burt Galaway eds., 1989); Caren Flaten, *Victim-Offender Mediation: Application with Serious Offenses Committed by Juveniles, in* RESTORATIVE JUSTICE: INTERNATIONAL PERSPECTIVES 387 (Burt Galaway & Joe Hudson eds., 1996).

794. Strang & Sherman, *supra* note 784, at 40.

795. *Id.*

796. Umbreit et al., *Victim-Offender Dialogue in Crimes of Severe Violence: A Multi-Site Study of Programs in Texas and Ohio,* at 2, *available at* http://ssw.che.umn.edu/rjp/ [hereinafter Umbreit et al., *Victim-Offender Dialogue*]; Umbreit & Vos, *supra* note 793, at 64.

797. Umbreit et al., *Victim-Offender Dialogue, supra* note 796, at 3, 9–10; Umbreit & Vos, *supra* note 793, at 70–74.

798. Umbreit et al., *Victim-Offender Dialogue, supra* note 796, at 17–18. Another offender indicated that the "forgiveness offered by his victim's mother was central." Umbreit & Vos, *supra* note 793, at 82.

799. Umbreit et al., *Victim-Offender Dialogue, supra* note 796, at 21.

800. Umbreit & Vos, *supra* note 793, at 78.

801. Umbreit et al., *Victim-Offender Dialogue, supra* note 796, at 18.

802. Tag Evers, *Blessed Are the Peacemakers,* ISTHMUS, Apr. 10, 1998.

803. Umbreit et al., *Victim-Offender Dialogue, supra* note 796, at 18.

804. Braithwaite, *A Future Where Punishment Is Marginalized, supra* note 779, at 1738–44; Lode Walgrave, *Imposing Restoration Instead of Inflicting Pain: Reflections on the Judicial Reaction to Crime, in* RESTORATIVE JUSTICE & CRIMINAL JUSTICE: COMPETING OR RECONCILABLE PARADIGMS? 61, 63–67 (Andrew von Hirsch et al. eds., 2003).

805. Anthony Duff, *Restoration and Retribution, in* RESTORATIVE JUSTICE & CRIMINAL JUSTICE: COMPETING OR RECONCILABLE PARADIGMS? 43, 43 (Andrew von Hirsch et al. eds., 2003); Wilson, *supra* note 116, at 546–47; *see also* Robinson, *supra* note 790, at 375; David Dolinko, *Restorative Justice and the Justification of Punishment,* 2003 UTAH L. Rev. 319, 321. As Elizabeth Kiss puts it, retributive and restorative processes largely overlap in part because criminally punishing wrongdoers constitutes a powerful way to affirm the dignity of victims. Kiss, *supra* note 88, at 79, 83. *See also* Charles Villa-Vicencio, *Restorative Justice: Dealing with the Past Differently, in* LOOKING BACK, REACHING FORWARD: REFLECTIONS ON THE TRUTH AND RECONCILIATION COMMISSION OF SOUTH AFRICA 68, 69, 72 (Charles Villa-Vicencio & Wilhelm Verwoerd eds., 2000) [hereinafter Villa-Vicencio, *Restorative Justice*].

806. Prosecutor v. Krstić, Case No. IT-98-33, Transcript, at 5818 (July 27, 2000).

807. Prosecutor v. Krstić, Case No. IT-98-33, Transcript, at 5769 (July 26, 2000) (testimony of witness DD). Davor Strinović, a Croatian forensic pathologist who examined the remains in the Ovcara massacre site, relates:

> Dealing with the mothers has been the most painful part of my work. For nearly five years, they waited for some kind of news. Is he alive? Is he dead? Some mothers expected a miracle to happen, something God-sent, which would magically return their child. Then the day comes when the body's been identified and I have to inform the mother. . . . All those years of hope are shattered in a matter of seconds.
>
> Eric Stover & Rachel Shigekane, *Exhumation of Mass Graves: Balancing Legal and Humanitarian Needs, in* MY NEIGHBOR, MY ENEMY: JUSTICE AND COMMUNITY IN THE AFTERMATH OF MASS ATROCITY 85, 90 (Eric Stover & Harvey M. Weinstein eds., 2004).

808. Nigel Biggar, *Making Peace or Doing Justice: Must We Choose?, in* BURYING THE PAST: MAKING PEACE AND DOING JUSTICE AFTER CIVIL CONFLICT 3, 9 (Nigel Biggar ed., 2003).

809. HAYNER, *supra* note 91, at 26.

810. Truth commission reports, for instance, are often sharply disputed. The report issued from El Salvador was vehemently opposed by the Salvadoran government, and the Guatemalan report was sharply criticized by right-wing groups. Rachel Sieder, *War, Peace, and the Politics of Memory in Guatemala, in* BURYING THE PAST: MAKING PEACE AND DOING JUSTICE AFTER CIVIL CONFLICT 209, 219–20 (Nigel Biggar ed., 2003). In South Africa, moreover, a last-minute lawsuit was filed by the ANC and the National Party seeking to prevent publication of the report. RICHARD J. GOLDSTONE, FOR HUMANITY: REFLECTIONS OF A WAR CRIMES INVESTIGATOR 69-70 (2000).

811. Hudson, *supra* note 792, at 180.

812. Community dissatisfaction with the amnesty granted to Jeffrey Benzien, for instance, was particularly strong. *See* Mark Sanders, *Renegotiating Responsibility after Apartheid: Listening to Perpetrator Testimony*, 10 AM. U. J. GENDER SOC. POL'Y & L. 587, 589 (2002). Further, in the notorious "ANC 37" case, the Amnesty Commission granted thirty-seven ANC leaders a collective amnesty without requiring specification of the acts committed and without treating each application individually. The TRC challenged the amnesties before the South African High Court, which overturned them. Lorna Mc-Gregor, *Individual Accountability in South Africa: Cultural Optimum or Political Façade*, 95 AM. J. INT'L L. 32, 39–40 (2001); *see generally* KROG, *supra* note 104, at 360–63.

813. GRAEF, *supra* note 776, at 27, 47; *see also* BRAITHWAITE, *supra* note 776, at 52.

814. *Biljana Plavšić: Serbian Iron Lady*, BBC NEWS, Feb. 27, 2003.

815. Alissa J. Rubin, *Former Serb Leader's Admission of Guilt Alienates Compatriots*, L.A. TIMES, Dec. 16, 2002.

816. Prosecutor v. Plavšić, Case No. IT-00-39&40/1, Transcript, at 609–11 (Dec. 17, 2002).

817. Sito-Sucic, *supra* note 12. Sulejman Tihic, a Bosniak member of the Bosnian presidency and a detainee in Serb detention centers, described Plavšić's plea as "'a highly moral act' which helps establish the truth about the kind of war that took place." Kebo, *supra* note 12.

818. *See* Elizabeth Latif, *Apologetic Justice: Evaluating Apologies Tailored toward Legal Solutions*, 81 B.U. L. REV. 289, 302–05 (2001); Deborah L. Levi, *The Role of Apology in Mediation*, 72 N.Y.U. L. REV. 1165, 1178 (1997).

819. Sim B. Sitkin & Robert J. Bies, *Social Accounts in Conflict Situations: Using Explanations to Manage Conflict*, 46 HUM. REL. 349, 359 (1993).

820. *See generally* Lee Taft, *Apology Subverted: The Commidification of Apology*, 109 YALE L.J. 1135 (2000).

821. "In Japan, offering apology and particularly letters of apology have been frequently used as an alternative to filing criminal charges. . . . A defendant's repentant and apologetic attitude may induce the police not to refer the case for prosecution to the Public Procurator's Office, it may lead the procurator not to prosecute or to demand a more lenient level of punishment, and it may lead the judges to impose a milder sentence." Hiroshi Wagatsuma & Arthur Rosett, *The Implications of Apology: Law and Culture in Japan and the United States*, 20 LAW & SOC'Y REV. 461, 482–83 (1986). *See also* John O. Haley, *The Implications of Apology*, 20 LAW & SOC'Y REV. 499, 501 (1986).

822. *See* Haley, *supra* note 821, at 499.

823. *See* Mark Bennett & Christopher Dewberry, *"I've Said I'm Sorry, Haven't I?" A Study of the Identity Implications and Constraints That Apologies Create for Their Recipients*, 13 CURRENT PSYCHOL. 10, 15–20 (1994).

824. O'Hara & Douglas Yarn, *supra* note 786, at 1147.

825. *See* Goodman, *supra* note 112, at 3. Cynthia Ngewu, the mother of another man who was killed in the same massacre, expressed similar sentiments: "We don't want [the perpetrators] to go to jail, but we do think they should help support these children." *Id.*; Lansing & King, *supra* note 116, at 769.

826. HAYNER, *supra* note 91, at 147.

827. Telephone Interview with Lars Waldorf, former researcher, Human Rights Watch (June 24, 2004).

828. The Argentine Truth Commission, for instance, sent questionnaires to former state officials, but it received no response in some cases, and it reported that none of the replies had been of use in clarifying the circumstances surrounding the disappearance of people or in helping to trace them. *See* ARGENTINA: NUNCA MAS: REPORT OF THE ARGENTINE NATIONAL COMMISSION ON THE DISAPPEARED, *reprinted in* 3 TRANSITIONAL JUSTICE: HOW EMERGING DEMOCRACIES RECKON WITH FORMER REGIMES, LAWS, RUL-INGS AND REPORTS 3, 17 (Neil J. Kritz ed., 1995) [hereinafter NUNCA MAS]. *But see* Sierra Leone TRC Report, *supra* note 101, at Vol. 2, Ch. 2, para. 568. William Schabas describes perpetrators who voluntarily came before the Sierra Leone TRC to tell their stories and in some cases to ask forgiveness. Schabas, *The Relationship between Truth Commissions and International Courts, supra* note 210, at 1051.

829. *See generally* Kiss, *supra* note 88; Villa-Vicencio, *Restorative Justice, supra* note 805, at 69; Villa-Vicencio, *Why Perpetrators Should Not Always Be Prosecuted, supra* note 107, at 205; McGregor, *supra* note 812, at 37; *see also* John M. Czarnetzy & Ronald J. Rychlak, *An Empire of Law, Legalism and the International Criminal Court*, 79 NOTRE DAME L. REV. 55, 84–85 (2003). For a critical analysis of the TRC's attempt to practice restorative justice, see Wilson, *supra* note 116.

830. *Bosnian TV Reports on Rajić Guilty Plea Fallout in Croatia*, BBC WORLDWIDE MONITORING, Nov. 6, 2005.

831. Jeevan Vasagar, *Body of Genocide Witness Found in River*, THE GUARDIAN, Dec. 24, 2005.

832. *Prosecution Witness Assassinated in Rwanda*, HIRONDELLE NEWS AGENCY, Oct. 20, 2004; Modestus Kessy, *Genocide Witness Killed after Testifying*, THE GUARD-IAN (Dar es Salam), Oct. 22, 2004; Nasser Ega-Musa, *Another Failure of Justice in Africa*, WASH. POST, Mar. 6, 1997, at A21.

833. Antije Krog describes the psychiatric view that realizing that actions that one perceived to be appropriate were in fact wrong requires a psychiatric breakthrough be-cause "it is almost impossible to acknowledge that the central truth around which your life has been built is a lie. At the risk of the disintegration of your self-image, you would rather keep on denying any wrongdoing." *See* KROG, *supra* note 104, at 120.

834. MINOW, *supra* note 16, at 59; Justin M. Swartz, *South Africa's Truth and Recon-ciliation Commission: A Functional Equivalent to Prosecution*, 3 DEPAUL DIG. INT'L L. 13, 26 (1997). Similarly, Brigadier Cronje, testifying about certain murders, implicated Spe-cial Forces commander Major General Joep Joube, South African Defence Forces Chief of Staff Lieutenant-General Ian Gleeson, and two other officials in the cover-up of the murders. Further, when Colonel Venter testified about the Pebco Three incident, victims' lawyers asked him for the names of participants or those who had information about the incident, and Venter supplied the names of four police officers, who were subsequently subpoenaed. McCarthy, *supra* note 106, at 242–43.

835. Sikirica Sentencing Judgement, *supra* note 319, at paras. 118, 153, 200.

836. At trial, forty-one prosecution witnesses testified about Kolundžija's efforts. Prosecutor v. Sikirica, Case No. IT-95-8-T, Transcript, at 5773 (Oct. 9, 2001).

837. In a somewhat similar vein, after the ICTY convicted Radislav Krstić, deputy commander of the Drina Corps, of genocide and sentenced him to forty-six years' imprisonment for his role in the Srebrenica massacres, lower-level Bosnian Serb Army officers Momir Nikolić and Dragan Obrenović saw fit to plead guilty to helping plan those massacres once the prosecution agreed to withdraw the genocide charges pending against them.

838. George P. Fletcher, With Justice for Some: Protecting Victims' Rights in Criminal Trials 191 (1996); LaFave et al., *supra* note 9, at 961.

839. Warren Burger, *The State of the Judiciary—1970*, 56 A.B.A. J. 929, 931 (1970).

840. Alschuler, *Defense Attorney's Role, supra* note 752, at 1249–51.

841. Marlise Simons, *In a Startling Plea, a Serbian Policeman Confesses to Atrocities*, N.Y. Times, July 27, 2003; Interview with Emir Suljagić, IWPR reporter and Srebrenica survivor, The Hague (Sept. 12, 2003).

Chapter 9

842. For a discussion contrasting Japanese and Western views on apologies, see Nicholas Tavuchis, Mea Culpa: A Sociology of Apology and Reconciliation 37–44 (1991). For a discussion contrasting Western and African views regarding apologies, see McGregor, *supra* note 812, at 37–38. *See also* Letitia Hickson, *The Social Context of Apology in Dispute Settlement: A Cross-Cultural Study*, 25 Ethnology 283 (1986); Shoshana Blum-Kulka et al., *Investigating Cross-Cultural Pragmatics: An Introductory Overview, in* Cross-Cultural Pragmatics: Requests and Apologies 1 (Shoshana Blum-Kulka et al., eds. 1989).

843. Kipnis, *supra* note 750, at 103.

844. For a discussion of Argentine human-rights violations, see Nunca Mas, *supra* note 828; Nino, *supra* note 14, at 53–66; Paul H. Lewis, Guerrillas and Generals (2002); Luis Roniger & Mario Sznajder, The Legacy of Human-Rights Violations in the Southern Cone: Argentina, Chile, and Uruguay 7–50 (1999).

845. Carlos Nino, for instance, describes the torture of Susan Caride, who was subjected to "simulated execution, electric shocks, beatings, and the 'cleansing' of wounds with salt water," and he describes the especially harsh treatment meted out to Jews, who were detained in rooms designated with Nazi insignia, forced to shout "I love Hitler," and paint their bodies with swastikas. Nino, *supra* note 14, at 55–56.

846. For a detailed description of these flights, see Verbitsky, *supra* note 60, at 24–25, 48–52 (1996). For a victim's account of the fear inspired by those flights, see *id.* at 85–89.

847. Paula K. Speck, *The Trial of the Argentine Junta*, 18 Inter-Am. L. Rev. 491, 498 (1984).

848. In December 1977, military president Jorge Rafael Videla asserted, "I categorically deny that there exist in Argentina any concentration camps or prisoners being held in military establishments beyond the time absolutely necessary for the investigation of

a person captured in an operation before they are transferred to a penal establishment."
Nine months later, General Roberto Viola reiterated: "There are no political prisoners
in Argentina, except for a few persons who may have been detained under government
emergency legislation and who are really being detained because of their political activity.
There are no prisoners being held merely for being political, or because they do not share
the ideas held by the Government." NUNCA MAS, *supra* note 828, at 10.

849. *Id.* at 31–32. Indeed, lawyers became reluctant even to present habeas corpus
appeals after a number who dared to do so were themselves disappeared. RONIGER &
SZNAJDER, *supra* note 844, at 25.

850. Jaime Malamud-Goti, *Punishing Human Rights Abuses in Fledgling Democracies: The Case of Argentina, in* IMPUNITY AND HUMAN RIGHTS IN INTERNATIONAL LAW
AND PRACTICE 160, 161 (Naomi Roht-Arriaza ed., 1995); RONIGER & SZNAJDER, *supra* note
844, at 21.

851. NUNCA MAS, *supra* note 828, at 22. Ten percent of the women who were disappeared were pregnant. The babies born to these women before their murders were given
to other families. *Id.* at 23; RONIGER & SZNAJDER, *supra* note 844, at 205.

852. NUNCA MAS, *supra* note 828, at 22; *see also* RONIGER & SZNAJDER, *supra* note 844,
at 21–24.

853. "[M]any [victims] were merely relatives or friends of those involved in [left-wing]
activity. Others were lawyers who filed habeas corpus petitions for those illegally detained, journalists who complained of the regime's abuses, psychoanalysts and writers
considered dangerous, members of human rights groups, trade unionists . . . who opposed
the regime's economic policy, and politicians who were deemed dangerous." NINO, *supra*
note 14, at 57; *see also* RONIGER & SZNAJDER, *supra* note 844, at 21. As General Ramon put
it: "'First, we will kill the guerrillas. Then, we will kill the guerrillas' families. Then we
will kill the friends of their families, and the friends of their friends, so that there will be
no one left to remember who the guerrillas were.'" Thomas C. Wright, *Human Rights in
Latin America: History and Projections for the Twenty-First Century,* 30 CAL. W. INT'L L.J.
303, 311 (2000).

854. NINO, *supra* note 14, at 80; Larry Rohter, *Argentina Nears Repeal of "Dirty War"
Amnesty,* INT'L HERALD TRIB., Aug. 21, 2003.

855. NUNCA MAS, *supra* note 828, at 13.

856. RONIGER & SZNAJDER, *supra* note 844, at 112 (quoting Emilio Mignone).

857. HAYNER, *supra* note 91, at 160.

858. For a discussion of the trial, *see generally* Speck, *supra* note 847. For a discussion
of the unrest and the pardons that followed, *see* NINO, *supra* note 14, at 90–104; Malamud-
Goti, *supra* note 850, at 162; Naomi Roht-Arriaza, *State Responsibility to Investigate and
Prosecute Grave Human Rights Violations in International Law,* 78 CAL. L. REV. 449, 459
(1990).

859. Human Rights Watch, *Truth and Partial Justice in Argentina: An Update,* 1991, at
69; *see also* VERBITSKY, *supra* note 60, at 7.

860. *See* Andrew S. Brown, Note, *Adios Amnesty: Prosecutorial Discretion and Military Trials in Argentina,* 37 TEX. INT'L L.J. 203, 206 (2002).

861. For a discussion of the history of ethnic violence in the Balkans, see Tom Gallagher, Outcast Europe: The Balkans, 1789–1989: From the Ottomans to Milošević
(2001); Scharf, *supra* note 2, at 21–24; Bassiouni & Manikas, *supra* note 48, at 5-25.

862. Tadić Judgement, *supra* note 297, at para. 65. *But see* Susan L. Woodward, Balkan Tragedy: Chaos and Dissolution after the Cold War 21–22 (1995). The people
of the former Yugoslavia were also united in their fear of a Soviet invasion. Tito developed a new military doctrine, termed "Total National Defense," that was designed to
defeat a Soviet invasion by mobilizing all of the nation's cultural, societal, and military
resources. Bassiouni & Manikas, *supra* note 48, at 15; Delalić Judgement, *supra* note 281,
at para. 93.

863. Krstić Judgement, *supra* note 327, at para. 9; Bassiouni & Manikas, *supra*
note 48, at 26–32, 39–41; Zimmermann, *supra* note 42, at 140–46, 152–61.

864. For a discussion of the war and the atrocities that took place during the war, *see
generally Final Report of the Commission of Experts Established Pursuant to Security Council Resolution 780*, U.N. Doc. S/1994/674 (1994); Bassiouni & Manikas, *supra* note 48, at
25–63; Steven L. Burg & Paul S. Shoup, The War in Bosnia-Herzegovina: Ethnic
Conflict and International Intervention 3–127 (1999); Lenard J. Cohen, Broken
Bonds: Yugoslavia's Disintegration and Balkan Politics in Transition (1993);
Tom Gallagher, The Balkans after the Cold War: From Tyranny to Tragedy
(2003); Century of Genocide: Critical Essays and Eyewitness Accounts 415–47
(Samuel Totten et al. eds., 2004).

865. In Bosnia, the prewar population consisted of approximately 44 percent Muslim,
31 percent Serb, and 17 percent Croat. Krstić Judgement, *supra* note 327, at para. 7.

866. Bassiouni & Manikas, *supra* note 48, at 33. For a discussion of the goal of a
"Greater Serbia" and the propaganda campaign to realize it, see Tadić Judgement, *supra*
note 297, at paras. 85–96. On the basis of the observations of his special envoy, then secretary-general of the U.N. Boutros Boutros-Ghali reported to the U.N. Security Council
that the Bosnian Serbs, with help from the JNA (Yugoslav People's Army), were making
"a concerted effort . . . to create 'ethnically pure regions'" by seizing "territory by military force and intimidation of the non-Serb population." *Further Report of the Secretary-
General Pursuant to Security Council Resolution 749*, para. 5. U.N. Doc. S/23900 (May 12,
1992).

867. Bassiouni & Manikas, *supra* note 48, at 51.

868. *See* Delalić Judgement, *supra* note 281, at paras. 146–57; Blaškić Judgement, *supra*
note 136, at paras. 384–428.

869. For detailed treatments of the Dayton Peace Accords, see Paola Gaeta, *The Dayton Agreements and International Law*, 7 Eur. J. Int'l L. 147 (1996); John R. W. D. Jones,
*The Implications of the Peace Agreements for the International Criminal Tribunal for the
former Yugoslavia*, 7 Eur. J. Int'l L. 226 (1996).

870. For a discussion of rapes during the Bosnian war, see generally Beverly Allen, Rape Warfare: The Hidden Genocide in Bosnia-Herzegovina and Croatia
(1996).

871. Power, *supra* note 20, at 251.

872. *Memorandum to the High Representative, supra* note 164.

873. For a discussion of the conditions prevailing in these camps, see Tadić Judgement, *supra* note 297, at paras. 154–79; Kvočka Judgement, *supra* note 405, at paras. 443–67; Stakić Judgement, *supra* note 343, at paras. 159–200; Dragan Nikolić Sentencing Judgement, *supra* note 11, at paras. 57–59; Sikirica Sentencing Judgement, *supra* note 319, at paras. 52–78; Banović Sentencing Judgement, *supra* note 285, at paras. 23–25.

874. Tadić Judgement, *supra* note 297, at para. 160.

875. For a discussion of the violence perpetrated against camp prisoners, see Dragan Nikolić Sentencing Judgement, *supra* note 11, at para. 60; Banović Sentencing Judgement, *supra* note 285, at paras. 26–27; Tadić Judgement, *supra* note 297, at paras. 163–67, 171, 175; Stakić Judgement, *supra* note 343, at paras. 201–50; Sikirica Sentencing Judgement, *supra* note 319, at paras. 79–103; Kvočka Judgement, *supra* note 405, at paras. 49–50, 68–109, 114–17.

876. Tadić Judgement, *supra* note 297, at para. 164.

877. Stakić Judgement, *supra* note 343, at paras. 203–06; Sikirica Sentencing Judgement, *supra* note 319, at paras. 101–03.

878. Stakić Judgement, *supra* note 343, at paras. 208–09.

879. For a detailed description of the siege of Sarajevo, *see* Galić Judgement, *supra* note 343; Tom Gjelten, Sarajevo Daily 124–25 (1995); Janine Di Giovanni, The Quick and the Dead: Under Siege in Sarajevo (1995); Zlatko Dizdarević, Sarajevo: A War Journal (1993).

880. Galić Judgement, *supra* note 343, at para. 230.

881. Gjelten, *supra* note 879, at 124–25.

882. Galić Judgement, *supra* note 343, at paras. 219–20.

883. See Mark R. von Sternberg, *Per Humanitatem ad Pacem: International Humanitarian Norms as a Jurisprudence of Peace in the Former Yugoslavia* 3 Cardozo J. Int'l & Comp. L. 357, 372 (1995).

884. Galić Judgement, *supra* note 343, at para. 215 (quoting Morten Hvall, a Norwegian journalist who covered the conflict from September 1992 to August 1994).

885. Galić Judgement, *supra* note 343, at para. 222. Janine Di Giovanni describes ten elderly people who froze to death in an abandoned nursing home and whose bodies could not be removed for fear of sniper fire. Di Giovanni, *supra* note 879, at 9–19.

886. Adam LeBor, *20 Years for Sarajevo Siege General*, The Times (London), Dec. 6, 2003; Charles J. Russo, *Religion and Education in Bosnia: Integration not Segregation?*, 2000 BYU L. Rev. 945, 953.

887. For a detailed description of the fall of Srebrenica and the subsequent massacres, see Jan Willem Honig & Norbert Both, Srebrenica: Record of a War Crime (1996); David Rohde, Endgame: The Betrayal and Fall of Srebrenica, Europe's Worst Massacre Since World War II (1997).

888. Krstić Judgement, *supra* note 327, at paras. 233–34; Honig & Both, *supra* note 887, at 48–66.

889. Prosecution v. Momir Nikolić, Case No. IT-02-60/1-PT, Joint Motion for Consid-

eration of Plea Agreement between Momir Nikolić and the Office of the Prosecutor at Tab A to Annex A, Statement of Facts and Acceptance of Responsibility, para. 13 (May 7, 2003).

890. Samir Krilic, *Report Finds Massacre Planned*, A.P., Nov. 8, 2004.

891. Prosecutor v. Deronjić, Case No. IT-02-61-S, Transcript, 206–07 (Jan. 28, 2004); Deronjić Sentencing Judgement, *supra* note 319, at para. 257; *see also* Prosecutor v. Deronjić, Case No. IT-02-61-S, Transcript, 208–10 (Jan. 28, 2004).

892. Krilic, *supra* note 890; Daria Sito-Sucic, *West Wants Serb Action after Srebrenica Report*, REUTERS, Nov. 8, 2004.

893. Gordana Katana, *Bosnian Serb "Forced" into Atrocity Admission*, IWPR's TRIBUNAL UPDATE, No. 363, June 18, 2004; *see also Ashdown Sacks Bosnian Serb Army Chief for Obstructing Srebrenica Probe*, AGENCE FRANCE-PRESSE, Apr. 16, 2004; Gordana Katana, *Bosnian Serbs Still in Denial over Srebrenica*, IWPR's TRIBUNAL UPDATE, No. 354, April 23, 2004. Srebrenica represents the latest in a long history of denials in the Balkans. During World War II, Croatia's fascist regime established the Jasenovac concentration camp at which Serbs, Jews, and Gypsies were murdered. Serbia puts the death toll at 750,000, while some Croatian historians claim that only 50,000 were killed. *Sanander Condemns "Croatia's Auschwitz,"* AGENCE FRANCE-PRESSE, Mar. 16, 2004.

894. Comprehensive histories of the Rwandan genocide, its causes and it aftermath can be found in LEAVE NONE TO TELL THE STORY, *supra* note 286; PRUNIER, *supra* note 283; MELVERN, *supra* note 52. *See also* ROMEO DALLAIRE, SHAKE HANDS WITH THE DEVIL: THE FAILURE OF HUMANITY IN RWANDA (2003); PAUL J. MAGNARELLA, JUSTICE IN AFRICA: RWANDA'S GENOCIDE, ITS COURTS, AND THE UN CRIMINAL TRIBUNAL (2000); MORRIS & SCHARF, ICTR, *supra* note 52, at 47–73.

895. LEAVE NONE TO TELL THE STORY, *supra* note 286, at 78.

896. *Id.* at 88. Mark Drumbl, in addition, tells of a "staged attack on Kigali, in which Habyarimana soldiers fired into the air to create the illusion of an attack." Drumbl, *Rule of Law*, *supra* note 283, at 559.

897. For a comprehensive treatment of Hutu hate propaganda, see LEAVE NONE TO TELL THE STORY, *supra* note 286, at 65–95; *see also* MELVERN, *supra* note 52, at 204–09. As Prunier put it, the radio station RTLM "poured out a torrent of propaganda, mixing constant harping on the old themes of 'majority democracy,' fears of 'Tutsi feudalist enslavement' and ambiguous 'calls to action.'" PRUNIER, *supra* note 283, at 200. The so-called Media Trial, which convicted radio and newspaper officials of genocide and direct and public incitement to commit genocide, also discusses in detail the substantial role of the media in inciting the population to genocide. *See generally* Nahimana Judgement, *supra* note 3.

898. LEAVE NONE TO TELL THE STORY, *supra* note 286, at 67.

899. Akayesu Judgement, *supra* note 137, at para. 126; LEAVE NONE TO TELL THE STORY, *supra* note 286, at 5.

900. GOUREVITCH, *supra* note 287, at 18.

901. Statement of Mr. Bicamumpaka (Rwanda) at 4, U.N. Doc. S/PV.3377 (May 16, 1994). Some foreign observers, however, believe that President Habyarimana was killed by

Hutu extremists in his own military who were disgruntled by his entering into the Arusha Accords. For a discussion of various hypotheses regarding the culprits, see PRUNIER, *supra* note 283, at 213–29; LEAVE NONE TO TELL THE STORY, *supra* note 286, at 181–85. Former RPF leader, and current Rwandan president Paul Kagame was again accused in 1994 of the assassination. *Kagame Accused over Plane Attack*, BBC NEWS, Mar. 10, 2004.

902. Akayesu Judgement, *supra* note 137, at para. 110; LEAVE NONE TO TELL THE STORY, *supra* note 286, at 9–10.

903. "The use of machetes often resulted in a long and painful agony and many people, when they had some money, paid their killers to be finished off quickly with a bullet rather than being slowly hacked to death." PRUNIER, *supra* note 283, at 255–56.

904. *Id.* at 254–55.

905. *Id.* at 141, 245. Not all scholars agree. Lars Waldorf calls the authoritarian thesis into question by pointing to, for instance, "instances of disobedience and resistance to state authority under a succession of regimes." Lars Waldorf, *Mass Justice for Mass Atrocity, Rethinking Local Justice as Transitional Justice*, TEMP. L. REV. (forthcoming 2006).

906. LEAVE NONE TO TELL THE STORY, *supra* note 286, at 231.

907. *Id.* at 231–34; *see also* PRUNIER, *supra* note 283, at 244.

908. "When the national authorities ordered the extermination of Tutsi, tens of thousands of Hutu responded quickly, ruthlessly and persistently. They killed without scruple and sometimes with pleasure." LEAVE NONE TO TELL THE STORY, *supra* note 286, at 260.

909. PRUNIER, *supra* note 283, at 247.

910. LEAVE NONE TO TELL THE STORY, *supra* note 286, at 237, 11; PRUNIER, *supra* note 283, at 248.

911. LEAVE NONE TO TELL THE STORY, *supra* note 286, at 7–8, 10–11, 214, 236, 251, 265.

912. *Id.* at 262; PRUNIER, *supra* note 283, at 259.

913. MORRIS & SCHARF, ICTR, *supra* note 52, at 58; Madeline H. Morris, *The Trials of Concurrent Jurisdiction: The Case of Rwanda*, 7 DUKE J. COMP. & INT'L L. 349, 350–52 (1997).

914. For a discussion of the East Timorese colonial period, see Fox, *supra* note 247, at 8–23.

915. *See Report of the International Commission of Inquiry on East Timor to the Secretary-General*, para. 5, U.N. Doc. A/54/726-S/2000/59 (Jan. 31, 2000) [hereinafter *Commission of Inquiry on East Timor*].

916. Joseph Nevins, *The Making of "Ground Zero" in East Timor in 1999*, 42 ASIAN SURVEY 623, 626 (2002); *see also* Carsten Stahn, *Accommodating Individual Criminal Responsibility and National Reconciliation: The UN Truth Commission for East Timor*, 95 AM. J. INT'L L. 952, 952 (2001); *Situation of Human Rights in East Timor: Note by the Secretary-General*, para. 16, U.N. Doc A/54/660 (Dec. 10, 1999) [hereinafter *U.N. 1999 Human Rights Report on East Timor*].

917. Dionísio Babo-Soares, *Political Developments Leading to the Referendum*, in OUT OF THE ASHES: DESTRUCTION AND RECONSTRUCTION OF EAST TIMOR 53, 60–62 (James J. Fox & Dionísio Babo-Soares eds., 2003) [hereinafter Babo-Soares, *Political Developments*]; *see generally* Grayson J. Lloyd, *The Diplomacy on East Timor: Indonesia, the*

United Nations and the International Community, in OUT OF THE ASHES: DESTRUCTION AND RECONSTRUCTION OF EAST TIMOR 74, 79–86 (James J. Fox & Dionísio Babo-Soares eds., 2003).

918. *Commission of Inquiry on East Timor, supra* note 915, at paras. 135–41; *U.N. 1999 Human Rights Report on East Timor, supra* note 916, at paras. 26, 63; *see also* Chandra Lekha Sriram, *Revolution in Accountability: New Approaches to Past Abuses,* 19 AM. U. INT'L. L. REV. 301, 401 (2003). The *Leite* case described the more than twenty-five militia groups operating in East Timor and the support given to them by the Indonesian military. Prosecutor v. Sabino Gouveia Leite, Dili District Court, Special Panels for Serious Crimes, Case No. 04b/2001, Judgement, paras. 82–83 (Dec. 7, 2002) [hereinafter Sabino Leite Judgement].

919. *U.N. 1999 Human Rights Report on East Timor, supra* note 916, at para. 26; *Commission of Inquiry on East Timor, supra* note 915, at paras. 41–42; Babo-Soares, *Political Developments, supra* note 917, at 64.

920. Suzannah Linton, *Rising from the Ashes: The Creation of a Viable Criminal Justice System in East Timor,* 25 MELB. U. L. REV. 122, 128–29 (2001) [hereinafter Linton, *Rising from the Ashes*].

921. JUSTICE FOR TIMOR-LESTE, *supra* note 204, at § 2.1; Linton, *Rising from the Ashes, supra* note 920, at 129; Strohmeyer, *Collapse and Reconstruction of a Judicial System, supra* note 213, at 50.

922. *See* Sabino Leite Judgement, *supra* note 918, at para. 101; *see also* Prosecutor v. João Franca da Silva et al., Case No. B0-06.1-99-SC, Indictment, para. 36 (May 25, 2001).

923. *Commission of Inquiry on East Timor, supra* note 915, at para. 130.

924. Hansjöerg Strohmeyer, *Policing the Peace: Post Conflict Judicial System Reconstruction in East Timor,* 24 U. NEW SOUTH WALES L.J. 171, 172 (2001); Dionísio Babo-Soares, *Law and Order: Judiciary Development in East Timor,* at 9, CONFERENCE PAPER FOR CONFERENCE ON COMPARING EXPERIENCES WITH POST-CONFLICT STATE BUILDING IN ASIA AND EUROPE, Denpasar, Bali-Indonesia, Oct. 15–17, 2001.

925. Linton, *Rising from the Ashes, supra* note 920, at 130. Indonesia agreed to permit the entry of this force only after the United States threatened to withhold billions of dollars in loans and aid. *Id.*

926. S.C. Res. 1272, U.N. Doc. S/RES/1272 (Oct. 25, 1999).

927. Tanja Hohe & Rod Nixon, *Reconciling Justice: "Traditional" Law and State Judiciary in East Timor,* Paper prepared for the United States Institute of Peace and delivered at the workshop on the Working of Non-State Justice Systems, held at the Development Institute, Brighton U.K., at 32 (Mar. 6–7, 2003).

928. Strohmeyer, *Collapse and Reconstruction of a Judicial System, supra* note 213, at 54, 57; UNTAET Regulation 1999/3 on the Establishment of a Transitional Judicial Service Commission (Dec. 3, 1999).

929. The Baucau District Court closed for three months, for instance, when judges and prosecutors failed to return from Dili because their houses in Baucau had no furnishings. Judicial System Monitoring Programme, *Justice in the Districts 2003,* at 15 (December 2003), *available at* http://www.jsmp.minihub.org/Reports/jsmpreports/Justice%20in%20

District%20Reports/Justice%20in%20Districts%20_E_.pdf [hereinafter *Justice in the Districts 2003*].

930. *Id.* at 18.

931. Press Release, JSMP, Results of Judges' Evaluations Released, Jan. 26, 2005.

932. David Mearns, *Looking Both Ways: Models for Justice in East Timor*, AUSTRALIAN LEGAL RESOURCES INTERNATIONAL PUBLICATION at 69–70 (Nov. 2002) (on file with author).

933. *Justice in the Districts 2003*, *supra* note 929, at 42.

934. UNTAET Regulation 2000/11, *supra* note 215, at § 7.

935. Shane Marshall, Speech, *The East Timorese Judiciary: At the Threshold of Self-Sufficiency?*, Conference of Supreme and Federal Court Judges, Darwin, Australia, January 2005. An amendment to Regulation 14 of 2000 reduced the number of district Courts to four.

936. *Justice in the Districts 2003*, *supra* note 929, at 16.

937. Mearns, *supra* note 932, at 41.

938. Dionísio Babo-Soares, Nahe Biti: *The Philosophy and Process of Grassroots Reconciliation (and Justice) in East Timor*, 5 ASIA PAC. J. ANTHROPOLOGY 15, 30 (2004) [hereinafter Babo-Soares, Nahe Biti].

939. United Nations Development Programme, Report, *The Community Reconciliation Process of the Commission for Reception, Truth and Reconciliation*, at 24 (April 2004), *available at* http://www.undp.east-timor.org/documentsreports/governance_capacity development/Piers%20report%20Final.pdf [hereinafter UNDP Report on the Community Reconciliation Process]; Hohe & Nixon, *supra* note 927, at 7.

940. Dionísio Babo-Soares, *Challenges for the Future, in* OUT OF THE ASHES: DESTRUCTION AND RECONSTRUCTION OF EAST TIMOR 262, 267 (James J. Fox & Dionísio Babo-Soares eds., 2003); Mearns, *supra* note 932, at 28–30; Hohe & Nixon, *supra* note 927, at 45–46; UNDP Report on the Community Reconciliation Process, *supra* note 939, at 26.

941. Fox, *supra* note 247, at 1; Babo-Soares, Nahe Biti, *supra* note 938, at 23. Space constraints prevent me from providing anything more than a bare-bones summary here.

942. Hohe & Nixon, *supra* note 927, at 13. The Wife Taker gives cattle, buffalo, and money to the Wife Giver while the Wife Giver gives gold weavings and pigs to the Wife Taker. Each of these goods symbolizes certain desirable attributes that the one family gives the other through marriage. *Id.* For more on the relationship between Wife Givers and Wife Takers, see ELIZABETH G. TRAUBE, COSMOLOGY AND SOCIAL LIFE: RITUAL EXCHANGE AMONG THE MAMBAI OF EAST TIMOR 13 (1986); Brigitte Clamagirand, *The Social Organization of the Ema of Timor, in* THE FLOW OF LIFE: ESSAYS ON EASTERN INDONESIA 134, 140 (James J. Fox ed., 1980).

943. Hohe & Nixon, *supra* note 927, at 14.

944. *Id.* at 18, 24; Mearns, *supra* note 932, at 39; Babo-Soares, Nahe Biti, *supra* note 938, at 21.

945. Hohe & Nixon, *supra* note 927, at 24. In some communities, the *liurai* takes the final decision, while in others the final decision is taken by the ritual authority. *Id.*

946. UNDP Report on the Community Reconciliation Process, *supra* note 939, at 26.

947. Hohe & Nixon, *supra* note 927, at 19.

948. Mearns, *supra* note 932, at 43; Hohe & Nixon, *supra* note 927, at 23.

949. Hohe & Nixon, *supra* note 927, at 17.

950. Mearns, *supra* note 932, at 44–45; Babo-Soares, Nahe Biti, *supra* note 938, at 22.

951. Hohe & Nixon, *supra* note 927, at 18.

952. Babo-Soares, Nahe Biti, *supra* note 938, at 15–16.

953. Mearns, *supra* note 932, at 43, 54; UNDP Report on the Community Reconciliation Process, *supra* note 939, at 11, 28.

954. Hohe & Nixon, *supra* note 927, at 20.

955. UNDP Report on the Community Reconciliation Process, *supra* note 939, at 26–27.

956. Hohe & Nixon, *supra* note 927, at 22–23. The East Timorese consider the communal meal so important that a portion of the limited budget of East Timor's Community Reconciliation Process, which will be discussed in further detail in Chapter 8, had to be set aside for food and drink, despite the fact that many international observers considered these expenditures extravagant. UNDP Report on the Community Reconciliation Process, *supra* note 939, at 63.

957. Hohe & Nixon, *supra* note 927, at 64. During the Indonesian period, for instance, serious matters were supposed to be handled by state courts, but these were not regarded as legitimate bodies to resolve disputes: "These courts remained inaccessible and alien, as they did not involve traditional leaders or the conflicting parties, they were not cost effective or time efficient, and did not result in 'appropriate' sanctions or incorporate the important notion of compensation." UNDP Report on the Community Reconciliation Process, *supra* note 939, at 25.

958. Isabelle Wesselingh & Arnaud Vaulerin, Speech, *Eleven Years after Ethnic Cleansing and Four Trials by the ICTY Later, Life between Denial and Hope in Prijedor (Bosnia)*, Feb. 5, 2004, T.C.M. Asser Institute, The Hague. The denial is quite understandable because little freedom of press exists in many parts of Bosnia; thus, evidence of Serb crimes is not well-publicized. *Id.*

959. *See generally* VERBITSKY, *supra* note 60, at 17–64, 152–57 (reproducing transcripts of interviews between a journalist and a navy officer who threw live prisoners from airplanes); *id.* at 13 (describing the confessions of two navy officers before the Argentine Senate).

960. *Id.* at 70; Speck, *supra* note 847, at 502–03.

961. *Fury over Pinochet "Angel" Claim*, BBC ONLINE NEWS REPORT, Nov. 25, 2003, *available at* http://news.bbc.co.uk/1/hi/world/americas/3237740.stm; Brett, *supra* note 4; Jonas, *supra* note 265, at 36; *see also* Alexandra Barahona de Brito, *Passion, Constraint, Law, and* Fortuna, *in* BURYING THE PAST: MAKING PEACE AND DOING JUSTICE AFTER CIVIL CONFLICT 177, 199 (Nigel Biggar ed., 2003) (observing that "the Chilean armed forces remain unapologetic").

962. Juan Forero, *Ex Generals and Others Protest Peru Report on Rebel Conflict*, N.Y. TIMES, Sept. 8, 2003, at A4.

963. Jean Ruremesha, *Rwanda: Should the Bones Be Silenced?*, INTER-PRESS SERVICE (Johannesburg), Aug. 5, 2004; Marc Lacey, *10 Years Later in Rwanda, the Dead Are Ever Present*, N.Y. TIMES, Feb. 26, 2004, at A8.

964. Delalić Judgement, *supra* note 281, at para. 686.

965. Kvočka Judgement, *supra* note 405, at para. 439.

966. *See Witnesses from the "Other Side,"* SENSE NEWS AGENCY, Mar. 1, 2004; *A Suspect Speaks Out*, SENSE NEWS AGENCY, Feb. 24, 2004. Sometimes, subordinates do not testify as planned. In the *Milošević* case, the prosecutor attempted to cross-examine his own witness, Dragan Vasilković, after Vasilković changed his story under Milošević's cross-examination and disavowed a written statement. Prosecutor v. Milošević, Case No. IT-02-54, Transcript, at 16727 (Feb. 21, 2003).

967. In the judgment convicting high-level junta members, the "court pointed to the organized and uniform methods used in the kidnappings . . . [and] observed that subordinates could not have carried out such widespread operations without logistic support, cooperation from civilian authorities, and, most importantly, assurance of impunity." Speck, *supra* note 847, at 505.

968. VERBITSKY, *supra* note 60, at 27.

969. Speck, *supra* note 847, at 502 and n.67.

970. Nahimana Judgement, *supra* note 3, at paras. 429, 431, 444, 446–48; William A. Schabas, *International Decision*, Barayagwiza v. Prosecutor, 94 AM. J. INT'L L. 563, 564 (2000).

971. *See* PRUNIER, *supra* note 283, at 358; Gabriel Gabiro, *Confronting Genocide with Country's Regular Courts*, HIRONDELLE NEWS AGENCY, Sept. 17, 2003, *available at* http://allafrica.com/stories/200309170501.html.

972. The value of such participation would probably be limited as well because crimes featuring a high victim-perpetrator ratio are usually carried out quickly, efficiently, and without much personal contact. For the reasons discussed below, then, neither victims nor society would benefit greatly from a substantial number of such interactions. The participation of a few token victims, by contrast, may usefully highlight the importance of victim concerns and serve as symbolic empowerment.

973. A small number of Bosnian men targeted for execution at Srebrenica survived when the bodies of those killed fell on them and concealed the fact that they were still alive. Krstić Judgement, *supra* note 327, at para. 69; Momir Nikolić Sentencing Judgement, *supra* note 282, at para. 110.

974. Bosnian prisoners and guards often lived in the same communities before the conflict. Prosecutor v. Češić, Case No. IT-95-10/1-S, Transcript, at 118–19 (Nov. 27, 2003); Češić Sentencing Judgement, *supra* note 319, at para. 14; Prosecution v. Dragan Nikolić, Case No. IT-94-2-S, Transcript, at 257, 268, 278–79 (Nov. 3, 2003); Milan Simić Sentencing Judgement, *supra* note 319, at para. 70.

975. *See, e.g.*, Prosecutor v. Krstić, Case No. IT-98-33, Transcript, at 5759–60 (July 26, 2000); Momir Nikolić Sentencing Judgement, *supra* note 282, at paras. 112, 121.

976. John Carlin reported on a Hutu offender who allegedly killed approximately seven thousand people. *See* John Carlin, *Could You Share a Pint with a Man Who Killed Your Family?*, NEW STATESMAN, Sept. 15, 2003.

977. While domestic restorative-justice programs do aim at community restoration, they target their reconciliatory efforts at the individual victim and perpetrator. Because international crimes typically are committed on a society-wide scale pursuant to a hate-

based ideology, the restoration to be sought must extend beyond the particular individuals involved to society at large. The value of restorative measures will diminish over time only with respect to societal restoration. By contrast, the individuals involved in the last crime to be prosecuted are apt to gain nearly as much from restorative procedures as did those involved in the first crime to be prosecuted.

978. Galić Judgement, *supra* note 343, at paras. 565–66.

979. Defendant Blagojević was born in Bratunac municipality while Jokić was born in the Zvornik municipality. *See* Prosecutor v. Vidoje Blagojević & Dragan Jokić, Case No. IT-02-60-T, Amended Joinder Indictment, paras. 1, 12 (May 26, 2003). Obrenović was born in Rogatica. Obrenović Sentencing Judgement, *supra* note 319, at para. 1. Deronjić, who was not charged with crimes at Srebrenica but who admitted to participating in their coordination, was born in Bratunac municipality. Deronjić Sentencing Judgement, *supra* note 319, at para. 5.

980. Momir Nikolić Sentencing Judgment, *supra* note 282, at para. 2; Comment of Munira Subašić, *supra* note 272.

981. Assuming, that is, that minimum standards of due process are observed. As Chapter 9 will describe, Rwanda's Tutsi-led government made an early attempt to prosecute every last offender, but its efforts were characterized by grave due-process violations, including arbitrary and lengthy detention of defendants without charge.

982. GOUREVITCH, *supra* note 287, at 123.

983. *Id.* at 47.

984. *See generally* VERBITSKY, *supra* note 60.

985. *See* Weitekamp, *supra* note 271, at 99; *but see* Douglas J. Sylvester, *Myth in Restorative Justice History*, 2003 UTAH L. REV. 471, 474–75 (accusing restorative-justice proponents of distorting history).

986. UNDP Report on the Community Reconciliation Process, *supra* note 939, at 16.

987. *U.N. 1999 Human Rights Report on East Timor*, *supra* note 916, at paras. 29, 33, 35.

988. *See* DAVID HICKS, TETUM GHOSTS AND KIN: FIELDWORK IN AN INDONESIAN COMMUNITY 114–16 (1988).

989. Nevins, *supra* note 916, at 624–25.

990. Press Release, Serious Crimes Unit, Crimes against Humanity Charges for Former Indonesian Minister of Defense, Top Indonesian Military Commanders and East Timor Governor, Feb. 25, 2003.

991. Los Palos Judgement, *supra* note 702, at para. 688; UNDP Report on the Community Reconciliation Process, *supra* note 939, at 73.

992. Mearns, *supra* note 932, at 49.

Chapter 10

993. *See* Erdemović, Joint Separate Opinion of Judge McDonald and Judge Vohrah, *supra* note 311, at para. 2; *see also* Prosecutor v. Erdemović, Case No. IT-96-22-A, Separate and Dissenting Opinion of Judge Cassese, para. 8 (Oct. 7, 1997). The *Sikirica* panel likewise observed that "by entering a plea of guilt before the commencement of his trial, an

accused will save the International Tribunal the time and effort of a lengthy investigation and trial." Sikirica Sentencing Judgement, *supra* note 319, at para. 149.

994. Todorović Sentencing Judgement, *supra* note 319, at para. 81; Sikirica Sentencing Judgement, *supra* note 319, at para. 149.

995. Erdemović, Joint Separate Opinion of Judge McDonald and Judge Vohrah, *supra* note 311, at para. 2; Todorović Sentencing Judgement, *supra* note 319, at para. 80.

996. Erdemović Second Sentencing Judgement, *supra* note 321, at para. 16(ii).

997. Momir Nikolić Sentencing Judgement, *supra* note 282, at para. 67. The *Obrenović* panel reaffirmed these views. *See* Obrenović Sentencing Judgement, *supra* note 319, at para. 118.

998. Deronjić Sentencing Judgement, *supra* note 319, at para. 236.

999. Obrenović Sentencing Judgement, *supra* note 319, at para. 111 ("The Trial Chamber finds that Dragan Obrenović's guilty plea is indeed significant and can contribute to fulfilling the Tribunal's mandate of restoring peace and promoting reconciliation"); Momir Nikolić Sentencing Judgement, *supra* note 282, at para. 145 ("The Trial Chamber finds that Momir Nikolić's guilty plea is significant and can contribute to fulfilling the Tribunal's mandate of restoring peace and promoting reconciliation").

1000. Plavšić Prosecution's Sentencing Brief, *supra* note 360, at para. 24.

1001. The two joint witnesses were Madeleine Albright, U.S. secretary of state during President Clinton's administration, and Dr. Alex Boraine, deputy chairman of the South African TRC. Both witnesses, like the prosecution, praised Plavšić's guilty plea for the contribution it made to reconciliation in Bosnia. *See* Prosecutor v. Plavšić, Case No. IT-00-39&40/1-S, Transcript, at 520–22, 562–66 (Dec. 17, 2002).

1002. Prosecution v. Obrenović, Case No. IT-02-60/2-S, Prosecutor's Brief on the Sentencing of Dragan Obrenović, para. 28 (July 30, 2003) (on file with author) [hereinafter Obrenović, Prosecutor's Sentencing Brief].

1003. *See* Prosecutor v. Obrenović, Case No. IT-02-60/2-S, Transcript, at 1531–36 (Oct. 30, 2003); Prosecutor v. Momir Nikolić, Case No. IT-02-60/1-S, Transcript, at 1642–48 (Oct. 29, 2003). *See also* Češić, Prosecution's Sentencing Brief, *supra* note 449, at paras. 51–54 . In *Banović*, the prosecution asserted that Banović's guilty plea "serves as a catharsis for victims and all people impacted by the war to start the healing process and to halt the cycle of personal or group retaliation in the area of conflict, thereby promoting reconciliation between the warring factions." Prosecutor v. Banović, Case No. IT-02-65/1-S, Transcript, at 112 (Sept. 3, 2003). Prosecution v. Miodrag Jokić, Case No. IT-01-42/1-S, Transcript, at 206 (Dec. 4, 2003) ("The fact of the plea is very significant for reconciliation.").

1004. *How to Punish Crime and Reward Guilty Pleas and Cooperation*, SENSE NEWS AGENCY, Apr. 2, 2004.

1005. Rachel S. Taylor, *Babić May Get Off Lightly*, IWPR's TRIBUNAL UPDATE, No. 351, Apr. 2, 2004.

1006. Prosecution v. Babić, Case No. IT-03-72-S, Transcript, at 234 (Apr. 2, 2004). Babić's defense counsel quoted prosecutor Alex Whiting's statement that "[i]t is an uncomfortable reality . . . that only by hearing the testimony of those who were on the inside, those who played a role in the crimes themselves that the full truth of what happened and who was responsible will be known." *Id.* at 244. The prosecution's sentencing brief likewise so praised Babić that it reads, rather, like a defense sentencing brief.

1007. These are Banović, Deronjić, Momir Nikolić, Obrenović, Češić, Jokić, Babić, Bralo, and Rajić. The prosecution did, however, include some victim-impact statements with its sentencing brief in *Češić* and *Bralo*. Prosecutor v. Češić, Case No. IT-95-10/1-S, Prosecution's Sentencing Brief, at Annexes A–D (Nov. 12, 2003); Bralo Prosecution's Sentencing Brief, *supra* note 485, at Attachments G–M, and it provided some background information about the victims in the *Jokić* case, Prosecution v. Miodrag Jokić, Case No. IT-01-42/1-S, Transcript, at 238–41 (Dec. 4, 2003). The sentencing hearings of Mrđa and Dragan Nikolić did feature victim testimony. *See* Chris Stephen, *What Price Justice?*, IWPR's TRIBUNAL UPDATE, No. 332, Nov. 7, 2003; *see also* Prosecution v. Banović, Case No. IT-02-65/1, Transcript (Sept. 3, 2003). In the Momir Nikolić sentencing hearing, prosecutors called no witnesses at all. Momir Nikolić Sentencing Judgement, *supra* note 282, at para. 22.

1008. Prosecutor v. Dragan Nikolić, Case No. IT-94-2-S, Transcript, at 239–40 (Nov. 3, 2003).

1009. *Id.* at 247.

1010. *Id.* at 257; *see also* Emir Suljagić, *Sušica Camp Chief Names Mass Grave Site*, IWPR's TRIBUNAL UPDATE, No. 332, Nov. 7, 2003.

1011. *See* Sikirica Plea Agreement, *supra* note 398; Kolundžija Plea Agreement, *supra* note 398; Došen Plea Agreement, *supra* note 398; Sikirica Sentencing Judgement, *supra* note 319, at para. 111.

1012. Babić Plea Agreement, *supra* note 319, at para. 8; Momir Nikolić Plea Agreement, *supra* note 11, at para. 9; Obrenović Plea Agreement, *supra* note 11, at para. 9; Deronjić Plea Agreement, *supra* note 11, at para. 12; Češić Plea Agreement, *supra* note 11, at para. 10; Banović Plea Agreement, *supra* note 11, at Annex 2; Jokić Sentencing Judgement, *supra* note 11, at para. 9; Mrđa Sentencing Judgement, *supra* note 11, at para. 69.

1013. Babić Plea Agreement, *supra* note 319, at para. 8; Momir Nikolić Plea Agreement, *supra* note 11, at para. 9; Obrenović Plea Agreement, *supra* note 11, at para. 9; Deronjić Plea Agreement, *supra* note 11, at para. 12; Rajić Plea Agreement, *supra* note 319, at para. 17.

1014. Babić Plea Agreement, *supra* note 319, at para. 8; Banović Plea Agreement, *supra* note 11, at Annex 2; Momir Nikolić Plea Agreement, *supra* note 11, at para. 9; Obrenović Plea Agreement, *supra* note 11, at para. 9; Deronjić Plea Agreement, *supra* note 11, at para. 12; Češić Plea Agreement, *supra* note 11, at para. 10.

1015. Momir Nikolić Plea Agreement, *supra* note 11, at para. 10; Obrenović Plea Agreement, *supra* note 11, at para. 10.

1016. Prosecutor v. Momir Nikolić, Case No. IT-02-60/1, Prosecutor's Brief on the Sentencing of Momir Nikolić, paras. 30, 39 (July 14, 2003) (on file with author); Obrenović, Prosecutor's Sentencing Brief, *supra* note 1002, at para. 40.

1017. Momir Nikolić Sentencing Judgement, *supra* note 282, at 156; Interview with FF, Dec. 5, 2003.

1018. Goran Jungvirth, *Bosnian Croat Insider Awaits Sentence*, IWPR's TRIBUNAL UPDATE, No. 448, Apr. 13, 2006.

1019. Nikolić testified on September 22, 23, 25, 26, 29, 31 and October 1, 2003, while Obrenović testified on October 1, 2, 6–9, and 10, 2003.

1020. Prosecution v. Krstić, Case No. IT-98-33-A, Transcript, at 173–80 (Nov. 21, 2003).

1021. Jokić testified on March 22 through 25 and on March 29.

1022. Prosecutor v. Milošević, Case No. IT-02-54, Transcript (Nov. 18–22, 25, 26, 2002, and Dec. 2–4, 6, 9, 2002).

1023. Prosecution v. Deronjić, Case No. IT-02-61-S, Transcript, at 237 (Jan. 28, 2004).

1024. Deronjić testified in the *Krstić* appeal, *see* Prosecutor v. Krstić, Case No. IT-98-33-A, Transcript, at 101–71 (Nov. 21, 2003), in the *Milošević* trial, *see* Prosecution v. Milošević, Case No. IT-02-54, Transcript (Nov. 26–27, 2003), in the *Blagojević* trial, Prosecutor v. Blagojević & Jokić, Case No. IT-02-60-T, Transcript, at 6305–92 (Jan. 21, 2004), and in the *Krajišnik* trial, Prosecutor v. Krajišnik, Case No. IT-00-39-Transcript (Feb. 12, 13, 16, 18, 19, 2004).

1025. *Insider Links Milošević to War in Croatia*, CIJ Report, Nov. 20, 2002.

1026. Prosecution v. Milošević, Case No. IT-02-54, Transcript, at 13166–67 (Nov. 20, 2002); Prosecution v. Milošević, Case No. IT-02-54, Transcript, at 13168–70 (Nov. 21, 2002).

1027. *The Case Is Almost Proved: Insider Says Milošević Was Responsible*, CIJ Report, Nov. 27, 2002.

1028. *See generally* Prosecution v. Milošević, Case No. IT-02-54, Transcript (Nov. 26–27, 2003); *see also* Prosecutor v. Krajišnik, Case No. IT-00-39-T, Transcript (Feb. 12–13, 2004).

1029. *See generally* Prosecutor v. Krajišnik, Case No. IT-00-39-T, Transcript (Feb. 12–13, 2004).

1030. *Bosnian TV Reports on Rajić Guilty Plea Fallout in Croatia*, BBC Worldwide Monitoring, Nov. 6, 2005.

1031. Rajić asserts, for instance, that his superior Slobodan Praljak ordered Rajić and others to "[s]ort out the situation in Vareš showing no mercy towards anyone," Rajić Factual Basis, *supra* note 497, at para. 16, and that during 1993, a state of international armed conflict existed in Bosnia involving "the Republic of Croatia and its government, armed forces, and representatives in an armed conflict against Bosnian Muslims on the territory of" Bosnia, *id*. at para. 43(b).

1032. *Id*. at paras. 32–38.

1033. Prosecution v. Blagojević, Case No. IT-02-60-T, Transcript, at 2126–31 (Sept. 29, 2003); Chris Stephen, *Key Srebrenica Witness Apologises for Lies*, IWPR's Tribunal Update, No. 327, Oct. 4, 2003. As part of his false statement, Nikolić asserted that another ICTY suspect—Ljubomir Borovcanin—was present at the executions with him; even after admitting his lie, Nikolić continued to maintain that he had heard of Borovcanin's presence through other sources. Prosecution v. Blagojević, Case No. IT-02-60-T, Transcript, at 2138–42 (Sept. 29, 2003).

1034. Prosecution v. Blagojević, Case No. IT-02-60-T, Transcript, at 2126–27 (Sept. 29, 2003).

1035. Prosecution v. Blagojević, Case No. IT-02-60-T, Transcript, at 6405–07 (Jan. 22, 2004).

1036. Karen Meirik, *Srebrenica Prosecution Blow*, IWPR's TRIBUNAL UPDATE, No. 340, Jan. 23, 2004; Stacy Sullivan, *Krajišnik "Helped Mastermind" Serb Crimes*, IWPR's TRIBUNAL UPDATE, No. 342, Feb. 9, 2004.

1037. 18 U.S.C.A. § 3553(e) (West Supp. 2003); U.S. Sentencing Guidelines Manual § 5K1.1 (2003).

1038. *See* Ellen Yaroshefsky, *Cooperation with Federal Prosecutors: Experiences of Truth Telling and Embellishment*, 68 FORDHAM L. REV. 917, 929 (1999). *See also* Timothy Hollis, Note, *An Offer You Can't Refuse?* United States v. Singleton *and the Effects of Witness/Prosecutorial Agreements*, 9 B.U. PUB. INT. L.J. 433, 446 (2000).

1039. Ellen Yaroshefsky concluded that "prosecutors' reliance on inaccurate cooperator testimony is a problem within the criminal justice system," Yaroshefsky, *supra* note 1038, at 921, and she set forth nine "bases for prosecutors' false beliefs in cooperator truthfulness": (1) insufficient corroboration, (2) lack of investigation, (3) insufficient evidence, (4) trust of cooperators, (5) rigid theory of guilt, (6) cultural barriers, (7) attitudes of individual assistants, (8) lack of prosecutorial experience, and (9) problems related to proffer sessions, *id.* at 931–62. *See also* United States v. Singleton, 144 F.3d 1343, 1360 (1998) (noting that the "temptation, even if unconscious, is to color or falsify one's testimony in favor of the donor"); United States v. Kimble, 719 F.2d 1253, 1255 (5th Cir. 1983) (noting that the cooperator "candidly stated that he was testifying only because of the lenient nature of the sentence he was to receive in return for his cooperation").

1040. Prosecutor v. Todorović, Case No. IT-95-9/1, Transcript, at 801–03, 805–06, 812–14 (Jan. 19, 2001).

1041. Prosecutor v. Momir Nikolić, Case No. IT-02-60-PT, Transcript (May 6, 2003). In response to this objection, the prosecution agreed to withdraw the genocide charges upon the acceptance of the guilty plea. *Id.*

1042. Prosecutor v. Krajišnik, Case No. IT-00-39-T, Transcript (Feb. 12, 2004). Interestingly, although the Special Panels in the Dili District Court in East Timor were generally far less rigorous than the ICTY in adhering to due-process norms, even the Special Panels were unwilling to admit the testimony of a guilty-plea defendant against codefendants before the defendant pleading guilty had been sentenced. THE LOLOTOE CASE: A SMALL STEP FORWARD, *supra* note 232, at § 2.5.2.1.

1043. Prosecutor v. Češić, Case No. IT-95-10-PT, Transcript, at 74 (Oct. 8, 2003); Dragan Nikolić Sentencing Judgement, *supra* note 11, at para. 259.

1044. Prosecutor v. Momir Nikolić, Case No. IT-02-60/1-S, Transcript, at 1479 (Oct. 27, 2003).

1045. *See* Deronjić Plea Agreement, *supra* note 11.

1046. *See* Prosecution v. Deronjić, Case No. IT-02-61-PT, Transcript, at 196–204 (Jan. 28, 2004); Chris Stephen, *Deronjić Plea-Bargain Claims*, IWPR's TRIBUNAL UPDATE, No. 335, Nov. 28, 2003.

1047. Interview with SW, The Hague, Sept. 26, 2003.

1048. *See* Prosecutor v. Češić, Case No. IT-95-10/1-PT, Third Amended Indictment, para. 17 (Nov. 26, 2002); Prosecutor v. Češić, Case No. IT-95-10/1-PT, Factual Basis, para. 18 (Oct. 8, 2003).

1049. Prosecutor v. Češić, Case No. IT-95-10/1-S, Transcript, at 98 (Nov. 27, 2003).

1050. *Id.* at 97–106.

1051. Banović Plea Agreement, *supra* note 11, at paras. 15–17.

1052. *See* Suljagić & Kebo, *supra* note 12.

1053. *Association "Women from Podrinje" Disappointed with Deronjić's Sentence*, NTV HAYAT (Sarajevo Radio Station), Mar. 31, 2004 (translation provided by Tuzla Night Owl, *available at* http://www.tfeagle.army.mil/tfeno/Feature_Story.asp?Article=81109).

1054. *See* Prosecution v. Dragan Nikolić, Case No. IT-94-2-PT, Transcript, at 176–96 (Sept. 4, 2003); Prosecution v. Deronjić, Case No. IT-02-61-PT, Transcript, at 47–64 (Sept. 30, 2003). Other Trial Chambers have not generally placed so high a value on publicizing the facts, but Judge Orie, presiding judge of Chamber I, did read out most of Ranko Češić's factual basis. Prosecutor v. Češić, Case No. IT-95-10/1-PT, Transcript, at 64–67 (Oct. 8, 2003).

1055. Prosecution v. Deronjić, Case No. IT-02-61-PT, Transcript, at 64–83 (Sept. 30, 2003).

1056. Prosecution v. Deronjić, Case No. IT-02-61-S, Transcript, at 131–71 (Jan. 27, 2004). For instance, the factual basis states that Deronjić "took positive and concrete actions, including affirmative actions, and related to the use of force to remove non-Serbs from Serb-designated territories," and Judge Schomburg asked Deronjić to explain exactly what he meant by "use of force." *Id.* at 134–39. Similarly, Judge Schomburg pressed Deronjić to explicate his role in the disarming of the Muslim community in Glogova, *id.* at 142–43, and in the decision to shell the houses of Muslims, *id.* at 145–49.

1057. Prosecution v. Deronjić, Case No. IT-02-61-PT, Transcript, at 248–50 (Mar. 5, 2004).

1058. Prosecutor v. Banović, IT-02-65/1, Transcript, at 111 (Sept. 3, 2003). Judge Schomburg concurred in this view, stating that "it is of high importance and relevance that the names of those killed at that time are mentioned in open court." Prosecution v. Deronjić, Case No. IT-02-61-PT, Transcript, at 79 (Sept. 30, 2003).

1059. Prosecutor v. Rajić, Case No. IT-95-12-PT, Defence Sentencing Brief, para. 18 (Mar. 6, 2006) [hereinafter Rajić Sentencing Brief]; Prosecutor v. Rajić, Case No. IT-95-12-S, Transcript, at 228 (Apr. 7. 2006). The plea agreement in fact refers to thirty-seven murder victims. Rajić Factual Basis, *supra* note 497, at para. 26.

1060. Rajić Factual Basis, *supra* note 497, at para. 26.

1061. Prosecutor v. Rajić, Case No. IT-95-12-S, Transcript, at 228 (Apr. 7. 2006).

1062. Rajić Factual Basis, *supra* note 497, at para. 34.

1063. Prosecutor v. Rajić, Case No. IT-95-12-S, Transcript, at 232 (Apr. 7. 2006); Rajić Sentencing Brief, *supra* note 1059, at para. 29.

1064. Prosecution v. Češić, Case No. IT-95-10/1-S, Ranko Češić's Sentencing Brief, paras. 42–43 (Nov. 12, 2003); Češić Sentencing Judgement, *supra* note 319, at para. 95. The Trial Chamber rejected this assertion as a mitigating circumstance on a balance of the probabilities. *See id.* at para. 97.

1065. Mrđa's Sentencing Brief, *supra* note 386, at para. 84.

1066. Prosecutor v. Banović, IT-02-65/1, Transcript, at 97 (Sept. 3, 2003).

1067. *Id.*

1068. Prosecution v. Mrđa, Case No. IT-02-59-S, Transcript, at 104 (Oct. 22, 2003).

1069. *Id.* at 105.

1070. *Id.* at 106–07.

1071. Prosecutor v. Banović, IT-02-65/1, Transcript, at 102 (Sept. 3, 2003).

1072. Prosecutor v. Rajić, Case No. IT-95-12-S, Transcript, at 235–36 (Apr. 7, 2006).

1073. Prosecutor v. Todorović, Case No. IT-95-9/1, Transcript, at 59 (May 4, 2001).

1074. *Id.* at 59–60.

1075. Prosecution v. Sikirica, Case No. IT-95-8-T, Transcript, at 5718–19 (Oct. 8, 2001). *See id.* at 5736–37 (Došen's statement of remorse).

1076. Immediately after apologizing to victims, Mrđa asserted: "I did not commit this because I wanted to commit this or I enjoyed doing this. I did not hate these people. I did it because I was ordered to do so. My commander, who enjoyed great respect and had a lot of authority, was present personally and issued these orders. In those moments, I could not muster up enough courage to disobey the order. I can tell you now what would have happened had I refused to carry out the order; I assure you that they would have killed me right then." Prosecution v. Mrđa, Case No. IT-02-59-S, Transcript, at 137 (Oct. 22, 2003). He went on to tell the judges of the dignified way that he behaved at other battlefields. *Id.* at 138.

1077. Prosecutor v. Rajić, Case No. IT-95-12-S, Transcript, at 244, 246 (Apr. 7, 2006).

1078. Prosecutor v. Češić, Case No. 95-10/1-S, Transcript, at 114–15 (Nov. 27, 2003).

1079. Dragan Nikolić Sentencing Judgement, *supra* note 11, at para. 241. Other defendants have issued similar statements. Momir Nikolić stated in part:

I sincerely wish before this Chamber and before the public, especially the Bosniak public, to express my deep and sincere remorse and regret because of the crime that occurred and to apologise to the victims, their families, and the Bosniak people for my participation in this crime. I am aware that I cannot bring back the dead, that I cannot mitigate the pain of the families by my confession, but I wish to contribute to the full truth being established about Srebrenica and the victims there and for the government organs of Republika Srpska, and all the individuals who took part in these crimes should follow in my footsteps and admit to their participation and their guilt, that they should give themselves in and be held responsible for what they have done.

Prosecutor v. Momir Nikolić, Case No. IT-02-60/1-S, Transcript, at 1677 (Oct. 29, 2003).

1080. Mrđa Sentencing Judgement, *supra* note 11, at para. 87; Češić Sentencing Judgement, *supra* note 319, at para. 66; Obrenović Sentencing Judgement, *supra* note 319, at para. 121; Dragan Nikolić Sentencing Judgement, *supra* note 11, at paras. 241–42; Momir Nikolić Sentencing Judgement, *supra* note 282, at para. 161; Jokić Sentencing Judgement, *supra* note 11, at paras. 89–92; Deronjić Sentencing Judgement, *supra* note 319, at para. 263.

1081. Banović Sentencing Judgement, *supra* note 285, at paras. 71–72.

1082. *See, e.g.,* Prosecution v. Dragan Nikolić, Case No. IT-94-2-A, Transcript, at 55–57

(Nov. 29, 2004); Prosecution v. Jokić, Case No. IT-01-42/1-A, Transcript, at 365–66 (Apr. 26, 2005).

1083. Predrag Banović stated:

> Your Honours, I have pleaded unequivocally as guilty. My guilty plea was an expression of sincere remorse concerning the events in Prijedor, and especially the Keraterm camp. I gave an interview about my role in this to the investigators of the Tribunal. Today, I wish to add only the following: My arrest and transfer to The Hague, as well as that of my brother, was something I experienced with great fear, mostly because the propaganda was always that The Hague was a place for the quiet murder of the Serbs. Fortunately, very soon, I came to the conclusion that this propaganda was a lie.
>
> Through the proceedings up to this point, I have experienced enlightenment. I have gathered the strength to face the truth and myself. This is why I made the decision to change my plea. I deplore the period of war and hatred, and I regret that I did not find a way to avoid mobilisation and my role in the camp. I feel sorry for all the victims, and I curse my own hands for having inflicted pain in any way on innocent people. I wish my sincere words to be understood as a balm for those wounds and as a contribution to the reconciliation of all people in Prijedor and the restoration of the situation that existed before the war.

Prosecution v. Banović, Case No. IT-02-65/1-S, Transcript, at 128–29 (Sept. 3, 2003).

1084. Telephone Interview with Refik Hodzić, formerly ICTY Outreach Program director for Bosnia (July 28, 2004).

1085. *See Pleading Repentance*, BALKAN RECONSTRUCTION REPORT, Feb. 2, 2004.

1086. Telephone Interview with Refik Hodzić, formerly ICTY Outreach Program director for Bosnia (July 28, 2004).

1087. Mark A. Drumbl, *Law and Atrocity: Settling Accounts in Rwanda*, 31 OHIO N.U. L. REV. 41, 47 (2005).

1088. Samantha Power, *Rwanda: The Two Faces of Justice*, 50 N.Y. REV. BOOKS No. 1, Jan. 16, 2003.

1089. *Id.*

1090. *See* Bisengimana Judgement, *supra* note 597, at para. 127; Prosecutor v. Rutaganira, Case No. ICTR-95-1C-T, Transcript, at 29 (Jan. 17, 2005).

1091. Prosecutor v. Rugambarara, Case No. ICTR-2000-59-I, Indictment, para. 2.3 (July 10, 2000).

1092. Rugambarara's indictment, for instance, alleges that Rugambarara, Bisengimana, and Semanza attended various meetings at which the audience was encouraged to exterminate the Tutsi. *Id.* at paras. 3.13, 3.14(i), 3.14(ii). Rugambarara is also alleged to have worked with Bisengimana and Semanza to recruit youths for Rwandan militias, *id.* at para. 3.15, to transport soldiers and militia to massacre Tutsi at the Musha church, *id.* at para. 3.28, to personally kill victims, *id.* at 3.29, and to organize mass burials, *id.* at 3.31(ii).

1093. Prosecutor v. Semanza, Case No. ICTR-97-20-I, Transcript, at 14 (Oct. 16, 2000).

1094. *ICTR/Serugendo—Serugendo's Guilty Plea Bargain Settled on a Prison Sentence of 6 to 10 Years*, HIRONDELLE NEWS AGENCY, June. 1, 2006; Serugendo Press Release, *supra* note 650.

1095. Serushago Plea Agreement, *supra* note 558, at paras. 18–23, 25, 28–28, 31–33.

1096. Serushago Sentence, *supra* note 554, at para. 25(iii); *see also id.* at paras. 25(vii), (xv)–(xvii).

1097. *Id.* at para. 25(vi).

1098. *Id.* at para. 25(xxiv).

1099. *Id.* at para. 41.

1100. Serushago also testified in the Military I trial. *See* Prosecutor v. Serushago, Case No. ICTR-98-39-A, Order for the Continued Detention of Omar Serushago in the ICTR Detention Facility in Arusha (Apr. 3, 2001). *See* Mary Kimani, *Media Trial: "Hassan Ngeze Did Not Want Me to Testify," Genocide Convict Claims*, INTERNEWS, Nov. 15, 2001, *available at* http://www.internews.org/activities/ICTR_Reports/ICTRNewsNov01.html1115a.

1101. For a discussion of Serushago's credibility problems, *see generally* Nahimana Judgement, *supra* note 3, at paras. 817–24.

1102. Lars Waldorf, *Silent Partner*, DIPLOMATIE JUDICIAIRE, Nov. 27, 2001.

1103. Nahimana Judgement, *supra* note 3, at para. 821.

1104. *Id.* at para. 824.

1105. Ruggiu Plea Agreement, *supra* note 573, at paras. 2–24.

1106. Ruggiu Judgement, *supra* note 568, at para. 44(i).

1107. Ruggiu Plea Agreement, *supra* note 573, at paras. 210–12.

1108. Nahimana Judgement, *supra* note 3, at para. 549; *Convicted Ex-Radio Presenter Has Mental Problems, Defence Suggests*, HIRONDELLE NEWS AGENCY, Mar. 5, 2002.

1109. Nahimana Judgement, *supra* note 3, at paras. 548–49.

1110. Kambanda Prosecutor's Pre-Sentencing Brief, *supra* note 542, at 23.

1111. *Id.* at 22–23.

1112. *See, e.g.*, MELVERN, *supra* note 52, at 172, 191–92, 194–95.

1113. *ICTR/Karemera—MRND Leaders Want Uwilingiyimana's Statements Made Public*, HIRONDELLE NEWS AGENCY, Feb. 23, 2006.

1114. Palmer, *supra* note 666.

1115. MELVERN, *supra* note 52, at 2.

1116. Kambanda Judgement, *supra* note 276, at paras. 51–52.

1117. Prosecutor v. Bisengimana, Case No. ICTR-2000-60-S, Transcript, at 45–46 (Jan. 19, 2006).

1118. Prosecutor v. Rutaganira, Case No. ICTR-95-1C-T, Sentencing Judgement, para. 157 (Mar. 14, 2005) (author's translation from the French version of the judgment).

1119. Ruggiu Transcript, *supra* note 568, at 250.

1120. Serushago Transcript, *supra* note 555, at 38–44; *ICTR/Former Rwandan Militia Leader Asks for the Forgiveness of Rwanda*, INTERNEWS, Jan. 29, 1998; *Militia Leader Who Confessed to Genocide Gets Fifteen Years in Prison*, INTERNEWS, Feb. 5, 1998.

1121. Helena Cobban, *Healing Rwanda: Can an International Court Deliver Justice?*, BOSTON REVIEW 10, 16 (Dec. 2003/Jan. 2003).

1122. *See* THE LOLOTOE CASE: A SMALL STEP FORWARD, *supra* note 232, at 3, n.5.

1123. Judicial System Monitoring Programme, Case Summary, *available at* http://www
.jsmp.minihub.org/courtmonitoring/spsccaseinformation2000.htm.

1124. Telephone Interview with Essa Faal, chief of prosecutions, Special Panels for
Serious Crimes (July 30, 2004).

1125. Telephone Interview with Mohamed Othman, former prosecutor general for
East Timor (Aug. 4, 2004).

1126. The Judicial System Monitoring Programme opined, for instance, that "to date
there has been little if any communal involvement in a process whose main function is to
bring healing and reconciliation to the people of Timor Leste." Press Release, JSMP, Conference on the Future of the Serious Crimes Process for Timor-Leste (Sept. 22, 2004).

1127. *See* Fausto Belo Ximenes, *The Unique Contribution of the Community-Based Reconciliation Process in East Timor* at 14 (May 28, 2004) *available at* http://www.easttimor-
reconciliation.org/jsmpReport-prk-summary.html.

1128. Telephone Interview with Alan Gutman, defense counsel, Special Panels for Serious Crimes (July 30, 2004).

1129. JSMP, THE LOS PALOS CASE REPORT, *supra* note 223, at § 3.2.3.

1130. Judicial System Monitoring Programme, *The Continuation of the Final Closing
Statement in the Case of Carlos Soares*, Nov. 17, 2003.

1131. THE LOLOTOE CASE: A SMALL STEP FORWARD, *supra* note 232, at § 3.4.

1132. Los Palos Judgement, *supra* note 702, at para. 1121.

1133. Augusto Dos Santos Judgement, *supra* note 731, at para. 56(b).

1134. Sabino Leite Trial Notes, Nov. 18, 2002 (on file with author).

1135. Jhoni Franca Trial Notes, Oct. 24, 2002 (on file with author).

1136. Agustinho Atolan Judgement, *supra* note 733, at 7–8.

1137. Drumbl, *Rule of Law, supra* note 283, at 571; Penal Reform International, *PRI Research Team on Gacaca: Report IV*, at 3 (Jan. 2003), *available at* http://www.penalreform
.org/download/Gacaca/Jan2003.pdf [hereinafter *PRI Report IV*]. The arrests were widely
condemned as arbitrary. "In the months immediately following the installation of the new
government in July 1994, primarily soldiers, but also local authorities (sometimes issued
blank warrants by their public prosecutor's offices), unlawfully detained thousands of individuals on the basis of uninvestigated oral accusations. There were few arrest warrants,
individuals were detained for longer than the lawful period of police custody and persons
released by judicial authorities for lack of evidence were frequently rearrested by soldiers."
AMNESTY INTERNATIONAL, GACACA: A QUESTION OF JUSTICE, Dec. 17, 2002, at III, *available at* http://web.amnesty.org/library/Index/ENGAFR470072002?open&of=ENG-RWA
[hereinafter GACACA: A QUESTION OF JUSTICE]. Drumbl also reports that some Rwandan
prisoners "were randomly rounded up, even at refugee camps. . . . Sometimes the original
arrest took the form of a minor offense (for example, not having a driver's license) and,
once in custody, the detainees were simply not released." Drumbl, *Rule of Law, supra*
note 283, at 608–09.

1138. Organic Law No. 08/96 of August 30, 1996, on the Organization of Prosecutions
for Offences Constituting the Crime of Genocide or Crimes against Humanity committed

since October 1, 1996, art. 2, *available at* http://www.preventgenocide.org/law/domestic/ rwanda.htm.

1139. *Id.* at art. 6. Category 1 perpetrators are eligible for a sentence reduction only when the perpetrator offers a legally valid confession before his or her name appears on a list of Category 1 offenders.

1140. *Id.* at arts. 14(b), 15(a), 16(a).

1141. *Id.* at art. 6(a) and (b).

1142. *Id.* at art. 6(c).

1143. William A. Schabas, *Genocide Trials and* Gacaca *Courts*, 3 J. INT'L CRIM. JUST. 879, 889 (2005) [hereinafter Schabas, *Genocide Trials*].

1144. Gabiro, *supra* note 971.

1145. Drumbl, *Rule of Law, supra* note 283, at 589–90. Defendants were not the only ones who lacked familiarity with the guilty-plea procedure. Major Peter H. Sennett, whose work with the International Training Detachment brought him to Rwanda in 1996, reported that, as a result of their civil-law background, Rwandan prosecutors also lacked adequate familiarity with "the guilty plea, and how it aids the justice system" and at times engaged in "guilty plea interrogations (or providence inquiries) that were almost as lengthy as full-blown trials." Peter H. Sennett, *Working with Rwanda toward the Domestic Prosecution of Genocide Crimes*, 12 ST. JOHN'S J. LEGAL COMMENT. 425, 443 (1997).

1146. Carla J. Ferstman, *Domestic Trials for Genocide and Crimes Against Humanity: The Example of Rwanda*, 9 AFR. J. INT'L & COMP. L. 857, 870 n.38 (1997); *see also* William A. Schabas, *Justice, Democracy, and Impunity in Post Genocide Rwanda: Searching for Solutions to Impossible Problems*, 1996 CRIM. L.F. 523, 533 (1996); GACACA: A QUESTION OF JUSTICE, *supra* note 1137, at V(1).

1147. Mark Drumbl, who provided legal representation to Rwandan prisoners through Legal Aid Rwanda, observed that "[m]ost of the lesser educated prisoners had never met with the Prosecution, had no idea with what they were charged, and did not even know whether a dossier had been prepared. . . . In total, about 40% of the prisoners with whom I personally met knew some or all of the charges against them, 10% did not know of any charges but knew that they had a dossier, and 50% claimed they knew neither whether there were any charges nor whether a dossier had been prepared." Drumbl, *Rule of Law, supra* note 283, at 604–05.

1148. *Id.* at 591. Fear of retaliation is not unfounded since witnesses have been killed to prevent their giving testimony or retaliation for it. *See* PRUNIER, *supra* note 283, at 358; Alan Zarembo, *Rwanda's Genocide Witnesses Are Killed as Wheels of Justice Slowly Begin Turning*, CHRISTIAN SCIENCE MONITOR, Jan. 23, 1997, at 7; *see also Hit Squad Kills Man Who Laid Trap against Genocide Suspect*, THE NATION (Nairobi), Jan. 21, 2003.

1149. GACACA: A QUESTION OF JUSTICE, *supra* note 1137, at V(1); Ferstman, *supra* note 1146, at 872.

1150. *See* Drumbl, *Rule of Law, supra* note 283, at 591.

1151. *Id.* at 591, 607.

1152. Schabas, *Genocide Trials, supra* note 1143, at 9.

1153. U.N. Economic and Social Council, Commission on Human Rights, E/CN.4/ 1999/33, *Report on the Situation of Human Rights in Rwanda Submitted by the Special Representative, Mr. Michel Moussalli, pursuant to Resolution 1998/69*, para. 42.

1154. GACACA: A QUESTION OF JUSTICE, *supra* note 1137, at 18.

1155. United Nations High Commissioner for Human Rights Field Operation in Rwanda (UNHRFOR), *Genocide Trials to 30 June 1997 status report as at 15 July 1997.*

1156. Gabiro, *supra* note 971. Human Rights Watch reported in 2001 that the Rwandan government had "some 119,000 persons in jail, fewer than 4000 of them tried and convicted." Human Rights Watch, Press Release, *Rwanda*, Feb. 1, 2001, *available at* http://www.hrw.org/backgrounder/africa/rwanda-bck-0131.htm.

1157. Organic Law No. 40/2000 of 26 January 2001 Establishing *Gacaca* Jurisdictions for the Prosecution of Genocide Offences and Crimes against Humanity Committed between 1 October 1990 and 31 December 1994.

1158. Leah Werchick, *Prospects for Justice in Rwanda's Citizen Tribunals*, HUM. RTS. BRIEF, Vol. 8, No. 3, at 15, 15 (2001).

1159. 2004 Revised *Gacaca* Law, *supra* note 769, at arts. 34(7), 41, 42, 43, 51.

1160. *Id.* at art. 34(1); Penal Reform International, *Research on the Gacaca: Report V*, at 47 (Sept. 2003) (table documenting the lists), *available at* http://www.penalreform.org/download/Gacaca/september2003.pdf [hereinafter *PRI Report V*].

1161. 2004 Revised *Gacaca* Law, *supra* note 769, at art. 34(6); Penal Reform International, *PRI Research Team on Gacaca Report III*, at 4 (Apr.–June 2002), *available at* http://www.penalreform.org/download/Gacaca/Apr-Jun2002.pdf [hereinafter *PRI Report III*].

1162. Waldorf, *Mass Justice for Mass Atrocity, supra* note 905.

1163. 2004 Revised *Gacaca* Law, *supra* note 769, at arts. 72–73.

1164. *Id.* at art. 73. Defendants performing community-service work will work three days a week in such enterprises as construction and repair of roads, bridges, and schools. Presidential Order, No. 26/01 of 10/12/2001 Relating to the Substitution of the Penalty of Imprisonment for Community Service, arts. 25, 32. Lars Waldorf reports, however, that by July 2005 the government had done very little to establish a community-service administration. Waldorf, *Mass Justice for Mass Atrocity, supra* note 905.

1165. 2004 Revised *Gacaca* Law, *supra* note 769, at art. 54.

1166. *Id.* at arts. 6, 8, 12.

1167. Schabas, *Genocide Trials, supra* note 1143, at 16.

1168. 2004 Revised *Gacaca* Law, *supra* note 769, at arts. 18, 23.

1169. *PRI Report III, supra* note 1161, at 12.

1170. *Id.* More recently, *gacaca* officials have compiled lists before the meetings, and those lists are discussed during the meetings. Telephone Interview with Lars Waldorf, former researcher, Human Rights Watch (Oct. 10, 2005).

1171. Victoria Brittain, *Letter from Rwanda*, THE NATION, Aug. 14, 2003.

1172. *PRI Report V, supra* note 1160, at 46.

1173. *See* Brittain, *supra* note 1171.

1174. Allison Corey & Sandra F. Joireman, *Retributive Justice: The* Gacaca *Courts in Rwanda*, 103 AFR. AFF. 73, 84 (2004).

1175. *See* Waldorf, *Mass Justice for Mass Atrocity*, *supra* note 905. Waldorf not only points out *gacaca*'s practical problems and structural weaknesses but also questions more fundamentally whether Western-style truth can emerge in the "small face-to-face communities" that characterize Rwanda, where "cultural constraints and 'the micropolitics of local standing'" impede the willingness of participants to provide truthful testimony.

1176. Approximately 50 percent of the judges in many districts are illiterate, and in some districts only 10 percent know how to read and write correctly. GACACA JUSTICE, *supra* note 290, at 9–10.

1177. For complaints about the quality of the instruction, see *id.* at 7; *PRI Report III*, *supra* note 1161, at 9.

1178. *Rwanda/Gacaca: Over 1000 Gacaca Judges Have Resigned over Genocide Allegations*, HIRONDELLE NEWS AGENCY, June 24, 2005; *see also* Penal Reform International, *Research Report on the* Gacaca, *Report VI: From Camp to Hill, the Reintegration of Released Prisoners* 56 (May 2004).

1179. GACACA JUSTICE, *supra* note 290, at 22, 30–33.

1180. Filip Reyntjens, *Rwanda, Ten Years On: From Genocide to Dictatorship*, 103 AFR. AFF. 177, 194 (2004).

1181. Waldorf notes that some amendments to the 2001 *gacaca* law were inspired by the desire to prevent discussion of RPF crimes during *gacaca* proceedings. Waldorf also describes the consequent frustration of Hutu victims of RPF crimes. Waldorf, *Mass Justice for Mass Atrocity*, *supra* note 905.

1182. Catherine Honeyman et al., *Gacaca Jurisdictions: Transitional Justice in Rwanda, Interim Report of Observations, June 10–August 8, 2002*, at IV(D), *available at* http://www .angelfire.com/journal2/honeymandocs/PDF_Gacaca_Report.pdf [hereinafter Harvard *Gacaca* Report]; *PRI Report III*, *supra* note 1161, at 8, 12. For a discussion of Inyangamugayo's resentment of *gacaca*'s jurisdictional one-sidedness, see GACACA JUSTICE, *supra* note 290, at 28–30.

1183. Waldorf, *Mass Justice for Mass Atrocity*, *supra* note 905; *PRI Report V*, *supra* note 1160, at 7–8.

1184. Harvard *Gacaca* Report, *supra* note 1182, at IV(A); GACACA JUSTICE, *supra* note 290, at 53; *PRI Report V*, *supra* note 1160, at 24, 30, 31.

1185. *Gacaca Exodus?*, INTERNEWS, June 13, 2005; Mary Kimani, *600 Tried, Thousands Flee*, INT'L JUST. TRIB., May 23, 2005.

1186. Waldorf, *Mass Justice for Mass Atrocity*, *supra* note 905.

1187. *PRI Report V*, *supra* note 1160, at 23; *Gacaca Justice*, *supra* note 290, at 53; Waldorf, *Mass Justice for Mass Atrocity*, *supra* note 905.

1188. 2004 Revised *Gacaca* Law, *supra* note 769, at art. 29.

1189. Telephone Interview with Lars Waldorf, researcher, Human Rights Watch (Oct. 2, 2003). Some prisoners have complained that their confessions were distorted and that they were pressured to sign inaccurate statements. *PRI Report IV*, *supra* note 1137, at 4.

1190. Waldorf, *Mass Justice for Mass Atrocity*, *supra* note 905.

1191. Schabas, *Genocide Trials, supra* note 1143, at 4; *see also* Andrew Meldrum, *One Million Rwandans to Face Killing Charges in Village Courts*, THE GUARDIAN, Jan. 15, 2005.

1192. Penal Reform International, *Research Report on* Gacaca *Courts:* Gacaca *and Reconciliation: Kibuye Case Study* 12 (May 2004), *available at* http://www.penalreform .org/download/Gacaca/Rapport%20Kibuye%20II_EN.pdf; *PRI Report IV, supra* note 1137, at 8.

1193. *PRI Report III, supra* note 1161, at 15; *see also PRI Report IV, supra* note 1137, at 4.

1194. Human Rights Watch, *World Report 2003, Rwanda, available at* http://www.hrw .org/wr2k3/africa9.html; GACACA: A QUESTION OF JUSTICE, *supra* note 1137, at VIII; *see also* Daly, *supra* note 286, at 356.

1195. *See* Alana Erin Tiemessen, *After Arusha: Gacaca Justice in Post-Genocide Rwanda*, 8 AFR. STUD. Q. 57, 66 (2004); Reyntjens, *supra* note 1180; Waldorf, *Mass Justice for Mass Atrocity, supra* note 905.

1196. UNDP Report on the Community Reconciliation Process, *supra* note 939, at 15, 20, 77; Babo-Soares, Nahe Biti, *supra* note 938, at 16.

1197. Babo-Soares, Nahe Biti, *supra* note 938, at 16.

1198. *Id.* at 20, 26–27.

1199. UNTAET Regulation No. 2001/10, On the Establishment of a Commission for Reception, Truth and Reconciliation in East Timor (July 13, 2001) [hereinafter UNTAET Regulation No. 2001/10].

1200. *Id.* at §§ 1(c), 3.1.

1201. Commission for Reception, Truth, and Reconciliation in Timor-Leste, *CAVR Update/Dec 2003–Jan 2004*, at 8, *available at* http://www.easttimor-reconciliation.org/ cavrUpdate-Dec03Jan04-en.html [hereinafter *CAVR Dec 2003–Jan 2004 Update*].

1202. *Id.* at 1.

1203. Commission for Reception, Truth, and Reconciliation in Timor-Leste, *CAVR Update/June–July 2003*, at 5, *available at* http://www.easttimor-reconciliation.org/cavr Update-JunJuly2003-en.pdf.

1204. Commission for Reception, Truth, and Reconciliation in Timor-Leste, *CAVR Update/April–May 2003* at 1, *available at* http://www.easttimor-reconciliation.org/cavr Update-AprilMay2003-eng.pdf.

1205. UNTAET Regulation No. 2001/10, *supra* note 1199, at §§ 13(c) and (d). CAVR's report was due in July 2005. At the time of this writing, in October 2005, the report had not yet been released.

1206. Not all people who sought reconciliation through the CRP were "offenders": some chose to participate in the CRP because, although they did not commit any offenses, they had some affiliation with militia groups that made them fearful of community reaction. *Id.* at 79–80. Consequently, the UNTAET legislation neutrally labels the people wishing to participate in the process "deponents." UNTAET Regulation No. 2001/10, *supra* note 1199, at § 23.1.

1207. UNTAET Regulation No. 2001/10, *supra* note 1199, at § 23.

1208. *Id.* at § 23.3. Schedule 1 of UNTAET Regulation No. 2001/10 provides guidance in determining the types of offenses suitable for a Community Reconciliation Process. For a discussion of the relationship between the CRP, the Serious Crimes Unit, and the Office of the General Prosecutor, see UNDP Report on the Community Reconciliation Process, *supra* note 939, at 33–39.

1209. UNTAET Regulation No. 2001/10 provides that the CRP panel shall hear from the "deponent." UNTAET Regulation No. 2001/10, *supra* note 1199, at § 27.1.

1210. UNDP Report on the Community Reconciliation Process, *supra* note 939, at 72.

1211. *Id.* at 53–54.

1212. UNTAET Regulation No. 2001/10, *supra* note 1199, at § 27.

1213. UNDP Report on the Community Reconciliation Process, *supra* note 939, at 65.

1214. *Id.* at 66.

1215. *Id.* at 73.

1216. *See* Ximenes, *supra* note 1127, at 17.

1217. UNDP Report on the Community Reconciliation Process, *supra* note 939, at 67–68.

1218. Commission for Reception, Truth, and Reconciliation in Timor-Leste, *CAVR Update/Oct–Nov 2003*, at 3, *available at* http://www.easttimor-reconciliation.org/cavr Update-OctNov2003-en.pdf [hereinafter *CAVR Oct–Nov 2003 Update*]. In another hearing, offenders were required to pay $100 over three months to fund construction of a village office. Commission for Reception, Truth, and Reconciliation in Timor-Leste, *CAVR Update/August–September 2003*, at 7, *available at* http://www.easttimor-reconciliation.org/cavrUpdate-AugSep2003-en.pdf [hereinafter *CAVR August–September 2003 Update*].

1219. *CAVR Dec 2003–Jan 2004 Update*, *supra* note 1201, at 7–8; *CAVR August–September 2003 Update*, *supra* note 1218, at 7; *CAVR Oct–Nov 2003 Update*, *supra* note 1218, at 3.

1220. UNTAET Regulation No. 2001/10, *supra* note 1199, at § 27.8.

1221. The CRP staff had to conduct some 120 hearings, involving eight hundred offenders, during the last three months of the program. *CAVR Dec 2003–Jan 2004 Update*, *supra* note 1201, at 7.

1222. Beth S. Lyons, *Getting Untrapped, Struggling for Truths: The Commission for Reception, Truth, and Reconciliation (CAVR) in East Timor, in* INTERNATIONALIZED CRIMINAL COURTS: SIERRA LEONE, EAST TIMOR, KOSOVO, AND CAMBODIA 99, 111 (Cesare P. R. Romano et al. eds., 2004).

1223. UNDP Report on the Community Reconciliation Process, *supra* note 939, at 84.

1224. *Id.* at 82.

1225. For example, at one hearing in the Balibar Suco, "one of the victims was in the full throes of malaria and had to be supported while he gave his testimony and raised his questions. He explained how important it was for him to be able to look into the eyes of the man he had suspected for so long and at last hear the truth." *Id.* at 68.

1226. *Id.* at 82.

1227. UNTAET Regulation No. 2001/10, *supra* note 1199, at Schedule 1.

1228. UNDP Report on the Community Reconciliation Process, *supra* note 939, at 35.

Conclusion

1229. Sanders, *supra* note 812, at 589.

1230. Thompson, *supra* note 64.

1231. *See* Ivković, *supra* note 2, at 323; Paul Roberts, *Restoration and Retribution in International Criminal Justice: An Exploratory Analysis, in* RESTORATIVE JUSTICE & CRIMINAL JUSTICE: COMPETING OR RECONCILABLE PARADIGMS? 115, 124–25 (Andrew von Hirsch et al. eds., 2003).

1232. *See* Combs, *Copping a Plea to Genocide, supra* note 8, at 37–46.

Bibliography

Articles

Akhavan, Payam, *Beyond Impunity: Can International Criminal Justice Prevent Future Atrocities?*, 95 AM. J. INT'L L. 7 (2001).

———, Current Developments, *The International Criminal Tribunal for Rwanda: The Politics and Pragmatics of Punishment*, 90 AM. J. INT'L L. 501 (1996).

———, *Justice and Reconciliation in the Great Lakes Region of Africa: The Contribution of the International Criminal Tribunal for Rwanda*, 7 DUKE J. COMP. & INT'L L. 325 (1997).

Aldana-Pindell, Raquel, *In Vindication of Justiciable Victims' Rights to Truth and Justice for State-Sponsored Claims*, 35 VAND. J. TRANSNAT'L L. 1399 (2002).

Aldrich, George H. & Chinkin, Christine M., Symposium, *The Hague Peace Conferences*, 94 AM. J. INT'L L. 1 (2000).

Alschuler, Albert W. *The Changing Plea Bargaining Debate*, 69 CAL. L. REV. 652 (1981).

———, *The Defense Attorney's Role in Plea Bargaining*, 84 YALE L.J. 1179 (1975).

———, *Implementing the Criminal Defendant's Right to Trial: Alternatives to the Plea Bargaining System*, 50 U. CHI. L. REV. 931 (1983).

———, *The Prosecutor's Role in Plea Bargaining*, 36 U. CHI. L. REV. 50 (1968).

———, *The Trial Judge's Role in Plea Bargaining*, Part I, 76 COLUM. L. REV. 1059 (1976).

Alvarez, Jose E., *Rush to Closure: Lessons from the Tadić Judgment*, 96 MICH. L. REV. 2031 (1998).

Amann, Diane Marie, *Medium as Message in Sierra Leone*, 7 ILSA J. INT'L & COMP. L. 237 (2001).

Arakawa, Mari, *A New Forum for Comfort Women: Fighting Japan in United States Federal Court*, 16 BERKELEY WOMEN'S L.J. 174 (2001).

Babo-Soares, Dionísio, *Law and Order: Judiciary Development in East Timor*, Conference Paper for Conference on Comparing Experiences with Post-Conflict State Building in Asia and Europe, Denpasar, Bali-Indonesia, Oct. 15–17, 2001.

————, *Nahe Biti: The Philosophy and Process of Grassroots Reconciliation (and Justice) in East Timor*, 5 Asia Pac. J. Anthropology 15 (2004).

Baldwin, John & McConville, Michael, *Plea Bargaining and Plea Negotiation in England*, 13 Law & Soc'y Rev. 287 (1979).

Baruch, Chad, *Through the Looking Glass: A Brief Comment on the Short Life and Unhappy Demise of the Singleton Rule*, 27 N. Ky. L. Rev. 841 (2000).

Bassiouni, M. Cherif, *From Versailles to Rwanda in Seventy-Five Years: The Need to Establish a Permanent International Criminal Court*, 10 Harv. Hum. Rts. J. 11 (1997).

Bazyler, Michael J., *Reexamining the Doctrine of Humanitarian Intervention in Light of the Atrocities in Kampuchea and Ethiopia*, 23 Stan. J. Int'l L. 547 (1987).

Bennett, Mark & Dewberry, Christopher, *"I've Said I'm Sorry, Haven't I?" A Study of the Identity Implications and Constraints That Apologies Create for Their Recipients*, 13 Current Psychol. 10 (1994).

Bibas, Stephanos, *Judicial Fact-Finding and Sentence Enhancements in a World of Guilty Pleas*, 110 Yale L.J. 1097 (2001).

————, *The Right to Remain Silent Helps Only the Guilty*, 88 Iowa L. Rev. 421 (2003).

Bibas, Stephanos & Bierschbach, Richard A., *Integrating Remorse and Apology into Criminal Procedure*, 114 Yale L.J. 85 (2004).

Binder, Guyora, *Punishment Theory: Moral or Political?*, 5 Buff. Crim. L. Rev. 321 (2002).

Braithwaite, John, *A Future Where Punishment Is Marginalized: Realistic or Utopian?*, 46 UCLA L. Rev. 1727 (1999).

————, *Restorative Justice: Assessing Optimistic and Pessimistic Accounts*, 25 Crime & Just. 1 (1999).

Brody, Reed, *The Prosecution of Hissène Habré—An "African Pinochet,"* 35 New Eng. L. Rev. 321 (2001).

Brown, Andrew S., Note, *Adios Amnesty: Prosecutorial Discretion and Military Trials in Argentina*, 37 Tex. Int'l L.J. 203 (2002).

Bryan, Chad W., *Precedent for Reparations? A Look at Historical Movements for Redress and Where Awarding Reparations for Slavery Might Fit*, 54 Ala. L. Rev. 599 (2003).

Buergenthal, Thomas, *The United Nations Truth Commission for El Salvador*, 27 Vand. J. Transnat'l L. 497 (1994).

Burger, Warren, *The State of the Judiciary—1970*, 56 A.B.A. J. 929 (1970).

Burke-White, William W., *Reframing Impunity: Applying Liberal International Law Theory to an Analysis of Amnesty Legislation*, 42 Harv. Int'l L.J. 467 (2001).

Bush, Darren, *Law and Economics of Restorative Justice: Why Restorative Justice Cannot and Should Not Be Solely about Restoration*, 2003 Utah L. Rev. 439.

Cassel, Douglass, *Lessons from the Americas: Guidelines for International Response to Amnesties for Atrocities*, L. & Contemp. Probs., Autumn 1996, at 197.

Cissé, Catherine, *The International Tribunals for the Former Yugoslavia and Rwanda: Some Elements of Comparison*, 7 Transnat'l L. & Contemp. Probs. 103 (1997).

Cochran, Robert F., Jr., *The Criminal Defense Attorney: Roadblock or Bridge to Restorative Justice*, 14 J. L. & Religion 211 (1999–2000).

Cohen, David, *Seeking Justice on the Cheap: Is the East Timor Tribunal Really a Model for the Future? in* Asia Pacific Issues No. 61 (East-West Center 2002).

Combs, Nancy Amoury, *Copping a Plea to Genocide: The Plea Bargaining of International Crimes*, 151 U. PENN. L. REV. 1 (2002).

——, *Procuring Guilty Pleas for International Crimes: The Limited Influence of Sentencing Discounts*, 59 VAND. L. REV. 69 (2006).

Corey, Allison & Joireman, Sandra F., *Retributive Justice: The* Gacaca *Courts in Rwanda*, 103 AFR. AFF. 73 (2004).

Czarnetzy, John M. & Rychlak, Ronald J., *An Empire of Law, Legalism and the International Criminal Court*, 79 NOTRE DAME L. REV. 55 (2003).

Daly, Erin, *Between Punitive and Reconstructive Justice: The Gacaca Courts in Rwanda*, 34 N.Y.U. J. INT'L L. & POL. 355 (2002).

——, *Reparations in South Africa: A Cautionary Tale*, 33 U. MEM. L. REV. 367 (2003).

Damaška, Mirjan, *Models of Criminal Procedure*, 51 ZBORNIK PRAVNOG FAKULLETA U ZAGREBU 477 (2001).

D'Amato, Anthony, Editorial Comment, *Peace vs. Accountability in Bosnia*, 88 AM. J. INT'L L. 500 (1994).

Dana, Shahram, *Revisiting the* Blaškić *Sentence: Some Reflections on the Sentencing Jurisprudence of the ICTY*, 4 INT'L CRIM. L. REV. 321 (2004).

Dolinko, David, *Restorative Justice and the Justification of Punishment*, 2003 UTAH L. REV. 319.

Drumbl, Mark A., *Law and Atrocity: Settling Accounts in Rwanda*, 31 OHIO N.U. L. REV. 41 (2005).

——, *Rule of Law Amid Lawlessness: Counseling the Accused in Rwanda's Domestic Genocide Trials*, 29 COLUM. HUM. RTS. L. REV. 545 (1998).

Ellis, Mark S. & Hutton, Elizabeth, *Policy Implications of World War II Reparations and Restitution as Applied to the Former Yugoslavia*, 20 BERKELEY J. INT'L L. 342 (2002).

Ensalaco, Mark, *Truth Commissions for Chile and El Salvador: A Report and Assessment*, 16 HUM. RTS. Q. 656 (1994).

Fabian, Kellye L., Note and Comment, *Proof and Consequences: An Analysis of the Tadić & Akayesu Trials*, 49 DEPAUL L. REV. 981 (2000).

Ferstman, Carla J., *Domestic Trials for Genocide and Crimes against Humanity: The Example of Rwanda*, 9 AFR. J. INT'L & COMP. L. 857 (1997).

Fisher, George, *Plea Bargaining's Triumph*, 109 YALE L.J. 857 (2000).

Frase, Richard S. & Weigend, Thomas, *German Criminal Justice as a Guide to American Law Reform: Similar Problems, Better Solutions?*, 18 B.C. INT'L & COMP. L. REV. 317 (1995).

Gaeta, Paola, *The Dayton Agreements and International Law*, 7 EUR. J. INT'L L. 147 (1996).

Garvey, Stephen P., *Restorative Justice, Punishment, and Atonement*, 2003 UTAH L. REV. 303.

Goldstone, Richard, *Conference Luncheon Address*, 7 TRANSNAT'L L. & CONTEMP. PROBS. 1 (1997).

Goodman, David, *Why Killers Should Go Free: Lessons from South Africa*, 22 WASH. Q. 1 (1999).

Haley, John O., *The Implications of Apology*, 20 LAW & SOC'Y REV. 499 (1986).

Hannum, Hurst, *International Law and Cambodian Genocide: The Sounds of Silence*, 11 HUM. RTS. Q. 82 (1989).

Hayner, Priscilla B., *Fifteen Truth Commissions—1974 to 1994: A Comparative Study*, 16 HUM. RTS. Q. 597 (1994).

Heasley, Nathanial, et al., *Impunity in Guatemala: The State's Failure to Provide Justice in the Massacre Cases*, 16 AM. U. INT'L L. REV. 1115 (2001).

Henquet, Thomas, *Mandatory Compliance Powers vis à vis States by the Ad Hoc Tribunals and the International Criminal Court: A Comparative Analysis*, 12 LEIDEN J. INT'L L. 969 (1999).

Herrmann, Joachim, *Bargaining Justice—A Bargain for German Criminal Justice?*, 53 U. PITT. L. REV. 755 (1992).

Hickson, Letitia, *The Social Context of Apology in Dispute Settlement: A Cross-Cultural Study*, 25 ETHNOLOGY 283 (1986).

Hohe, Tanja & Nixon, Rod, *Reconciling Justice: "Traditional" Law and State Judiciary in East Timor*, Paper prepared for the United States Institute of Peace and delivered at the workshop on the Working of Non-State Justice Systems, held at the Development Institute, Brighton U.K. (March 6–7, 2003).

Hollis, Timothy, Note, *An Offer You Can't Refuse? United States v. Singleton and the Effects of Witness/Prosecutorial Agreements*, 9 B.U. PUB. INT. L.J. 433 (2000).

Ivković, Sanja Kutnjak, Justice by the International Criminal Tribunal for the Former Yugoslavia, 37 STAN. J. INT'L L. 255 (2001).

Jenkins, Catherine, *After the Dry White Season: The Dilemmas of Reparation and Reconstruction in South Africa*, 16 S. AFRICAN J. HUM. RTS. 415 (2000).

Johnson, D. H. N., *The Draft Code of Offences against the Peace and Security of Mankind*, 4 INT'L & COMP. L. Q. 445 (1955).

Jonas, Stacie, *The Ripple Effect of the Pinochet Case*, HUM. RTS. BRIEF, Vol. 11, No. 3, at 36 (2004).

Jones, John R. W. D., *The Implications of the Peace Agreements for the International Criminal Tribunal for the Former Yugoslavia*, 7 EUR. J. INT'L L. 226 (1996).

Katzenstein, Suzanne, Note, *Hybrid Tribunals: Searching for Justice in East Timor*, 16 HARV. HUM. RTS. J. 245 (2003).

Keller, Andrew N., *To Name or Not to Name? The Commission for Historical Clarification in Guatemala, Its Mandate, and the Decision Not to Identify Individual Perpetrators*, 13 FL. J. INT'L L. 289 (2001).

Kipnis, Kenneth, *Criminal Justice and the Negotiated Plea*, 86 ETHICS 93 (1976).

——, *Plea Bargaining: A Critic's Rejoinder*, 13 LAW & SOC'Y REV. 555 (1979).

Landsman, Stephan, *Alternative Responses to Serious Human Rights Abuses: Of Prosecution and Truth Commissions*, 59 L. & CONTEMP. PROBS. 81 (1996).

Lansing, Paul & King, Julie C., *South Africa's Truth and Reconciliation Commission: The Conflict between Individual Justice and National Healing in the Post-Apartheid Age*, 15 ARIZ. J. INT'L & COMP. L. 753 (1998).

Latif, Elizabeth, *Apologetic Justice: Evaluating Apologies Tailored toward Legal Solutions*, 81 B.U. L. REV. 289 (2001).

Latore, Roseann M., *Coming Out of the Dark: Achieving Justice for Victims of Human Rights Violations by South American Military Regimes*, 25 B.C. INT'L & COMP. L. REV. 419 (2002).

Lepper, Steven J., *Remarks to the American Society of International Law on Prosecuting and Defending Violations of Genocide and Humanitarian Law: The International Tribunal for the Former Yugoslavia*, 88 PROC. AM. SOC. INT'L L. 239 (1994).

Levi, Deborah L., *The Role of Apology in Mediation*, 72 N.Y.U. L. REV. 1165 (1997).

Linton, Suzannah, *Cambodia, East Timor and Sierra Leone: Experiments in International Justice*, 12 CRIM. L.F. 185 (2001).

——, *Correspondents' Reports*, 2 Y.B. OF INT'L HUM. LAW 471 (2000).

——, *Rising from the Ashes: The Creation of a Viable Criminal Justice System in East Timor*, 25 MELB. U. L. REV. 122 (2001).

Linton, Suzannah & Reiger, Caitlin, *The Evolving Jurisprudence and Practice of East Timor's Special Panels for Serious Crimes on Admissions of Guilt, Duress and Superior Orders*, 4 Y.B. OF INT'L HUM. L. 167, 185 (2001).

Loubser, Max, *Linguistic Factors into the Mix: The South African Experience of Language and the Law*, 78 TUL. L. REV. 105 (2003).

Lutz, Ellen & Sikkink, Kathryn, *The Justice Cascade: The Evolution and Impact of Foreign Human Rights Trials in Latin America*, 2 CHI. J. INT'L L. 1 (2001).

Lynch, David, *The Impropriety of Plea Agreements*, 19 LAW & SOC. INQUIRY 115 (1994).

MacDermot, Niall, *Crimes against Humanity in Bangladesh*, 7 INT'L. LAW. 476 (1973).

Mack, Kathy & Anleu, Sharyn Roach, *Choice, Consent and Autonomy in a Guilty Plea System*, 17 L. CONTEXT 75 (1999).

——, *Sentence Discount for a Guilty Plea: Time for a New Look*, 1 FLINDERS J. L. REFORM 123 (1997).

McCarney, Willie, *Restorative Justice: An International Perspective*, 3 J. CENTER FOR FAMILIES, CHILD. & CTS. 3 (2001).

McCarthy, Emily H., Symposium Note, *South Africa's Amnesty Process: A Viable Route toward Truth and Reconciliation?*, 3 MICH. J. RACE & L. 183 (1997).

McDonald, Gabrielle Kirk, *Problems, Obstacles and Achievements of the ICTY*, 2 J. INT'L CRIM. JUST. 558 (2004).

McGregor, Lorna, *Individual Accountability in South Africa: Cultural Optimum or Political Façade*, 95 AM. J. INT'L L. 32 (2001).

Minow, Martha, *The Role of Forgiveness in the Law*, Symposium, 27 FORDHAM URB. L.J. 1347 (2000).

Morris, Madeline H., *The Trials of Concurrent Jurisdiction: The Case of Rwanda*, 7 DUKE J. COMP. & INT'L L. 349 (1997).

Mulcahy, Aogán, *The Justifications of "Justice:" Legal Practitioners' Accounts of Negotiated Case Settlements in Magistrates' Courts*, 34 BRIT. J. CRIMINOLOGY 411 (1994).

Mundis, Daryl A., *From 'Common Law' towards 'Civil Law': The Evolution of the ICTY Rules of Procedure and Evidence*, 14 LEIDEN J. INT'L L. 367 (2001).

——, *The Judicial Effects of the "Completion Strategies" on the Ad Hoc International Criminal Tribunals*, 99 AM. J. INT'L L. 142 (2005).

——, *New Mechanisms for the Enforcement of International Humanitarian Law*, 95 Aм. J. Int'l L. 934 (2001).

Murphy, John F., *Civil Liability for the Commission of International Crimes as an Alternative to Criminal Prosecution*, 12 Harv. Hum. Rts. J. 1 (1999).

Murphy, Sean D., ed., *Contemporary Practice of the United States Relating to International Law*, 95 Aм. J. Int'l L. 387 (2001).

Nevins, Joseph, *The Making of "Ground Zero" in East Timor in 1999*, 42 Asian Survey 623 (2002).

Nugent, William R. et al., *Participation in Victim-Offender Mediation and the Prevalence and Severity of Subsequent Delinquent Behavior: A Meta-Analysis*, 2003 Utah L. Rev. 137.

O'Hara, Erin Ann & Yarn, Douglas, *On Apology and Consilience*, 77 Wash. L. Rev. 1121 (2002).

Penrose, Mary Margaret, *Lest We Fail: The Importance of Enforcement in International Criminal Law*, 15 Aм. U. Int'l L. Rev. 321, 382 n.225 (2000).

Poulson, Barton, *A Third Voice: A Review of Empirical Research on the Psychological Outcomes of Restorative Justice*, 2003 Utah L. Rev. 167.

Reyntjens, Filip, *Rwanda, Ten Years On: From Genocide to Dictatorship*, 103 Afr. Aff. 177 (2004).

Robinson, Paul H., *The Virtues of Restorative Processes, the Vices of "Restorative Justice,"* 2003 Utah L. Rev. 375.

Roht-Arriaza, Naomi, *Reparations Decisions and Dilemmas*, 27 Hastings Int'l & Comp. L. Rev. 157 (2004).

——, *State Responsibility to Investigate and Prosecute Grave Human Rights Violations in International Law*, 78 Cal. L. Rev. 449 (1990).

Russo, Charles J., *Religion and Education in Bosnia: Integration Not Segregation?*, 2000 B.Y.U. L. Rev. 945.

Sanders, Mark, *Renegotiating Responsibility after Apartheid: Listening to Perpetrator Testimony*, 10 Aм. U. J. Gender, Soc. Pol'y & L. 587 (2002).

Sansani, Inbal, *The Pinochet Precedent in Africa: Prosecution of Hissène Habré*, Hum. Rts. Brief, Vol. 8, No. 2, at 32 (2001).

Schabas, William A., *Follow up to Rome: Preparing for Entry into Force of the International Criminal Court Statute*, 20 Hum. Rts. L.J. 157 (1999).

——, *Genocide Trials and Gacaca Courts*, 3 J. Int'l Crim. Just. 879 (2005).

——, *International Decision*, Barayagwiza v. Prosecutor, 94 Aм. J. Int'l L. 563 (2000).

——, *Justice, Democracy, and Impunity in Post Genocide Rwanda: Searching for Solutions to Impossible Problems*, 1996 Crim. L.F. 523.

——, *The Relationship between Truth Commissions and International Courts: The Case of Sierra Leone*, 25 Hum. Rts. Q. 1035 (2003).

——, *Sentencing by International Tribunals: A Human Rights Approach*, 7 Duke J. Comp. & Int'l L. 461 (1997).

Schulhofer, Stephen J., *Plea Bargaining as Disaster*, 101 Yale L.J. 1979 (1992).

———, *A Wake-Up Call from the Plea Bargaining Trenches*, 19 LAW & SOC. INQUIRY 135 (1994).

Sennett, Peter H., *Working with Rwanda toward the Domestic Prosecution of Genocide Crimes*, 12 ST. JOHN'S J. LEGAL COMMENT. 425 (1997).

Shuman, Daniel W., *The Role of Apology in Tort Law*, 83 JUDICATURE 180 (2000).

Simonović, Ivan, *The Role of the ICTY in the Development of International Criminal Adjudication*, 23 FORDHAM INT'L L.J. 440 (1999).

Sitkin, Sim B. & Bies, Robert J., *Social Accounts in Conflict Situations: Using Explanations to Manage Conflict*, 46 HUM. REL. 349 (1993).

Speck, Paula K., *The Trial of the Argentine Junta*, 18 INTER-AM. L. REV. 491 (1984).

Sriram, Chandra Lekha, *Revolution in Accountability: New Approaches to Past Abuses*, 19 AM. U. INT'L L. REV. 301 (2003).

Stahn, Carsten, *Accommodating Individual Criminal Responsibility and National Reconciliation: The UN Truth Commission for East Timor*, 95 AM. J. INT'L L. 952 (2001).

Strang, Heather & Sherman, Lawrence W., *Repairing the Harm: Victims and Restorative Justice*, 2003 UTAH L. REV. 15.

Strohmeyer, Hansjörg, *Collapse and Reconstruction of a Judicial System: The United Nations Missions in Kosovo and East Timor*, 95 AM. J. INT'L L. 46 (2001).

———, *Policing the Peace: Post Conflict Judicial System Reconstruction in East Timor*, 24 U. NEW SOUTH WALES L.J. 171 (2001).

Supernor, Christopher M., *International Bounty Hunters for War Criminals: Privatizing the Enforcement of Justice*, 50 A.F.L. REV. 215 (2001).

Swartz, Justin M., *South Africa's Truth and Reconciliation Commission: A Functional Equivalent to Prosecution*, 3 DE PAUL DIG. INT'L L. 13 (1997).

Sylvester, Douglas J., *Myth in Restorative Justice History*, 2003 UTAH L. REV. 471.

Taft, Lee, *Apology Subverted: The Commidification of Apology*, 109 YALE L.J. 1135 (2000).

Tiemessen, Alana Erin, *After Arusha: Gacaca Justice in Post-Genocide Rwanda*, 8 AFR. STUD. Q. 57 (2004).

Tomuschat, Christian, *International Criminal Prosecution: The Precedent of Nuremberg Confirmed*, 5 CRIM. L.F. 237 (1994).

Umbreit, Mark S. et al., *The Impact of Victim-Offender Mediation: Two Decades of Research*, 65 FED. PROBATION 29 (2001).

———, *Victim-Offender Dialogue in Crimes of Severe Violence: A Multi-Site Study of Programs in Texas and Ohio*, available at http://ssw.che.umn.edu/rjp/.

Umbreit, Mark S. & Vos, Betty, *Homicide Survivors Meet the Offender prior to Execution: Restorative Justice through Dialogue*, 4 HOMICIDE STUD. 63 (2000).

van Zyl, Paul, *Dilemmas of Transitional Justice: The Case of South Africa's Truth and Reconciliation Commission*, 52 J. INT'L AFF. 647 (1999).

Varney, Howard & Sarkin, Jeremy, *Failing to Pierce the Hit Squad Veil: An Analysis of the Malan Trial*, 10 SOUTH AFRICAN J. CRIM. L. 141 (1997).

Villa-Vicencio, Charles, *Why Perpetrators Should Not Always Be Prosecuted: Where the International Criminal Court and Truth Commissions Meet*, 49 EMORY L.J. 205 (2000).

von Sternberg, Mark R., *Per Humanitatem ad Pacem: International Humanitarian Norms as a Jurisprudence of Peace in the Former Yugoslavia*, 3 CARDOZO J. INT'L & COMP. L. 357 (1995).

Wagatsuma, Hiroshi & Rosett, Arthur, *The Implications of Apology: Law and Culture in Japan and the United States*, 20 LAW & SOC'Y REV. 461 (1986).

Waldorf, Lars, *Mass Justice for Mass Atrocity, Rethinking Local Justice as Transitional Justice*, TEMP. L. REV. (forthcoming 2006).

Wedgewood, Ruth, *The Evolution of United Nations Peacekeeping*, 28 CORNELL INT'L L.J. 631, 638 (1995).

Werchick, Leah, *Prospects for Justice in Rwanda's Citizen Tribunals*, HUM. RTS. BRIEF, Vol. 8, No. 3, at 15 (2001).

Williams, Sharon A., *Remarks to the American Society of International Law on the Draft Code of Offenses against the Peace and Security of Mankind*, 80 AM. SOC. INT'L PROC. 120 (1986).

Willis, John, *New Wine in Old Bottles: The Sentencing Discount for Pleading Guilty*, 13 L. IN CONTEXT 39 (1995).

Wilson, Christina M., Note, *Argentina's Reparation Bonds: An Analysis of Continuing Obligations*, 28 FORDHAM INT'L L.J. 786 (2005).

Wilson, Stuart, *The Myth of Restorative Justice: Truth, Reconciliation and the Ethics of Amnesty*, 17 S. AFR. J. HUM. RTS. 531 (2001).

Wippman, David, *Atrocities, Deterrence, and the Limits of International Justice*, 23 FORDHAM INT'L L.J. 473 (1999).

Wright, Thomas C., *Human Rights in Latin America: History and Projections for the Twenty-First Century*, 30 CAL. W. INT'L L.J. 303 (2000).

Ximenes, Fausto Belo, *The Unique Contribution of the Community-Based Reconciliation Process in East Timor* (May 28, 2004) available at http://www.easttimor-reconciliation.org/jsmpReport-prk-summary.html.

Yaroshefsky, Ellen, *Cooperation with Federal Prosecutors: Experiences of Truth Telling and Embellishment*, 68 FORDHAM L. REV. 917 (1999).

Yasuaki, Onuma, *Japanese War Guilt and Postwar Responsibilities of Japan*, 20 BERKELEY J. INT'L L. 600 (2002).

Zacharias, Fred C., *Justice in Plea Bargaining*, 39 WM. & MARY L. REV. 1121 (1998).

Zacklin, Ralph, *The Failings of Ad Hoc International Tribunals*, 2 J. INT'L CRIM. JUST. 541 (2004).

Books

ALLEN, BEVERLY, RAPE WARFARE: THE HIDDEN GENOCIDE IN BOSNIA-HERZEGOVINA AND CROATIA (1996).

BASSIOUNI, M. CHERIF & MANIKAS, PETER, THE LAW OF THE INTERNATIONAL CRIMINAL TRIBUNAL FOR THE FORMER YUGOSLAVIA (1996).

BORAINE, ALEX, A COUNTRY UNMASKED (2000).

BRAITHWAITE, JOHN, RESTORATIVE JUSTICE AND RESPONSIVE REGULATION (2002).

Braswell, Michael et al., Corrections, Peacemaking and Restorative Justice (2001).

Burg, Steven L. & Shoup, Paul S., The War in Bosnia-Herzegovina: Ethnic Conflict and International Intervention (1999).

Cayley, David, The Expanding Prison: The Crisis in Crime and Punishment and the Search for Alternatives (1998).

Christie, Kenneth, The South African Truth Commission (2000).

Cohen, Lenard J., Broken Bonds: Yugoslavia's Disintegration and Balkan Politics in Transition (1993).

Conquest, Robert, The Great Terror: A Reassessment (1990).

———, The Great Terror: Stalin's Purge of the Thirties (rev. ed. 1973).

Dallaire, Romeo, Shake Hands with the Devil: The Failure of Humanity in Rwanda (2003).

de Brito, Alexandra Barahona, Human Rights and Democratization in Latin America: Uruguay and Chile (1997).

Des Forges, Alison, Human Rights Watch, Leave None to Tell the Story: Genocide in Rwanda (1999).

Di Giovanni, Janine, The Quick and the Dead: Under Siege in Sarajevo (1995).

Dizdarević, Zlatko, Sarajevo: A War Journal (1993).

Dyzenhaus, David, Judging the Judges, Judging Ourselves: Truth, Reconciliation and the Apartheid Legal Order (1998).

Edelstein, Jillian, Truth & Lies: Stories from the Truth and Reconciliation Commission in South Africa (2002).

Elliott, Elizabeth, New Directions in Restorative Justice: Issues, Practice, Evaluation (2005).

European Forum for Victim-Offender Mediation and Restorative Justice, ed., Victim-Offender Mediation in Europe: Making Restorative Justice Work (2000).

Fisse, Brent & Braithwaite, John, Corporations, Crime and Accountability (1993).

Fletcher, George P., With Justice for Some: Protecting Victims' Rights in Criminal Trials (1996).

Gallagher, Tom, The Balkans after the Cold War: From Tyranny to Tragedy (2003).

———, Outcast Europe: The Balkans, 1789–1989: From the Ottomans to Milošević (2001).

Gjelten, Tom, Sarajevo Daily 124–25 (1995).

Gobodo-Madikizela, Pumla, A Human Being Died That Night: A South African Story of Forgiveness (2003).

Goldstone, Richard J., For Humanity: Reflections of a War Crimes Investigator (2000).

Gourevitch, Philip, We Wish to Inform You That Tomorrow We Will Be Killed with Our Families: Stories from Rwanda (1998).

GRAEF, ROGER, WHY RESTORATIVE JUSTICE? REPAIRING THE HARM CAUSED BY CRIME (2001).

GRAYBILL, LYN S., TRUTH & RECONCILIATION IN SOUTH AFRICA: MIRACLE OR MODEL? (2002).

GUEST, IAIN, ON TRIAL, THE UNITED NATIONS, WAR CRIMES, AND THE FORMER YUGOSLAVIA (1995).

HAYNER, PRISCILLA B., UNSPEAKABLE TRUTHS: FACING THE CHALLENGE OF TRUTH COMMISSIONS (2002).

HICKS, DAVID, TETUM GHOSTS AND KIN: FIELDWORK IN AN INDONESIAN COMMUNITY (1988).

HONIG, JAN WILLEM & BOTH, NORBERT, SREBRENICA: RECORD OF A WAR CRIME (1996).

JOHNSTONE, GERRY, RESTORATIVE JUSTICE: IDEAS, VALUES, DEBATES (2002).

KIERNAN, BEN, THE POL POT REGIME: RACE, POWER, AND GENOCIDE IN CAMBODIA UNDER THE KHMER ROUGE, 1975–1979 (1996).

KOMMERS, DONALD P., THE CONSTITUTIONAL JURISPRUDENCE OF THE FEDERAL REPUBLIC OF GERMANY (1989).

KROG, ANTIJE, COUNTRY OF MY SKULL: GUILT, SORROW, AND THE LIMITS OF FORGIVENESS IN THE NEW SOUTH AFRICA (1999).

KUPER, LEO, GENOCIDE: ITS POLITICAL USE IN THE TWENTIETH CENTURY (1981).

LAFAVE, WAYNE R. ET AL., CRIMINAL PROCEDURE (3d ed. 2000).

LEWIS, PAUL H., GUERRILLAS AND GENERALS (2002).

MAGNARELLA, PAUL J., JUSTICE IN AFRICA: RWANDA'S GENOCIDE, ITS COURTS, AND THE UN CRIMINAL TRIBUNAL (2000).

MEARNS, DAVID, LOOKING BOTH WAYS: MODELS FOR JUSTICE IN EAST TIMOR, Australian Legal Resources International Publication (November 2002).

MELVERN, LINDA, CONSPIRACY TO MURDER: THE RWANDAN GENOCIDE (2004).

MEREDITH, MARTIN, COMING TO TERMS: SOUTH AFRICA'S SEARCH FOR TRUTH (1999).

MERON, THEODOR, WAR CRIMES LAW COMES OF AGE (1998).

MINOW, MARTHA, BETWEEN VENGEANCE AND FORGIVENESS: FACING HISTORY AFTER GENOCIDE AND MASS VIOLENCE (1998).

MORRIS, VIRGINIA & SCHARF, MICHAEL P., THE INTERNATIONAL CRIMINAL TRIBUNAL FOR RWANDA, Vol. 1 (1998).

MURPHY, JEFFRIE G. & HAMPTON, JEAN, FORGIVENESS AND MERCY (1988).

NINO, CARLOS SANTIAGO, RADICAL EVIL ON TRIAL (1996).

OSIEL, MARK, MASS ATROCITY, COLLECTIVE MEMORY, AND THE LAW (1997).

POWER, SAMANTHA, A PROBLEM FROM HELL (2002).

PRUNIER, GÉRARD, THE RWANDA CRISIS: HISTORY OF A GENOCIDE (1995).

ROCHE, DECLAN, ACCOUNTABILITY IN RESTORATIVE JUSTICE (2003).

ROHDE, DAVID, ENDGAME: THE BETRAYAL AND FALL OF SREBRENICA, EUROPE'S WORST MASSACRE SINCE WORLD WAR II (1997).

RONIGER, LUIS & SZNAJDER, MARIO, THE LEGACY OF HUMAN-RIGHTS VIOLATIONS IN THE SOUTHERN CONE: ARGENTINA, CHILE, AND URUGUAY (1999).

SCHABAS, WILLIAM A., GENOCIDE IN INTERNATIONAL LAW (2000).

——, AN INTRODUCTION TO THE INTERNATIONAL CRIMINAL COURT (2001).

SCHARF, MICHAEL P., BALKAN JUSTICE (1997).

SHEA, DOROTHY, THE SOUTH AFRICAN TRUTH COMMISSION (2000).

SLUITER, GÖRAN, INTERNATIONAL CRIMINAL ADJUDICATION AND THE COLLECTION OF EVIDENCE: OBLIGATIONS OF STATES (2002).

STRANG, HEATHER, REPAIR OR REVENGE: VICTIMS AND RESTORATIVE JUSTICE (2002).

——, RESTORATIVE JUSTICE: PHILOSOPHY TO PRACTICE (2000).

SULLIVAN, DENNIS & TIFFT, LARRY, RESTORATIVE JUSTICE: HEALING THE FOUNDATIONS OF OUR EVERYDAY LIVES (2001).

TAVUCHIS, NICHOLAS, MEA CULPA: A SOCIOLOGY OF APOLOGY AND RECONCILIATION (1991).

TEITEL, RUTI G., TRANSITIONAL JUSTICE (2002).

TOTTEN, SAMUEL ET AL., EDS., CENTURY OF GENOCIDE: CRITICAL ESSAYS AND EYEWITNESS ACCOUNTS (2004).

TRAUBE, ELIZABETH G., COSMOLOGY AND SOCIAL LIFE: RITUAL EXCHANGE AMONG THE MAMBAI OF EAST TIMOR (1986).

TWADDLE, MICHAEL, ED., EXPULSION OF A MINORITY: ESSAYS ON UGANDAN ASIANS (1975).

UMBREIT, MARK S. ET AL., VICTIM MEETS OFFENDER: THE IMPACT OF RESTORATIVE JUSTICE AND MEDIATION (1994).

VERBITSKY, HORACIO, THE FLIGHT: CONFESSIONS OF AN ARGENTINE DIRTY WARRIOR (1996).

VILLA-VICENCIO, CHARLES & VERWOERD, WILHELM, EDS., LOOKING BACK, REACHING FORWARD: REFLECTIONS ON THE TRUTH AND RECONCILIATION COMMISSION OF SOUTH AFRICA (2000).

VON HIRSCH, ANDREW ET AL., CRIMINAL DETERRENCE AND SENTENCE SEVERITY (1999).

VON HIRSCH, ANDREW ET AL., EDS., RESTORATIVE JUSTICE & CRIMINAL JUSTICE: COMPETING OR RECONCILABLE PARADIGMS? (2003).

WALGRAVE, LODE, RESTORATIVE JUSTICE AND THE LAW (2002).

WOODWARD, SUSAN L., BALKAN TRAGEDY: CHAOS AND DISSOLUTION AFTER THE COLD WAR (1995).

ZEHR, HOWARD, CHANGING LENSES: A NEW FOCUS FOR CRIME AND JUSTICE (1990).

ZEHR, HOWARD & TOEWS, BARBARA, EDS., CRITICAL ISSUES IN RESTORATIVE JUSTICE (2004).

ZIMMERMANN, WARREN, ORIGINS OF A CATASTROPHE: YUGOSLAVIA AND ITS DESTROYERS (rev. ed. 1999).

Book Chapters

Abdullah, Ibrahim & Muana, Patrick, *The Revolutionary United Front of Sierra Leone*, in AFRICAN GUERRILLAS 172 (Christopher Clapham ed., 1998).

Aquino, Belinda A., *The Human Rights Debacle in the Philippines*, in IMPUNITY AND HUMAN RIGHTS IN INTERNATIONAL LAW AND PRACTICE 231 (Naomi Roht-Arriaza ed., 1995).

Babo-Soares, Dionísio, *Challenges for the Future*, in OUT OF THE ASHES: DESTRUCTION
    AND RECONSTRUCTION OF EAST TIMOR 262 (James J. Fox & Dionísio Babo-Soares
    eds., 2003).

———, *Political Developments Leading to the Referendum*, in OUT OF THE ASHES: DE-
    STRUCTION AND RECONSTRUCTION OF EAST TIMOR 53 (James J. Fox & Dionísio Babo-
    Soares eds., 2003).

Biggar, Nigel, *Making Peace or Doing Justice: Must We Choose?*, in BURYING THE PAST:
    MAKING PEACE AND DOING JUSTICE AFTER CIVIL CONFLICT 3 (Nigel Biggar ed., 2003).

Blum-Kulka, Shoshana et al., *Investigating Cross-Cultural Pragmatics: An Introductory
    Overview*, in CROSS-CULTURAL PRAGMATICS: REQUESTS AND APOLOGIES 1 (Shoshana
    Blum-Kulka et al., eds. 1989).

Cassel, Jr., Douglass W., *International Truth Commissions and Justice*, in TRANSITIONAL
    JUSTICE: HOW EMERGING DEMOCRACIES RECKON WITH FORMER REGIMES 326 (Neil
    J. Kritz ed., 1995).

Clamagirand, Brigitte, *The Social Organization of the Ema of Timor*, in THE FLOW OF LIFE:
    ESSAYS ON EASTERN INDONESIA 134 (James J. Fox ed., 1980).

Daly, Kathleen, *Mind the Gap: Restorative Justice in Theory and Practice*, in RESTORATIVE
    JUSTICE & CRIMINAL JUSTICE: COMPETING OR RECONCILABLE PARADIGMS? 219 (An-
    drew von Hirsch et al. eds., 2003).

de Brito, Alexandra Barahona, *Passion, Constraint, Law, and Fortuna*, *in* BURYING THE
    PAST: MAKING PEACE AND DOING JUSTICE AFTER CIVIL CONFLICT 177 (Nigel Biggar
    ed., 2003).

Duff, Anthony, *Restoration and Retribution*, in RESTORATIVE JUSTICE & CRIMINAL
    JUSTICE: COMPETING OR RECONCILABLE PARADIGMS? 43 (Andrew von Hirsch et al.
    eds., 2003).

Etcheson, Craig, *The Persistence of Impunity in Cambodia*, in Reining in Impunity for
    International Crimes and Serious Violations of Fundamental Human Rights: Pro-
    ceedings of the Siracusa Conference 17–21 September 1998, 231 (Christopher C. Joyner
    ed., 1998).

Flaten, Caren, *Victim-Offender Mediation: Application with Serious Offenses Committed
    by Juveniles*, in RESTORATIVE JUSTICE: AN INTERNATIONAL PERSPECTIVE 387 (Burt
    Galaway & Joe Hudson eds., 1996).

Fox, James J., *Tracing the Path, Recounting the Path: Historical Perspectives on Timor*, in
    OUT OF THE ASHES: DESTRUCTION AND RECONSTRUCTION OF EAST TIMOR 1 (James J.
    Fox & Dionísio Babo-Soares eds., 2003).

Goldstone, Richard J., *50 Years after Nuremberg: A New International Criminal Tribunal
    for Human Rights Criminals*, in CONTEMPORARY GENOCIDES: CAUSES, CASES, CONSE-
    QUENCES 215 (Albert J. Jongman ed., 1996).

Gordin, Jeremy, *Foreword to* EUGENE DE KOCK, A LONG NIGHT'S DAMAGE (1998).

Guariglia, Fabricio, *Investigation and Prosecution*, in THE INTERNATIONAL CRIMINAL
    COURT: THE MAKING OF THE ROME STATUTE 227 (Roy S. Lee ed., 1999).

Hamber, Brandon, *Does the Truth Heal? A Psychological Perspective on Political Strategies
    for Dealing with the Legacy of Political Violence*, in BURYING THE PAST: MAKING PEACE
    AND DOING JUSTICE AFTER CIVIL CONFLICT 155 (Nigel Biggar ed., 2003).

Hesse, Carla & Post, Robert, *Introduction to* HUMAN RIGHTS IN POLITICAL TRANSITIONS: GETTYSBURG TO BOSNIA 16 (Carla Hesse & Robert Post eds., 1999).

Hudson, Barbara, *Victims and Offenders*, in RESTORATIVE JUSTICE & CRIMINAL JUSTICE: COMPETING OR RECONCILABLE PARADIGMS? 177 (Andrew von Hirsch et al. eds., 2003).

Jung, Heike, *The Criminal Process in the Federal Republic of Germany—An Overview*, in THE CRIMINAL PROCESS AND HUMAN RIGHTS: TOWARD A EUROPEAN CONSCIOUSNESS 59 (Mireille Delmas-Marty & Mark A. Summers eds., 1995).

Kiss, Elizabeth, *Moral Ambition Within and Beyond Political Constraints: Reflections on Restorative Justice*, in TRUTH V. JUSTICE 68 (Robert I. Rotberg & Dennis Thompson eds., 2000).

Liebmann, Marian & Masters, Guy, *Victim-Offender Mediation in the UK*, in VICTIM-OFFENDER MEDIATION IN EUROPE: MAKING RESTORATIVE JUSTICE WORK 337 (The European Forum for Victim-Offender Mediation and Restorative Justice ed., 2000).

Liera, Socorro Flores, *Publications, Languages, and Translation*, in THE INTERNATIONAL CRIMINAL COURT: ELEMENTS OF CRIMES AND RULES OF PROCEDURE AND EVIDENCE 314 (Roy S. Lee ed., 2001).

Lloyd, Grayson J., *The Diplomacy on East Timor: Indonesia, the United Nations and the International Community*, in OUT OF THE ASHES: DESTRUCTION AND RECONSTRUCTION OF EAST TIMOR 74 (James J. Fox & Dionísio Babo-Soares eds., 2003).

Lyons, Beth S., *Getting Untrapped, Struggling for Truths: The Commission for Reception, Truth and Reconciliation (CAVR) in East Timor*, in INTERNATIONALIZED CRIMINAL COURTS: SIERRA LEONE, EAST TIMOR, KOSOVO, AND CAMBODIA 99 (Cesare P. R. Romano et al. eds., 2004).

Malamud-Goti, Jaime, *Punishing Human Rights Abuses in Fledgling Democracies: The Case of Argentina*, in IMPUNITY AND HUMAN RIGHTS IN INTERNATIONAL LAW AND PRACTICE 160 (Naomi Roht-Arriaza ed., 1995).

McDonald, William F. et al., *Prosecutorial Bluffing and the Case against Plea-Bargaining*, in PLEA BARGAINING 1 (William F. McDonald & James A. Cramer eds., 1980).

Mochochoko, Phakiso, *International Cooperation and Judicial Assistance*, in THE INTERNATIONAL CRIMINAL COURT: THE MAKING OF THE ROME STATUTE 305 (Roy S. Lee ed., 1999).

Orr, Wendy, *Reparation Delayed Is Healing Retarded*, in LOOKING BACK, REACHING FORWARD: REFLECTIONS ON THE TRUTH AND RECONCILIATION COMMISSION OF SOUTH AFRICA 239 (Charles Villa-Vicencio & Wilhelm Verwoerd eds., 2000).

Pelikan, Christa, *Victim-Offender Mediation in Austria*, in VICTIM-OFFENDER MEDIATION IN EUROPE: MAKING RESTORATIVE JUSTICE WORK 125 (The European Forum for Victim-Offender Mediation and Restorative Justice ed., 2000).

Pion-Berlin, David, *To Prosecute or to Pardon? Human Rights Decisions in the Latin American Southern Cone*, in TRANSITIONAL JUSTICE: HOW EMERGING DEMOCRACIES RECKON WITH FORMER REGIMES, Vol. 1, 82 (Neil J. Kritz ed., 1995).

Pirouet Louise, *Refugees in and from Uganda in the Post-Colonial Period*, in UGANDA NOW 246 (Holger Bernt Hassen & Michael Twaddle eds., 1988).

Popkin, Margaret & Roht-Arriaza, Naomi, *Truth as Justice: Investigatory Commissions in Latin America*, in TRANSITIONAL JUSTICE: HOW EMERGING DEMOCRACIES RECKON WITH FORMER REGIMES, Vol. 1, 262 (Neil J. Kritz ed., 1995).

Roberts, Paul, *Restoration and Retribution in International Criminal Justice: An Exploratory Analysis*, in RESTORATIVE JUSTICE & CRIMINAL JUSTICE: COMPETING OR RECONCILABLE PARADIGMS? 115 (Andrew von Hirsch et al. eds., 2003).

Roht-Arriaza, Naomi, *The Need for Moral Reconstruction in the Wake of Past Human Rights Violations: An Interview with José Zalaquett*, in HUMAN RIGHTS IN POLITICAL TRANSITIONS: GETTYSBURG TO BOSNIA 195 (Carla Hesse & Robert Post eds., 1999).

Rotberg, Robert I., *Truth Commissions and the Provision of Truth, Justice, and Reconciliation*, in TRUTH V. JUSTICE 6 (Robert I. Rotberg & Dennis Thompson eds., 2000).

Schiff, Mara, *Models, Challenges and the Promise of Restorative Conference Strategies*, in RESTORATIVE JUSTICE & CRIMINAL JUSTICE: COMPETING OR RECONCILABLE PARADIGMS? 315 (Andrew von Hirsch et al. eds., 2003).

Scott, Colleen, *Combating Myth and Building Reality*, in LOOKING BACK, REACHING FORWARD: REFLECTIONS ON THE TRUTH AND RECONCILIATION COMMISSION OF SOUTH AFRICA 107 (Charles Villa-Vicencio & Wilhelm Verwoerd eds., 2000).

Shapland, Joanna, *Restorative Justice and Criminal Justice: Just Responses to Crime?* in RESTORATIVE JUSTICE & CRIMINAL JUSTICE: COMPETING OR RECONCILABLE PARADIGMS? 195 (Andrew von Hirsch et al. eds., 2003).

Sieder, Rachel, *War, Peace, and the Politics of Memory in Guatemala*, in BURYING THE PAST: MAKING PEACE AND DOING JUSTICE AFTER CIVIL CONFLICT 209 (Nigel Biggar ed., 2003).

Slye, Ronald, *Justice and Amnesty*, in LOOKING BACK, REACHING FORWARD: REFLECTIONS ON THE TRUTH AND RECONCILIATION COMMISSION OF SOUTH AFRICA 174 (Charles Villa-Vicencio & Wilhelm Verwoerd eds., 2000).

Smith, Kathleen E., *Destalinization in the Former Soviet Union*, in IMPUNITY AND HUMAN RIGHTS IN INTERNATIONAL LAW AND PRACTICE 113 (Naomi Roht-Arriaza ed., 1995).

Stover, Eric & Shigekane, Rachel, *Exhumation of Mass Graves: Balancing Legal and Humanitarian Needs*, in MY NEIGHBOR, MY ENEMY: JUSTICE AND COMMUNITY IN THE AFTERMATH OF MASS ATROCITY 85, 90 (Eric Stover & Harvey M. Weinstein eds., 2004).

Teitel, Ruti, *Bringing the Messiah through the Law*, in HUMAN RIGHTS IN POLITICAL TRANSITIONS: GETTYSBURG TO BOSNIA 177 (Carla Hesse & Robert Post eds., 1999).

Umbreit, Mark S., *Violent Offenders and Their Victims*, in MEDIATION AND CRIMINAL JUSTICE 337 (Martin Wright & Burt Galaway eds., 1989).

van Zyl, Paul, *Justice without Punishment: Guaranteeing Human Rights in Transitional Societies*, in LOOKING BACK, REACHING FORWARD: REFLECTIONS ON THE TRUTH AND RECONCILIATION COMMISSION OF SOUTH AFRICA 42 (Charles Villa-Vicencio & Wilhelm Verwoerd eds., 2000).

Villa-Vicencio, Charles, *Getting on with Life: A Move towards Reconciliation*, in LOOKING BACK, REACHING FORWARD: REFLECTIONS ON THE TRUTH AND RECONCILIATION

Commission of South Africa 1 99 (Charles Villa-Vicencio & Wilhelm Verwoerd eds., 2000).

———, *Restorative Justice: Dealing with the Past Differently*, in Looking Back, Reaching Forward: Reflections on the Truth and Reconciliation Commission of South Africa 68 (Charles Villa-Vicencio & Wilhelm Verwoerd eds., 2000).

Walgrave, Lode, *Imposing Restoration Instead of Inflicting Pain: Reflections on the Judicial Reaction to Crime*, in Restorative Justice & Criminal Justice: Competing or Reconcilable Paradigms? 61 (Andrew von Hirsch et al. eds., 2003).

Weitekamp, Elmar G. M., *Research on Victim-Offender Mediation: Findings and Needs for the Future*, in Victim-Offender Mediation in Europe: Making Restorative Justice Work 99 (The European Forum for Victim-Offender Mediation and Restorative Justice ed., 2000).

Cases, Case Summaries, and Documents

Akayesu, Prosecutor v., Case No. ICTR-96-4-I, Amended Indictment, (June 17, 1997).

———, Case No. ICTR-96-4-T, Judgement (September 2, 1998).

———, Case No. ICTR-96-4-T, Sentence (October 2, 1998).

Aleksovski, Prosecutor v., Case No. IT-95-14/1-A, Judgement (March 24, 2000).

Atolan, Agustinho, Prosecutor v., Dili District Court, Special Panels for Serious Crimes, Case No. 3/2003, Judgement (June 9, 2003).

Babić, Prosecutor v., Case No. IT-03-72-I, Indictment (November 6, 2003).

———, Case No. IT-03-72-I, Amendment to the Joint Motion for Consideration of Plea Agreement between Milan Babić and the Office of the Prosecution Pursuant to Rule 62 *ter*, Tab 1 (January 22, 2004).

———, Case No. IT-03-72-I, Amendment to the Joint Motion for Consideration of Plea Agreement between Milan Babić and the Office of the Prosecutor Plea Agreement (January 22, 2004).

———, Case No. IT-03-72-I, Transcript (January 27, 2004).

———, Case No. IT-03-72-S, Transcript (April 2, 2004).

———, Case No. IT-03-72-S, Sentencing Judgement (June 29, 2004).

———, Case No. IT-03-72-A, Transcript (April 25, 2005).

———, Case No. IT-03-72-A, Judgement on Sentencing Appeal (July 18, 2005).

Bagaragaza, Prosecutor v., Case No. ICTR-2005-86-R11*bis*, Decision on the Prosecution Motion for Referral to the Kingdom of Norway (May 19, 2006).

Banović, Prosecutor v., Case No. IT-02-65/1, Transcript (September 3, 2003).

———, Case No. IT-02-65-1-S, Sentencing Judgement (October 28, 2003).

Barayagwiza, Prosecutor v., Case No. ICTR-97-17-AR72, Decision (November 3, 1999).

———, Case No. ICTR-97-17-AR72, Decision (Prosecutor's Request for Review or Reconsideration) (March 31, 2000).

Bere, Manuel Gonçalves, Prosecutor v., Dili District Court, Special Panels for Serious Crimes, Case No. 10/2000, Judgement (May 15, 2001).

Bisengimana, Prosecutor v., Case No. ICTR-2000-60-I, Indictment (July 1, 2000).

——, Case No. ICTR-2000-60-I, Plea Agreement between Mr. Paul Bisengimana and the Office of the Prosecutor (October 19, 2005).

——, Case No. ICTR-00-60-1, Amended Indictment (October 31, 2005).

——, Case No. ICTR-2000-60-I, Transcript (November 17, 2005).

——, Case No. ICTR-00-60-1, Amended Indictment (November 23, 2005).

——, Case No. ICTR-00-60-I, Joint Motion for Consideration of a Guilty Plea Agreement between Paul Bisengimana and the Office of the Prosecutor (November 30, 2005).

——, Case No. ICTR-2000-60-I, Transcript (December 7, 2005).

——, Case No. ICTR-2000-60-S, Transcript (January 19, 2006).

——, Case No. ICTR-00-60-T, Judgement and Sentence (April 13, 2006).

Blagojević, Prosecutor v., Case No. IT-02-60-T, Transcript (September 29, 2003).

——, Case No. IT-02-60-T, Transcript (January 22, 2004).

Blagojević, Vidoje & Jokić, Dragan, Prosecutor v., Case No. IT-02-60-T, Amended Joinder Indictment (May 26, 2003).

——, Case No. IT-02-60-T, Transcript (January 21, 2004).

Blaškić, Prosecutor v., Case No. IT-94-14-T, Judgement (March 3, 2000).

——, Case No. IT-95-14-A, Appeal Judgement (July 29, 2004).

Bralo, Prosecutor v., Case No. IT-95-17-PT, Indictment (November 2, 1995).

——, Case No. IT-95-17-PT, Plea Agreement (July 18, 2005).

——, Case No. IT-95-17-PT, Transcript (July 19, 2005).

——, Case No. IT-95-17-S, Prosecution's Sentencing Brief (October 10, 2005).

——, Case No. IT-95-17-S, Transcript (October 20, 2005).

——, Case No. IT-95-17-S, Sentencing Brief on behalf of Miroslav Bralo (November 25, 2005).

——, Case No. IT-95-17-S, Statement of Mehmed Ahmic, reprinted in Sentencing Brief on behalf of Miroslav Bralo (November 25, 2005).

——, Case No. IT-95-17-S, Sentencing Judgement, para. 97 (December 7, 2005).

——, Case No. IT-95-17-A, Appeal Brief on Behalf of Miroslav Bralo (May 26, 2006).

Brđanin, Prosecutor v., Case No. IT-99-36-T, Judgement (September 1, 2004).

Carmona, Carlos Soares, Prosecutor v., Dili District Court, Special Panels for Serious Crimes, Case No. 03 C.G. 2000, Judgement (April 19, 2001).

Carvalho, Lino de v. Prosecutor General, Court of Appeal of East Timor, Criminal Appeal No. 25 of 2001, Judgement of Fredrick Egonda-Ntende (October 29, 2001).

Cato v. United States, 70 F. 3d 1103 (1995).

Češić, Prosecutor v., Case No. IT-95-10/1-PT, Third Amended Indictment (November 26, 2002).

——, Case No. IT-95-10/1-S, Transcript (October 8, 2003).

——, Case No. IT-95-10/1-PT, Factual Basis (October 8, 2003).

——, Case No. IT-95-10/1-PT, Plea Agreement (October 8, 2003).

——, Case No. IT-95-10/1-S, Prosecution's Sentencing Brief (November 12, 2003).

——, Case No. IT-95-10/1-S, Ranko Češić's Sentencing Brief (November 12, 2003).

——, Case No. IT-95-10/1-S, Transcript (November 27, 2003).

————, Case No. IT-95-10/1-S, Sentencing Judgement (March 11, 2004).

Correia, Abilio Mendez, Prosecutor v., Dili District Court, Special Panels for Serious Crimes, Case No. 19/2001, Admissions by Abilio Mendez Correia (March 2, 2004).

————, Dili District Court, Special Panels for Serious Crimes, Case No. 19/2001, Disposition of the Decision (March 3, 2004).

da Costa, Agustinho, Prosecutor v., Dili District Court, Special Panels for Serious Crimes, Case No. 07/2000, Judgement (October 11, 2001).

Da Costa Nunes, Damiao, Prosecutor v., Dili District Court, Special Panels for Serious Crimes, Case No. 1/2003, Indictment (December 17, 2002).

————, Dili District Court, Special Panels for Serious Crimes, Case No. 1/2003, Dissenting Opinion of Judge Siegfried Blunk (December 10, 2003).

————, Dili District Court, Special Panels for Serious Crimes, Case No. 1/2003, Judgement (December 10, 2003).

de Deus, Marcurious José, Prosecutor v., Dili District Court, Special Panels for Serious Crimes, Case No. PID.C.G/13/2001, Sentence (April 18, 2002).

Delalić and Others, Prosecutor v., Case No. IT-96-21-T, Judgement (November 16, 1998).

Deronjić, Prosecutor v., Case No. IT-02-61-I, Indictment (July 3, 2002).

————, Case No. IT-02-61-PT, Amended Indictment (November 29, 2002).

————, Case No. IT-02-61-I, Second Amended Indictment (September 29, 2003).

————, Case No. IT-02-61-PT, Plea Agreement and Factual Basis (September 29, 2003).

————, Case No. IT-02-61-PT, Transcript (September 30, 2003).

————, Case No. IT-02-61-S, Miroslav Deronjić's Sentencing Brief (December 18, 2003).

————, Case No. IT-02-61-PT, Transcript (January 27, 2004).

————, Case No. IT-02-61-S, Transcript (January 27, 2004).

————, Case No. IT-02-61-PT, Transcript (January 28, 2004).

————, Case No. IT-02-61-S, Transcript (January 28, 2004).

————, Case No. IT-02-61-PT, Transcript (March 5, 2004).

————, Case No. IT-02-61-S, Transcript (March 5, 2004).

————, Case No. IT-02-61-S, Dissenting Opinion of Judge Schomburg (March 30, 2004).

————, Case No. IT-02-61-S, Sentencing Judgement (March 30, 2004).

————, Case No. IT-02-61-A, Judgement on Sentencing Appeal (July 20, 2005).

Dos Santos, Augusto, Prosecutor v., Dili District Court, Special Panels for Serious Crimes, Case No. 06/2001, Judgement (May 14, 2002).

Dos Santos Laku, Francisco, Prosecutor v., Dili District Court, Special Panels for Serious Crimes, Case No. 8/2001, Judgement (July 25, 2001).

Došen, Prosecutor v., Case No. IT-95-8-T, Joint Submission of the Prosecution and the Accused Damir Došen Concerning a Plea Agreement and Admitted Facts (September 6, 2001).

Erdemović, Prosecutor v., Case No. IT-96-22-T, Sentencing Judgement (November 29, 1996).

————, Case No. IT-96-22-A, Joint Separate Opinion of Judge McDonald and Judge Vohrah (October 7, 1997).

————, Case No. IT-96-22-A, Judgement (October 7, 1997).

———, Case No. IT-96-22-A, Separate and Dissenting Opinion of Judge Cassese (October 7, 1997).

———, Case No. IT-96-22-Tbis, Transcript (January 14, 1998).

———, Case No. IT-96-22-Tbis, Sentencing Judgement (March 5, 1998).

Fernandes, João, Prosecutor v., Dili District Court, Special Panels for Serious Crimes, Case No. 01/00.C.G.2000, Judgement (January 25, 2001).

Fernandes, João, Prosecutor v., Court of Appeal of East Timor, Criminal Appeal No. 2001/02 (June 29, 2001).

———, Court of Appeal of East Timor, Criminal Appeal No. 2001/02, Judgement of Egonda-Ntende, Judge (June 29, 2001).

Fernandes, Julio, Prosecutor v., Dili District Court, Special Panels for Serious Crimes, Case No. 02 C.G. 2000, Judgement (March 1, 2000).

Fernandes, Julio v. Prosecutor General, Court of Appeal of East Timor, Criminal Appeal No. 7 of 2001, Judgement of Fredrick Egonda-Ntende (June 29, 2001).

Franca da Silva, João, Prosecutor v., Dili District Court, Special Panels for Serious Crimes, Case No. 04a/2001, Judgement (December 5, 2002).

Franca da Silva, João et al., Prosecutor v., Case No. B0-06.1-99-SC, Indictment (May 25, 2001).

Gacumbitsi, Prosecutor v., Case No. ICTR-2001-64-T, Judgement (June 17, 2004).

Galić, Prosecutor v., Case No. IT-98-29-T, Judgement (December 5, 2003).

Haradinaj et al., Prosecutor v., Decision on Defence Motion on Behalf of Ramush Haradinaj to Request Re-assessment of Conditions of Provisional Release Granted 6 June 2005, Case No. IT-04-84-PT (October 12, 2005).

Janković, Prosecutor v., Case No. IT-96-23/2-PT, Decision on Referral of Case under Rule 11 bis (July 22, 2005).

Jelisić, Prosecutor v., Case No. IT-95-10-PT, Amended Indictment (March 3, 1998).

———, Case No. IT-95-10-T, Transcript (November 25, 1999).

———, Case No. IT-95-10-T, Judgement (December 14, 1999).

———, Case No. IT-95-10-A, Appeal Judgement (July 5, 2001).

Jokić, Prosecutor v., Case No. IT-01-42-PT, Order on Miodrag Jokić's Motion for Provisional Release (February 20, 2002).

———, Case No. IT-01-42, Second Amended Indictment (August 27, 2003).

———, Case No. IT-01-42-PT, Transcript (August 27, 2003).

———, Case No. IT-01-42/1-S, Miodrag Jokić's Sentencing Brief (November 14, 2003).

———, Case No. IT-01-42/1-S, Transcript (December 4, 2003).

———, Case No. IT-01-42/1-S, Sentencing Judgement (March 18, 2004).

———, Case No. IT-01-42/1-A, Transcript (April 26, 2005).

———, Case No. IT-01-42/1-A, Judgement on Sentencing Appeal (August 30, 2005).

Kajelijeli, Prosecutor v., Case No. ICTR-98-44A-T, Judgement and Sentence (December 1, 2003).

Kambanda, Prosecutor v., Case No. ICTR-97-23-1, Plea Agreement between Jean Kambanda and the Office of the Prosecutor (April 29, 1998).

———, Case No. ICTR-97-23-I, Prosecutor's Pre-Sentencing Brief (August 31, 1998).

———, Case No. ICTR-97-23-I, Transcript (September 3, 1998).

———, Case No. ICTR-97-23-S, Judgement and Sentence (September 4, 1998).

———, Case No. ICTR-97-23-A, Provisional Appellant's Brief and Motions for Extension of the Time-Limits and for Admission of New Evidence on Appeal Pursuant to Rules 115 and 116 of the Rules of Procedure and Evidence (March 29, 2000).

———, Case No. ICTR-97-23-A, Judgement (October 19, 2000).

Kamuhanda, Prosecutor v., Case No. ICTR-95-54A-T, Judgement and Sentence (January 22, 2004).

Kayishema, Prosecutor v., Case No. ICTR-95-1-T, Judgement and Sentence (May 21, 1999).

Kayishema & Ruzindana, Prosecutor v., Case No. ICTR-95-1-T, Judgement, at Sentence (May 21, 1999).

Kayishema et al., Prosecutor v., Case No. ICTR-95-1-I, First Amended Indictment (April 29, 1996).

Kolundžija, Prosecutor v., Case No. IT-95-8-T, Admitted Facts Relevant to the Plea Agreement for Dragan Kolundžija (September 4, 2001).

Kordić, Prosecutor v., Case No. IT-95-14/2-T, Judgement (February 26, 2001).

Kovacević, Prosecutor v., Case No. IT-01-42/2-I, Order on the Prosecutor's Request for Referral to National Authorities under Rule, 11 *bis* (January 20, 2005).

Krajišnik, Prosecutor v., Case No. IT-00-39, Transcripts (February 12, 13, 16, 18, 19, 2004).

Krajišnik & Plavšić, Prosecutor v., Case No. IT-00-39&40-PT, Factual Basis for Plea of Guilt (September 30, 2002).

Krstić, Prosecutor v., Case No. IT-98-33, Transcript (July 26, 2000).

———, Case No. IT-98-33, Transcript (July 27, 2000).

———, Case No. IT-98-33, Judgement (August 2, 2001).

———, Case No. IT-98-33-A, Transcript (November 21, 2003).

———, Case No. IT-98-33-A, Judgement (April 19, 2004).

Kvočka et al., Prosecutor v., Case No. IT-98-30/1-T, Judgement (November 2, 2001).

Leite, Sabino Gouveia, Prosecutor v., Dili District Court, Special Panels for Serious Crimes, Case No. 04b/2001, Judgement (December 7, 2002).

Leki, Gaspar, Prosecutor v., Dili District Court, Special Panels for Serious Crimes, Case No. 05/2001, Judgement (September 14, 2002).

Leki, Joseph, Prosecutor v., Dili District Court, Special Panels for Serious Crimes, Case No. 5/2000, Judgement (June 11, 2001).

Marques, Joni et al., Prosecutor v., Dili District Court, Special Panels for Serious Crimes, Case No. 09/2000, Judgement (December 11, 2001).

Martins, Anastacio & Gonçalves, Domingos, Prosecutor v., Dili District Court, Special Panels for Serious Crimes, Case No. 11/2001, Judgement (November 13, 2003).

Meakić et al., Prosecutor v., Case No. IT-02-65-PT, Joint Motion for the Consideration of a Plea Agreement between Predrag Banović and the Office of the Prosecutor, Annex 1 (June 18, 2003).

Mendonça, Domingos, Prosecutor v., Dili District Court, Special Panels for Serious Crimes, Case No. 18a/2001, Disposition of the Decision (October 13, 2003).

Milošević, Prosecutor v., Case No. IT-02-54, Transcripts (November 18–22, 25–27, 2002, and December 2–4, 6, 9, 2002).

———, Case No. IT-02-54, Transcript (February 21, 2003).

Mrđa, Prosecutor v., Case No. IT-02-59-I, Indictment (April 16, 2002).

———, Case No. IT-02-59-PT, Transcript (July 24, 2003).

———, Case No. IT-02-59-S, Amended Indictment (August 4, 2003).

———, Case No. IT-02-59-S, Darko Mrđa's Sentencing Brief (October 13, 2003).

———, Case No. IT-02-59-S, Transcript (October 22, 2003).

———, Case No. IT-02-59-S, Sentencing Judgement (March 31, 2004).

Mucić, Prosecutor v., Case No. IT-96-21-T*bis*-R117, Sentencing Judgement (October 9, 2001).

Musema, Prosecutor v., Case No. ICTR-96-13, Judgement and Sentence (January 27, 2000).

Nahimana et al., Prosecutor v., Case No. ICTR-99-52-T, Judgement and Sentence (December 3, 2003).

Naletilić & Martinović, Prosecutor v., Case No. IT-98-34-T, Judgement (March 31, 2003).

Nikolić, Dragan, Prosecutor v., Case No. IT-94-2-PT, Second Amended Indictment (January 7, 2002).

———, Case No. IT-94-2-PT, Transcript (September 4, 2003).

———, Case No. IT-94-2-PT, Third Amended Indictment (October 31, 2003).

———, Case No. IT-94-2-S, Transcript (November 3, 2003).

———, Case No. IT-94-2-S, Sentencing Judgement (December 18, 2003).

———, Case No. IT-94-2-A, Prosecution Respondent's Brief (August 9, 2004).

———, Case No. IT-94-2-A, Transcript (November 29, 2004).

———, Case No. IT-94-2-A, Judgement on Sentencing Appeal (February 4, 2005).

Nikolić, Momir, Prosecutor v., Case No. IT-02-60-PT, Transcript (May 6, 2003).

———, Case No. IT-02-60-PT, Joint Motion for Consideration of Plea Agreement between Momir Nikolić and the Office of the Prosecutor, at Tab A to Annex A, Statement of Facts and Acceptance of Responsibility (May 7, 2003).

———, Case No. IT-02-60/1, Prosecutor's Brief on the Sentencing of Momir Nikolić (July 14, 2003).

———, Case No. IT-02-60/1-S, Transcript (October 27, 2003).

———, Case No. IT-02-60/1-S, Transcript (October 29, 2003).

———, Case No. IT-02-60/1-S, Sentencing Judgement (December 2, 2003).

———, Case No. IT-02-60/1-A, Judgement on Sentencing Appeal (March 8, 2006).

Ndindabahizi, Prosecutor v., Case No. ICTR-2001-71-I, Judgement and Sentence (July 15, 2004).

Ngeze, Prosecutor v., Case No. ICTR-99-52-T, Judgement and Sentence (December 3, 2003).

Niyitegeka, Prosecutor v., Case No. ICTR-96-14-T, Judgement and Sentence (May 16, 2003).

Ntagerura et al., Prosecutor v., Case No. ICTR-99-46-T, Judgement and Sentence (February 25, 2004).

Ntakirutimana Gérard and Elizaphan, Prosecutor v., Case Nos. ICTR-96-10 & ICTR-96-17-T, Judgement and Sentence (February 21, 2003).

Obrenović, Dragan, Prosecutor v., Case No. IT-02-60-PT, Joint Motion for Consideration of Plea Agreement between Dragan Obrenović and the Office of the Prosecutor, Annex A, Plea Agreement (May 20, 2003).

Obrenović, Prosecutor v., Case No. IT-02-60-T, Joint Motion for Consideration of Plea Agreement between Dragan Obrenović and the Office of the Prosecutor, at Tab A to Annex A, Statement of Facts as set out by Dragan Obrenović (May 20, 2003).

——, Case No. IT-02-60/2-S, Prosecutor's Brief on the Sentencing of Dragan Obrenović (July 30, 2003).

——, Case No. IT-02-60/2-S, Transcript (October 30, 2003).

——, Case No. IT-02-60/2-S, Sentencing Judgement (December 10, 2003).

Plavšić, Prosecutor v., Case No. IT-00-39&40/1-S, Prosecution's Brief on the Sentencing of Biljana Plavšić (November 25, 2002).

——, Case No. IT-00-39&40/1-S, Transcript (December 17, 2002).

——, Case No. IT-00-39&40/1-S, Transcript (December 18, 2002).

——. Case No. IT-00-39&40/1, Sentencing Judgement (February 27, 2003).

Rajić, Prosecutor v., Case No. IT-95-12-PT, Amended Indictment, para. 15 (January 13, 2004).

——, Case No. IT-95-12-PT, Decision for Further Information in the Context of the Prosecutor's Motion for Referral of the Case under Rule 11bis (September 8, 2005).

——, Case No. IT-95-12-PT, Plea Agreement (October 25, 2005).

——, Case No. IT-95-12-PT, Factual Basis, (October 25, 2005).

——, Case No. IT-95-12-PT, Defence Sentencing Brief (March 6, 2006).

——, Case No. IT-95-12-S, Transcript (April 7, 2006).

——, Case No. IT-95-12-S, Sentencing Judgement (May 8, 2006).

Rugambarara, Prosecutor v., Case No. ICTR-2000-59-I, Indictment (July 1, 2000).Ruggiu, Prosecutor v., Case No. ICTR-97-32-I, Amended Indictment (December 18, 1998).

——, Case No. ICTR-97-32-DP, Plea Agreement between Georges Ruggiu and the Office of the Prosecutor (April 11, 2000).

——, Case No. ICTR-97-32, Transcript (May 15, 2000).

——, Case No. ICTR-97-32-I, Judgement and Sentence (June 1, 2000).

Rutaganda, Prosecutor v., Case No. ICTR-96-3, Judgement and Sentence (December 6, 1999).

Rutaganira, Prosecutor v., Case No. ICTR-95-1C-T, Transcript (January 17, 2005).

——, Case No. ICTR-95-1C-T, Sentencing Judgement (March 14, 2005).

Sarmento, Benjamin et al., Prosecutor v., Dili District Court, Special Panels for Serious Crimes, Case No. 18/2001, Disposition of the Decision Relating to the Conviction of the Accused Benjamin Sarmento and Romeiro Tilman (July 16, 2003).

Semanza, Prosecutor v., Case No. ICTR-97-20-T, Transcript (October 16, 2000).

——, Case No. ICTR-97-20-T, Transcript (November 7, 2000).

——, Case No. ICTR-97-20-T, Transcript (December 6, 2000).

——, Case No. ICTR-97-20-T, Transcript (February 27, 2001).

——, Case No. ICTR-97-20-T, Transcript (March 7, 2001).

——, Case No. ICTR-97-20-T, Transcript (June 18, 2002).

————, Case No. ICTR-97-20-T, Judgement and Sentence (May 15, 2003).

Serugendo, Prosecutor v., Case No. ICTR-2005-84-I, Corrigendum of Indictment (July 21, 2005).

Serushago, Prosecutor v., Case No. ICTR-98-37, Plea Agreement between Omar Serush-ago and the Office of the Prosecutor (December 4, 1998).

————, Case No. ICTR-98-37-I, Indictment (October 8, 1998).

————, Case No. ICTR-98-39, Transcript (January 29, 1999).

————, Case No. ICTR-98-39-S, Sentence (February 5, 1999).

————, Case No. ICTR-98-39-A, Order for the Continued Detention of Omar Serushago in the ICTR Detention Facility in Arusha (April 3, 2001).

Sikirica, Prosecutor v., Case No. IT-95-8-T, Judgement on Defence Motions to Acquit (September 3, 2001).

————, Case No. IT-95-8-T, Joint Submission of the Prosecution and the Accused Duško Sikirica Concerning a Plea Agreement and Admitted Facts (September 6, 2001).

————, Case No. IT-95-8-T, Transcript (October 8, 2001).

————, Case No. IT-95-8-T, Transcript (October 9, 2001).

Sikirica et al., Prosecutor v., Case No. IT-95-8-T, Sentencing Judgement (November 13, 2001).

Simić, Milan, Prosecutor v., Case No. IT-95-9/2-T, Prosecutor's Brief on the Sentencing of Milan Simić (July 15, 2002).

————, Interview with Milan Simić, March 2, 1998, at 15, reprinted as Annex A to Case No. IT-95-9/2-T, Prosecutor's Brief on the Sentencing of Milan Simić (July 15, 2002).

————, Case No. IT-95-9/2, Sentencing Judgement (October 17, 2002).

Simić et al., Prosecutor v., Case No. IT-95-9, Transcript (October 23, 2001).

————, Case No. IT-95-9, Transcript (November 2, 2001).

————, Case No. IT-95-9, Fourth Amended Indictment (January 9, 2002).

————, Case No. IT-95-9-T, Judgement (October 17, 2003).

Soares, Carlos, Prosecutor v., Dili District Court, Special Panels for Serious Crimes, Case No. 12/2000, Judgement (May 31, 2001).

Soares, Marcelino, Prosecutor v., Dili District Court, Special Panels for Serious Crimes, Case No. 11/2003, Judgement (December 11, 2003).

Stakić, Prosecutor v., Case No. IT-97-24-T, Judgement (July 31, 2003).

————, Case No. IT-97-24-A, Judgement, at Disposition (March 22, 2006).

Strugar, Prosecutor v., Case No. IT-01-42-T, Judgement, Annex IV (January 31, 2005).

Strugar & Kovacević, Prosecutor v., Case No. IT-01-42, Second Amended Indictment (October 17, 2003).

Strugar et al., Prosecutor v., Case No. IT-01-42, Indictment (February 22, 2001).

————, Case No. IT-01-42, Amended Indictment (March 31, 2003).

Tadić, Prosecutor v., Case No. IT-94-1-T, Opinion and Judgement (May 7, 1997).

Todorović, Prosecutor v., Case No. IT-95-9/1, Transcript (December 13, 2000).

————, Case No. IT-95-9/1, Transcript (January 19, 2001).

————, Case No. IT-95-9/1, Transcript (May 4, 2001).

————, Case No. IT-95-9/1, Sentencing Judgement (July 31, 2001).

United States v. Kimble, 719 F. 2d 1253 (5th Cir. 1983).

United States v. Singleton, 144 F. 3d 1343 (1998).

Valente, Jose, Prosecutor v., Dili District Court, Special Panels for Serious Crimes, Case No. 3/2001, Judgement (June 19, 2001).

Vasiljević, Prosecutor v., Case No. IT-98-32-T, Judgement (November 29, 2002).

Conferences

Conference, Plea Agreements and Guilty Pleas at the ICTY and Related Practice in National Systems, December 5–6, 2003, Sarajevo, Bosnia-Herzegovina.

International Criminal Law Network Conference, *Establishing the International Criminal Court*, The Hague, December 16–18, 2002.

Editorials and Newspaper and Online Articles

Apologies All Around, TRANSITIONS ONLINE (Prague), September 9–15, 2003.

Annan Proposes Assessed Dues to Close Sierra Leone Court's Budget Gap, March 11, 2004, available at http://www.un.org/apps/news/storyAr.asp?NewsID=10044&Cr=sierra&Cr1=&Kw1=assessed&Kw2=dues&Kw3=sierra.

Archer, Lincoln, "*We Feel We've Been Robbed*," BBC NEWS, September 20, 2004.

Ashdown Sacks Bosnian Serb Army Chief for Obstructing Srebrenica Probe, AGENCE FRANCE-PRESSE, April 16, 2004.

Association "Women from Podrinje" Disappointed with Deronjić's Sentence, NTV HAYAT (Sarajevo radio station), March 31, 2004, available at http://www.tfeagle.army.mil/tfeno/Feature_Story.asp?Article=81109).

Beresford, David & Rossouw, Rehana, *Generals Avoid Justice as System Struggles to Cope*, MAIL & GUARDIAN (South Africa), September 29, 1995.

Biljana Plavšić: Serbian Iron Lady, BBC NEWS, February 27, 2003.

Blaškić's Sentence Cut Down from 45 to 9 Years in Prison, SENSE NEWS AGENCY, July 29, 2004.

Bosnian Muslims Protest "Shameful" War Crimes Sentence, AGENCE FRANCE-PRESSE, October 29, 2003.

Bosnian Serb "Monster" Todorović to Be Released from Prison, AGENCE FRANCE-PRESSE, June 29, 2005.

Bosnian State Judiciary Faces Funding Crisis as Donations Dwindle, BBC MONITORING EUROPE, June 4, 2006.

Bosnian TV Reports on Rajić Guilty Plea Fallout in Croatia, BBC WORLDWIDE MONITORING, November 6, 2005.

Bosnian Women's Association Calls Serb Camp Guard Sentence "Insult," BBC WORLDWIDE MONITORING, October 29, 2003.

Bravin, Jess, *Tribunal in Africa May Serve as Model for Trial of Hussein*, WALL STREET JOURNAL, February 12, 2003.

Brett, Sebastian, *Justice a Step Closer in Chile*, THE OBSERVER, May 30, 2004.

Brittain, Victoria, *Letter from Rwanda*, THE NATION, August 14, 2003.

Brody, Reed, *Idi Amin at Death's Door: Despots Should Not Rest in Peace*, INTERNATIONAL HERALD TRIBUNE, July 25, 2003.

Carlin, John, *Could You Share a Pint with a Man who Killed Your Family?*, NEW STATESMAN, September 15, 2003.

The Case Is Almost Proved: Insider Says Milošević Was Responsible, COALITION FOR INTERNATIONAL JUSTICE REPORT, November 27, 2002.

Cevallos, Diego, *Rights-Mexico: Extradition of Accused Argentine Torturer Approved*, INTERPRESS SERVICE, June 10, 2003.

Chhatbar, Sukhdev, *Priest Dismisses Rwanda Genocide Charges, Says He's Praying for the Victims*, CANADIAN PRESS, September 27, 2004.

——, *Rwandan Pleads Innocent to Genocide Charge*, ASSOCIATED PRESS, September 30, 2005.

Chile Torture Victims Win Payout, BBC NEWS, November 29, 2004.

Cobban, Helena, *Healing Rwanda: Can an International Court Deliver Justice?*, BOSTON REVIEW 10 (December 2003/January 2003).

Convicted Ex-Radio Presenter Has Mental Problems, Defence Suggests, HIRONDELLE NEWS AGENCY, March 5, 2002.

Court Sentences Former Regime's Security Chief to Death, ETHIOPIAN HERALD, August 11, 2005.

Croatia's Top Court Orders War Crimes Retrial, REUTERS, August 19, 2004.

Cruvellier, Thierry, *Confessions—A Key to Wrapping Up Trials in ICTR*, INTERNATIONAL JUSTICE TRIBUNE, March 27, 2006.

——, *Sierra Leone: The Cost of a Mixed Model*, INTERNATIONAL JUSTICE TRIBUNE, No. 27, June 13, 2005.

Darehshori, Sara, *Inching toward Justice in Rwanda*, NEW YORK TIMES, September 8, 1998.

Dixon, Robyn, *A Decade after Apartheid: The Official Truth Falls Short for Many*, LOS ANGELES TIMES, May 30, 2004.

DR Congo Rebel in Landmark Trial, BBC NEWS, March 20, 2006.

Dupont, Gilbert, Mutilé et éviscéré, LA DERNIERE HEURE, December 24, 2005.

——, *Rien ne contredit le suicide*, LA DERNIERE HEURE, February 7, 2006.

Ega-Musa, Nasser, *Another Failure of Justice in Africa*, WASHINGTON POST, March 6, 1997.

Egan, Louise, *Victims: Chile's Human Rights Plan Soft on Military*, REUTERS, August 13, 2003.

Evers, Tag, *Blessed Are the Peacemakers*, ISTHMUS, April 10, 1998.

Forero, Juan, *Ex Generals and Others Protest Peru Report on Rebel Conflict*, NEW YORK TIMES, September 8, 2003.

Former Bosnian Serb President Complains about Prison Conditions in Sweden, AGENCE FRANCE-PRESSE, October 17, 2003.

Former Rwandan Minister's Body Found in Belgium, ASHEVILLE GLOBAL REPORT, No. 363, December 29–January 4, 2006.

Furney, William J., *East Timor Atrocities: Submit to International Tribunal*, Straits Times (Singapore), August 15, 2003.

Fury over Pinochet "Angel" Claim, BBC Online News Report, November 25, 2003, available at http://news.bbc.co.uk/1/hi/world/americas/3237740.stm.

Gabiro, Gabriel, *Confronting Genocide with Country's Regular Courts*, Hirondelle News Agency, September 17, 2003.

Gacaca Exodus?, Internews, June 13, 2005.

Habré Allowed to Stay in Senegal, BBC News, November 27, 2005.

Hate Radio Presenter Set to Plead Guilty to Genocide Charges, Hirondelle News Agency, May 9, 2000.

Hit Squad Kills Man Who Laid Trap against Genocide Suspect, The Nation (Nairobi), January 21, 2003.

How Belgian Journalist Became Involved in Hate Media, Internews, May 15, 2000, available at http://www.internews.org/activities/ICTR_Reports/ICTRNewsMay00.html.

How to Punish Crime and Reward Guilty Pleas and Cooperation, SENSE News Agency, April 2, 2004.

I Lied in My Book to Protect RTLM, Says Convicted Radio Presenter, Hirondelle News Agency, February 28, 2002.

ICTR: Looking for the Secrets of the Akazu, International Justice Tribune, September 12, 2005.

ICTR and Rwanda Argue over Plea Bargains, Hirondelle News Agency, April 22, 2006.

ICTR/Bisengimana—Former Mayor Who Pleaded Guilty Sentenced to 15 Years, Hirondelle News Agency, Apr. 13, 2006.

ICTR/Former Rwandan Militia Leader Asks for the Forgiveness of Rwanda, Internews, January 29, 1998.

ICTR/Judges/Prosecution—ICTR Hampers Prosecution Strategy Again, Hirondelle News Agency, May 25, 2006.

ICTR/Karemera—MRND Leaders Want Uwilingiyimana's Statements Made Public, Hirondelle News Agency, Feb. 23, 2006.

ICTR/Prosecution—Synthesis: Prosecutors at the ICTR, Hirondelle News Agency, October 28, 2003.

ICTR/Rusatira—General Rusatira's Release Heightens Tension between Rwanda and the ICTR, Hirondelle News Agency, October 29, 2003.

ICTR/Serugendo—Serugendo's Guilty Plea Bargain Settled on a Prison Sentence of 6 to 10 Years, Hirondelle News Agency, June 1, 2006.

ICTR/Uwilingiyimana—Many Questions in Arusha after the Announcement of Uwilingiyimana's Death, Hirondelle News Agency, December 23, 2005.

ICTR/Uwilingiyimana—Uwilingiyimana's Death Threatens to Hamper Prosecutor's Work, Hirondelle News Agency, Jan. 17, 2006.

Impunity Bears the Germ of Future Conflicts, SENSE News Agency, October 11, 2004.

Insider Links Milošević to War in Croatia, Coalition for International Criminal Justice Report, November 20, 2002.

Jelacić, Nerma & Stephen, Chris, *Anger at Short Sentence for Prison Killer*, IWPR's TRIBU-
NAL UPDATE, No. 331, November 1, 2003.

Jungvirth, Goran, *Bosnian Croat Insider Awaits Sentence*, IWPR's TRIBUNAL UPDATE,
No. 448, April 13, 2006.

Kagame Accused over Plane Attack, BBC NEWS, March 10, 2004.

Kampschror, Beth, *Bosnia to Try Its War Criminals, But Is New Court Up to the Job?*,
CHRISTIAN SCIENCE MONITOR, December 23, 2003.

Kandić, Natasa, *How to Protect Witnesses Who Are Seen by Public and Police as Traitors*,
February 6, 2004 (on file with author).

Katana, Gordana, *Bosnian Serb "Forced" into Atrocity Admission*, IWPR's TRIBUNAL UP-
DATE, No. 363, June 18, 2004.

———, *Bosnian Serbs Still in Denial over Srebrenica*, IWPR's TRIBUNAL UPDATE, No. 354,
April 23, 2004.

Kebo, Amra, *Regional Report: Plavšić Sentence Divides Bosnia*, IWPR's TRIBUNAL UP-
DATE, No. 302, February 24–28, 2003.

Kessy, Modestus, *Genocide Suspects Call Off Protest*, THE SUNDAY OBSERVER (Tanzania),
September 26, 2004.

———, *Genocide Witness Killed after Testifying*, THE GUARDIAN (Dar es Salaam), October 22, 2004.

Kimani, Mary, *Former Rwandan Militia Leader Asks for the Forgiveness of Rwanda*, IN-
TERNEWS, January 29, 1998, available at http://internews.org/activities/ICTR_reports/
ICTRnewsJAN99.html.

———, *Media Trial: "Hassan Ngeze Did Not Want Me to Testify," Genocide Convict Claims*,
INTERNEWS, November 15, 2001, available at http://www.internews.org/activities/
ICTR_Reports/ICTRNewsNov01.html.

———, *600 Tried, Thousands Flee*, INTERNATIONAL JUSTICE TRIBUNE, May 23, 2005.

Kratovac, Katarina, *Thousands Bid Farewell to Ultranationalist War Crimes Suspect*, AS-
SOCIATED PRESS, February 23, 2003.

Krilic, Samir, *Report Finds Massacre Planned*, ASSOCIATED PRESS, November 8, 2004.

Lacey, Marc, *10 Years Later in Rwanda, the Dead Are Ever Present*, NEW YORK TIMES,
February 26, 2004.

Lawyer for the Former Rwandan Prime Minister Argues for Light Sentence, INTERNEWS,
September 4, 1998, available at http://www.internews.org/activities/ICTR_reports/
ICTRNewsSep98.html.

LeBor, Adam, *20 Years for Sarajevo Siege General*, THE TIMES (London), December 6, 2003.

Lindsey, Reed, *Taking on the Past, Argentina Repeals Amnesty*, BOSTON GLOBE, August 22, 2003.

Madra, Ek, *U.N., Cambodia Look to Khmer Rouge Trial in 2007*, REUTERS, February 9,
2006.

Maykuth, Andrew, *A Watershed Trial in South Africa: Did an Ex-Defense Minister and
Others Train an Apartheid Hit Squad?*, PHILADELPHIA INQUIRER, April 22, 1996.

McLoughlin, Patrick, *Serb War Criminal Plavšić Goes to Swedish Jail*, REUTERS,
June 27, 2003.

———, *War Criminal's Conditions Rile Guards*, REUTERS, August 1, 2003.

Meirik, Karen, *Srebrenica Prosecution Blow*, IWPR's TRIBUNAL UPDATE, No. 340, January 23, 2004.

Meldrum, Andrew, *One Million Rwandans to Face Killing Charges in Village Courts*, THE GUARDIAN, January 15, 2005.

Metcalf, J. Coll, *An Interview with United Nations' Chief War Crimes Prosecutor, Carla del Ponte*, INTERNEWS, February 15, 2000.

Mexico to Extradite "Dirty War" Argentine to Spain, NEW YORK TIMES, June 10, 2003.

Militia Leader Who Confessed to Genocide Gets Fifteen Years in Prison, INTERNEWS, February 5, 1998.

Mothers' Association Urges Re-examination of All Aspects of Srebrenica Massacre, BBC WORLDWIDE MONITORING, October 10, 2003.

Murder Sentence Changes Unveiled, BBC NEWS, September 20, 2004.

9 Convicted of Kidnap of War-Crimes Suspect, NEW YORK TIMES, December 12, 2000.

Onishi, Norimitsu, *Japan Apologizes to China for Injuries from Remnants of War*, NEW YORK TIMES, August 13, 2003.

Palmer, Karen. *Justice in Jeopardy*, TORONTO STAR, March 27, 2006.

Petit, Franck, *Cameroonian Intrigues*, INTERNATIONAL JUSTICE TRIBUNE, March 5, 2001.

Pleading Repentance, BALKAN RECONSTRUCTION REPORT, February 2, 2004.

Political Parties in Croatia Differ on President's Apology for War Crimes, BBC WORLDWIDE MONITORING, September 12, 2003.

Pomfret, John & Hockstader, Lee, *In Bosnia, a War Crimes Impasse*, WASHINGTON POST, December 9, 1997.

Portrait of Georges Ruggiu, Journalist Who Incited Genocide, HIRONDELLE NEWS AGENCY, May 14, 2000.

Power, Samantha, *Rwanda: The Two Faces of Justice*, 50 NEW YORK REVIEW BOOKS No. 1, January 16, 2003.

Prosecution Witness Assassinated in Rwanda, HIRONDELLE NEWS AGENCY, October 20, 2004.

Prosecutor Steps Up Pressure on the Akazu, INTERNATIONAL JUSTICE TRIBUNE, December 5, 2005.

Redressing Injustices of the Past Back on Chile's Agenda, TAIPEI TIMES, September 8, 2003.

Restrictions on Vojislav Šešelj's Communication Privileges Extended, SENSE NEWS AGENCY, June 10, 2004.

Rohter, Larry, *Argentina Announces Deal on Its Debt Default*, NEW YORK TIMES, March 4, 2005.

———, *Argentina Nears Repeal of "Dirty War" Amnesty*, INTERNATIONAL HERALD TRIBUNE, August 21, 2003.

———, *Now the Dirtiest of Wars Won't Be Forgotten*, NEW YORK TIMES, June 18, 2003.

———, *Default Reopens "Dirty War" Wounds*, NEW YORK TIMES, MARCH 12, 2002.

Rubin, Alissa J., *Former Serb Leader's Admission of Guilt Alienates Compatriots*, LOS ANGELES TIMES, December 16, 2002.

Ruremesha, Jean, *Rwanda: Should the Bones Be Silenced?*, INTER-PRESS SERVICE (Johannesburg), August 5, 2004.

Rwanda: Government Wants Acquitted Bagambiki to Surrender in Order to Face Rape Trial, HIRONDELLE NEWS AGENCY, May 4, 2006.

Rwanda Pressing UN to Drop Del Ponte as Prosecutor: Spokeswoman, AGENCE FRANCE-PRESSE, July 24, 2003.

Rwanda Unhappy with Ruggiu Sentence, HIRONDELLE NEWS AGENCY, June 1, 2000.

Rwanda/Gacaca: Over 1000 Gacaca Judges Have Resigned over Genocide Allegations, HIRONDELLE NEWS AGENCY, June 24, 2005.

Sadović, Merdijana, *Teething Problems for Bosnian Courts*, IWPR's TRIBUNAL UPDATE, No. 358, May 15, 2004.

Sanader Condemns "Croatia's Auschwitz," AGENCE FRANCE-PRESSE, March 16, 2004.

Saponja-Hadzić, Milanka, *Hague Deals Reduce Impact*, IWPR's TRIBUNAL UPDATE, No. 321, July 24, 2003.

——, *Serbia Tries Hague's Patience*, IWPR's TRIBUNAL UPDATE, No. 362, June 11, 2004.

——, *Surprise at Babić Indictment*, IWPR's TRIBUNAL UPDATE, No. 334, November 22, 2003.

Scheffer, David, *A Rare Chance to Try These Architects of Atrocity*, FINANCIAL TIMES (London), August 16, 2004.

Schreinemacher, Elisabeth, *Sierra Leone War-Crimes Court Running Out of Money*, MAIL & GUARDIAN, October 6, 2005.

Sengupta, Somini, *African Held for War Crimes Dies in Custody of a Tribunal*, NEW YORK TIMES, July 31, 2003.

Sentence against Bisengimana to Discourage Further Confessions, HIRONDELLE NEWS AGENCY, April 20, 2006.

Serb Leader Alleges Prison Conspiracy, THE INDEPENDENT (London), October 18, 2003.

Sierra Leone: Special Court Registrar Announces Resignation But Urged to Stay, IRIN NEWS, August 4, 2004.

Sierra Leone War Crimes Prosecutors Gather Witnesses Ahead of Trials, AGENCE FRANCE-PRESSE, May 5, 2004.

Simons, Marlise, *In a Startling Plea, a Serbian Policeman Confesses to Atrocities*, NEW YORK TIMES, July 27, 2003.

——, *War Crimes Court Takes It Easy on a Cooperative Bosnian Serb*, NEW YORK TIMES, August 1, 2001.

Simpson, Daniel, *U.N. Tribunal, with Surprise Guilty Plea, Rivets Bosnians*, NEW YORK TIMES, October 4, 2002.

Sipress, Alan, *Khmer Rouge Trials Stalled by Political Deadlock*, WASHINGTON POST, May 5, 2004.

Sito-Sucic, Daria, *Muslim Victims Outraged, Say Plavšić Sentence Low*, REUTERS, February 27, 2003.

——, *West Wants Serb Action after Srebrenica Report*, REUTERS, November 8, 2004.

State to Halt Legal Aid for "Third Force," MAIL & GUARDIAN (S. Afr.), April 4, 1997.

Stephen, Chris, *Deronjić Plea-Bargain Claims*, IWPR's Tribunal Update, No. 335, November 28, 2003.

———, *Key Srebrenica Witness Apologises for Lies*, IWPR's Tribunal Update, No. 327, October 4, 2003.

———, *What Price Justice*, IWPR's Tribunal Update, No. 332, November 7, 2003.

Suljagić, Emir, *Sušica Camp Chief Names Mass Grave Site*, IWPR's Tribunal Update, No. 332, November 7, 2003.

———, *Truth at The Hague*, New York Times, June 1, 2003.

Suljagić, Emir & Kebo, Amra, *Mrđa Guilty Plea Sparks Anger*, IWPR's Tribunal Update, No. 322, August 1, 2003.

Sullivan, Stacy, *Krajišnik "Helped Mastermind" Serb Crimes*, IWPR's Tribunal Update, No. 342, February 9, 2004.

A Suspect Speaks Out, SENSE News Agency, February 24, 2004.

Taylor, Rachel S., *Babić May Get Off Lightly*, IWPR's Tribunal Update, No. 351, April 5, 2004.

Thompson, Ginger, *South Africa to Pay $3900 to Each Family of Apartheid Victims*, New York Times, April 16, 2003.

Tobar, Hector, *Argentine Court Voids Amnesty in Dirty War*, Los Angeles Times, June 15, 2005.

Tribunal Throws Out Motion to Have Bagaragaza's Transfer to Norway, Hirondelle News Agency, May 19, 2006.

U.N. War Crimes Court to Try 20 Suspects in Sierra Leone, New York Times, January 4, 2002.

The Uwilingiyimana Mystery, International Justice Tribune, January 23, 2006.

Vasagar, Jeevan, *Body of Genocide Witness Found in River*, The Guardian, December 24, 2005.

Vergara, Eva, *Chilean President Plans to Up Reparations*, Associated Press, August 13, 2003.

Waldorf, Lars, *Memoirs of a Snitch*, Diplomatie Judiciaire, November 27, 2001.

———, *Silent Partner*, Diplomatie Judiciaire, November 27, 2001.

Warrant Issued for Ex-Chad Leader, BBC News, September 29, 2005.

Wax, Emily, *In Exile, Taylor Exerts Control: Liberian Ex-President Exercises Influence from Nigeria*, Washington Post, September 17, 2003.

Witnesses from the "Other Side," SENSE News Agency, March 1, 2004.

Witte, Eric, *The Cost of Impunity for Liberian Ex-Leader*, IWPR African Reports, No. 44, October 17, 2005.

Woodd, Richard & Sokheng, Vong, *US Senate Moves to Block KR Trial Funds*, Phnom Penh Post, October 8, 2004.

Wroclavsky, Damian, *Argentina Says It Would Extradite "Angel of Death,"* Reuters, October 11, 2003.

Zarembo, Alan, *Rwanda's Genocide Witnesses Are Killed as Wheels of Justice Slowly Begin Turning*, Christian Science Monitor, January 23, 1997.

Interviews

BH, Sarajevo, Bosnia (December 4, 2003).

BM, The Hague (November 8, 2004).

FF, Sarajevo, Bosnia (December 5, 2003).

SW, The Hague (September 26, 2003).

McDonald, Gabrielle Kirk, former president of the ICTY, The Hague (September 15, 2003).

Suljagić, Emir, IWPR reporter and Srebrenica survivor, The Hague (September 12, 2003).

Telephone Interviews

SK (December 1 and 10, 2004).

Bowers, Terree, former ICTY senior trial attorney (October 30, 2001).

Faal, Essa, chief of prosecutions, Special Panels for Serious Crimes (July 30, 2004).

Gutman, Alan, defense counsel, Special Panels for Serious Crimes (July 30, 2004).

Harmon, Mark, ICTY prosecutor (February 24, 2005).

Hodzić, Refik, former ICTY outreach program director for Bosnia (July 28, 2004).

Kostić, Nicola, ICTY defense counsel (October 25, 2001).

Koumjian, Nicholas, deputy prosecutor for serious crimes, Special Panels for Serious Crimes (July 29, 2004).

Morrison, Howard, ICTR defense counsel (December 2, 2004).

Othman, Mohamed, former prosecutor general for East Timor (August 4, 2004).

Othman, Mohamed, former ICTR prosecutor (August 27, 2005).

Waldorf, Lars, researcher, Human Rights Watch (October 2, 2003).

Waldorf, Lars, former researcher, Human Rights Watch (June 24, 2004).

Waldorf, Lars, former researcher, Human Rights Watch (October 10, 2005).

Zecević, Slobodan, ICTY defense counsel (December 17, 2002).

Zecević, Slobodan, ICTY defense counsel (September 1, 2005).

Radio Interview

Eric Migamba, Juvénal Uwilingiyimana's son, by Phil Taylor, January 9, 2006, available at http://www.taylor-report.com/audio/index.php?month=2006-01.

Letters

Letter of Juvénal Uwilingiyimana, available at http://cirqueminime.blogcollective.com/blog/_archives/2005/12/27/1523635.html.

Press Releases, Remarks, and Speeches

Bicamumpaka, Mr., Statement of (Rwanda), U.N. Doc. S/PV.3377, at 4 (May 16, 1994).

Brammertz, Serge, Speech, *Challenges Faced during an Investigation*, March 10, 2005, Grotius Center, The Hague.

Clinton, President William J., *Remarks in Apology for Study Done in Tuskegee*, May 16, 1997, available at http://www.cmh.pitt.edu/presremarks.html.

Corell, Hans, Statement by U.N. Legal Counsel, *Negotiations between the U.N. and Cambo-dia Regarding the Establishment of the Court to Try Khmer Rouge Leaders*, February 8, 2002, available at http://www.un.org/News/dh/infocus/cambodia/corell-brief.htm.

Human Rights Watch, Press Release, *Rwanda*, February 1, 2001, available at http://www.hrw.org/backgrounder/africa/rwanda-bck-0131.htm.

International Criminal Tribunal for Rwanda (ICTR), Press Release, *President and Pros-ecutor Update Security Council on Completion Strategy*, ICTR/INFO-9-2-394(a).EN (July 6, 2004).

———, Press Release, *Joseph Serugendo Sentenced to Six Years Imprisonment*, ICTR/INFO-9-2-478.EN (June 2, 2006).

International Criminal Tribunal for the former Yugoslavia (ICTY), Press Release, *Ad-dress by Carla Del Ponte, Chief Prosecutor of the International Criminal Tribunal for the Former Yugoslavia, to the United Nations Security Council*, CT/P.I.S./863-e, June 30, 2004.

———, Press Release, *Address by His Excellency, Judge Claude Jorda, President of the International Criminal Tribunal for the Former Yugoslavia, to the United Nations Security Council*, JDH/P.I.S./690-e, July 26, 2002, available at http://www.un.org/icty/pressreal/p690-e.htm.

———, Press Release, Address by his Excellency, Judge Claude Jorda, President of the International Criminal Tribunal for the Former Yugoslavia, to the United Nations Security Council, JDH/P.I.S./708-e, October 30, 2002, available at http://www.un.org/icty/pressreal/p708-e.htm.

———, Press Release, Address by the Prosecutor of the International Criminal Tribu-nals for the Former Yugoslavia and Rwanda, Mrs. Carla del Ponte, to the United Na-tions Security Council, JJJ/P.I.S/709-e, October 30, 2002, available at http://www.un.org/icty/pressreal/p709-e.htm.

———, Press Release, Address to the United Nations Security Council by the Prosecutor of the International Criminal Tribunals for the Former Yugoslavia and Rwanda, Carla Del Ponte, to the U.N. Security Council, GR/P.I.S/642-E, November 27, 2001.

———, Press Release, Indictment against Miroslav Bralo Made Public, JL/P.I.S./902-e, October 13, 2004.

———, Press Release, *Registry Imposes Communications Restrictions on Detainees with regard to Political Campaigning in the Media from the Tribunal's Detention Unit*, JL/P.I.S./810-e, December 12, 2003.

———, Press Release, *Statement by Judge Theodor Meron, President, International Crimi-nal Tribunal for the Former Yugoslavia, to the Security Council*, TM/MOW/976e, June 13, 2005.

Judicial System Monitoring Programme, *The Continuation of the Final Closing Statement in the Case of Carlos Soares*, November 17, 2003.

———, Press Release, *Conference on the Future of the Serious Crimes Process for Timor-Leste*, September 22, 2004.

———, Press Release, *Results of Judges' Evaluations Released*, January 26, 2005.

Marshall, Shane, Speech, *The East Timorese Judiciary: At the Threshold of Self-Sufficiency?*, Conference of Supreme and Federal Court Judges, Darwin, Australia, January 2005.

Rapoza, Phillip, *The Serious Crimes Process in Timor-Leste: Accomplishments, Challenges and Lessons Learned*, speech delivered at the International Symposium on U.N. Peace-keeping Operations in Post-Conflict Timor-Leste: Accomplishments and Lessons Learned, J. Special Panel for Serious Crimes, April 28, 2005.

Sarmento, Tiago A., *The Future of Serious Crimes*, Victoria University, June 16–18, 2005.

Serious Crimes Unit, indictee file, available at http://socrates.berkeley.edu/~warcrime/Serious%20Crimes%20Unit%20Files/suspects/MVIS-65KAKY.html.

———, Information Release, *SCU Indicts Suai Church Massacre Commanders*, November 30, 2004.

———, Press Release, *Crimes against Humanity Charges for Former Indonesian Minister of Defense, Top Indonesian Military Commanders and East Timor Governor*, February 25, 2003.

Statement by the President of the ICTR to the United Nations General Assembly, October 28, 2002, available at http://69.94.11.53/ENGLISH/speeches/pillay281002ga.htm.

Wesselingh, Isabelle & Vaulerin, Arnaud, Speech, *Eleven Years after Ethnic Cleansing and Four Trials by the ICTY Later, Life between Denial and Hope in Prijedor (Bosnia)*, February 5, 2004, T.C.M. Asser Institute, The Hague.

Reports

African Rights, Gacaca Justice: A Shared Responsibility, January 2003.

Amnesty International, *Bosnia-Herzegovina: Memorandum to the High Representative of Bosnia-Herzegovina*, AI Index: EUR 63/009/2002, August 1, 2002, available at http://web.amnesty.org/library/index/engeur630092002.

———, The Criminal Justice System and the Protection of Human Rights in South Africa: The Role of the Prosecution Service, AI Index: AFR 53/001/1998, February 11, 1998.

———, Ethiopia, Accountability Past and Present: Human Rights in Transition, April 1995.

———, Gacaca: A Question of Justice, December 17, 2002, available at http://web.amnesty.org/library/Index/ENGAFR470072002?open&of=ENG-RWA.

———, International Criminal Tribunal for Rwanda: Trials and Tribulations, April 1, 1998, available at http://web.amnesty.org/ai.nsf/index/ior400031998?OpenDocument&of=THEMES/INTERNATIONAL+JUSTICE.

———, Public Statement, Justice for Timor-Leste: Victims Await Further Action from the Security Council to Ensure Perpetrators Are Held to Account (April 29, 2005).

———, Memorandum to the High Representative of Bosnia-Herzegovina, AI Index: EUR 63/009/2002, August 1, 2002.

———, Report 2004—Bosnia and Herzegovina, available at http://web.amnesty.org/report2004/bih-summary-eng.

———, Rwanda: The Troubled Course of Justice, AI Index: AFR 47/010/2000, April 4, 2000.

Amnesty International & Human Rights Watch, Truth and Justice: Unfinished Business in South Africa, AI Index: AFR 53/001/2003, February 2003.

AMNESTY INTERNATIONAL & JUDICIAL SYSTEM MONITORING PROGRAMME INDONESIA AND TIMOR-LESTE, JUSTICE FOR TIMOR-LESTE: THE WAY FORWARD, AI Index: ASA 21/006/2004, April 1, 2004.

Argentine National Commission on the Disappeared, *Nunca Mas: Report of the Argentine National Commission on the Disappeared*, reprinted in TRANSITIONAL JUSTICE: HOW EMERGING DEMOCRACIES RECKON WITH FORMER REGIMES, LAWS, RULINGS AND REPORTS, Vol. 3, 3 (Neil J. Kritz ed., 1995).

Binaifer Nowrojee, *"Your Justice Is Too Slow?" Will the ICTR Fail Rwanda's Rape Victims?* Occasional Paper 10, UNITED NATIONS RESEARCH INSTITUTE FOR SOCIAL DEVELOPMENT 14–17 (November 2005).

Coalition for International Criminal Justice, *Frequently Asked Questions- ICTR*, available at http://www.cij.org/index.cfm?fuseaction=faqs&tribunalID=2#q7.

———, *Status of U.S. Bilateral Immunity Agreements*, April 14,, 2006, available at http://www.iccnow.org/documents/CICCFS_BIAstatusCurrent.pdf.

Commission for Reception, Truth, and Reconciliation in Timor-Leste, CAVR Update/April–May 2003, available at http://www.easttimor-reconciliation.org/cavrUpdate-AprilMay2003-eng.pdf.

———, CAVR Update/August–September 2003, available at http://www.easttimor-reconciliation.org/cavrUpdate-AugSep2003-en.pdf.

———, CAVR Update/June–July 2003, available at http://www.easttimor-reconciliation.org/cavrUpdate-OctNov2003-en.pdf.

———, CAVR Update/December 2003–January 2004, available at http://www.easttimor-reconciliation.org/cavrUpdate-Dec03Jan04-en.html.

Final Report of the Commission of Experts Established Pursuant to Security Council Resolution 780, U.N. Doc. S/1994/674 (1994).

Guatemalan Commission for Historical Clarification, *Guatemala: Memory of Silence*, available at http://shr.aaas.org/guatemala/ceh/report/english/intro.html.

Hirst, Megan & Vareny, Howard, International Center for Transitional Justice, *Justice Abandoned? An Assessment of the Serious Crimes Process in East Timor*, June 2005.

Honeyman, Catherine et al., *Gacaca Jurisdictions: Transitional Justice in Rwanda, Interim Report of Observations, June 10–August 8, 2002*, available at http://www.angelfire.com/journal2/honeymandocs/PDF_Gacaca_Report.pdf.

Human Rights Watch, *Bringing Justice: The Special Court for Sierra Leone, Accomplishments, Shortcomings and Needed Support*, Vol. 16, No. 8(A), September 2004.

———, *Croatia: Conviction Spotlights Justice Failings*, July 19, 2004, available at http://hrw.org/english/docs/2004/07/19/croati.9083.htm.

———, *Discreet Path to Justice?: Chile Thirty Years after the Military Coup*, Briefing Paper, September 2003, available at http://hrw.org/backgrounder/americas/chile/chile0903.pdf.

———, *Getting Away with Murder, Mutilation, Rape*, (1999), available at http://www.hrw.org/reports/1999/sierra.

———, *The Trial of Dominik Ilijasević*, BALKANS JUSTICE BULLETIN, January 2004, available at http://hrw.org/backgrounder/eca/balkans0104.htm.

———, *Truth and Partial Justice in Argentina: An Update*, 1991.

——, *World Report 2003, Rwanda*, available at http://www.hrw.org/wr2k3/africa9.html.

HUMAN RIGHTS WATCH AFRICA, Vol. 6, No. 11, ETHIOPIA: RECKONING UNDER THE LAW, December 1994.

Human Rights Watch News, *Chile: Court Ruling May Define Future of Rights Prosecutions*, May 27, 2004, available at http://www.hrw.org/english/docs/2004/05/27/chile8622.htm.

International Criminal Tribunal for the former Yugoslavia (ICTY), ICTY at a Glance, General Information, updated May 8, 2006, available at http://www.un.org/icty/glance-e/index.htm (Follow General Information hyperlink).

Ivanisević, Bogdan & Mattioli, Géraldine, *Real Progress in The Hague*, March 29, 2005, available at http://hrw.org/english/docs/2005/03/29/serbia10386.htm.

Judicial System Monitoring Programme, *Departure of International Judge Means Special Panels for Serious Crimes in East Timor Unable to Function*, April 21, 2003, available at http://www.jsmp.minihub.org/News/News/21_04_03nb.htm.

——, *The Future of the Serious Crimes Unit*, JSMP Issue Report, January 2004.

——, *The General Prosecutor v. Joni Marques and 9 Others* (The Los Palos Case), JSMP Trial Report (March 2002).

——, THE LOLOTOE CASE: A SMALL STEP FORWARD (July 2004), available at http://www.jsmp.minihub.org/Reports/jsmpreports/Lolotoe%20Reports/Lolotoe%20report%20%20FINAL.pdf.

——, *Justice in the Districts 2003*, December 2003, available at http://www.jsmp.minihub.org/Reports/jsmpreports/Justice%20in%20District%20Reports/Justice%20in%20Districts%20_E_.pdf.

——, Special Panels for Serious Cases—Weekly Report, January 27–31, 2003 (January 27–31 2003) available at http://www.jsmp.minihub.org/Reports/spscweeksumm/SPSC27-31Jan03jr10feb03.pdf.

——, *The Special Panels for Serious Crimes Hear Their Final Case*, JUSTICE UPDATE, Issue 12/2005 (2005), available at http://www.jsmp.minihub.org/Justice%20update/2005/May%202005/050520_JSMP_JUissue12(e).pdf.

Human Rights First, A HUMAN RIGHTS FIRST REPORT ON THE ICTR AND NATIONAL TRIALS, 1997, available at http://www.humanrightsfirst.org/pubs/descriptions/rwanda.htm.

Office of the Deputy General Prosecutor for Serious Crimes Timor Leste, *Serious Crimes Unit Update*, April 30, 2004.

ORGANIZATION FOR SECURITY AND CO-OPERATION IN EUROPE, MISSION TO CROATIA, BACKGROUND REPORT: DOMESTIC WAR CRIME TRIALS 2003, JUNE 22, 2004.

——, MISSION TO CROATIA: SUPPLEMENTARY REPORT: WAR CRIME PROCEEDINGS IN CROATIA AND FINDINGS FROM TRIAL MONITORING, June 22, 2004.

PENAL REFORM INTERNATIONAL, PRI RESEARCH TEAM ON GACACA: REPORT III (April–June 2002), available at http://www.penalreform.org/download/Gacaca/Apr-Jun2002.pdf.

——, PRI RESEARCH TEAM ON GACACA: REPORT IV (January 2003), available at http://www.penalreform.org/download/Gacaca/Jan2003.pdf.

———, RESEARCH ON THE GACACA: REPORT V (September 2003), available at http://www .penalreform.org/download/Gacaca/september2003.pdf.

———, RESEARCH REPORT ON GACACA COURTS: GACACA AND RECONCILIATION: KIBUYE CASE STUDY (May 2004), available at http://www.penalreform.org/download/Gacaca/ Rapport%20Kibuye%20II_EN.pdf.

———, RESEARCH REPORT ON THE GACACA, REPORT VI: FROM CAMP TO HILL, THE RE-INTEGRATION OF RELEASED PRISONERS (May 2004).

SIERRA LEONE TRUTH AND RECONCILIATION COMMISSION, REPORT, Vol. 2 (2004), available at http://www.trcsierraleone.org/pdf/FINAL%20VOLUME%20TWO/VOLUME %202.pdf.

Status of Detainees, available at http://69.94.11.53/default.htm.

TRUTH AND RECONCILIATION COMMISSION OF SOUTH AFRICA, REPORT, Vol. 1 (2003).

UNITED NATIONS DEVELOPMENT PROGRAMME, REPORT, THE COMMUNITY RECONCILI-ATION PROCESS OF THE COMMISSION FOR RECEPTION, TRUTH, AND RECONCILIA-TION, April 2004, available at http://www.undp.east-timor.org/documentsreports/ governance_capacitydevelopment/Piers%20report%20Final.pdf.

United Nations Commission on the Truth for El Salvador, *Report: From Madness to Hope*, U.N. Doc. S/25500, Annexes (1993).

United Nations High Commissioner for Human Rights Field Operation in Rwanda (UNHRFOR), *Genocide Trials to 30 June 1997*, Status Report at July 15, 1997.

U.S. Department of State, *Country Reports on Human Rights Practices—2004, Ethiopia*, available at http://www.state.gov/g/drl/rls/hrrpt/2004/41603.htm.

Zalaquett, José, *Introduction* to Chilean National Commission on Truth and Reconcilia-tion, Report, Vol. 1 (Philip Berryman trans., 1993).

Treaties and Other International Agreements

Agreement between the United Nations and the Government of Sierra Leone on the Es-tablishment of a Special Court for Sierra Leone, January 16, 2002, available at http:// www.specialcourt.org/documents/Agreement.htm.

Agreement between the United Nations and the Royal Government of Cambodia Con-cerning the Prosecution under Cambodian Law of Crimes Committed during the Pe-riod of Democratic Kampuchea, June 6, 2003.

Agreement for the Prosecution and Punishment of the Major War Criminals of the Eu-ropean Axis Powers, August 8, 1945, 54 Stat. 1544, 82 United Nations Treaty Series 280.

Charter of the International Military Tribunal for the Far East, January 19, 1946, Treaties and Other International Acts Series No. 1589, 4 Bevans 20 (as amended April 26, 1946, 4 Bevans 27).

Code of Offenses against the Peace and Security of Mankind, U.N. General Assembly Resolution 177 (II), U.N. Doc. A/CN.4/4 (1947).

Convention against Torture and Other Cruel, Inhuman or Degrading Treatment or Pun-ishment, December 10, 1984, United Nations Treaty Series 85, U.N. General Assembly Resolution 39/46, U.N. Doc. A/39/51 (1984).

Convention (No. IV) Respecting the Laws and Customs of War on Land, with Annex of Regulations, October 18, 1907, 36 Stat. 2277, TS No. 539.

Convention on the Prevention and Punishment of the Crime of Genocide, December 9, 1948, 102 *U.S. Statutes at Large* 3045, 78 United Nations Treaty Series 277.

Definition of Aggression, U.N. General Assembly Resolution 3314 (XXIX), December 14, 1974, Supp. No. 31, U.N. Doc. A/9631.

Draft Code of Crimes against the Peace and Security of Mankind, Report of the International Law Commission on its Forty-eighth Session, May 6–July 26, 1996, Supp. No. 10, U.N. Doc. A/51/10.

1874 Declaration of Brussels, Project of an International Declaration Concerning the Laws and Customs of War, August 27, 1874, 4 Martens Nouveau Recueil (ser. 2) 219.

Federal Republic of Germany and German Democratic Republic, Treaty on the Establishment of German Unity, *done at* Berlin, August 31, 1990, reprinted in 30 I.L.M. 457 (1991).

Geneva Convention for the Amelioration of the Condition of the Wounded, Sick and Shipwrecked Members of Armed Forces at Sea, August 12, 1949, 6 U.S. Treaties and Other International Agreements 3217, 75 United Nations Treaty Series 85.

Geneva Convention for the Amelioration of the Condition of the Wounded and Sick in Armed Forces in the Field, August 12, 1949, 6 U.S. Treaties and Other International Agreements 3114, 75 United Nations Treaty Series 31.

Geneva Convention for the Amelioration of the Condition of the Wounded of Armies in the Field, August 22, 1864, 18 Martens Nouveau Recueil (ser. 1) 607.

Geneva Convention Relative to the Protection of Civilian Persons in Time of War, August 12, 1949, 6 U.S. Treaties and Other International Agreements 3516, 75 United Nations Treaty Series 287.

Geneva Convention Relative to the Treatment of Prisoners of War, August 12, 1949, 6 U.S. Treaties and Other International Agreements 3316, 75 United Nations Treaty Series 135.

International Convention on the Suppression and Punishment of the Crime of Apartheid, November 30, 1973, 1015 United Nations Treaty Series 243.

1950 Convention for the Suppression of the Traffic in Persons and of the Exploitation of the Prostitution of Others, March 21, 1950, 96 United Nations Treaty Series 271, 274.

1956 Supplementary Convention on the Abolition of Slavery, the Slave Trade, and Institutions and Practices Similar to Slavery, September 7, 1956, 18 U.S. Treaties and Other International Agreements 3201, 266 United Nations Treaty Series 3.

Rome Statute of the International Criminal Court, July 17, 1998, U.N. Doc. A/Conf.183/9.

St. Petersburg Declaration, Declaration Renouncing the Use, in Time of War, of Explosive Projectiles under 400 Grammes Weight, November 29, 1868, 18 Martens Nouveau Recueil (ser. 1) 474.

Statute of the International Criminal Tribunal for the Former Yugoslavia, art. 29(2), adopted by U.N. Security Council Resolution 827, U.N. Doc. S/RES/827 (May 25, 1993).

Statute of the Special Court for Sierra Leone, January 16, 2002, available at www.sc-sl.org/scsl-statute.html.

Statutes, Statutory Materials, and Constitutions

Chile
Law of Amnesty, No. 2.191 (April 18, 1978).

Czech and Slovak Federal Republic
Law on Extrajudicial Rehabilitation (*"Large Restitution Law"*), 1991, reprinted in CENTRAL AND EASTERN EUROPEAN LEGAL TEXTS (March 1991).
International Criminal Court (ICC), RULES OF PROCEDURE AND EVIDENCE 183, available at http://www.iccnow.org/documents/RulesofProcedureEvidence_English.pdf.

International Criminal Tribunal for the Former Yugoslavia (ICTY)
RULES OF PROCEDURE AND EVIDENCE 28 (2004), available at available at http://www .un.org/icty/legaldoc-e/basic/rpe/ITo32Rev37e.pdf.
RULES OF PROCEDURE AND EVIDENCE 62(iii).
RULES OF PROCEDURE AND EVIDENCE 62*bis* (December 4, 1998).
RULES OF PROCEDURE AND EVIDENCE 62*ter* (December 13, 2001).

International Criminal Tribunal for Rwanda (ICTR)
RULES OF PROCEDURE AND EVIDENCE 15*bis* (2003), available at http://69.94.11.53/ ENGLISH/rules/index.htm.
RULES OF PROCEDURE AND EVIDENCE 62(A)(iii) (October 6, 1995).
RULES OF PROCEDURE AND EVIDENCE 62(B)(iii) (July 1, 1999).
RULES OF PROCEDURE AND EVIDENCE 62*bis* (May 27, 2003).

Rwanda
Organic Law No. 08/96 of August 30, 1996, on the Organization of Prosecutions for Offences Constituting the Crime of Genocide or Crimes against Humanity Committed Since October 1, 1996, available at http://www.preventgenocide.org/law/domestic/ rwanda.htm.
Organic Law No. 16/2004 of June 19, 2004, Establishing the Organisation, Competence and Functioning of *Gacaca* Courts Charged with Prosecuting and Trying the Perpetrators of the Crime of Genocide and Other Crimes against Humanity Committed between October 1, 1990 and December 31, 1994.
Organic Law No. 40/2000 of January 26, 2001, Establishing *Gacaca* Jurisdictions for the Prosecution of Genocide Offences and Crimes against Humanity Committed between 1 October 1990 and 31 December 1994.
Presidential Order No. 26/01 of October 12, 2001, Relating to the Substitution of the Penalty of Imprisonment for Community Service.

South Africa
Constitution of the Republic of South Africa, available at http://www.polity.co.za/html/ govdocs/constitution/saconst.html.
Promotion of National Unity and Reconciliation Act, No. 34, of 1995, available at www .doj.gov.za/trc/legal/act9534.htm.

Restitution of Land Rights Act 22 of 1994, assented to November 17, 1994, available at http://www.info.gov.za/acts/1994/a22-94.pdf.

United Nations Transitional Administration of East Timor (UNTAET)

UNTAET Regulation 1999/3 on the Establishment of a Transitional Judicial Service Commission (December 3, 1999), available at http://www.pict-pcti.org/courts/pdf/eastimor/19993.htm.

UNTAET Regulation 2000/11 on the Organization of the Courts in East Timor (March 6, 2000), available at http://www.pict-pcti.org/courts/pdf/eastimor/200011.pdf.

UNTAET Regulation No. 2000/15 on the Establishment of Panels with Exclusive Jurisdiction over Serious Criminal Offenses (June 6, 2000), available at http://www.un.org/peace/etimor/untaetR/Reg0015E.pdf.

UNTAET Regulation 2000/30 on the Transitional Rules of Criminal Procedure (September 25, 2000) available at http://www.un.org/peace/etimor/untaetR/reg200030.pdf.

UNTAET Regulation No. 2000/30 on the Transitional Rules of Criminal Procedure, as amended by Regulation 2001/25 of September 14, 2001, available at http://www.un.org/peace/etimor/untaetR/2001-25.pdf.

UNTAET Regulation No. 2001/10 on the Establishment of a Commission for Reception, Truth, and Reconciliation in East Timor (July 13, 2001), available at http://www.un.org/peace/etimor/untaetR/Reg10e.pdf.

United States

Apologizing for Those Who Suffered as Slaves under the Constitution and Laws of the United States until 1865, U.S. House, H.R. Con. Res. 96, 105th Cong. (1997).

Civil Liberties Act of 1988, Public Law No. 100-383, 102 *U.S. Statutes at Large* 903 (1988), codified at 50 *U.S. Code* § 1989B (2000).

Foreign Operations, Export Financing, and Related Programs Appropriations Act, U.S. House, H.R. 4818, § 5054(e), 108th Cong. (2004).

Foreign Operations, Export Financing, and Related Programs Appropriations Act, U.S. Senate, S. 2812 § 554(e), 108th Cong. (2004).

Torture Victims Protection Act of 1991, Public Law No. 102-256, 106 *U.S. Statutes at Large* 73 (1992).

U.S. Code Annotated 18 § 3553(e) (West Supp. 2003).

U.S. Code 28 § 1350 (2000).

U.S. Sentencing Guidelines Manual § 5K1.1 (2003).

United Nations Documents

Annan, Kofi A., Letter dated 12 July 2001 from the Secretary-General addressed to the President of the Security Council, U.N. Doc. S/2001/693 (July 12, 2001).

Annex to the Letter dated 9 August 2000 from the Permanent Representative of Sierra Leone to the United Nations addressed to the President of the Security Council, U.N. Doc. S/2000/786, Annex (August 10, 2000).

Completion Strategy of the International Criminal Tribunal for Rwanda, U.N. Doc. S/2003/946, Enclosure to Letter from Erik Møse, President, ICTR, to the Secretary-General, Letter Dated 3 October 2003, Annex, (October 6, 2003).

Financing the International Criminal Tribunal, Report of the Secretary-General on the Activities of the Office of Internal Oversight Services, U.N. Doc. A/51/789 (February 6, 1997).

International Commission of Inquiry on East Timor, *Report of the International Commission of Inquiry on East Timor to the Secretary-General*, U.N. Doc. A/54/726-S/2000/59 (January 31, 2000).

International Criminal Tribunal for the Prosecution of Persons Responsible for Genocide and Other Serious Violations of International Humanitarian Law Committed in the Territory of Rwanda and Rwandan Citizens Responsible for Genocide and Other Such Violations Committed in the Territory of Neighbouring States between 1 January and 31 December 1994, Fifth Annual Report, U.N. Doc. A/55/435-S/2000/927 (October 2, 2000).

———, Sixth Annual Report, U.N. Doc. A/56/351-S/2001/863 (September 14, 2001).

———, Seventh Annual Report, U.N. Doc. A/57/163-S/2002/733 (July 2, 2002).

———, Tenth Annual Report, U.N. Doc. A/60/229-S/2005/534 (August 15, 2005).

International Law Commission, Report on the Work of Its Sixth Session, U.N. Doc. A/2693 (June 3–July 28, 1954), reprinted in [1954] 2 Y.B. INT'L L. COMM'N 140, U.N. Doc. A/CN.4/SER.A/1954.

International Tribunal for the Prosecution of Persons Responsible for Serious Violations of International Humanitarian Law Committed in the Territory of the Former Yugoslavia since 1991, Report, U.N. Doc. A/49/342 (August 29, 1994).

———, Ninth Annual Report, Summary, U.N. Doc. A/57/379-S/2002/985 (August 14, 2002).

———, Eleventh Annual Report, U.N. Doc. A/59/219, S/2004/627 (August 13, 2004).

Lasso, José Ayala, Report of the United Nations Commissioner for Human Rights, Mr. José Ayala Lasso, on his Mission to Rwanda, May 11–12, 1994, U.N. Doc. E/CN.4/S-3/3 (1994).

Letter dated 22 December 2000 from the President of the Security Council Addressed to the Secretary-General, U.N. Doc. S/2000/1234 (December 22, 2000), available at http://documents-dds-ny.un.org/doc/UNDOC/GEN/N00/812/77/pdf/N0081277.pdf?OpenElement.

Meron, Theodor, Assessments and Report of Judge Theodor Meron, President of the International Criminal Tribunal for the Former Yugoslavia, provided to the Security Council pursuant to paragraph 6 of Security Council Resolution 1534, U.N. Doc. S/2004/420, Enclosure (May 24, 2004).

Møse, Erik, Letter dated 30 April 2004 from the President of the International Criminal Tribunal for the Prosecution of Persons Responsible for Genocide and Other Serious Violations of International Humanitarian Law Committed in the Territory of Rwanda and Rwandan Citizens Responsible for Genocide and Other Such Violations Committed in the Territory of Neighbouring States between 1 January and 31 December 1994 addressed to the President of the Security Council, U.N. Doc. S/2004/341 (May 3, 2004).

———, Letter dated 5 December 2005 from the President of the International Criminal Tribunal for the Prosecution of Persons Responsible for Genocide and Other Serious

Violations of International Humanitarian Law Committed in the Territory of Rwanda and Rwandan Citizens Responsible for Genocide and Other Such Violations Committed in the Territory of Neighbouring States between 1 January and 31 December 1994 addressed to the President of the Security Council, U.N. Doc. S/2005/782 (Dec. 14, 2005).

Report of the Secretary-General on the Establishment of a Special Court for Sierra Leone, U.N. Doc. S/2000/915 (October 4, 2000).

Report of the Secretary-General on the Establishment of the Commission of Experts Pursuant to Paragraph 1 of Security Council Resolution 935 (1994) of July 1, 1994, U.N. Doc. S/1994/879 (July 26, 1994).

Report of the Secretary-General Pursuant to Security Council Resolution 749, U.N. Doc. S/23900 (May 12, 1992).

Report on the Operation of the International Criminal Tribunal for the Former Yugoslavia Submitted by Judge Claude Jorda, President, on Behalf of the Judges of the Tribunal, U.N. Doc. A/55/382-S/2000/865, Annex I (May 12, 2000), available at http://www.un.org/icty/pressreal/RAP000620e.htm.

Secretary-General, The Rule of Law and Transitional Justice in Conflict and Post-Conflict Societies, delivered to the Security Council, U.N. Doc. S/2004/616 (August 23, 2004).

Secretary-General's Report on Aspects of Establishing an International Tribunal for the Prosecution of Persons Responsible for Serious Violations of International Humanitarian Law Committed in the Territory of the Former Yugoslavia, U.N. Doc. S/25704 (1993).

Security Council, Resolution 1272, U.N. Doc. S/RES/1272 (October 25, 1999).

——, Resolution 764, U.N. Doc. S/RES/764 (July 13, 1992).

——, Resolution 260B (III), G.A. Res. 260B (III), U.N. Doc. A/760 (December 9, 1948).

——, Resolution 771, U.N. Doc. S/RES/771 (August 13, 1992).

——, Resolution 780, U.N. Doc. S/RES/780 (October 6, 1992).

——, Resolution 781, U.N. Doc. S/RES/781 (October 9, 1992).

——, Resolution 808, U.N. Doc. S/RES/808 (February 22, 1993).

——, Resolution 955, Annex, art. 1, U.N. Doc. S/RES/955 (November 8, 1994).

——, Resolution 1166, U.N. Doc. S/RES/1166 (May 13, 1998).

——, Resolution 1315, U.N. Doc. S/RES/1315 (August 14, 2000).

——, Resolution 1329, U.N. Doc. S/RES/1329 (November 30, 2000).

——, Resolution 1411, U.N. Doc. S/RES/1411 (May 17, 2002).

——, Resolution 1431, U.N. Doc. S/RES/1431 (August 14, 2002).

——, Resolution 1481, U.N. Doc. S/RES/1481 (2003).

——, Resolution 1503, U.N. Doc. S/RES/1503 (August 28, 2003).

——, Resolution 1534, U.N. Doc. S/RES/1534 (March 26, 2004).

Situation of Human Rights in East Timor: Note by the Secretary-General, U.N. Doc A/54/660 (Dec. 10, 1999).

U.N. Economic and Social Council, Commission on Human Rights, E/CN.4/1999/33, Report on the Situation of Human Rights in Rwanda Submitted by the Special Representative, Mr. Michel Moussalli, pursuant to Resolution 1998/69, U.N. Doc. E/CN.4/1999/33 (1999).

Index

acknowledgment of crimes: by paying reparations, 19, 147; truth-telling, 163, 172; value of, 178, 183, 186, 187. *See also* confessions
Adeogun-Phillips, Charles, 103–4, 105
African National Congress (ANC), 23
aggression, defined, 233n22
Ahmići municipality, 70, 83, 131
Akayesu, Jean-Paul, 106
akazu, inner circle in Rwanda, 108–10, 206
Akhavan, Payam, 229n1
Aleksovski, Zlatko, 72–73
Allende, Salvador, 13
Alschuler, Albert, 127, 282n756
Alywin, Patricio, 13, 21
Amin, Idi, 5, 12
amnesty: in Argentina, 229n4; in Chile for Pinochet, 13, 43–44, 230n4; disclosure requirements, 150–51; in Latin American countries, 234n32, 235n38; in South Africa, 23, 42, 52, 130, 150–51
Annan, Kofi, 36
apartheid, 17
apologies, 6; in restorative-justice programs, 138, 144–48; as symbolic reparations, 19–21, 175. *See also* confessions; statements of remorse
apologies as restorative element in guilty-plea processes: in Argentina, 177–78; in Bosnia, 180–82, 199–202; in East

Timor, 211, 221; in Rwanda, 185, 208–9, 213
appeals: in ICTY guilty-plea cases, 86–90
Argentina: optimal restorative-justice guilty-plea system, 177–79; reparations, 17; summary of atrocities, 157–59; Truth Commission, 158
Argentine forced disappearances: financial burdens on victims, 175; restorative justice values, 172, 173, 174; summary of, 157–59
Argentine junta trial, creating collective memory, 56
Argentine military junta: prosecutions using hierarchy of, 173; role in disappearances, 157–59, 184; secrecy of crimes, 177
arrest and surrender, 34, 35
Arusha, Tanzania, 94, 108, 112, 113, 203
Arusha Accords, 163
Asian Women's Fund, 20
Atolan, Agustinho, 123, 124–25, 212
Australian view of plea bargaining, 282n746

Babić, Milan: apology of, 202; inculpating other defendants, 82, 193; plea bargain, 81–83, 87, 88, 89, 90; reconciliation and truth-telling of guilty plea, 190
Babo-Soares, Dionísio, 169

Bagambiki, Emmanuel, 101, 105
Bagaragaza, Michel, 108–9, 112–13, 206
Banović, Predrag: no prior criminal
    record, 257n285; plea bargain, 75, 87;
    statement of remorse, 202; truth-
    telling as restorative element, 196, 197,
    198–99; victim reaction to lenient sen-
    tence, 132, 133
Barayagwiza, Jean-Bosco, 112
Baruch, Chad, 128
Bassiouni, M. Cherif, 160, 236n47–48
Basson, Dr. Wouter, 42
Baucau District Court, 168, 297n929
Belgian canal death, 109
Benzien, Jeffrey, 24, 289n812
Berbić, Saha, 70
Bere, Manuel, 121
Bigogwe military camp, 164
Bikumbi commune, 102, 204
Bisengimana, Paul: plea bargain, 101–6,
    111, 112; restorative elements in guilty-
    plea process, 203–4, 208
Blagojević, Vidoje, 78, 192, 193
Blair, Tony, 19
Blaškić, Tihomir, 28, 83
Bobonaro, 222
Borovcanin, Ljubomir, 304n1033
Bosanski Šamac, 63, 64, 71, 76
Bosnia: acknowledgment of crimes, 172,
    179; Federal Commission of Missing
    Persons, 83; optimal restorative-justice
    guilty-plea system, 179–82; refugee
    returns, 132; summary of atrocities,
    159–63
Bosnia-Herzegovina: and historical re-
    cord, 54; special court, 30–31; steps to-
    ward independence, 14, 159, 160, 161
Bosnian Croat army, 85, 193–94
Bosnian Croat Defense Council, 70
Bosnian Croats: at Bosanski Šamac, 63,
    64; in Bosnian war, 160–61; in Bralo
    case, 83; in ethnic-cleansing campaign,
    73–74; Plavšić apology, 144–45
Bosnian Muslims: acknowledgment of
    massacres, 179–80; at Bosanski Šamac,
    63, 64; in Bosnian war, 160–61; in Bralo
    case, 70; in Deronjić case, 69, 88; in
    ethnic-cleansing campaign, 73–74; at

Luka detention camp, 61; Plavšić apol-
    ogy, 144–45; at Srebenica massacres,
    60, 76; at Stupni Do, 85
Bosnian Serb Army, 78, 79
Bosnian Serb Police Reserve Unit, 74–75
Bosnian Serbs: in Bosnian war, 160–61;
    confronted by victims, 174; in ethnic-
    cleansing campaign, 73–74; in Jelisić
    case, 61; Plavšić apology, 144–45; Ser-
    bia's arming of, 67, 193; siege of Sara-
    jevo, 162; in Simić case, 63; at Srebenica
    massacres, 60. See also ethnic-cleansing
    campaigns in Bosnian war
Bosnian war: deterrence goal of ICTY,
    47–48; numbers of victims, 161; role in
    international justice, 14. See also Sre-
    brenica massacres
Botha, P. W., 24, 42, 151
Braithwaite, John, 49, 137, 140
Bralo, Miroslav, 70–71, 83–85, 131
Bratunac Brigade, 76
Bratunac municipality, 67–68, 88, 195
Brazil amnesty, 234n32
Brčko, Bosnia, 61
Brčko Police Station, 75
Brđanin case, 28
bride price in East Timor, 168, 298n942
British view of plea bargaining, 282n746
Burger, Warren, 152
burials. See funerals
Bush, George H. W., 19

Cambodia, 2, 5, 16, 40, 252n238
Canada, apologies to Aboriginals, 19
Cardoso, José, 209
Caride, Susan, 291n845
Carvalho, Lino de, 120
Cassese, Antonio, 60
Catholic apology, 19
Čelebići prison camp, 73, 173
cell-level gacacas, 214–16
census process in Rwanda, 215–16, 218
ceremonial handover on Timorese border,
    219
Češić, Ranko, 74–75, 80, 181, 196, 198, 201
Chad, and Hissène Habré, 12
charge bargaining: Bisengimana case,
    103–6; in East Timor, 119–20; at ICTY,

63–71; prosecutor abuses, 127–28; *Ruta-ganira* case, 99–101; in Rwanda, 97–110, 111–12

Child-Friendly Version of truth commission report, 22

child soldiers, 36

Chile: domestic court system, 43–44; financial constraints, 3; and Pinochet, 12–13, 43–44, 172; reparations, 17, 237n59

circle sentencing, 286n778

claim of compulsion: in East Timor cases, 187, 211; in Rwandan cases, 184–85

Clemente Noel, Roberto, 172

Clinton, Bill, 19

Cobban, Helena, 208

code of international crimes, 11

Cold War, role in international justice, 14

collective memory, 55–56

comfort women, apology to, 20

Commission for Reception, Truth, and Reconciliation (CAVR), 186, 219–20

community participation, in *gacaca*, 217–18

Community Reconciliation Agreement, 221

Community Reconciliation Process (CRP), 220–22, 299n956

community service, 147, 176, 185, 215, 221

compensation: East Timorese obligation, 175, 187, 221. *See also* reparations

complementarity principle, 31–32

compulsion, acting under. *See* claim of compulsion

confessions: in Rwanda, 183, 213–16, 218. *See also* guilty pleas

context of domestic vs. international crimes: plea bargaining in, 129–30; summary, 224–25

context of large-scale violence, 45, 131

Contreras, Manuel, 230n4

conventions on human rights, 11–12

Corey, Allison, 216

Ćorić, Valentin, 193

corporate crime, deterrence of, 49

Correia, Abilio Mendez, 120

Counter-Reformation apology, 19

courtroom morality plays, 55

cover-ups by governments, 74, 194, 197

crime, concept of in East Timor, 169–70

crimes against humanity, 11

crimes against the peace, 11

criminal accountability, 2, 16; in amnesty process, 24; and plea bargaining, 130; and political constraints, 176–77; in restorative-justice guilty-plea system, 141–43. *See also* restorative justice, model guilty-plea system; restorative justice, optimal guilty-plea systems

Croatia: apology from, 20; domestic court transfers, 30; involvement in Bosnian war, 193; secession declaration, 81; steps toward independence, 159, 160, 161

Croatian Serbs, 81–82

Croats in Bosnia. *See* Bosnian Croats

Cronje, Brigadier, 290n834

culpability: Organic Law categories, 212. *See also* inculpating other defendants

Cvjetan, Sasa, 30

Czechoslovakia, restitution and reparations, 17

da Costa, Agustinho, 121

da Costa, João, 116, 122

da Costa, Paolo, 122–23

Da Costa Nunes, Damiao, 125

Dayton Peace Accords, 30, 161

Debelo Brdo, 192

de Deus, Marcurious José, 119, 123

defendants: historical record and rights of, 54–55; untrue testimony, 194–95

defense attorneys: abusing the system, 128; appointed vs. retained, 128; and resource constraints, 38–39

de Kock, Eugene, 20–21, 42, 253n249

Delalić, Zejnil, 173

Delić, Hazim, 73

Del Ponte, Carla, 31, 47, 112

democratization: of Latin America, 12–13; and public reckoning of mass violence, 55

De Morais, Dora Martins, 124

deponents, 314n1206

Dergue regime in Ethiopia, 43

Deronjić, Miroslav: appeal of, 87; charge bargaining, 67–69; restorative elements in guilty-plea process, 190, 193, 194–95, 196, 197; sentence bargaining, 80–81

detention: East Timorese view of, 170; of Rwandan suspects, 153

detention centers in Argentina, 158

deterrence, 47–49, 131

Di Giovanni, Janine, 294n885

Dili, East Timor, 167

Dili District Court, East Timor, 37–40, 210

disappearances: in Argentina, 157–59, 172, 173, 174; in Latin America, 24, 130

disclosure requirements: of amnesty, 23–24; in restorative-justice programs, 149–51

do Carmo, Antonio Helder Viera, 124

domestic courts: transfer of cases in Bosnia-Herzegovina, 83, 153; transfer of cases in Rwanda, 30, 108–9. *See also* hybrid international-domestic courts

domestic criminal justice system: and restorative-justice programs, 138–41; threat of prosecution, 152–53

domestic prosecutions, 41–44; and plea bargaining, 129

domestic rehabilitation, 51–52

Došen, Damir, 72, 75, 151

Dos Santos, Augusto, 119, 123, 211

Drina Corps, 75

Drina River incident, 265n425

Drumbl, Mark, 311n1147

Dubrovnik, Croatia, 66–67

Eastern Europe, restitution and reparations, 17

East Timor: Community Reconciliation Process (CRP), 220–22, 299n956; financial burdens on victims, 175; judicial system, 167–68; local justice system, 168–70, 175, 185, 219, 222; optimal restorative-justice guilty-plea system, 185–87; summary of atrocities, 166–70; vote of independence, 16, 114, 166. *See also* plea bargaining at Special Panels in East Timor; Special Panels in East Timor

East Timorese defendants: confronted by victims, 174; guilty pleas of, 224

East Timorese militias: organization and direction of, 173; violence of, 167, 186

East Timor hybrid court, 37–40, 41, 42

Egonda-Ntende, 115–16

Eichmann trial, creating collective memory, 56

El Salvador: amnesty, 234n32; Commission on the Truth, 22

Ena, Umbertus, 281n741

Erdemović, Dražen, 58, 60–61, 85, 86, 189

Ethiopia: domestic court system, 43; and Mengistu Haile Miriam, 12

ethnic-cleansing campaigns in Bosnian war: of Ahmići village, 70; Babić's role in Krajina region, 81, 88; of Bosanski Šamac and Odžak, 71; in Bratunac municipality, 195; financial burdens on victims, 175; pattern of, 160–63; Plavšić's role, 73, 144–45; prison camps in Bosnia, 161–62; and refugee returns, 132; by Serbs, 67–68

extradition, 34

Extraordinary Chambers in Cambodia, 2, 16, 40

Faal, Essa, 280n714

family group conferencing, 286n778

fear of retaliation, 149–50, 213, 217

Federal Republic of Yugoslavia, 160

Fernandes, João, 115–16, 117, 119, 121, 124

financial compensation, as reparations, 16–17, 18, 19, 147, 175–76

financial realities, 27–44; Cambodia courts, 40–41; domestic prosecutions, 41–44; funding of tribunals, 2, 15, 247n165; guilty pleas in ICTY, 189–90; ICC, 31–35; ICTY and ICTR, 27–31; for judicial system in East Timor, 167–68; obstacle in guilty-plea system, 152–54; Special Court for Sierra Leone, 35–37; Special Panels in East Timor, 37–40, 209

Fisse, Brent, 49

Florit, Francesco, 124

Foca municipality, 73

Franca, Jhoni, 118, 120, 211

France, 109

funerals: desired by victims' relatives, 186, 192; in siege of Sarajevo, 162

gacaca courts in Rwanda: compared to ICTR victim participation, 203; description of, 214–19; motivating guilty pleas, 133, 153–54; reason to establish, 43
general strikes, 152
Geneva Conventions, 11, 41, 98, 232n18, 232n21
genocide, charges of: in Rwanda, 96, 97–98, 111–12; in Srebenica massacres, 74; of Timorese by Indonesia, 166; withdrawn in ICTY cases, 65
Genocide Convention, 11, 15
Germany, 237n58; reparations, 17; unification of East and West, 17. *See also* Nuremburg tribunal
Gikoro commune, 101–6
Gisenyi prefecture massacres, 204
Gleeson, Ian, 290n834
Glogova village, 68, 88, 195
goals of prosecutions, 45–56; deterrence, 47–49; incapacitation, 49–51; rehabilitation, 51–53; retribution, 46–47; specific to societies emerging from violence, 53–56
Gobodo-Madikizela, Pumla, 20
Goldstone, Richard, 229n1
Gonçalves, Domingos, 120, 124
Gorbachev, Mikhail, 233n26
Gourevitch, Philip, 51, 164, 183
Graybill, Lyn, 21
Guatemala: amnesty, 235n38; inability to prosecute, 13; Truth Commission, 21–22, 238n70
guilty pleas: and compensation caps, 128; completion strategy of ICTY, 29; history of, 127; role of, 4–6; and truth telling, 130–31; and victim dissatisfaction, 74, 132–35. *See also* confessions; plea bargaining at ICTR; plea bargaining at ICTY; plea bargaining at Special Panels in East Timor; restorative justice, model guilty-plea system; restorative justice, optimal guilty-plea systems
guilty pleas and restorative elements in

current prosecutions: in East Timor's CAVR, 219–22; in East Timor Special Panels, 209–12; in ICTR, 202–9; in ICTY, 188–202; in Rwandan domestic and *gacaca* courts, 212–19
Gutman, Alan, 280n715, 280n718

Habibie, B. J., 166
Habré, Hissène, 12, 234n30
Habyarimana, Juvénal, 95, 108, 163–64, 295n901
Hadzić, Habiba, 191–92
The Hague, 1, 189
The Hague detention facilities, 108, 113
The Hague Peace Conferences, 232n18
Hampton, Jean, 255n270
Haradinaj, Ramush, 257n284
hate propaganda in Rwanda, 50, 52, 164, 165, 184
Hayner, Priscilla, 23, 239n92
healing of society, 26
Hecter, Jacques, 241n115
Herman, Judith, 147
hierarchical structures of mass violence, 173, 179
high-level perpetrators: implicated by ICTR defendants, 204; incapacitating hostile conduct of, 49–50; in Indonesia, 115; plea agreements and truth-telling, 196; prosecuted by testimony of subordinates, 173; retribution desired by victims, 46–47; victims' wrath at, 54. *See also* offenders
historical record: distortions of, 66, 207; established by Rwandan *gacacas*, 215; established by truth-telling commissions and trials, 24, 54–55; failure to develop at Special Panels, 209; and plea bargaining, 77
Hrastov case, 30
human-rights prosecutions. *See* prosecutions of international crimes
human-rights treaties, 11
Human Rights Watch, 43
Hunt, David, 194–95
Hutu, 15; close relationships to Tutsi, 183–85; community-service requirements,

147–48; disillusionment of *gacaca* justice, 217; executions of convicts, 214; historical summary, 163–66; incapacitation of perpetrators, 50; incarceration of, 52; incitement in genocide, 101, 164, 165, 205; numbers of perpetrators, 48–49, 212

hybrid international-domestic courts, 35–41; in Cambodia, 40; in East Timor, 37–40, 41; in Sierra Leone, 35–37, 41

Ibrahimefendić, Teufika, 142
ICC. *See* International Criminal Court
ICTR. *See* International Criminal Tribunal for Rwanda
ICTY. *See* International Criminal Tribunal for Yugoslavia
Ilomska River, 257n285
impunity, 11–14
incapacitation, 49–51
inculpating other defendants: insider testimony in ICTR cases, 204–7; insider testimony in ICTY cases, 179, 181, 192–95; value of truth-telling, 173
Indonesia: domestic prosecutions, 251n216; East Timor vote of independence, 37, 114, 166–67; invasion of East Timor, 166
Indonesian Criminal Code, 38, 114
Indonesian military (TNI), 166, 186
insider testimony. *See* testimony
Interahamwe militia: in *Bisengimana* case at Musha church, 101, 103, 104, 106; in *Ruggiu* case, 205; in *Serugendo* case, 106–7, 108; in *Serushago* case, 94
intergenerational justice, 18
International Criminal Court (ICC), 1, 16, 31–35
International Criminal Tribunal for Rwanda (ICTR): domestic court transfers, 30; establishment of, 1, 15–16, 27–28; funding of, 27–31; procedural rules for guilty pleas, 58; restorative elements in guilty-plea process, 202–9; retaliation against truth-telling defendants, 150. *See also* plea bargaining at ICTR
International Criminal Tribunal for Yugoslavia (ICTY): accounting of crimes in

plea bargains, 142; completion strategy, 29; deterrence goal, 47–48; domestic court transfers, 30; embrace of plea bargaining, 4; enforcement cooperation, 33–34; establishment of, 1, 14–15, 27–28; Evidence and Procedure rules, 58, 84; funding of, 27–31; and historical record, 54; insider testimony, 192–95; public expectations of guilty-plea system, 134–35; restorative elements in guilty-plea process, 188–202; retaliation against truth-telling defendants, 149; and rule of law, 53; sentencing leniency, 132, 133–34; statute articles 7(1) and 7(3), 87; summary, 224. *See also* plea bargaining at ICTY
International Law Commission (ILC), 232n22
international tribunals. *See* tribunals
interpreters/translators, 33, 38, 41, 168, 211
Inyangamugayo village elders, 214
Ivković, Sanja, 46
Izetbegović, Alija, 235n42

Japan apologies, 19–20
Japanese American internments, 18, 19
Japanese criminal justice system, and apologies, 146, 289n821
Jasenovac concentration camp, 295n893
Jelisić, Goran, 61–62, 63, 75, 86
Jews, harsh treatment of, 291n845
Jim Crow laws, 18
John Paul II, Pope, 19
Joireman, Sandra, 216
Jokers special-forces unit, 70
Jokić, Miodrag, 66–67, 80, 87, 88–89, 193
Joube, Joep, 290n834
judges: East Timor shortage of, 167; and resource constraints, 39
justice: East Timorese concept of, 168–70; establishing tribunals, 14–16; impunity norms, 11–14; in plea bargaining, 129, 130; reparations schemes, 16–21; in restorative-justice programs, 148; truth-telling commissions, 21–26
just sentence, defined by Alschuler, 282n756

Kambanda, Jean: plea bargain, 92–94, 110, 113; restorative elements of case, 202, 208, 209
Kampala, Uganda, 203
Kangara newspaper, 164
Kaonik prison, 73
Karadžić, Radovan, 73
Karemera et al., 207
Karlshoven, Fritz, 236n48
Keller, Andrew, 22
Keraterm detention camp: in *Banović* case, 75, 196, 197; mass execution at, 162; in *Sikirica* case, 72–73, 151, 200
Khmer Rouge, 5, 16, 40, 252n238
Khrushchev, Nikita, 233n26
Kigali, Rwanda, 107, 203
Kigese, Rwanda, 216
Kinyarwanda language, 203
Kipnis, Kenneth, 157
Kirchner, Néstor, 229n4
Kiss, Elizabeth, 21, 283n764, 288n805
Knin, industrial town, 81
Kolundžija, Dragan, 72, 73, 75, 151
Kordić & Čerkez trial, 28
Koricanske Stijene, 69–70, 196
Kosovar Albania, 48
Koumjian, Nicholas, 119, 280n716
Kovacević, Vladimir, 66–67
Krajina region, 81, 193
Krajišnik, Momčilo, 73, 193, 195
Kratine village, 70
Kravica warehouse executions, 194
Krog, Antije, 290n833
Krstić, Radislav, 66, 75, 142, 193
Kvočka case, 173

Lagos, Ricardo, 44, 237n59, 255n268
Land Claims Court, 18
language translation: in East Timor, 38, 41, 168, 210–11; at ICTY and ICTR, 33; in Rwanda, 203
Latin America: democratization of, 12–13; forced disappearances, 24, 130, 172. *See also* Argentine forced disappearances
laws of war, 11
leftist guerrillas, 178
legal counsel, lack of in Rwanda, 43, 213, 218

Leite, Sabino, 211
Leki, Gaspar, 116, 279n699
Leki, Joseph, 121
lian nain, 169
Liberia. *See* Taylor, Charles
life sentences, 93, 133, 134
Lille, France, 109
Liquica church, 166
Liu Daqun, 77
liurai, 169
local justice in East Timor, 168–70, 219, 222
Lolotoe case, 39, 117
Los Palos case, 279n702; guilty pleas, 116, 117; lack of resources, 38, 39, 209, 210; sentences imposed, 121–23
low-level perpetrators: Bralo and Erdemović, 85; custody of, in East Timor, 115, 210; deterrence of, 48–49; incapacitating hostile conduct of, 50; plea agreements and truth-telling, 196; retribution desired by victims, 46–47; using testimony to prosecute high-level offenders, 173; victims' wrath at, 54. *See also* offenders
Ludji & Pereira case, 119–20
Luka detention camp, 61, 75

Macedonia, 159, 160
machetes, 164, 165, 167, 187, 296n903
Malan, Magnus, 42, 253n246
Mali imprisonment, 93, 109
Manikas, Peter, 160
Marques, Joni, 119, 121–23
Martins, Anastacio, 124
Martins & Gonçalves case, 120, 124
martyrs, creation of, 54
massacre, determination of in Rwanda, 97–98
mass atrocities, 3; difficulty of prosecuting, 12–13
mass executions: in Argentine disappearances, 158; in Bosnian prison camps, 162; in Rwanda, 165
mass graves, 163, 172
Max Planck Institute, 79–80
Mayan genocides, 22
Mbeki, Thabo, 17

McDonald, Gabrielle Kirk, 189
media coverage, 23
Media Trial, 1, 94, 205–6, 295n897
Medina, Hugo, 234n32
Melvern, Linda, 206
Mengistu Haile Miriam, 12
Mesić, Stjepan, 20
mid-level perpetrators: deterrence of,
    48–49; incapacitating hostile conduct
    of, 51; using testimony of to prosecute
    high-level offenders, 173; victims'
    wrath at, 54. See also offenders
Mignone, Emilio, 159
militias. See paramilitary groups
Milošević, Slobodan, 1; and Babić case, 81;
    incapacitating hostile conduct of, 50;
    lack of deterrence of ICTY, 48; rise to
    power, 160; testimony of other defen-
    dants, 193; witnesses giving informa-
    tion, 49
mine-clearing, 83
Minow, Martha, 20, 21, 25, 54
Missing Persons, Federal Commission, in
    Bosnia, 83
missing persons in Argentina. See Argen-
    tine forced disappearances
Miya, Eunice, 147
monetary payments, as reparations, 16–17,
    18, 19
Montenegro, 159
monuments in Bosnia and Croatia, 160–61
Mothers of Srebrenica and Zepa, 255n272
Mrđa, Darko: appeal of, 87; charge bar-
    gain, 69–70; no prior criminal record,
    257n285; plea bargain, 196; sentence
    bargain, 80, 198–99; statement of re-
    morse, 200
Mthimkulu, Joyce, 143
Mubuga church massacre, 98–100
Mubuga sector, 98
Murayama, Tomiichi, apology by, 19–20
Musha church massacre, 101–6
Muslims, in Bosnia. See Bosnian Muslims

Nairobi, Kenya, 94, 203
naming names in truth-telling commis-
    sions, 22

national security and enforcement coop-
    eration, 34
NATO in Bosnia-Herzegovina (SFOR),
    Todorović case, 62
neighborhood sanctioning boards,
    286n778
New Zealand model of family group con-
    ferencing, 286n778
Ngewu, Cynthia, 289n825
NGO reports, 117
Nice, Geoffrey, 193
Nikolić, Dragan: appeal of, 86, 87, 89–90;
    charge bargain, 70; indictment read by
    judge, 197; no prior criminal record,
    257n285; sentence bargain, 79–80, 83;
    statement of remorse, 201; victim-of-
    fender interaction, 191–92
Nikolić, Momir: appeal of, 86, 89–90;
    charge bargain, 65–66; familiarity with
    victims, 180; guilty plea and truth tell-
    ing, 131; restorative elements in guilty-
    plea process, 189, 190, 192, 193, 194, 195;
    sentence bargain, 75, 76–79, 83
Nino, Carlos, 12, 291n845
no-fly zone over Bosnia, 14
nonprosecutorial mechanisms: repara-
    tions schemes, 16–21; truth-telling
    commissions, 21–26
Norway, courts of, 108–9, 113
Nuremburg tribunal, 11, 49, 55–56, 258n298

Obrenović, Dragan: appeal of, 86; charge
    bargain, 65–66; guilty plea and truth
    telling, 131; inculpating other defen-
    dants, 193; reconciliation and truth-
    telling of guilty plea, 190, 195; sentence
    bargain, 75, 78–79
Odžak, ethnic cleansing of, 71
Oecusse court, 168
offenders: benefits of reparations, 147; de-
    nying their crimes, 163, 172, 181; guilty
    pleas and truth-telling, 143; refugees
    returning to East Timor, 219, 222; in
    restorative-justice systems, 136–39. See
    also high-level perpetrators; low-level
    perpetrators; mid-level perpetrators
O'Hara, Erin Ann, 146

Ohio study of victim-offender mediation, 139–40
Omarska camp, 73, 162, 173
Opstina Prijedor conflict, 54
Organic Law, Rwanda, 212, 215
Osiel, Mark, 3, 55
Ovcara massacre, 288n807

paramilitary groups: Argentine military junta, 157–59; in Bosnia, 161; in East Timor, 167, 173
Pebco Three incident, 290n834
Penal Reform International Report, 216, 218
penological goals. *See* goals of prosecutions
Pereira, José, 120
Perón, Isabel, 157
perpetrators. *See* offenders
persecution as crime against humanity, 63–64
Peru, 172, 234n32
Petković, Milivoj, 193
Pinochet, Augusto, 12–13, 43–44, 172, 230n4, 234n34
Plavšić, Biljana: apology, value of, 144–45; factual agreement of plea agreement, 196; guilty plea, 65–66, 73–74, 84; reaction to lenient sentence, 74, 132, 133; reconciliation and truth-telling of guilty plea, 21, 92, 131, 190; summary, 224
plea bargaining: completion strategy of ICTY, 29; criticisms of, 129, 132; domestic vs. international use of, 5; in East Timor, 39, 119–25; in Ethiopia, 43; increasing criminal prosecutions, 127–35; pros and cons of, 77; and rehabilitation of defendants, 52; summary, 223–26; use of in common-law vs. civil-law states, 4. *See also* restorative justice, model guilty-plea system; restorative justice, optimal guilty-plea systems
plea bargaining at ICTR, 91–113; *Bisengimana* case, 101–6; charge bargaining, 97–110; early guilty pleas, 92–97; *Kambanda* case, 92–94; negotiations for in-

formation, 108–10; *Ruggiu* case, 95–97; *Rutaganira* case, 98–101; sentence bargaining, 97–110; *Serugendo* case, 106–8; *Serushago* case, 94–95; summary of, 110–13, 125–26
plea bargaining at ICTY, 4, 57–90; appeals in guilty-plea cases, 86–90; charge bargaining, 63–71; completion strategy, 29; early guilty pleas, 59–62; guilty-plea procedures, 58–59; sentence bargaining, 71–86; summary of, 125–26
plea bargaining at Special Panels in East Timor, 114–26; early guilty pleas, 114–18; evolution of, 119–25; restorative elements in process, 209–11; summary of, 125–26
political constraints and criminal accountability, 176–77
Pol Pot, 5
Portugal, 166, 167
Portuguese language, 211
potato famine, in Ireland, 19
Poulson, Barton, 137
Power, Samantha, 203
Praljak, Slobodan, 193, 304n1031
Prcać, Dragoljub, 73, 173
Presidential Guard, 164
pretrial detention, 28, 39
Prijedor municipality, 73, 200
Prijedor Police "Intervention Squad," 69–70
prison camps in Bosnia, 161–62; denial by Serbs, 172, 180–81
Prlić, Jadranko, 193
propaganda in Rwanda, 50, 52, 164, 165, 184
prosecutions of international crimes: difficulty of, 12–13; establishment of tribunals, 14–16; financial obstacles to threat of prosecution, 152; introduction to, 1–6; Osiel's theory of collective memory, 55–56; reparations schemes, 16–21; in restorative-justice programs, 148; truth-telling commissions, 21–26; using plea bargaining to increase numbers, 127–35. *See also* goals of prosecutions; inculpating other defendants;

restorative justice, minimal role in current prosecutions

prosecutors: abusing the system, 127–28; threatening prosecution, 152–53

public condemnation, 24, 216, 221

public defenders: in America, and general strikes, 152; in Indonesia, and resource constraints, 38–39

public expectations of guilty-plea system, 134–35

Public Prosecution Department, Rwanda, 214

punishment: in restorative-justice programs, 140–41

Pušić, Berislav, 193

radio broadcasts in Rwanda, 50, 95–96, 106–7, 164, 173, 205

radios, distribution of, 164

Radio Television Libre des Mille Collines (RTLM), 95–96, 106–7, 205

Rajić, Ivica: facing retaliation back home, 149; government cover-up of crimes, 194; guilty plea, 83, 85–86, 87; inconsistent assertions, 197, 199; inculpating other defendants, 193; statement of remorse, 200

Ramon, General, 292n853

rape. *See* sexual assaults

Reagan, Ronald, 19

recidivism, 51, 139

reconciliation: in amnesty process, 24; and Argentine disappearances, 159; and guilty pleas, 131; in ICTY cases, 190–91; of offenders in Rwanda, 214–15; in restorative-justice programs, 138; restoring social order in East Timor, 169–70, 187; summary, 223, 224; through East Timor's CAVR, 219–22; through Rwanda's domestic courts, 212–19; value of apologies, 21, 144–46, 175; value of material reparations, 175–76. *See also* restorative justice, model guilty-plea system; restorative justice, optimal guilty-plea systems

refugees: returning to Bosnia, 132, 147; returning to East Timor, 219, 222

rehabilitation, 51–53

remorse of defendants, 90

reparations: in Bosnia, 180–82; in East Timor, 187, 211, 221; government-funded, 6; in restorative-justice programs, value of, 144–48; in Rwanda, 185; symbolic, 6, 19; value in different factual contexts, 175–76

reparations schemes, 16–21; in Argentina, 17; in Chile, 17; in Germany, 17; results of, 19; in South Africa, 17–18

Republika Srpska Bureau of Government, 163

Resolution 764, 235n43

Resolution 771, 235n43

Resolution 780, 14

Resolution 955, 15, 236n56

Resolution 1272, 37

Resolution 1315, 249n195

Resolution 1534, 31

restitution: in domestic restorative-justice programs, 147; in reparations schemes, 17–18

Restitution of Land Rights Act, 17–18

restorative justice, 6–7, 136, 231n16

restorative justice, applying principles in aftermath, 155–87; optimal guilty-plea systems, 176–87; summary of atrocities, balancing retribution and restoration, 157–70; values in different contexts, 170–76. *See also* retribution balanced with restoration

restorative justice, minimal role in current prosecutions, 188–222; in East Timor's CAVR, 219–22; in East Timor Special Panels, 209–12; in ICTR, 202–9; in ICTY, 188–202; in Rwandan domestic and *gacaca* courts, 209–19

restorative justice, model guilty-plea system, 136–54; apologies, 144–46; potential obstacles, 149–53; programs described, 137; reparations, 144–48; theory of, 136–41; truth-telling, 141–43; values combined, 148–49; victim participation, 144

restorative justice, optimal guilty-plea systems, 156, 176–87; in Argentina, 177–79; in Bosnia, 179–82; in East Timor, 185–87; in Rwanda, 182–85

retaliation, fear of, 149–50, 213, 217
retribution: as penological goal, 46–47; in restorative-justice programs, 140–41; in Rwanda *gacacas*, 215; through reparations, 19
retribution balanced with restoration, 157–70; in Argentina, 157–59; in Bosnia, 159–63; in East Timor, 166–70; in Rwanda, 163–66
revictimization, 138
Robinson, Peter, 207
Rome Statute: deterrence as goal, 47; and establishment of ICC, 2–3, 16; and ICC, 32, 33, 34, 35
RPF. *See* Rwandan Patriotic Front
RTLM radio station, 95–96, 106–7, 205, 295n897
Rugambarara, Juvénal, 204
Ruggiu, Georges: arrest of, 94; plea bargain, 95–97, 111, 113; restorative elements of case, 202, 204, 205–6, 208
Ruhanga Protestant church and school, 102, 103
rule of law, in societies emerging from violence, 53
Rusanganwa (Tutsi man), 102, 103, 104
Rutaganira, Mrs. Vinccent, 100
Rutaganira, Vincent: plea bargain, 98–101, 103, 111; restorative elements in guilty-plea process, 202, 203, 208
Rwanda: establishment of tribunal, 15–16; financial constraints, 3; genocide determination, 97–98; guilty pleas and sentencing, 133; imprisonment after genocide, 50; Office of Tourism and National Parks, 109; optimal restorative-justice guilty-plea system, 182–85; Organic Law, 212, 215; summary of atrocities, 163–66. *See also* International Criminal Tribunal for Rwanda (ICTR); plea bargaining at ICTR
Rwanda domestic justice system: detention and guilty pleas, 153–54; disrepair after mass violence, 43; government prosecutions, 100–101, 105, 106; reconciliation and restoration in guilty-plea procedures, 212–19; transfers, 30, 109. *See also gacaca* courts in Rwanda

Rwandan genocide: importance of testimony of subordinates, 173; incapacitating hostile conduct of perpetrators, 50; numbers of perpetrators, 48–49, 212; rehabilitation goal, 51–52
Rwandan government: acknowledgment of crimes, 172; community-service requirements on Hutu, 147–48; military clashes, 163–66; opposition to transferring cases to Norway, 108–9, 113
Rwandan Patriotic Front (RPF), 95, 96, 163, 166, 205, 217
Rwendeye, Colonel, 205

sacred house in East Timor, 169
Sandici executions, 194
Sankoh, Foday, 250n200
Sarajevo, siege of, 162, 179
Sarmento, Benjamin, 117–18, 120
Saudi Arabia, 12
Schomburg, Wolfgang, 68–69, 80–81, 196–97
Scilingo, Adolfo, 184
scorched earth campaign in East Timor, 37, 167
search and seizure powers, 22
secret police in Yugoslavia, 160
Semanza, Laurent, 102, 104–5, 204
Senegal, 12, 234n30
Sennett, Peter H., 311n1145
sentence bargaining: in East Timor, 119–23; at ICTY, 71–86; leniency and severity of, 132–34
sentence discounts: 50 percent reduction, 124–25; *Rutaganira* case, 99; in Rwanda, 97–110; summary, 224, 225; *Todorović* case, 62
Serb Crisis Staff and War Presidency, 63
Serbia: domestic court transfers, 30; as republic in Yugoslavia, 159
Serbian Autonomous Region of Krajina in Croatia, 193
Serbian Communist Party, 160
Serbian Croats, 81–82
Serbian Democratic Party in Croatia, 81
Serbian Democratic Party of Bosnia and Herzegovina, 67

Serbian Republic of Bosnia and Herze-
govina, 73, 160
Serious Crimes Unit, 114–15, 119, 186, 209
Serugendo, Joseph, 106–8, 204
Serushago, Omar: plea bargain, 94–95, 110,
113; restorative elements of case, 204–5,
207, 208
Šešelj, Vojislav, 50, 256n282, 256n284
sexual assaults in prison camps in Bosnia,
161–62
Shahabuddeen, Mohamed, 90
Sherman, Lawrence, 139
siege of Sarajevo, 162, 179
Sierra Leone: hybrid court, 35–37, 41;
Truth and Reconciliation Commission
(TRC), 22. See also Special Court for
Sierra Leone
Sikirica, Duško, 72–73, 75, 151, 200
Simić, Milan, 63–65, 71–72, 76, 86
Simón, Julio "El Turco Julian," 159
slavery, 11–12, 18, 20, 239n81
Slovenia, 159, 160
Soares, Carlos, 121, 210
Soares, Marcelino, 281n741
social order in East Timor, 168–70
South Africa: amnesty requirements, 52,
150–51; domestic prosecutions and
amnesty, 42–43; financial constraints,
3; historical account of apartheid,
24; Land Claims Court, 18; language
translations, 41–42; Promotion of National Unity and Reconciliation Act,
17, 23; reparations, 17–18; Restitution
of Land Rights Act, 17–18; victim testimony, 25–26
South Africa Truth and Reconciliation Commission (TRC): Amnesty
Committee, 149; apartheid victims
confronted tormentors, 174; financial
constraints, 42; plea bargaining and
prosecutions, 130; public expectations
of guilty-plea system, 134–35; Reparation and Rehabilitation Committee,
149, 238n70; reparations recommendations, 17; restorative-justice practices,
148–49; truth-telling of guilty-plea
defendants, 22–26, 143; value of apolo-

gies by amnesty applicants, 20–21, 145;
victim participation, 144
Special Court for Sierra Leone: establishment of, 2, 16, 249n195; gaining information from witnesses, 49; procedural
rules for guilty pleas, 59; Truth and
Reconciliation Commission, 22; warrant on Charles Taylor, 48
Special Panels in East Timor: establishment of, 2, 16; financial constraints,
37–40, 168; procedural rules for guilty
pleas, 59; restorative elements in
guilty-plea process, 186, 209–12; Serious Crimes Unit, 114–15, 119, 186, 209.
See also plea bargaining at Special Panels in East Timor
Special War Crimes Court in Sarajevo,
85
Srebrenica massacres: acknowledgment
of crimes, 179, 180; constituted genocide, 65; defendants in, 67–68, 74, 75,
76, 78; denial by Serbs, 163, 172, 180;
Erdemović case, 58, 60–61; financial
burdens on victims, 175; guilty pleas
and truth-telling, 130–31; history of,
162–63; lack of deterrence of ICTY, 48;
psychologist testimony, 142; testimony
of Momir Nikolić, 194, 195. See also
Bosnian war
staffing issues, 33
Stalin's purges, 12, 233n26
statements of remorse: in East Timor
Special Panels, 211; in ICTR cases,
208–9; in ICTY cases, 199–202. See also
apologies
Stojić, Bruno, 193
Strang, Heather, 139
Strinović, Davor, 288n807
Strugar, Pavle, 66–67, 193
Stupni Do (Bosnian Muslim town), 85,
194, 197
Suai District Court, 168
Subašić, Munira, 255n272
subpoena powers, 22, 35
survivors. See victims
Sušica detention camp, 70, 79, 191, 201
Swedish imprisonment, 74

symbolic reparations, 6, 19, 144, 175
symbolism of apologies, 20
syphilis study apology, 19

Taba commune, 106
Tadić, Duško, 1, 54, 71
Taft, Lee, 146
Tavares, Augusto, 121
Taylor, Charles, 48
tea industry in Rwanda, 108
Team Alfa militia, 121
Teitel, Ruti, 26, 53
testimony: inconsistencies in ICTR cases, 206; inconsistencies in ICTY cases, 197–99; inculpating other defendants in ICTR cases, 204–7; inculpating other defendants in ICTY cases, 192–95
Texas study of victim-offender mediation, 139–40
Tihic, Sulejman, 289n817
Tilman, Romeiro, 118
Timor: West Timor, 219. *See also* East Timor
Tito, Josip Broz, 160, 293n862
Todorović, Stevan: charge bargain, 63; plea bargain, 62; sentence bargain, 71, 86; statement of remorse, 199–200; testimony and plea bargain, 194–95
Tokyo tribunal, 11, 56
Tomuschat, Christian, 22
torture: in Argentine disappearances, 158; in prison camps in Bosnia, 161–62
translators/interpreters, 33, 38, 41, 168, 211
tribunals: establishment of, 14–16; financial obstacles to threat of prosecution, 152, 153; financial support of, 1, 2; introduction to, 1–10; jurisdiction over crimes, 11; length and cost of, 28–29; revising procedural rules, 245n142. *See also* financial realities
truth-telling: and guilty pleas, 130; and historical record, 24, 54; obstacle of disclosure requirement, 149–51; in restorative-justice guilty-plea systems, 141–43; value in different factual contexts, 171–73
truth-telling as restorative element in

guilty-plea systems: in Argentina, 177–79; in Bosnia, 179–82, 190, 192–99; in East Timor, 186; in Rwanda, 182–83, 203–7
truth-telling commissions: in Chile, 13; described, 21–26; value of, 6, 143, 148
Tutsi, 15; close relationships to Hutu, 183–85; community-service requirements on Hutu, 148; government-organized genocide, 182–84; historical summary, 163–66; incapacitation of perpetrators, 50; incitements to kill, 92, 95, 106–7, 205; Mubuga church massacre, 98–100; Musha church massacre, 101–6; numbers of victims, 48–49; roadblocks to capture, 92, 94
Tutu, Desmond, 21, 26

Uganda: and Idi Amin, 5, 12; numbers of victims, 233n27
Umbreit, Mark, 137
U.N. Commission on Human Rights, 15
UNESCO World Cultural Heritage, 67
United States: Alien Tort Claims Act, 19; Public Health Service study on syphilis, 19; *Todorović* case, 62
U.N. peacekeeping forces, 15
U.N. Security Council: completion pressure, 91, 125, 207; completion strategies, 29, 31; deterrence goal, 47–48; domestic court transfers, 30; enforcement cooperation, 33–34; establishment of ad hoc tribunals, 1, 14–16; establishment of UNTAET, 167; financial support of tribunals, 2; hybrid courts and funding, 36–37. *See also resolutions*
U.N. Transitional Administration in East Timor (UNTAET): and CAVR, 219, 220, 222; establishment of, 37, 114, 167; establishment of Special Panels, 57; Regulation 2000/11, district courts, 168
Uruguay amnesty, 234n32
Uwilingiyimana, Juvénal, 108, 109–10, 150, 206–7

Valente, Jose, 121
van der Merwe, Johan, 21, 151

Vareš (town), 85
Vasiljević, Mitar, 76
Vasilković, Dragan, 300n966
vengeance. *See* retribution
Venter, Colonel, 290n834
Verbitsky, Hector, 159
victim involvement as restorative element
    in guilty-plea processes: in Argentine
    disappearances, 177–78; in East Timor
    Special Panels, 187, 210–11; in ICTR,
    202–3; in ICTY, 180–82, 191–92
victim-offender mediation study in Texas
    and Ohio, 139–40
victim participation: in restorative-jus-
    tice programs, 144; restorative role of
    dialogue in Rwanda, 183–85; value in
    different factual contexts, 174; victim-
    offender interactions, 144
victims: in Argentine disappearances, 158;
    desire for retribution, 46–47; dissatis-
    faction of, 223; empowerment of, 24,
    25; financial burdens of, 175, 180, 181;
    individualizing justice, 54; informa-
    tion for families, 195–96; perception of
    sentence leniency, 132, 133; protection
    of, 42; public expectations of guilty-
    plea system, 134–35; reactions to plea
    agreements, 196; refugees returning
    home, 132, 147; restitution value, 147;
    in restorative-justice programs, 137–38;
    testimonies of, 25
Videla, Jorge Rafael, 159, 172, 291n848
Vincent, Robin, 37
Viola, Roberto, 292n848
Vohrah, Lal Chand, 189

Wagga model of family group conferenc-
    ing, 286n778

Waldorf, Lars, 313n1189
war crimes, 11
West Timor, 219
Wilson, Stuart, 283n764
Wippman, David, 5
Wiranto, General, 186
Wisconsin restorative-justice program,
    139
witnesses, motivations to give informa-
    tion, 49
witness-protection program, 22–23, 42,
    213
women: Asian Women's Fund, 20; Japa-
    nese comfort women, 20; Mothers of
    Srebrenica and Zepa, 255n272; Muslim
    widows, 175, 180; as victims of Ar-
    gentine disappearances, 158, 292n851;
    Women from Podrinje, 196
World War II: German reparations, 17;
    prosecutions compared to ICTY, 53;
    tribunals of, 11

Yarn, Douglas, 146
Yaroshefsky, Ellen, 305n1039
Yugoslav Army, 81
Yugoslavia: composition of republics,
    159; deterrence goal of ICTY, 47–48;
    domestic court transfers, 30; establish-
    ment of tribunal, 14–15; and histori-
    cal record, 54. *See also* International
    Criminal Tribunal for Yugoslavia
    (ICTY); plea bargaining at ICTY
Yugoslav National Army, 160
Yugoslav People's Army (JNA), 160

Zimbabwe, 12
Zvornik Brigade, 79, 80

The authorized representative in the EU for product safety and compliance is:
Mare Nostrum Group
B.V Doelen 72
4831 GR Breda
The Netherlands

www.ingramcontent.com/pod-product-compliance
Lightning Source LLC
Chambersburg PA
CBHW021548210326

41599CB00010B/353